CHILD LAW

AUSTRALIA
Law Book Co.
Sydney

CANADA and USA
Carswell
Toronto

HONG KONG
Sweet & Maxwell Asia

NEW ZEALAND
Brookers
Wellington

SINGAPORE and MALAYSIA
Sweet & Maxwell Asia
Singapore and Kuala Lumpur

CHILD LAW

Geoffrey Shannon

B.Comm., LL.B., LL.M., Solicitor

THOMSON ROUND HALL
2005

Published in 2005 by
Thomson Round Hall
43 Fitzwilliam Place
Dublin 2
Ireland

Typeset by
Gough Typesetting Services
Dublin

Printed by
MPG Books, Cornwall

ISBN 1-85800-399-7 hbk
ISBN 1-85800-352-0 pbk

A catalogue record for this book
is available from the British Library

© Geoffrey Shannon 2005

FOREWORD

This new work by Geoffrey Shannon is both remarkable and welcome. It is remarkable in its scope and comprehensiveness. It is welcome in that it reflects what the author describes as "a gradual but decisive shift in attitudes to children" which has taken place in recent decades. Until relatively recently the law regarding children was viewed as a subsidiary aspect of matrimonial law or, on the public law side, as a matter of providing a suitable destination for children in need of care and protection. Today, as Mr Shannon points out, children are viewed "as people with rights rather than objects of concern".

Child Law covers a legal spectrum reaching far beyond the traditional area of family law. It deals with the law of contract as it affects children, with children as tortfeasors, and with children in the workplace. There are comprehensive chapters on education, on the workings of the Child Care Act 1991, and on adoption. There is a full discussion of the Children Act 2001 and the general area of juvenile justice.

The author has a particular interest in the separate representation of children themselves in the court process and he highlights how this has developed both in this jurisdiction and through the influence of international instruments and conventions. We have moved a long way from the point where provision for the appointment of a guardian *ad litem* was added, almost as an afterthought, in a late amendment to the Child Care Act 1991.

A feature of *Child Law* which will be particularly valuable to practitioners is the author's treatment of the various relevant international instruments, ranging from the 1980 Hague Convention on the Civil Aspects of International Child Abduction and the 1989 United Nations Convention on the Rights of the Child to the Revised Brussels II Regulation (Brussels II bis) which will apply in its entirety in this jurisdiction from March 1, 2005. Mr Shannon has a depth of expertise in this area which is rare among Irish lawyers and he presents a telling analysis of both the advantages and the possible difficulties which may arise from the operation of this new Regulation.

In the context both of changes in domestic law and of the international provisions, the opening chapter of this book, which deals with the Constitution, the family and the child, is relevant not alone to lawyers but to Government and to the general public. Mr Shannon draws attention to the fact that Art.41 of the Constitution lacks a child focus and fails to recognise the child as a juristic person with individual rights. He draws attention to the recommendations for constitutional change made by the Kilkenny Incest Investigation Committee in 1993, by the Constitution Review Group in 1996 and more recently by the United Nations Committee on the Rights of the Child. His comments are illustrated by an analysis of the relevant case law. One cannot but hope that his criticisms will help to bring about change in this area of basic law.

Child Law will be an indispensable resource for all those who practise in this area. The author and the publishers are to be congratulated on their achievement.

The Hon. Mrs Justice Catherine McGuinness

PREFACE

The past decades have witnessed a gradual but decisive shift in attitudes to children. No longer does the ancient Roman *patria potestas* prevail. Today, children are now viewed as people with rights rather than objects of concern. The law relating to children in Ireland is growing and developing at an unprecedented rate. For example, the Children Act 2001 brought about a fundamental revolution in the law relating to juvenile justice and will continue to influence law and practice for many years to come.

Child Law provides a detailed text with full analysis and commentary, offering an assessment of the law together with suggested approaches to its practice. Because of the scope of the topics covered, it has not been possible to treat each of them in depth. As far as the construction of the book is concerned, the first chapter attempts to set out the framework in which the law relating to children operates, covering the Irish Constitution and the general law. Chapters 2 to 11 examine critically, in what I hope is a logical progression, the private and public law governing the care and upbringing of children in Ireland. Chapter 12 concludes with an examination of the international law dealing with children. I felt the need to include such a chapter as we have recently witnessed the increasing internationalisation of child law. This chapter considers the impact of the proliferation of international instruments on domestic child law. Currently, there are three bodies generating such instruments, namely, the Hague Conference, the Council of Europe and the EU Commission. International regulation is therefore becoming increasingly complex, which may serve to undermine the very objectives that such regulation seeks to confer. Nowhere is this more evident than in the area of child abduction: see Chapter 10. For example, complete automatic enforcement is the basis of the new Council Regulation repealing the Brussels II Regulation (known as the revised "Brussels II Regulation"). While the revised Brussels II Regulation will take precedence where the child is within the European Union, the 1980 Hague Convention is to apply where the child is outside the European Union. This should make for some interesting "forum shopping" by personal litigants.

It is clear from some of the developments detailed in this book that factors beyond the textbook law have been responsible for shaping and constructing our child law system. Unfortunately, empirical evidence is in short supply. Indeed, one of the great difficulties encountered in the writing of this book was the lack of available statistics. The figures which have been provided furnish little information. The time is therefore ripe to review the manner in which we gather and collate statistical information. I hope this book will provide the impetus for this review.

I am honoured to have a foreword written by the Hon. Mrs Justice Catherine

McGuinness of the Supreme Court who has been synonymous with the development of child law in Ireland. The proliferation of her judgments cited in this title is evidence of her contribution to the development of the law relating to children. I am most grateful to her.

I am indebted to a large number of people who have assisted me with this book. In particular, I would like to acknowledge Sarah Farrell, Rosemary Horgan, and Fergus Ryan who all contributed to a previous publication *Children and the Law* (Thomson Round Hall, 2001) out of which this work has emerged. In addition, I would also like to acknowledge the enormous assistance afforded by Catherine Dolan of Thomson Round Hall. Her professionalism, expertise and advice over a lengthy period have greatly enhanced this work. Special thanks to Susan Rossney of Thomson Round Hall. Thanks are also due to Margaret Byrne, Librarian; Mary Gaynor, Assistant Librarian; Ann-Marie O'Neill; and Eddie Mackey of the Law Society library. I would also like to thank Justine Kelly for her assistance.

When commencing this book the main objective was to focus attention on the cataclysmic developments in child law over the last decade and to provide practitioners in particular with a user-friendly resource to help them practise in the area of child law. My hope is that this book has, in some way, achieved this.

While every effort has been made to ensure that the text is accurate I would be pleased to receive any comments on the material included and invite suggestions as to areas that might be addressed in future editions. The law and practice are stated as at September 1, 2004, but it has been possible to include new developments since that date.

Geoffrey Shannon
October 2004

TABLE OF CONTENTS

APPENDICES

Appendices to Chapter 1

Appendices to Chapter 2

Appendices to Chapter 3

Appendices to Chapter 5

Appendices to Chapter 6

Appendices to Chapter 9

Appendices to Chapter 10

Appendices to Chapter 11

Appendices to Chapter 12

TABLE OF CASES

Child Law

TABLE OF LEGISLATION

IRELAND

UK ACTS

EUROPE

INTERNATIONAL

STATUTORY INSTRUMENTS

THE LEGAL STATUS OF THE CHILD IN IRISH SOCIETY

PART I

INTRODUCTION

1–01   One of the founding documents of the State, the Proclamation of Easter 1916, promised to cherish all the children of the nation equally. Equality of treatment, however, can hardly be said to characterise the care of children in Ireland today. How many of the laws, structures, institutions and practices established to protect children and their welfare actually do so?

This work attempts to evaluate the entire Irish child law system. The subject matter contained in the following chapters provides an opportunity for examining the relationship that exists, or ought to exist, between child welfare and parental rights. It examines the rights and duties of parents and children in respect of each other. It considers how best to balance the welfare of children who may require care, with the right of children—and their families—to protection from unwarranted State intervention.

This book does not contain the implicit claim that only the most important and vital areas of child law have been selected for discussion; but it does focus on some of the most pressing, significant and interesting issues in this branch of the law. It provides evidence that injustice, inequality, hypocrisy and the denial of human rights occur in many areas of child law.

1–02   The paramountcy of parental rights in Ireland is considered alongside the invisibility of children, most notably in judicial separation and divorce proceedings. Often in these proceedings, where neither adult appears incontestably correct, parents seem locked in a power struggle with each other, using the child as a weapon or trophy, but ignoring his needs.

It is only with difficulty that the law has advanced from its position of regarding children as possessions. Even in acknowledging that the "best interests of the child" are its central concern, it has made false promises to children. The US Supreme Court, as far back as 1969, in the case of *Tinker v Des Moines Independent School District*,[1] acknowledged children as persons under the Constitution with rights that should be protected by the State. This stands in contrast to some recent Supreme Court pronouncements in this

---

[1]   393 U.S. 503 (1969).

jurisdiction, most notably in *Sinnott v Minister for Education and Others*[2] and *North Western Health Board v H.W. and C.W.*[3] In the former case, one Supreme Court judge questioned the very notion that the child in question had the rights that he claimed. The effect of the latter judgment is to maintain the Irish family as a type of independent republic.

The rights of children should be taken seriously. Despite protestations to the contrary, the law in the area of child rights in this jurisdiction still falls far short of our international obligations, including the requirements of the United Nations Convention on the Rights of the Child 1989.

1–03   The ratification of international instruments is only a beginning: it is a signal of a commitment to the recognition of children's rights, which requires implementation in practice. In fact, unimplemented domestic and international law create false expectations and do children more harm than good. Inherent in this argument is the view that rights without resources are meaningless.

Notwithstanding the recent economic boom, 8 per cent of children are living in "consistent poverty", while 24 per cent are living in "relative income poverty". Poverty in childhood can prevent children from reaching their full potential development, and can negatively affect their health, education and life chances. In fact, a significant cause of child placement in this jurisdiction is poverty or some factor related to it. The provision of preventative services to avoid the necessity of children being taken into care should be a priority.

That children have rights is beyond doubt: the importance and nature of these rights is explored throughout this book. It suffices to state at this juncture that the present law concerning children is somewhat patchwork in appearance and beset with uncertainties. Therefore, what is now needed is reformulation and clarification of children's rights in both the Constitution and legislation.

The Constitution and the family

1–04   The principal source of fundamental rights in the family law arena in Ireland is the Constitution. Articles 41 and 42 of the Constitution have had a profound impact on the manner in which family legislation has been enacted and family law judgments delivered. Article 41 of the Irish Constitution of 1937 concerns the family and "recognises the family as the natural and primary unit group of society" and further guarantees "to protect the family in its constitution and authority".

1–05   The rights guaranteed by Art.41 are recognised as belonging not to individual members of the family, but to the family unit as a whole. An individual on behalf of the family may invoke them but, as Costello J. notes in *Murray v Ireland*,[4] they "belong to the institution in itself as distinct from the personal rights which each individual member might enjoy by virtue of membership of the family".

---

[2]   [2001] 2 I.R. 598
[3]   [2001] I.R. 622.
[4]   [1985] I.L.R.M. 542 at 547.

Article 41 lacks a child focus. It fails to recognise the child as a juristic person with individual rights. This is in no small measure attributable to the principle of parental autonomy created by Art.41 of the Constitution. This article establishes a private realm of family life, which the State can enter only in exceptional circumstances, which are detailed in Art.42.5 of the Constitution. Article 42 provides as follows:

"1. The State acknowledges that the primary and natural educator of the child is the Family and guarantees to respect the inalienable right and duty of parents to provide, according to their means, for the religious and moral, intellectual, physical and social education of their children.

[...]

5. In exceptional cases, where the parents for physical or moral reasons fail in their duty towards their children, the State, as guardian of the common good, by appropriate means shall endeavour to supply the place of the parents, but always with due regard for the natural and imprescriptible rights of the child."

Clearly, this article provides that only in exceptional cases, where parents, for physical or moral reasons, fail in their duty towards their children, can the State, as guardian of the common good, endeavour to supply the place of the parents.

1–06 The Irish Constitution is unique. Whereas most other Western constitutions have a public/private divide, the family unit in Ireland has autonomy over and above that of the individual members of the family. In fact, the individual rights of the constituent members of the family are both directed and determined by the family as an entity in itself. Consequently, membership of the constitutional family in Ireland subordinates the rights of the individual members. This is true specifically of the rights of children and manifests itself glaringly in Supreme Court judgments on the issue.

Article 42 has in fact more to do with the family than with the substantive right to education (which is discussed in Chapter 3). In many respects, it is an addendum and subordinate to Art.41. It deals with education in a wider sense than scholastic education. When it refers to education, it is alluding to the upbringing of the child, which it holds not only to be a right, but a duty, of parents. This article reinforces the decision-making autonomy of the family. This can be observed on examining the intellectual structure of Art.42, which assigns a strong sense of priority to parental autonomy.

1–07 Article 42.5 of the Constitution is of particular importance in that it addresses the complete inability of some parents to provide for their children's education. It has been interpreted as being confined not just to a failure by the parents of a child to provide education for him and her, but may in exceptional circumstances extend to failure in other duties necessary to satisfy the personal rights of the child. This interpretation supports the assertion that the right to education in Art.42 is a mere extension of the concept of "the family" in Art.41.

Articles 41 and 42 of the Constitution together render the rights of married parents in relation to their children "inalienable". Article 41 alludes to the inalienable and imprescriptible rights of the family. Article 42 refers to the rights and duties of married parents. Only if the circumstances satisfy the constitutional caveat on inalienability in Art.42.5 of the Constitution, is there scope for the legal supplantation of the rights of the married parents.

1–08   Section 3 of the Guardianship of Infants Act 1964, discussed in detail in Chapter 2, makes it abundantly clear that in considering an application relating to guardianship, custody or upbringing, the court must have regard to the welfare of the child concerned. This, the section states, is "the first and paramount consideration". The Supreme Court, however, has determined that the welfare of a child must, unless there are exceptional circumstances or other overriding factors, be considered to be best served by its remaining part of its marital family. This was dictated, the court considered in a number of cases, by the constitutional preference for the marital family exhibited in Art.41.3 of the Constitution and requirement that the family be protected from attack.[5] There is, therefore, an uneasy tension between, on the one hand, the provisions of Arts 41 and 42 of the Constitution and, on the other, the welfare principle outlined in s.3 of the Guardianship of Infants Act 1964.

1–09   This apparent contradiction has been correctly reconciled by the judiciary by holding that the welfare of the child is to be found within the confines of the Constitution.[6] This is a negative definition of child welfare. The focus is not on actively promoting the welfare interests of the child, but merely on ensuring that these interests are not seriously impaired. This approach is attributable to the wording of Arts 41 and 42 of the Constitution. It could therefore be argued that the current constitutional position in Ireland embodies a "seen but not heard" approach to the concept of children's rights. In its concluding observations on Ireland's implementation of the UN Convention on the Rights of the Child 1989 (CRC), the United Nations Committee on the Rights of the Child was critical of this approach to children's rights. It held that the implementation of the recommendations of the *Report of the Constitution Review Group*[7] should be accelerated to reinforce "the status of the child as a full subject of rights". The *Report of the Constitution Review Group* recommended, *inter alia*, in 1996 that an express statement of identified

---

[5]   See, for example, *Re JH (An Infant)* [1985] I.R. 375 and *North Western Health Board v H.W. and C.W.* [2001] 3 I.R. 635.

[6]   *North Western Health Board v H.W. and C.W.* [2001] 3 I.R. 635. See, however, *Southern Health Board v C.H.* [1996] 1 I.R. 231, where O'Flaherty J. observed, in a case concerning the admissibility of a video-taped interview containing allegations of parental abuse, that: "it is easy to comprehend that the child's welfare must always be of far graver concern to the court. We must, as judges, always harken to the constitutional command which mandates, as prime consideration, the interests of the child in any legal proceedings".

[7]   Constitution Review Group, *Report of the Constitution Review Group* (The Stationery Office, Dublin, 1996).

rights of children be incorporated into the Constitution. Further, the Kilkenny Incest Investigation Committee[8] recommended:

"… that consideration be given by the Government to the amendment of Articles 41 and 42 of the Constitution so as to include a statement of the constitutional rights of children".

INCREASING FOCUS ON THE CHILD BY THE STATE

The Constitution and the child

1–10 The courts have, in the past, accepted that children have certain personal, unenumerated rights under Arts 40 and 42 of the Constitution.

In the case of *G. v An Bord Úchtála*, Finlay P. held that the child "has a constitutional right to bodily integrity and has an unenumerated right to an opportunity to be reared with due regard to her religious, moral, intellectual, physical and social welfare".[9] O'Higgins C.J. in the Supreme Court expanded Finlay P.'s statement when he stated:

"The child also has natural rights. … [T]he child has the right to be fed and to live, to be reared and educated, to have the opportunity of working and of realising his or her full personality and dignity as a human being. These rights of the child (and others which I have not enumerated) must equally be protected and vindicated by the State. In exceptional cases the State, under the provisions of Article 42.5 of the Constitution, is given the duty, as guardian of the common good, to provide for a child born into a family where the parents fail in their duty towards that child for physical or moral reasons. In the same way, in special circumstances the State may have an equal obligation in relation to a child born outside the family to protect that child, even against its mother, if her natural rights are used in such a way as to endanger the health or life of the child or to deprive him of his rights."[10]

1–11 In the same case, Walsh J. stated that "[t]here is nothing in the Constitution to indicate that in cases of conflict the rights of the parent are always to be given primacy."[11] He went further by analysing the rights of children in the following terms:

"Not only has the child born out of lawful wedlock the natural right to have its welfare and health guarded no less well than that of a child born in lawful wedlock, but *a fortiori* it has the right to life itself and the right to be guarded against all threats directed to its existence whether before

---

[8] Kilkenny Incest Investigation: Report presented to Mr Brendan Howlin TD, Minister for Health by South Eastern Health Board (The Stationery Office, Dublin, May 1993).

[9] [1980] I.R. 32 at 44.

[10] *ibid.* at 69.

[11] *ibid.* at 78.

or after birth. The child's natural rights spring primarily from the natural right of every individual to life, to be reared and educated, to liberty, to work, to rest and recreation, to the practice of religion, and to follow his or her conscience. ... It lies not in the power of the parent who has the primary natural rights and duties in respect of the child to exercise them in such a way as intentionally or by neglect to endanger the health or life of the child or to terminate its existence. The child's natural right to life and all that flows from that right are independent of any right of the parent as such."[12]

1–12 In the case of *O.G. v Eastern Health Board*, Denham J., in a laudable judgment, held that the child had "the right to be reared with due regard to his religious, moral, intellectual, physical and social welfare; to be fed, accommodated and educated; to suitable care and treatment; to have the opportunity of working and of realising his personality and dignity as a human being."[13]

Recently, however, the Supreme Court has veered away from enumerating children's rights by holding that the project of articulating the rights of children was a matter for the Government. This approach can be gleaned from four landmark judgments of the Supreme Court in the past four years on children's rights: *North Western Health Board v H.W. and C.W.*;[14] *Sinnott v Minister for Education and Others*;[15] *T.D. v Minister for Education and Others*[16] and *Lobe and Osayande v Minister for Justice, Equality and Law Reform*.[17] They concern the children in society who are most in need; children who are dependent on the State for their education, health, welfare and citizenship. Such children now inhabit a legal limbo. These cases will discussed throughout the book in the discrete areas where they arise.

1–13 In summary, the foregoing judgments signpost a shift to conservatism by the Supreme Court both legally and in terms of social policy.[18] That said, the judgments could also indicate a desire on the part of the Supreme Court to respect the principle of the doctrine of the separation of powers. Whatever interpretation one affords to the recent approach of the Supreme Court regarding children's rights, there is a lacuna in the current legislative framework where children's rights are concerned. The Supreme Court has, as previously outlined, recognised that the Constitution protects children's rights. Clearly, the State is bound to uphold these rights. That said, if the State fails to protect the rights of individual children, and the Supreme Court refuses to step in as guardians of the Constitution (save in exceptional circumstances), to uphold such rights, on whom does this duty now fall?

---

[12] *ibid*. at 69.

[13] [1998] 1 I.L.R.M. 241 at 262.

[14] [2001] 3 I.R. 622.

[15] [2001] 2 I.R. 598.

[16] [2001] 4 I.R. 259.

[17] [2003] 1 I.R. 1.

[18] See, however, the recent judgment of Finlay-Geoghegan J. in *F.N. and E.B. v C.D., H.D. and E.H.*, unreported, High Court, Finlay-Geoghegan J., March 26, 2004.

The Constitution and the right to citizenship

1–14　Article 2 of the Irish Constitution, introduced as part of the British-Irish Agreement (*i.e.* the Belfast Agreement), provides that:

> "It is the entitlement and birthright of every person born in the island of Ireland, which includes its islands and seas, to be part of the Irish nation".

The automatic entitlement to Irish citizenship was removed (on June 11, 2004) when the Irish people passed by a large majority a new provision into the Constitution at Art.9, which provides as follows:

> "Notwithstanding any other provision of this Constitution, a person born in the island of Ireland, which includes its islands and seas, who does not have, at the time of his her or her birth, at least one parent who is an Irish citizen or entitled to be an Irish citizen, is not entitled to Irish citizenship or nationality, unless otherwise provided by law."

1–15　Irish citizenship can now only be acquired at birth by an Irish-born child of non-national parents if one of the parents has been legally resident in Ireland for three of the four years prior to the birth of the child. This amendment to Art.9 of the Constitution has changed the entire basis on which citizenship has been conferred in this jurisdiction by replacing the *jus solis* system (citizenship by reason of birth) with the *jus sanguinis* system (citizenship through bloodline).

1–16　The Irish Nationality and Citizenship Bill 2004,[19] published on September 30, 2004, details the citizenship rights of children born in Ireland to non-nationals. The aforementioned Constitutional change facilitated the introduction of this legislation. Section 4 of the 2004 Bill is of particular significance in that it inserts a new s.6A(2)(c) into the Irish Nationality and Citizenship Act 1956, which provides that where one of its parents is a British citizen, a child born in the island of Ireland will be entitled to citizenship irrespective of the length of stay of his parents. The 2004 Bill also includes a provision designed to ensure that the former scheme of investment-based naturalisation cannot be re-instated.

State intervention and the child

1–17　Notwithstanding the aforementioned difficulties, in vindicating the rights of children under the Irish Constitution, the past decades have witnessed a gradual but decisive shift in the dominant concerns of family law. Where once the relationship between husband and wife prevailed as the focus of most attention, the centre of gravity in family law globally has moved to the child.[20] A perusal of any modern family law publication will bear this out.

---

[19] S.I. No.40 of 2004.
[20] See Dewar, "Policy Issues in Law and the Family" in Wilson (ed.), *Frontiers of Legal*

1–18 Historically, courts and state officials alike tended to prove reticent about interfering with the upbringing of a child. The dominant rule in judicial circles was that "father knew best". In custody disputes, for instance, the principle of "*patria potestas*" (roughly translated as "paternal precedence") precluded any sustained debate about the fate of children: invariably it was the father who would be granted custody. Since 1950, however, all this has changed. The decision of the Supreme Court in *Re Tilson, Infants: Tilson v A.G.*[21] asserted for the first time in this jurisdiction that in relation to the upbringing of their children, a husband and wife had equal say. In other words, the rearing of children was a joint endeavour. Neither husband nor wife could claim the final exclusive say in how a child should be brought up.[22]

1–19 Reform, however, has not merely been internal to the family. The State, too, has gradually asserted a greater role in safeguarding the welfare of children. But there are restrictions in this regard. The family based on marriage, in particular, as previously stated, enjoys certain privileges from State intervention. The State may not, for instance, dictate how many children a family should have or by what means (other than abortion) they should regulate family size.[23] It may not, furthermore, as will be discussed in Chapter 3, force parents to make their children attend a particular school.[24] Subject to requirements as to a minimum standard of education, the parents may provide for their children's education in whatever way they see fit.

1–20 The State, as "guardian of the common good" has the right under the Constitution to intervene on behalf of a child, where there is a total failure on the part of the parents to vindicate the rights of the child and where the welfare of the child requires such intervention.[25] The State need not stand idly by

---

Scholarship (Chancery Law Publishing, Chichester, 1995), Chap.5, in particular, pp.64–67.

[21] [1951] I.R. 1.

[22] On gender equality in the family see also *T. O'G. v A.G. and An Bord Uchtála* [1985] I.L.R.M. 61 and *McKinley v Minister of Defence* [1992] 2 I.R. 333.

[23] *McGee v A.G.* [1974] I.R. 284.

[24] Arts 42.2 and 42.3 of the Constitution of Ireland 1937.

[25] See, however, *North Western Health Board v H.W. and C.W.*, unreported, Supreme Court, November 4, 2001, where it was held that the refusal of parents to permit a "PKU blood test" on a new-born infant, for religious reasons, did not justify the State (*i.e.* health board) intervening. The parental refusal was not unlawful and the intervention sought was not justified. Denham J. took the view that to order the PKU test in this case would establish a very low threshold for court intervention in future cases relating to children. Such intervention only arises in exceptional circumstances. What constitutes exceptional circumstances will depend upon the facts of a case; they include an immediate threat to the health or life of the child. Denham J. held that the "exceptional circumstances" test should be maintained. On this basis she concluded that this was not an exceptional case. Murphy J. agreed, stating that to substitute the court's judgment for that of the parents would "damage the long term interests of the child by eroding the interest and dedication of the parents in the performance of their duties". Hardiman and Murray JJ. also agreed, with the latter noting that to permit too readily State intervention in this case would "result ultimately in the court [becoming involved] in a sort of micro-management of the family". Keane C.J. dissented.

when the interests of children are at stake. The welfare of a child is a matter not merely of private concern. It is strongly asserted that the community at large has an interest in seeing that all children are treated with dignity and respect and given every opportunity to develop as rounded individuals and members of society. Thus, Art.42 of the Constitution is careful to speak not only of the rights of parents in respect of their children, but also of their duties. In exceptional cases where parents fail in these duties, for moral or physical reasons, it is open to the State to intervene, with a view to defending the welfare of children.[26] This it has done with increasing frequency by means, for instance, of care and supervision orders, designed to vindicate the interests of children at risk. International law also imposes certain obligations. In *Z. & Ors. v U.K.*,[27] discussed in detail in Chapter 12, the European Court of Human Rights (ECt.HR) held that Art.3 of the European Convention on Human Rights (ECHR), in certain circumstances, imposes a positive obligation on the State to take preventative measures to protect a child at risk.

1–21 A more subtle means of intervention occurs where the parents of children part company, particularly in cases of marital breakdown. In many cases, the key element of negotiations to work out a separation agreement after the breakdown of a marriage relates to the fate of the children. In most cases the parents will agree among themselves as to custody and access arrangements, and invariably the courts will respect such settlements. Where agreement is not possible, however, the principle of spousal equality precludes either parent from unilaterally determining such matters. In such cases the matter falls to the court to decide.

1–22 It is easy in such highly combative circumstances to view the children as merely an award for the legal victor. In fact, in child law generally, the dominant concern is not with the interests of either parent or adult third party. Should a decision be favourable to any such party, this is merely incidental. In child law proceedings, the invariable rule is that the child's interests and welfare take precedence over all other matters. In theory, then, it is the child who is placed firmly at the centre of such proceedings. The court's dominant concern must lie with promoting his or her best interests.

PART II

CHILDREN AND THE LAW

Introduction

1–23 Children are among the most vulnerable members of society. For this reason the law has extended protections to this group until they are deemed to be of an age at which they can interact with other members of society as adults.

---

[26] *ibid.*, Art.42.5.
[27] [2001] 2 F.L.R. 612.

Both the common law and statute law recognise the inexperience and immaturity of minors, and seek to prevent the exploitation of these attributes by those who have the advantage of greater knowledge and experience. This concern is particularly relevant in the areas of contract, family, employment, tort and succession law. From birth, children are dependent on adults, usually their parents, to provide them with the necessities of life. For this reason, obligations are imposed on parents in succession law, to ensure that their moral obligation to properly provide for their child is met. Further, provision of necessities is one exception to the general rule that contracts entered into by a child are voidable. Statute also extends protection to minors by limiting the extent that they can enter into binding obligations in contracts of employment and marriage, and the age at which it is possible to apply for certain licenses. However, minors can still be held responsible for their actions, as illustrated in the law of tort. It should be noted that all claims arising out of public liability, road traffic accidents and personal injuries must now be submitted to the Personal Injuries Assessment Board (PIAB) under the Personal Injuries Assessment Act 2003. The remainder of this chapter considers the rights and responsibilities that are conferred on children by the law.

LAW OF CONTRACT

1–24   The law of contract seeks to prevent the exploitation of the inexperience and immaturity of children and teenagers under the age of 18. The age of majority was reduced from 21 to 18 by the Age of Majority Act 1985. This change has been reflected in the decline of litigation in this area, as it was in the three years between 18 and 21 that most young people were likely to enter into contracts. Now that this group has been accorded the freedom and responsibility to act as adults with full legal capacity, far fewer conflicts arise out of contracts involving children. As well as the prevention of exploitation, the law seeks to ensure that the legal rules protecting children are not themselves abused by children. These rules also facilitate adults and children in doing business which is fair and in the child's best interests. Under common law, this has been achieved by the general rule that contracts involving children are voidable, save in respect of contracts for "necessaries" which are binding. A distinction is made between contracts that are void and others that are voidable. In some cases the contracts will be valid unless repudiated by the child within a reasonable time; in others, the contracts will be considered void unless adopted within a reasonable time of reaching the age of majority.

Necessaries

1–25   Section 2 of the Sale of Goods Act 1893 defines necessaries as "goods suitable to the condition in life of such infant or minor ... and to his actual requirements at the time of sale and delivery." What amounts to a "necessary" will be decided by the judge on the circumstances of the case. A number of types of goods are excluded because they amount to luxury or recreational items. This can be a fine distinction. The Law Reform Commission's *Report* *on Minors' Contracts*[28] provides such an example. A computer, needed for his studies, supplied to a 17-year-old student of computer science would be a necessity, whereas the same computer supplied to a 17-year-old who wanted it to play computer games would not be. Much will turn on the facts of the case. However, the common law is very restrictive in the area of trading contracts, which are not enforceable even when contributing to the minor's livelihood.[29]

1–26 Further, even if it is shown that the goods are necessaries, there are still hurdles to establishing that the contract is enforceable. In *Nash v Inman*,[30] for example, the supplier failed to show that the minor did not have a sufficient supply of the necessary in question. Therefore, the contract for 11 waistcoats ordered by the minor was not valid. Section 2 of the 1893 Act also provides that the minor need only pay a "reasonable price" for the necessary. If a contract is not drafted in a manner advantageous to the minor it will not be enforceable against him or her. A relevant and instructive case is that of *Keays v The Great Southern Railway*[31] where a 12-year-old girl injured in an accident had purchased a season ticket for travelling to and from school. Hanna J. held the terms of the ticket to be unfair, as they excluded liability for negligence, allowing the girl to repudiate the contract.

Services such as such as education[32] and legal advice[33] may also be within the definition of necessaries if they are beneficial to the child. Similarly, contracts of service providing a livelihood will also be generally enforced in so far as a livelihood is beneficial to a minor.

Beneficial contracts of service

1–27 Contracts of service is one area where litigation can arise, particularly in cases involving high-earning children in sports or entertainment. Generally, if a contract of service, viewed in its entirety, is beneficial for the child, then the contract will be upheld. This is the situation even if certain provisions in the contract are not beneficial. This was the reasoning of the English Court of Appeal in the leading case of *Doyle v White City Stadium*.[34] Doyle, the plaintiff, had been disqualified for throwing a low punch and forfeited his purse under one of the rules set by the British Boxing Board of Control. He argued that the forfeiture was an unfair term of his licence. However, the Court rejected this, holding that rules set by the Boxing Board protected the child plaintiff by discouraging and penalising breach of the rules, and were for his overall benefit—even though they sometimes operated against him.

---

[28] Law Reform Commission, *Report on Minors' Contracts* (The Law Reform Commision, Dublin, 1985), p.15.
[29] *Cowern v Nield* [1912] 2 K.B. 419, *Mercantile Union v Ball* [1937] 2 K.B. 498.
[30] [1908] I.R. 534.
[31] [1941] I.R. 534.
[32] *Roberts v Gray* [1913] 1 K.B. 520.
[33] *Helps v Clayton* (1864) 17 C.B. (N.S.) 53.
[34] [1935] 1 K.B. 110.

1–28 In *Chaplin v Leslie Frewin (Publishers) Ltd*[35] the Court of Appeal took a similar view. The 19-year-old alienated son of Charlie Chaplin entered a contract with the publishers to produce and publish a book about life with his parents in collaboration with ghost writers, for which he received an advance payment. He later sought to stop publication arguing that the book was potentially libellous. He held that the contract had been a contract of service which was not for his overall benefit. The Court, by a majority decision, agreed it should be viewed as a contract of service, but upheld the contract, focusing on the financial benefits for the plaintiff.[36]

1–29 These decisions can be contrasted with the Canadian case of *Toronto Marlboro Hockey Club v Tonelli*.[37] The Ontario Court of Appeal held that a contract between the defendant, a young player, and the club was unfair even though the player obtained training as part of the deal. The only route to becoming an ice hockey player was through a junior hockey club. The contract entered into provided for the payment of a percentage of earnings on expiry of his contract if the player should be signed by a senior professional team. Although all clubs had similar terms, in a majority decision the Court held the defendant was not bound by the contract.

Voidable contracts

1–30 In contracts with children involving ongoing obligations, the common law will not enforce the contract unless the child fails to repudiate the contract within a reasonable time of either entering the contract or after reaching the age of majority. Such contracts have been identified by Clark[38] as falling into five distinct categories:

(1) insurance contracts involving payment by regular instalments;

(2) payment for shares and of calls on shareholders;

(3) partnership agreements;

(4) family settlements and settlements made in contemplation of marriage; and

(5) leases.

1–31 The courts have had to deal with the issue of value obtained by the child before the contract was repudiated. Varying approaches have been taken according to the facts of the case; the courts holding that existing payments were forfeited in some cases, while in others holding the contract void *ab initio*, so monies paid by a child, or owing before repudiation, were not due.

---

[35] [1966] Ch. 71.

[36] The dissenting judgment of Lord Denning MR focused on the damage which could be done by publication.

[37] (1979) 96 D.L.R. (3d) 135.

[38] R. Clark, *Contract Law in Ireland* (4th ed., Round Hall, Sweet & Maxwell, Dublin, 1998), p.379.

Such issues may not arise so much now, as the cases on which these categories have been formulated are quite dated, with many going back to the nineteenth century and to the time when 21 was the age of majority.

Infants Relief Act 1874

1–32 This Act concerns contracts for the purchase of goods, making absolutely void all contracts by which money is lent to minors and goods, which are not necessaries, supplied. The Act has been much criticised, with many problems arising over interpretation, identified in the litigation that has arisen from the purported purchase of goods by children.[39] Further, s.2 of the Infants Relief Act 1874, dealing with minors' promises to pay on reaching majority, is not clearly drafted. Essentially such contracts cannot be ratified, even with payment of new consideration. A wholly new contract must be entered into with the important psychological element of recognising that the under-age agreement is not valid, and that there is a real choice to be free of it.[40]

Remedies

1–33 Where a contract with a minor cannot be enforced, it may be attractive to bring a claim in tort against the minor, as many actions can result in concurrent liability. Although minors can be liable in tort under certain conditions[41] the courts have been reluctant to allow tort remedies to be used to undermine the prohibition on enforcing minors' contracts. That said, if there has been a fundamental breach of a term of the contract, so that the act could be considered as totally outside the terms of the contract, the minor may be liable in tort. For example, in *Ballett v Mingay*,[42] an 18-year-old bailee was able to be sued for conversion when he was not able to return the amplifier and microphone he was renting because he had lent it to a third person, contrary to the express terms of the contract of bailment.

1–34 Equitable remedies may also be available where contracts are invalid due to age. The court can order restitution where property transferred as a result of a void contract with a minor is still in his or her possession.[43] However, this remedy is limited to situations where the property has not been parted with or consumed by the minor, even where the minor still has the proceeds of

---

[39] See Clark's discussion on the Act in R. Clark, *Contract Law in Ireland* (5th ed., Thomson Round Hall, Dublin, 2004), where he identifies and comments on some of the issues raised by the Act. The full title of the Act is "An Act to amend the law as to the Contracts of Infants 1874" (38 & 38V. c.61).

[40] s.5 of the Betting and Loans (Infants) Act 1892 provides that a fresh promise given after coming of age to pay a loan contracted during minority, such loan being void at law, and any negotiable instrument given in respect of such a loan, is void against all persons.

[41] *O'Brien v McNamee* [1953] I.R. 86: if the tortfeasor is of sufficient age to have an intention; if the tort does not require malice to be shown; and if it does not arise out of breach of contract involving a minor. See later discussion of minors' liability in tort at para.1–48 *et seq.*

[42] [1943] K.B. 281.

[43] *R. Leslie v Shiells* [1914] 3 K.B. 607.

sale. This is due to the principle that restitution ends where repayment begins. This lack of discretion can lead to the unjust enrichment of the child.[44] An action may also be brought in *quasi* contract for recovery of money paid or property transferred, if it is still in the child's possession. Here, the minor is not being required to perform the contract—only its restitution.

1–35   A further equitable remedy may apply where property was obtained as a result of fraud; for example, fraud as to the true age of the minor. There has been some divergence in decisions on whether it is possible that equity would require a minor to account for the proceeds if he or she has parted with the goods. It was supported in the case of *Stocks v Wilson*[45] but rejected in *R. Leslie v Shiells*[46] by the Court of Appeal.[47] The Irish courts have not been required to directly adjudicate on the matter. However, it has been established that equitable estoppel will not operate against a child, even though he does not "come to court with clean hands", and has committed a fraud.[48]

The European Communities (Unfair Terms in Consumer Contracts) Regulations 1995 and 2000

1–36   These regulations[49] can be used to protect minors from manifestly unfair terms of trade in consumer contracts. Certain consumer contracts or terms within such contracts can be invalid if they are unfair and cause significant imbalance in the parties' rights and obligations under the contract to the detriment of the consumer. Under the regulations, the schoolgirl plaintiff from *Keays v The Great Southern Railway*[50] would be able to sever the restrictive term from the contract for her railway ticket as an unfair term.[51] That said, the protection offered is limited to consumer issues and does not address the overall position of children in relation to the law of contract.

Advertising Code

1–37   A code on children's advertising, introduced by the Broadcasting Commission of Ireland, will come into force in January 2005. It will require television advertisements to include warnings on fast food and foods containing sugar, and will also set down guidelines for children appearing in advertising.
   The code will only apply to home-based broadcast media.

---

[44]   s.3(1) of the UK Minors Contracts Act 1987 attempts to prevent unjust enrichment by giving the court the discretion to require the child to return property acquired under the void contract, or any property representing it.

[45]   [1913] 2 K.B. 235.

[46]   [1914] 3 K.B. 607.

[47]   A contrary decision was made in the Australian case of *Campbell v Ridgely* (1887) 13 V.L.R. 701.

[48]   *Levene v Brougham* (1909) 25 T.L.R. 265.

[49]   S.I. No. 27 of 1995 and S.I. No. 307 of 2000.

[50]   [1941] I.R. 534.

[51]   Schedule 3 provides a non-exhaustive sample list of unfair terms including a term "excluding or limiting the legal liability of a seller or supplier in the event of the death of a consumer or personal injury to the latter resulting from an act or omission of that seller or supplier".

CHILDREN AND MARRIAGE

1–38   The law has also restricted the age at which a person may enter into a valid contract of marriage. The age at which society considers young people responsible enough to enter into marriage has changed over the past century, in line with changing beliefs on the issue. Prior to January 1, 1975, a boy of 14 years and a girl of 12 years could contract a valid marriage.[52] With effect from August 1, 1996, both parties to a marriage must be at least 18 years old.[53] This change occurred in response to a series of long-standing recommendations from a number of quarters, including the Joint Oireachtas Committee on Marital Breakdown and the Law Reform Commission.[54]

1–39   The present minimum age applies to all marriages celebrated within the Republic of Ireland and, in addition, to all marriages, wherever celebrated, where either one or both of the parties at the time of the marriage, is/are ordinarily resident in the Republic of Ireland. Subject to the exception outlined below, a marriage contracted in contravention of the minimum age requirement will be null and void from the date of its apparent inception.[55] By virtue of s.31(2) of the 1995 Act, any person (*e.g.* the registrar, minister, priest or rabbi) who has been called on to solemnise a particular marriage may, at his or her discretion, ask for evidence that the party or parties fulfil the minimum age requirements. Should the parties refuse to furnish such evidence, the person requesting it is at liberty to refuse to celebrate the marriage, and cannot legally be called to account for such refusal. Where such evidence is produced, but shows that either one or both of the parties is/are younger than the required minimum age, the law requires that solemnisation not take place.

1–40   A person may be convicted of a summary offence and fined up to a maximum of IR£500 (€635) for a breach of this section. Section 31(4) states that a person who knowingly marries or knowingly solemnises the marriage of a minor, or allows the solemnisation of such marriage to take place, in breach of the section, will be guilty of an offence. The fact that any party alleged to have committed an offence is tried and acquitted, however, does not serve to validate a marriage otherwise invalided for lack of age.

1–41   Where either or both or both of the parties is/are under the age of 18 years, it is nonetheless possible to contract a valid marriage where an exemption has been obtained under s.33 of the Family Law Act 1995. The Circuit Court or High Court may only grant such exemption on application being made by, or on behalf of, both parties prior to the solemnisation of the marriage. Waiver

---

[52] The age was raised to 16 by the Marriages Act 1972.
[53] s.31 of the Family Law Act 1995 (S.I. No. 26 of 1995).
[54] See respectively, the *Report of the Joint Oireachtas Committee on Marital Breakdown*, Pl.3084, para.3.4.7 and The Law Reform Commission, *Report on the Age of Majority, the Age of Marriage and Some Connected Subjects* (Law Reform Commission, Dublin, 1983).
[55] Family Law Act 1995, s.31(1)(a)(i) and (c).

of the age requirement may, it should be noted, only be obtained prior to the marriage ceremony and not subsequent thereto. An application under s.33 must be made by, or on behalf of, both parties. It may, however, be made informally. The Court is not entitled to charge a fee but may not, however, grant such exemption lightly. It must be shown that the exemption is "justified by serious reasons and is in the interests of the parties to the intended marriage". Sections 3 and 38(4) of the 1995 Act cumulatively require that where an exemption is sought from the Circuit Court, it should only be granted by a judge of the circuit in which either of the parties "ordinarily resides or carries on any business, profession or occupation".

Children in the workplace

1–42   Legislation recognises the vulnerability of children under 18 years of age entering the workplace. There is a comprehensive body of legislation to prevent children from being exploited, which recognises the inexperience of children starting work.

Dismissal

1–43   Certain categories of trainees and probationers may be excluded from the Unfair Dismissals Acts 1977–1993. Termination of employment on the expiry of an apprenticeship may not be an unfair dismissal, being justified as being for some other substantial reason justifying dismissal.

Protection of Young Persons (Employment) Act 1996

1–44   The Safety, Health and Welfare at Work Act 1989 obliges employers to provide safe places and systems of work for all staff, including young persons. The Protection of Young Persons (Employment) Act 1996 in effect limits the employment of young persons between the ages of 16 and 18 and restricts the employment of children under 16. In general, no child under the age of 13 is permitted to work without a licence from the Minister for Enterprise, Trade and Employment who must take cognisance of such matters as the safety, health, welfare and education of the child before granting such a licence.

1–45   The Protection of Young Persons (Employment) Act 1996 outlines restrictions on the type of work, periods and hours allowed to be worked, and the breaks required depending on the child's age. There are general rules imposed by the Act pertaining to the employment of children. For example, the Act requires the employer to receive a copy of the person's birth certificate and, in the case of children, written permission from the parent or guardian, prior to the commencement of employment. The employer must maintain a register of employed young persons (including children) which outlines the times of attendance at work for each day, the rate of pay and the total amount paid in wages. Section 36 of the Organisation of Working Time Act 1997 amends the Protection of Young Persons (Employment) Act 1996 to extend to situations where a young person has more than one job.

1–46   Double employment[56] resulting in the legal periods of work being exceeded is prohibited although it is a good defence for an employer to show that he had not knowledge of the other employment. Breaches of the legislation is a criminal offence prosecutable within 12 months and punishable by a fine of 1,200 (€1,523.69) and further daily fines where the breach continues. The Act also provides that the young person, any parent or guardian aiding and abetting the employer, and the employer, may each be guilty of an offence.[57] Any offences under the Act may be prosecuted summarily by the Minister or, in most cases, a trade union.[58] The employee's trade union or a parent may also sue an employer in contract for any sum due to the child.[59]

Safety, Health and Welfare at Work (Children and Young Persons) Regulations 1998[60]

1–47   The Safety, Health and Welfare at Work (Children and Young Persons) Regulations 1998 (the "1998 Regulations") elaborate on the basic requirements detailed in the Safety, Health and Welfare at Work Act 1989 and the Safety, Health and Welfare at Work (General Application) Regulations 1993. The 1998 Regulations require the employer to carry out a risk assessment that takes cognisance of the particular risks to young persons or children to be employed. The risk assessment is to include an assessment of the exposure to certain physical, chemical and biological agents, as well as particular work activities, which are detailed in the Schedule to the 1998 Regulations. In *National Authority for Occupational Safety and Health v Carabine Joinery Ltd*,[61] the defendant company was convicted of a breach of the 1998 Regulations. The case resulted from an accident where a 17-year-old seriously injured his left hand when he was removing a spanner from an automatic spindle-moulder machine. Judge Devins fined the defendant company €2,000 and awarded costs and expenses totalling €1,065. This case highlights not only the dangers associated with machinery, but how important it is for all employers to address the specific risk to the safety and health of a young employee. The level of any such risk should be assessed for each workplace as part of the process of preparing a safety statement.[62]

1–48   The risk assessment must not only take cognisance of the safety and health of the child or young person, but should also take account of his physical

---

[56] s.35 of the Organisation of Working Time Act 1997 amends the Protection of Young Persons (Employment) Act 1996 to extend to situations where a young person has more than one job.

[57] s.10.

[58] Enforcement of the transitional and non-penalisation provision in ss.13 and 17 is by way of complaint to a rights commission. Proceedings take place in private, with the right of appeal to the Employment Appeals Tribunal and eventual enforcement by the District Court.

[59] s.9.

[60] S.I. No. 504 of 1998.

[61] Ballina District Court, February, 12, 2002.

[62] See Chap.3, para.3–48.

and mental development. The employer must provide protective and preventative measures and consult any child or young person employed in relation to these measures and the risks from which they are being protected. The parent or guardian is also to be informed of these risks and preventative measures taken. Where the results of a risk assessment confirm that particular work activities may cause harm to a child or young person, he or she shall not be employed in any such activity.[63] Where an assessment shows that a child or young person may be exposed to a risk to his physical or mental development, health surveillance must be made available to him without charge.

1–49   If the job involves night work, the employer must provide health assessment without charge prior to the commencement of night work and at regular intervals thereafter.[64] The parents or guardians of children must be informed of the results of these health surveillances or assessments.

Safety, Health and Welfare at Work (Night Work and Shift Work) Regulations 2000[65]

1–50   The principal elements of the 1993 EC Working Time Directive, 93/104/EC, were implemented by the Organisation of Working Time Act 1997. Arts 9 and 13 of the 1993 Directive were implemented by the Safety, Health and Welfare at Work (Night Work and Shift Work) Regulations 1998,[66] which became law on February 1, 1999. The Safety, Health and Welfare at Work (Night Work and Shift Work) Regulations 2000 (the "2000 Regulations") revoke and replace the Safety, Health and Welfare at Work (Night Work and Shift Work) Regulations 1998. Their purpose is to avoid any ambiguity as regards the application of the provisions of Regulation 6 of the Safety, Health and Welfare at Work (Night Work and Shift Work) Regulations 1998 to night workers. The 2000 Regulations do not impose new obligations or conditions not intended in the Safety, Health and Welfare at Work (Night Work and Shift Work) Regulations 1998.

In summary, the 2000 Regulations oblige employers to take such steps as are approriate, having regard to the nature of the work, for the protection of the health and safety of night workers and shift workers. Regulation 6 of the 2000 Regulations requires an employer to carry out a risk assessment to determine if any night workers are exposed to special hazards or a heavy physical strain.[67] The risk assessment must take account of the specific effects and hazards of night work and have regard to the risk assessment requirements detailed in s.12 of the Safety, Health and Welfare at Work Act 1989.

---

[63] Regulation 3(d).
[64] However, under the Protection of Young Persons (Employment) Act 1996, young persons are expressly precluded from being employed after 11pm or before 7am. Similarly, children cannot be employed after 8pm or before 8am the next morning.
[65] S.I. No. 11 of 2000.
[66] S.I. No. 485 of 1998.
[67] See also ss.16(2)(a) and 16(2)(b) of the Organisation of Working Time Act 1997.

1–51 Regulation 7(1) of the 2000 Regulations obliges prospective and ongoing employers of night workers to make available to the employee, free of charge, an assessment of the effects of night work, if any, on the employee's health before and at regular intervals during employment. Regulation 7(2) states that the health assessment must be conducted by a registered medical practitioner or a person acting under his or her supervision. The employer and employee are to be advised by the person carrying out the assessment of his opinion as to whether the employee is fit or unfit to perform the night work concerned.[68] If the person carrying out the assessment is of the opinion that the employee is unfit both parties are to be informed of the person's opinion of what changes could be made which may result in the employee being considered fit to perform that work.[69] Regulation 7(4) provides that the health assessment must comply with the requirements of medical confidentiality. Regulation 7(5) requires employers, whose night workers become ill or otherwise exhibit symptoms of ill-health which are recognised as being connected with the fact that they perform night work, to re-assign such workers to day work suited to them whenever possible.

Protection of Young Persons (Employment) Act 1996 (Employment of Licensed Premises) Regulations 2001[70]

1–52 The Protection of Young Persons (Employment) Act 1996 (Employment of Licensed Premises) Regulations 2001 not only reinforce the working hours as detailed in the 1996 Act but also contain a detailed code of practice concerning the employment of young persons in licensed premises, the terms of which are set out in the Schedule of the Regulations.

Protection of Young Persons (Employment) Act 1996 (Bar Apprentices) Regulations 2001[71]

1–53 The Protection of Young Persons (Employment) Act 1996 (Bar Apprentices) Regulations 2001 relax the restricted hours of work for full-time bar apprentices, permitting 16- and 17-year-old bar apprentices to work in a bar until midnight, provided they are supervised by an adult and they are not starting work prior to 8am the next morning.

Minimum Wage Act 2000

1–54 This Act applies to all employees including children, with some exceptions for relations and apprentices.[72] For children and those aged 18 and older, if it is their first entry into employment, sub-minimum rates of pay apply.

---

[68] Regulation 7(3)(b).
[69] Regulation 7(3)(b).
[70] S.I. No. 350 of 2001.
[71] S.I. No. 351 of 2001.
[72] s.5(b)—apprentices within the meaning of or under the Industrial Training Act 1967 or the Labour Services Act 1987.

For those under 18, the minimum wage is 70 per cent of the standard minimum wage. Those first entering employment after 18 or who continue in employment on reaching 18 are entitled to 80 per cent of the minimum wage for one year, and 90 per cent in the following year.[73] For people who undergo training during working hours, sub-minimum rates are also permitted. For the first third of the training period the pay rate is at 75 per cent of the national minimum wage; rising to 80 per cent in the second third and 90 per cent in the final third of training.[74]

CHILDREN AS TORTFEASORS

1–55   One of the most influential factors in determining whether to bring an action in tort against a child will be fiscal realities. Generally, a child does not have the resources to make litigation worthwhile. However, a remedy may be sought up to six years, or two years in the case of personal injury, after the tortious act was committed. Further, the remedy may be enforced within six years or sometimes longer, after that.[75] During this time the minor may have acquired sufficient assets to warrant an action, or a judgment may be made payable by instalments which the minor can afford to pay requiring that the court address the issues arising from tortious acts committed by minors. Whether a minor may be liable in tort turns mainly on the nature of the tort alleged. The major determining factor is the intent required to prove the tort. A child may be liable for trespass, where it has been held that no intent is required.[76] However, for torts such as defamation or malicious prosecution, which require an intention, it is unlikely children or older minors would be liable. Difficulties have arisen in relation to the liability of minors for negligence and contributory negligence, and have tended to turn on the age, understanding and maturity of the minor in question.

Negligence

1–56   The test for negligence is based on the standard of the reasonable person, which is not necessarily appropriate when determining the liability of a child. The judgement of a reasonable person is not usually expected of children or at times older minors. The preponderance of the case law in this area has been in relation to issues of contributory negligence by children, but the same principles should apply to negligence by a child. The three main issues that have arisen for determination are age, the appropriate standard to be used, and parental liability. Parental liability is a dominant theme in the Children Act 2001.[77]

---

[73] s.15.

[74] The maximum period for any sub-minimum rate is 12 months.

[75] Glanville, *The Enforcement of Judgements* (Round Hall Sweet & Maxwell, Dublin, 1999), p.21.

[76] *O'Brien v McNamee* [1953] I.R. 86.

[77] See Chap.11.

Age is an important factor when determining whether a child can be (contributory) negligent. Young children cannot be expected to take precautions for their own safety, but children from about the age of nine years have generally been found to be capable of contributory negligence. Decisions in cases involving children between these ages have varied. O'Brien J. in *Fleming v Kerry County Council*[78] summarised the principles involved in determining whether a child has been negligent and the test to be applied:

"In cases where contributory negligence is alleged against a child, it is the duty of the trial Judge to rule, in each particular case, whether the plaintiff, having regard to his age and mental development, may properly be expected to take some precautions for his own safety and consequently be capable of being guilty of contributory negligence. Having ruled in the affirmative, it becomes a question of fact for the jury, on the evidence, to determine whether he has fallen short of the standard which might reasonably be expected from him having regard to his age and development. In the case of an ordinary adult person, the standard is what should be expected from a reasonable person. In the case of a child, the standard is what may reasonably be expected having regard to the age and mental development of the child and the other circumstances of the case."

1–57   There is a lack of uniformity in the case law in this area, so that decisions have varied between an objective and subjective test in relation to the age of the child in question. Children can vary considerably in their development and once the issue of capacity has been positively decided, this subjective element is usually taken into account in deciding whether the child was contributory negligent.[79] However, other decisions have varied on this point, though the Supreme Court decisions of *McNamara v ESB*[80] and *Brennan v Savage Smith & Co.*[81] show a preference for a subjective standard. It would seem logical and consistent that the subjective test should also be applied when deciding whether a child is capable of non-contributory negligence. The Law Reform Commission[82] agreed, and has further recommended abandoning the preliminary issue of age regarding whether the child was of an age to be capable of (contributory) negligence. Instead, it was suggested that the court should retain the subjective test of the child's age, intelligence and experience, for children up to the age of 16, after which the child's (contributory) negligence should no longer be judged by subjective standards.

---

[78] [1955–56] Ir. Jur. Rep. 71 at 72.
[79] McMahon & Binchy, *Law of Torts* (3rd ed., Butterworths, Dublin, 2000), p.1049.
[80] [1975] I.R. 1 at 16–18.
[81] [1982] I.L.R.M. 223.
[82] On the liability in tort of minors and the liability of parents for damage caused by minors, see Law Reform Commission, *Report on the Liability in Tort of Minors and the Liability of Parents for Damage Caused by Minors* (Law Reform Commission, Dublin, 1985).

Parental responsibility and liability

1–58   Parents or others in charge of children are not liable for a child's dangerous acts, unless the child was directed, authorised or, possibly, had his act ratified by the carer, or if the child was acting as a servant or an agent of the carer.[83] It should be stated that a parent or carer may also be liable for his own negligence where he exposed others to the dangers represented by the child. For example, a farmer was found liable for leaving a gun loaded and cocked, leaning against a fence on a path to his house in *Sullivan v Creed*.[84] His 15-year-old son, not realising the danger, picked it up and pointed it at the plaintiff in jest, seriously wounding him. The farmer was found negligent, not because the boy was his son, but for leaving the gun where he could anticipate others finding it and possibly misusing it. Negligence has also been found in a case of a carer insufficiently supervising a small child who escaped onto the road causing a traffic accident,[85] and a driver failing in his duty to take reasonable care to prevent negligent conduct by a passenger, his 13-year-old daughter.[86]

1–59   A parent can also be found liable where he or she knows of a child's dangerous disposition and does not act. Such behaviour could be a tendency to steal,[87] to set fire to property,[88] or where the child has previously attacked someone.[89] Whether liability will be established will depend on the actions taken by the parent to guard against the behaviour recurring. This might include disciplining the child, encouraging reform, removing what amounts to be a potential risk and warning a possible victim. A parent is not required to guarantee a child's good behaviour[90] so where the parent has taken all reasonable steps liability will not be imposed. Liability will also be influenced by factors such as the age of the child, and the seriousness of the act.

   The responsibilities and obligations on parents to participate in the control and welfare of their child will be modified by ss.111 to 114 of the Children Act 2001, which are not yet fully in force. These sections are discussed in Chapter 11.

Trespass

1–60   Issues have also arisen in relation to children's liability in trespass. The tort of trespass requires two elements: an act of trespass, as well as a state of mind in which the act is done intentionally or negligently.[91] Once the plaintiff

[83] *Gibson v O'Keeney* [1928] N.I. 66.
[84] [1904] 2 I.R. 317 (Court of Appeal).
[85] *Carmarthenshire Co. Council v Lewis* [1955] A.C. 549 and Chap.7, para.7–63.
[86] *Curley v Mannion* [1965] I.R. 543.
[87] *Steifel v Stroz*, 11 D.L.R. (2d) 667 (B.C. Sup. Ct., Whittaker J., 1957).
[88] *Thibodeau v Cleff*, 24 O.L.R. 214 (Div. Ct., 1911), *Agensini v Olsen*, 277 App. Div. 1006, 100 N.Y.S. 2d. 338 (App. Div. 2nd Dept., 1950).
[89] *Goreley v Codd* [1967] 1 W.L.R. 19, *Court v Wyatt, The Times*, June 24, 1960.
[90] *Zuckerbrod v Burch* 88 N.J. Super. 1, 210 A. 2d. 425 (Sup. Ct. App. Div., 1965).
[91] McMahon & Binchy, *op. cit.*, pp. 653, 668.

establishes that there was an act physically constituting trespass, the onus then falls to the defendant to prove that he did not have the requisite state of mind. The trespass must be voluntary, as was found in *O'Brien v McNamee*[92] where a seven-year-old carried a lighted paper into a neighbour's barn, leading to its destruction. Davitt P. held that as no intention was required for the tort of trespass, the act merely had to be "voluntary", even though the child would not have appreciated the danger of his actions. In contrast, if the child had been carried into the barn, rather than walking in on his own, he would not have trespassed.

1–61   The Law Reform Commission has considered how comparable the voluntary nature of a child's act is to that of an adult.[93] The Commission argued that it is unrealistic to impute the same quality of voluntariness to a young child as to an adult who is differently aware of the dangers and implications of a "voluntary" act. The Commission therefore suggested a test similar to that used for negligence:

> "that in proceedings against a child under sixteen for trespass where it has been established that the child's action is voluntary and intentional, liability should be imposed unless the child can show, to the satisfaction of the Court, that, having regard to his or her age, mental development and experience, he or she had not such personal responsibility for the action that it would be just to impose liability on the child for the action."[94]

1–62   The onus of showing that ordinary standards should not apply is therefore placed on the child who wants to rely on this.

The Commission also considered torts involving malice such as defamation or malicious prosecution did not require reform as they did not usually involve minors.

Occupiers' liability

1–63   The occupier of a premises is obliged to take reasonable precautions in terms of the general condition of the premises. This is termed occupiers' liability and is largely governed by the Occupiers' Liability Act 1995, which Act was signed by the President and came into force on July 17, 1995. It constituted a sweeping reformation of the existing law at that time and created three new categories of entrants: visitors, recreational users and trespassers.

1–64   A visitor is a person whose presence on the premises is lawful. The term covers those invited onto a premises by an occupier as well as those permitted by the occupier to be there. The status of visitor is conferred by

---

[92] [1953] I.R. 86.

[93] Law Reform Commission, *Report on the Liability in Torts of Minors and the Liability of Parents for Damage Caused by Minors* (Law Reform Commission, Dublin, 1985).

[94] See the previous discussion of the Law Reform Commission recommendations in relation to the question of minors' liability in negligence and contributory negligence.

virtue of the purpose of the visit. Section 3 of the 1995 Act establishes the duty of care which is owed by occupiers' of premises to visitors. In summary, the duty is the "common duty of care". Consequently, there is an obligation on the occupier to take reasonable care to ensure that the visitor does not suffer personal injury or damage to his or her property, as a result of any danger existing on the premises. The discharge of this duty is facilitated by the use of a notice on the premises identifying the hazards on the premises. Regard will be had, however, "to the care which a visitor may reasonably be expected to take for his or her own safety and, if the visitor is on the premises in the company of another person, the extent of the supervision and control the latter person may reasonably be expected to exercise over the visitor's activities".[95] This section would apply to children who are visitors under the control of their parents or other person. The test reflects the expectation that parents or other minders of children have primary responsibility for ensuring their safety. For example, on school tours (discussed in Chapter 3), the expectation is that teachers accompanying the children will exercise a reasonable level of supervision. However, the protection afforded to the occupier may be limited, as the courts have traditionally been reluctant to relieve an occupier of any duty of care towards a child, particularly in the event of serious injury.

1–65 Recreational users are those persons who, without payment of any charge, enter onto premises to engage in a recreational activity which is carried out in the open air. A trespasser is defined in s.1(1) of the 1995 Act as an entrant other than a recreational user or visitor. Section 4(1) of the 1995 Act provides that an occupier owes recreational users or trespassers on a premises a restricted duty not to impose injury or cause injury to be imposed on them. Further, he owes them a duty not to damage their property intentionally and not to act with reckless disregard for them or their property unless, and in so far as, the occupier has extended his duty in accordance with s.5 of the 1995 Act. Section 4(2)(i) (which broadly mirrors s.3(2) of the 1995 Act) transfers some responsibility to parents and guardians (who are either recreational users or trespassers) in the care and control of children, which has the practical implication of reducing, however slight, the onus or duty of a care on occupiers. The 1995 Act does not state that an occupier owes a child a common duty of care. Nor does it mention that the occupier is strictly liable for whatever accident may befall such an entrant. Indeed, the Act introduced additional criteria which make it clear that in circumstances where a child is on the premises and is in the company of another person, the extent of the supervision and control which that person might reasonably be expected to exercise over the child's activities will be relevant in determining whether an occupier is liable.

Modification of occupiers' duties to entrants

1–66 Section 5(2) of the 1995 Act provides that an occupier may restrict, modify or exclude his duty towards visitors. In effect, by complying with the

---

[95] s.3(2) of the 1995 Act.

section, occupiers may reduce the duties they owe to visitors to the level owed to recreational users and trespassers. The duty owing to a visitor may never fall below that owing to recreational users or trespassers. In summary, an occupier is precluded from excluding liability.

1–67 Under s.5(2)(b) a modification or exclusion *shall not* be binding on a visitor unless: (1) it is reasonable in all the circumstances, and (2) the occupier has taken reasonable steps to bring the notice to the attention of the visitor. An occupier shall be presumed, unless the contrary is shown, to have taken reasonable steps to bring a notice to the attention of a visitor if it is prominently displayed at the normal means of access to the premises.

1–68 Section 5(5) of the 1995 Act has particular relevance to children. It provides:

> "Where injury or damage is caused to a visitor or property of a visitor by a danger of which the visitor has been warned by the occupier or another person, the warning is not, without more, to be treated as absolving the occupier from liability unless, in all the circumstances, it was enough to enable the visitor, by having regard to the warning, to avoid the injury or damage so caused."

It would appear from the foregoing that a permanently displayed notice may not be sufficient in the case of younger children who cannot read or understand the significance of such warnings.

1–69 The effect of a proper notice, assuming it is effective and binding, can only operate to reduce the duty of care owed to visitors to that lower and more restricted duty which is owed to recreational users and trespassers. In *Baldwin v Foy and Forest Way Riding Holdings Ltd*,[96] Laffoy J. considered two notices posted up at a premises. The first notice from the Association of Irish Riding Establishments stated that the Association did not accept liability for any accident arising out of the operation of the riding establishment. The second notice stated:

> "Riding is a risk sport. Your choice to ride is voluntary. We take care to provide suitable and safe horses and ponies for our customers, but all animals can be unpredictable. We strongly advise you to take out full personal accident cover."

1–70 Laffoy J. held that the foregoing notices did not exclude liability for negligence. It would appear therefore that any notice placed on a premises attempting to reduce the liability of occupiers from the common law duty of care to the reckless disregard standard must be clear, unambiguous and specific.

---

[96] unreported, High Court, Laffoy J., July 1, 1997.

1–71   As a matter of general observation, occupiers do not appear to have utilised the possible benefits to them of the 1995 Act. It may be the case that as occupiers become more aware of the benefits available under the Act, perhaps through the passage of time or the public attention consequent on a future High Court case, this will change.

Guidelines for drafting a notice restricting liability under the Occupiers' Liability Act 1995

1–72   Notices should clearly specify the relevant information. This includes identifying the category of entrant and what duty the occupier intends to exclude. It is clear from s.5(3) of the Occupiers' Liability Act 1995 that the effect of a proper notice can only operate to reduce the duty of care owed to visitors to that lower and more restricted duty which is owed to recreational users and trespassers.[97]

MINORS AND LICENCES

1–73   The inexperience and immaturity of minors is recognised in limitations imposed by the law in the application for licenses. Statutes impose explicit or implicit restriction on young people applying for driving licences and liquor licences. However, other legislation has not addressed the possibility of minors applying for a license.

Driving licences

1–74   The ages at which people can obtain provisional and full driving licences for different categories of vehicles have been defined by regulations made under Pt III of the Road Traffic Act 1961.[98] Sixteen is the minimum age for Classes A1, M and W:

> A1   motor cycles with an engine capacity not exceeding 125 cubic centimetres and with a power rating not exceeding 11 kilowatts;[99]
>
> M   mopeds;
>
> W   work vehicles and land tractors.

Seventeen is the prescribed minimum age for Classes B and EB:

> B   vehicles (other than motorcycles, mopeds, work vehicles or land tractors) having a design gross vehicle weight not exceeding 3,500

---

[97] See Appendix 3 for sample notice.

[98] Road Traffic (Licensing of Drivers) Regulations 1999, S.I. No 352 of 1999, Art.8.

[99] Road Traffic (Licensing of Drivers) (Amendment) Regulations 1999, S.I. No. 366 of 1999 establish the general rule that first-time provisional licence holders will be restricted to riding motor cycles not exceeding 25kw engine power until two years after taking out a full licence in Category A.

kg, and having passenger accommodation for not more than eight persons;

EB combinations of vehicles with drawing vehicles in category B.

All other categories of vehicle require the licence applicant to be at least 18 years of age.

Liquor licensing

1–75 Section 20 of the Excise Management Act 1827 provides that no entry of licensed premises into the General Entry Book can be made in the name of a person less than 21 years of age. Further, a minor is implicitly excluded from holding a licence, as an applicant must clearly be involved in the management, supervision and control of the business[100] and this is precluded by restrictions on the employment of young people and their presence on licensed premises.[101] If a minor were to inherit an enterprise involving a liquor licence, it appears that a nominee may not apply to hold the licence on his or her behalf.[102] If this were to happen, the premises and licence would have to be put in the name of the executor or other trustee until the heir reached the age of majority.

Casual trading licenses

1–76 The granting of casual trading licences devolves to local authorities by virtue of the Casual Trading Act 1995. There is no requirement for age in s.4, which deals with licences. However, s.4(1)(a) provides the granting authority with a wide discretion to prescribe the form of the application and the information required. For example, the Dublin City Council issues two types of licence, one on an annual basis and one for events. While neither application has an age limit, each requires a Personal Public Service (PPS) number, which most children do not have until entry into the taxation system through employment, although the number may be allocated at any age. While the Civil Registration Act 2004 provides for the allocation of a PPS number to every new born baby upon registration of its birth, the past use of the PPS number was no guarantee that an applicant for a casual trading licence was over 18.

Charitable collections and charitable trading

1–77 The Street and House to House Collections Act 1962 governing charitable collections does not specify an age limit under which people may not apply for a permit. The regulations[103] introduced pursuant to the Act require

---

[100] C. Cassidy, *The Licensing Acts* (Thomson Round Hall, Dublin, 2001), para.3.20.7.
[101] See Pt IV of the Intoxicating Liquor Act 1988, also McGrath, *Liquor Licensing Law* (Butterworths, Dublin, 2001), p.869.
[102] Finance Act 1992, s.242.
[103] Street and House to House Collections (Prescribed Forms) Regulations 1962, S.I. No. 134 of 1962.

basic information about the applicant and organisation to be included in the application for a licence. That said, the issuer of the permit is the Garda Chief Superintendent of the area in which the collection is to be made, and he or she may attach conditions, or refuse a permit on discretionary grounds. This discretion could conceivably cover an application from a child. Under s.15, children under the age of 14 are prohibited from collecting and to allow them to do so is an offence. However, there have been no reports of the absence of an age limit presenting a problem in practice.[104]

A casual trading licence is not required for charitable trading.[105] Accordingly, charitable fundraisers selling anything do not need a permit. Such charitable fundraisers can be of any age.

Children's succession rights

1–78   The vulnerability of children is particularly apparent on the death of a parent or guardian. Further, the succession rights of children can cause difficulty in the distribution of a parent's estate. The primary reason for this is the competing right to succession of the deceased's spouse.

1–79   The Succession Act 1965 sets out mostly non-discretionary rules of intestate succession,[106] adapting approaches developed in other jurisdictions. The intestacy rules have been influenced by the prevailing philosophy that a surviving spouse should remain financially independent in his or her existing home, or an alternative. However, the primacy given to the surviving spouse can have serious implications where the children are still young.

1–80   Part VI of the Succession Act 1965 deals with intestacy, providing that the estate of a deceased person is divided between a surviving spouse, if any, and the deceased's children, or their children if the deceased's children have died before the deceased.[107] Since the Status of Children Act 1987 came into effect, non-marital children have the same rights to inheritance as children born in a marriage. Further, adopted children have the same rights as natural children under the Adoption Act 1952. However, step-children and other children to whom the deceased was *in loco parentis* are not regarded as having the same rights.

1–81   Succession rights on the death of a testator are governed by Pt IX of the Succession Act 1965, as amended. Section 111 provides a minimum entitlement for a spouse but none for the children. Should the deceased have children, the surviving spouse is entitled to one-third of the estate, even if no provision or a lesser provision was made in the will. Should the deceased die without children, the spouse's legal share is one half.

---

[104] See Law Society's Law Reform Committee, *Charity Law: The Case for Reform* (Law Society of Ireland, 2002), p.167.

[105] See s.2(2) of the Casual Trading Act 1995.

[106] s.56(10) affords an element of discretion to enable a widowed spouse to retain the family home.

[107] s.67(2).

1–82 Regardless of the mode of inheritance, the surviving spouse is entitled to require his or her home and household chattels, if part of the estate of the deceased, to be appropriated to his or her share of the estate. Should that share not be sufficient, he or she may also require the share of any infant for whom he or she is a trustee to be appropriated also.[108] Thus the entitlements of the surviving spouse will impact on the property remaining for the children.

Provision for children on application to the court under s.117

1–83 Section 117(1) of the Succession Act 1965, as amended, allows a child who has not been properly provided for by a deceased parent to apply to the court for a discretionary award from the estate, where the court is of the opinion that the testator failed in his or her moral duty. The court must consider the application from the point of view of a prudent and just parent, taking into account all the circumstances to be as fair as possible to all the children.[109] However, such an application cannot affect the entitlement or legal share of the surviving spouse.[110] The rationale underpinning this is that a surviving natural parent owes a moral obligation to provide for the child. A child will have a right to claim under s.117 if the surviving spouse is a step-parent or if the child is a non-marital child of the deceased, unless the step-parent's legal right share would be affected.

1–84 An application under s.117 must be made within six months from the first taking out of representation of the deceased's estate,[111] the period for which cannot be extended. Although this has the advantage of speeding up the administration of estates, there is some concern that such a short period can lead to injustice, especially for young children whose lack of capacity and experience may leave them ignorant of their rights under the Act and the time limit. This may be exacerbated by a conflict between the child and the personal representative or carer for the child. A Supreme Court decision on a comparable subsection[112] of the Civil Liability Act 1961 has raised doubts over the compatibility of s.117 with the Constitution. This is particularly in regard to the lack of flexibility in the time limit and the absence of a duty on the part of the personal representative to notify possible claimants. In *O'Brien v Keogh*,[113] the Supreme Court considered a provision where the ordinary limitation period for the making of a personal injury compensation claim on behalf of a child

---

[108] s.56.

[109] s.117(2). Cases dealing with s.117(2) include: *Browne v Sweeney and McCarthy* [1998] 4 I.R. 527; *D.E.B. v D.E.B.* [1991] 2 I.R. 105; *B.(S.) (orse M.(S.)) v Bank of Ireland*, unreported, High Court, Blayney J., July 27, 1988; *C. & F. v (C.(W.) & C.(T.)* [1990] 2 I.R. 143, [1989] I.L.R.M. 815; *B.(E.) v S.(S.) & G.(McC)* [1998] 4 I.R. 553, [1998] 2 I.L.R.M. 141; *MacDonald v Norris* [1999] 4 I.R. 313, [2000] 1 I.L.R.M. 382; *C.(K.) & F.(B.C.) v F.(C.)*, unreported, High Court, Carroll J., December 16, 2003; *S.(D.) v M.(K.) & D.*, unreported, High Court, Carroll J., December 19, 2003.

[110] s.117(3).

[111] Family Law (Divorce) Act 1996, s.46.

[112] s.49(2)(a)(ii).

[113] [1972] I.R. 144.

could only be extended where the child was without a parent or guardian to act for him. The Supreme Court held this to be unconstitutional in that it failed to adequately protect the interests of the child in circumstances where there could be a conflict of interest between the parent or guardian, and the child. This decision raises strong arguments in favour of greater safeguards for children being incorporated into the Succession Act.

1–85   The changing nature of the family also provides challenges for the Succession Act. At present, foster children, step-children and grandchildren dependent on the deceased do not have succession rights, nor are they entitled to institute proceedings under s.117 of the Succession Act 1965. Assisted conception techniques, such as surrogacy and artificial insemination, also present challenges.

CONCLUSION

1–86   The Courts will not look favourably on those who take advantage of others unable to protect themselves, as evidenced by the extensive body of legislation and case law developed to protect children. The law, particularly in the areas of contract and employment, imposes obligations on those dealing with children to ensure that they are not unfairly disadvantaged or exploited due to their immaturity and lack of experience. However, restrictions are also placed on children, with limitations in their ability to enter into certain contracts, marriage and some licences before they are ready for the responsibility entailed in such actions. Further, depending on factors such as age and intent, a child may be liable in areas of tort such as trespass and negligence. One of the earliest lessons to be learned by the child is that with rights, come responsibilities.

Guardianship, Custody, Welfare and Access: Protecting the Welfare of the Child in Family Disputes

2–01   By virtue of s.11 of the Guardianship of Infants Act 1964,[1] any guardian of a child may apply to the court for an order on any question relating to the welfare of that child. A child, for these purposes, is defined in s.2 of the 1964 Act as "a person who has not attained full age". By virtue of s.2 of the Age of Majority Act 1985,[2] a person reaches full age at 18. Once its jurisdiction has been invoked, the court may make such order relating to the welfare of the child in question as it thinks proper. Typically, such an order would concern guardianship and custody of, or rights of access to, the child. Any order made is interlocutory in nature as s.12 of the 1964 Act allows such an order to be varied or discharged (see District Court Rules 1997, Ord.58, r.6).

The Court may also make an order requiring either the father or mother to make such maintenance payments as it considers reasonable.[3] In determining the level of payment, however, the court must have regard to the means of the parent making the payment. It seems also that there is no provision in the Act for the making of a lump sum payment; s.11(2)(b) refers only to a "weekly or other periodical sum".

2–02   An order may be made under s.11 even if both parents, at the time the order is made, reside together. However, such an order shall not be enforceable and no liability shall attach or accrue from it for so long as the parents of the child in question continue to cohabit.[4] Indeed, should the parents continue to reside together for a period of at least three months after an order under s.11 is made, that order will cease to have effect.

2–03   While the legislation, at first glance, refers to a "father" and "mother" respectively, it is clear that the precise relative legal rights of each party depend on the status of their relationship. Where the parties are married at the time of the child's birth, both are conferred with joint and equal guardianship rights.[5] Where the parents are not married, rather different considerations apply. While

---

[1] No. 7 of 1964, hereinafter "the 1964 Act". See District Court Rules 1997, Ord. 58, r.5.
[2] No. 2 of 1985.
[3] s.11(2)(b).
[4] s.11(3).
[5] See s.6 of the Guardianship of Infants Act 1964.

the natural mother of a child is deemed automatically to be his or her guardian, a natural father, who is not the husband of the mother, is not considered to be a guardian unless one of three conditions is met:[6]

(i) a man, who is not married to the mother of his child at the time of its birth, may subsequently acquire guardianship by marriage to the aforementioned mother;

(ii) alternatively, the natural father may apply to the court under s.6A of the 1964 Act (inserted by s.12 of the Status of Children Act 1987) for an order conferring on him the status of guardianship;[7]

(iii) the third, and probably simplest option, is for the parties, by agreement, to make a statutory declaration stating that while not married to each other, they are indeed father and mother respectively of the child in question, and that they have agreed that the natural father should be appointed guardian. The father must be registered as father on the birth certificate of the child in question to utilise this procedure.[8] Such a declaration must be made in the form prescribed by the Guardianship of Children (Statutory Declaration) Regulations 1998.[9] The parties must, furthermore, have made arrangements regarding the custody of and/or access to, the child in question.

2–04 In fact, the term "father" as used in the Act is deemed by s.2 generally to exclude (with certain exceptions) "the father of a child who has not married that child's mother". That said, even where the natural father does not have guardianship rights, he may nonetheless apply to the court (by virtue of s.11(4) of the 1964 Act—see District Court Rules 1997, Ord.58, r.5) for an order regarding the custody of, or access to, his natural child. Thus, notwithstanding s.2, a reference in s.11 to the father or parent of a child may indeed include the non-marital father of a child, although it seems that such person may only apply for an order of custody or access. The Act seems to preclude such person from applying for an order of maintenance in respect of the child.

Welfare

2–05 The meaning of the term "welfare", for the purposes of the Guardianship of Infants Act 1964, is quite widely defined. It includes, according to s.2, the religious, moral, intellectual, physical and social welfare of the child in question. Section 3 of the Act makes it abundantly clear that in considering an application relating to the guardianship, custody or upbringing of a child, or to the administration of property belonging to, or held in trust for, that child, or to the application of the income of the child, the court must have regard to the

---

[6] See further below at para.2–43.
[7] See *K. v W.* [1990] I.L.R.M. 121 and *W. O'R v E.H.* [1996] 2 I.R. 248.
[8] See s.2(4) of the 1964 Act.
[9] S.I. No. 5 of 1998.

welfare of the child. This, the section states, is "the first and paramount consideration". It is not the only relevant consideration, but it is, apparently, the most important. In the course of his judgment in *G. v An Bord Uchtála*,[10] Walsh J. stated as follows:

> "The word 'paramount' by itself is not by any means an indication of exclusivity: no doubt if the Oireachtas had intended the welfare of the child to be the sole consideration it would have said so. The use of the word 'paramount' certainly indicates that the welfare of the child is to be the superior or the most important consideration, in so far as it can be, having regard to the law or the provisions of the Constitution applicable to any given case."[11]

2–06 The ostensible rule then (although this has been qualified by the constitutional preference for the marital family),[12] is that where there is a conflict between the welfare of the child and other considerations (such as the rights of parents), the welfare of the child takes precedence over all other matters. This is sometimes known as the "best interests test", although s.3 refers specifically to the welfare of the child.[13] The principle that the best interests of the child must take precedence in all matters concerning the child's welfare, is in line with Ireland's international obligations, in particular with the UN Convention on the Rights of the Child 1989.[14] O'Flaherty J., in applying this principle in *Southern Health Board v C.H.*,[15] stated that:

> "It is easy to comprehend that the child's welfare must always be of far graver concern to the court. We must, as judges, always harken to the constitutional command which mandates, as a prime consideration, the interests of the child in any legal proceedings."

Later in his judgment, O'Flaherty J. observed that "the first point to note about this case is that the judge is in essence required to inquire as to what is in the best interests of the child".

2–07 For the purposes of clarity, the various constituent factors making up the concept of welfare shall be dealt with in turn. This is not to suggest that each of these factors must of necessity be considered in a vacuum. As noted by Walsh J. in *M.D.D.S. v P.D.O.S.*,[16] it is essential that the court consider all

---

[10] [1980] I.R. 32 at 76.
[11] See also the dicta of McDermott L.J. considering the corresponding English provision in *J. v C.* [1970] A.C. 668 and Henchy J. in *MacD. v MacD.* (1979) 114 I.L.T.R. 66.
[12] See Chap.1 and below at para.2–26.
[13] See Walsh J. in *G. v An Bord Uchtála, op. cit.* at 76, who appears to suggest that the two terms may differ in meaning in certain contexts. It is submitted, with utmost respect, that the distinction suggested is perhaps rather fine.
[14] The UN Convention on the Rights of the Child 1989 was ratified by Ireland on September 21, 1992.
[15] [1996] 2 I.L.R.M. 142.
[16] (1974) 110 I.L.T.R. 57.

of these factors collectively and as a whole, rather than as a series of distinct matters:

> "[A]ll the ingredients which the Act stipulates ... are to be considered globally. This is not ... to be decided by the simple method of totting up the marks which may be awarded under each of the five headings. It is the totality of the picture presented which must be considered ... the word 'welfare' must be taken in its widest sense."[17]

The opinion of Walsh J. was cited with approval by McGuinness J. in *C.(C.) v C.(P.)*,[18] the latter reiterating the need to adopt an overall view of the child's welfare.[19]

Religious welfare

2–08   In determining the matter of custody, the court must have regard to the religious upbringing of the child. Generally, the courts have proved anxious not to disturb the religious and moral formation of the child in question. Thus, the courts have often refused to give custody to a parent who was in a relationship with a person of a religious persuasion different to that of the child. In this respect the courts have an unenviable task to perform. On the one hand, they must be seen to respect the initial decision of the parents regarding the child's religious upbringing. On the other hand, it can hardly be regarded as acceptable that a person will be denied custody of a child on the basis, even in part, of their religious persuasion. Here, as in other areas, one detects the serious tension between the constitutional preference for the promotion of free practice of religion, and the constitutional rule against discrimination on the basis of religious profession, status or belief.[20]

2–09   A different religious inclination is not, however, an absolute bar to custody. One possible solution is to grant custody subject to a condition as to religious upbringing. In *Cullen v Cullen*,[21] a mother was granted custody of her child notwithstanding the husband's assertion that this would be to the detriment of the child's religious welfare. The mother, at the time of the order, was not an active member of the church in which the child was being reared. She nonetheless had promised the court that she would ensure that the child in question would receive religious instruction and formation, in particular that he would "say his prayers."

---

[17] See also the *dicta* of Finlay P. in *MacD. v MacD.* (1979) 114 I.L.T.R. 66.

[18] [1994] 3 Fam. L.J. 85.

[19] See also *D.F. O'S. v C.A.*, unreported, High Court, McGuinness J., April 20, 1999.

[20] Article 44.2.1° and 44.2.3° respectively. See *Quinn's Supermarket v A.G.* [1972] I.R. 1; *McGrath and O Ruairc v Maynooth College* [1979] I.L.R.M. 166; *Campaign to Separate Church and State v Ireland* [1998] 3 I.R. 321, all of which seem to suggest a preference for buttressing the free practice of religion.

[21] unreported, Supreme Court, May 8, 1970.

2–10   In *MacD. v MacD.*,[22] the Supreme Court granted custody of a child being reared as a Roman Catholic to his Protestant mother. The mother, furthermore, was at the time residing with a Protestant man. The Supreme Court accepted the mother's agreement that she would bring the child up as a Roman Catholic, despite her and her partner's religious preferences. It is hard, nonetheless, to dispute the fact, as noted in Griffin J.'s dissent, that despite the best intentions of the mother, it is difficult in the extreme to raise a child in a faith for which one has little enthusiasm or appreciation. This concern is tempered somewhat by the provision of access to the father, during which time the latter would have the opportunity to monitor and supplement the children's religious formation. Barron J. in *A.H.S. v M.S.*[23] hinted at a similar solution, suggesting (albeit *obiter*) that there would be no difficulty with a father professing the Islamic faith bringing up his child as a Roman Catholic. Ultimately, custody was awarded to the child's Roman Catholic mother, although religious persuasion seems not to have been of significance in this regard.

2–11   It is suggested then, and with respect to the religious sensibilities of the parties involved, that this factor must be considered in the light of the overall welfare of the child. It is obvious, for instance, that a parent who is otherwise unsuited to have custody of a child, should not be allowed to use religious difference as a "trump card", displacing all other considerations.

Moral welfare

2–12   In addition to his or her spiritual well-being, the court should have regard to the appropriate moral formation of the child. Formerly, it was considered that where a parent was residing with a person not his or her spouse, the lifestyle of such parent was not conducive to the moral welfare of the child. In *J.J.W. v B.M.W.*,[24] for instance, the Supreme Court refused to award custody of three children to a woman who had committed adultery. By virtue of her conduct, the court believed that the father was the party more likely to safeguard the children's welfare than the mother. Fitzgerald J. observed that:

> "The fact is, however, that the home which [the mother] has to offer to her children is one in which she continues an adulterous association with a man who has deserted his own wife and his own two children. A more unhealthy abode for the three ... children would be difficult to imagine."[25]

It is not at all clear how the mere fact of a parent's marital status affects the moral sensibilities of the child. It is suggested, with respect, that the opinion expressed by the learned Chief Justice betrays an overly narrow view of moral well-being, one unduly focused on sexual matters, to the virtual exclusion of

---

[22] (1979) 114 I.L.T.R. 59.
[23] unreported, High Court, Barron J., November 12, 1982.
[24] (1971) reported in (1976) 110 I.L.T.R. 45.
[25] *ibid.* at 52. See also *S. v S.* [1992] I.L.R.M. 732.

more general considerations of morality. Indeed, of late, the courts have tended to veer away from attributing moral unworthiness to parties in second relationships following marriages. In particular, the courts have accepted that custody cannot be seen as a prize for a wholesome and chaste sexual lifestyle. This more circumspect attitude is evidenced by the decision of Walsh J. in *E.K. v M.K.*,[26] where he observed that:

> "... custody is awarded not as a mark of approbation or disapprobation of paternal conduct but solely as a judicial determination of where the welfare of the children lies."

2–13   In *M.O'B. v P.O'B.*,[27] Kenny J. remarked in a similar vein that "an award of custody is not reward for good behaviour". This tendency has become more marked with the passage of time. In *S. v S.*,[28] Finlay C.J. in the Supreme Court stated that the conduct of the parents is relevant only in so far as it affects the welfare of the child.[29]

A similar tendency has evolved in Britain, if not yet in Ireland, in relation to parents living in same-sex (homosexual) relationships. At one point it seemed that a homosexual or transsexual orientation was, in practice, virtually a complete bar to custody.[30] In *Re T., petitioner*,[31] however, a Scottish court made an order of adoption notwithstanding the fact that the adopting party was living with his male partner in a homosexual relationship.[32] In fact, Lord Clyde of the British House of Lords has gone so far as to approve a reference to such a union (albeit *obiter*) as constituting a "family".[33]

It is again suggested that, although the moral welfare of children remains a factor of importance, considerations of moral propriety cannot displace the overall function of the court in determining what solution is in the best interests of the child.

Intellectual welfare

2–14   This factor concerns the educational and intellectual prospects of the child. That is not to say, however, that the court must award custody to the more learned or better-educated parent. The court must endeavour to ensure that its decision, as best it can, ensures that the child will have adequate opportunities for education and formation as best promote the child's development towards adulthood. It is suggested, in this connection, that the

---

[26] unreported, Supreme Court, July 31, 1974.

[27] unreported, High Court, Kenny J., January 5, 1971.

[28] [1992] I.L.R.M. 732.

[29] Although he did add that such conduct is relevant in considering the priorities of the parents in relation to the child. See also *P.C. v C.G.*, unreported, High Court, Ellis J., July 1983.

[30] See for instance *Re D. (Consent to Adoption)* [1977] A.C. 602; *C. v C. (Custody Appeal)* [1991] 1 F.L.R. 223, CA.

[31] (1997) S.L.T. 724.

[32] See also *Re W. (A minor)* [1998] Fam. L.J. 58.

[33] *Fitzpatrick v Sterling Housing Association* [1999] 3 W.L.R. 1113 at 1135.

term "education" comprises not merely the formal instruction of a child in intellectual matters, but also his or her general formation as a responsible and competent adult. Where intellectual or psychological welfare is at issue, the practitioner should always adduce professional evidence from a child psychologist in establishing where the psychological welfare lies.

Physical welfare

2–15 A further consideration is the extent to which the order of the court will promote the physical well-being and health of a child. The courts have tended, in this regard, to consider, at least in relation to a child of "tender years" (approximately seven years old or younger), that physical welfare is best served by the mother.[34] More recent cases, however, have tended to dilute this inclination, although the courts continue generally to regard the mother, all else being equal, as the more appropriate and competent care-giver.[35]

Social welfare

2–16 This final factor relates to the social formation of children. It is perhaps best explained by a quote from Finlay P. in *J.C. v O.C.*[36] as "… their capacity to mix with and enter into and become part of the society in which they will be brought up...." The learned judge noted in particular that the social development of siblings tends best to be promoted by their remaining as part of one residential unit.[37]

OTHER RELEVANT CONSIDERATIONS

2–17 No individual factor can, in itself, be considered conclusive. This was highlighted by Walsh J. in his judgment in *S. v S.*[38] which was quoted favourably by McGuinness J in *C.C. v P.C.*,[39] wherein the learned judge stressed the merits of assuming an overall view:

> "[A]ll the ingredients which the Act stipulates are to be considered globally. This is not to be decided by the simple method of totting up the marks which may be awarded under each of the five headings. It is the totality of the picture presented which must be considered … the word "welfare" must be taken in its widest sense."[40]

---

[34] See further below at para.2–19.
[35] See dicta of McGuinness J. in *D.F. O'S. v C.A.*, unreported, High Court, McGuinness J., April 20, 1999 and the discussion below at para.2–20.
[36] unreported, High Court, July 10, 1980.
[37] See further the discussion concerning the desirability of "keeping siblings together" below, para.2–25.
[38] (1974) 110 I.L.T.R. 57.
[39] [1994] 3 Fam. L.J. 85.
[40] See also *D.F.O'S. v C.A.*, unreported, High Court, McGuinness J., April 20, 1999.

The welfare of a child must be judged by reference to all relevant matters. While the welfare of the child, as defined by the Guardianship of Infants Act 1964, is deemed to be a paramount consideration, it is nonetheless possible (and sometimes necessary) to look outside the strict confines of the definition in s.2 of the 1964 Act. Other factors have been found relevant to the consideration of the court and are discussed below.

Emotional welfare

2–18   A factor not mentioned in the 1964 Act, but nonetheless of importance, is the question of emotional welfare. This was highlighted most recently by the decision of McGuinness J. in *D.F.O'S. v C.A.*[41] There the learned judge, referring to supporting precedent, noted the recognition of this added factor.[42] This "most important aspect of welfare", though not explicitly mentioned in the 1964 Act, should be taken into account in determining applications under the Act. In the instant case, McGuinness J. suggested that the emotional welfare of the child would be better served by their attending counselling sessions.

"Tender years" principle

2–19   It has generally been accepted where a child is of "tender years" (generally under the age of seven), that, all else being equal, the child in question should reside in the custody of its mother. In *B. v B.*,[43] for instance, O Dálaigh C.J. ruled that "… in view of his tender age, there can be no doubt that the younger son [of the parties] should continue in the custody of his mother."

The more generally applicable comments of Budd J. in *B. v B.*[44] reveal the reasoning behind the court's decision noting that "young children are notoriously nearer to their mother than their father".[45] His later comments seem to suggest that he believed that only the mother in that case could attend to her son's physical needs and give him the attention he needs. Indeed, at one point, the principle seemed to have evolved into something approaching a presumption of law.[46] In *H. v H.*,[47] Parke J. noted the "ample judicial support" for the proposition that "a child of tender years should be entrusted to the custody of his mother unless she has so gravely failed in her duty as a mother as to forfeit such right". In *MacD. v MacD.*,[48] Henchy J. expressed the preference for the mother as follows:

> "In the case of very young children … the person *prima facie* entitled to their custody, where the parents are estranged, is the mother, for by reason

---

[41] unreported, High Court, April 20, 1999.
[42] See also *M.B. O'S. v P.D. O'S.* (1974) 110 I.L.T.R. 57; *MacD. v MacD.* (1979) 114 I.L.T.R. 66, *per* Griffin J.; *S. v S.* [1992] I.L.R.M. 732.
[43] [1975] I.R. 54 at 59.
[44] *ibid.* at 67.
[45] See also his comments, *ibid.* at 70.
[46] See also the dicta of Walsh J. in *E.K. v M.K.*, unreported, Supreme Court, July 31, 1974.
[47] unreported, High Court, Parke J., February 4, 1976.
[48] (1979) 114 I.L.T.R. 66.

of her motherhood she will usually be the person primarily and uniquely capable of ministering to their welfare".

2–20 In more recent times, however, this approach has been somewhat more restrained. It is arguable that this principle, besides compounding gender stereotypes, ignores the growing prevalence and acceptance of men who play an enhanced parenting role in their respective families. In fact the principle is not invariable, and in light of changing parenting patterns the courts have proved increasingly willing, as in *J.J.W. v B.M.W.*,[49] to make an order of custody relating even to young children in favour of their father. In this regard, a recent dictum of McGuinness J. is most instructive. In *D.F.O'S. v C.A.*,[50] the learned judge, in deciding to grant joint custody of a four-year old child, noted that she:

> "... [did] not entirely accept the old *tender years* principle: modern views and practices of parenting show the virtues of shared parenting and the older principles too often meant the automatic granting of custody to the mother virtually to the exclusion of the father".

Parental capacity

2–21 The question of parental capacity is closely allied to the last factor, although it relies on the surer footing of individual characteristics rather than resorting to crude gender stereotypes. The court is required to ensure that the parent being granted guardianship, custody or access has sufficient mental and physical resources to perform the duties envisaged. This is not to say that the more capable spouse will always be granted custody. Nor should it suggest that parents with needs of their own, owing for instance to disabilities, should be denied custody. In *E. v E.*[51] and *A.H.S. v M.S.*,[52] for instance, custody was granted to women who, despite a history of mental illness, were shown to have overcome their difficulties to an extent sufficient to allow their having custody.[53]

Where a parent, however, is manifestly incapable of carrying out this role, the court will lean heavily against such an order. In *C.(C.) v C.(P.)*,[54] McGuinness J. declined to make an order of custody in favour of a father. The evidence showed that the roles of child and parent had largely reversed in this case. In response to his father's difficulties, the child, it seemed, had taken on the role of parent, generally looking out for and protecting his father. In such a case there was a danger, in the judge's words, of the child becoming "parentified", of taking on the mantle of responsibility for a family well before his time.

---

[49] (1971) 110 I.L.T.R. 49.
[50] unreported, High Court, McGuinness J., April 20, 1999.
[51] unreported, High Court, February 3, 1977.
[52] unreported, High Court, November 12, 1982.
[53] Although in the former case the order was made subject to subsequent review.
[54] [1994] 3 Fam. L.J. 1985.

The wishes of the child

2–22   Considering that the court must act in the best interests of a child who is the subject of an application under the 1964 Act, it seems self-evident that where the child is of sufficient age and maturity, the court should have regard to his or her wishes. This should especially be so where a child harbours a particular animosity towards a particular parent. Indeed, s.25 of the 1964 Act[55] allows the court, where it thinks appropriate and practicable with regard to the age and understanding of the child, to take account of his or her wishes in any proceedings to which s.3 of the 1964 Act relates:

> "In any proceedings to which section 3 [of the 1964 Act] applies, the Court shall, as it thinks appropriate and practicable having regard to the age and understanding of the child, take into account the child's wishes in the matter."

This will generally be done only where the child is of sufficient age and maturity. In *Cullen v Cullen*[56] for instance, the wishes of a 17-year-old girl seemed to have played a significant part in the decision of the court to award custody to her mother. Similarly, in *P.C. v C.G. (No.2)*,[57] the court refused an application for custody by the mother of a 13-year-old boy, Ellis J. noting the strong preference of the latter to remain in the care of his father.[58]

2–23   Some care is needed, however, to ensure that impressionable children are not unduly influenced by a parent. The case of *J.C. v O.C.*[59] concerned the custody of three young children, aged 11, nine and five respectively. The father argued that if the children were interviewed, they would, most likely, be subject to the persuasion of their mother. The court accepted that the children should only be interviewed by the judge after the decision regarding custody had been made by the court.

Arguably there will be situations where the court has little option but to heed the wishes of the child. In *W. v W.*,[60] for instance, the Supreme Court dismissed an appeal against an order of the High Court granting custody of two boys to their father. The main reason for this decision lay in the fact that the two boys, aged 11 and 14 respectively, had categorically stated that they did not want to live with their mother and would run away if she was granted custody. The court should, in this as in other areas, be slow in making orders that in practice will be near impossible to enforce. In this regard, Finlay-Geoghegan J. held that children aged 13 and 14 were of an age and maturity to have their wishes taken into account in the recent case of *F.N. and E.B. v C.D.*,

---

[55] Formerly s.17(2) – see s.11 of the Children Act 1997 (No. 40 of 1997).
[56] unreported, High Court, November 12, 1982.
[57] unreported, High Court, Ellis J., July, 1983.
[58] See also *M.W. v D.W.*, unreported, High Court, June 6, 1975 and *N.A.D. v T.D.* [1985] I.L.R.M. 153.
[59] unreported, High Court, July 10, 1980.
[60] unreported, Supreme Court, June 1975.

H.D. and E.K.[61] This is a significant judgment which draws a useful link between the personal right of a child under Art.40.3 of the Constitution to have a decision made in accordance with natural and constitutional justice, and the provisions of the Guardianship of Infants Act 1964:

> "[S]ection 25 [of the 1964 Act] should be construed as enacted for the purpose of, *inter alia*, giving effect to the procedural right guaranteed by Article 40.3 to children of a certain age and understanding to have their wishes taken into account by a court in making a decision under the Act of 1964, relating to the guardianship, custody or upbringing of a child."

2–24　The case of *A.S. (orse A.B.) v. R.B.*[62] should also be noted on the issue of a judge seeing a child in chambers. Keane C.J. urged caution with regard to doing this, noting that the only evidence that should be received by a trial judge is that on oath in the presence of the parties. He was, however, of the view that interviews may help the judge in determining the wishes of the child.

Keeping siblings together

2–25　Considering the upheaval often caused by marital breakdown, it is obvious that the court should concern itself with ensuring maximum stability for the children in question. As a general rule the courts tend to prefer not to split up siblings, if possible allowing them to remain in the family home. In *J.C. v O.C.*,[63] for instance, Finlay P. noted that the social development of a family is often best promoted by allowing brothers and sisters to reside in a common household. In that case the learned judge refused to grant custody of two young boys to their father, partly on the basis that to do so would cause them to be separated from their sister, a factor that he considered "by no means insignificant".

In a similar vein, Ó Dálaigh C.J. in *B. v B.*[64] observed that:

> "[a]fter the separation of the parents, there remain two lesser points of unity around which one would wish, if possible, to build: the first of these is the unity or comradeship of the three children, and the second is the family home where these three children have grown up together."

Constitutional considerations

2–26　Where there is a conflict between the provisions of a statute and the requirements of the Constitution of Ireland 1937, the latter generally prevail.[65] The provisions of the Constitution place significant restrictions on the State in

---

[61] unreported, High Court, Finlay-Geoghegan J., March 26, 2004.

[62] [2002] 2 I.R. 428.

[63] unreported, High Court, July 10, 1980.

[64] [1975] I.R. 54 at 59.

[65] The two exceptions are where the provisions of the statute are necessitated by our membership of the European Union (Art.29.4.7° of the Constitution) and in situations envisaged by the emergency provisions of Art.28.3.3°.

its dealings with the children of marital families. Adoption of such children, for instance, is permitted only in the most extreme of circumstances as contemplated by the Adoption Act 1988.[66]

2–27 In *Re J.H. (An Infant)*,[67] the Supreme Court added a further restriction. In that case, the court had to consider which of two sets of parents should have custody of a child. The child in question was born to parents who were then unmarried and was placed for adoption at an early stage in life. Before the adoption could go ahead, however, the child's natural parents married and proceeded to recover custody. For technical reasons the adoption could not proceed.[68] The prospective adoptive parents claimed nonetheless that they should retain custody of the child, as to allow otherwise would cause him significant trauma. The child, at this stage, had spent at least two of its most formative years with the prospective adopters.

2–28 On this basis, Lynch J., in the High Court, refused to make an order of custody in favour of the natural parents. In doing so, he looked to the welfare of the child as the paramount consideration. The Supreme Court, however, rejected this approach as inadequate. Finlay C.J. in the Supreme Court[69] observed that:

> "... it does not seem to me that s.3 of the Act of 1964 can be construed as meaning simply that the balance of the welfare as defined in s.2 of the Act of 1964 must be the sole criterion for the determination by the court of the issue as to custody of the child ..."

The court noted that while the best interests of the child are to take precedence over all other matters, the welfare of a child must, unless there are exceptional circumstances or other overriding factors, be considered to be best served by its remaining as part of its marital family. This was dictated, the court considered, by the constitutional preference for the marital family exhibited in Art.41.3 and the requirement therein that it be protected from attack.

2–29 Thus there was a presumption that the child's best interests were served by its being returned to the now married natural parents. This result could only be displaced by evidence of exceptional circumstances or other compelling reasons that justified the rebuttal of the presumption.[70] Despite a lengthy absence from the natural parents, Lynch J. (on a rehearing in the High Court) was not satisfied that the potential for psychological damage was sufficiently well proven. He thus awarded custody to the natural parents.

---

[66] No. 30 of 1988.

[67] [1985] I.R. 375 (HC); 390 (SC).

[68] See Chap.9 on adoption.

[69] *ibid.* at 394.

[70] The mention of "exceptional circumstances" mirrors the terms of Art.42.5 and seems thus to be closely modelled on it. See *Southern Health Board v An Bord Uchtála* [1995] 2 I.L.R.M. 369 and *Southern Health Board v An Bord Uchtála*, unreported, Supreme Court, June 10, 1999.

2–30 This decision represents an uneasy compromise between, on the one hand, the provisions of Arts 41 and 42 of the Constitution and, on the other, the welfare principle outlined in s.3 of the 1964 Act. It is suggested that, despite its child-friendly veneer, it is ultimately pro-parent and has thus significantly dented the operation of the welfare principle. The court's rhetoric disguises a tendency that is unavoidably parent-centred—in effect, if not in form—and is hardly in keeping with the spirit of the 1964 Act. The net outcome, it seems, is that married parents, involved in a custody dispute with persons not being the marital parents of the child, will only be denied custody in exceptional circumstances or for other "compelling reasons". Indeed, this parental preference is reflected in s.3(2)(b) of the Child Care Act 1991,[71] where a health board charged with promoting the welfare of children in its jurisdictional area must have regard "to the rights and duties of parents, whether under the Constitution or otherwise."[72]

2–31 In *Southern Health Board v C.H.*,[73] however, the Supreme Court reiterated that the primacy of considerations centred on the welfare of the child, rather than the interests of its parents. O'Flaherty J. observed, in this case which concerned the admissibility of a video-taped interview containing allegations of paternal abuse, that:

> "… it is easy to comprehend that the child's welfare must always be of far graver concern to the court. We must, as judges, always harken to the constitutional command which mandates, as prime consideration, the interests of the child in any legal proceedings".[74]

2–32 In essence, he continues, "the judge is … required to inquire as to what is in the best interests of the child. …" The Court's primary concern, he stated, was with the welfare of the child. It is noteworthy that the Supreme Court fails even to mention its earlier decision in *K.C. v A.C.*[75] The ethos of this case is decidedly child-centred. The constitutional fiction that a child is always best served by a ruling that promotes the interests of its married parents is ignored in favour of a perspective that looks solely to the child's own best interests. This more child-centred tendency displaces one of the enduring ironies of *K.C. v A.C.*, namely that under it, the welfare of the non-marital child is arguably accorded more respect than that of the marital child. Abolishing the rule in *K.C.*, then, can only help matters in this regard, by restoring the principle of equality between children, regardless of the circumstances of their birth.

2–33 The majority Supreme Court decision in *North Western Health Board v H.W. and C.W.*,[76] discussed in Chapter 1, has, however, veered away from

---

[71] No. 17 of 1991.
[72] See Duncan, "The Child's Right to a Family-Parental Rights in Disguise" (1986) 8 D.U.L.J. 76.
[73] [1996] 1 I.R. 219.
[74] *ibid.* at 238.
[75] [1985] I.R. 375.
[76] [2001] 3 I.R. 622.

this approach and has set the threshold for State intervention in the family at a very high level. In that case Denham J. established the requisite text for State intervention in the following terms:

> "The question is whether the defendants, while exercising their responsibility and duty to P. [the child, and subject matter of the proceedings in this case] under the Constitution (Article 41), failed in their duty to him, so that his constitutional rights (including the right to life and bodily integrity) were or are likely to be infringed. In analysing this, P.'s rights to and in his family are a factor. Consideration has to be given as to whether the State (whether it be a health board or other institution of the State) as guardian of the common good should by appropriate means endeavour to supply the place of the parents to ensure that the welfare of the child is the paramount consideration, but always with due regard to the natural and imprescriptible rights of the child including his rights in and to his family.
>
> The decision as to the P.K.U. test is one of the very, very many which parents make about their children every day. These decisions, medical and otherwise, are usually not challenged by anyone even if they are not in accordance with specific expert advice. It is only in exceptional circumstances that courts have intervened to protect the child to vindicate the child's constitutional rights. The court will only intervene, and make an order contrary to the parents' decisions, and consent to procedures for the child, in exceptional circumstances. An example of such circumstances in relation to medical matters may be a surgical or medical procedure in relation to an imminent threat to life or serious injury."[77]

2–34   The comments of Denham J. in the last sentence should be noted in the context of the recent decision of Abbot J. in the High Court.[78] In that case the Court directed that a five-month-old baby undergo heart surgery, overruling opposition on religious grounds from her mother, who was a member of the Jehovah's Witness community.

2–35   The comments of Hardiman J. in *North Western Health Board v H.W. and C.W.* should also be noted:

> "Article 42.5 is in the nature of a default provision. Under its terms, the State may, in exceptional circumstances, upon a failure of parental duty for physical or moral reasons, become a default parent. The sub-article does not constitute the State as an entity with general parental powers ... I do not view a conscientious disagreement with the public health authorities as constituting either a failure in duty or an exceptional case justifying State intervention."[79]

---

[77] *ibid*. at p.727.
[78] unreported, High Court, August 5, 2004.
[79] *ibid*. at p.757.

2–36 Murray J. in the same case stated:

"It would be impossible and undesirable to seek to define in one neat rule or formula all the circumstances in which the State might intervene in the interests of the child against the express wishes of the parent. It seems however, to me, that there must be some immediate and fundamental threat to the capacity of the child to continue to function as a human person, physically, morally or socially, deriving from an exceptional dereliction of duty on the part of the parents to justify such an intervention."[80]

2–37 Murphy J. adopted the following approach:

"In my view the subsidiary and supplemented powers of the State in relation to the welfare of children arise only where either the general conduct or circumstances of the parent is such as to constitute a virtual abdication of their responsibilities or alternatively the disastrous consequences of a particular parental decision are so immediate and inevitable as to demand intervention and perhaps call into question either the basic competence or devotion of the parents."[81]

2–38 Keane C.J., as he then was, held:

"I do not accept the submission advanced on behalf of the defendants that, because of the particular provisions of the Constitution upholding the authority and constitution of the family, the court, in a case such as this, is obliged to allow the wishes of the parents, however irrational they may be, to prevail over the best interests of P., which must be the paramount concern of the court under the Constitution and the law. Far from giving effect to the values enshrined in Article 42, such an approach would greatly endanger his right, so far as human endeavour can secure it, to a healthy and happy life and would be a violation of those individual rights to which he is entitled to as a member of the family and which the courts are obliged to uphold."[82]

2–39 Some suggestion has been made that the Constitution itself should be amended to contain a provision respecting the precedence of the "best interests test." It is submitted that such a reform would bring much needed clarity to the present situation regarding the principle. Such a proposal was introduced in late 1999, by Deputy Roisín Shortall T.D. The Twenty-First Amendment of the Constitution (No. 5) Bill 1999 proposed that a new Art.41.4 be inserted after Art.41.3. This new measure would require the State, as far as practicable, to defend and vindicate the rights of the child, in particular the right to have the child's best interests regarded as the first and paramount consideration in

---

[80] *ibid.* at pp.740–741.
[81] *ibid.* at p.733.
[82] *ibid.* at pp.705–706.

welfare proceedings relating to him or her. Though not ultimately accepted by
the Dáil, it is suggested that the proposal indicates a growing awareness of the
need to place the child at the centre of child law proceedings.

GUARDIANSHIP

2–40   Guardianship is a concept often confused with custody. In fact, it is
not necessary that the guardian of a child be also its custodian and day-to-day
caregiver. Guardianship is altogether a more global responsibility. The concept
of guardianship relates not to the specific matters of a child's daily life, but to
its overall welfare and upbringing. Guardianship, in other words, concerns
matters of overriding seminal importance to a child's upbringing, *e.g.* where
he or she is educated, according to which religious belief he or she is to be
reared, and whether the child should undergo serious medical treatment.

Guardianship should not be seen solely as a right. It entails both rights and
duties, in particular the duty to ensure that a child is properly cared for and
that decisions relating to the child are made with his or her best interests at
heart.

Who can be a guardian?

2–41   Certain parties are, by law, deemed automatically to be the guardian(s)
of a child. The identity of the guardian(s) is determined primarily by reference
to the circumstances of the child's birth; that is, whether its parents were, or
were not, married to each other at the time of birth.

Marital children

2–42   In the case of all children born to parents who, at the relevant time, are
married to each other, s.6(1) of the 1964 Act confers joint and equal rights of
guardianship on both the father and the mother. If either parent should die
during the lifetime of the other, the latter will be deemed guardian of their
children either alone or together with such person as is appointed by the
deceased spouse or by the court.[83]

Non-marital children

2–43   Where a child, by contrast, is born to parents who are not married to
each other at the time of birth, only the natural mother will be deemed to be a
guardian. The hardship of this rule is obviated by a series of exceptions:

(a) a natural father may become guardian of his child upon marriage to the
    mother thereof, notwithstanding the fact that this occurs after the birth of
    the child;

(b) since 1988, the natural father of a child may, notwithstanding the fact that

---

[83] See s.6(2) and (3) of the 1964 Act.

he is not married to its mother, apply to the court to be appointed a guardian under s.6A of the 1964 Act.[84] Such appointment, however, shall not affect the guardianship status of any other person in relation to the child who is the subject of the order.

Despite these new powers, the court is not obliged to grant guardianship status to every natural father. The decision in *J.K. v V.W.*[85] underlines this point. There the Supreme Court held that while a father is entitled by virtue of s.6A to apply to be made guardian, it did not confer any automatic right to be appointed as such. In a similar vein, the Court noted that the insertion of s.6A did not, despite the spirit of equality inspiring the Status of Children Act 1987, confer upon the natural father of a child the automatic rights of guardianship enjoyed by a father of a child born within marriage. In the course of his decision, Finlay C.J. observed that:

> "... [t]he discretion vested in the Court on the making of such an application must be exercised regarding the welfare of the infant as the first and paramount consideration. The blood link between the infant and the father and the possibility for the infant to have the benefit of the guardianship by and the society of its father is one of the many factors which may be viewed by the court as relevant to its welfare ...".[86]

The matters that will be taken into account in proceedings under s.6A were alluded to in the Supreme Court decision in *W.O'R. v E.H and An Bord Uchtála*.[87] That case, like *J.K. v V.W.*,[88] involved the adoption of a non-marital child. Amongst the matters that arose was the character and extent of the rights that the natural father had in respect of his child. The Supreme Court, while reiterating the predominant position of the child's welfare in such proceedings, did also consider the weight to be given to the blood link between father and child. This blood link alone, it noted, was not a factor sufficient of itself to give rise to a judgment favourable to the father in an application to be appointed guardian under s.6A. Where, however, the child had been born into a stable and established home environment and had been cared for by both father and mother, the Court suggested that the father's prospects of success were considerably stronger. The blood link, combined with the interest and concern that arose from the father's close connection to the child, might give rise to more substantial rights in respect of the child. In a disputed application to be appointed a guardian under s.6A, the Court generally looks at a variety of factors, including:

- the circumstances surrounding the birth of the child;
- the relationship between the parents;

---

[84] As inserted by s.12 of the Status of Children Act 1987. See also District Court Rules 1997, Ord. 58, r.4.
[85] [1990] 2 I.R. 437.
[86] *ibid.* at 447.
[87] [1996] 2 I.R. 248.
[88] [1990] 2 I.R. 437.

- the way in which parental responsibilities have been shared to date;
- the history of access up to the date of the application.

(c) by far and away the simplest procedure for a non-marital father to become guardian of his child is that set out in s.2(4) of the 1964 Act. This section was inserted only recently by s.4 of the Children Act 1997 and allows the mother and father by agreement to make a statutory declaration conferring upon the father the status of guardian. The declaration must be made by reference to procedures laid down by the Guardianship of Children (Statutory Declarations) Regulations 1998.[89] Both parties must have agreed to the appointment and are required to have made arrangements concerning the custody of and/or access to the child in question. The natural father must be named as father on the birth certificate of the child. There are practical difficulties with the operation of this section. For example, where does one "file" the declaration? Furthermore, if the father is not registered on the birth certificate and presents the statutory declaration to the Registrar, it is likely that the Registrar will not accept the declaration and will require a court order.[90] The main difficulty, of course, arises when the father's wish and application to be appointed a joint guardian is contested by the natural mother. The position in relation to these applications has not been altered by s.4 of the 1997 Act.

(d) a natural father may also be appointed guardian on the death of the natural mother or other guardian.[91]

Guardianship and a void or voidable marriage

2–44 Where the parents are party to a void or voidable marriage, special rules as to guardianship apply. These are now set out in s.2(1) and 2(3) of the Guardianship of Infants Act 1964 but took effect only in 1988, having been inserted into the Act by s.9 of the Status of Children Act 1987 and s.4 of the Children Act 1997. In the case of marriages that are voidable, the parents will continue to be treated as joint guardians of their child or children, provided that the decree of nullity is granted at a time after, or at some time during the period of 10 months before, the birth of the infant. Thus if a child is born, or could have been conceived, before a decree is granted in respect of a voidable marriage, both parents will be guardians.

2–45 For instance, Mary and Pat go through a ceremony of marriage in 1984. The marriage is voidable but only voided in 1989. They have three children, John, born 1986, James, born 1988 and Joanne, born 1991. As a decree of nullity was obtained in 1989, after John and James were born but before Joanne's birth, Mary and Pat will continue to be joint guardians of John and

---

[89] S.I. No. 5 of 1998. See also Appendix 7.

[90] See Ord.59 of the Circuit Court Rules 2001 (S.I. No. 510 of 2001) which requires the father to be registered as the father in a register maintained under the Births and Deaths Registration Acts 1863–1996.

[91] See discussion below at para.2–47.

James. By contrast, Mary alone will be guardian of Joanne. Had Joanne been born within 10 months of the granting of the decree, both parents would have been deemed guardians. There was, however, a two-year gap between the decree and the birth of Joanne.

2–46 Where the parents are party to a void marriage, they will be treated as joint guardians notwithstanding this fact, provided that the father reasonably believed that the marriage was valid at the relevant time. Such reasonable belief may be due to a mistake of law or of fact, or both. The relevant time for these purposes is:

(a) where the marriage ceremony occurred before the birth of the child, at some time during the period of 10 months before that birth (that is, at some time when it was possible that the child was conceived); or

(b) where the ceremony occurred after the birth of the child, at the time of the marriage ceremony.

For these purposes, there is a presumption, valid until the contrary is shown, that the father in question reasonably believed that the marriage ceremony referred to above resulted in a valid marriage. This preference can be displaced by evidence that the father in fact knew of the invalidity; where, for instance, he received legal advice more than 10 months before the baby was born to the effect that the marriage was void.

Testamentary guardianship

2–47 Any parent who is also the guardian of a child may, by deed or will, appoint any person or persons to take the former's place as guardian or guardians in the case of the death of that parent.[92] Such appointee (the "testamentary guardian") shall, on the death of the parent in question, act together with any other surviving guardians. A surviving parent may, however, object to such appointment. In this case the testamentary guardian cannot act as guardian unless, on application to the court, the court grants an order that the testamentary guardian shall act as guardian either jointly with the surviving parent or indeed to the latter's exclusion.[93] In making such an order, the court may also, at its discretion, make such orders relating to the custody of, or access to, the children concerned.[94]

If both parents die without naming a testamentary guardian, it shall be open to any person to apply to the court to appoint a guardian to act in that capacity for the children. If a testamentary or court-appointed guardian has been appointed, but either dies or no longer wishes to act in that capacity for the children, any person can apply to the court to appoint another guardian.

---

[92] s.7 of the 1964 Act.
[93] s.8(5).
[94] s.8(6).

Where an infant has no guardian

2–48   Where an infant has no guardian any person or persons may, by virtue of s.8(1) of the 1964 Act, apply to the court to be appointed as guardian(s) of the child (see District Court Rules 1997, Ord.58, r.4). The court may similarly appoint a guardian when a deceased parent of a child has not appointed a testamentary guardian, or alternatively, where the latter appointee has refused to act as such.[95] In such a case the person appointed by the court acts as joint guardian with the surviving parent. In appropriate circumstances, the court can, however, allow the new appointee to act to the exclusion of the surviving parent. A relevant and instructive case is the recent High Court decision of Finlay-Geoghegan J. in *F.N. and E.B. v C.O., H.O. and E.K.*,[96] where the applicant maternal grandparents were appointed guardians over two children (aged 13 and 14). The learned judge held that while the Oireachtas did not detail the factors to be taken into account when making a decision under s.8(2) of the Guardianship of Infants Act 1964, the provisions of ss.3 and 25 of the 1964 Act were applicable. Significantly, the High Court held that the appointment of a guardian under s.8(2) does not extinguish the constitutional rights of the surviving parent. The applicant's maternal grandparents in this case also sought, and were granted, sole custody of the children, notwithstanding the opposition of the marital father, his new wife and the paternal grandfather. It is to be noted that the children had effectively resided with the maternal grandparents since their mother died in 1995. Their father had separated from the mother prior to her death, and had remarried.

2–49   Where a guardian appointed under s.8 is acting jointly with a surviving parent, the latter's death will not affect the former's right to continue as guardian.

Removal of a guardian

2–50   Provision is made for the removal of certain guardians appointed by will or deed or under s.2(4) or s.8 of the 1964 Act.[97] Such removal may only occur by order of the court and may be accompanied by an order appointing a new guardian in replacement. A guardian who holds office other than by virtue of the above may not, it seems, be removed by the court. Section 8(4), for instance, does not seem to apply to marital parents who enjoy rights of guardianship by virtue of s.6 of the 1964 Act.

Rights and duties of a guardian

2–51   Section 10(1) of the 1964 Act states that a guardian under the Act shall be a guardian both in respect of the person and of the estate of the child. This means that the guardian will be entitled to make decisions, together with any

---

[95] s.8(2).
[96] unreported, High Court, Finlay-Geoghegan J., March 26, 2004.
[97] s.8(4) of the 1964 Act.

other guardians, regarding the education, religion and overall care and welfare of the child. Where the guardian has been appointed by deed, will or order of the court, these rights may be curtailed by the terms of such appointment.

A guardian, acting as such under the 1964 Act, is prima facie entitled to the custody of the child in respect of whom he or she is guardian, as against any other person not also being a guardian, in respect of the child. This is subject to the express terms of any deed, will or court order in respect of the child. Section 10(2)(a) further allows the guardian to take proceedings to recover custody of the child from any person who has unlawfully taken away or detained the child. In doing so, the guardian may recover damages for any injury or trespass against the person of the child. In this capacity, the guardian acts strictly on behalf of the child. In other words, such damages are to be held for the benefit of the child.

2–52 The guardian is also entitled to the possession and control of all property, real and personal, of the child. The guardian shall manage such property and receive all rents and profits on behalf of and for the benefit of the child. He or she remains responsible for the estate until the child has reached the age of 18 or for such shorter period as is stipulated by deed, will or court order.[98] For these purposes, the guardian may take such proceedings in relation to the estate of the child as may be brought by any guardian of the latter's estate.

Passport applications

2–53 Where the non-marital father is a joint guardian of the child, his consent is required for any passport application made in respect of the child. Otherwise the consent of the non-marital father is not required for passport purposes.

CUSTODY

2–54 Whereas guardianship is concerned with the enduring, global interests of the child, custody comprises the right and duty of a parent to exercise, on a day-to-day basis, the physical care of and control over a child.[99] These concepts are, nonetheless, connected. Any guardian (see above) is entitled, as against all other non-guardians, to custody of the child. Thus as a general rule a natural mother of a non-marital child, being sole guardian, is prima facie entitled to the sole custody of her children.[100] The married parents of a child, by the same token, are prima facie entitled to the custody of their children, but jointly and equally so (as joint guardians).[101] As such, a guardian may take proceedings

---

[98] See changes made by the Age of Majority Act 1985, s.2(3).

[99] See the House of Lords decision in *J. v C.* [1970] A.C. 668, quoted with approval by Denham J. in *W.O'R. v E.H.* [1996] 2 I.R. 248 at 289.

[100] See ss.6(4) and 10(2)(a) of the Guardianship of Infants Act 1964 and the dicta of O'Higgins C.J. in *G. v An Bord Uchtála* [1980] I.R. 32 at 55.

[101] See s.6(1) and s.10(2) of the Guardianship of Infants Act 1964 and the dicta of Henchy J. in *G. v An Bord Uchtála* [1980] I.R. 32 at 86.

against any person who wrongfully takes away or detains the child. Furthermore, a guardian may sue for the recovery of damages for any injury to or trespass against the child, although such damages must be retained or used for the benefit of the child in question.

Notwithstanding this general rule, however, it is nonetheless possible for a father, who is not guardian of a child, to be awarded custody. Section 11(4) of the 1964 Act allows a father to make an application for custody despite the absence of guardianship status (see District Court Rules 1997, Ord.58, r.5).

Section 14 and 16 of the 1964 Act provide for the forfeiture of custody in very limited circumstances by a parent.

2–55 On the granting of a decree of nullity it is open to the court, by virtue of s.46 of the Family Law Act 1995,[102] to declare either of the spouses unfit to have custody "of any dependent member of the family who is a minor." This will have the effect of precluding an order granting custody to the person so named. Even on the death of the other spouse, indeed, a spouse in respect of whom such a declaration is made will not be entitled as of right to the custody of that minor.

Custody orders in matrimonial proceedings

2–56 It is possible to make an order for custody not only in proceedings taken under the 1964 Act, but also in the course of certain matrimonial proceedings. In particular, it is not necessary in such proceedings, where custody or access is sought, for a separate application to be made under s.11 of the Act of 1964. In proceedings for judicial separation, the court is empowered to make, prior to deciding whether to grant or refuse a decree of judicial separation, a preliminary order relating to custody or access or any other matter relating to the welfare of a child.[103] On the granting of a decree of divorce, the court is empowered in a similar manner by s.5 of the Family Law (Divorce) Act 1996. This allows the court, upon divorce, to give directions as if an application under s.11 of the 1964 Act had been made. These would relate to any matter regarding the welfare, custody of, or access to, any dependent member of the family who is an "infant" within the meaning of 1964 Act.

Where a decree of nullity, judicial separation or divorce is granted by a court, the court is further enabled to make an order as to the unfitness of either of the spouses to have custody of a dependent child of the family.[104] The court may thus declare either of the spouses unfit to have custody "of any dependent member of the family who is a minor."[105] This is a draconian remedy, and is only likely to be ordered in the most extreme of circumstances, such as child abuse.

---

[102] No. 26 of 1995.
[103] s.6 of the Family Law Act 1995.
[104] s.46 of the Family Law Act 1995 (No. 26 of 1995), s.41 of the Judicial Separation and Family Law Reform Act 1989 (No. 6 of 1989), and s.41 of the Family Law (Divorce) Act 1996 (No. 33 of 1996) respectively.
[105] See para.2–53.

The effects of an order of custody

2–57   An order of custody necessarily involves some element of residential care; in other words, a child in the custody of a parent will be expected to live under that parent's roof. This does not, however, negate the rights of the non-custodial parent. The latter is entitled to apply for (and invariably will be granted) access and of course, if a guardian, will retain the right to make decisions concerning the overall upbringing and welfare of the child. It is difficult, nonetheless, to shake the perception that custody is an "all or nothing" solution to marital breakdown. The prevalence of this perception has, it is submitted, led to many heated custody disputes.

Joint custody

2–58   Section 11A of the 1964 Act[106] makes it clear that, should any doubt exist, it is possible even where a couple is separated, to award custody to both the father and mother jointly ("joint custody"). Joint custody involves a child residing with each parent for a stipulated period of time, *e.g.* spending weekdays with the mother and weekends with the father. In *B. v B.*,[107] for instance, Ó Dálaigh C.J. appeared to suggest that joint custody was a desirable option in certain cases, suggesting that the unity of the children in this instance would be best served "by allowing them to reside for half the year with one parent, and the other half with the other." Such an arrangement should not, however, be such as to cause significant disruption to a child's life; for instance, where one parent lives a significant distance from the school at which the children normally attend.

Each decision depends, of course, on the individual facts of the case. Joint custody tends, however, to be the exception rather than the rule. Most custody agreements and orders require that children reside with only one parent with access to the second. In particular, as noted by McGuinness J. in *E.P. v C.P.*,[108] joint custody is ill-advised where there is significant acrimony between the parents. In such circumstances, she felt, joint custody was not suitable. The reason for this is outlined further by the same learned judge in *D.F.O'S. v C.A.*,[109] McGuinness J. noting that:

> "As a general rule where there is deep hostility between the parents I am very reluctant to make an order granting joint custody, due to the probable inability of the parents to co-operate in caring for the child."

2–59   The existence of inter-parental conflict, however, is by no means an absolute bar to joint custody. In the latter case, for example, and notwithstanding the existence of conflict and acrimony between the parents, McGuinness J. made an order granting joint custody to both parents. She did so in the hope that the conferral of joint responsibility would encourage them to "put their

---

[106] As inserted by s.9 of the Children Act 1997.
[107] [1975] I.R. 54.
[108] unreported, High Court, November 27, 1998.
[109] unreported, High Court, April 20, 1999.

antagonisms behind them". The learned judge feared, moreover, that the award of sole custody to either parent could exacerbate the sense of bitterness and resentment already existing between them. Referring to expert evidence submitted at the trial, McGuinness J. observed that despite their tempestuous marital relationship, both parties had maintained an excellent personal relationship with their daughter and that, under the circumstances, joint custody was the most appropriate solution.[110] A similar approach was adopted by Herbert J. in *D.McA. v K.McA.*,[111] where he granted joint custody of their children to a father and mother—although he did express the view that the everyday routine of the children should not be circumscribed by the arrangement.

ACCESS

2–60 Where a parent who is a guardian does not obtain custody, he or she may nonetheless apply for access to the child. Access may conveniently be described as a right and duty of visitation, allowing the person with access to visit and communicate with a child on a temporary basis. Access should not be confused with joint custody; the latter confers a right and duty, albeit shared, to the care of a child. By contrast, the care-giving functions involved in access rights are merely incidental, and it is clear that the parent in question is neither obliged nor entitled to usurp the role of the primary care-giver.

While the order for access is often coined in terms of parental rights, it is probably more accurate to see access as a right of the child. Access, it is suggested, is the right of the child rather than of the parents. This has long been the case in England and Wales. In *M. v M.*,[112] for instance, Wrangham J. stated that access to a parent should not be denied to the child unless the interests of the *child* so required. In *N.A.D. v T.D.*,[113] Barron J., in a similar vein, remarked that his function "is to see whether or not it would be for the *benefit of these children* to see their mother."[114]

2–61 Until the 1990s, however, the Irish Supreme Court seemed to consider access as one of the rights of parents, rather than a basic right of the child.[115] The tenor of the language in access cases in this jurisdiction remained predominantly parent-centred until the judgment of Carroll J. in *M.D. v G.D.*[116] In that case, Carroll J. held, *inter alia*, that the welfare of the child being the paramount consideration in this area, the court is concerned with the right of the child to access rather than the right of the adult. In *W.(S). v W.(F.)*,[117] a

---

[110] See also *E.H. v J.M.*, unreported, High Court, Kinlen J., April 4, 2000 and *C.F. v J.D.F.*, unreported, High Court, O'Sullivan J., May 16, 2002.
[111] unreported, High Court, Herbert J., December 17, 2002.
[112] [1973] 2 All E.R. 81 (Fam. Div.).
[113] [1985] I.L.R.M. 153 at 156.
[114] Emphasis added.
[115] See *State (D. &. D.) v G.* [1990] I.L.R.M. 19 and *State (F.) v Superintendent, B. Garda Station* [1990] I.L.R.M. 243.
[116] unreported, High Court, July 30, 1992.
[117] [1995] 1 F.L.J.

Circuit Court decision, McGuinness J. made an order restraining the respondent from bringing further applications for custody/access without leave of the court. McGuinness J. pointed out that access is primarily the right of the children to enable them to maintain a relationship with the non-custodial parent, and an order is made strictly on the basis of the welfare of the children.

2–62 This sentiment largely mirrors that expressed by the European Court of Human Rights in cases concerning the proper approach to cases involving child custody and access.[118] In *Eriksson v Sweden*,[119] for instance, the aforementioned court held that the natural family relationship is not terminated by reason of the fact that a child is taken into public care or otherwise taken from the custody of a person. The Court seemed to indicate that access is an automatic right of the child and must not be denied unless there is clear evidence that it is contrary to the welfare of the child.

2–63 In keeping with this theme, it is worth noting that recent legislation reinforces upon the Irish courts the duty to consider all matters of access primarily by reference to what is in the child's best interests. Section 9 of the Children Act 1997 added a new s.11D to the Guardianship of Infants Act 1964. This requires that the court, in considering making any order under ss.6A, 11, 14 or 16 of the 1964 Act, have regard to whether the child's best interests would be promoted by maintaining personal relations and direct contact with both his or her father and mother on a regular basis. Therefore, it seems that the legislature now regards access to both parents as invariably being in the interests of a child. It is, indeed, exceptionally uncommon for an application of access to be refused. Where it is felt that unsupervised access may, for whatever reason, be unwise, it is the standard practice of the court to grant access subject to the condition that it be supervised. In *O'D. v O'D.*,[120] for instance, the High Court granted supervised access to the father where there was a reasonable suspicion that he might have sexually abused his child.

2–64 The strong judicial tendency in favour of granting access is exemplified by *A. MacB. v A.G. MacB.*[121] There, a father was granted access to his children despite strong evidence that the children were afraid of him. Additionally, access was given despite the fact that the father was alleged to have caused malicious damage to property. Barron J., nonetheless, considered that it was "essential that the children know that they have a father and ... that their father is able to take the place of a father in their lives".[122]

Occasionally an order of access will be made with conditions. In *B. v B.*,[123]

---

[118] See, for instance, *Hendricks v Netherlands* (1983) 5 E.H.R.R. 223; *W. v U.K.* (1988) 10 E.H.R.R. 29; *R. v U.K.* (1988) 10 E.H.R.R. 74; *O. v U.K.* (1988) 10 E.H.R.R. 82; *H. v U.K.* (1988) 10 E.H.R.R. 95; *McMichael v U.K.*, Application No. 16424/90; and *Olsson v Sweden* (1988) 11 E.H.R.R. 259.

[119] (1989) 12 E.H.R.R. 200.

[120] [1994] 3 Fam. L.J. 81.

[121] unreported, High Court, Barron J., June 6, 1984.

[122] *ibid.* at 13.

for instance, an order allowing a mother access to her children at her house was made conditional on the absence of her new male partner during visitation. The case is clearly a product of its time, the court being concerned that exposure to a non-marital relationship would be damaging to the moral welfare of the children. It is unlikely that such a decision would be made today considering the relaxation in attitudes towards alternative family units. In *O'D. v O'D.*,[124] the High Court made it a condition of access by a father accused of sexual abuse of his child that one of the father's four sisters be present at all times.

2–65   The general rule seems to be that contact between a child and his parent is to be maintained wherever practical. Where immediate direct contact cannot be ordered, supervised or indirect contact is the more likely order.[125]

Where conditions are to be attached to an access order they should be properly related to the issue of access rather than injunctive type orders designed mainly to appease the custodial parent's need for protection. For example, in the English case of *Re D. (A Minor) (Contact Orders: Conditions)*,[126] the Court of Appeal held that it was wholly inappropriate to impose conditions on the parent exercising access which had no direct bearing on the implementation of the contact order.

Very occasionally, however, access will be refused, as in the English case of *Re C. (Contact: No Order for Contact)*,[127] where Connell J. upheld an order refusing a father access and even indirect contact on the basis of the father's absence over a period of three years; inconsistent attempts by him at indirect contact; and the child's extreme adverse reaction to his father.

It is not uncommon for all access issues to be remitted to the District Court for further determination. In *S. v S.*,[128] O' Flaherty J. noted that where a situation is ongoing, the matter should be remitted to the District Court or Circuit Court for the purposes of monitoring progress at an easily accessible local venue.

Access—some practical problems

2–66   Children are very sensitive to conflict between their parents. Disagreement is normal in any family but can become polarised and damaging in a family where the parents live separately. Separated parents can sometimes over compensate for their lack of "living time" with their child. Access orders do not come with guidelines for parents exercising access, and parents find it hard to access such advice. Common pitfalls include non-custodial parents:

- overcompensating by giving expensive holidays and presents, which tend to spoil the children and engender resentment in the custodial parent;

---

[123] unreported, High Court, December, 1973.
[124] [1994] 3 Fam. L.J. 81.
[125] See *Re. B. (A Minor) (Contact: Stepfather's Hostility)* [1997] 2 F.L.R. 579.
[126] [1997] 2 F.L.R. 797.
[127] http://www.familylaw.co.uk.
[128] [1992] 2 I.L.R.M. 732.

- upsetting the children's routine too abruptly;
- continuing the conflict by covertly forcing the children to take sides;
- not allowing the children to express their anger or sadness over the separation;
- negatively commenting on the custodial parent;
- failing to show consistency;
- pumping the child for information;
- declining to avail of access, as there is not enough money to take the children somewhere special.

2–67 Custodial parents and parents exercising access can deal with common access problems by giving themselves, their former spouse and their children time to readjust. By positive re-enforcement to the children of the message that they are not to blame for the break-up, and that they are not being rejected or abandoned, mutual respect should replace lost affection between the parents. Children must be enabled to talk about their feelings without being encouraged to take sides, or burdened with too much information on the circumstances of the break-up. Neither should information be demanded of the children. Access should be a positive thing for the adult and for the child.[129] When the practitioner is consulted, every effort should be made to reduce the conflict between parents; to rephrase the problem in child-centred terms; to find common ground; to build on existing common ground; and to encourage the client to establish a pattern for separate parenting which ensures the best interests of the child.

Parental alienation syndrome

2–68 Practitioners will be familiar with situations where a child absolutely refuses to have access to a non-custodial parent. This alienation can be due to overt or covert actions by the custodial parent designed to turn the child against the absent parent. The custodial parent may maintain that he or she is in favour of access but will not force the child to go if the child does not wish to do so. He or she may be unwilling to obey a court order for access, citing the distress of the child, even though he or she may acknowledge that in the long term it is better for the child to have access to, and contact with, the other parent. Although access is increasingly viewed as the right of the child to see a non-custodial parent, what can a court do where the child refuses all such contact?

2–69 In the English case of *Re O. (Contact: Imposition of Conditions),*[130] the court appealed to the parents to recall that they were once close enough to conceive the child in question, but also warned that the court would not simply

---

[129] See advice material produced by the Family Mediation Service and One Family (formerly Cherish).

[130] [1995] 2 F.L.R. 124. See also *Re O (Contact: Withdrawal of Application* [2004] 1 F.L.R. 1258; *Re D. (Intractable Contact Dispute: Publicity)* [2004] 1 F.L.R. 1266; and *Re C. (Prohibition on Further Applications)* [2002] 1 F.L.R. 1136.

abdicate its responsibility to grant access in the face of a recalcitrant parent. However, the options of the court on breach of an access order are quite limited. It may fine or imprison the parent in breach of an order for access.[131] A summons may have the desired effect of alerting the custodial parent to the fact that he or she is obliged to comply with a court order and facilitate access as ordered to the non-custodial parent. The court may also award custody to the other parent. The duty of the court in custody disputes is the review of the factors defining "welfare" as set out in s.2 of the Guardianship of Infants Act 1964, which might bear on the respective qualifications of the parents as custodians. When the debits and credits on each side have been taken into account, the court makes the order that can be predicted to be in the best interests of the child. The ability of a parent to put the child's needs over and above his or her own is a very important issue. It is clearly of significant concern, then, if the custodial parent is unable to promote the welfare of the child by encouraging access to the non-custodial parent, because of personal antipathy towards that parent. In practical terms, however, as the focus is on the "welfare of the child", this will, in most cases, tilt the balance in favour of the existing custodial parent.

2–70   If the child steadfastly refuses to comply with the order, the court must consider an application to take into account the wishes of the child.[132] The child may request to be present for the hearing of any application which relates to him or her, and the court must grant this request unless it appears to it that, having regard to the age of the child or the nature of the proceedings, acceding to the request would not be in the child's best interests.[133] The court may soon be in a position to appoint a guardian *ad litem* for the child and arrange for separate representation of the guardian.[134] In many cases a child may need expert counselling to overcome parental alienation without destabilising his or her relationship with the custodial parent.

Access to parties other than parents

2–71   In the rough and tumble of custody proceedings, it is often forgotten that the granting of sole custody may effectively preclude access by a child or children to their grandparents, and other persons related to the non-custodial parent. Until January 9, 1998, only a parent or guardian of a child could apply for access to a child. Since the commencement of s.9 of the Children Act 1997, however, certain additional persons may now apply to the court to be afforded access to a child. These persons include the relative of a child or a

---

[131] Courts Act (No.2) 1986, s.5 created the offence of failure of, or refusal to comply with, the requirements of a direction given in an order under ss.7 or 11 of the Guardianship of Infants Act 1964. On conviction the court may impose a fine of £200 (€254) and/or imprisonment of six months: see District Court Rules 1997, Ord.58, r.8.

[132] s.25 of the Guardianship of Infants Act 1964 (as amended).

[133] s.27(2) of the Guardianship of Infants Act 1964 (as amended).

[134] s.28 of the Guardianship of Infants Act 1964 (as amended) is one of two sections of the Children Act 1997 not yet in force.

person who has acted *in loco parentis* in respect of the relevant child. This is made possible by s.11B of the 1964 Act.[135] By virtue of S.I. No. 125 of 1999, Ord.58, r.3, such application must "be preceded by the issue and service of a notice ... upon each guardian of the child". Form Number 58.19 of Sch.C outlines the form that such notice should take.[136]

While initial drafts of the legislation confined the meaning of "relative" to persons related by blood only, this definition was subsequently abandoned. For these purposes, then, the term "relative" includes such persons as are related to the child by marriage or adoption as well as by blood, for instance, a relative of the child's adoptive parents. A person *in loco parentis* may include, for instance, a former foster parent, or the cohabiting partner of a parent. The degree of care required of a person in *loco parentis* is not clear, although it is submitted that this subsection does not include persons in *loco parentis* by virtue of their occupation; for instance, day-care minders and teachers.

2–72 Any such order may be accompanied by terms and conditions as the court sees fit. Such an application is, however, conditional upon the court initially granting leave to apply to make such an application. In deciding whether to grant such leave, the court will have regard to all relevant circumstances including, but not restricted to, the nature of the relationship and connection between the applicant and the child. This may include the risk, if any, that the application would disturb the child to the extent that the latter would be harmed. The court must also have regard to the wishes of the child's guardians. The reasons for this two-tier process are not obvious, and it is arguable that the insertion of the "application for leave" stage creates an added burden and expense on the relatives of a child. It is submitted, however, that this additional requirement is useful in filtering out claims of an unmeritorious nature.

By virtue of S.I. No. 125 of 1999, Ord.59, r.5(1), such application for leave must in turn "be preceded by the issue and service of a notice ... upon each guardian of the child". Form Number 58.15 of Sch.C outlines the form that such notice should take. Despite the requirement of notice, however, it is submitted that the application for leave stage should be made *ex parte* and should not involve the guardians of the child.

2–73 Despite these welcome reforms, some problems remain. It is technically not possible, for instance, for a court to grant indirect access, *e.g.* by means of letters, cards or e-mail exchanged for example between grandparents and grandchildren separated by a great distance. A second drawback is that while s.11B extends the right to apply for access, it affords no similar right to apply for custody. It is, at least, arguable that in some cases (for instance, where the parents of a child are manifestly unfit to have custody of the child) the most appropriate person to assume custody may in fact be the grandparents or other

---

[135] As inserted by s.9 of the Children Act 1997.
[136] It does not seem to be required that the applicants notify the non-marital natural father of the child unless he has been appointed guardian thereof. This is arguably in conflict with the spirit of the judgment of the European Court of Human Rights in *Keegan v Ireland* (1994) 18 E.H.R.R. 341.

relatives of the child. Any grandparent seeking custody must, however, still revert to the zealously protected wardship jurisdiction unless he or she, as previously stated, can make an application under s.8(2) of the Guardianship of Infants Act 1964.

Grandparents/relatives: access check-list and miscellaneous matters

2–74   The following is a summary of the proceedings in applying for access under s.11B of the 1964 Act:

1.   Issue and service of notice on guardians of intention to seek leave to apply.

2.   Application for leave to apply.

3.   Issue and service of notice on guardians of intention to apply for access.

4.   Application for access proper.

Variation of custody and access orders

2–75   All custody and access decisions are "interlocutory" by nature. Thus a decision is never final and conclusive but is open to variation, should the welfare of the child so demand. The original decision may be changed should altered circumstances or new information require it. Indeed, s.12 of the Guardianship of Infants Act 1964 enables a court to vary or discharge any previously made custody or access order in respect of a child. This led O'Flaherty J. in *S. v S.*[137] to remark that:

> "There must be a better solution to cases of this kind than to have protracted High Court proceedings with an appeal to the Supreme Court. As the situation was ongoing, the matter should be remitted to the District Court or Circuit Court for the purpose of monitoring progress at any easily accessible, local venue."

Denham J. further underlined the variable nature of orders made under the Act of 1964 when she noted in *C. v B.*[138] that:

> "[t]he decision relating to custody of a child, especially a baby … is never final but evolves with the child, retaining in changing times the fundamental concept of the welfare of the child".

2–76   A grandparent may receive child benefit if he or she has custody of a grandchild, who must be residing with him or her. Form CB1, which is available from post offices, should be completed. A grandparent who is a lone parent may apply for the One-Parent Family Payment if he or she has custody of a grandchild who lives with him or her. Form OFP1, which is available from post offices, should be completed.

---

[137] [1992] I.L.R.M. 732.
[138] [1996] 1 I.L.R.M. 63.

Custody/access orders in matrimonial/domestic-violence proceedings

2–77   In proceedings for judicial separation/divorce, solicitors are obliged to direct the client to the benefits of resolving matters either through counselling or mediation. They must also provide the client with a list of appropriate services in that regard. Clients may, for whatever reason, prefer to ask the court to determine the custody dispute in the course of the matrimonial proceedings. The court is empowered to make (without the institution of separate proceedings under the Guardianship of Infants Act 1964), an order relating to custody or access or any other matter relating to the welfare of a child as a preliminary order.[139] Similarly, under the Domestic Violence Act 1996, the court can make such an order when hearing domestic-violence proceedings.[140]

Allegations of abuse arising in the course of matrimonial proceedings

2–78   It is not uncommon for allegations of sexual abuse to arise in the context of private law guardianship, custody or access litigation. Once the allegation is made it must be taken very seriously and investigated by the relevant health board. Invariably the health board will seek to stop all contact with the alleged abuser until the investigation has been completed and the abuse either validated or discounted by the Sexual Abuse Unit investigating the allegation. In the case of *O'D. v O'D. (C.) & Others*,[141] Geoghegan J. pointed out that the primary matter to be considered by the court in determining access rights to a child was the welfare of the child. A substantial risk of abuse would have to be taken into account, but a parent's "right to access" cannot be made dependent upon a finding of whether there was or was not sexual abuse. A genuine risk, falling well short of probability, has to be considered relevant in the exercise of discretion in the determination of access rights, unless it is possible to exclude the possibility of sexual abuse on the balance of probabilities. This poses obvious difficulties for the parent accused of misbehaviour towards their child. It may take considerable time to investigate the allegation, and in the intervening period, the parent making the allegation may have exclusive care and control of the child. This can be surmounted in the intervening period by the granting of supervised access. In exercising its discretion in making orders for access, the court must separate the determination of any issue of sexual abuse from the exercise of such discretion. The *O'D. v O'D. (C.) & Others* case followed with approval an English case of *H. v H. and C.*[142]

2–79   In practice, however, once an allegation of child sexual abuse is made against a parent by the other parent, the access of the accused parent to the child in question is either suspended or made subject to strict supervision pending the investigation of the allegation. Supervised access facilities are, unfortunately, practically non-existent, and unless an agreed supervisor can be found it is likely that there will be no access pending the completion of the

---

[139] See s.6 of the Family Law Act 1995 and s.5 of the Family Law (Divorce) Act 1996.
[140] See s.9 of the Domestic Violence Act 1996.
[141] [1994] 3 Fam. L.J. 81.
[142] [1989] 3 All E.R. 740.

investigation. Although practice varies, it is important that the parent against whom the allegation is made is also included in the investigation process. The European Court of Human Rights has determined that the right to a fair hearing cannot be interpreted restrictively merely because an issue must be determined in a family law context.[143] This includes the principle of equality of arms, freedom from self-incrimination, access to justice, presence in court, adversarial argument and reasons for the judgment.[144] In the case of *M.Q. v Gleeson*,[145] an action for judicial review of the Eastern Health Board and Dublin V.E.C. was considered by the High Court on the issue of whether the obligations of natural justice were owed to alleged wrongdoers in such situations. Barr J. held that in serious cases, the complaint should be put to the alleged abuser in the course of the investigations and he or she should be given an opportunity of responding to the allegation. Allegations of abuse, which are subsequently validated, should be recorded. Where the allegation is found to be positively false, recording the identity of the alleged abuser would be unfair to the person who had been falsely accused, and so his or her identity should not be recorded. In the case of *M.Q. v Gleeson*, the court noted that unfounded complaints could be a source of great injustice and harm, not only to the person complained of, but perhaps also to the particular child. A false complaint of child abuse, if incorrectly interpreted by a health board, could involve the destruction of a family unit by wrongfully having the children taken into care. It could also destroy or seriously damage a good relationship between husband and wife or long-standing partners.

2–80   The case of *D.McA. v K.McA.*[146] in which the High Court failed to take false allegations of sexual abuse into account when reaching a decision on custody should be noted. The allegations in this case had been made by the mother against the father, though it was clear from the expert evidence adduced at the trial that these allegations were wholly without foundation.

2–81   The case of *State (D. & D.) v Groarke*[147] set down certain procedural safeguards to be applied in cases where allegations of child sexual abuse are made. In that case, the Supreme Court stated that the court must have before it the basic evidence from which a conclusion of child sexual abuse has been drawn. The lawyers acting for the parents are also entitled to have, in good time for the trial, reports or summaries of the evidence which is to be given, and an examination of any video recording made. Where anatomically correct dolls have been used, then a demonstration of the precise use and the expert witness's belief in the meaning of the use by the child of the dolls should be given. The revised set of child protection guidelines, issued by the Department of Health and Children in September 1999, entitled *Children First*,[148] detail

---

[143] See *McMichael v UK* (1995) 20 E.H.R.R. 205 and *T.P. and K.M. v UK* [2001] 2 F.L.R. 549.

[144] See Art.6 of the European Convention on Human Rights.

[145] unreported, High Court, Barr J., February 13, 1997; [1998] 1 I.J.F.L. 30.

[146] unreported, High Court, Herbert J., December 17, 2002.

[147] [1990] 1 I.R. 305.

[148] *Guidelines for the Protection and Welfare of Children*, Department of Health and

the procedure to be followed in interviewing a child in the course of child protection proceedings.[149] The child must be in a position to consent to the interview, which should normally be conducted with parental permission. Where a parent is requested to attend a case conference by a health board, he or she is not generally legally represented at that conference; however, this practice may, in fact, be questionable.[150]

In *R. v Cornwall County Council, ex parte L.H.*,[151] the court declared unlawful both a policy of Cornwall County Council in refusing to provide parents with copies of the minutes of a child protection conference which they had attended, and a policy of refusing to allow parents to be accompanied by solicitors at a child protection conference.

Split hearings

2–82 Where allegations of abuse arise in the context of other proceedings, such allegations are dealt with by way of enquiry rather than a separate "*lis inter partes*". Whilst the rights of the alleged abuser must be safeguarded within that enquiry, the welfare of the child must take precedence over those individual rights. The Supreme Court emphasised the "best interests of the child" as the overreaching objective when dealing with such enquiries in the case of *Southern Health Board v C.H.*[152] In effect, this case dealt with the admissibility of a videotape interview with the child, and the purpose for which the court could view the interview. Was the video recording the hearsay evidence of the child or was it part of the expert testimony? The court determined that the videotape interview was part of the expert testimony to be given by the social worker.[153]

In the case of *Re M.K., S.K. and W.K. Minors; Eastern Health Board*,[154] the Supreme Court referred to the videotape interview as simply back-up material to the testimony of the social worker, in the same way that a doctor might rely on a medical report. The President of the High Court who heard both cases classified the evidence as hearsay evidence that he deemed admissible due to the nature of the proceedings.

Discovery

2–83 Where information is not made available to the solicitor acting for the

---

Children (1999), *Children First: Guidelines for the Protection and Welfare of Children* (Department of Health, Dublin).

[149] Para.8.12.

[150] See also *State (M.F.) v Superintendent Ballymun Garda Station and Others* [1990] 10 I.L.R.M 767 and *State (D.C.) v Midland Health Board* [1990] 7 F.L.J. 10.

[151] unreported, Queen's Bench Division, Scott-Baker J., November 4, 1999: http://www.familylaw.co.uk/upd.

[152] [1996] 1 F.L.R. 101; [1996] 2 I.L.R.M. 142.

[153] However, this decision sits unhappily with the earlier decision of the Supreme Court in *K.C. & A.C. v An Bord Uchtála* [1985] I.L.R.M. 302; *sub nom. Re J.H. an Infant* [1985] I.R 375. In the latter case, the Supreme Court appeared to give precedence to parental rights over children's rights when balancing competing rights.

[154] [1996] 1 I.L.R.M 370; [1999] 2 I.L.R.M. 321.

alleged wrongdoer, it is now possible to seek discovery in the District Court pursuant to the District Court (Discovery of Documents) Rules 1998.[155] In the case of *W.W. (A Minor) v P.B.*,[156] a headmaster who was accused by a former pupil of sexual assault brought a motion for discovery against the former pupil seeking to discover, *inter alia,* all counselling notes and records relating to, or touching on, the issues raised or the alleged assaults between the date the former pupil entered the school and the date he consulted a solicitor about his complaints against the defendant. It was held that the material was prima facie discoverable as it came into existence prior to the date when the plaintiff first consulted a solicitor about his allegations. It was held that all or some of the documents could contain information which could be helpful to the defendant in making his defence to the allegations, and therefore it would be unjust to deprive him of that potential advantage. The plaintiff, having brought a civil action against the defendant claiming damages for alleged sexual abuse, did not have the right to confidentiality *vis-à-vis* the defendant and his advisors in respect of remedial treatment of harm allegedly suffered by him on foot of such abuse prior to the date when he first consulted his solicitor in that regard.

2–84   Delay between the alleged incident(s) of abuse and the making of a complaint by the victim of that abuse can create serious difficulties for both the person seeking redress in respect of the abuse and the person seeking to defend themselves from such allegations. However, delay is frequently explained by the exercise of dominion by the alleged perpetrator over the complainant. Where power imbalance is found to characterise the relationship between the alleged perpetrator and the victim, the courts have been unwilling to hold that such delay of itself and without more can justify prohibiting a trial.[157] However, the right of the alleged wrongdoer to fair procedures is superior to the community's right to prosecute.[158]

2–85   In the case of *Re M.K., S.K. and W.K., (Infants)*,[159] Costello P. noted that where bitter matrimonial disputes exist, the court may consider it unsafe to act on an accusation of wrongdoing made by a child against one parent where the risk of undue influence by the other is a very real one.[160]

---

[155] S.I. No. 285 of 1999.

[156] unreported, High Court, Barr J., March 18, 1999.

[157] *D. v DPP* [1994] 2 I.R. 465; *Z. v DPP* [1994] 2 I.R 496; *Hogan v President of the Circuit Court* [1994] 2 I.R. 513; *G. v DPP* [1994] 1 I.R. 374; *B. v DPP* [1997] 2 I.L.R.M 118; and *M.O'H. v DPP*, unreported, High Court, O'Sullivan J., March 25, 1999.

[158] *Per* Denham J. in *D. v DPP* [1994] 2 I.R. 465 at 474.

[159] [1996] 1 I.L.R.M. 370 at 381.

[160] See, generally, Green, "True and False Allegations of Sexual Abuse in Child Custody Disputes" (1988) *Journal of the American Academy of Child Psychiatry* 25 at 4:445–456; Spencer and Flin, *The Evidence of Children, the Law and the Psychology* (2nd ed., Blackstone Press Limited, London, 1993), and Memon, Vrij and Bull, *Psychology and the Law Truthfulness, Accuracy and Credibility* (McGraw-Hill Publishing Company, London, 1998).

2–86   Allegations of child sexual abuse take a considerable length of time to investigate and the procedures set out in Guidelines on Procedures for the Identification, Investigation and Management of Child Abuse also take time.[161] In addition, once the allegation has been made, the Gardaí are notified in accordance with the Guidelines on the Notification of Suspected Cases of Child Abuse between Health Boards and Gardaí.[162] Ultimately, if the allegations transpire to be "unfounded" or not established, there is very little which the "wronged party" can do from a practical point of view. The Protection of Persons Reporting Child Abuse Act 1998[163] effectively provides immunity from suit to anyone reporting child abuse, as long as the person reporting is acting reasonably and in good faith both in forming the opinion and in reporting it. Parents who make false allegations can, however, expect serious censure. In the case of *S. v S.*,[164] the Supreme Court upheld the award of custody of three children to the husband, in a case where the High Court judge had considered that the wife had attempted to make false allegations of improper sexual behaviour against the husband.

The manner of the investigation of allegations of child sexual abuse has led to significant litigation, a Report of Inquiry and new legislation in the neighbouring jurisdiction. The *Report of the Inquiry into Child Abuse in Cleveland 1987*[165] led to the introduction of the Children Act 1989.

2–87   The Cleveland Report suggested a blueprint for the investigation of allegations of child abuse and made very specific recommendations for practice in such investigations. As a result of these recommendations, the methods used in diagnostic interviews have been significantly refined, partly in response to some very strong judicial criticism.[166] Much criticism was made of the use of leading questions and coercive methods, which encouraged the child to say that sexual abuse had taken place. Refinement of the interviewing techniques, however, were later noted with approval, and seem to have diminished significantly the number of leading or hypothetical questions in favour of spontaneous statements by the child with regard to what had happened.[167] The courts have noted the benefit of such evidence.[168]

---

[161] See Department of Health Guidelines (1987).
[162] Department of Health (1995).
[163] No. 49 of 1998.
[164] [1992] I.L.R.M. 733.
[165] (H.M.O., July 1988); see in particular Chap.12, "Listening to the Child"; Chap.13 "Social Work Practice"; Chap.16 "The Courts"; and Part Three, "Conclusions and Recommendations".
[166] *Re E.* [1987] 1 F.L.R. 269; *Re N.* [1987] 1 F.L.R. 280; *Re G.* [1987] 1 F.L.R. 310; *C. v C.* [1987] 1 F.L.R. 321.
[167] *Eastern Health Board v M.K. & M.K.*, unreported, Supreme Court, January 29, 1999; *C. v C.* [1988] F.C.R. 458; [1988] 1 F.L.R. 462.
[168] *Re M. (A Minor) (Child Abuse: Evidence)* [1987] 1 F.L.R. 293; *H. v H.: K. v K.* [1990] Fam. 86; *Re E. (Child Abuse: Evidence)* [1990] F.C.R. 793; *Re Z. (Minors) (Child Abuse: Evidence)* [1989] F.C.R. 440; *R. v Hove Justices, ex parte W.* [1989] F.C.R. 286; *Re C. (A Minor) (Care: Balancing Exercise)* [1992] F.C.R. 65.

The practitioner and custody and access applications

2–88 The success of the custody or access application will largely depend on the information obtained and imparted prior to the application to the court. An applicant for custody who is not routinely involved in the day-to-day care of the child prior to the application is unlikely to be successful in an application for sole custody, save in exceptional circumstances. For example, a client who is not well informed about practical matters concerning the child, is unlikely to impress the court that he or she has performed a "hands on" role in the rearing of the child to date. It is important to ascertain whether the client has possession of some or all of the following information:

- where the child goes to school;
- who his or her teacher is;
- what class the child is in;
- whether the child has had a full inoculation program;
- who the child's doctor/dentist is;
- games played;
- normal bedtime;
- favourite food.

To aid the practitioner in this process, some fact-gathering sheets are included in Appendix 1 to this book.

Alternative means of dispute resolution

2–89 Even with the best will in the world, court proceedings involving the proper custody of children have a tendency to become acrimonious. It is obviously desirable for all parties then that, if at all possible, a solution be reached by means other than court proceedings. To this end, s.11 of the Children Act 1997 introduced a variety of measures designed to promote alternative means of dispute resolution. These are contained in ss.20 to 24 of the Guardianship of Infants Act 1964. In certain respects, they mirror similar provisions contained in ss.5 to 7 of the Judicial Separation and Family Law Reform Act 1989 and ss.6 to 8 of the Family Law (Divorce) Act 1996.

2–90 Section 20 of the 1964 Act relates to advice that should be given to an applicant in proceedings under s.6A (provision for the natural father to be appointed guardian in respect of a child), s.11 and s.11B (access to relatives) of the 1964 Act. It places a positive duty upon a solicitor acting on behalf of the applicant to discuss the existence of alternative means of dispute resolution including:

(a) the possibility of counselling to assist in coming to an agreement regarding guardianship, custody or access or any other question affecting the welfare of a child. For this purpose the solicitor should furnish the names and addresses of persons suitably qualified to give such counselling;

(b) the possibility of mediation to assist in coming to such an agreement. For this purpose the solicitor should furnish the names and addresses of persons suitably qualified to provide a mediation service;

(c) the possibility of entering into an agreement with the respondent, by deed or otherwise in writing, dealing with matters of custody, access or any question affecting the welfare of the child.

A similar requirement is outlined in s.21 of the 1964 Act in respect of a solicitor who has received instructions from a respondent involved in proceedings under s.6A, 11 or 11B of the Act.

2–91 Sections 20(3) and 21(3) of the 1964 Act require the respective solicitors involved to furnish evidence of compliance with the requirements of ss.20(2) and 21(2) of the Act. When the solicitor for the applicant is lodging the original documents to initiate proceedings, a certificate, signed by the solicitor, indicating that he or she has observed the requirements of the relevant section, must accompany these documents. A copy of this certificate should accompany any copy of the original documents served on any person in respect of the proceedings. In a similar manner, the solicitor for the respondent, when formally responding to the institution of proceedings, must indicate in writing that the obligation placed on him or her by s.21(2) has been fulfilled. A copy of the certificate indicating compliance should be delivered to the applicant in the proceedings. In both cases, however, compliance will not be necessary where the parties have already satisfied s.5(2) of the Judicial Separation and Family Law Reform Act 1989 or s.6(4) of the Family Law (Divorce) Act 1996.[169] These sections place a comparable duty on solicitors in proceedings for judicial separation and divorce, respectively. This saver, thus, prevents unnecessary duplication of advice regarding alternative means of dispute resolution.

2–92 Further provision is made where proceedings under s.6A, 11 or 11B of the 1964 Act have already commenced. If it appears to the court during the course of proceedings that agreement between the parties may be possible, s.22 of the 1964 Act allows the court to adjourn proceedings with a view to facilitating such agreement. This is in addition to, and not as a substitute for, any other power that the court may have to adjourn proceedings. Where an adjournment is obtained under s.22, the parties may make attempts, either unaided or with the assistance of a third party, to seek an agreed solution to the matter being considered by the court. Such adjournment will end, however, where either party requests that the court resume hearing the proceedings—as obvious an indication as any that the negotiations have failed.[170]

2–93 In order to encourage attempts at agreement, s.23 of the 1964 Act stipulates that certain oral or written communications between a party to the proceedings and any third party will not be admissible as evidence in the proceedings to which they relate. Any record of such communication is equally inadmissible. The communications contemplated are those made for the

---

[169] See ss.20(4) and 21(4) of the 1964 Act.
[170] This, of course, is subject to any other power of the court to adjourn the proceedings.

purposes of seeking help to reach agreement regarding matters of custody, access or any question relating to the welfare of a child. This will be so, regardless of whether such communication was known to, or made in the presence of, the other party to the proceedings.

Any agreement resulting from the negotiations contemplated by Pt IV of the 1964 Act can be made a rule of court by virtue of s.24 of the Act. This gives such an agreement the force and application of a court order, and may be especially effective where there are strong fears of non-compliance. The agreement must relate either to the custody rights of the parties or to access arrangements agreed by them, or both. In such a case, either party may apply to the court for an order rendering the agreement a rule of court. The court may only accede to such a request, however, if it is satisfied that the agreement is fair and reasonable and, in all the circumstances, adequately protects the interest of the parties and the child. Any such order shall be deemed to be an order under either s.11(2)(a) or 11B of the 1964 Act, as appropriate.

Separation agreements and parenting plan

2–94   Where parents are separating by agreement, it is desirable that they attend mediation in order to work out a comprehensive parenting plan. A parenting plan is a written agreement between parents covering the practical arrangements which must be made because they have separate lives and residences post-separation. It covers such issues as:

- with whom will the children reside?
- when can the absent parent spend time with the children?
- how can the absent parent continue to be a part of the big decisions?
- education;
- holidays;
- religious and medical matters;
- how can financial responsibility be shared?
- how can changes be incorporated without problems?
- how to incorporate any wishes expressed by the child;
- the nature of the relationship between children and significant others;
- shared arrangements.

Drawing up the plan helps parents focus positively on child care arrangements. It also re-enforces stability for children. Once the practical issues are dealt with, parents are frequently less concerned with terms of art such as "custody", "sole custody", "joint custody" and "access".

Move away applications

2–95   Where a custodial parent wishes to move away from the country to live elsewhere, the decision is rarely accompanied with the blessing of the parent exercising access unless provision is made for some other form of access which preserves the relationship between the absent parent and the child. This can often be achieved by arrangements for generous holiday access, provision for the absent parent to exercise access in the new country of residence, and generous indirect contact. Where there is disagreement, however, the advice must be "apply, don't fly", where the parents exercise "rights of custody" as defined by the Hague Convention.[171] It should be noted that the Irish courts adopt a unified approach and return the child speedily to the country of habitual residence for the courts there to determine what orders should be made in respect of the child. Refusal to return is only considered where there is a grave risk and the return would place the child in imminent danger or in a truly intolerable situation.[172] Child abduction legislation, incorporating the Hague, and Luxembourg Conventions on International Child Abduction, make it very easy for the absent parent with "rights of custody" to secure the return of the children to the country of ordinary residence for the courts to determine the issue. Such a parent, however, cannot seek the summary return of the child to the jurisdiction unless there is a legally binding agreement giving him "rights of custody". The right must not be "stale" but must actually be exercised in practice.[173] The right also arises if proceedings have been instituted seeking custody rights and the removal takes place before such proceedings have been determined.

2–96 All that a parent can do in relation to access rights is to apply to the Central Authority to assist in the enforcement of these rights[174] and the Central Authority is bound to "promote the peaceful enjoyment of access rights and the fulfillment of any conditions to which the exercise of these rights may be subject". In this regard the Central Authority may either directly or indirectly initiate or assist in the institution of proceedings to protect the rights of access involved.[175] The parent left behind who has rights of custody can secure "free" legal aid, which may not be available so readily to the abducting parent.

2–97 It is worth noting that the right to a fair hearing within a reasonable time in accordance with Art.6 of the European Convention on Human Rights is likely to be raised by parents seeking to resist applications for the summary return of their children under the Hague Convention. It may be argued that procedural delays preventing the expeditious determination of the application may result in the issue being determined on a factual rather than a legal basis.[176] They may also seek to prevent the matter being determined in a summary manner by insisting on a right to call oral evidence and to cross-examine.

2–98 The Irish courts have stated that the parent with sole custody has the

---

[171] See Chap.10.
[172] See Chap.10, para.10–54.
[173] See Art.3(1)(b) of the Hague Convention and *C.M. and O.M. v Delegacion de Malaga and Others* [1999] 2. I.R 363.
[174] *W.P.P. v S.R.W.,* unreported, Supreme Court, April 14, 2000.
[175] See Art.21 of the Hague Convention and para.10–30.
[176] See *W. v UK* (1987) 10 E.H.R.R. 29.

right to determine the residence of the child as part of their "rights" as custodial parent.[177] A parent who does not have physical custody of the child, but has the right to determine the place of residence of the child has, under Art.5, a right of custody which is protected by the Convention.[178] An unmarried parent with "rights of access" only cannot seek the summary return of the child to the country of habitual residence in order to enforce such rights of access.[179] Where a parent is not actually exercising "rights of custody", but merely holds the rights "on paper", the onus is on the parent asserting such rights to show that they are actually exercised.[180] Removal of the child by one party during the course of an application (under the Guardianship of Infants Act 1964) to determine issues of child custody and guardianship in the District Court is not permissible.[181]

2–99 Where a parent applies to court for permission to relocate, the court determines the question under the general heading of "best interests of the child" as a paramount consideration. However, the court must also consider other matters such as the question of freedom of movement. Where an individual's rights are in conflict, the court must balance the interests of the parties carefully and conscientiously.[182] In the case of *Re M (Leave to Remove Child from Jurisdiction)*,[183] Hale J. considered the application by an asylum-seeking Bulgarian mother for leave to remove herself and her child to Canada. The mother was likely to be given a work permit and right of residence in Canada due to the high level of her computing skills. The Nigerian father, who faced deportation to Nigeria, objected. However, the court held that it was manifestly in the child's best interests that the mother be allowed to reside in Canada. There were compelling reasons for her application and the mother demonstrated good sense and responsibility in making the application at an early stage. Although there appears to be no Irish case determining the matter, other jurisdictions with very similar legal provisions have considered the issue.

2–100 In Australia, for example, the test appears to be for the court to focus on what is best for the child. It determines what benefits the child will have, what detriments the child will suffer in a move, and the consequences that will follow from an order restricting movement. In determining such cases the courts in Australia have evolved the following principles:

---

[177] See *W. v W.* [1993] 2 I.R. 476; *H.I. v M.G.* [1999] 2 I.L.R.M. 22; and *W.P.P. v S.R.W.* [2001] 1 I.L.R.M. 371.
[178] See *W.P.P. v S.R.W.* [2001] 1 I.L.R.M. 371, where the order of the Californian court gave the left-behind parent access only. In such circumstances the removal by the custodial parent was not "wrongful" even though it was in breach of his access rights.
[179] See *S. v H. (Abduction: Access rights)* [1997] 1 F.L.R. 971 and *V-B (Abduction: Rights of Custody)* [1999] 2 F.L.R. 192.
[180] See McGuinness J. in *C.M. and O.M. v Delegacion de Malaga and Others* [1999] 2 I.R. 363.
[181] See *H. (Abduction: Rights of Custody)* [2000] 1 F.L.R. 201.
[182] *G-A (Permission to Remove from Jurisdiction: Human Rights)*, (CA) February 29, 2000. See www.familylaw.co.uk/Upd.
[183] [1999] 2 F.L.R. 334.

- The welfare or best interests of the child remains of paramount importance but is not the sole consideration.

- A court cannot require the applicant for the child's relocation to demonstrate "compelling reasons" for the relocation. Similarly, the party opposing relocation will not be required to show "compelling reasons" for opposing it. Neither party bears such an onus.

- It is necessary for the court to evaluate each of the proposals advanced by the parties.

- A court cannot proceed to determine the issues in a way which separates the issue of relocation from that of residence and the best interests of the child. There can be no dissection of the case into discrete issues such as a primary issue as to who should have residence and a further issue or separate issue as to whether the relocation should be permitted.

- The evaluation of the competing proposals must weigh the evidence and submissions as to how each proposal would hold advantages and disadvantages for the child's best interests.

- The statutory criteria must be considered.

- The issue of freedom of movement must be weighed.

- Where granting leave to relocate, the court must, if necessary, devise a regime which adequately fulfils the child's right to regular contact with the parent no longer living permanently in close physical proximity.[184]

Where a custodial parent wishes to relocate for bona fide reasons, it is suggested that these principals may well be considered, if not adopted, by the Irish courts.

---

[184] See *A.M.S. v A.I.F.; A.I.F. v A.M.S.* (1999) F.L.C. 92-852; *Paskandy v Paskandy* (1999) F.L.C. 92-878; and *A. v A. (Relocation Approach)* [2000] Fam. C.A. 751.

CHAPTER 3

EDUCATION

PART I

CONSTITUTIONAL RIGHT TO EDUCATION

Introduction

3–01   Article 42 of the Irish Constitution provides for the right to education. In particular, Art.42.4 is the core provision and is in the following terms:

> "The State shall provide for free primary education and shall endeavour to supplement and give reasonable aid to private and corporate educational initiative, and when the public good requires it, provide other educational facilities or institutions with due regard however, for the rights of parents, especially in the matter of religious and moral formation."

3–02   Ó Dálaigh C.J. in *Ryan v Attorney General*[1] defined education as referred to in the Constitution in the following terms:

> "Education is the teaching and training of a child to make the best possible use of his inherent and potential capacities, physical, mental and moral."

3–03   Article 42 of the Constitution requires the State to "provide for" free primary education. This constitutional obligation applies to the education of all children, including those with disabilities. In his judgment, O'Hanlon J. in *Paul O'Donoghue v Minister for Health and Others*,[2] implies that, in the case of persons with disabilities, primary education can continue for so long as "the ability for further development is discernible". The right to education of a physically disabled and profoundly mentally handicapped eight-year-old child who needed special schooling was considered in this case. No place was available for the plaintiff. Consequently, the plaintiff's mother cared for him at home at her own expense. When the plaintiff finally secured a place in a special school, the absence of appropriate facilities was such that the High Court concluded that the State had failed to discharge its constitutional obligations.

O'Hanlon J. held that the applicant child in this case could benefit from education and that the State had failed in the duty it had in respect of this child

---

[1]   [1965] I.R. 294.
[2]   [1996] 2 I.R. 20.

to provide for his primary education. The learned judge outlined the position as follows:

> "I conclude having regard to what has gone before that there is a constitutional obligation on the State by the provisions of Article 42.4 of the Constitution to provide for free basic elementary education of all children and that this involves giving each child advice, instruction and teaching as will enable him or her to make the best possible use of his or her inherent and potential capacities, physical, mental and moral, however limited these capacities may be."

A further relevant and instructive case is *Comerford v Minister for Education*.[3]

3–04   In the case of *Jamie Sinnott (suing by his mother and next friend Kathryn Sinnott) v Minister for Education, Ireland and the Attorney General*,[4] the plaintiff was an adult with a moderately severe form of autism, a condition that profoundly inhibits normal communication and social development in the sufferer. While the plaintiff secured a place in a variety of special schools, these for the most part amounted to what Keane C.J. described as "baby-sitting services", with the result that over 22 years, he received less than three years' of meaningful education. It was argued on behalf of the plaintiff that he was entitled as a matter of constitutional right to free primary education beyond the age of 18.

The case did not concern a child as such, the applicant being 23 at the time of the Supreme Court hearing. That said, the issue for consideration in the case was the scope of the constitutional right to education, the only express rights guaranteed to children under the Irish Constitution.

3–05   In summary, the facts of the case were as follows: James Sinnott, a 23-year-old man, been diagnosed as autistic at an early age. Despite representations from his mother, the State failed to provide him with an adequate primary education. In fact, up to the hearing of the case, the State had provided him with a total of two years' primary education. It was claimed that the State had failed in its constitutional obligation to provide free primary education to the plaintiff. A mandatory injunction was sought directing the State to provide free primary education to the plaintiff for as long as he could benefit from such education.

3–06   In the High Court, Barr J. held that the plaintiff was entitled to continuous education for so long as this was of discernible benefit to him. He rejected the argument advanced by the State that there was an implicit age limit contained in Art.42.4, and held that, owing to the mandatory nature of the provision, the State was obliged to provide free primary education to all children. Such a right, the learned judge stated, was not age-related and did not cease at any particular age. In fact, Barr J., in alluding to the aforementioned

---

[3]   [1997] 2 I.L.R.M. 134.
[4]   unreported, Supreme Court, July 12, 2001.

O'Donoghue case stated:

> "It is impossible to avoid the conclusion that such grounds of appeal [the Department of Education's appeal against the *O'Donoghue* decision] were persisted in against an overwhelming tide of national and international expert opinion without any hope of success in the appeal but with the intention of delaying the implementation of the *O'Donoghue* judgment for as long as possible. In the event, there was no compliance with it under 1998—five years after the judgment. Even then nothing was done for those suffering from autism."

3–07   The State appealed to the Supreme Court, submitting that the right to free primary education continued only for so long as the plaintiff remained a child, and not, under any circumstances, beyond the age of 18. It did not, however, challenge the fact that it had failed to provide adequate education to James Sinnott, nor did it challenge the award of damages made in the High Court.[5]

3–08   The majority of the Supreme Court ruled that the right to a free primary education continued only for so long as the beneficiary of this duty remained a "child". It further held that on reaching the age of 18, an individual can no longer be categorised as a "child". This conclusion may have been technically correct, but is unduly formalistic, treating adulthood as a functional rather than chronological issue. Article 42 of the Constitution is not limiting as to the age at which childhood is deemed to end and adulthood begin. Indeed, childhood has always proved markedly fluid in statute law. For example, the Family Law Acts define child as "any person under the age of 18 years or if the child has attained that age ... is receiving full-time education ... and is under the age of 23 years". The former Chief Justice, Keane C.J., acknowledges the fluid nature of childhood in his judgment in the following manner:

> "No principled basis exists either in law or in the evidence for the contention ... that a person in [the plaintiff's] position ceases to be in need of primary education at age 18, or age 22, or at any age in the future which can now be identified with any precision."

3–09   In fact, the decision of the Supreme Court sits uneasily beside s.7 of the Education Act 1998, which creates a right to education for all persons, regardless of age.

On the mandatory injunction issue, the Supreme Court adopted a very strict interpretation of the separation of powers doctrine. It held that it would only be in the most exceptional circumstances, such as if the Government ignored a constitutional imperative and defied a court declaration that the court could mandate another branch of the State to carry out a particular task.

---

[5]   It should also be noted that the State appealed the decision of Barr J. to award damages of the mother of James Sinnott, Kathryn Sinnott.

PART II

THE EDUCATION ACTS

Introduction

3–10   The Irish system of education has undergone a major upheaval in the past decade. The legislative landscape has been transformed, particularly by the Education Act 1998 (the "1998 Act") and the Education (Welfare) Act 2000 (the "2000 Act"). Education is a fundamental human right recognised as such in the European Convention on Human Rights (ECHR), the UN Bill of Rights and, as previously stated, the Constitution. In general, these instruments require that children should not be denied access to education and that parents have the right to ensure that the education of their children is in accordance with their religious and philosophical beliefs. The Education Acts give practical effect to the State's constitutional and international obligations. The Acts seek to increase the openness of the education system, making schools more accountable, particularly in decision-making areas such as admissions and disciplinary actions. The issue of attendance has also been an area of reform, with a change in philosophy from previous legislation which focused on punitive measures to enforce attendance, to the Education (Welfare) Act which now seeks to encourage attendance using a multi-disciplinary approach. This seeks to address individual recalcitrant students and identify weakness in the system as a whole. The significant changes to the education system as a result of recent legislative developments will be considered in the following paragraphs.

The Education Act 1998

3–11   The Education Act 1998 provides a statutory framework for primary and post-primary education. The Act seeks to bring the previously ad hoc system under statutory control, enabling a more transparent and accountable system of education. It gives statutory recognition to the rights and functions of the key shareholders in the educational process; provides for the establishment of the Inspectorate on a statutory basis; and imposes an obligation on a board of management to arrange for the preparation of a school plan. Section 6 of the 1998 Act sets out the objectives of the Act and effectively provides the statutory expectations of a school. In summary, these are to give practical effect to the constitutional rights of all children, to promote access and opportunities to an appropriate level of education, and to contribute to the achievement of national policies in an open system. These objectives are mirrored in the functions of a school provided in s.9 of the 1998 Act.

Admissions

3–12   Section 9 of the 1998 Act requires a school to establish and maintain an admissions policy which provides for the maximum accessibility to the school. One measure to achieve this, and to also increase the transparency of the admissions system, is the provision that the board of management publish:

"the policy of the school concerning admission to, and participation in, the school, including the policy of the school relating to the expulsion and suspension of students and admission to and participation by students with disabilities or who have other special educational needs, and ensure that as regards that policy, principles of equality and the right of parents to send their children to a school of the parents' choice are respected and such directions as may be made from time to time by the Minster, having regard to the characteristic spirit of the school and the constitutional rights of all persons concerned, are complied with."[6]

In light of the above provision, the admissions policy must have regard to children who have disabilities or other special educational needs, and must further comply with the provisions of the Equal Status Act 2000, as amended by the Equality Act 2004.[7]

The school plan

3–13 Section 2(1) of the 1998 Act provides that the board of management is to prepare a "school plan" and is to ensure that the plan is regularly reviewed and updated. The school plan sets down the objectives of the school "relating to the equality of access to and participation in the school and the measures which the school proposes to take to achieve those objectives including equality of access to and participation in the school by students with disabilities or who have other special educational needs". The recently published Disability Bill 2004[8] should be noted. The school plan must be prepared in consultation with the parents, patron, staff and students of the school and the Department of Education and Science.

Grievance procedure

3–14 Section 28 of the 1998 Act, which provides for a grievance procedure, states that:

"(a) the parent of a student or, in the case of a student who has reached the age of 18 years, the student, may appeal to the board against a decision of a teacher or other member of staff of a school,

(b) grievances of students, or their parents, relating to the students' school (other than those which may be dealt with under *paragraph (a)* or *section 29*) shall be heard, and

(c) appropriate remedial action shall, where necessary, be taken as a consequence of an appeal or in response to a grievance."[9]

This section had not yet been commenced as of October 24, 2004.

The Ombudsman for Children Act 2002, discussed in Chapter 8, should also be noted, as the Ombudsman for Children is empowered to investigate

---

[6] s.15(2)(d) of the Education Act 1998.
[7] No. 24 of 2004.
[8] No. 39 of 2004.
[9] s.28(1).

any action taken in relation to the performance of administrative functions, by or on behalf of a school, in connection with its functions under s.9 of the Education Act 1998.[10] Schools not registered under s.10 of the 1998 Act do not fall for consideration by the Ombudsman, who is also excluded, pursuant to s.49 of the Education Act 1998, from involvement in a matter relating to the State examinations. The Ombudsman for Children may only investigate an action under s.28(1)(a) of the 1998 Act[11] where the procedures detailed in that section are operational and have been exhausted. Section 29 grievances are excluded from the remit of the Ombudsman in that there is no provision in the Ombudsman for Children Act 2002 for the Ombudsman to accept a referral where an appeal already exists to a body other than the school. The examination and investigation of complaints by the Ombudsman are considered in Chapter 8.

Appeals procedure

3–15 Section 29 of the 1998 Act gives parents the right to appeal certain decisions taken by the board of management of the school, or taken by a person acting on behalf of the board of management, to the Secretary General of the Department of Education and Science. Section 29 restricts the decisions that can be the subject of an appeal to:

(a) permanent expulsions of a student from a school;

(b) a suspension of a student which would bring a cumulative period of suspension to 20 school days in any one school year; or

(c) a refusal to enrol a child in a school.[12]

In the case of a Vocational Education Committee (VEC) school, an appeal against the decision of the board of management of the school must first be made to the VEC during the 20-day period if the board has serious concerns arising out of the behaviour of a disruptive student. Such an appeal will generally be taken "to ensure that good order and discipline are maintained in the school concerned and that the safety of students is secured."[13]

3–16 A decision may be appealed by the parent of the student, an adoptive parent, a guardian, a foster parent or other person acting *in loco parentis*, the National Educational Welfare Board, or by a student who is 18 years of age or older. They may appeal either orally or in writing within 42 days of the parent being notified of the decision. Schools must also advise of the right to appeal.

Section 29 envisages a three-step process. First, the school and parents will be asked if accommodation can be achieved at a local level. Secondly, failing such accommodation being achieved, the appeals committee established by the Minister will recommend a facilitator where it is of the view that a

---

[10] s.9 of the Ombudsman for Children Act 2002 (No. 22 of 2002).

[11] s.28 of the 1998 Act had not been commenced by October 24, 2004.

[12] At this stage no other grounds of appeal have been determined by the Minister under s.29(1)(d).

[13] s.29.

possible agreement can be reached. Thirdly, if no agreement can be reached, a hearing will take place. The parties are notified of those attending three days prior to the hearing. The appeal is determined by a majority vote, with the chairperson of the committee having a casting vote in the event of an equal division of votes.[14] This system has been in place since December 23, 2000, although most appeals have been dealt with at local level.

Appeals process

3–17   Appeals are to be made in writing on the Section 29 Appeals Application Form, which can be obtained from the school or from the Appeals Administration Unit in the Department of Education and Science. The application must be addressed to the Appeals Administration Unit, and at the same time the appellant should notify the school of the appeal. Where the application is by fax or email, the appellant should send a signed copy by post as well. Section 29(4) requires that appeals be concluded within 30 days of receipt by the Secretary General, subject only to an extension of 14 days. Where an appeal is inadmissible, a letter is issued stating the grounds on which the appeal cannot be heard. If the appeal is admissible, the Minister must appoint an Appeals Committee, comprising three persons. These persons will include an Inspector and two other persons, who in the opinion of the Minister would be appropriate in light of their experience, expertise and independence to hear the appeal.[15]

3–18   In order to guarantee a certain minimum education, where an appeal in s.26 is unsuccessful and a student is permanently excluded or not enrolled, the board is required to employ all reasonable efforts to have the student enrolled at another recognised school.[16] If this attempt fails, the board may look at alternative arrangements, such as enrolment at an unrecognised school or private school, only with the consent of the child's parents and the Minister. The board is then required to continue to monitor the child's progress. The Act does not, however, address the course of action to be taken if the consent of the child's parent is refused, or whether consent could be dispensed with.

The Education (Welfare) Act 2000

3–19   The Education (Welfare) Act 2000 provides a national system for compulsory school attendance which will ensure that children of schoolgoing age attend school, or if they fail to do so, otherwise receive at least a minimum standard of education. It imposes a statutory duty on schools to adopt a more proactive approach to the problem of truancy, and introduces State supervision of the aforementioned minimum education in recognised schools or otherwise.

Attendance was previously regulated by the School Attendance Act 1926,

---

[14] s.29(3).
[15] s.29(2).
[16] s.27(1).

which, through the use of sanctions, sought to compel children between six and 15 years of age to attend school every day it was open for instruction.[17] Fines levied on recalcitrant parents were one means of enforcing the obligation of attendance. In the event of persistent non-attendance, the child could be removed from the family and placed either in an industrial school or the care of a relative or other fit person.[18] This 1926 Act was enforced by An Garda Síochána or the local school-attendance committee. The 1926 Act was framed negatively rather than positively, focusing "on punishing offenders, rather than assessing the causes of non-attendance".[19] Difficulties also arose with Article 42 of the Constitution which guarantees that "the primary and natural educator of the child is the Family". In contrast, the 2000 Act aims to provide "a supportive infrastructure to help every element of the system to make its own contribution to tackling school attendance difficulties".[20] Research has consistently demonstrated a link between early school-leaving and anti-social behaviour, social deprivation and underachievement generally.[21]

3–20   The 2000 Act requires a parent to ensure that his or her child attends a recognised school on each school day subject to certain exceptions.[22] It departs from the definition of a child in the 1926 Act, which Act sought to compel children between six and 15 years of age to attend school. A child is now defined as a person who has reached the age of six and who has not reached the age of 16 years or has not completed three years of post-primary education, which ever comes later, up to a maximum of 18 years. This new definition guarantees that each person receives a minimum of three years of post-primary education. A number of limited exceptions to the parents' duty to ensure that their children go to a recognised school exist where:

(a) the child is registered with the National Educational Welfare Board for education provided outside the recognised system under s.14;

(b) the child is being educated outside the State or is taking part in a programme of education, training, instruction or work experience prescribed by the Minister under s.14(19);

(c) the child is receiving a certain minimum education in accordance with s.27(2); or

(d) another sufficient cause exists for the child's non-attendance.

---

[17] s.4 of the School Attendance Act 1926.
[18] s.174 of the 1926 Act.
[19] Mr William O'Dea, *Dáil Debates*, Col.838, October 5, 1999.
[20] *ibid.*
[21] See D. Glendenning, "School Attendance, The Common Good and the Education (Welfare) Act 2000" (May 2001) *Bar Review* 381; D. Stokes, "Youthreach: An Overview-Development and Future Trends" (Department of Education, 1994); Dr Paul O'Mahony, "Punishing Poverty and Personal Adversity", in Professor Ivanna Bacik and Dr Michael O'Connell (eds.), *Crime and Poverty in Ireland* (Round Hall Sweet and Maxwell, Dublin, 1998). See also *Report of the Working Group on Foster Care* (May 2001), p.39.
[22] s.17 of the Education (Welfare) Act 2000.

3–21   The 2000 Act also imposes a statutory duty on schools, assisted by the National Educational Welfare Board, to adopt a pro-active approach to the problem of truancy by students. There is a clear management reporting structure for the effective operation of the Act, as the National Educational Welfare Board, schools and their boards of management have defined duties under the legislation, and are to be assisted by the education welfare officers and liaison officers.

National Education Welfare Board

3–22   The 2000 Act attempts to address the problem of truancy and non-attendance at school through the establishment of a National Education Welfare Board ("the Board"). The Board is given a wide mandate under the Act, with its principal function being to ensure that each child receives a certain minimum education either in a recognised school or otherwise, and to assist and advise on the formation and implementation of Government policy in this area.[23] Section 10 illustrates the multi-disciplinary approach adopted in the 2000 Act, with the Board required to address issues relating to truancy at an individual level, school level, through to society in general. However, the functions of the Board are not confined to tackling non-attendance, but are also directed at student misbehaviour. The Board is to advise and assist children (and their parents) who exhibit problems relating to behaviour in school[24] and also to advise schools on matters relating to the good conduct of students generally.[25]

3–23   The Board also has the authority to require a child to undergo an assessment as to his or her intellectual, emotional and physical development by such person as may be determined.[26] Where a parent refuses to consent to such an assessment, the Board may apply to the Circuit Court for an order requiring the assessment, of the child. The Circuit Court will grant such an order only if the Court is satisfied the assessment is warranted due to the child's behaviour, lack of educational progress, or where he or she is regularly absent from school without reasonable excuse. This is a far-reaching power. In light of the privacy and family provisions in the Constitution, it is questionable whether it would survive a constitutional challenge. A relevant and instructive case is *North Western Health Board v H.W. and C.W.*,[27] discussed in Chapter 1, where Murphy J. held that to substitute the court's judgment for that of the parents would "damage the long-term interests of the child by eroding the interest and dedication of the parents in the performance of their duties."[28]

3–24   The Act does not address the situation where a child is unwilling to

---

[23] s.10.

[24] s.10(1)(f).

[25] s.10(1)(d).

[26] s.10(4).

[27] [2001] I.R. 622.

[28] See, however, the recent High Court case of August 5, 2004 where Abbot J. directed that a five-month-old girl was to undergo heart surgery, overruling opposition on religious grounds from her mother, who was a member of the Jehovah's Witnesses community.

submit to an assessment under s.10(4) of the 2000 Act, notwithstanding the parents' consent to the assessment. Should this contingency arise, there is no facility under the Act to apply to the court for an order that the assessment be carried out, an oversight that should be addressed by amending legislation.

Education welfare officers

3–25 In order to implement the 2000 Act in practice, the Board has the power to appoint education welfare officers.[29] Their functions are outlined in Pt III of the Act and allow welfare officers to wield extensive power in relation to school attendance, as detailed below. Further, s.29 imposes duties on the Board to register and monitor children who are in employment. In order to give effect to s.29, education welfare officers have powers of forcible entry under warrant to get information.[30] A person who impedes an officer in fulfilling this function may be liable on summary conviction to either a fine or imprisonment for up to six months, or both.[31]

Education of children not at a recognised school

3–26 Parents have a choice of whether to educate their child in a recognised school or not. Article 42.2 of the Irish Constitution states:

> "Parents shall be free to provide education in their homes or in private schools or in schools recognised or established by the State."

That said, s.14 of the 2000 Act places an obligation on a parent who decides not to educate their child at a recognised school to apply to the Board to have the child placed on a register of children in receipt of education in a place other than a recognised school. Inclusion in the register exempts the child from the attendance provisions of the 2000 Act, though the Board may test the quality of the education received by the student to ensure that "a certain minimum education, moral, intellectual and social" is given to the child as guaranteed in Art.42.3.2° of the Constitution. Registration is contingent on the Board being satisfied that the child concerned is receiving a certain minimum education.[32]

3–27 On receipt of an application under s.14 of the 2000 Act, for a child to be placed on the Register of Children in receipt of education in a place other than a recognised school, the Board is required to commission an authorised person, such as an education welfare officer, to assess and report on the education and materials being provided, and the time spent in the provision of such education. If further information is required, the Board can cause that person, with the consent of the parent, to enter and observe the premises, the materials and the education being received by the child. Also subject to

---

[29] s.11(1).
[30] s.30.
[31] S 30(7).
[32] s.14(10)(a).

examination is the intellectual, emotional and physical development of the child, including his or her knowledge and proficiency in such exercises as the authorised person deems appropriate. The precise minimum education required has never been defined by either the Constitution or statute though the Superior Courts have been careful not to require too high a standard. For example, Denham J. has stated:

> "minimum education must be conducive to the child achieving intellectual and social development and not such as to place the child in a discriminatory position".[33]

3–28   When sufficient information has been obtained, the Board may include the child in the register, register the child subject to conditions to ensure he or she receives a certain minimum education, or refuse to register the child. Where the Board refuses registration or imposes conditions, a parent may appeal against the decision within 21 days by notice to the Minister.[34]

Children attending special schools or institutions do not come within the ambit of the 2000 Act.[35]

3–29   In September of 2003, the Department of Education and Science issued guidelines for the education of chlidren in a place other than a recognised school, including private schools and the home.[36]

Children attending a recognised school

3–30   The 2000 Act requires compulsory school attendance for all children not exempt by entry in the register. Parents are required to ensure their children attend school, and where the child is absent, the parent must notify the principal of the reason for the child's absence, in accordance with procedures specified in the school's code of behaviour.[37] Compulsory attendance under the 2000 Act also requires that children have open access to a recognised school. This mandatory policy of openness, requiring that the board of management of a school does not refuse to admit a student, is subject only to s.15(2)(d) of the 1998 Act to the extent that it is incompatible with the published admissions policy of the school.[38] If admission is refused, an appeal may be made, pursuant to s.29 of the 1998 Act, to the Secretary General of the Department of Education, who is required to set up an appeals committee to hear the appeal.[39] These steps are designed to promote open access to all schools.

3–31   The principal is required to enter the child's name into a register of all

---

[33] See *DPP v Best* [2000] 2 I.R. 32; [2000] 2 I.L.R.M. 1.

[34] s.15(1).

[35] See Mental Treatment Act 2001 at para.7–06.

[36] *Guidelines on the Assessment of Education in Places Other Than Recognised Schools* (Department of Education and Science, September 2003).

[37] s.18.

[38] s.19(1).

[39] See discussion of appeals at para.3–16.

students attending the school on the first day of attendance.[40] In the past, inter-school transfers were somewhat haphazard; the 2000 Act addresses this issue by requiring principals to inform a child's previous school in writing of the transfer, so that the latter school can de-register the child. The 2000 Act also requires that information on the child is furnished to the new school, to inform it of issues relating to school attendance, or other matters pertaining to the child's educational progress.[41]

3–32 The principal of a school is obliged to maintain school attendance records that not only note the fact of non-attendance but also the reason for it. The register provides the basis on which the educational welfare officer is notified of poor attendance. It is then the responsibility of the officer to encourage the recalcitrant child to attend school. At the end of each school year, the school's board of management must submit a report on the level of attendance for the preceding year to the welfare officer and the local parents' association if one is established.[42] The school also has an active role in encouraging attendance through the development and adoption of strategies to promote an appreciation of learning and regular attendance. Section 22 requires a "statement of the strategies and measures … for the purposes of fostering an appreciation of learning among students attending that school and encouraging regular attendance". It embodies the change in philosophy from the 1926 Act in recognising that schools need to make efforts to attract students. The most innovative provision allows a school to alter the Minister's prescribed curriculum to facilitate regular attendance.[43]

School attendance notice

3–33 Under s.25 of the 2000 Act the Board can serve a notice on the parents of a child not attending school. Prior to serving the notice the Board must make all reasonable efforts to consult with the parents of the child and the principal of the recognised school in question. Should the parents ignore the notice and not then send the child to school, they are guilty of an offence and liable on summary conviction to a fine or imprisonment for up to one month, or both. Surprisingly, at the notice stage there is no involvement of the relevant Health Board. The involvement only occurs after the parents have been convicted of an offence or where, in the prosecution for such an offence, the parents have shown that they have taken all reasonable steps to have the child attend school.

Code of behaviour

3–34 In addition to a statement of strategies, a recognised school is required to have a code of behaviour. The High Court, in the case of *Murtagh v Board of Management, St Emer's NS*,[44] recommended that a school have a code of

---

[40] s.20(1).
[41] s.20(5).
[42] s.21(6).
[43] s.22(g)(i) and (ii).
[44] [1991] 1 I.R. 482.

conduct. Pursuant to s.23, it is now mandatory for each school to have one. The code must adhere to guidelines issued by the Board[45] and be prepared after consultation with the principal, parents, teachers and the assigned educational welfare officer.[46] Section 23(2) of the 2000 Act also specifies five matters that must be addressed in the code:

> "(*a*) the standards of behaviour that shall be observed by each student attending the school;
> (*b*) the measures that may be taken when a student fails or refuses to observe these standards;
> (*c*) the procedures to be followed before a student may be suspended or expelled from the school concerned;
> (*d*) the grounds for removing a suspension imposed in relation to a student; and
> (*e*) the procedures to be followed relating to notification of a child's absence from school."

3–35   The code of behaviour should form part of the school plan and should include an anti-bullying and anti-harassment policy, policies which are discussed in greater detail later in this chapter. An obligation is placed on the principal of the school to ensure that parents see and accept the code in writing before their child can be registered at the school. In accepting the code, the parent is also confirming that he or she will make "all reasonable efforts to ensure compliance with such code by the child."[47] A number of concerns have been raised about this requirement, as schools may be subject to claims by parents that they signed under duress or without fully appreciating what they were signing.

School discipline

3–36   In August 1997, the Non-Fatal Offences Against the Person Act 1997 outlawed the use of corporal punishment. Any physical chastisement of a student by a teacher will now expose the teacher to a criminal prosecution for assault under the 1997 Act.

Expulsion

3–37   The right of schools to expel students where their behaviour is not compatible with the code of behaviour of the school was recognised in *The State (Smullen) v Duffy*,[48] as part of the board of management's duty to the school and other students. This common law right has been retained by the Act through s.24. Where the board of management, or a "person acting on its behalf" (*i.e.* school principal), wishes to have a student expelled, it must notify the education welfare officer with reasons of its opinion that the child should

---

[45] s.23 (3).
[46] s.23(1).
[47] s.23(4).
[48] [1980] I.L.R.M. 46 at 52.

be expelled. The education welfare officer is then obliged to employ all reasonable efforts to ensure "that provision is made for the continued education" of the student concerned. Section 24(4) provides that a student must be left in the school for 20 school days following notification of the education welfare officer[49] while the officer convenes a meeting with the stakeholders, that is, the student's parents and the principal, in an effort to have the expulsion order lifted,[50] as the officer has a duty to secure the continued education of the student. The difficulty arises for the school in that it is required to have the expelled student on the school premises for 20 days. That said, as previously stated, the Board is empowered to take "reasonable measures" to ensure the safety, good order and discipline of students,[51] which makes it lawful to suspend a disruptive student during the 20-day period if the Board has serious concerns about the behaviour of a disruptive student "to ensure that good order and discipline are maintained in the school concerned and that the safety of students is secured."[52]

3–38 Section 26 of the 2000 Act amends s.29 of the 1998 Act to allow the Board to appeal the decision of a school to expel on behalf of the student concerned. This appeal facility is independent of an appeal brought under s.29 by the student or his or her parents. While it would be unlikely for the Board to act where an appeal was being brought by parents or a student, this amendment allows it to act where neither the parents nor the child are sufficiently motivated or interested to act. Section 26 restricts the powers of the Board to bring an appeal relating to a permanent exclusion or where there has been a refusal to enrol a student at all. Where an appeal is brought by the student or parents, the Board has the discretion to make submissions to the Appeals Committee if it considers this to be appropriate.[53]

Personal information

3–39 Section 28 of the 2000 Act clearly sets out the circumstances in which a school may supply "personal data". These are limited to requests in relation to educational purposes. The prescribed purposes are the supply of information for recording a person's education history so that he or she may be assisted in availing of opportunities to develop his or her full educational potential,[54] and to allow research assessing the effectiveness of education programmes and the extent to which a certain minimum education is being provided.[55]

Conclusion

3–40 Problematic behaviour leading to truancy can arise as a result of any number of factors: family breakdown; problems within the school system;

---

[49] s.24(4).
[50] s.24(3).
[51] s.24(5).
[52] *ibid.*
[53] s.26(2). The Board may exercise its discretion where it wishes to add its weight to the voices of the parents or the student at the hearing.
[54] s.28(3)(a).
[55] s.28(3)(b).

bullying; because of unidentified special needs; learning disabilities; or emotional or mental disorders. The Education Acts acknowledge the futility of a punitive approach in response to the problem and are more "child-centred". The legislation requires a partnership approach involving parents, schools, the Board and its officers, to encourage attendance, rather than enforce it. Schools are required to be more transparent in their practices and processes, especially with regard to admissions and decisions to permanently exclude pupils, as the mechanisms through which parents can appeal such decisions have been strengthened. The Acts also require the Board and its officers to take a proactive approach to the issues of attendance and misbehaviour, vesting extensive powers in this body to achieve these aims. The success of the Education Acts is highly contingent on resources. It is hoped that the current low numbers of education welfare officers will be increased to facilitate the full implementation of the statutory duties imposed on the Board by the 2000 Act.

Education for Persons with Special Educational Needs Act 2004[56]

3–41 The Education for Persons with Special Educational Needs Act 2004 is to be fully implemented over a five-year period.[57] It introduces targeted support for people with special educational needs. Section 1 of the Act defines special educational needs to mean, in relation to a person, "a restriction in the capacity of the person to participate in and benefit from education on account of an enduring physical, sensory, mental health or learning disability, or any other condition which results in a person learning differently from a person without that condition".

3–42 Section 2 of the Act establishes as a general principle a requirement that children with special educational needs be educated in an inclusive environment. It provides:

"A child with special educational needs shall be educated in an inclusive environment with children who do not have such needs unless the nature or degree of those needs of the child is such that to do so would be inconsistent with—

(*a*) the best interests of the child as determined in accordance with any assessment carried out under this Act, or

(*b*) the effective provision of education for children with whom the child is to be educated."

The Act establishes a system whereby children who are not benefiting from conventional education can be referred for assessment of their educational

---

[56] No. 30 of 2004.

[57] s.53(a) provides the that Act "shall come into operation on such day or days as the Minister may appoint by order or orders either generally or with reference to any particular purpose or provision and different days may be so appointed for different purposes or different provisions."

needs. Following the expert assessment, the school principal must cause a plan (known as an "education plan"[58]) to be prepared and reviewed at least annually for the appropriate education of the student.

3–43 Section 19 provides for the establishment of a National Council for Special Education. The functions of the Council are detailed in s.20 and include the dissemination to schools and parents of information relating to the education of children with special educational needs. The Council will also be required to plan and co-ordinate the provision of the necessary support services to children with special educational needs.

PART III

Health and Safety in the School—Emerging Issues

Introduction

3–44 In the last number of years there has been a considerable amount of detailed regulation of health and safety. Such regulation has as much relevance to the safety of the child in school as it does to the safety of the employee in the workplace. Indeed, for the purposes of the following paragraphs, the school is treated as a workplace with references to employer and employee duties. While students/pupils are not directly implicated, they must also be considered, as can be seen from s.7 of the Safety, Health and Welfare at Work Act 1989. Onerous obligations are imposed on the board of management and, in some instances, the owner or patron. The employing body will require the principal teacher to discharge certain duties in order to comply with its duties. As well as obligations under statute law, a common law duty of care also arises. For example, a specific duty exists to provide a safe school premises, independently of any duty under the health and safety legislation.

The legal framework

3–45 The significant health and safety statutes are:
- the Factories Act 1955;
- the Safety in Industries Act 1980;
- the Fire Services Act 1981;
- the Safety, Health and Welfare at Work Act 1989;
- the Safety, Health and Welfare at Work (General Application) Regulations 1993, and the 2001 and 2003 amendment Regulations;
- the Maternity Protection Act 1994 and associated Regulations and Orders;

---

[58] s.11.

- the Safety, Health and Welfare at Work (Chemical Agents) Regulations 2001;
- the Organisation of Working Time Act 1997;
- the Children Act 2001;
- the Safety, Health and Welfare at Work (Construction) Regulations 2001 and 2003.

3–46   The Safety, Health and Welfare at Work Act 1989 ("the 1989 Act") is the principal statute. It was a groundbreaking piece of legislation. Unlike previous Acts, which were aimed at defining the circumstances whereby liability was imposed, this Act is proactive in seeking to prevent accidents by obliging employers to assess and address potential risks in their place of work and by establishing a regulatory body with enforcement powers. Generally, the 1989 Act provides only for criminal liability for breaches of its provisions (though it is likely to change under the recently published Safety, Health and Welfare at Work Bill 2004). That said, s.28 of the 1989 Act allows for the making of Regulations that attract civil liability.

The 1989 Act focuses responsibility not just on the school but also on the individuals who operate and control the school. An individual can be charged where he or she fails to comply with a specific health and safety duty or fails to take such measures as are "reasonably practicable" to protect the health and safety of others, more of which later.

General duties imposed by the 1989 Act

3–47   Part II of the 1989 Act, ss.6 to 11, establishes the general duties imposed upon persons under the Act.

General duties of employers to their employees

3–48   Section 6(1) of the 1989 Act provides that it shall be the duty of every employer to ensure, so far as is reasonably practicable, the safety, health and welfare at work of all his or her employees. Ten specific matters which an employer must consider when fulfilling the duty imposed by s.6(1) of the Act are referred to in s.6(2). It is important to note that this list is not exhaustive and is merely an expanded statement of the common law position.[59] Further, the duties imposed under the 1989 Act cannot be taken by employers as granting them a licence to implement draconian measures under the guise of purported compliance with the 1989 Act. The actions of the employer in each particular case must be reasonable in the circumstances.

General duties of employees

3–49   Section 9 sets down the duties on all employees while at work. The employees' primary duty is to take reasonable care for their own and others'

---

[59] The common law duty owed by employers to employees is broadly stated as to provide a safe place of work, a safe system of work, proper equipment and competent staff.

safety, health and welfare. There is also a duty on an employee to co-operate with his or her employer, to use the protective equipment and clothing provided to him or her, and to report dangerous risks of which he or she becomes aware.

"Reasonably practicable"

3–50   It was previously stated that the principal teacher will be required to take such steps as are "reasonably practicable" to protect the health and safety of others. That said, what is "reasonably practicable"? Asquith L.J. classically defined the "reasonably practicable" standard in *Edwards v National Coal Board*[60] in the following manner:

> "'[r]easonably practicable' is a narrower term than 'physically possible' and seems to me to imply that a computation must be made by the owner in which the *quantum* of risk is placed on one scale and the sacrifice involved in the measures necessary for averting the risk (whether in money, time or trouble) is placed in the other, and that, if it be shown that there is a gross disproportion between them-the risk being insignificant in relation to the sacrifice-the defendants discharge the onus on them. Moreover, this computation falls to be made by the owner at a point of time anterior to the accident...."

3–51   It is important to distinguish between the concept of negligence, discussed in Chapter 1, and that of "reasonably practicable". A defendant may avoid liability in negligence for failing to fulfil certain duties merely by demonstrating that the burden imposed upon him [time and/or cost] by taking those precautions outweighs the scale of the loss, taking into account the chance of that loss occurring. It is clear from Lord Asquith in the *Edwards* case that reasonable practicability is an altogether different creature. For reasonable practicability there must be a gross disproportion. In *Daly v Avonmore Creameries Limited*,[61] McCarthy J., in the Supreme Court, considered "reasonably practicable" at p.131:

> "I am not to be taken as supporting a view that, where lives are at stake, considerations of expense are any more than vaguely material...."[62]

3–52   It would appear, therefore, that in monetary terms the monies required to be expended by a school would have to be very significant before it would not be "reasonably practicable" to take the precautions. This is a matter for each individual principal teacher, however, as pursuant to s.50 of the 1989 Act, in any prosecution for an offence consisting of a failure to comply with a duty to do something, so far as it was practicable or "reasonably practicable", the principal teacher will have to prove that it was not practicable or was not "reasonably practicable" to do more than was in fact done to satisfy this duty

---

[60] [1949] 1 All E.R. 743 (C.A.).
[61] [1984] I.R. 131.
[62] See also *Kirwan v Bray UDC*, unreported, Supreme Court, July 30, 1969.

or requirement. The Supreme Court reinforced this view in *Boyle v Marathon Petroleum Ireland Limited.*[63]

Approved codes of practice

3–53   Another source of guidance for the principal teacher as to what may be regarded as "reasonable" are approved codes of practice. Section 30 of the 1989 Act empowers the Health and Safety Authority, with the consent of the Minister for Labour, Trade and Consumer Affairs, to issue technical specifications in the form of approved codes of practice to support the detailed statutory provisions. A failure to observe any part of a code of practice will not of itself render a person liable to criminal proceedings. That said, a code of practice can be used in evidence in criminal proceedings as well as in civil cases.

It can be seen from s.31 of the 1989 Act that the special legal standing accorded to the code of practice means that if you are prosecuted for a breach of health and safety law, and it is proven that you did not adhere to the relevant statutory provisions or the code of practice, you will need to demonstrate that you have complied with the law in some other manner or a court will find you liable.

Safety statements

3–54   Under s.12 of the 1989 Act every principal teacher must, as soon as possible, prepare or cause to be prepared in writing a "safety statement". This statement specifies the manner in which safety, health and welfare shall be secured in the school. It should contain a summary of the school's safety and health goals and objectives, assignment of responsibilities and means of achieving the aims and objectives.

The purpose of the safety statement is to require the principal teacher to assess the school over which he or she has control and to identify the hazards to safety, health and welfare at that school. It must also specify the arrangements made and the resources provided for safeguarding the school staff and pupils. The requirement of a written risk assessment was amplified in the General Application Regulations 1993. Regulation 10 states as follows:

"10. Risk Assessment

It shall be the duty of every employer in preparing a safety statement–

   (a) to be in possession of an assessment in writing of the risks to safety and health at the place of work as required under section 12(3) of the Act, such risks to include any which put groups of employees at unusual risk, and
   (b) to decide on any protective measures to be taken and, if necessary, the protective equipment to be used."

The safety statement must therefore be based on a systematic and compre-

---

[63] unreported, Supreme Court, January 12, 1999.

hensive identification of hazards. Risk assessment must be followed by the implementation of risk-reduction measures.

3–55 The risk assessments undertaken in the preparation of a safety statement take the form of a systematic informed evaluation of the risk or danger associated with school tasks. They are a vital planning and management tool to which the phrase *premonitus premunitus* (forewarned is forearmed) is directly applicable. Thus, the emphasis that the enforcement authorities place on such assessments cannot be overestimated. Risk assessments are, therefore, a key mechanism for achieving and maintaining safety in the school. The Health and Safety Authority (HSA) has published very helpful guidance on the drafting of a safety statement.[64]

3–56 A safety statement must also identify the co-operation required from other school staff and include the names of the persons responsible for the safety tasks assigned to them under the Act. In addition, the principal must bring the terms of the safety statement to the attention of both school staff and pupils. While, as previously stated, the obligation to make the safety statement available is confined to staff members, s.7 of the 1989 Act imposes an obligation on the principal teacher to provide pupils with information in relation to how particular activities "might affect their safety or health".

Failure to comply with the s.12 safety statement requirement attracts both criminal and civil liability, as s.12 is not included in the civil liability embargo contained in s.60 of the 1989 Act.

3–57 For guidelines on the drafting of a safety statement and examples of risk assessments, see Appendix 9.

Regulations implemented under the Safety, Health and Welfare at Work Act 1989

3–58 Section 28 of the 1989 Act empowers the Minister to make regulations in respect of a very wide range of topics as well as any other matters necessary to give effect to the Act.[65] Their primary importance derive from the fact that breach of the regulations incur civil liability.

To date, numerous regulations have been implemented under the 1989 Act. The main Regulations are the Safety, Health and Welfare at Work (General Application) Regulations 1993 (the "1993 Regulations").

Bullying and stress as a health and safety issue under the 1993 Regulations

3–59 An employer's duty of care to look after the health and safety of employees includes the reasonable prevention of bullying and stress-related injury in the workplace.

---

[64] See *Guidelines on Preparing your Safety Statement and Carrying out Risk Assessments* (Health and Safety Authority, 2000).
[65] See Fourth Schedule to the 1989 Act.

Bullying

3–60   The 1989 Act provides that employers shall carry out a risk assessment
at their place of work in the preparation of a safety statement. Such an
assessment should include the risks associated with bullying. Procedures or
preventative measures should follow this risk assessment in order to eliminate
the risk or reduce the level of risk to an acceptable level. Regulation 10 of the
1993 Regulations requires employers to document the results of the risk
assessment.

3–61   There is no statute addressing bullying in the workplace, as there is
with most other causes of action in employment law. Indeed, one of the problems
with bullying is the absence of an accepted definition. The Health and Safety
Authority (HSA) has published a booklet on bullying which provides a
definition:

> "Bullying in the workplace is repeated aggression, verbal, psychological
> or physical, conducted by an individual or group against another person
> or persons. Bullying is where aggression or cruelty, viciousness, intimi-
> dation, or a need to humiliate dominate the relationships".[66]

The definition goes on to emphasise that bullying is aggressive behaviour which
is systematic and ongoing and does not relate to isolated, one-off incidents of
aggression.

3–62   Bullying behaviour affects not only the victim and perpetrator but every
child/person in the school and should be proactively addressed through a range
of school-based initiatives and strategies. It may not be deliberate. For example,
a teacher may, through using sarcasm or humiliating an academically weak
student, facilitate a bullying environment.

   An anti-bullying policy should form an integral part of the code of behaviour
in the school plan.[67] This policy should include a procedure for the formal
noting of and reporting of an incident of bullying in the school. Any such
procedure should provide for the early detection of bullying. Serious cases of
bullying should be dealt with immediately by the principal or vice-principal.
A written record should be kept of all investigations of bullying. This could
include giving the victim and/or perpetrator an opportunity to write down his
account of the incident. Parents of the victim and perpetrator should be told by
the principal or vice-principal at the earliest possible opportunity.

3–63   In *Mulvey (A Minor) v McDonagh*,[68] it was held that the standard of
care owed by a teacher to his pupils was that which would be owed to children
of similar age and in similar circumstances by a prudent parent acting
reasonably. As the board of management, in the instant case, through its agent,
the school principal, had acted as a reasonable parent would have done in the

---

[66] See also *Saehan Media Ireland v A Worker* [1999] E.L.R. 41.
[67] See para.3–33.
[68] [2004] I.E.H.C. 48 (March 26, 2004).

circumstances, the High Court concluded that it had discharged its duty of care towards a child whose parent had claimed that the board of management had been negligent in not shielding the child from bullying at the school.

3–64 The national child protection guidelines, "Children First", imposes obligations on the school management to deal with bullying and states:

> "It is imperative that school management boards should have in place a policy to deal with bullying. In a situation where the incident is serious and where the behaviour is regarded as potentially abusive, the school should consult the relevant health board with a view to drawing up an appropriate response such as a management plan".[69]

Stress

3–65 The HSA defines workplace stress as arising "when the demands of the job and the working environment on a person exceeds their capacity to meet them".[70] An employer's duty is not to provide a stress-free environment but to take reasonably practicable steps to shield employees from exposure to stress and from the consequences of unreasonably stressful working conditions.

3–66 Employers have both a statutory and common law duty of care to protect their staff against stress. Whilst there have been few cases decided on this point, the potential for litigation in this area is growing. This can be seen from the case of *Saehan Media Ireland Ltd. v A Worker*,[71] where the Labour Court acknowledged work-related stress as a health and safety issue and held that "employers have an obligation to deal with instances of its occurrence which may be brought to their attention".

3–67 Health and safety law requires risks to be eliminated or reduced so far as is reasonably practicable—a concept previously discussed at length. The 1989 Act also requires employers to conduct risk assessments. Any such risk assessments should include assessments of activities that could potentially cause unreasonable stress to workers. Regulation 10 of the 1993 Regulations provides that the results of these assessments should be documented.

3–68 Workers claiming compensation for stress in England and Wales were required to satisfy strict new rules laid down by the Court of Appeal in February 2002 that made it clear that no job is inherently dangerous to an employ-

---

[69] *Children First: National Guidelines for the Protection and Welfare of Children* (The Stationery Office, Dublin, September 1999) at para.11.7.1, p.107.

[70] *Workplace Stress* (Health and Safety Authority, 1992). The British Health and Safety Executive (HSE) defines stress as "people's natural reaction to excessive pressure". See also the document of the Commission of the European Union (EU), *Guidance on work-related stress*, which defines work-related stress as "the emotional, cognitive, behavioural and physiological reaction to aversive and noxious aspects of work, work environments and work organisations". Work-related stress, the EU Commission document states, "is characterised by high levels of arousal and distress and often by feelings of not coping".

[71] [1999] E.L.R. 41.

ee's mental health. In judgments that appeared to signpost a sea-change in compensation awards for stress, the Court of Appeal overturned damages claims by three workers totalling nearly £200,000. Lady Justice Hale opined that it should not be the responsibility of an employer to make exhaustive investigations into the mental health of employees. Instead, the onus was on the stressed worker to decide whether to leave the job or carry on working and accept the risk of a mental breakdown.

3–69 On April 1, 2004, the House of Lords overturned the Court of Appeal's judgment (in *Barber v Somerset County Council*, which had been one of the four cases heard as a composite appeal by the Court of Appeal).[72] While the House of Lords approved the practical guidance issued by the Court of Appeal, it held that the Court had erred in concluding that the senior management team were not in breach of the employer's duty of care:

> "The senior management team should have made inquiries about [the appellant's] problems and seen what they could do to ease them, in consultation with officials at the County Council's Education Department, instead of brushing him off unsympathetically … or sympathising but telling him to prioritise his work...."

3–70 The House of Lords, quoting with approval the dicta of Swanwick J. in *Stokes v Guest, Keen and Nettlefold (Bolts and Nuts) Ltd*,[73] held that each case will depend on its own facts:

> "… the overall test is still the conduct of the reasonable and prudent employer, taking positive thought for the safety of his workers in the light of what he knows or ought to know; where there is a recognised and general practice which has been followed for a substantial period in similar circumstances without mishap, he is entitled to follow it, unless in the light of common sense or newer knowledge it is clearly bad; but, where there is developing knowledge, he must keep reasonably abreast of it and not be too slow to apply it; and where he has in fact greater than average knowledge of the risks, he may be thereby obliged to take more than the average or standard precautions. He must weigh up the risk in terms of the likelihood of injury occurring and the potential consequences if it does; and he must balance against this the probable effectiveness of the precautions that can be taken to meet it and the expense and inconvenience they involve. If he is found to have fallen below the standard to be properly expected of a reasonable and prudent employer in these respects, he is negligent."

Minimising liability

3–71 There is a detectable movement towards encouraging employers to manage health and safety issues and this is particularly pertinent when

---

[72] [2004] U.K.H.L. 13.
[73] [1968] 1 W.L.R . 1776 at 1783.

addressing the identification of bullying and stress in the school. Such an approach involves, *inter alia*, the principal teacher (or someone nominated by him) carrying out a risk assessment on an ongoing basis. The risk assessment should form part of the safety statement. This statement should aver not merely to the physical hazards but also to the potential damage of stress and bullying.

3–72 Bullying procedures and policies are essential in the defence of a bullying and stress claim by an employee. The sanctions to be taken against those found to be in breach of the anti-bullying policy should be clearly stated. A recommendation of the Task Force Report on the Prevention of Workplace Bullying is that every workplace should have a "Dignity in the Workplace" Charter in addition to a separate and specific written anti-bullying policy designed to suit each organisation's requirements.[74] A code of practice on the Prevention of Workplace Bullying has also been published. It details procedures for identifying, preventing and processing allegations of bullying in the workplace. In particular, the code provides instruction on preparing an anti-bullying policy. It also outlines procedures for addressing allegations of workplace bullying. Such procedures include written complaints being examined by a designated member of management, culminating in an investigation either by management or an agreed third party.

The Department of Education and Science has issued guidelines for dealing with bullying in both primary and post-primary schools.[75] Given the consequences of bullying for both the child and school, these guidelines are reproduced almost in full in Appendix 8.

3–73 Formal grievance procedures should be put in place to ensure access to management. Such procedures are central to the avoidance of bullying and stress-related claims in that they impose an obligation on the employee to alert the employer to the existence of a bullying- and stress-related problem. Each complaint must be comprehensively investigated. Failure to adopt this approach can have serious consequences. A relevant and instructive case is *A. v Shropshire County Council*.[76] The case arose as a result of the introduction by a new head teacher of new disciplinary procedures for students, which were a failure. The lack of discipline that followed the introduction of the new regime led to the plaintiff suffering stress symptoms that endured for some time. The plaintiff's employers ignored the warning signs. The plaintiff was eventually diagnosed as having suffered a nervous breakdown. A substantial settlement of £300,000 was made in the case.

3–74 Not only should grievance procedures be spelled out for school staff alleging bullying or harassment, a pupil against whom an allegation of

---

[74] The *Task Force Report on the Prevention of Workplace Bullying* was established by the then Minister for Labour, Trade and Consumer Affairs, Mr Tom Kitt T.D., in September 1999, under the auspices of the HSA, and the report of its findings was launched on April 10, 2001. Minister Fahy has recently announced a further initiative in this area.

[75] See Department of Education's 1993 Guidelines on bullying in post-primary schools.

[76] English High Court, June, 2000.

wrongdoing is made is also entitled to the benefit of fair procedures.[77] Kearns J. in *Student A and Student B v Dublin Secondary School* noted that the expulsion of two pupils, caught using cannabis, as part of the school's zero-tolerance policy on drugs occurred before "either the students or the parents had an opportunity of making representations prior to the imposition of the most severe penalty to be imposed.... This is an essential element of fair procedures."[78]

The school's code of conduct should specify the grounds of misconduct on which a pupil may be suspended and on which the pupil may ultimately be expelled. Even where the complaint of bullying, for example, is supported by an investigation, disciplinary procedures should include a number of steps.[79] In particular, the sanction will have to be measured so as to meet the circumstances of the particular case.[80]

3–75 Where an employer becomes aware that an employee is exposed to work-related stress, the employer should relieve the employee of his or her duties on full salary and obtain advice from health professionals. It is also essential that employers comply with the Organisation of Working Time Act 1997 as regards daily, weekly and annual breaks.

Part III – Workplace

3–76 Regulation 16 defines a place of work to include schools and colleges. Regulation 17 and the Second Schedule of the 1993 Regulations cover a number of workplace standards on ventilation, room temperature, natural and artificial room-lighting, space allocation and sanitary facilities that must be in place.[81]

The smoking ban

3–77 The Tobacco Smoking (Prohibition) Regulations 2003 (the "2003 Regulations"),[82] and the amendments thereto, came into force on March 29, 2004. The 2003 Regulations ban smoking in the school building as did the now-revoked Tobacco (Health Promotion and Protection) Regulations 1995.[83]

3–78 The 2003 Regulations add to a number of existing legal requirements applicable to smoking in the workplace. Significantly, the Public Health (Tobacco) (Amendment) Act 2004 provides that "smoking" includes sucking, sniffing or chewing any tobacco product. As "tobacco product" includes "any

---

[77] See *McKenna (a Minor) v Ó Ciarain*, unreported, Ó Caoimh J., November 30, 2001.
[78] See *Student A and Student B v Dublin Secondary School*, unreported, Kearns J., November 25, 1999.
[79] See *James Wright and Alexander Wright v The Board of Management of Gorey Community School*, unreported, O'Sullivan J., March 28, 2000.
[80] See *Timmons v Oglesby and Butler Ltd* (1999) E.L.R. 119.
[81] See also Safety, Health and Welfare at Work (Miscellaneous Welfare Provisions) Regulations 1995 (S.I. No. 358 of 1995) and Guidelines (Health and Safety Authority, Dublin, 1995).
[82] S.I. No. 481 of 2003.
[83] S.I. No. 359 of 1995, made under the Tobacco (Health Promotion and Protection) Act 1988.

cigarette paper or filter", having an unlit cigarette in your mouth would render you liable under the legislation.[84]

The legislation covers only enclosed areas and does not apply to outdoor work areas. An outdoor work area is defined as a place or premises, or part of a place or premises, "covered by a fixed or movable roof, provided that not more than 50 per cent of the perimeter is surrounded by one or more walls or similar structures (inclusive of windows, doors, gates or other means of access to or egress from that part)".[85]

3–79 The smoking ban in the workplace has enjoyed a high level of compliance to date with authorised officers under the Public Health (Tobacco) Act 2002 having responsibility for the enforcement of the smoking ban. A fine of up to €3,000 can be imposed for failing to comply with the legislation. It is a defence to any proceedings in respect of an offence under the Public Health (Tobacco) Acts 2002 and 2004 for an employer to show that "he or she made all reasonable efforts to ensure compliance" with the smoking ban.[86]

Smoking policy

3–80 Every school principal should formulate a policy on smoking that is to be followed by teachers and other staff working in the school. The purpose of such a policy is to determine the manner in which the school manages tobacco smoking. Any dismissal resulting from a breach of the smoking policy should be executed in accordance with the schools' disciplinary procedure. It should be noted that an employer is not obliged to provide an outdoor smoking facility. If such a facility is provided, the HSA recommends that it should not be within "six metres of all entrance(s), exit(s), open windows, ventilation intake systems and covered entryways of any building".[87] Moreover, it should be noted that the sale of cigarettes to a child under 18 years of age is an offence. Part 3 of the Children Act 1908, as amended by the Tobacco (Health and Protection) Act 1988, imposed a maximum fine of £2 for selling cigarettes to a child under 16 years of age. This was amended by the said Tobacco (Health and Promotion) Act 1988.

Part IV – Use of work equipment

3–81 This part of the 1993 Regulations addresses the issue and use of work equipment. Regulation 18 defines the use of work equipment as "any activity involving work equipment". Regulation 19 outlines the duties of employers, which cover responsibilities such as risk assessment [subsection (b)] and the provision of training relating to the proper use of the work equipment [subsection (e)].

3–82 The Safety, Health and Welfare at Work (General Application) (Amend-

---

[84] See s.2 of the Public Health (Tobacco) (Amendment) Act 2004.

[85] See s.16 of the 2004 Act.

[86] *ibid.*

[87] See HSA Guidance.

ment) Regulations 2001 ("the 2001 Regulations")[88] amend Pt IV of the 1993 Regulations. The 2001 Regulations set down new requirements, such as ergonomic risk assessments, in respect of all work equipment.

3–83 All equipment supplied must be maintained to the requisite standard throughout its life. The onerous duty imposed upon employers in relation to work equipment was addressed in the case of *Eamon Stakelum v Governor and Company of the Bank of Ireland*.[89] In summary, the High Court held that employers have a duty to ensure that any equipment used by an employee in the course of his work is free from defects and suitable for the purposes for which it is used. O'Donovan J. placed particular emphasis on the employer's duty to submit equipment used by an employee in the course of his employment to risk/safety assessment.

This part of the regulations is particularly relevant to the PE teacher. Sport equipment should be checked with a view to deciding if it can cause risk and how any such risk might be prevented. In particular, weights should be subject to regular inspections by a known specialist.

Part V – Personal protective equipment

3–84 This part of the 1993 Regulations requires employers, where risk to health and safety cannot be avoided by technical measures and procedures, to provide personal protective equipment for use by their employees. It would appear that the Regulations do not impose a duty on an employer to enforce the use of the personal safety equipment that he is obliged to provide to his employees. A common law duty is imposed on an employer in this regard, however, through the tort of negligence.

The 1993 Regulations do not apply to pupils as they are not employees. That said, in discharging its duty of care, the school should specify particular equipment types and ensure that pupils wear such equipment while engaged in sports activities; for example, shin guards, shoulder pads or mouth guards.

Part VI – Manual handling of loads

3–85 Regulation 27 defines what constitutes the manual handling of loads:

> " 'Manual handling of loads' means any transporting or supporting of a load by one or more employees, and includes lifting, putting down, pushing, pulling, carrying or moving a load, which, by reason of its characteristics or of unfavourable ergonomic conditions, involves risk, particularly of back injury, to employees."

Part VI envisages the manual handling of loads by employees as a last resort. Where such handling is required, an employer is obliged to minimise the risk involved and provide, where possible, information concerning the weight and centre of gravity of a load to the employee.[90]

[88] S.I. No. 188 of 2001.
[89] unreported, High Court, O'Donovan J., July 5, 1999.
[90] See Reg.28.

3–86 The Eighth Schedule details the four factors that must be taken into account by an employer for the manual handling of loads. These are:

1. the characteristics of the load;

2. the physical effort required;

3. the characteristics of the working environment; and

4. the requirements of the activity.

3–87 In *Fiona Stone v Metropolitan Police Commissioner*,[91] the plaintiff, a 28-year-old woman, was awarded Stg£400,000 for the soft-tissue lower-back injury she suffered as a result of lifting and transporting heavy loads whilst at work. This was a cumulative injury over time and not a single event. Significantly, Reg.28 and the Eighth Schedule anticipate such injuries.

The Ninth Schedule identifies individual risk factors in the manual handling of loads. This schedule provides that an employee may be at risk if he is physically unsuited to perform the task in question, is wearing unsuitable clothing, and/or does not have the adequate or appropriate knowledge or training.[92]

Regular manual handling training will reduce the exposure of an employer to a claim under this part of the Act. A relevant and instructive case is *Gorry v British Midland Airways Ltd*.[93] Judge Dunne, citing Pt VI of the General Application Regulations 1993, noted that all reasonable precautions were required. The learned judge held that, even where employees were performing a task regularly, they acquired bad habits and needed to be reminded from time to time to execute their tasks safely.

Part IX – First aid

3–88 Part IX of the Regulations imposes a duty on an employer in respect of first aid. Regulation 54 provides a definition for first aid:

"'first-aid' means–

(a) in a case where a person requires treatment from a registered medical practitioner or a registered general nurse, treatment for the purpose of preserving life or minimising the consequences of injury or illness until the services of such a practitioner or such a nurse are obtained, or

(b) in a case of minor injury which would otherwise receive no treatment or does not need treatment by a registered medical practitioner or registered general nurse, treatment of such an injury;..."

---

[91] Milton Keynes County Court, Serota J., September 16, 1999 L.T.L.P.I. September 27, 1999.

[92] The Ninth Schedule provides that wearing unsuitable footwear or other personal effects may also put an employee at risk.

[93] (1999) 17 I.L.T. 224. On training, see also Reg.13 of the 1993 Regulations.

In defining "occupational first-aider", Reg.54 also identifies the need for the training of first-aiders. The recently introduced Safety, Health and Welfare at Work (General Application) (Amendment) (No.2) Regulations 2003 explicitly require that the first-aid equipment provided to be used by occupational first-aiders is adequate.[94]

Every teacher should have easy access to first-aid boxes, kits and facilities. First-aid needs can only be determined by the carrying out of a risk assessment at the school.[95]

Part X – Notification of accidents and dangerous occurrences

3–89   Part X and the Twelfth Schedule to the 1993 Regulations impose requirements with respect to the notification of accidents and the maintenance of records relating to accidents.[96]

Safety, Health and Welfare at Work (Miscellaneous Welfare Provisions) Regulations 1995[97]

3–90   The Safety, Health and Welfare at Work (Miscellaneous Welfare Provisions) Regulations 1995 provide for a number of employer duties. This S.I., along with Reg.17 and the Second Schedule of the 1993 Regulations, imposes an obligation on employers to provide a safe and comfortable place of work. The employer's duties include, *inter alia*, the provision of adequate and suitable facilities for taking meals and an adequate supply of drinking water.

Fire and emergencies

3–91   The Fire Services Act 1981 places a responsibility on the occupiers' or owners' of buildings to safeguard against the outbreak of fires on the premises and to ensure the safety of persons on the premises in the event of an outbreak of fire. In practice, this will involve the enforcement of a fire-prevention policy. It will also involve ensuring the following are adequate:

1.   fire alarm(s);

2.   emergency procedures;

3.   emergency exits (including emergency lighting if appropriate); and

4.   available fire-fighting equipment.

---

[94] S.I. No. 53 of 2003.

[95] See *Guidelines on First Aid* (Health and Safety Authority, Dublin, 1994) and *Guide to the 1989 Act and the 1993 Regulations* (Health and Safety Authority, Dublin, 2000).

[96] See Approved Forms for Reporting Accidents and Dangerous Occurrences: IR 1 and IR 3. The HSA have recently introduced a new Form IR 1 for the reporting of work-related accidents with extended explanations as to what is reportable and not reportable. The new form obliges the designated responsible person to include details relating to what caused the accident and how the person was injured. See also *Guidelines for Reporting Accidents and Dangerous Occurrences* (Health and Safety Authority, Dublin, 1995).

[97] S.I. No. 358 of 1995.

Part II of the Safety, Health and Welfare at Work (General Application) Regulations 1993 imposes an obligation on employers to prepare and communicate any emergency procedures (which would include the contingency of a fire).

The Safety, Health and Welfare at Work (Signs) Regulations 1995[98] specify the type of signs to be used for prohibiting activities causing a fire hazard (*e.g.* "no smoking" signs), as well as emergency escape and fire-fighting signs.

Chemical agents and dangerous substances

3–92 The Safety, Health and Welfare at Work (Chemical Agents) Regulations 2001[99] came into force on December 19, 2001 and now form a basic framework for all legislation relating to chemical agents, including carcinogens, lead, asbestos and flammable/explosive materials. They should be read in conjunction with the 2002 Code of Practice for the Safety, Health and Welfare at Work (Chemical Agents) Regulations 2001. In summary, the Safety, Health and Welfare at Work (Chemical Agents) Regulations 2001 require that before any worker is exposed to a hazardous substance, he or she is to be subject to an assessment so that appropriate precautions can be taken. As paint and solvents used in the teaching of art are chemical agents, a risk assessment must be carried out on all such chemicals used as detailed in the 2001 Regulations.

Regulation 4 of the 2001 Regulations imposes a duty to determine what substances in the school constitute a risk to health, and Regs 5 and 6 require either the elimination of such a risk or its reduction to an acceptable level. Regulation 7 imposes duties in respect of the proper use of personal protective equipment while Reg.9 requires the provision of information and training in relation to the risks associated with the use of any chemical agent and the means whereby such risks are reduced (including the correct use of personal protective equipment). Regulation 8 of the 2001 Regulations imposes a duty to make arrangements to deal with accidents, incidents and emergencies.

Enforcement under the 1989 regime

3–93 The sanctions provided under the Safety Health and Welfare at Work Act 1989 are primarily criminal, although this will change under the recently published Safety, Health and Welfare at Work Bill 2004. Given the fact that breaches would be technical in nature, it was logical to vest responsibility for enforcement in an administrative body, namely the National Authority for Occupational Safety and Health, better known as the Health and Safety Authority (HSA). Part III of the 1989 Act establishes the HSA, while Pts V, VI, VII and VIII provide that body with its metaphorical teeth. Health and safety inspectors from the HSA normally enforce the health and safety statutory provisions.

Both individuals and bodies corporate may be prosecuted. Section 48(19) of the 1989 Act specifically provides for the prosecution of management. The

---

[98] S.I. No. 132 of 1995.
[99] S.I. No. 445 of 2001.

application of s.48(19) in this jurisdiction can be seen as far back as the November 1998 case of *National Authority for Occupational Safety and Health v Noel Frisby Construction Ltd and Noel Frisby.*[100]

Insurance

3–94 Appropriate insurance should be taken out to ensure that the school is protected against staff- and pupil-related claims, arising from an accident taking place in the school or during an out-of-school activity.

Overview

3–95 It is clear from the foregoing that there has been a powerful movement towards greater protection of the safety, health and welfare of staff, teachers and pupils at school. It is probable that many more regulations affecting all aspects of the school and all those persons connected with it will be introduced pursuant to s.28 of the 1989 Act. These regulations will, no doubt, impose more extensive obligations on the principal teacher as will the Safety, Health and Welfare at Work Bill 2004 when it is enacted.

The leading question that remains to be addressed is what duty of care will be imposed in the future. Currently, the protection afforded by statute is in excess of that presently afforded by the common law. Several provisions of the 1989 Act require the high standard of reasonable practicability from employers. In fact, the 1993 Regulations impose certain absolute duties.

3–96 It has been suggested that the duty of care imposed under future regulations should be one of absolute liability.[101] A number of reasons for this approach are proffered. Most regulations commence life as Directives from Europe, which this State is obliged, pursuant to its treaty obligations, to implement. Directives set down minimum standards, not maximum ones, and do not preclude the imposition of a higher duty of care. Accordingly, it is always open to a court to hold that the regulations impose a higher standard than that provided for under the 1989 Act. In addition, in some cases, absolute duties have already been in existence in Irish law since the Factories Act 1955, and to withdraw or recoil from that now would be to reduce the level of protection available under the 1989 Act. This would be totally contrary to the intention of the legislature and the spirit of the legislation. Further, many of the regulations are general in nature and, indeed, vague in parts. This would and should militate against too strict an interpretation of the regulations by the courts.

3–97 With the passage of time, the 1989 Act, the regulations implemented

---

[100] See the Health and Safety Authority's annual report of 1998, p.17.

[101] Strict liability is not to be equated with absolute liability. Defences may be pleaded in respect of a strictly liability standard whereas no defence is available to a standard of absolute liability. This standard is higher than that of reasonable practicability under the 1989 Act.

under that Act and the Occupiers' Liability Act 1995 will improve the health and safety standards which staff, teachers and pupils enjoy in the school. This should result in fewer accidents. Consequently, the number and cost of claims should fall. This increased protection may raise the expectations of society as a whole in so far as safety, health and welfare at work are concerned. It may serve in time to impact upon the common law duty of care. In other words, what is reasonable now may not be deemed reasonable in the future. In summary, the greater protection afforded by statute may become no more than merely declaratory of the common law position.

CHILD PROTECTION

3–98　The national child protection guidelines, *Children First*,[102] provide that schools have a vital role in child protection: The guidelines state:

"Boards of Management, principals and senior management teams have primary responsibility for the care and welfare of their pupils. Management arrangements within primary and post-primary schools should provide for the following:

(i)　the planning, development and implementation of an effective child protection programme;

(ii)　the continuous monitoring and evaluation of the effectiveness of such provision;

(iii) the effective implementation of agreed reporting procedures;

(iv) the planning and implementation of appropriate staff development and training programmes."[103]

3–99　*Children First* outlines the responsibilities of the school management in the following terms:

"It is the responsibility of the Board of Management of each school to do the following:

(i)　have clear procedures which teachers and other school staff must follow where they suspect, or are alerted to, possible child abuse, including where a child discloses abuse;

(ii)　designate a senior member of staff to have specific responsibility for child protection. In the case of primary schools, the designated liaison person for dealing with outside agencies should be the Principal or other person designated by the Board. The Principal/designated person is responsible for ensuring that the standard reporting procedure is followed so that suspected cases of child abuse are referred to the local health board or An Garda Síochána;

---

[102] *Children First: National Guidelines for the Protection and Welfare of Children* (The Stationery Office, Dublin, September 1999).
[103] *ibid.* at para.6.8.1, pp.50–51.

(iii) monitor the progress of children considered to be at risk;
(iv) contribute to the prevention of child abuse through curricular provision;
(v) promote in-service training for teachers and members of Boards of Management to ensure that they have a good working knowledge of child protection issues and procedures;
(vi) have clear written procedures in place governing action to be taken where allegations are received against school employees."

Paragraph 6.8.1 considers the position of teachers in the protection of children:

"Teachers have a general duty of care to ensure that arrangements are in place to protect children and young people from harm. In this regard, young people need to be facilitated to develop their self-esteem, confidence, independence of thought and the necessary skills to cope with possible threats to their personal safety both within and outside the school."[104]

3–100   With reference to school staff generally, it is clear from paragraph 6.8.3, entitled "Personal Responsibilities of School Staff", that everyone has a duty to protect children:

"If a child discloses [allegations] to a teacher or to other school staff that (s)he is being harmed by a parent/carer or any other person, the person who receives the information should listen carefully and supportively. This applies equally where the child implies that (s)he is at risk of being harmed by a parent/carer or any other person. It also implies equally if a parent/carer or any other person discloses that (s)he has harmed or is at risk of harming a child. The child or young person should not be interviewed formally; the teacher/staff member should obtain only necessary relevant facts if and when clarification is needed. *Confidentiality must never be promised to a person stating a disclosure* and the requirement to report to the school board must be explained in a supportive manner. The discussion should be recorded accurately and the record retained. The teacher or other staff member should then inform the principal or designated person who is responsible for reporting the matter to the health board or An Garda Síochána."[105]

Guidelines for child protection in primary schools, similar to those detailed in *Children First*, were issued by the Department of Education and Science in 2001. Similar guidelines and procedures were also commenced for post-primary schools.

---

[104] *ibid.* at p.50.
[105] *ibid.* at p.51.

The Equality Act 2004[106]

3–101   The Equality Act 2004, which was commenced on July 18, 2004, amends both the Employment Equality Act 1998 and the Equal Status Act 2000. The Employment Equality Acts 1998–2004 apply to schools as employers. The Equal Status Acts are applicable as education is a service covered by the Acts. They have been effective in the creation of an inclusive school and affect both primary and post-primary schools, particularly in ensuring that one child is not treated less favourably than another.

There are a number of exceptions to the obligations imposed by the Equal Status Acts, one of which is religious ethos. A school whose objective is to educate "in an environment which promotes certain religious values" is allowed to favour in its admissions policy students of a particular religious denomination where "it is prove[n] that the refusal is essential to maintain the ethos of the school."

The 2004 Act contains discrete onerous provisions on disability. In particular, the requirement of "reasonable accommodation" under the Employment Equality Acts has been replaced with a provision obliging the adoption of appropriate measures "unless the measures would impose a disproportionate burden". Reasonable accommodation continues to be the test under the Equal Status Acts. The provisions of the recently published Disability Bill 2004,[107] as previously stated, should also be noted.

PART IV

CONCLUSION

3–102   It is necessary to have some regard to international instruments such as the UN Convention on the Rights of the Child (CRC) and the ECHR when considering the developments that have taken place in the education sector. In practice, international instruments are rarely relied on by the Irish courts due to the dualist nature we adopt to the incorporation of such instruments.[108] That said, in *O'Donoghue v Minister for Health*,[109] O'Hanlon J. in the High Court referred to the CRC and ECHR to lend support to his determination that a child with disabilities had a right to education in order to enable him to maximise his inherent potential capacities, however limited those capacities might be. The CRC has a strong influence on policy and legislation and the ECHR has been incorporated into domestic law, albeit at a sub-Constitutional level, by the ECHR Act 2003.

3–103   While the CRC may not be binding on individual schools, it does set down standards of best practice, which, if implemented, could enhance the educational experience. For example, Art.12 of the CRC states that every child

---

[106] No. 24 of 2004.
[107] No. 39 of 2004.
[108] See Chap.12.
[109] [1996] 2 I.R. 20.

has the right to be heard and to have his or her views given due weight in accordance with his or her age and maturity. This principle is reflected in s.27 of the Education Act 1998, which provides that a school should encourage and facilitate students of a post-primary school in establishing a student council. In addition to Art.12, the other guiding principles of the CRC are Art.2, guaranteeing the right of every child to enjoy Convention rights without discrimination; and Art.3, requiring that the best interest of the child be a primary consideration in all matters concerning children. In regard to education, Art.28 clearly establishes a right to education for all, while Art.29 details the aims of such education. Schools play a central role in the development of children; therefore, the rights articulated in the CRC should not only be implemented in the process and procedures of the school, but also taught to its students.

3–104   The ECHR (in Art.2 of the Protocol) makes particular reference to education in providing that no person shall be denied the right to education. The ECHR recognises that no rights are absolute and a basic premise of this international instrument is the principle of proportionality. The test of this is whether the interference with the right in the form of the disadvantage suffered by the individual is excessive in relation to the legitimate aim being pursued. This involves a balancing of considerations. The principles in the ECHR impinge on many practices in education; for example, Art. 3 prohibits treatment or punishment that is inhuman or degrading. Schools must take measures to protect pupils from such treatment regardless of who inflicts it—staff, members of the board of management or other pupils. Since 1997 corporal punishment has not been permitted in Irish schools;[110] however, Art. 3 may require schools to protect children from abuse and bullying. Schools should, as previously stated, therefore have anti-bullying policies that are brought to the attention of pupils, and procedures allowing complaints to be addressed as a matter of best practice. A similar obligation is imposed on authorities to protect teachers and other staff from ill-treatment. The issue was further explored in the discussion on the health and safety obligations imposed on the school management.

3–105   Article 6 of the ECHR provides for the right to a fair trial, which includes the right to a hearing in the presence of the parties involved; a right to be heard; a right to a hearing within a reasonable time; and a reasoned judgment on conclusion. These rights and the principles of natural justice are supported by Art.40.3 of the Constitution as well as by case law.[111] O'Sullivan J. stated that fair procedures require that:

> "the accused should be given a reasonable opportunity to hear the case (*i.e.* charges and an account of the evidence) against him, to respond to it with evidence of his own if he wishes and to address the deciding body. I also consider that such a reasonable opportunity includes being given

---

[110] Non-Fatal Offences Against the Person Act 1997.

[111] *Re Haughey* [1970] I.R. 217, *Garvey v Ireland and Others* [1981] I.R. 750.

advance notice of the charges and the gist of the evidence upon which they are based, so as to enable a considered response to be given, if necessary after taking legal advice."[112]

In the education context it would appear from the decided case law that legal representation is not required if fair procedures are followed. The foregoing principles are particularly relevant in relation to a school's decision to suspend or expel a student, especially in light of the parents' right of appeal provided in s.29 of the Education (Welfare) Act 2000.

---

[112] *James Wright (a minor) suing by his Mother and Next Friend Helen Wright and Alexander Wright (a minor) suing by his Mother and Next Friend v The Management of Gorey Community College*, unreported, High Court, O'Sullivan J., March 28, 2000.

CHAPTER 4

SAFEGUARDING THE WELFARE OF CHILDREN IN NEED

DUTIES OF THE STATE

4–01   Questions of child welfare arise primarily in disputes between guardians, parents and the State. The general welfare of the child is a matter of concern, not only to his or her family but also to society at large. It is no longer accepted that the State should defer to the autonomy of the family in all matters relating to children. There are clearly defined circumstances in which the State is not merely entitled but obliged to intervene with a view to safeguarding children from harm, even from within their own families.

4–02   The conventional image of the child at risk is where allegations of child sexual abuse arise. Children may equally be at risk by reason of serious physical and emotional abuse, on a continuous basis, often by persons who are specifically charged with promoting the child's welfare. In such cases, the State intervenes not by invitation of the parties (as where there is a dispute as to custody) but on its own initiative. Such intervention may comprise the initiation of criminal proceedings. However, the obligation of the State is not fulfilled simply by the punishment of wrongdoers. In order to protect the welfare of the child, it may be necessary to take further measures independent of any criminal proceedings.

4–03   To this end, the Child Care Act 1991[1] has introduced a definitive legal structure designed to allow the health boards to take a range of steps to best promote the welfare of children.[2] It replaces a legal framework that was best described as "skeletal." In fact, between 1908 and 1991 there was little in the line of substantial reform in this area, leaving the health boards to rely on a rather haphazard and outdated range of remedies.

4–04   Prior to the enactment of the 1991 Act, the Children Act 1908 provided for the protection of children who were at risk. Section 131 of the 1908 Act distinguished between a child and a young person; a child was under the age of 15 years while a young person was between 15 and 17 years of age. Part II of the 1908 Act provided for the "prevention of cruelty to children and young persons".

---

[1]   No. 17 of 1991.

[2]   This Act is hereinafter referred to as "the 1991 Act".

4–05 In *M.F. v The Superintendent of Ballymun Garda Station, the Eastern Health Board and Another*, Finlay C.J. stated that there was a need for a "modern Children Act making a more efficient and simpler procedure for the protection of children available to the courts".[3] This modern Children Act came in the form of the 1991 Act, which Act abolished the distinction between "young person" and "child", putting in their place a new definition of child which is a person under the age of 18 years who has not been married.

4–06 The 1991 Act represents a significant improvement in terms of child protection remedies on those available under the legislation that it replaced. However, the Act not only modernises the child protection measures available; it also imposes a positive duty on health boards to promote the welfare of children in its area who are not receiving adequate care and protection and to set up mechanisms for the identification of such children. The Act also recognises the rights and duties of parents, under the Constitution or otherwise, and the fact that it is generally in the best interests of a child to be brought up in his or her own family. In that context the act goes on to acknowledge the primacy of the child's welfare. The Act reflects, then, not only constitutional imperatives but also those of the European Convention of Human Rights.

JURISDICTION AND OTHER MATTERS OF GENERAL APPLICATION

4–07 Part I of the 1991 Act defines the persons whose welfare is to be considered. The health boards are required to look to the welfare of children, a "child" being defined as a person under the age of 18. Excluded from this definition, however, are all persons who, though under the stipulated age, are or have been married. In practice the latter qualification will rarely be of relevance. The minimum age for marriage is, since 1996, 18.[4] Although parties of a younger age may marry by consent of the Circuit Court, this can only occur where the circumstances are such as to render such a step necessary in the interests of the parties. Interestingly, the definition of child is restated in s.3(1) of the Children Act 2001,[5] although s.271 thereof provides for the exclusion from the definition of persons under 18 years of age who are enlisted members of the Defence Forces. Both of these sections came into operation on May 1, 2002.[6] Should there be any doubt as to the age of a child for the purposes of the 1991 Act, the court may make such inquiries as it sees fit to determine his or her age.[7] The court's final determination, until the contrary is shown, shall be presumed to be the correct age of the child.

4–08 The primary forum for the proceedings contemplated by the Act is the

---

[3] [1990] I.L.R.M. 767.
[4] s.31 of the Family Law Act 1995 and Chap.1.
[5] S.I. No. 24 of 2001.
[6] See Children Act 2001 (Commencement) Order 2002 (S.I. No. 151 of 2002).
[7] s.32 of the Act of 1991.

District Court.[8] Normally, this court will have jurisdiction over the area in which the child resides or is to be found for the time being, although where this is not possible, an alternative district may be regarded as having jurisdiction. It is possible to appeal the decision of the District Court to a sitting of the Circuit Court. No sitting under this Act, however, whether in the District Court or Circuit Court, shall coincide with an ordinary sitting of the court. It is clearly stipulated that sittings should take place at different places, times or days from ordinary sittings. In other words a special time, place or setting should be set aside for such hearings. The concern here is obviously to set the child care process apart from the normal court process, both physically and symbolically, a step that may lead ultimately to the establishment of a separate children's court.[9]

4–09   The conduct of child care proceedings, too, is intended to be markedly different from the normal court case. All proceedings under the Act, as with virtually all proceedings concerning children, will be heard other than in public.[10] The conduct of such proceedings shall be as informal as is possible, to the extent that this is consistent with the requirements of natural justice. In particular, the judges and legal personnel are not permitted to wear wigs or gowns during such proceedings.[11] It is also possible for the court to proceed in the absence of the child to whom the proceedings relate.[12] The court may do so either on its own initiative or on the request of a party, but only where it is satisfied that this is necessary for the proper disposal of the case. Where a child requests to be present, however, the court will refuse this request only where it appears that it would not be in the child's interests to grant this request. In deciding whether to accede to such a request, the court should have regard to such matters as the age of the child and the nature of the proceedings.

In camera

4–10   The *in camera* rule applies to proceedings heard under Pts III, IV of VI of the 1991 Act. In particular, s.31 of the 1991 Act preserves the anonymity of children and states that "no matter likely to lead members of the public to identify a child who is or has been the subject of proceedings under Pts III, IV of VI shall be published in a written publication available to the public or be broadcast." Section 31, therefore, sets out restrictions on the publication of matter likely to result in members of the public identifying a child who is or has been the subject of proceedings under the 1991 Act. Any breach of this section is a summary offence, which attracts a penalty of 12 months' imprisonment or a fine of IR£1,000 (€1,270) or both. There is also the possibility

---

[8]   s.28 of the Act of 1991.

[9]   A new Children's Court was established under Pt 7 of the Children Act 2001 to deal with matters of juvenile justice.

[10]   s.29(1).

[11]   s.29(2) of the 1991 Act incorporates, by reference, the requirements of ss.33 and 45 of the Judicial Separation and Family Law Reform Act 1989.

[12]   s.30.

of the person who is in breach of this section being found in contempt of court.

Welfare of the child

4-11   The overriding concern of the health board and court alike, in all cases to which the 1991 Act relates, is to promote the welfare of the child.[13] Significantly, the word "welfare" is not defined in the 1991 Act. In *State (Kavanagh) v Sullivan and in the Matter of John Martin Kavanagh and William Kavanagh*,[14] Kennedy C.J. held that the word "welfare" of a child could not be "measured by money only, nor by physical comfort only". The word "welfare" he stated "must be taken in its widest sense". He contined:

> "The moral and religious welfare of the child must be considered as well as its physical well-being. Nor can the ties of affection be disregarded ... every circumstance must be taken into consideration, and the Court must do what under the circumstances a wise parent acting for the true interests of the child would or ought to do."[15]

4-12   In *O'B. v O'B.*,[16] Griffin J. stated:

> "The word 'welfare' ordinarily refers to health and well-being and, in respect of a spouse, this would include both physical and emotional welfare; in the case of a child, it would in addition include moral and religious welfare."[17]

4-13   While there is also a requirement that the court give due consideration to the rights and duties of parents, whether under the Constitution or otherwise, the 1991 Act is clear that the child's interests are "the first and paramount consideration". The court may take into account, as far as practicable, the wishes of the child in question and these will be given due consideration having regard to the age and level of understanding of the child in question.

The reference in ss.3 and 24 to the rights conferred by the Constitution underpins an important consideration of general application. Article 42 of the Constitution, as stated in Chapter 1, confers on the parents of a child, provided they are married to each other, inalienable rights and duties in respect of the child. The parents in particular are deemed to be the primary educators of the child. There is a presumption that the welfare of a child is to be found within his or her marital family. A health board contemplating the removal of a child from his or her home must establish a very clear prospect of harm which justifies the steps it proposes. It should in particular be mindful of the possibility that in some cases the solution may cause more harm than the ill it seeks to cure.

---

[13]   See ss.3 and 24 of the 1991 Act.
[14]   [1933] I.R. 618 at 630.
[15]   *ibid.*
[16]   [1984] I.R. 182.
[17]   *ibid.* at 194.

4–14   Parenting in any case is an inexact science. Clearly the various health boards are required to provide support services for vulnerable families, where possible, in order to obviate compulsory action being necessary to protect the interests of children. Even the most diligent parent makes mistakes and the health board should take care to avoid being over-zealous in the steps it takes. Some tension may arise, however, where parents have adopted means of parenting that are considered unconventional. However, well-meaning the parents, the health board may take the attitude that such a parenting approach is detrimental to the welfare of the child. In such a case, the health board should proceed with caution and only where it is satisfied that the approach taken has, in fact, put the child at serious risk. Where such intervention is taken by health boards, the courts must balance the competing rights involved by reference to the incremental nature of the remedies and relief available which ensure child welfare interests, whilst protecting the privacy and autonomy of the family unit, where possible.[18]

4–15   In *A. and B. v Eastern Health Board, District Judge Mary Fahy and C.*,[19] the High Court considered the statutory recognition given to the rights of parents by s.24 of the 1991 Act. In upholding the validity of s.24 of the 1991 Act, Geoghegan J. stated that while s.24 provides that in any proceedings before a court under the 1991 Act the Court must both regard the welfare of the child as the first and paramount consideration and give due regard to the wishes of the child, it must do so within a constitutional framework. The learned judge also cautioned that intervention should only occur when all other avenues have been exhausted, including family support services pursuant to s.3(3) of the 1991 Act.[20]

General functions and duties of the health board

4–16   Part II of the 1991 Act relates to the functions of the health board. Section 3 is particularly important in this regard. It sets out the basic function of health boards as follows:

> "1. It shall be the function of every health board to promote the welfare of children in its area who are not receiving adequate care and protection.
> 2. In the performance of this function, a health board shall–
>   (a) take such steps as it considers requisite to identify children who are not receiving adequate care and protection and co-ordinate information from all relevant sources relating to children in its area;
>   (b) having regard to the rights and duties of parents, whether under the Constitution or otherwise–

---

[18] See *North Western Health Board v H.W. and C.W.* [2001] 1 I.R. 622, discussed in Chap.1.
[19] [1998] 1 I.R. 464.
[20] See also *K and T v Finland*, judgment of April 27, 2000 and Chap.12, para.12–44.

(i) regard the welfare of the child as the first and paramount consideration, and

(ii) in so far as is practicable, give due consideration, having regard to his age and understanding, to the wishes of the child; and

(c) have regard to the principle that it is generally in the best interests of a child to be brought up in his own family."

4–17 Section 3 of the 1991 Act places upon the health board the overriding duty to promote the welfare of all children within its functional area, who are not receiving adequate care and protection. This is significant for several reasons. First, and arguably most important, is the framing of the section in terms of "duty" rather than "power". The health board is not merely entitled but obliged to provide such protection where it is not otherwise being provided. The second notable feature is that the legislation applies regardless of whether the child is a "resident" of the functional area. Any child who is found "in" the functional area of the health board is deemed to be its responsibility. This obviates the possibility of a health board disclaiming responsibility for a child on the grounds, for instance, that he or she has run away from a family home situated in another functional area.

4–18 The extent of the health board's duties under the 1991 Act have been given a broad interpretation. In *Eastern Health Board v E.A. and A.*,[21] Laffoy J. held that the role of the health board extended to intervention in an attempt by the mother of a child to place her child with strangers in a private adoption, in that the placement seriously compromised the welfare of the child.[22]

4–19 While the board is required generally to carry out certain tasks, there is some leeway regarding the precise measures that it should take in any particular case. The board has some autonomy then as to whether and to what extent it should act in any particular case, but subject to the overriding requirement, that it should do something. Its discretion is subject, as with all public bodies, to the requirement that it act reasonably, with reference to all relevant considerations and ignoring irrelevant and extraneous matters, and that it act at all times with utmost good faith and impartiality. Where it fails to exercise its discretion in a case where it is obvious that a child is in need, it would be open to a person affected to proceed by means of judicial review for an order of *mandamus* requiring it to take steps to secure the welfare of a child.

(a) Child care and support services

4–20 Section 3(3) of the 1991 Act places on the health board a general obligation to make available child care and family support services. For these purposes, it may provide and maintain premises and make such other provision

---

[21] [2000] 1 I.R. 430.

[22] Since s.7 of the Adoption Act 1998, it is now an offence to make a private placement of a child with a view to adoption.

as it sees fit. This is subject to the overall power of the Minister for Health and Children, by virtue of s.69 of the Act, to give general direction to health boards regarding their functions and duties under this Act.

4–21   Each health board is also required to put in place a committee (or more than one committee should the Minister consent) that will monitor its overall performance in this area. These are called "Child Care Advisory Committees" and are dealt with by s.7 of the Act. This requires the health board to establish such a committee composed of a selection of persons with a special expertise and interest in child welfare and child care. This may include members of voluntary child care services and family-support agencies. In particular, the body is required to report on the provision of services to children and families in its functional area, with particular reference to children who are not receiving adequate care and protection. In doing so it is empowered to obtain all non-personal information in relation to child care and family-support services in the relevant area and to consult with voluntary bodies providing child care and family-support services in the area in question.

4–22   A key drawback is that while there is provision for payment of expenses, it is not possible to pay the members of this committee for the performance of their tasks. With respect, despite the goodwill of volunteers, there should at least be provision for the payment of such persons. The danger is that otherwise, because of a shortage of well-qualified people willing to do the job for free, the committees may end up being comprised of those already in the employment of the health board. While the latter are no doubt well-qualified, even with the best will in the world such a situation would obviously fetter the committee's functioning as an independent monitor of the health board's functions.

(b) Identifying children in need

4–23   A health board cannot be satisfied simply to react to the initiatives of others. The board is under a specific duty actively to identify children in need of care and protection.[23] To this end it is required to take such steps as it deems necessary to identify children not receiving adequate care and protection. The function of primary co-ordinator of all information relating to the child is placed in the hands of the health board.

(i) Homeless children

4–24   The Act, should there be any doubt, is also clearly and especially applicable to children who are homeless. While there is no specific definition of "homeless" in the Act, s.5 refers to a situation where "there is no accommodation available to [the child] which he can reasonably occupy." In deciding whether such accommodation is available, it is not enough to conclude that the child has a family home. The conditions in the family home may be precisely the reason why the child is homeless. For instance, a child may have run away

---

[23] s.3(2)(a).

from home because of abuse or maltreatment and the board should take these factors into account when deciding whether the child may "reasonably occupy" the accommodation available. Returning a child to a place without adequately dealing with the factors that caused the child to leave that place in the first instance is no solution to the problem of homelessness.

4–25 In addition to the general requirement that the welfare of all children in need be safeguarded, the health board is under a specific requirement to ensure that the homeless child is adequately accommodated. Where it appears to the board that a child is homeless, the board will be obliged to make enquiries to verify this impression. Should it find that there is no adequate accommodation available to the child that he or she can reasonably occupy, the board is under an obligation to provide suitable accommodation for that child.

4–26 Scarcity of resources made available to health boards from central government has been cited as being central to the problem of youth homelessness. This was highlighted by a case involving a 16-year old girl who had been tortured and raped by her father.[24] In July 2000, press and media reports emerged that, despite her ordeal, she had been left without suitable accommodation for several months. Following the public outrage arising from the media reports, the State moved swiftly to redress the particular situation relating to the girl in that case. The Eastern Regional Area Health Authority[25] admitted to grave dissatisfaction with the problem of youth homelessness in its area. It also sounded a note of concern with some aspects of child care provision.

4–27 The underlying cause of youth homelessness, however, is not solely due to lack of resources. The supply of suitable and adequate accommodation is clearly a major issue for health boards. That said, the underlying difficulties which propel a child or young person onto the streets in the first place are more complex. A child or young person may leave home because of abuse or maltreatment, serious disagreement with parents or other custodians, mental or psychological problems, issues with sexuality, and a myriad of other reasons.

(ii) Abandoned and lost children

4–28 Where it appears to the health board that a child has been lost or abandoned, the health board must act as it would in relation to any child in need of care and protection. The board is additionally required by s.4(4), however, to do all that it reasonably can do to reunite the child with its family, should this appear to the board to be in the child's best interests.

---

[24] See *Irish Times*, July 11, 2000.
[25] The body with overall responsibility for the East Coast, Northern and South Western Health Boards, and the relevant authority in that particular case.

(iii) Children with special needs

4–29 The State has persistently failed to provide high support units for
children with special needs. This is a reflection of the low political priority
given to this issue. It constitutes contempt for the State's obligations under
international law. The duty to provide accommodation for children in need
was first highlighted in the case of *F.N. (a minor) v Minister for Education
and Others*,[26] which involved a 12-year old boy with a hyper-kinetic conduct
disorder. Geoghegan J. outlined the position as follows:

> "[W]here there is a child with very special needs which cannot be provided
> by the parents or guardian there is a constitutional obligation on the State
> under Article 42 Section 5 of the Constitution to cater for those needs in
> order to vindicate the constitutional rights of the child."

4–30 The constitutional obligation has been raised in a number of high-profile
cases since then, two of which involved injunctions compelling the State to
build high support units for children with special needs.[27] In the case of *T.D.
(a minor) v Minister for Education, Ireland, the AG, the Eastern Health Board
and the Minister for Health and Children*,[28] Kelly J. made orders against the
administrative branch of the Government by holding that there was a default
of its constitutional obligations to provide for the accommodation needs of
children with special needs.[29] This decision was overturned by the Supreme
Court,[30] where it was held that the orders made by the High Court were
inconsistent with the distribution of powers under the separation of powers
doctrine. Keane C.J. held as follows:

> "The difficulty created by the order of the High Court in this case is not
> simply that it offends in principle against the doctrine of the separation
> of powers, though I have no doubt that it does. It also involves the High
> Court in effectively determining the policy which the executive is to
> follow in dealing with a particular social problem. … I find the conclusion
> inescapable that, since the High Court first began the difficult task of
> grappling with this problem, a Rubicon has been crossed, clearly from
> the best motives, in which it is moving to undertake a role which is
> conferred by the Constitution on the other organs of State, who are also
> entrusted with the resources necessary to discharge that role in the interests
> of the common good."[31]

4–31 In relation to the right of the child to high support accommodation,
Keane C.J. stated that although no such right is expressly recognised by the
Constitution as such, "to the extent that it does exist, it must be as one of the

[26] [1995] 1 I.R. 409.
[27] See also *D.B. v Minister for Justice* [1999] 1 I.L.R.M. 93.
[28] unreported, High Court, February 25, 2000.
[29] See also *D.B. v Minister for Justice* [1999] 1 I.L.R.M. 93.
[30] [2001] 4 I.R. 259.
[31] At pp.53–55.

unenumerated personal rights guaranteed under Article 40.3.1° of the Constitution...."

4–32 Indeed, Murphy J. stated:

"With the exception of Article 42 of the Constitution, under the heading 'Education', there are no express provisions therein cognisable by the courts which impose an express obligation on the State to provide accommodation, medical treatment, welfare or any other form of socio-economic benefit for any of its citizens."[32]

4–33 Hardiman J., while acknowledging that the State owed children a duty under Art.42.5 of the Constitution, stated:

"It is, of course, manifest that, pursuant to Article 42.5 of the Constitution, the State has grave and particular obligations towards children ... In the case of very young children, this obligation can often in practice be discharged only by assuming full responsibility, directly or vicariously, for their shelter, feeding, health, education and general nature. As the child gets older, however, and passes the age of reason, and the age of criminal responsibility, the State's duties are complimented by a reciprocal duty on the part of the child or young person to engage and co-operate with the facilities and services made available to him. It is neither realistic nor legally necessary to treat a young person up to his eighteenth birthday as an entirely passive recipient of services, whether provided by his parents or by the State, without responsibility of any description for his own behaviour and formation."[33]

In summary, the Supreme Court held that only when the State failed in its duty in an "exemplary fashion" could the Supreme Court, as guardian of the Constitution, intervene and remedy the situation.

VOLUNTARY CARE

4–34 Section 4 of the 1991 Act provides a mechanism whereby parents/guardians may voluntarily place a child in the care of the health board without the need for a court order. A health board is obliged to take a child into care where it appears that that child requires care and protection and where such care and protection is unlikely to be provided in the child's present environment. The key difference between this provision and those outlined below is that it cannot be activated without the consent of each parent having custody of the child and of other persons acting *in loco parentis* in respect of the child. In other words, s.4 envisages a situation where the parents and health board alike

---

[32] [2001] 4 I.R. 259.
[33] *ibid.*

recognise the risk posed to the child and further acknowledge the need for health-board assistance. This should not necessarily be viewed as an admission of wrongdoing on the part of any parent. It may simply be an acknowledgement of special difficulties being experienced by the parent because of medical, psychological or other circumstances. A pertinent example might be the situation of a drug-dependent parent who requires special treatment for addiction, or that of a single parent with serious medical problems and little family support. The key advantage of this provision is that at any time the parent in question may resume caring for the child, and for this purpose, custody of a child must be restored to the parent when he or she so requests. Voluntary care ceases, in other words, at such time as the parent demands that his or her children be returned into his or her custody.

4–35 Where a child is taken into care under s.4, the board must maintain the child in care until such time as it appears that the child's welfare no longer requires such action. In line with the prevailing ethos of the section, the board must at all times have regard to the wishes of the original custodians of the child (and, of course, the child must be returned to the latter whenever the latter so requests).

EMERGENCY SITUATIONS

4–36 Where a child is at immediate risk of harm or injury, swift action is required. Part III of the 1991 Act deals with the protection of children in such emergency situations, giving both the relevant health board and An Garda Síochána the power to act with a view to safeguarding the welfare of the child in the short term.

Power of the Garda Síochána to take a child into safety

4–37 Section 12 of the 1991 Act envisages certain circumstances where a member of the Garda Síochána is permitted to remove a child to safety. This may happen where:

(i) there are reasonable grounds for believing that there is an immediate and serious risk to the health or welfare of the child; and

(ii) there are reasonable grounds for believing that it would be insufficient, for the purpose of obviating such risk, to wait for the health board to apply for an emergency care order under s.13 of the Act.

4–38 In order to remove the child from danger, the garda is fully empowered to enter any house or other place without the need for a warrant. In doing so, the garda may be accompanied by such other persons as are considered necessary (including, presumably, other gardaí) and may use such force as is deemed necessary in achieving the removal of the child. For these purposes, a "house or other place" includes any building or part thereof, a tent, caravan or other temporary or moveable structure. It is also possible to remove a child from any vehicle, vessel, aircraft or hovercraft. This power is without prejudice to any other power that the Gardaí may also possess—in other words, it complements, rather than replaces, such other powers.

4–39 This measure is clearly intended to be used only in extreme circumstances. The normal protocol for communication between An Garda Síochána and health boards is now set out in the revised set of child protection guidelines entitled *Children First*.[34] It is clear, therefore, that the circumstances in which the child is removed by a garda must exceed those where the normal protocol for the notification of cases of child abuse between health boards and An Garda Síochána would have ensured the welfare and protection of the child.

It is also clear that it is not the responsibility of the Gardaí indefinitely to accommodate the child in question. Their obligation is to deliver the child into the custody of the health board in whose functional area the child is at that time "as soon as possible". At this point the health board has two options. First, it may return the child to the parent or guardian having custody of the child. Alternatively it must make an application for an emergency care order.[36] The application should be made at the next sitting of the local District Court. If no such sitting is scheduled for any of the three days following the date on which the child has been delivered up to the health board, a special sitting of the court must be arranged in compliance with s.13(4) of the 1991 Act. That sitting must occur within three days. Pending the hearing of the application, it shall be lawful for the health board to retain custody of the child. Presumably, by implication, it would be unlawful for any person to remove the child from the custody of the health board during such time without the consent of the latter.

4–40 The tight time-frame envisaged by the Act is arguably deliberate. The requirement of swift delivery to the health board prevents the scenario of children being held in custody by the Gardaí, a prospect neither conducive to the child's welfare nor desired by the already-busy law-enforcers. The further requirement that an emergency care order be applied for within three days of delivery prevents the child from entering into a care-related "limbo" where his or her ultimate care needs are not addressed. The provision is after all, intended for emergency situations. As with all emergencies, speed is of the essence.

Emergency care orders

4–41 Section 13 of the 1991 Act allows a judge of the District Court to make an emergency care order (which provides short-term emergency protection) on the application of a health board, where:

(i) there is an immediate and serious risk to the health or welfare of the child which necessitates his being placed in care of a health board; or

---

[34] *Children First: Guidelines for the Protection and Welfare of Children* (The Stationery Office, Dublin, September 1999).
[35] s.12(4).

(ii) there is likely to be such a risk if the child is removed from the place where he is for the time being.

4–42 An emergency care order need not be preceded by the removal of a child by a garda as envisaged by s.12, although a s.12 removal must necessarily be followed by an application for an emergency care order, except where the child has been returned to the lawful custodian. The health board must make an application to a District Court judge. The judge must be a judge for the district in which the child resides, or is for the time being residing, although where such judge is not immediately available, an application may be heard by any District Court judge.[36] The court must be satisfied on two issues under s.13: first, the question of immediacy, and second, the seriousness of the risk. The judge must be of the "opinion" that these threshold criteria have been met in the particular case before the order can be granted. The risk must be an immediate and serious one and must be current or prospective in nature. Past harm is not sufficient to ground the application but may be relevant to the extent that it indicates future risk. The second or alternative leg of the criteria refers to the "likely risk" of immediate and serious harm unless the child is removed. The risk involved is directly related to the gravity of the harm anticipated.

4–43 An application should usually be made only after notice has been given to the parents of other custodians of the child in question. It is possible, however, for such application to be made *ex parte,* should the judge be satisfied that the urgency of the matter requires it.[37] It may even be the case that the identity of the child's custodians is not known. The Act explicitly contemplates a situation where the name of a child is unknown. In such a case it will not be necessary to name the child in any application or order made under s.13.[38] It is also possible, where considered necessary, to hear the case and make an order other than at a public sitting of the District Court. In such a case, the judge must be satisfied that the urgency of the matter requires this step.

4–44 The effect of the emergency care order is to place the child in the care of the health board for a period of not more than eight days.[39] A shorter period may be specified in the order. When considering this matter, however, the Oireachtas rejected a motion to reduce this eight-day period to four days, considering the latter time period to be too short. Deputy Treacy[40] considered that the period of eight days:

> "strikes a reasonable balance between giving the health board time to prepare an application for a care order and ensuring that the parties are not deprived of the custody of their children for too long before having an opportunity to put their side to the court."

---

[36] s.13(4).
[37] s.13(4)(c).
[38] s.13(6).
[39] s.13(2).
[40] 304 *Dáil Debates* Col.2129.

An appeal may be taken from the making of this order but any appeal does not have the effect of staying the operation of such an order. The effect of an emergency order cannot then be undermined simply by the lodging of an appeal. Considering the tight time-frame in which s.13 operates, an effective appeal would thus have to be made and heard with maximum speed.[41]

4–45   Where the court makes an emergency care order, it may also issue a search and find warrant. This may be necessary for the purpose of giving effect to the emergency care order and may authorise a member of An Garda Síochána to remove the child from any place.[42] In so doing, the judge may grant a warrant allowing the garda, and any other garda or person as may be necessary, to enter any house or other place specified in the warrant where a child is, or where there are reasonable grounds to believe that the child may be. This may include a building or part thereof, a tent, caravan or other temporary or moveable structure, vessel, vehicle, aircraft or hovercraft. As under s.12, the garda is required to deliver the child, once removed, into the custody of the health board.

4–46   There are some differences between the provisions in s.12 and those in s.13. For example, under s.13 the garda may only enter a premises on foot of a warrant; no such warrant is required under s.12. Section 13 also explicitly notes, in contrast to s.12, that other members of An Garda Síochána may accompany the garda. It is suggested that this would also be possible under s.12, the garda being entitled to be accompanied by such "other persons" as are considered necessary. The difference in wording is nonetheless confusing and may, on certain interpretations, suggest that under s.12 the garda must act without the aid of his colleagues.[43]

4–47   Section 13(7) allows the court to give various directions ancillary to the making of an emergency care order. Any such direction may be made at any time during the currency of the order. These may be made following application by any person or on the judge's own initiative. A judge may give direction as to:

(i)   whether the location at which a child is to be kept should be concealed from the parents or custodians of a child or from any other person;

(ii) whether the child should have access to any named persons and if so, under what conditions, if any, such access should be allowed;

(iii) whether it is necessary to carry out a medical or psychological examination or assessment of the child;

(iv) whether it is necessary to treat the child for medical or psychiatric reasons.

---

[41] s.13(6).

[42] s.13(3).

[43] It might be argued that, by inclusion in one section and exclusion in another, the facility was intended only to be available in the former case.

4–48   While there is a preference for informing the parents of the location of the child,[44] this should, it is suggested, not be done where there is a risk that the parents or other persons will attempt by illegal means to recover custody of the child. It should be acknowledged, however, that access to his or her parents may, notwithstanding the risk that activated the making of an emergency care order, remain a very important element of the child's continued welfare. In *State (D. & D.) v Groarke*,[45] the Supreme Court noted that parental access would in most cases remain "a very necessary ingredient in the welfare of the child."[46]

Consent

4–49   The Act of 1991 has no provision obliging parents to co-operate in the medical examination/treatment of a child outside of the context of a care order or a supervision order. The making of an order which provides for the medical or psychiatric examination, treatment or assessment of a child on the making of an emergency care order makes no provision for the consent of either the parents/guardians of the child or, indeed, the consent of the "mature" child. Section 23 of the Non-Fatal Offences Against the Person Act 1997[47] provides that children over 16 can give full consent to medical examination and treatment as if they were of full age.

It states:

> "1. The consent of a minor who has attained the age of 16 years to any surgical, medical or dental treatment which, in the absence of consent, would constitute a trespass to his or her person, shall be as effective as it would be if he or she were of full age; and where a minor has by virtue of this section given an effective consent to any treatment it shall not be necessary to obtain any consent for it from his or her parent or guardian.
> 2. In this section, "surgical, medical or dental treatment" includes any procedure undertaken for the purposes of diagnosis, and this section applies to any procedure (including, in particular, the administration of an anaesthetic) which is ancillary to any treatment as it applies to that treatment.
> 3. Nothing in this section shall be construed as making ineffective any consent which would have been effective if this section had not been enacted."

4–50   The Irish Medical Council guide, *A Guide to Ethical Conduct and Behaviour*, states:

> "Children are as entitled to considerate and careful medical care as are

---

[44] See *State (D. & D.) v Groarke* [1990] I.L.R.M. 10, wherein it was held that parents are generally entitled to know the whereabouts of the child.

[45] [1990] 1 I.R. 305.

[46] *Per* Finlay C.J. at 319.

[47] No. 26 of 1997.

adults. If the doctors feel that a child will understand a proposed medical procedure, information or advice this should be explained fully to the child. Where the consent of parents or guardians is normally required in respect of a child for whom they are responsible, due regard must be had to the wishes of the child. The doctor must never assume that it is safe to ignore the parental/guardian interest."[48]

4–51   In *A. and B. v Eastern Health Board*,[49] Geoghegan J. held that the termination of pregnancy was "medical treatment" within the meaning of the 1991 Act. The case concerned a child, pregnant as a result of rape, who was the subject of an interim care order. The parents objected to the termination of the pregnancy. While Geoghegan J. rejected the contention that the District Judge had failed to take cognisance of the parents wishes, he stated:

> "[T]he court must undoubtedly have regard to the welfare of the child as the first and paramount consideration … but it must do so within a constitutional framework."[50]

4–52   The rights of the "mature child" when in conflict with the rights of parents were examined in the case of *Gillick v West Norfolk and Wisbech AHA*.[51] In that case a doctor was held to have discretion to prescribe contraceptives to a girl under 16 without the knowledge or permission of her parents, as she had reached an age and had sufficient understanding and intelligence which rendered her capable of fully understanding what was involved. The House of Lords, by a majority, held that parental rights yield to those of competent children, even those under 16. Lord Scarman stated that it will be a question of fact in each case whether a child has sufficient understanding of what is involved to give a valid consent.[52] Whether such a conclusion would be reached in Ireland is an open question. Arguably, the constitutional rights of parents under Art.42 might preclude such a result.

4–53   In practical terms, a health board would be obliged to respect the refusal by a mature child to undergo any examination/treatment ordered in the context of an emergency care order. Where such examination/treatment was deemed to be important for the welfare of the "mature child", the health board could face practical problems in the case of such a child refusing to co-operate. The non-consenting child could of course insist on being present at a court

---

[48] The Medical Council, *A Guide to Ethical Conduct and Behaviour* (5th ed., Irish Medical Council, Dublin, 1998).
[49] [1998] 1 I.L.R.M. 460.
[50] *ibid.* at p.475.
[51] [1986] A.C. 112.
[52] See also *Re S (A minor)*, *The Independent*, July 9, 1992, where the Court of Appeal upheld a decision that a 10-year-old was sufficiently mature to object to being returned to France from where she had been abducted by her mother. That said, in *Re J. (A minor)(Medical Treatment)*, *The Independent*, July 14, 1992, the Court of Appeal declared that a 16-year-old anorexic's decision to refuse medical treatment could be overruled by her parents and doctors in life-and-death situations.

application for directions on the matter. The power of the court to join a child as a party to the proceedings or to appoint a guardian *ad litem* is, however, only available in the context of proceedings under Pts IV or VI of the 1991 Act. Any direction made on the granting of an emergency care order or made at any time during the currency of the order may be varied or discharged on the application of any person. The lack of provision for the representation of the "mature" child at the "emergency" stage of proceedings under the Act could create practical problems for both health boards and "mature children".

MATTERS APPLICABLE TO BOTH SS.12 AND 13

Notification requirements

4–54   Where a child, under ss.12 or 13 of the 1991 Act, has been placed in the custody of the health board, the health board should take certain steps. These are primarily to ensure that the child's parents or custodians or any person acting *in loco parentis* in respect of such child is/are made aware of this fact as soon as possible.[53] This requirement may be avoided, naturally, where such persons cannot, by reasonable means, be located. Where s.13 applies, a person shall furthermore be deemed to have been informed of the health board having custody of a child if either:

(i)   he or she has been shown a copy of an emergency care order made under s.13; or

(ii) he or she was present at the court hearing at which such an order was considered.

Notification to be given by health board

4–55   Section 14 provides for notification to be given by the health board "as soon as possible" to the parent having custody of the child taken into care or the person acting *in loco parentis* in respect of that child. The duty to inform parents as soon as possible arises when the child has been delivered to or placed into the custody of the health board, either pursuant to s.13 or s.12 on an *ex parte* basis.

The term "as soon as possible" was considered in the case of the *State (at the prosecution of D.C.) v Midland Health Board.*[54] Keane J., commenting on the emergency nature of the powers concerned in the earlier statute, noted that such powers, although clearly essential in the interest of children who are at risk for a variety of reasons, are also a serious abridgement of the rights of parents. Any statutory scheme which did not keep to a minimum the interval of time which may necessarily elapse between the removal of the child from his or her parents and the determination of its future custody by the court would constitute, in his view, an impermissible violation of parental rights. In

---

[53] s.14 of the 1991 Act.

[54] [1990] 7 Fam. L.J. 10.

effect, the law must strike the correct balance between upholding the rights of parents to due process and safeguarding children from actual or potential significant harm. The foregoing comments of the Chief Justice are instructive in the context of the concerns expressed in respect of the extension in the Children Act 2001 of the lifespan of the interim care order.[55]

4–56 The practical problem facing practitioners who are consulted by parents who have been served with an emergency care order is how to prepare an adequate case in so short a period of time. This dilemma was noted also in the case of *M.F. v Superintendent Garda Station, B.*[56] In this case, it was held that the return date on the summons to take children into care should be as short as possible, having regard to the necessity for both applicant and respondent to have an opportunity of preparing for a proper hearing of the application for a fit persons order (under the earlier legislation).

While the issue of the separate representation of the child cannot arise in an application for an emergency care order, the health board must be in a position to establish that it has given due consideration to the wishes of the child. The obligation on a health board to give due consideration to the wishes of the child, having regard to his age and understanding, is one of its primary functions under s.3 of the 1991 Act.

Accommodation

4–57 While a child is in the custody of the health board by virtue of either ss.12 or 13, it is required by s.15 of the 1991 Act to make adequate provision for the temporary accommodation of the child. To this end, arrangements may be made with the proprietor of a registered children's residential centre or with any other appropriate person (*e.g.* a foster parent who has agreed to provide short-term care for such children.) The responsibility for making such arrangements lies with the relevant health board. It should be noted in particular that it is not appropriate, where s.12 applies, for a child to be kept in the custody of the Gardaí for any longer than is strictly necessary. The undoubted kindness of the Gardaí notwithstanding, the child may otherwise be left with the impression that he or she has done something wrong and is being punished.

Should intervention be mandatory?

4–58 It is notable that, by contrast with Pt IV of the 1991 Act, s.12 and 13 merely empower the relevant authorities to act in appropriate circumstances. Whereas under Pt IV a health board would be obliged to take action where a child is at long-term risk, no such duty exists under Pt III where a child is believed to be in imminent danger. Without suggesting that either the Gardaí or health authorities would ignore a child in obvious need, this divergence seems strange. There is some argument that the discretion of the authorities should not be unduly fettered, especially when considering delicate situations

---

[55] See s.267(1)(a) of the Children Act 2001 and Chap.11 of this book.
[56] [1991] 1 I.R. 189.

involving the welfare of a child. It might nonetheless be suggested that if the health boards are under a duty to act to promote the welfare of children in need within its functional area, this duty should be deemed considerably weighty where a child is in especially urgent need. Such proceedings as are envisaged by Pt III are obviously intended to be of temporary nature only; a stopgap pending further proceedings. The long-term welfare of a child may require that steps be taken to provide for the care of a child outside its parental or normal home environment.

GENERAL GUIDELINES FOR CARE PROCEEDINGS

Emphasis on co-operation

4–59   The philosophy of the 1991 Act is that families and children should be supported with the aim of enabling the child to be brought up within his or her own family. The emphasis on co-operation between health boards and vulnerable families is also contained in the Departmental guidelines on procedures for the identification, investigation and management of child abuse published in 1995 (and revised in 1997 and again in 1999).[57] Some health boards have published a manual of child protection procedures which outline the protocol to be followed by the health board in child care cases. The departmental guidelines place significant emphasis on the case conference being convened. The guidelines provide that parents/guardians should be made aware of the general approach being adopted in the case.

The case conference

4–60   Case conferences are mechanisms whereby information is exchanged between agencies and individual professionals so that co-ordinated decisions can be taken based on such information. The report of the Kilkenny incest investigation noted that the case conference serves a number of broad purposes, including:

(i)   it will bring together relevant professions involved with the particular child so that they can pool information about his or her circumstances so as to develop a clearer picture of the risks to the child;

(ii) it will also reach decisions as to what action is to be taken and appoint a key care-worker to manage the case. A subsequent case conference will also be used to review the intervention decided upon;

(iii) it will pool information which may be used in legal proceedings and recommend that the child's name should or should not be included in the list of children at risk.

---

[57] The most recent guidelines are available on the internet at www.doh.ie.

The report recommended the following:

(i) where a case is being referred to the DPP with a view to prosecution, the case conference should formulate a view on the effect that this will have on the welfare of the child and this view should be transmitted to the DPP with the garda file;

(ii) the agenda and the purpose of the case conference should be set out in advance and circulated with the invitation to those who are expected to attend;

(iii) all health professionals who have had previous dealings with the case should bring their records to the conference and should have prepared a written summary of the case history for the initial conference. Facts should be distinguished from opinions;

(iv) the minutes of the case conference should set out clearly the conclusions reached, recommendations made, and the information upon which they are based. Action to be taken should be noted.

4–61   The report is silent on the vexed question of the attendance of parents at the case conference. It may be argued that if parents are present throughout the case conference, there will be a less frank exchange of information between professionals.[56] Excluding parents from participation at case conferences where major decisions are taken with regard to their children must be justified or otherwise may well constitute an interference with respect for family life under the Constitution and the European Convention on Human Rights. Sometimes parents are excluded from the case conference entirely, only being invited in to hear the conclusions of the conference. British research on parental attendance at case conferences found "partial attendance" to be the least desirable form of inclusion. Sometimes parents are invited to participate at later case conferences, in particular where their co-operation is a necessary feature of the child care plan. The English case of *R. v Cornwall County Council, ex parte L.H.*[59] held that local authority policies of refusing to allow parents to be accompanied by solicitors at child protection conferences, and the policy of refusing to provide parents with copies of the minutes of conferences which they had attended, were unlawful. The European Court of Human Rights, in the case of *W. v U.K.*,[60] decided that the State must ensure that the decision-making process involves parents to a degree sufficient to provide them with a requisite protection of their interests. This must be done in order to give effect to Art.8, which protects family life from unlawful and arbitrary State interference. It should be noted, however that it is possible to take a child into *voluntary care* with the co-operation of the parents.[61]

---

[58] Thoburn, "Working Together and parental attendance at case conferences" (1992) 4 J. Ch. L. 11 and Thompson, "Parents at Case Conferences—A Legal Advisor's Viewpoint" (1992) 4 J. Ch. L. 15.

[59] [2000] L.G.R. 180; see www.familylaw.co.uk/upd

[60] (1987) 10 E.H.R.R 29. See also Chap.12, n.31.

[61] s.4.

The outcome of the case conference consists of recommendations to individual agencies for action. The timing of the first case conference depends upon the urgency of the particular case under investigation. The guidelines clearly envisage a case conference being held, in most cases, in advance of court action.

CARE PROCEEDINGS

4–62   Part IV of the 1991 Act allows for the making of various orders designed to protect, in the medium to long term, a child who is believed to be in danger, whether currently or in the past. Part IV is notable in that it not only empowers but, rather obliges the health board in whose functional area a child resides or is found, to make an application for a care or supervision order (as it sees fit) in the following circumstances:

(i)   where the child in question is in need of care or protection; and

(ii) where the child is unlikely to receive such care or protection unless such an order is made.

4–63   The two key orders that may be made in these circumstances are as follows:

(i)   care order—this allows a child to be committed to the care of the health board. For these purposes, the child may be removed from the care of its parents or other custodians;

(ii) supervision order—this allows a child, while remaining in the custody of his or her parents or other custodian, to be visited periodically by the health board.

4–64   Only a health board may apply for such orders to be made. Where the health board fails to fulfil the duty laid out in s.5 of the 1991 Act in respect of a particular child, it will not thus be possible for a third party to invoke the jurisdiction of the court in granting any such order. It may be possible, however, to seek, by means of judicial review, an order of *mandamus* requiring the health board to take such proceedings. A number of High Court cases which involved a challenge to the State for failure to provide proper services for children demonstrated the willingness of that Court to oblige the State to fulfil its obligations to vulnerable children.[62] The High Court case of *T.D. (A minor) v Minister for Education & Ors*[63] alluded to earlier in this chapter, held that the Court was entitled to expect that bureaucratic haggling would not delay

---

[62] See *D.D. (A minor) v Eastern Health Board & Ors*, unreported, High Court (Costello J.), May 3, 1995; *D.T. v Eastern Health Board*, unreported, High Court (Geoghegan J.), March 24, 1995; *F.N. v Minister for Education* [1995] 1 I.R. 409; [1995] 2 I.L.R.M. 297; *D.G. v Eastern Health Board* [1998] 1 I.L.R.M. 241; *D.B. v Minister for Justice, Minister for Education & Ors* [1999] 1 I.L.R.M. 93.

[63] [2000] 2 I.L.R.M 321 and also at [2000] I.J.F.L. 28.

the addressing of children's rights. Kelly J. held that it was the duty of the Court to vindicate and defend the rights guaranteed by the Constitution. The learned judge held that the Court had the jurisdiction to make orders against the administrative branch of Government, where there was default of its constitutional obligations. Such orders are, however, not made lightly, as can be seen from the Supreme Court judgment which overturned, by a four-to-one majority, the High Court judgment of Kelly J.[64] The Supreme Court stated that the court's jurisdiction to intervene in policy decisions should be used sparingly and only where it is absolutely necessary to enable the court to carry out its constitutional duties.

4–65 The Supreme Court decision of *T.D. (a minor suing by his mother and next friend M.D. v Minister for Education, Ireland and the Attorney General, the Eastern Health Board and by order of the Minister for Health and Children*[65] has placed clear limitations on the court's power to intervene to protect the rights and welfare of children. Murray J., expressing the majority view of the Supreme Court, alluded to the exceptional circumstances that must be present before the court can order the executive to fulfil a legal obligation "where an organ or agency of the State has disregarded its constitutional obligations in an exemplary fashion":

> "In my view the phrase 'clear' disregard can only be understood to mean a conscious and deliberate decision by the organ of the State to act in breach of its constitutional obligation to other parties accompanied by bad faith or recklessness."[66]

4–66 Hardiman J. stated that such an order could only be made as an "absolutely final resort" in circumstances of great crisis. The learned judge referred to his judgment in *Sinnott v Minister for Education*[67] and opined as follows:

> "[I]f the courts (or either of the other organs of government) expand their powers beyond their constitutional remit, this expansion will necessarily be at the expense of the other organs of government ... If citizens are taught to look to the courts for remedies for matters within the legislative or executive remit, they will progressively seek further remedies there, and progressively cease to look to the political arms of government."

4–67 The decision in *F.N. v Minister for Education*[68] must now be appraised in light of the Supreme Court decision in *T.D.* in so far as it impacts on the ability of the courts to make orders against the administrative branch of the

---

[64] [2001] 4 I.R. 259.
[65] *ibid.*
[66] *ibid.*
[67] [2001] 2 I.R. 598.
[68] [1995] 2 I.L.R.M. 297.

Government where there is a default of its constitutional obligations. While the *T.D.* case calls into question the validity of the judgment of Geoghegan J. in *F.N.*, and whether the Constitution should be interpreted to include socio-economic rights, it reserves these issues until a case where the matters are fully argued.

Interim care orders

4–68   Pending the making of a full care order, it is open to the court to make such orders as it sees fit to make. This may be done only on the application of the relevant health board and, unless the judge directs otherwise, after notice has been given to the parents or other custodians of the child. The prescribed period of notice is detailed in Reg.11 of the District Court (Child Care) Rules 1995, and is at least seven days' notice prior to the making of an application.

A district judge may make such an order if each of the following three conditions is met:

(i)   that an application has been made, or is about to be made, for a care order in respect of the child. It is not necessary, however, that an emergency care order be in force at the time in question;

(ii) that he or she is satisfied that there is reasonable cause to believe that the child has been assaulted, neglected, sexually abused or otherwise ill-treated, or that the child's health, development or welfare has been, is being or is likely in the future to be avoidably impaired or neglected; and

(iii) that the judge considers it necessary, in order to protect the health or welfare of the child, that he or she be placed in the care of the health board, pending the full determination of the application for a care order.

4–69   An example of the threshold conditions necessary for the granting of an interim care order can be found in the judgment of the Court of Appeal in England and Wales in *Re D. (Minors)*.[69] The local authority in that case sought the order after reviewing a report from a consultant psychologist, who expressed the view that the mother of the children was suffering from paranoia. Critically, the psychologist advised that significant harm had come to the children from the parenting by the mother. The court granted the interim care order under s.38 of the English Children Act 1989, the section corresponding to s.17 of the Irish Child Care Act 1991.[70] A causal connection with the behaviour of the care providers must be established before the removal of a child can be sanctioned. This approach was followed by Browne-Wilkinson L.J. in *Re C. (A Minor) (Interim Care Order: Residential Assessment)*[71] where he stated that "... before the court can make an order it has to be satisfied that the harm being suffered or anticipated is attributable to the actual or anticipated care being received by the child, an issue likely to be dominated by the evidence as

---

[69] *Times Law Reports*, February 19, 1997.
[70] See also in *Re H. (A Child)* [1999].
[71] [1997] A.C. 489 at 499.

to the abilities and conduct of the parents and the relationship between the child and those parents".

4–70 The effect of an interim care order is to require the placement of the child in the care of the health board only for a period not exceeding 28 days.[72] This time period may, however, be extended with the consent of both the health board and any parent with custody of the child, or person acting *in loco parentis*. The district judge concerned may make a further extension on application of any of the parties. If such an extension is to exceed 28 days, the consent of all the aforementioned persons is still required.[73] Before such an extension is granted, the judge must be satisfied that the grounds upon which the original order was made still exist with respect to the child in question. In considering the power of the court to extend an interim care order, Thorpe L.J. in *Re B. (Minors)*[74] stated that once the trial judge had determined that the threshold criteria for the granting of a care order had been established, "it would have been an abuse of her statutory power thereafter to control the local authority's management of the child's life by a series of repeated interim orders covering a period as long as twelve months". Section 267(1) of the Children Act 2001 should reduce the frequency with which interim care order applications need to be renewed. It is to be noted that since this section came into effect by way of a Commencement Order[75] on May 1, 2002, the Court Services Board has withdrawn the second health board day every second week in the Children's Court in Dublin. Concerns arise in relation to the extended lifespan of the interim care order, which are discussed in Chapter 11.Where an interim order is made, the district judge is empowered to give such directions as may be made under s.13(7) of the 1991 Act. Brown-Wilkinson L.J. in *Re C. (A Minor)*[76] described the power to give directions on making an interim care order under the corresponding provisions of the Children Act 1989 in England and Wales as "the interaction between the powers of the local authority entitled to make decisions as to the child's welfare in the interim and the needs of the court to have access to the relevant information and assessments to be able to make the ultimate decision". If such directions are already in force (*i.e.* where the application for a care order was preceded by the making of an emergency order) the judge may require that they remain in force. These relate, *inter alia,* to whether the parents or other custodians should be informed of the whereabouts of the child in respect of whom the order has been made. In this context, the points made previously regarding the desirability of parental access are equally applicable.

4–71 Pending the determination of an application for a care order, s.18(6) allows a court to make further directions regarding the care and custody of a

---

[72] See s.267(1)(a) of the Children Act 2001 (S.I. No. 24 of 2001) and the Children Act 2001 (Commencement) Order 2002 (S.I. No. 151 of 2002).

[73] See s.17(2)(b) of the Child Care Act 1991 as amended by s.267(1)(a) of the Children Act 2001.

[74] [1998].

[75] S.I. No. 151 of 2002.

[76] [1997] A.C. 489.

child. This may include the making of a supervision order as permitted by s.19 of the 1991 Act. The difference between orders made under s.18 and the orders contemplated by s.17 is that the former, potentially, have a longer shelf-life. An order under s.18(6) will continue in force until such time as the determination of the application for a care order has been made. An interim care order will not, in normal circumstances, exceed 28 days in duration. A key advantage of s.17, however, is that orders may be made before a formal application for a care order has been made. A s.18(6) order may only be granted where a full care order application has been made.

Care orders

4–72   This is the more serious of the two non-interim orders that may be made by the court and, as such, should not be invoked lightly. A care order effectively allows a child in need to be removed from his or her parents or other custodians, and maintained or placed in the care of the relevant health board.

A health board in whose functional area a child resides or is otherwise found may make an application for such an order. Upon this application, a judge may make a court order if he or she is satisfied that the following conditions have been met:

(i)   the child has been assaulted, neglected, sexually abused or otherwise ill-treated; or the child's health, development or welfare has been, is being or is likely in the future to be avoidably impaired or neglected;

(ii) he or she considers that the child requires care or protection; and

(iii) he or she further believes that the child is unlikely to receive such care or protection unless an order is made under s.18.[77]

4–73   As previously stated, the threshold criteria encompass past and present assaults, ill-treatment, neglect or sexual abuse in addition to "likely" impairment or neglect to a child's health, development and welfare, past, present and future. There is no statutory definition of the terms "assault, ill-treatment, neglect or sexual abuse" under the 1991 Act. However, assault is defined in the Non-Fatal Offences Against the Person Act 1997, and ill-treatment may encompass emotional abuse such as being constantly shouted at, denigrated, criticised and rejected, or exposed to domestic violence. Such behaviour may be very difficult to prove. Neglect may be evidenced by a failure to thrive; however, this is sometimes also referable to some organic cause. Neglect has been defined in the child protection guidelines, *Children First*, as "persistent or severe neglect, whether wilful or unintentional", which results in significant harm or serious impairment of the child's health, development or welfare. It is defined in terms of an omission and need not be the result of intentional conduct by a parent or guardian. Harm, in turn, is defined in *Children First* as "the ill-treatment or the impairment of the health or development of a child".[78] The

---

[77] s.18(1).
[78] Para.3.2.2.

threshold of significant harm is achieved "when the child's needs are neglected to the extent that his or her well-being and development are severely affected".[79] Sexual abuse has been defined in the same document as "the use of children for sexual gratification". The examples of child sexual abuse cited in *Children First* include exposure to sexual organs; intentional touching or molesting of the body of the child; masturbation in the presence of the child or the involvement of the child in an act of masturbation; sexual intercourse with the child; sexual exploitation of a child by any of the methods specified; and consensual sexual activity involving an adult and an under-age child.[80] The court must be satisfied that an instance of assault, ill-treatment, neglect or sexual abuse has, in fact, taken place, or is taking place.

4–74 The threat to the health, development or welfare of the child is broader and may be based on past events, current events or apprehended events. However, such impairment must be "avoidable". The neglect or impairment can be to the child's health, development or welfare. Health can include both physical and mental health (psychiatric and psychological). The child protection guidelines, *Children First*, note that emotional abuse occurs when a child's need for affection, approval, consistency and security are not met.[81] The document cites "exposure to domestic violence"[82] as an example of emotional abuse of children.[83] Emotional abuse was held to come within the term "development" in the English case of *F. v Suffolk County Council*.[84] It is not necessary to prove any malevolence on the part of the parents/guardians, and the neglect may arise by force of circumstances. The term "likely to be" involves a prospective element. There must, however, be a real possibility that the child would suffer.[85]

Section 47 provision

4–75 Section 47 provides:

> "Where a child is in the care of a health board, the District Court may, of its own motion or on the application of any person, give such directions and make such order on any question affecting the welfare of the child as it thinks proper and may vary or discharge any such direction or order."

4–76 The case of *Eastern Health Board v Judge McDonnell*[86] is worthy of note. This held that where the child is placed in the care of the health board following a care order, the District Court retains jurisdiction under the 1991

---

[79] *Children First*, para.3.2.3.
[80] Para.3.5.1.
[81] Para.3.3.1.
[82] Para.3.3.1 (x).
[83] See also *Re H. (Minors)* [1996] 1 All E.R. 1.
[84] (1981) F.L.R. 208.
[85] *Re H. and others (Minors)* [1996] 1 All E.R. 1.
[86] [1999] 1 I.R. 74; [1999] 2 I.J.F.L. 26.

Act to impose directions on the health board in relation to the child placed in care. The legislation entrusts the ultimate care of the child to the court.

4–77   In the aforementioned case, the court directed that there should be no change in the child's foster parents or social workers without leave of the court. The health board concerned argued that once the District Court had made the care order, the power of the court was spent. The function of the health board was to draw up a plan for the care of the child received into its custody. Section 47 of the 1991 Act, however, gives the Court a wide jurisdiction so that it may impose directions in relation to children whom it places in care.

McCracken J. stated the position as follows:

> "Section 47 is an all embracing and wide ranging provision which is intended to entrust the ultimate care of a child who comes within the Act in the hands of the District Court."

4–78   He qualified this statement, however, by stating:

> "This is not to say that the District Court should interfere in all day-to-day decisions made by a health board, but rather that whenever any matters of concern are brought to the attention of the District Court, which could reasonably be considered adversely to affect the welfare of the child, and only in such circumstances, should the District Court 'interfere'."[87]

4–79   The issue arose in the case of *Western Health Board v K.M.*,[88] which is discussed in Chapter 7. Finnegan J. in the High Court stated that the functions of the District Court under s.47 of the 1991 Act were not merely supervisory ones, but were to be considered in an expansive manner. McGuinness J. in the Supreme Court held that s.47 was to be looked at in the context of the Child Care Act 1991 as a whole, and that both the health board and the court must bear in mind that the child is in the care of the health board at all times when making any proposals for the future care of the child.

Care order and access

4–80   The child does not have the legal right, under s.37 of the 1991 Act, to apply to the Court for access to other siblings in care. That section requires the health board to facilitate reasonable access to the child by his parents or any person acting *in loco parentis* with a bona fide interest in the child. Access may include overnight or residential access. Where any person authorised by the section is dissatisfied with access arrangements, he or she may seek Court intervention on the matter.[89] In practice, children taken into care can be split up and access to each other can be severely restricted by questions of logistics

---

[87] *ibid.*
[88] [2001] 1 I.R. 729 (HC); [2003] 2 I.R. 493 (SC).
[89] s.37(2).

and resources. The articulation of such concerns can be achieved through separate representation of the children concerned.

Consequences of a care order

4–81 The effect of a care order, when made, is to cause the child concerned to be removed and placed or maintained in the care of the health board making the application. By such order, the health board is required to act as if it were a prudent and responsible parent of the child. In particular, the board shall exercise the same control over the child as if it were a parent and do all that is reasonable, under the circumstances, to safeguard and promote the child's health, development or welfare.[90] In so acting, the board is conferred with the authority to do the following:

(i) decide the type of care and accommodation that should be provided from the list of options outlined in s.36 of the Act (*e.g.* placement with a foster parent, with a relative, or in a residential care facility or children's residential centre);

(ii) consent to the child undergoing any necessary medical or psychiatric examination, treatment or assessment;

(iii) consent to the child being issued with a passport, or such other passport facilities as are considered necessary, in order to allow the child to travel abroad. Such absence from the State as is contemplated by this section is clearly temporary.

4–82 Where the board gives the consent noted at (ii), this will be deemed sufficient to allow the carrying out of such examination, treatment or assessment by a qualified health professional so permitted, notwithstanding the wishes of any other person. Likewise, where the board gives the consent contemplated by (iii) above, this will be sufficient to allow the provision of passport facilities (including the issuing of a passport) by any person authorised to make such provision.[91]

Care order—a measure of last resort

4–83 In considering whether to initiate care proceedings, the effect of a care order, detailed above, should be borne in mind. The severity of a care order requires that it be utilised only as a measure of last resort. Parents should be afforded every opportunity to demonstrate their intention and ability to provide a safe and secure environment for their child. Indeed, as the Supreme Court recently stated in *North Western Health Board v H.W. and C.W.*,[92] the Constitution necessitates such an approach. McCracken J. held that Art.41.1 of the Constitution places the marital family in a "very special position", being

---

[90] s.18(3).
[91] s.18(4).
[92] [2001] 3 I.R. 635.

the primary and fundamental unit group of society, and it "also provides that the family possesses rights which are antecedent and superior to all positive law". Finlay C.J. in *K.C. and A.C. v An Bord Uchtála*[93] noted "that the welfare of the child … is to be found within the family unless the court is satisfied that there are compelling reasons why this cannot be achieved".[94] In *Lancashire County Council and Another v Barlow and Another*,[95] the House of Lords stated that the application for a care order calls for immense caution and restraint. Clyde L.J. noted that "the stress which care proceedings may well impose on the parents may even itself be damaging to the child". Significantly, he also alluded to the provisions of Art.8 of the European Convention on Human Rights, which underline "the need for caution and restraint" in applying for a care order.

4–84   Due to the far-reaching consequences that attach to the making of a care order, the 1991 Act requires that a court may only make such an order on the basis of proven facts. Nicholls L.J. in *Re H. and R. (Child sexual abuse: Standard of proof)*[96] summarised the position in the following terms:

> "[Parents] are not to be at risk of having their children taken from them and removed into the care of the local authority on the basis only of suspicions, whether of the judge or of the local authority or anyone else. A conclusion that the child is suffering or is likely to suffer harm must be based on the facts, not just suspicion."

4–85   The child protection guidelines, *Children First*, make provision for a specialist examination or assessment.[97] Permission must be obtained from the child's parents to conduct such an examination or assessment, and they should be afforded an opportunity to attend. If permission is refused, the parents should be informed of the health board's option to seek an emergency care order.

4–86   In *Re H. and R. (Child sexual abuse: Standard of proof)*,[98] the House of Lords considered the standard of proof required to establish the threshold conditions for the making of a care order. It was held that the threshold condition for a care order was met if it was shown that there was a real possibility the children would suffer significant harm. According to Nicholls L.J. in *Re H. and R. (Child sexual abuse: Standard of proof)*,[99] the more improbable the event, the stronger must be the evidence that it did occur before, on the balance of probability, its occurrence will be established.

4–87   It is likely that the Irish courts will be guided by the principles of law

---

[93] [1986] 6 I.L.R.M. 65.
[94] See also *Southern Health Board v C.H.* [1996] 2 I.L.R.M. 142.
[95] [2000] 1 F.L.R. 583.
[96] [1996] A.C. 563 at 592.
[97] Para.8.13.
[98] [1996] A.C. 563; [1996] 1 F.L.R. 80.
[99] [1996] A.C. 563 at 592.

set down in *Re H. and R. (Child sexual abuse: Standard of proof)* in interpreting s.18 of the Child Care Act 1991. The ordinary civil standard of proof applies to s.18(1)(a) and (b). In s.18(1)(c), however, the court is assessing the risk of something happening in the future. In interpreting this section the Irish courts are likely to follow the approach adopted in *Re H. and R. (Child sexual abuse: Standard of proof)*, which case approved the decision of the Court of Appeal in *Newham London BC v A-G.*[100] The latter case held that the threshold test is met if, in the court's view, there is a real or substantial risk of significant harm in the future. "Likely to suffer significant harm" is not to be equated with "on the balance of probabilities". Therefore, it may be, that under s.18(1)(c), it is enough if the occurrence of impairment or neglect is a real possibility. Nicholls L.J. in *Re H. and R. (Child sexual abuse: Standard of proof)* summarised the position in the following terms:

> "It is, of course, open to a court to conclude there is a real possibility that the child will suffer harm in the future although harm in the past has not been established. There will be cases where, although the alleged maltreatment itself is not proved, the evidence does establish a combination of profoundly worrying features affecting the care of the child within the family. In such cases it would be open to a court in appropriate circumstances to find that, although not satisfied the child is yet suffering significant harm, on the basis of such facts as are proved there is a likelihood that he will do so in the future".[101]

4–88 A care order, once made, shall remain in effect until such time as the child ceases to be a child, that is until the child reaches the age of 18 or, if earlier, marries.[102] The latter possibility is slight, considering that since 1996 a person under the age of 18 may only marry with the consent of the Circuit Court and then only where this is seen to be in the interests of the parties marrying. The care order may operate for a shorter period, should the court so determine. In such a case, it shall nonetheless be possible, so long as the child is under the age of 18 and unmarried, to extend the shorter period. For this to occur, the relevant judge must be satisfied that the circumstances that led to the initial order being made still exist and require the continuation of the order. The judge may make such an order of his own motion or on the application of any person, including the health board. An application to extend the operation of a care order requires that the respondent be notified. The prescribed period of notice is detailed in Ord.84, r.11 of the District Court Rules 1997[103] and is at least seven days notice prior to the making of an application.

4–89 It is possible, where a care order is made, to require the parents of a child to make a contribution towards his or her maintenance.[104] This may

---

[100] *Re M. & R. (C.A.)* [1996] 2 F.L.R. 195.
[101] *ibid.*, judgment of Butler-Sloss L.J.
[102] s.18(2).
[103] S.I. No. 93 of 1997.
[104] s.18(7).

involve the payment of such weekly or other periodic sum as the court sees fit. Any order that is made may, however, be discharged or varied on application to the court by the debtor involved.[105] In making such an order for maintenance, the court should have regard to the means of the parties. It is suggested also that the court should take into account the care obligations of the parents, in particular whether there are other dependants still in their custody. It would be counter-productive to make a maintenance order in respect of one child that may be to the detriment of other children still in the custody of their parents. Order 4, r.15 of the District Court Rules 1997 provides that a copy of the order requiring contribution by a parent or parents must be served on the parent concerned. Under the 1997 Rules, seven days' notice of an application to vary or discharge a contribution order must be given to the health board.

4–90 Where the court decides, under s.18, that it should not make a care order, it is still open to it to make a supervision order under the provisions of s.19.[106] This may be done where the court considers that, its primary decision notwithstanding, it is still desirable that the child be visited periodically in his or her home. An initial proposal was put forward that the supervision order could only be made where the court was satisfied that this would adequately protect the child, but this proposal was not ultimately adopted by the Oireachtas. A supervision order made under s.18(5) must, by virtue of Ord.84, r.12 of the District Court Rules 1997, be served on the respondent.

4–91 Section 18(6) of the 1991 Act enables the court, pending the hearing of an application for a care order, of its own motion or on the application of any person, to give directions as to the care and custody of the child, or to make a supervision order in respect of the child. Order 84, rr.13 and 14 of the District Court Rules 1997 provide that a minimum of two days notice be given to the respondent of the intention to apply under s.18(6).

Supervision orders

4–92 A care order may involve the removal of a child from his or her home environment. This is a drastic step that requires strong evidence of maltreatment. It is possible, however, to make an order that will seek to enhance the welfare of a child without removing him or her from the home environment. This facility comes in the form of a supervision order. By virtue of s.19 of the 1991 Act, a court may grant such an order. Once granted, the health board may visit the child, on such periodic occasions as appear necessary to that board, with a view to monitoring the provision of care to the child.[107] Order 84, r.16 of the District Court Rules 1997 requires that notice of an application for a supervision order be served upon the parents, or the parent with custody of the child, or a person acting *in loco parentis*, at least seven days prior to the hearing of the

---

[105] s.18(8).
[106] s.18(5).
[107] s.19(2).

application. The supervision order made on such an application must be served by the applicant health board upon each respondent.

The criteria for granting a supervision order are less stringent than those applicable in the case of a care order. In the latter case, the court must be "satisfied" of the matters listed in s.18(1). Section 19(1), by contrast, requires only that the court be satisfied "that there are reasonable grounds for believing" the matters listed in the Act. This is closer, then, to the requirement that a *prima facie* case of harm be established; the health board need not have solid proof but may, instead, act on the basis of a reasonably founded suspicion.

4–93 The matters referred to in the previous paragraph are as follows. The court must be satisfied that there are reasonable grounds for believing that:

(i) the child has been assaulted, neglected, sexually abused or otherwise ill-treated; or the child's health, development or welfare has been, is being or is likely in the future to be avoidably impaired or neglected; and

(ii) that it is desirable that the child be visited periodically, either by or on behalf of the health board.

4–94 The visitation rights afforded by this section have a dual purpose. The first is primarily to monitor the child and his or her carers, to ensure that the child's welfare is being promoted. The second purpose allows for a more proactive approach, permitting the board to give any necessary parenting advice to the child's custodians or carers, with a view ultimately to improving the child's well-being.

4–95 In other words, the supervision order facilitates the monitoring of a child considered to be at risk. It is certainly less intrusive than the care order. In some cases, indeed, it may obviate the need for further proceedings. The knowledge that the authorities are "keeping an eye" on them may prompt some errant parents to take the necessary steps to mend their ways. The health board may, by contrast, find that their initial fears were unfounded, that the situation that led to the making of the order was not an accurate representation of the child's treatment in general, or that the parents simply need additional support in certain areas of care-giving. Indeed, the chance for supervision may also give the health board the opportunity to assess whether it may, by its actions, improve the situation of the parents or care-givers, in particular by supplementing the resources of the family in need. The supervision order has the added advantage of leaving a child's home environment intact, a solution that, if at all possible, should be rejected only in the most pressing of circumstances. Obviously, however, a supervision order is inappropriate where it is clear that a child will suffer significant emotional or physical harm if he or she is not removed from the home environment as soon as possible. For a supervision order to be effective in securing the welfare of a child, it is essential that there is a good working relationship between the parents and the health board.[108]

---

[108] See *Re D (A Minor) and D and A (Minors)*, *Times Law Reports*, August 5, 1997 and *Re M (A Minor)*, *Times Law Reports*, December 31, 1998.

4–96   Despite the advantages of the supervision order, its imposition will by
no means be welcomed by all. The prospect of parental dissent is obviously
high. Where a parent of a child who is the subject of a supervision order (or a
person acting *in loco parentis* in respect of such child) objects to the manner
in which the order is being executed, s.19(3) allows such person to apply to
the court. In this case the court may grant such direction as it sees fit and the
health board will be obliged to comply. A court should of course be aware that
a parent's primary concern might not be with the manner of exercise of the
order but with the very fact that such an order has been made. Once satisfied
that a supervision order is necessary, the court should be wary of imposing
restrictions that may effectively negate the order. Order 84, r.17 of the District
Court Rules 1997 requires that notice of an application for directions under
s.19(3) be served upon the respondent at least seven days prior to the hearing
of the application.

Section 19(4) allows the court to make further provision for the monitoring
of a child's welfare. This permits the court, in particular, to require that a child
who is the subject of a supervision order be submitted for medical or psychiatric
examination, treatment or assessment at any place (*e.g.* hospital, clinic)
specified by the court. The court is additionally entitled to make such further
direction pertaining to the child's care as it sees fit. It is clear from the nature
of the supervision order, however, that any direction should respect the custodial
rights of all relevant persons. Section 19(4) is obviously not an appropriate
avenue for making an order that would upset prevailing custody arrangements.
Order 84, r.18 of the District Court Rules 1997 requires that the applicant
health board provide seven days' notice to parents of the intention to apply for
directions under s.19(4).

4–97   A supervision order has a necessarily limited shelf-life, usually 12
months. Section 19(6) states that it shall cease to have effect on the occurrence
of any of the following events, whichever is earliest:

(i)   the end of a period of 12 months beginning on the date on which the order
      was made;

(ii) the end of a period shorter than 12 months, if stipulated by the court at the
      time the order is made;

(iii) the child's reaching the age of 18;

(iv) the child's marriage.

4–98   It is possible, however, except where the child is 18 or over or married,
to make a further supervision order on, or before, the expiration of another
such order.[109] This will take effect on the expiration of the previous order. It
appears from *Re A (a Minor)*[110] that the health board is not required, when it
applies for an extension of a supervision order, to re-establish the threshold
conditions detailed in s.19(1) of the 1991 Act. In any such application, the

---

[109]   s.19(7).
[110]   [1995] 1 W.L.R. 482; [1995] 3 All E.R. 401.

court is likely to be guided by the welfare requirements of the 1991 Act.

It is an offence to breach the terms of a supervision order.[111] Any person who:

(i) fails to comply with such an order; or

(iii) fails to comply with any additional directions made by the court; or

(iii) obstructs the carrying out of a supervision order; or

(iv) prevents any authorised person from visiting a child

shall be guilty of an offence. On conviction, the offender will be subject to a maximum fine of IR£500 (€630); a term of imprisonment not exceeding six months, or both.

Interim care order, care order and supervision order appeals

4–99 An appeal against an interim care order, a care order or supervision order will not serve to stay the operation of the order. That said, s.21 of the 1991 Act enables the court making the order to stay its operation on such terms, if any, as may be imposed by the court making the determination.

4–100 A court considering an appeal against an interim care order, care order or supervision order is not in a position to interfere with the original judge's findings unless "he was plainly wrong or that he took into account what he should not have taken into account or failed to take into account what he should have taken into account."[112] Normally, additional evidence, other than evidence to emerge subsequent to the original hearing, shall only be admitted on appeal in exceptional circumstances. This approach is evidenced in *Re H. (Minors)*[113] where Swinton-Thomas L.J. in the Court of Appeal in the neighbouring jurisdiction stated that before additional evidence is admitted, even in a child case, "it must be evidence which is of considerable importance and be capable of so affecting the case that it may result in a different answer to that reached by the judge".

Variation and discharge of care orders and supervision orders

4–101 The court, under s.22 of the 1991 Act, may of its own initiative or on the application of any person:

(a) vary or discharge a care order or a supervision order; or

(b) vary or discharge any condition or direction attaching to the order; or

(c) in the case of a care order, discharge the care order and make a supervision order.

---

[111] s.19(5).

[112] Butler-Sloss L.J. in *Re D. (Minors)* [1997].

[113] [1997] 2 W.L.R. 563.

Order 84, r.20 of the District Court Rules 1997 provides that a notice of intention to apply for an order under s.22 be served upon the respondent at least seven days prior to the date of the application. A copy of any order made must be served on every person affected by the order.

Invalid care orders

4–102   Section 23 of the 1991 Act details the powers of the court in cases where a care order proves to be invalid. If a court makes such a declaration of invalidity in any proceedings for whatever reason, this section enables the status quo concerning the child's care to be maintained whilst a new care order is obtained. It should only be applied where the court is of the opinion that it is not in the best interests of the child to be returned. The terms of s.23 are very broad, and allow for the child who is considered to require care to be safeguarded against technical or fundamental matters which invalidate care orders.

Special care orders

4–103   In addition to the measures noted above, the Children Act 2001[114] introduces a "special care order" designed to provide for the care of troubled and unruly children. The Children Act 2001, together with the Children Act 1941[115] and the Children (Amendment) Act 1957,[116] deals with the treatment of unruly children and those found to be in breach of the criminal law. It was signed by the President on July 8, 2001, though several of the provisions of the Act are not yet in force.[117] The Children Act 2001 contains 271 sections, designed primarily to overhaul the Children Act 1908. It will be discussed in detail in Chapter 11.

---

[114] S.I. No. 24 of 2001.
[115] S.I. No. 12 of 1941.
[116] S.I. No. 28 of 1957.
[117] See Children Act 2001 (Commencement) Order 2002 (S.I. No. 151 of 2002).

CHAPTER 5

OPTIONS FOR CARE: FOSTER CARE AND PLACEMENT WITH RELATIVES

INTRODUCTION

5–01 Where a child has been placed in the care of a health board, the board has a number of placement options. Section 36 of the Child Care Act 1991 (the "1991 Act") specifies three options: foster care, residential care and placement with relatives. By virtue of s.36(1)(c) of the 1991 Act, a health board can place a child who may be eligible for adoption "with a suitable person with a view to his adoption". Section 6(3) of the 1991 allows a health board to "take a child into its care with a view to his adoption and maintain him" until the child is placed for adoption. The 1991 Act also requires each health board to provide an adoption service. In reality this facilitates adoption under the Adoption Act 1988.[1]

The above listed options are not, however, exhaustive; s.36(1)(d) allows for other suitable arrangements to be made as the board thinks proper, making it clear that there is scope for creative solutions to child care needs.

FOSTER CARE

5–02 Over the past decade, the relative use of foster care as a substitute care facility has undergone a definite change and has been propelled to the centre of child care in this jurisdiction. In 2001, 3,260 of the 3,600 children in the care of the health boards were placed in foster care. There has been a concentrated effort to encourage people to become foster parents to children whose parents cannot care for them.

Foster care involves the placing of a child with a "foster parent". A foster parent is defined (by s.36(2) of the 1991 Act) as "a person other than a relative of the child who is taking care of the child on behalf of a health board in accordance with regulations made under s.39 of the [1991] Act". The key attribute of this form of care is that it involves the placement of a child with a person who is made responsible for the care of that child in a non-occupational capacity. In other words, a foster parent tends to be a person who cares for the particular foster child or children in his or her care other than as a child care professional specifically employed for that purpose.

---

[1] No. 30 of 1988.

5–03 There is no legislative definition of foster care. This is, perhaps, due to the complexity of foster care and the evolution of a broad spectrum of foster placements. Perhaps the most comprehensive definition of foster care in Ireland is given by Mollan and Lefroy, as it acknowledges the complexity of the foster placement, the rights of the natural parents, and the objectives of this mode of care. It states:

"In fostering, the natural parents retain their basic rights and their relationship with the child, but the care of the child is transferred for a long, short or a indeterminate period to the foster parents. The foster parents are normally given an allowance to assist with the expenses of looking after the child and they are responsible to the agency which arranges the fostering placement. Developing a relationship with the natural parents of the child can be a most important part of the fostering experience and the overall aim of fostering is often to work towards the return of the child to her own family".[2]

History of foster care

5–04 In order to understand or appreciate the present situation of foster care for children in Ireland, some brief discussion of its historical background is needed. Foster care was a regular practice of child care until approximately the seventeenth century. It features prominently in the Brehon Laws, where it was a means of caring for unwanted, abandoned or orphaned children.[3] The Brehon Laws operated as the legal system in Ireland for an estimated 700 years. They created two types of fosterage. One was what was called "*altramm serce*",[4] foster care for which no remuneration was given. The other type of fosterage provided a fee.

Under English law a form of fostering involving the boarding out of children was adopted in Ireland, and was looked upon by the English as a means of emancipating these children from what was perceived as the evil influence of their parents.

5–05 The current foster care system has its origins in the Irish Poor Law (Amendment) Act 1862 which empowered "Boards of Guardians" to "board out" children with families until the age of five years and in some circumstances until the age of eight.[5] The arrangements in this Act were designed "solely and exclusively in the interests of the health of very young children who lacked a mother's care at an age when it was essential".[6] This was the first piece of legislation in Ireland to acknowledge not only the bond between the child and

---

[2] Mollan and Lefroy, *New Families* (Turoe Press, Dublin, 1984), p.6.
[3] Kelly, *A Guide to Early Irish Law* (Institute for Advanced Studies, Dublin, 1988), pp.88–90.
[4] Meaning "fosterage for affection".
[5] An account of this is to be found in Robins, *The Lost Children: A Study of Charity Children in Ireland 1700–1900* (IPA, Dublin, 1980), pp.272–284.
[6] Report of the Poor Law Commissions (1871).

his parents, but the importance of maintaining that bond during the all-important impressionable years.

5–06 The genesis of State intervention in foster care can be traced to legislation in 1897,[7] which invested local authorities with power to appoint female inspectors who could visit and, if necessary, remove children placed in foster care.

Following the passage of the Children Act 1908, discussed in Chapter 6, placing children in foster care in Ireland developed on what can be described as an informal basis. Fostering and adoption were not legally differentiated, which led to a number of long-term foster-care placements becoming what are now called *de facto* adoptions.

The Health Act 1953 was the first major modern initiative in relation to foster care.[8] The 1953 Act was augmented by the Boarding Out of Children Regulations 1954, which were in turn repealed by the Boarding Out of Children Regulations 1983.

5–07 The shortcomings of foster care in Ireland in the 1960s were considered in the Tuairim report.[9] Staffing was isolated by the authors as one of the major problems then facing this genre of care. Tuairim expressed concerns about the lack of training of the early children's officers, because the placement of children with families:

> "is undertaken among many other duties by public health nurses, who have probably not the necessary time, experience or knowledge to make adequate investigations of the suitability and motives of prospective foster parents, nor the suitability and needs of individual children to be fostered".[10]

5–08 With the establishment of the Regional Health Board following the enactment of the Health Act 1970, the health boards became directly responsible for foster care. From 1980 onwards a positive, progressive foster-care system began to emerge. There was a renewed impetus for the use of foster care, leading to its increased presence as a form of placement for children in care. New regulations were introduced in the form of the Boarding Out of Children Regulations 1983, which repealed the 1954 Regulations. The health boards were now required to place a child in foster care and, unless this was not possible, could not place a child in residential care.[11]

---

[7] Infant Life Protection Act 1897 (60 & 61 Vict.) Ch.57.

[8] See s.55(1) of the 1953 Act.

[9] Tuairim, *Some of our Children—A Report of the Residential Care of the Deprived Child in Ireland* (London, 1966) at p.10. Tuairim, founded in 1954, was a society which encouraged the involvement of Irish citizens in public affairs. It had branches in the principal towns in Ireland. Its most important piece of work was the aforementioned report called *Some of our Children*, which took the form of cursory examination of child care as it stood in Ireland in the 1960s.

[10] *ibid.*

[11] Boarding Out of Children Regulations 1983 (S.I. No. 67 of 1983), s.5.

Modern foster care

5–09   Fostering is more than parenting. It is what can be termed "parenting plus", taking the form of a partnership with social workers, the health board and very often also with the natural parents. It has been advanced as an alternative to the "emotional vacuum" of residential care, providing what many would perceive as the proper environment in which a child can develop his or her physical, mental and social capabilities to the full.

Whereas substitute care in the form of foster care involves a change in legal custody of the child, substitute care in adoption involves going beyond a change in legal custody to a change in legal guardianship. It is the latter which severs the parents' tie to the child completely. However, it must be stated that while long-term foster placements have the veneer of *de facto* adoption, the fact that legal guardianship of the child has not transferred from the natural parents to the foster parents has very considerable implications for the nature of the relationship it creates between the foster child and foster family. Fostering allows for the return of the child to his or her natural home at any time. The foster child has dual family status – he belongs, in part, to both his foster family and his natural family. His "belonging" to the natural family is not only formal and legalistic, but fostering means that in name and kinship affiliation he is still part of that family.

5–10   "Family life" has been held by the European Court of Human Rights to include the relationship between a foster parent and a foster child, although the Court has noted that the content of family life may depend on the nature of the fostering arrangement.[12]

The foster parents

5–11   The insecurity of the fostering arrangement has made it a less attractive option than adoption. Foster parents have a number of duties and few rights. For example, when foster parents attempt to adopt a child without the approval of the health board under the Adoption Act 1988, the legislature in the guise of s.5 of that Act imposes on the foster parents the risk of costs being levied against them if they are unsuccessful.

Duty of care to foster parents

5–12   In *W. v Essex County Council*,[13] proceedings were brought by foster parents against the defendant local authority arising from abuse suffered by the children of the foster parents at the hands of another child placed in the family's care by the defendant council. The foster parents sought and were given oral assurances by Essex County Council that no child who was a known or suspected sexual abuser would be placed with them. The Court held the

---

[12] See *Gaskin v UK* (1989) 12 E.H.R.R. 36, para.49; *X v Switzerland*, Application No. 8257/78 (Dec), (July 10, 1978) 13 D.R. 248; and *Rieme v Sweden* (1992) 16 E.H.R.R. 155.

[13] [1997] 2 F.L.R. 535.

Council vicariously liable for the conduct of the social worker in the case, who had a duty of care to provide the information requested by the foster parents.

The natural parents

5–13 Acceptance of foster care by the natural parents involves acceptance of an anomalous position. They still retain the status of parents, but they can no longer practise directly the daily responsibilities of the role. They have to forfeit some of the prerogatives of parenthood to an alternative set of parents.

As far as the natural parents' rights in relation to a child in voluntary care are concerned, they retain all their rights in relation to their child and can reclaim the foster child at any time. Foster parents must deliver the child to the natural parents in the terms detailed in the Child Care (Placement of Children in Foster Care) Regulations 1995.[14]

The natural parents' rights in relation to a foster child committed though the courts may be outlined as follows:

(1) The natural parents' rights to the care of their child has been relinquished. They have the right to appeal the court's decision when they feel ready to assume the care of their child, but must prove that they are capable of resuming care of their child.

(2) The natural parents have the right of access to their child.

The foster child

5–14 Children in foster families do not have stability, save through court proceedings. They are not independently represented and orders can, and have been, made which have resulted in children being propelled from parents they have lived with for years to virtual strangers, without cognisance been given to their welfare. Article 12 of the United Nations Convention on the Rights of the Child 1989 and Art.6 of the European Convention on Human Rights require separate representation for children in proceedings of this nature. The delay in this jurisdiction in putting in place the infrastructure for the operation of a guardian *ad litem* system has deprived numerous children of this central right.

Child Care (Placement of Children in Foster Care) Regulations 1995

5–15 Section 39 of the 1991 Act requires the Minister for Health and Children to make regulations pertaining to foster care. These regulations were put in place in 1995, in the form of the Child Care (Placement of Children in Foster Care) Regulations 1995.[15] These regulations will be dealt with here under five distinct headings: the welfare of the child; the procedures to be carried out prior to placement; the duties of foster carers; the monitoring of placements; and the removal of children from placements. The National Standards for Foster

---

[14] S.I. No. 260 of 1995.
[15] Hereinafter termed "the 1995 Regulations".

Care, launched on April 29, 2003, will also be considered alongside the 1995 Regulations.[16] The development of the National Standards for Foster Care was one of the recommendations of the report of the Working Group of Foster Care.[17] The National Standards for Foster Care provide guidance on the provisions of quality foster care within the existing legislative framework.

(a) Welfare of the child

5–16 In keeping with the standard policy of child law, the overriding obligation on the health board in these matters is to promote the welfare of the child.[18] While the health board is required to pay special attention to the rights and duties of parents (more especially where they enjoy the "inalienable and imprescriptible" constitutional rights conferred by virtue of their marital status), the primary and paramount consideration is clear: the board must act first and foremost by reference to the welfare of the child. This may, in appropriate cases, require the health board to consult the child himself or herself in regard to his or her preferences. In particular, where a child is of sufficient age and maturity, it is stipulated that his or her wishes should be afforded due consideration.

(b) Pre-placement procedures

5–17 Part III of the 1995 Regulations lays down certain procedures that must be adopted and/or satisfied prior to the placement of a child with a foster parent.

Panel of foster parents

5–18 Under Art.5(1) of the 1995 Regulations, each health board is required to establish and maintain a list of persons willing and able to act as foster parents. To become a foster parent, a person must first be placed on such a panel. It is worth noting that a health board may place a child with foster parents who, while not on the panel maintained by that health board, have been placed on the panel of another health board.[19]

5–19 In order to be placed on such a panel, a prospective foster parent must first furnish to the board:

(i)   a written report from a registered medical practitioner regarding the state of the applicant's health;

(ii) the names and addresses of two referees, other than members of the applicant's family, who are willing and able, if asked, to comment upon the applicant's character and personality;

---

[16] *National Standards for Foster Care* (Government Publications, Dublin, April 2003).
[17] *Foster Care—A Child Centred Partnership* (Government Publications, Dublin, May 2001).
[18] See Pt II of the 1995 Regulations.
[19] Art.27.

(iii) such authorisations as are necessary to allow the health board to make enquiries with An Garda Síochána, in particular to establish whether the applicant or any member of his family has a criminal record;

(iv) any other information that the health board may reasonably require.

5–20 Once such information has been furnished, the board will appoint an authorised person to assess the suitability of the applicant. In carrying out his or her inquiries, that person is also required to visit the home of the applicant to ensure that it is suitable for the upbringing of children. Following this, the authorised person will submit a written report to a committee of persons established under Art.5(3) of the 1995 Regulations. That committee consists of persons with suitable experience and ability in the field of child care and in matters affecting the welfare of children.

Under Art.5(6) of the 1995 Regulations, the applicant is entitled to a written statement regarding the outcome of these proceedings. In addition, s.18 of the Freedom of Information Act 1997 allows the applicant to apply in writing to the head of the health board seeking reasons for the decision. In this case (subject to certain exceptions), the latter will be obliged to furnish such reasons within four weeks of receiving the application.

Eligibility of non-marital couples

5–21 While there may be a preference for placing a child with two parents, preferably living in a stable relationship, it does not seem to be legally necessary that a foster parent be married. Indeed, it is possible for one person alone to be a foster parent. In general, it is fair to say that the eligibility requirements applicable to foster care are not quite as exacting in practice as those applicable in the case of adoption. This is not, by any means, to be taken to imply that foster parents are not as capable as adoptive parents. In fact, in certain respects, the job of foster parent often proves the more difficult one of the two. Foster care involves greater flexibility than adoption. With provision for supervision and monitoring by the health board and the ever-present possibility that the child may be removed from their custody, foster parents must surely face the possibility of emotional and psychological strain on a scale not usually experienced by more traditional family units.

5–22 The flexibility of the foster-care system allows, however, for certain persons who would not normally be chosen as adoptive parents to act as foster parents. The preferred adoptive parent is usually married[20] and aged between 25 and 45. Many people are thus in practice effectively precluded from being adoptive parents. The small and decreasing number of children available for adoption compounds this situation, thus effectively rendering ineligible all but those who most closely meet the "ideal" (invariably young, married (and thus, heterosexual) couples). There are, by contrast, more children available for foster care and this allows for otherwise ideal parents, who may not meet

---

[20] Although there is, since 1991, provision for adoption by single persons; see s.10(2) of the Adoption Act 1991 (No. 14 of 1991).

the criteria for adoption, to take care of a child. Thus, people over the age of 45 and single people will usually find it easier to foster than to adopt. This factor also potentially facilitates creative solutions designed to deal with special circumstances. For instance, one novel approach, now becoming more common in Britain and in some parts of the United States, involves the placement of older teenagers, who have self-identified as gay or lesbian, in the foster care of a same-sex couple. This may occur where, for instance, a child has been placed in care following his or her parents' rejection of the child on the grounds of this professed sexual orientation. No doubt this approach may be considered by some to be controversial but ultimately, where carefully thought-out and planned, such creative solutions may be of benefit to a child's welfare.

Assessment of the child

5–23   Before a child is placed in foster care, the health board must carry out an assessment of his or her circumstances.[21] This will include a medical examination unless the board is satisfied that such an examination is not necessary. In deciding whether a medical examination is necessary, the board should have regard to such information and reports as are available to it. An assessment of the child's circumstances must usually be undertaken before the child is placed in foster care. In emergency situations, however, it is possible to postpone the assessment until after placement occurs. In these cases, the board must carry out an assessment as soon after placement as is practically possible.

Standard 6 of the National Standards provides as follows:

> "An assessment of the child's or young person's needs is made prior to any placement or, in the case of emergencies, as soon as possible thereafter".[22]

Selecting foster parents

5–24   Foster parents are to be chosen from the panels mentioned previously. In each case, Art.7 of the Regulations requires the board to take steps to ensure that the parents chosen from this panel have sufficient capacity to meet the needs of the child concerned. It is not necessary that the foster parents be of the same religious persuasion as the child. That said, the health board should endeavour to respect the wishes of the child's guardians regarding the religious upbringing of the child. If this is not possible, the board may make such arrangements for the care of the child as it considers reasonable. Presumably, this may include special arrangements for religious instruction and formation in the child's faith. Should the guardian remain dissatisfied regarding these arrangements, the health board is obliged to inform him or her of the right, under s.47 of the 1991 Act, to apply to the District Court for a direction as to the most appropriate approach.

---

[21] Art.6 of the 1995 Regulations.
[22] At p.17.

It is worth reiterating that while a child may be placed in the care of a relative under s.36(1)(d) of the 1991 Act, a foster parent may not be a relative of the child in his or her care. Presumably, this rule is intended to obviate the necessity for relatives of a child to be first placed on a panel of foster parents.

Contract between health board and foster parents

5–25   The making of arrangements for placement of a child with foster parents will be deemed to have effected a contract between the foster parents and the health board. A copy of this contract must be given to the foster parents in the form laid out in the First Schedule to the Regulations and in Appendix 10 of this book. This should be accompanied by a copy of the 1991 Regulations.

5–26   Before a child is placed with foster parents, it is necessary that the latter be furnished with information regarding the child.[23] This allows the parents to make appropriate arrangements for the care of the child. The information contemplated by Art.9 is as follows:

(i)   the name of the child, together with details of his or her sex, religion and date of birth;

(ii)   the reason why the child was admitted to the care of the health board;

(iii)   whether the child was put in care voluntarily or by means of a court order;

(iv)   whether the child has been placed in care before. If so, details of same should accompany the statement of information;

(v)   names and addresses of the child's parents;

(vi)   the names, ages and whereabouts of the child's sisters and/or brothers (if any);

(vii)   details of arrangements for access by parents or relatives;

(viii)   details of medical or nutritional requirements (*e.g.* is the child asthmatic or diabetic? Is the child a vegetarian?);

(ix)   details of arrangements for the child's attendance at school.

5–27   It is also possible to provide additional information, as required, to the foster parents. Indeed, it is arguable that personal information that may be necessary to help foster parents to understand children entrusted to their care, and to avoid dangers of which they would otherwise be unaware, should be disclosed to them under the terms of Art.8 of the European Convention on Human Rights. Private life under Art.8 of the Convention includes the right to establish and develop relationships with other human beings. In *Niemietz v Germany*,[24] the European Court of Human Rights stated:

---

[23] Art.9 of the 1995 Regulations.
[24] [1992] 16 E.H.R.R. 97.

"It would be too restrictive to limit the notion [of private life] to an 'inner circle' in which the individual may live his own personal life as he chooses and to exclude therefrom entirely the outside world not encompassed within that circle. Respect for private life must also comprise to a certain degree the right to establish and develop relationships with other human beings."[25]

Care and upbringing plan

5–28   Before a child is placed in foster care, it is incumbent on the health board to prepare a "care and upbringing" plan.[26] This plan should lay down specific aims and objectives for the placement, with details of the support to be provided by the health board to the child, the foster parents and the natural parents. This plan should also outline all access arrangements and provisions for review of the plan. In preparing the plan, the health board is required to consult with the foster parents, and, if appropriate, with the child and his or her guardian(s). Once completed, a copy of the plan should be delivered to the foster parents, and, in so far as it is practicable to do so, the child and guardians of the child.

The requirement for such a plan may be postponed where a child is in need of immediate placement. In this case, the plan should be drawn up as soon as practicable after the placement has been made. Addressing the issue of care planning, Standard 7 of the National Standards for Foster Care provides:

"Each child and young person in foster care has a written care plan. The child or young person and his or her family participate in the preparation of the care plan."[27]

(c) Duties of the foster parents

5–29   Once the placement has been made, the foster parents have lawful custody of the child until such time as the placement is ended. In the meantime, Art.16 of the Regulations contains details of the duties, general and specific, that are placed upon the foster parents. Article 16(1) places a general obligation on the foster parents to take all reasonable steps to promote the child's health, development and welfare.

5–30   In addition, however, several specific stipulations are contained in the regulations. Article 16(2) lists several duties of persons acting as foster parents:

(i)   where the health board considers it necessary in the interests of the child, it may authorise periodic visits to the child. This may be, for instance, for the purpose of assessing the child in care with a view to determining what is in his or her best interests. Where a person is so authorised, the

---

[25] *ibid.*, para.29.

[26] Art.11. See also *Eastern Health Board v Judge McDonnell and Others (with notice parties)*, unreported, High Court, McCracken J., March 5, 1999.

[27] At p.18.

foster parents must afford such persons reasonable access to the child, including the right to see the child and to visit the foster home for this purpose;

(ii) the foster parents are further required to co-operate with the person mentioned above, in particular by giving him or her all relevant information that may reasonably be required;

(iii) the foster parents are under a duty to maintain the confidentiality of any information given to them relating to the child, or his or her family, by the health board;

(iv) where a child suffers from injury or illness, the foster parents are required to take steps to see that the child receives appropriate medical treatment;

(v) foster parents should inform the health board, as soon as possible, of any significant event in the child's life;

(vi) the board should also be informed of any change in the circumstances of the foster parents that might affect their capacity to provide for the child in their care;

(vii) a care order or arrangement may be accompanied by directions or arrangements as to access by the child to his or her relatives. Foster parents are required to co-operate in giving effect to these arrangements;

(viii) where the foster parents intend to change residence, the board should be given at least 28 days' notice of such intended change;

(ix) where either the child or the foster parents are absent from the home, adequate ("good and proper") arrangements should be made by the latter for the care of the child;

(x) where such absence (by the child or the foster parents) is likely to exceed 72 hours (three days), the health board should be given prior notice.

Medical consent

5–31 The issue of medical consent in foster care is one which is fraught with difficulty. Articles 16(1) and 16(2)(d) of the 1995 Regulations set down the legal framework for dealing with this issue:

"(1) It shall be the duty of the foster parents who are taking care of a child on behalf of a health board in accordance with these regulations to take all reasonable measures to promote the child's health, development and welfare.
[...]
(2) Without prejudice to the generality of sub-article (1) of this article, foster parents shall in particular—
[...]
(d) seek appropriate medical aid for the child if the child suffers from illness or injury."

5–32   While the foregoing provisions address the issue of health care in a general fashion, they fail to provide sufficient guidance on the issue of medical consent. The National Standards for Foster Care, however, have addressed this issue by stating that "foster carers have the capacity to consent to urgent medical treatment" if "in the clinical judgement of the medical practitioner" it is necessary "in the interest of the child's welfare."[28]

In relation to non-urgent elective medical treatment for a child under 16 years of age in voluntary care, the health board must obtain the consent of the child's natural parents. Where this is not forthcoming, the health board should seek directions from the District Court under s.47 of the 1991 Act.

Where an emergency or interim care order is in place, the health board can seek direction from the court in relation to elective treatment of a child under 16 years of age under either s.13(7), s.17(4) or s.47 of the 1991 Act.[29] The health board can consent to the non-urgent medical treatment of a child under 16 years of age where a care order is in place in respect of the child and treatment is in the best interests of the child. For children 16 years old and over, s.23 of the Non-Fatal Offences Against the Person Act 1997 applies. This section is discussed in detail in Chapter 4 at para.4–49.

Financial support

5–33   Article 14(1) provides for the payment of a fostering allowance to be made to foster parents in respect of each foster child in the parents' care. The amount of such allowance is to be set from time to time by the Minister for Health and Children. It goes without saying that the existence of this allowance should not be the primary motivation for a person deciding to become a foster carer. The reality for many foster parents is that the child's overall well-being may require their footing the bill for certain expenses.

Article 14(2) allows the health board to provide additional financial or other assistance necessary for the care of any child. The decision as to such necessity is, however, to be determined by the health board. Disputes may arise, as to the amount of resources made available for the care of the child. In this regard, it is worth noting that any person may apply to the District Court to obtain its direction on any matter relating to the welfare of the child.[30]

(d) Monitoring of the child in a placement

Register

5–34   Each health board is required to keep a register of all children placed in foster care by the board.[31] This should include the following details in respect of each child:

---

[28] See Standard 11 (pp.25–26) and Appendix 2 (pp.60–62) of the National Standards for Foster Care.

[29] See para.4–72.

[30] See s.47 of the 1991 Act.

[31] Art.12 of the 1995 Regulations.

(a) his or her name, sex and date of birth;

(b) the names and address(es) of the child's parents;

(c) the names and address(es) of the foster parents;

(d) the date of the placement;

(e) the date, if appropriate, on which the placement shall end.

Case record

5–35 In respect of every child in foster care, the health board is additionally required to maintain an up-to-date case record containing certain documents as follows:

(i) all medical and social reports in respect of the child. This should include background information relating to the child's family, presumably including any inheritable disorders or ailments;

(ii) a copy of all orders made by a court in relation to the child or, alternatively, a copy of the parental consent permitting the placement of a child in voluntary care as the case may be;

(iii) the child's birth certificate;

(iv) a copy of the contract between the foster parents and the health board as contemplated by Art.9 of the Regulations, and of the care plan required by Art.11;

(v)   school reports and other documents regarding the educational development of the child;

(vi) written details of any access visits between the child and his or her parents;

(vii) notes or memos concerning any review of the child's case undertaken under the 1995 Regulations;

(viii) a note of all significant events that have affected the child. It should be noted that under Art.16(2)(e) of the 1995 Regulations, the foster parents of a child are required to notify the board of all such events.

Supervision and visitation

5–36 An authorised member of the health board may, by virtue of Art.17(1) of the Regulations, visit a child in foster care as often as is considered necessary by the board. Such visitation as occurs should be in line with the details of the care plan drawn up under Art.11 of the Regulations. Whatever specific arrangements are made, however, Art.17 requires that the child be visited at least once every three months during the first two years of the placement. The first visit must take place within one month of the date of the initial placement. After the initial two-year period has ended, the child should be visited at least once every six months.

A note of every visit should be entered in the case record of the child, as contemplated by Art.17(5) of the Regulations. Should such visit reveal that there has been any deviation from the requirements set out in the 1995 Regulations, the health board is obliged to take appropriate remedial action. Particulars of any action taken by the board in the wake of the visit should also be noted in the case record.

Case review

5–37   In the first two years after placement, the care plan drawn up in respect of a child should be reviewed by an authorised person at least every six months and, thereafter, at intervals of a year or less.[32] The health board should make arrangements for such periodic review. Where a health board commences any review, Art.18(4) requires that the health board give notice of this fact to the foster parents and, in so far as it is considered practically possible, to the child and guardian(s) of the child. Such persons as are so informed are entitled to be heard in person or otherwise consulted in the course of the review.

5–38   Each review should address the following matters:

(i)   is every reasonable effort being made to promote the welfare of the child?

(ii) is such care as is being presently provided suited to the current needs of the child?

(iii) have the circumstances of the child's parents changed to such an extent as to require reconsideration of the placement?

(iv) considering such changes, would the return of the child to its parents be conducive to the child's best interests?

(v)   is the child due to leave the care of the health board? If so, the health board should consider the child's need for aftercare as contemplated by s.45 of the Act of 1991.

When conducting the review, the board is obliged to have due regard to reports of authorised visits by health board officials; the child's most recent school report and any other information deemed relevant. In a similar vein, the board is required to consider any information furnished by the child, the foster parents or the natural parents in the course of the review, in addition to the expressed wishes of such persons. That said, it is, as ever, the welfare of the child that predominates.

5–39   A note of the review should be taken and kept, together with details of any action taken consequent upon the review, as part of the child's case record. Furthermore, any decisions taken as a result of the review shall be transmitted to the foster parents and, where applicable, to the child and his or her guardians. The board may also inform any other person that it considers ought to be informed.

Provision is also made for the initiation of a special review. Article 19 allows any person with a bona fide interest in the welfare of a child in foster

---

[32] Art.18 of the 1995 Regulations.

care to deliver a written statement to the health board requesting the making of such a review. The board must comply with such a request unless it considers such review unnecessary. Where the request is successful, a review shall take place in compliance with the procedures laid down in Art.18 as if it were a review conducted under that article. Where the request is rejected, the board must notify the maker of the request in writing. It is open to the latter, as in all cases, to seek the direction of the court and thus override this rejection.[33]

5–40 In certain cases a child will be the subject of several placements in succession. The short duration of such placements may not allow for the making of periodic reviews, as envisaged by the provisions noted above. It may thus be the case that the normal schedule for periodic reviews will not be activated. In such a case, the board should carry out regular reviews of the child's case, notwithstanding the brevity of its consecutive placements.

(e) The termination of a placement

5–41 The placement of a child in foster care will end where the child reaches the age of 18 or, alternatively, marries. At such point, after all, the person involved is no longer a "child" as defined by the Act and thus is not subject to the provisions of the Act. That said, there is nothing in law or otherwise preventing such a person and the foster parents from maintaining a continuing family relationship.

Where a person remains a "child" as defined by the Act, he or she may be removed from the placement by one of several methods listed below. These are contained in Pt V of the 1995 Regulations. The effect of such removal will be bring to an end the lawful custody of the child by its foster parents.

Removal at the request of the foster parents

5–42 The foster parents may request that a child in their care be removed. In such a case the board must, as soon as possible, take steps to provide alternative arrangements for the child's care with due regard, as always, to the best interests of the child. The foster parents in question will be required in such circumstances to sign a written declaration verifying that the child is being removed at their request. This declaration should be retained as part of the case record.

Termination of the placement by the health board

5–43 In the alternative, it is possible for the health board itself to terminate the placement of the child. This may be done, for instance, where the health board proposes to reunite the child with his or her original family. It is possible also to effect a termination where the board considers that the child's continued placement with the particular foster parents is no longer conducive to his or her welfare, or indeed, is no longer the most appropriate way of achieving the child's welfare.

---

[33] s.47 of the 1991 Act.

5-44   Obviously, the foster parents may object to such removal. If this happens, they will be given every opportunity to make representations to the health board. Should the board, notwithstanding these representations, decide to proceed with the removal, it shall be obliged to give a written statement of the decision to the foster parents, containing in particular the reasons for such a decision. This statement should be accompanied by a request that the child be returned to the custody of the health board at such place and time as is stipulated by the board. Should the foster parents refuse to comply, the health board may apply for a direction of the District Court, under s.43(2) of the 1991 Act, to the effect that the child be delivered up to the board. Non-compliance with such an order is, it should be reiterated, an offence under s.43(3) of the 1991 Act punishable by up to six months in prison or a fine not exceeding IR£500 (€630), or both. Such a refusal may also amount to a contempt of court.

Where a child is removed from the custody of foster parents under Pt V of the 1995 Regulations, the foster parents are, in appropriate circumstances, provided with counselling facilities by the health board.

(f) Other miscellaneous provisions

5-45   Part VI of the Regulations makes certain additional provisions of a miscellaneous nature. The board may, for instance, make arrangements with any competent and qualified voluntary body or person with a view to providing assistance in the performance of the health board's functions. Part VI also allows the Minister for Health and Children to appoint a person to monitor the practices and procedures relating to foster care services provided by a health board. To this end, the person so appointed may, *inter alia*, consult such records as may exist and interview any employee of the health board involved in the provision of foster-care services.

Similar rules apply in respect of the placement of children with relatives under the Child Care (Placement of Children with Relatives) Regulations 1995.[34]

Foster care and succession rights

5-46   Foster children have no legal entitlement to inherit any share of the estate of a deceased foster parent. If a foster parent wishes to make provision for a foster child, this can only be achieved by making a will. In summary, a will gives a foster parent the opportunity to provide for the devolution of some or all of his property to a foster child on his or her death.

5-47   The issue of the succession rights of foster children was considered by the Northern Circuit Court in February 2000.[35] The facts of the case highlight a lacuna in Irish family law. Although the foster children were clearly seen by the foster parents in this case as their children, they were regarded in law as

---

[34] See paras 5–78 to 5–98.
[35] See *Kevin O'Rourke and Gerry O'Rourke v Owen Gallagher* [2000] 2 I.J.F.L. 28.

strangers. Thus, in the absence of an express provision in the will of their foster father, the foster children had no entitlement under the Succession Act 1965 for provision out of the estate. While past discrimination in this area against non-marital children has been removed by the Status of Children Act 1987, no provision is specifically made for the foster family. At the root of this situation is the focus of the law on one particular family form: that of the family based on marriage with natural children. This narrow definition of the family is in conflict with the approach adopted by the European Court of Human Rights.[36]

Foster care and capital acquisitions tax

5–48   Sections 221 and 222 of the Finance Act 2001[37] have widened the category of "child" for the purposes of computing capital acquisitions tax. A child for this purpose now includes:

(a) a step child;[38]

(b) a child adopted under the Adoption Acts 1952–1998 or under a foreign adoption which is deemed to be a valid adoption within the meaning of the Adoption Act 1991 (as amended by the Adoption Act 1998);[39]

(c) a foster child;[40] and

(d) a natural (adopted) child.[41]

5–49   The extended category of "child" for the purposes of calculating capital acquisitions tax includes a foster child and a natural (adopted) child. That said, the definition of a "child" for the purposes of the capital acquisitions tax legislation remains unaffected by the foregoing development. The reliefs included in the Finance Act 2001 only apply to foster children and natural children adopted by others in terms of benefits received from the disponer, not for any other purpose.

5–50   A foster child is now classified as a child of the foster parents in limited circumstances for the calculation of capital acquisitions tax. Section 221 of the Finance Act 2001 adds a new s.59D to the Capital Acquisitions Tax Act 1976 by providing that a foster child (successor) will bear to the deceased foster parent (disponer), in relation to a gift or inheritance taken on or after December 6, 2000, the relationship of a "child" if the following conditions are met:

(a) the foster child must have been placed in the foster care of the deceased foster parent under the 1995 Regulations, or

---

[36] See Chap.12.
[37] No. 7 of 2001.
[38] Capital Acquisitions Tax Act 1976, s.2(1).
[39] Finance Act 1992, s.223(1).
[40] Finance Act 2001, s.221.
[41] Finance Act 2001, s.222.

(b) the foster child must have resided with the deceased foster parent for a
     period of five years before he or she reached 18 years ("the appropriate
     period") and must have been under the care of and maintained by the
     foster parent at the foster parent's own expense.

If these conditions are proven, the foster child will be deemed to bear to the
foster parent the relationship of a child for the purpose of computing the tax
payable on any gift or inheritance from the deceased foster parent, which
relationship now has a Group 1 threshold of €456,438. An independent witness
must corroborate the foster child's claim for Group 1 status.

Long-term foster care and adoption

5–51 For a significant number of children in foster care, rehabilitation within
the biological family unit is an unattainable goal. These children, although
they no longer have active access arrangements in place with their biological
parents, nevertheless legally "belong" to them and are not free for adoption.
Of necessity, then, they live in a twilight world—between a family that does
not want them and a family that cannot fully have them. These children should
be eligible for adoption.

5–52 Foster parents have always, theoretically, been capable of applying for
an adoption order. Prior to the enactment of the Adoption Act 1988, if the
foster parents with whom the child had been placed, believed that it was contrary
to the child's welfare to remove him or her from their custody, the only legal
option at their disposal was to have such a child made a ward of court and then
proceed to procuring an order for custody in their favour. This occurred in *Re
JL (A Minor)*, unreported, High Court, 1978. Other cases in which a similar
approach was adopted include *Re Farrell (minors)*,[42] and *Re Williams
(Minors)*.[43]

5–53 In order for an adoption to proceed under the 1988 Act, very stringent
requirements must be satisfied. In effect, the Act requires that the parents of
the child must have so comprehensively abandoned their parental duties in
such a manner as to indicate that the child is unlikely ever to receive even
minimal care from them. The Act lays down a two-tier process for non-
consensual adoptions. While an application must, initially, be made to the
Adoption Board, it must be followed by an order of the High Court permitting
such adoption.[44]

The reform of long-term foster care, in the guise of the Adoption Act 1988,
was most inadequate when viewed alongside the situation that exists in other
jurisdictions.

5–54 In response to the child's need for a set of parents whom he or she can

---

[42] unreported, High Court, January 1978.
[43] unreported, High Court, August 1978.
[44] For more information on adoption see Chap.9 of this book.

identify as his or her "own" with some promise of permanence, many states in the United States have moved to simplify the process of termination of parental rights in circumstances where the parents have abandoned their child to foster care. This enables termination of access and other rights in cases where parents show no consistent interest in the child and where there is no reasonable or foreseeable likelihood that the parents can, or will, plan for the rehabilitation of the child within the natural family. One of the earliest examples of such termination of parental rights occurred in New York in 1959, to free the "permanently neglected" child for adoption.[45] The net effect of the New York reform was that termination of parental rights without the natural parents' consent was made possible in circumstances where the natural parents had surrendered their rights to the child by failure to discharge the obligations of parenthood.[46] Previously, such children were available for adoption only in circumstances similar to the Adoption Act 1988. One of the real problems in New York manifested itself in the phrase "physically able". Some children remained in long-term foster care because their mothers were hospitalised for mental illness. There was strong resistance to terminating parental rights in such circumstances, because mental illness is not the fault of the parent. The Children's Bureau in that jurisdiction stated that, where mental illness is likely to continue for an extended period, the equivalent of our health board should be given the facility to press for the termination of parental rights so as to free the child for adoption. It is suggested that the aforementioned no-fault based approach would ideally apply not only to foster care but across the entire child care spectrum in Ireland.

5–55 In theory, foster care is a temporary means of providing care for a child in a family environment until his or her parents are in a position to provide care for their child. Unfortunately, the reality is often different, with the result that a considerable number of children remain in foster care indefinitely, drifting from one foster placement to the next. Many children remain in foster care due to the inadequacies of the adoption laws which, until the enactment of the Adoption Act 1988, confined adoption to non-marital or orphaned children. The adoption of non-marital children was allowed only in cases when this status could be legally proven. In fact, adoption was not legally possible even in circumstances where marital parents requested it.

5–56 As so many children spend long periods in foster care in this country, many foster parent-child relationships grow into relationships emotionally

---

[45] A "permanently neglected child" was defined as a child in foster care whose parents "failed substantially and continuously or repeatedly for a period of more than one year to maintain contact with, and plan for the future of the child, although physically and financially able to do so ...." (Polier, "Amendments to New York's Adoption Law: The Permanently Neglected Child" (1959) 38 *Child Welfare* 2).

[46] For a comprehensive account of the circumstances in which parental rights can be terminated in the United States, see: Pennypacker, "Reaching Decisions to Initiate Court Action to Free Children in Care for Adoption" (1961) 40 *Child Welfare*; Polier, *Parental Rights* (New York: Child Welfare League of America, 1958; and Polier, "Amendments to New York's Adoption Law: The Permanently Neglected Child", *ibid.*

indistinguishable from biological parent-child relationships, and the foster parent becomes a psychological parent. The inability to terminate parental rights, except in extreme circumstances, has resulted in a small number of these children remaining in foster care indefinitely. In Ireland, the protective curtain of the Constitution has merely been raised by the enactment of the Adoption Act 1988, but only to allow through a trickle of children from the public law domain.

Removal

5–57   Inappropriate placements result in unnecessary moves and inconsistency in children's lives. When moves are unavoidable they should always be planned to cushion the damaging impact on the child involved. In particular, a precipitous removal is to be avoided. When the child leaves foster care, it should be planned and occur as a result of mutual participation between the social worker, the natural parents, the foster child and the foster parents. If possible, any move should have the support of the foster parents, so that they can assist the child to move. If the child is being moved from the foster placement because of the inability of the foster parents to cope, the health board social worker must be alive and sensitive to the foster parents' feelings, and attempt to help them to perceive the removal as other than evidence of their failure. The health board is obliged to comply with the removal procedure detailed in Pt V of the 1995 Regulations. A very interesting provision manifests itself in s.15 of the Social Work (Scotland) Act 1969, which states that a natural parent who wishes to remove his child from foster care must give 28 days' notice in writing, where the child has been in care for a period of six months or more.

Swedish child law is similarly child-centred. Under s.28 of the Swedish Social Services Act 1980, the Social District Council may, where the interests of the child so require, prohibit the guardian from taking a child from a foster home, providing that there is a substantial risk of harm being occasioned to the child's physical or *mental* health if removed. The prohibition in this section is a temporary measure pending the arrival of an appropriate moment for transferring the child from the foster home without the risk of such detrimental effects as are specified in the section. The factors to be considered when deciding to issue a prohibition under s.28 of the Swedish Social Services Act 1980, include the child's age; degree of development; character; emotional ties; present and prospective living conditions; the time the child has been away from his or her parents; and his or her contacts with them when separated. This provision is aimed at safeguarding the interests of the child, in that it enables the child's interests to prevail regardless of whether they conflict with the guardian's interest in deciding where the child should live. It is child-welfare-centred to not tolerate, without good reason, repeated transfers and transfers that take place after a long time, when the child has developed strong attachments with the foster parents. It is therefore true to say that the problems associated with the removal of a child from a foster home and the possible detrimental effects on him or her of reunification with his or her natural parents are acknowledged in Swedish legislation. A provision analogous to s.28 would ensure greater stability and structure in long-term foster care in Ireland.

Foster care and the Constitution

5–58 If true change is to be brought about in the foster-care area, child care policy in Ireland must support the philosophy that, in any decision about a foster child's future, the welfare of the child should be the first and paramount consideration. If this necessitates the termination of parental rights, then that should be an option. However, the Irish Constitution presents a major obstacle to the achievement of this child-welfare approach. The paramountcy of the family unit in Art.41 of the Irish Constitution makes it impossible for the courts to give the foster child's welfare anything but a qualified consideration. Article 41 ensures the views of married parents are paramount in relation to the welfare of their child and has stifled legislative changes in regard to child welfare. The foster child in Ireland thus finds himself or herself in a family unit that makes it difficult for him or her to assert any rights. In fact, the absence of substantive child rights in Irish law is reminiscent of the perceived deficiencies of other liberal democratic regimes. The legal situation remains unchanged even after the implementation of the 1991 Act and the 1995 Regulations. In effect, the foster child will remain subordinate in the fostering process until a constitutional amendment is brought forward to delineate the welfare of children more clearly and in a manner that would be less prone to adverse Supreme Court interpretation than has been the case.

European Convention on Human Rights and foster care[47]

5–59 The case of *Olsson v Sweden*[48] illustrates the potential of the Convention for foster care. In this case, the applicant's daughter was placed in a foster home under the equivalent of a care order. Five years later the Swedish Court decided that there was no longer any need for the child to remain in public care. However, the health board equivalent issued a "prohibition" on the removal of the child from the foster home by the natural parents. The reasons for the prohibition were based on the expert opinion that the child was deeply rooted in the foster home and a transfer to her mother's home would jeopardise her mental health and development. Access to the child was limited to a visit in the foster home once every two months. Under Swedish legislation at the time, there was no administrative appeal against a decision by the health board equivalent to restrict access.

The Swedish Government argued that there was, in effect, a right to challenge through the ability to challenge the reasons for the prohibition on removal. The European Court disagreed:

> "In cases of the present kind, the question of access is quite distinct from the question whether or not to uphold the prohibition on removal; only if sufficient access is first permitted will there be real possibilities of having the prohibition on removal lifted. The recourse available in the administrative courts in the form of a challenge to the prohibition of removal

---

[47] See also Chap.12.
[48] (1989) 11 E.H.R.R. 250.

is thus not sufficient for the purpose of the mother's claim for access rights."[49]

The European Court of Human Rights held that the natural family relationship is not terminated by reason of the fact that a child is taken into care.

5–60 In *Olsson* the court noted that there was an obligation on national authorities to take appropriate practical measures to facilitate reunion with parents. The three Olsson children in that case were taken into foster care and placed with different foster parents a considerable distance from each other and from their parents. The geographical distance between the members of the family resulted in contact being cut off between them. The court found that this gave rise to a violation of Art.8 of the European Convention on Human Rights. More importantly, it attributed little weight to the administrative difficulties alluded to in the case, such as the lack of appropriate foster families. Unfortunately, the court did not provide instruction as to what is an acceptable distance by which children and parents can be separated.

Specialist foster care

5–61 All children needing substitute care, whatever their age, physical, mental or emotional disabilities, should have the opportunity to live in a foster family. Standard 22 of the National Standards for Foster Care should be noted in this regard:

> "Health boards provide for a special foster care service for children and young people with serious behavioural difficulties".[50]

One of the most serious problems facing social workers in the health boards is locating suitable placements for disturbed adolescents. Foster placements for disturbed adolescents appear highly fraught and susceptible to disruption. This is not surprising given the fact that troubled adolescents present the greatest challenge for those involved in the child care system. They often display serious behavioural problems and may have very serious needs. They present social workers with the task of locating appropriate, yet extremely scarce, placements. They also present a challenge to foster parents in terms of managing their needs and behaviour. Training for foster parents should be a prerequisite of this form of care before and during placement, and also for social workers involved in the supervision of these placements.

In order to assist foster parents in the challenge of caring for disturbed adolescents, supports must be constructed around this type of placement. This might take the form of:

(i) child care workers who can give foster parents a break or assistance in periods of acute stress;

---

[49] *ibid.*, paras 80 to 81.
[50] At p.46.

(ii) linking foster parents with residential centres which can give respite care and training/support;

(iii) extra allowances and monetary assistance; and

(iv) support from adolescent services, created by linking the efforts of current agencies and personnel in the field, *e.g.* health board and youth services.

5–62 It is vital in planning foster care for disturbed adolescents to be clear about the limits of foster care. International research and experience signposts the need for caution. Some young people have no desire to be placed in a family. Others have needs that cannot be satisfied in a family setting. It impacts negatively on the lives of young people and of foster families, and the overall perception of foster care, if these realities are ignored. The initial enthusiasm for foster care can blind many to its limitations. It has a critical and significant role to play in a network of services for adolescents at risk, but a policy that dictates that foster care can or should provide all placements in care for all adolescents is quite misguided. It is therefore necessary to develop a strong and cohesive residential care service alongside a thriving foster-care service.

Private foster care

5–63 Part 3 of the Children Act 2001,which came into force on September 23, 2004[51] (with the exception of s.23D), inserts a new tranche of provisions to deal with private foster care in the 1991 Act. Section 23P provides that a health board must be notified not less than 30 days before a private foster-care placement is effected. It imposes the obligation on all persons arranging or undertaking foster-care arrangements, as defined in s.23O, regardless of whether there is a reward. Section 23Q(1) details the information to be furnished to the health board at the time of notification. The information required by s.23Q(1) includes:

(a) the person's name and address;

(b) the name, sex, date and place of birth and address of the child concerned;

(c) the name and address of the parent or guardian of the child;

(d) if the child's residence is changed, the child's new address;

(e) if the private foster-care arrangement terminates, the reasons for its termination; and

(f) any other information that the health board may consider necessary in relation to any persons involved in the arrangement.

5–64 Section 23P(2) states that where a foster-care arrangement is undertaken in an emergency, those making and undertaking it have to notify the health board within 14 days. Under s.23R, it is the duty of any person arranging or

---

[51] Children Act 2001 (Commencement) (No.2) Order 2004 (S.I. No. 548 of 2004).

undertaking a private foster care arrangement to make all reasonable inquiries to ensure the safety, health and welfare of the child is secured. Section 23U allows the health board three types of interventions where it is of the opinion that a person has made or undertaken a private foster-care arrangement, without notifying the board, or the person is not taking all reasonable measures to secure the safety, health and welfare of the child concerned. The three remedies that the health board may obtain from the District Court under the 1991 Act are a supervision order, an order that the child be taken into care, or an order that the arrangement be terminated. Section 23V is worthy of particular attention and states:

> "23V.—(1) A person shall not arrange or undertake a private foster care arrangement for the purpose of adopting a child under the Adoption Acts, 1952 to 1998.
>
> (2) Any person undertaking a private foster care arrangement in respect of a child shall not apply under those Acts to adopt the child unless—
>
>> (a) the child is eligible for adoption under the Adoption Acts, 1952 to 1998, and
>> (b) the relevant health board has consented to the continuance of the arrangement pending the completion of an assessment of that person under those Acts.
>
> (3) If a health board believes that a person who is arranging or undertaking a private foster care arrangement is doing so in contravention of subs.(1) or (2), it may apply to the District Court for an order either—
>
>> (a) that the child be taken into its care under sections 13, 17 or 18, or
>> (b) that the arrangement be terminated and the child returned to his or her parents or guardian,
>
> and the Court may order accordingly."

5–65   The purpose of s.23V is clearly to prohibit people from using private foster care for the purpose of adopting a child under the Adoption Acts 1952 to 1998. It also provides that any person "undertaking a private foster care arrangement in respect of a child shall not apply under those Acts to adopt the child unless—(a) the child is eligible for adoption under the Adoption Acts 1952 to 1998, and (b) the relevant health board has consented to the continuance of the arrangement pending the completion of an assessment of that person under those Acts". Two main criteria must, therefore, be adhered to: that the child is available and eligible for adoption; and that the health board consents. This provision restricts the entitlement of foster parents to make application for adoption under the Adoption Act 1988, in that if a foster parent wishes to apply for adoption, he cannot do so without obtaining proper consent from the health board. This approach should be reviewed in the context of the approach adopted in the report of the working group on foster care, which addressed the issue in the following terms:

> "The working group is very concerned about the very high proportion of children in care for a period of two years or more and a number of

submissions identified the issue of allowing for adoption of children in long-term foster care....The working group is concerned that some children remain in long-term foster care when adoption may in fact be in their best interests. The working group recommends that health boards actively consider the option of adoption in the best interests of the individual child for all children in long-term foster care."[52]

Vicarious liability and allegations of abuse

5–66   Vicarious liability may be invoked by a plaintiff alleging abuse in foster care. It has not been pleaded to date in the Irish jurisdiction but, if accepted by the Irish courts, would enable the health board that selected the foster parents at the centre of the accusation, to be held accountable for the effects of the abuse. Vicarious liability has been imposed by the British Columbia Court of Appeal in cases of abuse involving foster parents. In *A.(C.) v Critchley*, McEachern J.B. held that the nature of the relationship between the foster parent and the Crown was sufficient to support vicarious liability, as the Crown delegated to the foster parents virtual 24-hour parental authority.[53] There was therefore a direct connection between the foster parents' authority and the wrongs committed, as they were all perpetuated when the boys were in the care of the foster parents. Further, in *KLB v British Columbia*,[54] the Crown was held vicariously liable for the abuse of the plaintiffs by the foster parents on the grounds that the social workers employed by the Crown were negligent in their inadequate supervision of the foster-care placement.

5–67   In *Koepf v County of York*,[55] the Supreme Court of Nebraska held that the placement of children in foster care and the supervision of their health and care thereafter must be accomplished by the welfare department (*i.e.* health board), and that the State could be held liable for breach of that duty.[56] The case of *Doe v New York City Department of Social Services*[57] addressed the continued mistreatment and sexual abuse of a child by her foster father. It was held that the State may be liable for omission where it demonstrates "deliberate indifference" to a known injury or risk, or it fails to carry out the duty to eliminate that risk. In summary, what is required is knowledge on the part of the state and the failure to act based on that knowledge.

5–68   The rationale for imposing liability on the state was explained in *B. v*

---

[52] *Foster Care—A Child Centred Partnership* (The Stationery Office, Dublin, May 2001), p.43.
[53] (1999) 1666 D.L.R. 4th 475 British Columbia Court of Appeal.
[54] (2001) B.C.C.A. 221, (2001) 197 D.L.R. 4th 431 British Columbia Court of Appeal.
[55] (1977) 198 Neb. 37, 251 NW 2d 866, 90 A.L.R. 3d 1208.
[56] See also *B.J.M. v State Department of Health and Rehabilitative Services* (1993, Fla. App. D3) 627 S02d 512, 18 F.L.W.D. 2147; *Newville v Dept. of Family Services* (1994, Mont.) 883 P2d 793 and *Jervis v McMullen* (8th Cir. 1999) 186 F.3d 1066.
[57] (1983, C.A. 2 N.Y.) 709 F2d 782, cert den. 464 U.S. 864, 78 L.Ed. 201 171,1045 Ct. 195.

Dane County,[58] the Supreme Court of Wisconsin noting that the state, in placing children in foster care, acts in the place of the children's parents. Accordingly, a special relationship exists between the child and the state. Unlike *Doe*, the Court concluded that the duty owed to foster children is based on a "professional judgement" standard, not the "deliberate indifference" standard. The "professional judgement" standard was elaborated upon in *Youngberg v Romeo*[59] as follows:

> "The decision, if made by a professional, is presumptively valid; liability may be imposed only when the decision by the professional is such a substantial departure from accepted professional judgement, practice, or standards as to demonstrate that the person responsible actually did not base the decision on such judgement."[60]

REFORM

5–69 Articles 41 and 42 of the Constitution, which recognise the natural rights and duties of marital parents in respect of their children, describe such rights and duties as "inalienable" and "imprescriptible". They essentially prevent marital parents from surrendering their parental rights to others. While Arts 41 and 42 represent a legal impediment to State-intrusion into the marital family, no such impediment arises in the context of the non-marital family. In this case, the best interests of a non-marital child will take precedence over all other matters.

The two principal treaties to which Ireland is a party and which are relevant to guardianship and adoption are the 1989 UN Convention on the Rights of the Child (CRC) and the 1950 European Convention on Human Rights (ECHR). While both instruments have been ratified by the State and are thus binding on it, the ECHR has also been given further effect in Irish law by virtue of the European Convention on Human Rights Act 2003. It should be noted, however, that the ECt.HR has alluded to the provisions of the CRC where ECHR-guidance is lacking.[61]

Article 2 of the CRC recognises the right of all children to enjoy all the rights of the ECHR without discrimination of any kind. The fact that a number of children in Ireland remain in long-term foster care indefinitely and cannot be adopted precisely because their parents are married is clearly at odds with this provision. Paragraph 3.40 of the report of the working group on foster care addresses the lack of permanency for children in long-term foster care.[62]

---

[58] Wis. 2d 140, 159-160, 555 D.W. 2d 630 (1996), Supreme Court of Wisconsin; 198 Wis. 2d 24, 61, 542 N.W. 2d 777 (Ct. App. 1995), *aff'd*, 205 Wis. 2d 140, 555 N.W.2d 630, 205, the Wisconsin Court of Appeals.

[59] 457 U.S. 307, at 232, 73 L. Ed. 2d 28, 102 S. Ct. 2452 (1982).

[60] See also *K.H. v Morgan* 914 F.2d 846, 845 (7th Cir. 1990).

[61] The almost universal ratification of the CRC has given it a moral authority beyond its legal force.

[62] *Foster Care—A Child Centred Partnership* (The Stationery Office, Dublin, 2001), p.43.

The report highlights the fact that a higher proportion of children remain in long-term foster care in Ireland "than is the case in either the UK or the USA".[63]

Article 20 of the CRC requires states to provide alternative care for a child deprived of his or her family environment and, in so doing, emphasises the desirability of continuity and stability in a child's upbringing.

New options

5–70 Currently, the options available to provide permanence for children in long-term care are very limited. Only adoption provides legal permanence, but it requires a complete severance of links with the child's natural family. Long-term fostering in Ireland is not legally secure and does not currently provide a child with stability and permanence. Working within the current constitutional framework and having regard to international law, a range of options promoting permanence for the child temporarily deprived of his or her family environment should be considered. One such option is guardianship.

1. Guardianship

5–71 Currently, adoption is the only option available to substitute parents to establish a stable legal relationship with a child. It is only possible for either a parent (including a non-marital father) or guardian to seek a custody order under the Guardianship of Infants Act 1964. The circumstances in which a non-parent may be appointed a guardian under the 1964 Act are very limited and are to be found in s.8 of that Act. Where a child has no guardian, any person or persons may, by virtue of s.8(1) of the 1964 Act, apply to the court to be appointed as guardians of the child. The court may similarly appoint a guardian when a deceased parent of a child has not appointed a testamentary guardian, or alternatively, where the latter appointee has refused to act as such.[64] In such a case, the person appointed by the court acts as joint guardian with the surviving parent. The court can, however, in appropriate circumstances, allow the new appointee to act to the exclusion of the surviving parent. The fact that adoption is the only mechanism by which to establish a stable legal relationship with a child raises the question as to whether it is the most appropriate option for a child.

Twenty years ago, the Report of the Review Committee on Adoption Services, chaired by the late Dr Joseph Robins (then Assistant Secretary at the Department of Health), recommended the availability of guardianship to substitute carers of children in long-term care:

> "We have examined guardianship only in the context of adoption applications because we understand that the new Children Bill may contain proposals for a legal procedure which would enable persons who are providing care for a child on a long-term basis to seek guardianship.

---

[63] R. Gilligan, "Children Adrift in Care—Can the Child Care Act rescue the 50% who are in care five years or more?" (1996) 14, 1 *Irish Social Worker* at 21.

[64] s.8(2).

We would welcome the introduction of such a procedure. While we consider that adoption is a beneficial arrangement for a child who lacks the security of a family, it is, as we have pointed out, quite inappropriate in some circumstances. A generally available means, short of adoption, by which persons who are bringing up a child, apart from his natural parents, could obtain a legal status in relation to the child, would have considerable merit."[65]

5–72   Legislation should be enacted to create greater stability for parents and children in long-term foster care by permitting some or all guardianship rights to be vested in the foster parents. That said, if such vesting were to involve a serverance of the natural marital parents' guardianship rights, such reform might be unconstitutional, involving as it does the transfer of "inalienable rights and duties". Any legislative proposal should therefore focus on suspending rather than supplanting rights.

Where a child has been in the care of a foster parent or parents for at least five continuous years, the foster parents should be permitted to apply to the Court for a "special guardianship" order. This would allow the foster parents to make relevant decisions regarding the child's upbringing. A similar provision could also apply to relatives, such as grandparents.[66]

For the length of time of the "special guardianship", the court would be in a position to suspend the guardianship rights of persons other than the foster parents. A special guardianship order would never be final and could always be altered by a court if changed circumstances so demanded.

A special guardianship order, intended to provide permanence for children for whom adoption is not appropriate, has been introduced in s.115 of the Adoption and Children Act 2002 in England and Wales. Section 115 of that Act introduces a number of new sections into the Children Act 1989. A foster parent with whom a child has lived for a period of at least one year preceding the application may apply for the order. The new s.14A of the Children Act 1989 sets out who may apply for a special guardianship order and the process for making an application. Applicants must give three months' written notice to the local authority of their intention to apply for the new order. The local authority must then investigate and prepare a report to the court about the suitability of the applicants. The matters covered by the report are set out in regulations. The court cannot make an order unless it has received a report covering the suitability of the prospective guardians.

This new guardianship order could bridge the gap between foster care and adoption. It would offer a positive new option for delivering permanence for children.

2. Long-term foster care

5–73   Rationale   Where a child has been in long-term foster care, he or she remains in a precarious legal position. Regardless of the length of foster care,

---

[65] *Report of the Review Committee on Adoption Services* (The Stationary Office, Dublin, 1984), p.84.
[66] *ibid.* at p.82.

the child may still be returned to its natural parents, thereby causing significant instability in his or her life.

Currently, long-term foster parents have no standing in adoption proceedings. In Northern Ireland, if the child has been in the care of foster parents for a period of five years or more, the prospective adopters acquire statutory rights, independent of their role as carers for the local authority.[67] As a consequence of this, the child can only be removed from the foster parents after their application for the granting of an adoption order has been heard. Further, the consent to apply for an adoption order is not contingent on the support of the local authority. Thus, we see a situation where the length of the placement confers rights on the foster parents and acknowledges the value of long-established ties.

5–74 Proposal A child who has been in foster care for at least five years may not be returned to his or her natural parents without the consent of a court.

3. Guardianship as an alternative to adoption

5–75 Adoption is not always appropriate for children. Frequently, older children, whose natural parents continue to have a positive involvement in their lives, may not wish to be separated legally from them. In such circumstances, guardianship would seem to be a legislative option that would provide permanence short of the legal separation involved in adoption. The Review Committee on Adoption Services recommended guardianship as such an option:

> "We recommend ... the ... Court should have power to grant applicants for an adoption order an alternative order appointing them to be the child's guardians and awarding them custody of the child where the Court is satisfied that in the circumstances, such an order would be more appropriate than an adoption order."[68]

---

[67] s.29 of the Adoption (NI) Order 1987 as amended:

"(1) While an application for an adoption order in respect of a child made by the person with whom the child has had his home for the five years preceding the application is pending, no person is entitled, against the will of the applicant, to remove the child from the applicant's [home] except with the leave of the court or under authority conferred by any enactment or on the arrest of the child.

(2) Where a person ("the prospective adopter") gives notice to the Board [or HSS trust] within whose area he has his home that he intends to apply for an adoption order in respect of a child who for the preceding five years has had his home with the prospective adopter, no person is entitled, against the will of the prospective adopter, to remove the child from the prospective adopter's [home], except with the leave of a court or under authority conferred by any enactment or on the arrest of the child, before–

　(a) the prospective adopter applies for the adoption order, or
　(b) the period of three months from the receipt of the notice by the Board [or HSS trust] expires,

whichever occurs first."

[68] *Report of the Review Committee on Adoption Services* (The Stationery Office, Dublin, 1984), at p.83.

Conclusion

5–76 The last decade has seen an upsurge of interest in foster care abroad. The adoption of the United Nations Convention on the Rights of the Child 1989 by the General Assembly of the United Nations on November 20, 1989 signposted a new era for foster care internationally. Indeed, it was the first time that foster care was recognised at this level.

Today, foster parents feel they have many responsibilities and few rights in relation to their children. Many perceive foster care as falling well short of a partnership with social workers, which may be due to the lack of power of foster parents in situations of conflict. Foster care as a child care practice must be upgraded, not only in monetary terms, but also in respect of decision making. The September 1991 edition of the English foster care journal acknowledges this:

> "Adequate maintenance for the child is one factor. Just as important for foster carers is the need for recognition of their knowledge and expertise, by acknowledging their status and involving them in decision making".[69]

5–77 Although fostering is merely a temporary arrangement, long-term foster parents should arguably be given rights akin to adoptive parents. After all, they are taking the place of natural parents in making day-to-day decisions. After a period of time, the foster parents' rights should progressively increase. They should have a right to seek custody, as well as a right to challenge the natural parents, not as a stranger would challenge them, but as substitute parents challenging the natural parents. In fact, in many cases the substitute parents are the only parents the child has ever known.[70] As regards short-term foster care, the inclusive fostering concept propounded by Robert Holman, which involves the social worker seeking to nurture a partnership between the natural parent and foster parent, is deserving of support. This would provide the child with "an accessible bridge" as well as providing a "window" for the child's "sense of identity".[71]

PLACEMENT WITH RELATIVES

5–78 As previously stated, for the purposes of foster-care arrangements, a child cannot be placed with a relative. It is possible, however, to place a child with a relative by virtue of s.36(1)(d) of the Child Care Act 1991. Section 41

---

[69] National Foster Care Association (September, 1991) *Foster Care* at 9.

[70] The necessity for this type of reform is evidenced by the findings of some research conducted by the writer in the residential care area. Out of a sample of 17 residential homes, 11 were in a position to furnish a figure on the number of children from broken-down fostering arrangements arriving into residential care. From that research, it emerges that just under 13% of children fall into that category. In one individual home, the figure was as high as 50%.

[71] N. Stone, "Out of sight but not out of mind. Increasing options for access" (1988) 18 *Family Law* 218.

of the 1991 Act specifically requires the Minister for Health and Children to formulate regulations for such placements. These were enacted in 1995 as the Child Care (Placement of Children with Relative) Regulations 1995.[72] With certain appropriate amendments, these regulations are virtually identical both in form and in substance to those enacted in respect of foster care, and much of what follows replicates what has been said before, with appropriate modifications.

It is suggested, however, that in practice, great caution must be exercised in opting for placement with relatives. The advantages, particularly where children are of a tender age, are clear. The children will be placed with persons familiar to them, perhaps a grandparent, aunt or uncle who has already cared for them on an occasional basis, and with whom they will be familiar. For the child, the sense of displacement from his or her family will surely be lessened. Practically speaking, access to parents will be easier. There may then be situations where it is entirely appropriate to place a child with members of his or her family. This is especially appropriate where a child has been placed in the care of the health board voluntarily. In subsequent discussions, it may transpire that the relatives are willing to take care of the child. Where all parties are on good terms this may be the ideal solution. In such cases, of course, arrangements may always be made privately between family members, although where a child is clearly at risk, the health board's obligations are not displaced by such arrangements.

5–79   Nevertheless, there must surely be some reticence about the option of placement with relatives, especially where a child has been removed from his or her parents against their will. In such a case, placing a child with relatives may be nothing short of a recipe for disaster. Where the family is on bad terms already, this may serve only to exacerbate the difficulties involved. Take, for instance, a child who is placed with paternal grandparents who passionately dislike the child's mother. Access arrangements in such cases would surely be fraught with ill-will. A health board, in such cases, would probably be well advised to steer clear of stirring up family politics and place the child with a neutral party.

The term "relative" for these purposes is not explicitly defined. It is implicit in Art.3(3) of the 1995 Regulations, however, that the primary meaning of the word is persons related by blood: grandparents, siblings, aunts, uncles and cousins among them. For the purposes of the 1995 Regulations, however, the term "relative" is deemed to include the spouse of a relative of the child and any person who has acted *in loco parentis* (presumably in respect of that child).

5–80   It should be noted, however, that these regulations only apply where a child has been placed in, or alternatively taken into, the care of a health board by virtue of the provisions of the 1991 Act. They do *not* apply where a child has been placed directly with a relative without the intervention of the health board. This may happen where, for instance, a parent feels that he or she is not

---

[72]   S.I. No. 261 of 1995.

ready to bring up a child and where, by independent agreement with a relative, the parent has placed the child directly with such relative, usually a grandparent, uncle or aunt of the child. These direct arrangements are, of course, without prejudice to the overall obligation placed on the health board by s.5 of the 1991 Act in respect of children needing care and protection. Indeed, even where such an independent arrangement has been made, the health board may still, in some cases, find it necessary to intervene with a view to promoting the child's best interests.

(a) Welfare of the child

5–81   The overriding obligation on the health board in these matters is, as ever, to promote the welfare of the child.[73] While the health board is indeed required to pay special attention to the rights and duties of parents (more, especially, where they enjoy the "inalienable and imprescriptible" constitutional rights, conferred by virtue of their marital status), the primary and paramount consideration is clear. The board must act first and foremost by reference to the welfare of the child. This may, in appropriate cases, require that the health board consult the child himself or herself in regard to his or her preferences. In particular, where a child is of sufficient age and maturity, it is stipulated that his or her wishes should be afforded due consideration.

In determining what the welfare of the child demands, it is suggested, following on the discussion above, that the health board should consider, in particular, the condition of intra-familial relationships. However suitable as parents the relatives may be, the prospect of family conflict will probably be detrimental to the child's overall welfare. Placing the child at the centre of such conflict should, if at all possible, be avoided.

(b) Pre-placement procedures

5–82   Part III of the 1995 Regulations lays down certain procedures that must be adopted and/or satisfied prior to the placement of a child with a relative. The key difference between these Regulations and those applicable to foster care is that in the case of relatives, there is no requirement to choose from a pre-determined panel of persons.

This does not, however, obviate the need for relatives intending to care for a child to satisfy the board as to their suitability as substitute carers. In particular, Art.5 requires that the relatives submit, prior to placement:

(i)   a written report from a registered medical practitioner regarding the state of the applicant or applicants' health;

(ii) the names and addresses of two referees, other than members of the applicant's family, who are willing and able, if asked, to comment upon an applicant's character and personality;

---

[73] See Pt II, Art.4 of the 1995 Regulations.

(iii) such authorisations as are necessary to allow the health board to make enquiries with An Garda Síochána, in particular to establish whether the applicant or any member of his family has a criminal record;

(iv) any other information that the health board may reasonably require.

5–83 Once such information has been furnished, the board will appoint an authorised person to assess the suitability of the applicant relative(s). In carrying out his or her inquiries, that person will also be required to visit the relatives' home in order to ensure that it is suitable for the upbringing of children. Following this, the authorised person will submit a written report to a committee of persons established under Art.5(3) of the 1995 Regulations. That committee should consist of persons with suitable experience and ability in the field of child care and in matters affecting the welfare of children.

Under Art.5(6) of the 1995 Regulations, the applicant is entitled to a written statement regarding the outcome of these proceedings. In addition, s.18 of the Freedom of Information Act 1997, as amended by s.13 of the Freedom of Information (Amendment) Act 2003, allows the applicant to apply in writing to the head of the relevant health board seeking reasons for the decision. In such a case (subject to certain exceptions) the latter will be obliged to furnish these reasons within four weeks of receiving the application.

Assessment of the child

5–84 Before a child is placed with relatives, the health board must carry out an assessment of the child's circumstances.[74] This will include a medical examination, unless the board is satisfied that the latter is not necessary. In deciding whether a medical examination is necessary, the board should have regard to such information and reports as are available to it.

An assessment of the child's circumstances must usually be undertaken before the child is placed with relatives. In emergency situations, however, it is possible to postpone the assessment until after placement occurs. In these cases, the board must carry out an assessment as soon after placement as is practically possible.

Contract between health board and relatives having care of a child

5–85 The making of arrangements for placement of a child with his or her relatives will be deemed to have effected a contract between the relatives and the health board.[75] A copy of this contract shall be given to the relatives in the form laid out in the First Schedule to the 1995 Regulations. This should be accompanied by a copy of the 1995 Regulations.

5–86 Before a child is placed with relatives, it is necessary that the latter be furnished with information regarding the child. Much of this, of course, may already be known to them, but this facility nonetheless allows the relatives to

---

[74] Art.7 of the 1995 Regulations.
[75] Art.9.

make appropriate arrangements for the care of the child. The information contemplated by Art.10 is as follows:

(i)   the name of the child, together with details of his or her sex, religion and date of birth;

(ii)   the reason why the child was admitted to the care of the health board;

(iii)   whether the child was put in care voluntarily or by virtue of a court order;

(iv)   whether the child has been placed in care before; if so, details of same should accompany the statement of information;

(v)   names and addresses of the child's parents;

(vi)   the names, ages and whereabouts of the child's sisters and/or brothers (if any);

(vii) details of arrangements for access by parents or relatives other than the child's carers;

(viii) details of medical or nutritional requirements;[76]

(ix)   details of arrangements for the child's attendance at school.

While some of this information[77] may seem superfluous, it is nonetheless required by the 1995 Regulations. It is possible also to provide additional information, as required, to relatives with whom a child has been placed.

Care and upbringing plan

5–87   Before a child is placed in the care of his or her relatives, it is incumbent on the health board to prepare a care and upbringing plan.[78] This care plan should lay down specific aims and objectives for the placement, with details of the support to be provided by the health board to the child, the relatives and the natural parents of the child. This plan should also outline all access arrangements and provisions for review of the plan. In preparing the plan, the health board is required to consult with the relatives and, if appropriate, with the child and his or her guardian(s). Once completed, it is also stated that a copy of the plan should be delivered to the relatives in question, and, in so far as it is practicable to do so, the child and guardians of the child.

The requirement for such a plan may be postponed where a child is in need of immediate placement. In this case, the plan may be drawn up as soon as practicable after the placement has been made.

---

[76] For example, whether or not the child is asthmatic or diabetic, or whether or not he or she is a vegetarian?

[77] For example, the names of the parents, which would, of course, be already known to the relatives.

[78] Art.11.

(c) Duties of the relatives

5–88 Once the placement has been made, the relatives in question shall have lawful custody of the child until such time as the placement is ended. In the meantime, Art.16 contains details of the duties, general and specific, that are placed upon the relatives. These are in terms that are virtually identical to the duties placed on foster parents. Article 16(1) places a general obligation on relatives with whom a child has been placed to take all reasonable steps to promote the child's health, development and welfare.

In addition, however, several specific stipulations are contained in the 1995 Regulations. Article 16(2) lists several duties of relatives acting as carers:

  (i) where the health board considers it necessary in the interests of the child, it may authorise periodic visits to the child. This may be, for instance, for the purpose of assessing the child in care with a view to determining what is in his or her best interests. Where a person is so authorised, the relatives must afford such persons reasonable access to the child, including the right to see the child and to visit the relatives' home for this purpose;

  (ii) the relatives are further required to co-operate with such person, in particular by giving him or her all relevant information that may reasonably be required;

  (iii) the relatives are under a duty to maintain the confidentiality of any information given to them by the health board relating to the child or his or her family;

  (iv) where a child suffers from injury or illness, the relatives are required to take steps to see that the child receives appropriate medical treatment;

  (v) relatives should inform the health board, as soon as possible, of any significant events in the child's life;

  (vi) the board should correspondingly be informed of any change in the circumstances of the relatives that might affect their capacity to provide for the child in their care;

  (vii) a care order or arrangement may be accompanied by directions or arrangements as to access by the child to his or her other relatives. The relatives with whom the child has been placed are required to co-operate in giving effect to these arrangements;

  (viii) where the relatives in question intend to change residence, the board should be given at least 28 days' notice of such intended change;

  (ix) where either the child or the relatives responsible for him or her are absent from the home, adequate ("good and proper") arrangements should be made by the latter for the care of the child;

  (x) where such absence (by the child or the relatives) is likely to exceed 72 hours (three days), the health board should be given prior notice of such absence.

Financial support

5–89   Article 14(1) provides for the payment of an allowance, similar to that made to foster parents, in respect of the child or children in the relatives' care. The amount of such allowance is to be set from time to time by the Minister for Health and Children.

Article 14(2) allows the health board to provide additional financial or other assistance where necessary for the care of any child. The decision as to such necessity is, however, to be determined by the health board and, as such, disputes may arise as to the amount of resources made available for the care of the child. In this regard, it is worth noting that any person may apply to the District Court to obtain its direction on any matter relating to the welfare of the child.[79]

(d) Monitoring of the child in placement

Register

5–90   Each health board is required (by Art.12 of the Regulations) to keep a register of all children placed in the care of their relatives by the board. This should include the following details in respect of each child:

(a) his or her name, sex and date of birth;

(b) the names and address(es) of the child's parents;

(c) the names and address(es) of the relatives with whom the child has been placed;

(d) the date of the placement;

(e) the date, if appropriate, on which the placement shall end.

Case record

5–91   In respect of every child placed in the care of relatives, the health board is additionally required[80] to maintain an up-to-date case record containing certain documents as follows:

(i)   all medical and social reports in respect of the child. This should include background information relating to the child's family, including, presumably, information on any inheritable disorders or ailments;

(ii)   a copy of all orders made by a court in relation to the child or, alternatively, a copy of the parental consent permitting the placement of a child in voluntary care;

(iii) the child's birth certificate;

(iv)   a copy of the contract between the relatives and the health board as contemplated by Art.9, and of the care plan required by Art.11;

---

[79] See s.47 of the 1991 Act.
[80] See Art.13.

(v) school reports and other documents regarding the educational development of the child;

(vi) written details of any access visits between the child and his or her parents;

(vii) notes or memoranda concerning any review of the child's case undertaken under the 1995 Regulations;

(viii) a note of all significant events that have affected the child. It should be noted that, under Art.16(2)(e), the relatives with whom the child has been placed, are required to notify the board of all such events.

Supervision and visitation

5–92 An authorised member of the health board may, by virtue of Art.17(1), visit a child placed in the care of his or her relatives as often as is considered necessary by the board. Such visitation as occurs should be in line with the details of the care plan drawn up under Art.11 of the 1995 Regulations. Whatever specific arrangements are made, however, Art.17 requires that the child be visited at least once every three months during the first two years of the placement. The first such visit must take place within one month of the date of the initial placement. After the initial two-year period has ended, the child should be visited at least once every six months.

A note of every such visit should be entered in the case record of the child, as contemplated by Art.17(5) of the 1995 Regulations. Should such visit reveal there has been any deviation from the requirements set out in the 1995 Regulations or care plan, the health board is obliged to take appropriate remedial action. Particulars of any action taken by the board in the wake of the visit should also be noted in the case record.

Case review

5–93 In the first two years after placement, the care plan drawn up in respect of a child should be reviewed by an authorised person at least every six months, and thereafter at intervals of a year or less.[81] The health board should make arrangements for such periodic review. Where a health board commences such a review, Art.18(4) requires that it give notice of this fact to the relatives with whom the child has been placed and, in so far as it is considered practically possible, the child and guardian(s) of the child. Such persons, as are so informed, are entitled to be heard in person or otherwise consulted in the course of the review.

Each review should address the following matters:

(i) is every reasonable effort being made to promote the welfare of the child?

(ii) is such care as is being presently provided suited to the present needs of the child?

---

[81] Art.18.

(iii) have the circumstances of the child's parents changed to such an extent as to require reconsideration of the placement?

(iv) considering such changes, would the return of the child to his or her parents be conducive to the child's best interests?

(v) is the child due to leave the care of the health board? If so, the health board should consider the child's need for aftercare as contemplated by s.45 of the 1991 Act.

5–94   When conducting the review, the board is obliged to have due regard to reports of authorised visits by health board officials, the child's most recent school report, and any other information deemed relevant. In a similar vein, the board is required to consider any information furnished by the child, by the relatives caring for him or her, or by the natural parents, in the course of the review, in addition to the expressed wishes of such persons. That said, it is, as ever, the welfare of the child that predominates.

A note of the review should be taken and kept, together with details of any action taken consequent upon the review, as part of the child's case record. Furthermore, any decisions taken as a result of the review must be transmitted to the relatives in question and, where applicable, to the child and his or her guardians. The board may also inform any other person that it considers ought to be informed.

Provision is also made for the initiation of a special review. Article 19 allows any person with a bona fide interest in the welfare of a child in care, to deliver a written statement to the health board, requesting the making of such a review. The board must comply with such a request unless it considers such review unnecessary. Where the request is successful, a review shall take place in compliance with the procedures laid down in Art.18, as if it were a review conducted under that article. Where the request is rejected, the board must notify the maker of the request in writing. It is open to the latter, as in all cases, to seek the direction of the court and thus override this rejection.[82]

5–95   Sometimes a child will be the subject of several placements in succession. The short duration of such placements may not allow for the making of periodic reviews as envisaged by the provisions noted above. It may thus be the case that the normal schedule for periodic reviews will not be activated. In such a case, the board should carry out regular reviews of the child's case, notwithstanding the brevity of its consecutive placements.[83]

(a) The termination of a placement

5–96   The placement of a child with his or her relatives will end where the child reaches the age of 18 or, alternatively, marries. At such point, after all, the person involved is no longer a "child" as defined by the Act and thus not

---

[82] s.47 of the 1991 Act.
[83] Art.20.

subject to the provisions of the Act. That said, there is nothing in law or otherwise preventing such person and the relatives from maintaining a continuing family relationship. Indeed, considering the family nexus already in place, this is to be expected.

Where a person remains a "child" as defined by the Act, he or she may be removed from the placement by one of several methods. These are contained in Pt V of the Regulations. The effect of such removal will bring to an end the lawful custody of the child by its relatives.

Removal at the request of the relatives

5–97 Relatives with whom a child has been placed may request that a child in their care be removed.[84] In such a case, the board must, as soon as possible, take steps to provide alternative arrangements for the child's care, with due regard, as always, to the best interests of the child. The relatives in question will be required, in such circumstances, to sign a written declaration verifying that the child is being removed at their request. This declaration should be retained by the health board as part of the child's case record.

Termination of placement by the health board

5–98 Alternatively, it is possible for the health board itself to terminate the placement of the child. This may be done, for instance, where the health board proposes to reunite the child with his or her parents. It is also possible to effect such termination where the board considers that the child's continued placement with the particular relatives is no longer conducive to the child's welfare, or indeed, is no longer the most appropriate way of achieving the child's welfare. This may occur, for instance, where the health board has noted that the placement of the child with its relatives has been the cause of significant intra-familial conflict and where such conflict has affected the emotional welfare of the child.

Obviously, the custodial relatives may object to such removal. If this happens, they will be given every opportunity to make representations to the health board. Should the board, notwithstanding these representations, decide to proceed with removal, it is obliged to give a written statement of such decision to the relatives with whom the child has been placed, containing in particular the reasons for such a decision. This statement should be accompanied by a request that the child be returned to the custody of the health board at such place and time as is stipulated by the board. Should the relatives in question refuse to comply, the health board may apply for a direction of the District Court, under s.43(2) of the 1991 Act, to the effect that the child be delivered up to the board. Non-compliance with such an order is, it should be noted, an offence under s.43(3) of the 1991 Act punishable by up to six months in prison or a fine not exceeding IR£500 (€630), or both. Such refusal may also amount to a contempt of court.

Where a child is removed from the custody of relatives under Pt V, the

---

[84] Art.21.

latter should, in appropriate circumstances, be provided with counselling facilities by the health board.[85]

Other miscellaneous provisions

5–99   Part VI makes certain additional provisions of a miscellaneous nature. The board may, for instance, make arrangements with any competent and qualified voluntary body or person with a view to providing assistance in the performance of the health board's functions.[86] Part VI also allows the Minister for Health and Children to appoint a person in order to monitor the practices and procedures relating to services provided to children placed with relatives by a health board.[87] To this end, the person so appointed may, *inter alia,* consult such records as may exist and interview any employee of the health board involved in the provision of such care services.

[85] Art.23.
[86] Art.24.
[87] Art.25.

CHAPTER 6

RESIDENTIAL CARE

PART I

1. Introduction

6–01　When the Reformatory and Industrial Schools Systems Report ("the Kennedy Report")[1] was published in 1970, an awareness and concern was created for the first time as to what was hidden behind the euphemistic words "residential child care". A chilling feature of the accounts of children who were in care in Ireland prior to the report emerged. So too did the unquestioned, and apparently unquestionable, moral authority of the care providers and the reckless disregard for the child-welfare concept. The Kennedy Report exposed the extent to which large residential care institutions, however well-intentioned they were, were largely unfit to meet the complex needs of children in care. Residential care units in Ireland face immense challenges in dealing with new demands in a rapidly changing society. Traditional forms of residential care no longer exist, and specialised residential care units have emerged. It is important now that residential care be valued as a distinct form of care, rather than as a form of care of last resort.

2. History of residential care

6–02　Residential care in Ireland was governed by what can only be described as a miscellany of legislation. Taking the Poor Law Act 1838 as a starting point offers an insight into how far legislative intervention has travelled in improving the welfare of the child in residential care. State control of child care in general in Ireland commenced after 1838, when:

> "... the workhouses became the main centres for charity children of all categories. While these new institutions were harsh and punitive in concept, the Irish Poor Law Commissioners and their successors, the Local Government Board for Ireland, were humane in outlook and genuinely concerned about the welfare of the work house child."[2]

---

[1]　Department of Health, *Report on the Reformatory and Industrial Schools System* (The Stationary Office, Dublin, 1970). This report was prepared by a committee on reformatory and industrial schools established by the Government in 1967. Its terms of reference were "to survey the Reformatory and Industrial Schools Systems and to make a report and recommendations to the Minister for Education", which terms were later extended to include all children in care. The Chairman of the committee was District Justice Eileen Kennedy of the Dublin Metropolitan Children's Court, and the report came to be known as "the Kennedy Report".

An 1858 legislative provision titled "An Act to Promote and Regulate Reformatory Schools for Juvenile Offenders in Ireland" signposted the evolution of the reformatory schools system, which was perceived as a means of addressing the problem created by an increasing number of destitute children. However, this provision was a reactive one and was stimulated by a desire to remove the problem of street children from sight, rather than out of a concern to provide for the welfare of such children.

6–03   It was not until 1868 that an Act providing for the extension of industrial schools to Ireland was placed on the statute books.[3] It was identical to the equivalent Acts in England and was designed to provide for the destitute child.[4] In practice, children were admitted to industrial schools for a number of reasons; some because of poverty; some because they were abandoned; while others were committed because of offences.

Industrial schools were considered delinquent-only institutions. This perception only began to change with the transfer of responsibility for industrial schools in 1928 from the Department of Justice to the Department of Education.

During this period there also developed a body of law showing a concern for the welfare of children. One of the most significant enactments was the Prevention of Cruelty and Protection of Children Act 1889, which provided for the punishment of persons ill-treating or neglecting children.

6–04   The next Act worthy of comment was enacted in August 1898 and was called "An Act to make further provision with respect to the Relief of Pauper Children in Ireland, and for other purposes connected therewith". It is significant in that it signposted a movement away from the institutional-care system, in that it made provision for the placing of destitute or orphaned children into the care of a nurse or boarding house.

The most significant Act in this area was enacted in 1908 and is called "An Act to Consolidate and Amend the Law relating to the Protection of Children and Young Persons, Reformatory and Industrial Schools, and Juvenile Offenders, and otherwise to Amend the Law with respect to Children and Young Persons". The Children Act 1908, also known as "The Children's Charter", co-ordinated and superseded previous legislation and will only be fully repealed when the Children Act 2001 is fully operational. The National Children's Office, which has the lead role in relation to the implementation of the Children Act 2001, has indicated that the Act may not be fully operational

---

[2]   Robins, *The Lost Children: A Study of Charity Children in Ireland 1700–1900* (I.P.A., Dublin, 1980) p.9.

[3]   The Act was called an "Act to Extend the Industrial Schools Act in Ireland". For an informative account on the operation of the industrial school system in Ireland, see *Report of Commission of Enquiry into the Reformatory and Industrial School System 1934–1936* (The Stationery Office, Dublin, 1936) p.6.

[4]   An interesting account on the introduction and intent behind the industrial school system is to be found in O'Sullivan, "Social Definitions in Child Care in the Irish Republic: Models of the Child and Child Care Intervention" (1979) 10, 3 *Economic and Social Review* 211.

until early 2008. The provisions of the Children's Charter of 1908 (hereinafter "the 1908 Act") dealt with infant life, protection, prevention of cruelty to children and young persons, juvenile smoking, reformatory and industrial schools, and juvenile justice.

6–05 The function of the child in society has changed significantly since 1908, and cognisance of this must be taken in our efforts to provide for this vulnerable section of society. Any examination of the modern residential care system in this country would be incomplete without a cursory examination of this statute. Part 1 of the Act covered the area of infant-life protection. It outlines the provisions governing the retaining of children for reward and has been amended eight times, particularly by the Health Act 1970[5] and the Children Act 2001.[6] The most relevant provisions, and probably the most controversial in Pts 2 and 3 of the 1908 Act, are to be found in ss.21, 38, 58 and 59. These provisions deal with the appointment of a "fit person" entrusted with the care of children or young people, and include: "… any society or body corporate established for the reception or protection of poor children or the prevention of cruelty to children". The Kennedy Report noted that no "fit persons" orders had been made by the Irish courts for some time and this may have stimulated the revival of these provisions.[7] That said, a Supreme Court decision of November 2, 1989 stated that a health board was not a "fit person".[8] This led to an immediate legislative response in the form of the Children Act 1989.

6–06 The law covering reformatory and industrial schools, which includes ss.44 to 93, is contained in Pt IV of the 1908 Act. The Committee on Young Offenders proposed in 1927 that the maximum age for the juvenile courts should be raised to 17, the critical factor being that children should be kept out of the courts system for as long as possible. Despite this proposal, the upper limit for the juvenile courts was only raised to 18 when Pt 7 of the Children Act 2001 came into force on May 1, 2002,[9] leaving us some 69 years behind the neighbouring jurisdiction that implemented the Committee on Young Offenders recommendation[10] in s.107 of their Children and Young Persons Act 1933. This issue is considered further in Chapter 11.

6–07 Section 44 of the 1908 Act refers to an industrial school as "a school for the industrial training of children, in which children are lodged, clothed and fed, as well as taught".[11] Considering the other provisions in Pt 4 of that Act, ss.45 to 51 provide for the certification and inspection of reformatory and

---

[5] See Stewart, "Young Offenders: Children and the Criminal Law" (1976) I.L.T. 229.

[6] See Chap.11.

[7] *Supra*, n.1.

[8] *State (D. & D.) v G. (No.1)* [1990] I.LR.M. 10.

[9] See Children Act 2001 (Commencement) Order 2002, S.I. No. 151 of 2002.

[10] Report of the Departmental Committee on the Treatment of Young Offenders (HMSO, Dublin, 1927). The report was published by the Committee on the Treatment of Young Offenders, which was chaired by Sir Thomas F. Moloney.

[11] Children Act 1908, s.44 (8 Edw. 7, c.67).

industrial schools, while ss.52 to 56 set out the powers and duties of the managers of such institutions. Section 58 of the 1908 Act details the categories of children liable to be committed to these schools: children found begging; wandering; destitute; under the care or in the company of reputed criminals or drunkards; residing in a house used by a prostitute; offenders under 12; or first offenders.[12] It also provided that the period of detention in the industrial schools was to be left to the courts to determine but was not, under any circumstances, to extend beyond the time when the child reached 16 years of age.[13] The remaining provisions in Pt 4 provide for the maintenance of children in certified schools.[14]

6–08 Sections 94 to 113 of the 1908 Act, deal with juvenile justice and is beyond the scope of this chapter. Following the 1908 Act little change occurred until the 1980s, prompting the 1970s Kennedy Report[15] to mention that child care law did not conform with modern thinking in the field.

The Children Act 1989,[16] previously alluded to, was enacted on November 9, 1989. This, as previously stated, was a reactive piece of legislation that was passed to bridge a gap in the 1908 Act, in relation to the expression "fit persons". This Act was rushed through both houses of the Oireachtas as a result of the Supreme Court's decision in the case of *State (D. & D.) v. G. (No.1)*,[17] which declared that health boards were not "fit persons". Section 1 of the 1989 Act was enacted to address the problem and states that the health boards are, and always have been, "fit persons".

PART II

RESIDENTIAL CENTRES AND MODERN RESIDENTIAL CARE

6–09 Section 38(1) of the Child Care Act 1991 ("the 1991 Act") requires a health board to make arrangements to ensure the existence of an adequate number of residential places for children in its care. To this end, a health board may make arrangements with the registered proprietors of children's residential centres or with other suitable persons. It may also, however, with the permission of the Minister for Health and Children, establish and maintain a residential centre or other premises for the provision of residential care for children.[18]

---

[12] These categories were amended and extended by s.10 of the Children Act 1941.

[13] It should noted, however, that s.12 of the Children Act 1941 permitted the extension by the Minister for Education of the period of detention of the child in an industrial school until such child reached the age of 17 years.

[14] Children Act 1908, s.75. This Section was later amended by s.22 of the Children Act 1941 and by s.9 of the Children Amendment Act 1957.

[15] *Supra*, n.1.

[16] This Act is titled "An Act to Amend and Extend the Children Act 1908 to 1957" (No. 18 of 1989).

[17] *Supra*, n.8.

[18] s.38(2) of the 1991 Act.

6–10 The Minister for Health and Children has, under powers conferred by s.38(3), made regulations relating to the operation of such homes operated by, or on behalf of, the health board. These are the Child Care (Placement of Children in Residential Care) Regulations 1995 ("the 1995 Residential Care Regulations").[19] The National Standards for Residential Care for Young People[20] should also be noted, and provide considerable guidance in interpreting the provisions relating to residential care in the 1991 Act. They should be considered alongside the 1995 Residential Care Regulations and the Child Care (Standards in Children's Residential Centres) Regulations 1996.[21]

6–11 For the purposes of the 1995 Residential Care Regulations, the term "residential centre" refers to "any home or other institution, whether operated by a health board, a voluntary body or other person which provides residential care for children in the care of a health board."[22] Further clarity comes in the statement that the definition specifically excludes:

(i) an institution managed by, or on behalf of, a minister of the Government, (this would presumably include a prison or secure facility for young offenders);

(ii) an institution in which a majority of the children are being treated for acute illnesses;

(iii) an institution for the care and maintenance of physically or mentally handicapped children;

(iv) a mental institution within the meaning of the Mental Treatment Acts 1945 to 1966; and

(v) an institution which is a "certified school" within the meaning of Pt IV of the 1908 Act,[23] functions in relation to which stand vested in the Minister for Education.

The provisions applicable to children placed in residential care centres are largely identical to those applicable in the case of children in foster care, with appropriate modifications.

(a) Promoting the welfare of the child

6–12 Should there be any doubt about the matter, Pt II of the Residential Care Regulations underlines the central aim of the residential care arrangements as are made under these regulations. This is that the welfare of the child be promoted as the first and paramount consideration in making any decision

---

[19] S.I. No. 259 of 1995.
[20] The National Standards for Residential Care for Young People (The Stationery Office, Dublin, 2004).
[21] S.I. No. 397 of 1996.
[22] Part I of the 1995 Residential Care Regulations.
[23] This Act will be repealed when all the provisions of the Children Act 2001 are fully in force. See Chap.11.

relating to a child in the care of the health board. The board must, as far as practicable, take account of the wishes of the child, and also pay due consideration to the rights and duties of the child's parents, but always subject to the primary duty to give precedence to what is in the child's best interests.

(b) Pre-placement requirements

6–13 *Care Plan* As in the case of a child in foster care, the placement of a child in residential care must, except in emergency situations, be preceded by the creation of a care plan in respect of that child. This care plan should list specific aims and objectives for the placement, with details of the support to be provided by the health board to the child, the residential centre and to any other named person. This plan should also outline all access arrangements and provisions for review of the plan. In preparing the plan, the health board is required to consult with the manager of the residential centre in which it is proposed that he or she will be placed and, if appropriate, with the child and his or her guardian(s). Once completed, it is also stated that a copy of the plan should be delivered to the manager of the residential centre and, in so far as it is practicable to do so, to the child and guardians of the child.

In emergency situations, a care plan need not precede placement, but should be drawn up as soon as possible thereafter.

6–14 Standard 5 of the National Standards for Residential Care for Young People makes reference to the care plan and provides:

"There should be a writen care plan for every young person in care."[24]

6–15 *Medical examination* On or before placement, the board is required to arrange for a medical examination of a child in its care to be carried out by a qualified medical practitioner. This requirement can be avoided only where the board is satisfied, on the basis of the information available to it, that no such examination is necessary.

(c) Standards and duties stipulated in the 1995 Residential Care Regulations

6–16 In addition to the general duties placed on the health board in respect of children in its care, it must be satisfied that the following standards are met in each residential centre over which it has jurisdiction.[25]

6–17 *1. Operational policies* Appropriate and suitable care practices and operational policies must be adopted, taking into account the number of children accommodated at the centre and the nature of their needs.[26]

---

[24] At p.11.
[25] Standard 10 of the National Standards for Residential Care for Young People should also be noted: "Residential centres should be in suitable and well-maintained buldings" (at p.26).
[26] Art.5 of the 1995 Residential Care Regulations.

6–18 *2. Staffing* The health board should be satisfied that there is an adequate number of suitably qualified and experienced staff available to work at each residential centre within its functional area.[27] A similar requirement exists in respect of a residential centre operated outside its jurisdiction, but in which the board has placed, or wishes to place, a child in care.

6–19 *3. Accommodation* Appropriate and suitable accommodation is to be provided.[28] Whether such accommodation is adequate will again depend on the number of children accommodated at the centre and their respective needs. The health board is obliged, in particular, to ensure that there is:

(a) adequate and suitable furniture, bedding and other furnishings;

(b) a sufficient number of lavatories, wash basins, baths and showers, with sufficient water, hot and cold. As far as practicable such arrangements should respect the need for privacy;

(c) adequate facilities for laundry (washing, drying and ironing);

(d) adequate light, heat and ventilation;

(e) sufficiently clean premises, appropriately decorated and maintained in good structural condition;

(f) adequate recreation facilities.

6–20 *4. Access arrangements* The health board should satisfy itself that adequate arrangements have been made to enable the child to have appropriate access to its parents, relatives, friends and to other persons with a genuine interest in the child.[29]

6–21 *5. Health care* Children at the centre should have access to the services of a general practitioner. It should be possible, furthermore, to refer a child, if required, for medical, psychological, dental, ophthalmic or other specialist treatment or assessment.

6–22 *6. Religion* Appropriate arrangements should be in place to facilitate the child in practising his or her religion. This may include provision for transport to weekend services and making appropriate arrangements for other religious events.[30]

6–23 *7. Food and cooking facilities* Adequate amounts of food should be supplied, having regard to the nutritional needs of the children at the centre. Such food should be properly prepared, wholesome and nutritious. There should be a sufficient element of variety and choice. The staff should in particular be mindful of dietary requirements and prescriptions.[31] Each centre should have

---

[27] Art.6.

[28] Art.7.

[29] Art.8.

[30] For example, First Holy Communion, Confirmation, and Bar/Bat Mitzvah.

[31] For example, vegetarianism, allergies, lactose-intolerance and such other conditions.

suitable and sufficient catering equipment, crockery and silverware/cutlery, proper refrigeration and other storage facilities. Such facilities and items should be maintained to a high standard of hygiene, in particular in relation to the storage and preparation of food and the disposal of domestic refuse.

6–24   *8. Fire precautions* Without prejudice to the detailed requirements of the Fire Services Act 1981, the Residential Care Regulations lay down specific stipulations as to fire safety.[32] A chartered engineer or suitably qualified architect with experience in fire safety design and management must give written confirmation that the premises used or to be used as a residential centre meets all relevant fire safety and building-control requirements. The authorised person should in particular check the following matters:

Fire safety check-list

(a) Have adequate steps been taken to prevent, as best one can, a fire occurring at the centre?

(b) In case of fire, are there adequate means of escape from the centre, including alternative routes of evacuation?

(c) Have adequate arrangements been made for the detection of a fire?[33]

(d) Are there adequate facilities for containing and extinguishing fires?[34]

(e) Have members of staff been equipped to use, in appropriate cases, these facilities?

(f) Is fire-fighting equipment adequately maintained?

(g) Have steps been taken to ensure that the materials contained in bedding and other furnishings are sufficiently fire-retardant and contain the lowest possible levels of toxicity?

6–25   Where structural alterations or extensions are made to the centre, further confirmation of the above is required in respect of such alterations or extensions.

The health board should, finally, satisfy itself that children and staff alike are made sufficiently aware of evacuation procedures in the case of a fire or other emergency, by means of fire drills and practices as necessary.

6–26   *9. Other safety precautions* Adequate arrangements should be made to ensure that the facilities are otherwise sufficiently safe, having regard to the age and maturity of the children housed there.[35] Every reasonable effort should be made to obviate the risk of injury upon the premises. Particular attention should be directed to the risk of injury from stairways, appliances, windows

---

[32] Art.12.

[33] For example, smoke alarms.

[34] For example, fire doors and fire extinguishers.

[35] Art.13.

and doors, glazing, the storage of medicines, and to cleaning and other materials. The health board should further be satisfied that appropriate arrangements have been made for the reporting and recording of accidents and injuries affecting resident children. In addition, each residential centre should be adequately insured in respect of any accident or injury that may affect children.

6–27 *10. Recording and reporting duties* Each residential centre must satisfy the health board that it is maintaining adequate records in respect of each child placed with it. These records should be available for examination by any authorised person appointed by the health board. The residential centre is specifically required to notify the health board of the occurrence of any significant event that might affect a child in its care. Adequate procedures should be in place to facilitate the prompt reporting of such matters.

6–28 *11. Overall supervision of standards* The health board is made primarily responsible for ensuring, in respect of all residential centres in its functional area, that these Regulations are being observed and upheld. With this in mind, the health board is empowered to permit authorised persons to enter the premises of a residential centre with a view to its inspection. Such inspection may be carried out at any reasonable time. If, having carried out an inspection, the board believes that one or more of the standards stipulated in the 1995 Residential Care Regulations are not being maintained in any centre, it is required to request that the manager of that centre take such steps as are necessary to rectify this. The board may, alternatively, remove the children from the facility in accordance with s.43 of the 1991 Act.

(d) Monitoring of placements

6–29 *Register* Each health board is required to keep a register of all children placed in residential care by the board. This should include the following details in respect of each child:

(a) his or her name, sex and date of birth;

(b) the names and address(es) of the child's parents;

(c) the name and address of the residential centre in which he or she has been placed;

(d) the date of such placement;

(e) the date on which the placement shall end.

Should any of these details change, the register should be altered accordingly.

6–30 *Case record* In respect of every child in residential care, the health board is additionally required to maintain an up-to-date case record containing certain documents as follows:

(i) all medical and social reports in respect of the child. This should include, where available, background information relating to the child's family, including, presumably, details of any inheritable disorders or ailments;

(ii)   a copy of all orders made by a court in relation to the child or, alternatively, a copy of the parental consent permitting the placement of a child in voluntary care;

(iii)   the child's birth certificate;

(iv)   a copy of the of the care plan required by Art.23 of the 1995 Residential Care Regulations;

(v)   school reports and other documents regarding the educational development of the child;

(vi)   written details of any access visits between the child and any other person;

(vii)   notes or memoranda concerning every review of the child's case undertaken under the regulations;

(viii) a note of all significant events that have affected the child. It should be noted that under the 1995 Residential Care Regulations, the residential centre is required to notify the board of all these events.

6–31   *Supervision and visitation* An authorised member of the health board is required, by virtue of Art.24, to visit a child in residential care as often as is considered necessary by the board. Such visitation as occurs should be in line with the details of the care plan drawn up under Art.23 of the Residential Care Regulations. Whatever specific arrangements are made, however, Art.24 requires that the child be visited at least once every three months during the first two years of the placement. The first such visit must take place within one month of the date of the initial placement. After an initial two-year period has ended, the child should be visited at least once every six months.

A note of every visit should be entered in the case record of the child.[36] Should such a visit reveal that there has been any deviation from the requirements set out in the Residential Care Regulations, the health board is obliged to take appropriate remedial action. Particulars of any action taken by the board in the wake of the visit should also be noted in the case record.

6–32   *Review of placements* Article 25 of the 1995 Residential Care Regulations requires that regular reviews should be undertaken in respect of each child placed in residential care by the relevant health board. In addition, in the first two years after placement, the care plan drawn up in respect of a child should be reviewed by an authorised person at least every six months, and thereafter, at intervals of a year or less. The health board should make arrangements for such periodic reviews. Where a health board commences a review, Art.25(4) of the Residential Care Regulations requires that it give notice of this fact to the manager of the residential centre in whose care the child has been placed and, in so far as it is considered practically possible, the child and guardian(s) of the child. Such persons as are so informed are entitled to be heard in person, or otherwise consulted in the course of the review.

---

[36] Art.24(5).

6–33 Each review should address the following matters:

(i) is every reasonable effort being made to promote the welfare of the child?

(ii) is such care as is being presently provided suited to the present needs of the child?

(iii) have the circumstances of the child's parents changed to such an extent as to require reconsideration of the placement?

(iv) considering such changes, would the return of the child to his or her parents be conducive to the child's best interests?

(v) is the child due to leave the care of the health board? If so, the health board should consider the child's need for aftercare, as contemplated by s.45 of the 1991 Act.

6–34 When conducting the review, the board is obliged to have due regard to the following:

(i) all views expressed by the child, his or her parents, the manager of the residential centre in which the child is being cared for, and of any other person consulted in the course of the review;

(ii) any information supplied by the parties listed above;

(iii) any report from the residential centre in which the child is being cared for;

(iv) a report of any visits to the child by a person authorised in accordance with Art.24(5) of the Regulations;

(v) where the child attends school, the most recent available school report in respect of the child;

(vi) any other information that is considered relevant to the review.

It is, as ever, the welfare of the child that should be considered the predominant factor in such a review.

A note of the review shall be taken and kept, together with details of any action taken consequent upon the review, as part of the child's case record. Furthermore, any decisions taken as a result of the review shall be transmitted to the manager of the residential centre in whose care the child has been placed and, where practicable, to the child and his or her guardians. The board may also inform any other person who it considers ought to be informed.

6–35 *Special review* Provision is also made for the initiation of a special review. Any person with a bona fide interest in the welfare of a child in care may deliver a written statement to the health board requesting the making of such a review. The board must comply with this request unless it considers such a review unnecessary. Where the request is successful, a review shall take place in compliance with the procedures laid down above as if it were a review conducted under the normal rules. Where the request is rejected, the board must notify the maker of the request in writing. It is open to the latter, as in all cases, to seek the direction of the court and thus override this rejection.

6–36 *Frequent changes in the child's care arrangements* An opportunity to review the case of a child should not be lost merely because a child is frequently moved between different care facilities. Where a child is placed in residential care 12 months or less after a previous placement in residential care (*i.e.* more than once in one period of 12 months), the board is obliged to carry out a review of the child's case.

(e) Removal of a child from residential care

6–37 In addition to the provisions noted above, the 1995 Residential Care Regulations make provision for the removal of a child from residential care. This may be done, for instance, where the health board considers that it is appropriate for a child to be reunited with his or her parents. It is also possible, however, for the board to decide that the child's continued placement is no longer conducive to his or her best interests. In any such case, the board should communicate its intention to remove the child from the centre to the manager of the centre in which the child resides for the time being. This should be accompanied by the reasons for this decision.

A manager who disagrees with this decision, once made, is to be given an adequate opportunity to address the board, making such representations as he or she sees fit. Where, in spite of such representations, the board refuses to alter its position, notice of the decision shall be delivered to the manager together with the reasons for such decision. The manager will, thereby, be asked to deliver up the child on a specific date. In the unlikely event that the manager should fail or refuse to comply with this direction, the health board may seek appropriate directions from the District Court, including, of course, an order under s.43 or s.46 of the 1991 Act.

(f) Other miscellaneous matters

6–38 Part V of the 1995 Residential Care Regulations deals with other miscellaneous matters pertaining to children in residential care. It requires, in particular, that the health board should provide all necessary support services to each residential centre in which it has placed children in care. It may, furthermore, enter into arrangements with competent and appropriately qualified voluntary bodies or other experienced persons, with a view to obtaining assistance in the performance of its functions.

6–39 *Inspections* Article 31 of the 1995 Residential Care Regulations allows the practices and procedures of the health board in relation to residential care to be subjected to periodic inspection. For this purpose, a person may be authorised by the health board to examine the board's practices and procedures relating to the provision of residential care. In doing so, the authorised person is entitled to enter any residential centre under the control of the health board for the purpose of inspecting the state of such centre and the management thereof and to oversee the treatment of children placed therein. In the course of his or her inquiries, the authorised person may examine the records of the centre and interview such members of staff as are involved in the residential care functions of the centre.

PART III

CHILDREN'S RESIDENTIAL CENTRES

6–40 Part VIII of the 1991 Act details the rules obtaining in respect of the registration, regulation and discontinuance of children's residential centres. This part of the Act came into force on December 18, 1996.[37]

Register of centres

6–41 By virtue of s.61 of the 1991 Act each health board is required to establish and maintain a register of all children's residential centres as exist within its jurisdiction. Section 60 of the same Act prohibits the establishment or running of any unregistered children's residential centre by any person, and requires further that no person should take charge of such an unregistered centre. The maximum penalty for infringement of this provision is a fine of IR£1,000 (€1,260) or a term of imprisonment of 12 months, or both.[38]

Registration

6–42 A health board may register, or refuse to register, a children's residential centre, or register a centre subject to conditions in relation to the carrying on of the centre.[39] It is to be noted that a health board may only refuse to register on limited grounds, including the following instances:[40]

- the premises do not comply with the Child Care (Standards in Children's Residential Centres) Regulations 1996;[41]

- the carrying on of the centre is not, or will not be, in compliance with the 1995 Residential Care Regulations;

- the registered proprietor or the person in charge of the centre has been convicted of any offence, including the carrying on of a children's residential centre that has not been registered;

- the applicant or registered proprietor has failed or refused to furnish or has furnished false information in a material particular to the health board;

- the registered proprietor has contravened a condition imposed by the health board up to one year prior to the date for the removal or registration in relation to the running on of a centre.

6–43 Article 4 of the Child Care (Standards in Children's Residential Centres) Regulations 1996 provides that the application for registration should be in

---

[37] Child Care Act 1991 (Commencement) Order 1996 (S.I. No. 399 of 1996).
[38] s.64 of the Child Care Act 1991.
[39] s.61(6) of the 1991 Act.
[40] s.61(5) of the 1991 Act.
[41] S.I. No. 397 of 1996.

the prescribed form included in the Schedule to the Regulations and in Appendix 11 of this book.

A renewal of registration of a children's residential centre must be made two months prior to the expiry of the registration, and is made under s.61(3) of the 1991 Act. In effect, the renewal procedure is identical to a first registration.

A health board must notify the applicant or registered proprietor of the following decisions and the reasons for any such decision:

(a) a refusal to register;

(b) attaching a condition to registration; and

(c) amending or revoking a condition.

6–44 Section 16(2) requires each decision to be accompanied by a statement informing the applicant or registered proprietor of his right to make representations to the health board within 21 days. The health board must consider any such representation and issue a decision and the reasons for it. A registered proprietor or applicant should also be advised that an appeal can be made to the District Court within 21 days of the health board's decision. Section 61(3) renders it an offence to breach a condition attaching to a registration.

6–45 Section 62 of the 1991 Act sets out the appeal procedure to the District Court from a health board's decision. Decisions that may be appealed include a decision of a health board:

• to refuse to register the children's residential centre;

• to remove the children's residential centre from the register;

• to amend or revoke a condition attached to the registration of the children's residential centre.

As previously stated, a decision of the health board must be appealed within 21 days and must be served on the health board not later than seven days before the date of the appeal hearing.[42] A centre is deemed to be registered during an appeal unless the centre is run by a person who is not a registered proprietor. Section 63(4) allows the health board, under Pt 8 of the 1991 Act and within six months of a person being convicted of an offence, to apply to the Circuit Court for an order disqualifying a person from carrying on, being in charge, or concerned with the management of any centre.

6–46 Two issues of concern arise under Pt 8 of the 1991 Act. The first concerns an ambiguity as to whether garda clearance is required for applicants wishing to open a children's residential centre. The second concerns the powers of the inspectorate in respect of an unregistered centre. For example, does

---

[42] See also r.34 of the District Court (Child Care) Rules 1995 (S.I. No. 338 of 1995) which requires a copy of the decision of the health board or notification of such decision to be lodged in the District Court.

s.63(2)(g) give powers of entry to an inspectorate to satisfy itself that a children's residential centre may be operational or even to discount such a suspicion.

The Child Care (Standards in Children's Residential Centres) Regulations 1996

6–47   The Child Care (Standards in Children's Residential Centres) Regulations 1996[43] set down strict guidelines for the quality of care provided in "children's residential centres". The latter is defined in Art.3 of the 1996 Regulations[44] as "any home or other institution for the residential care of children in the care of health boards or other children who are not receiving adequate care and protection". This excludes:

(i)   an institution managed by, or on behalf of, a Minister of the Government (this would presumably include a prison or secure facility for young offenders), or by a health board;

(ii)   an institution in which a majority of the children are being treated for acute illnesses;

(iii) an institution for the care and maintenance of physically or mentally handicapped children;

(iv)   a mental institution within the meaning of the Mental Treatment Acts 1945 to 1966; and

(v)   an institution which is a "certified school" within the meaning of Pt IV of the 1908 Act,[45] functions in relation to which stand vested in the Minister for Education.

6–48   It can be seen from the foregoing that the definition of a children's residential centre excluded an institution for the care and maintenance of physically or mentally handicapped children. This exclusion has been deleted by s.267(1)(b) of the Children Act 2001, which provides as follows:

> "The Act of 1991 is hereby amended—
>
>> in section 59 (definition for purposes of Part VIII), by the deletion of paragraph (c) from the definition of 'children's residential centre'."

Critically, however, there is no corresponding deletion in the 1996 Regulations introduced pursuant to ss.61, 63 and 68 of the Children Act 2001. This omission has the potential to render redundant any efforts to inspect an institution for the care and maintenance of physically or mentally handicapped children.

6–49   Exclusion (i) above is especially important. It indicates quite clearly

---

[43] Hereinafter the "1996 Regulations".

[44] See Pt I of the Regulations.

[45] This Act will be repealed when all the provisions of the Children Act 2001 are fully in force. See Chap.11.

that health board premises, that is, centres established and run by or under the authority of the health boards, are not subject to these 1996 Regulations. Such premises would, of course, be required to comply with the provisions of the Residential Care Regulations,[46] outlined previously, relating to all residential care centres.

These present (1996) Regulations, then, are designed to regulate the private and voluntary sections of child care not under the direct authority of the State. They are, it seems, additional to the 1995 Residential Care Regulations noted above.

Duties of and standards in residential centres

6–50   The registered proprietor and any person in charge of a residential centre are obliged to satisfy the health board that the residential centre meets the standards laid down in the 1996 Regulations as follows:

1. Operational policies

6–51   Appropriate and suitable care practices and operational policies must be adopted, taking into account the number of children accommodated at the centre and the nature of their needs.[47] There should, in particular, be a person who has overall control and responsibility for the centre, as outlined in Art.6.

2. Staffing

6–52   The health board should be satisfied that there is an adequate number of suitably qualified and experienced staff available to work at each residential centre within its functional area.[48] A similar requirement exists in respect of a residential centre operated outside its jurisdiction, but in which the board has placed or wishes to place, a child in its care.

3. Accommodation

6–53   Appropriate and suitable accommodation is to be provided.[49] Whether such accommodation is adequate will again depend on the number and needs of the children accommodated at the centre. The registered proprietor and any person in charge of a residential centre are obliged, in particular, to ensure that there is:

(a) adequate and suitable furniture, bedding and other furnishings;

(b) a sufficient number of lavatories, wash basins, baths and showers, with sufficient water, both hot and cold. As far as practicable such arrangements should respect the need for privacy;

(c) adequate facilities for laundry (washing, drying and ironing);

---

[46] S.I. No. 259 of 1995.

[47] Art.5.

[48] Art.7.

[49] Art.8.

(d) adequate light, heat and ventilation;

(e) sufficiently clean premises, appropriately decorated and maintained in good structural condition;

(f) adequate recreation facilities.

The foregoing are unduly vague and subjective. Additional guidance should be provided to assist both registered proprietors and inspectors in making judgements on these matters.

4. Access arrangements

6–54 The registered proprietor and persons in charge of the centre should make adequate arrangements to enable the child to have appropriate access to parents, relatives, friends and other persons with a bona fide interest in the child.[50] The obligations imposed in this regard are more onerous since the incorporation of the European Convention on Human Rights into Irish law.

5. Health care

6–55 Children at the centre should have access to the services of a general practitioner.[51] It should be possible, furthermore, to refer a child, if required, for medical, psychological, dental, ophthalmic or other specialist treatment or assessment. Consent is an issue that arises in considering health care and is discussed in Chapter 4 at para.4–49 and Chapter 5 at para.5–30. The National Standards for Residential Care for Young People should also be noted. Standard 8 provides as follows:

> "Young people in care should get the kind of health care they need and should be encouraged, as they grow older, to make their own decisions with regard to their health."[52]

6. Religion

6–56 Appropriate arrangements should be put in place to facilitate the child in practising his or her religion.[53] This may include provision for transport to weekend services and making appropriate arrangements for other religious events.[54]

7. Food and cooking facilities

6–57 Adequate amounts of food should be supplied.[55] Such food should be properly prepared, wholesome and nutritious. There should be a sufficient

---

[50] Art.9.
[51] Art.10.
[52] The National Standards for Residential Care for Young People (The Stationery Office, Dublin, 2004), p.24.
[53] Art.11.
[54] For example, First Holy Communion, Confirmation, and Bar/Bat Mitzvah.
[55] Art.12.

element of variety and choice. The staff should in particular be mindful of dietary requirements and prescriptions.[56] Each centre should have suitable and sufficient catering equipment, crockery and silverware/cutlery, proper refrigeration and other storage facilities. Such facilities and items should be maintained to a high standard of hygiene. Compliance with Art.12 and the provision of adequate food and cooking facilities may be determined by an environmental health officer.

8. Fire precautions

6–58   Without prejudice to the general requirements of fire safety legislation, certain fire safety steps should be taken by the registered proprietor and any person in charge of a residential centre.[57] A chartered engineer or suitably qualified architect must confirm that relevant fire-safety and building-control rules have been complied with. Such designated person should also check the following matters:

Fire-safety checklist

(a) Have adequate steps been taken to prevent, as best one may, a fire occurring at the centre?

(b) In case of fire, are there adequate means of escape from the centre, including alternative routes of evacuation?

(c) Have adequate arrangements been made for the detection of a fire?

(d) Are there adequate facilities for containing and extinguishing fires?

(e) Have members of staff been equipped to use, in appropriate cases, these facilities?

(f) Is fire-fighting equipment adequately maintained?

(g) Have steps been taken to ensure that the materials contained in bedding and other furnishings are sufficiently fire-retardant and contained the lowest possible levels of toxicity?

9. Safety precautions

6–59   Adequate arrangements should be made to ensure that the facilities are otherwise sufficiently safe, having regard to the age and maturity of the children housed there.[58] Particular attention should be directed to the risk of injury from stairways, appliances, windows and doors, storage of medicines, cleaning and other materials. The obligation imposed by Art.14 in respect of safety precautions should be discharged through the preparation of a safety statement.

---

[56] For example, vegetarianism, allergies, lactose-intolerance and other such conditions.
[57] Art.13.
[58] Art.14.

It should be noted that s.12 of the Safety, Health and Welfare at Work Act 1989 requires every employer to prepare or cause to be prepared a safety statement. The safety statement sets down the arrangements made and the resources allocated for safeguarding the children and staff at the childrens' residential centre. While the duty to make the safety statement available is confined to staff, s.7 of the 1989 Act imposes an obligation on the registered proprietor to provide children with information in relation to how particular activities that "might affect their safety or health".

10. Insurance

6–60 The health board should be satisfied that the centre is adequately insured against injury to any child resident at the centre.[59] Adequate insurance may include professional indemnity insurance and sufficient public liability insurance cover.

11. Other duties

6–61 The registered proprietor and person in charge of a residential centre have other miscellaneous duties. These include the requirement that the health board should be notified of significant events in the child's life.[60] Furthermore, appropriate records should be maintained and kept available in respect of each child at the facility.[61]

Power to inspect the premises

6–62 Article 18 of the Regulations allows any person so authorised by a health board to enter upon the premises of a residential centre for the purposes of inspection. The registered proprietor and members of staff are obliged to facilitate an inspection by authorised persons and allow them access to the facilities and to such relevant information as may be required. Such authorised persons are permitted, in particular, to examine all records relating to children at the centre and to take copies of these, if considered necessary. This excludes, however, medical records in respect of the child; only a duly authorised medical practitioner may consult such records.

6–63 Each health board is required and empowered to enforce these regulations in respect of all and each children's residential centre operating within its jurisdiction.[62]

---

[59] Art.15.
[60] Art.16.
[61] Art.17.
[62] Art.19.

PART IV

REDEFINING RESIDENTIAL CARE

Negative aspects of residential care

6–64   Currently residential care of any kind is viewed with extreme suspicion and antipathy. Frequently, it is seen as a part of the problem that manifests itself in the child care system and not part of the solution. The negative perception of residential care has not been helped and is nowhere more evident than in the current anti-residential sentiment engendered by recent child sexual abuse scandals.

Positive aspects of residential care

6–65   Notwithstanding the foregoing, one must not totally denigrate residential care, as in certain limited circumstances it may be the most desirable option for certain children. In fact, one of the main differences between the Danish and Irish child care systems is vested in the fact that, while family oriented caring is intensely pursued in Denmark, the planners and policy makers there have acknowledged the fact that some children will not be able to live in the natural or alternative family. Thus the Danish residential care system acknowledges residential care as a separate, discrete form of care and not a form of care of last resort.

6–66   Traditional forms of residential care are no longer suitable to accommo-date the needs of children/young people in need of institutional care. Therefore, new forms of residential care need to continue to evolve to ensure that the rights and needs of the child/young person are sensitively and comprehensively provided for. It is suggested, for example, that specialised residential centres continue to be constructed for more disturbed children and older young people. This will require highly trained personnel, and is a recommendation that was strongly advocated by the Task Force on Child Care Services, which stated that:

> "Some specialised residential provision will be needed for severely disturbed children, to create for them a therapeutic and nurturing environment in which help in relation to all their difficulties can be combined and in which the demands made on them can be limited to those to which they can respond at each stage of their progress".[63]

Conclusion

6–67   It is now 25 years since the Kennedy Report[64] was first published, and

---

[63] Department of Health, *Report of the Task Force on Child Care Services* (The Stationery Office, Dublin, 1980) at p.200.

[64] *Supra*, n.1.

while many important changes have taken place in the residential care sector in the intervening period, the shortcomings alluded to in this chapter still remain. It is submitted that residential care has a legitimate and valuable role to play in the overall provision of child care services. That said, this form of care should be provided as a form of care of choice. In summary, there is a need for the re-assertion of the values and importance of residential care in the spectrum of services for children and young people.

CHAPTER 7

CHILD CARE: GENERAL AND MISCELLANEOUS MATTERS

PART I

PROVIDING FOR CHILDREN IN CARE: GENERAL PROVISIONS

Introduction

7–01   Where a child has been placed in the care of a health board there are, as previously stated, several options open to the board in providing for his or her care. These are laid out in s.36 of the Child Care Act 1991 (the "1991 Act"). The health board may, subject to its control and supervision, place the child in foster care. This would involve the placing of a child with a foster parent. Alternatively, a child may be placed in residential care. This may take the form of a placement in a registered children's residential centre or in a residential home maintained by a health board. Each of these options has been dealt with in detail in Chapter 6.

7–02   In appropriate cases, the child may, if eligible, be placed for adoption, although this approach is likely to be used only in exceptional cases. It is worth noting at this juncture that a child of married parents may only be adopted in very extreme circumstances, and in compliance with the exceptionally exacting requirements of the Adoption Act 1988.[1] The adoption of a child born outside marriage is comparatively easier, although the board would in these circumstances be required to obtain certain consents. In particular, consent would be required of the natural mother and/or guardian of the child, and of any person who had care and control over the child at the relevant time. Provision is made for such consent to be dispensed with by a court, but this can only be done where this is, in the opinion of the court, in the best interests of the child. A less drastic solution would be to place a child with a relative; an option explicitly contemplated by s.36(1)(d) of the 1991 Act. The listed options are not, however, exhaustive; s.36(1)(d) allows for other suitable arrangements to be made as the board thinks proper, making it clear that there is scope for creative solutions to child care needs.

---

[1]   No. 30 of 1988. See also Chap.9.

Placement outside the State

7–03   In *Western Health Board v K.M.*,[2] the applicant health board applied to the District Court for a direction as to whether it was entitled to place T.K. with a relative in the United Kingdom. The District Court stated a case for the High Court, asking the following questions:

(i)   whether the health board had such a placement power under s.36 of the 1991 Act;

(ii)   whether the District Court could order such a placement under s.47 of the 1991 Act; and

(iii) if the answer to (i) and (ii) was in the affirmative, could the period of the placement be limited?

Finnegan J. answered the first question in the negative and the second and third question in the affirmative.

7–04   The High Court held that the powers of the heath board under s.36 of the 1991 Act must be read in conjunction with s.18(3) of that Act, which envisages a power to take children abroad but only in very limited circumstances, described by the High Court in the present case as holiday or medical situations. Finnegan J. held that s.47 of the 1991 Act enabled the District Court to do whatever it deemed appropriate to achieve the policy of the 1991 Act. Consequently, if a health board seeks to place a child outside the State, it must get an order from the District Court authorising that. As there is no limitation on the District Court's power under s.47 of the 1991 Act, it can direct a foreign placement with or without a time limit. The High Court provided little guidance regarding the circumstances in which a District Court should grant a request for a foreign placement, though it did refer to the objectives set out in s.24 of the 1991 Act regarding the welfare and wishes of the child. In affirming the decision of the High Court, McGuinness J. in the Supreme Court stated that the 1991 Act is "… a remedial and social statute …" that should be "… construed as widely and liberally as can fairly be done." She was of the opinion that s.47 of the 1991 Act could be used "to direct or permit the placement of a child outside the State where the evidence before the Court indicates that the placement is truly in the best interests of the child."[3]

7–05   McGuinness J. did, however, place a number of restrictions on the Court in considering the making of such an order. She held that the order for the placement of a child outside the State should be granted sparingly, and having regard to the following factors:

(1)   the constitutional rights of the child and parents;

---

[2]   [2001] 1 I.R. 729 (High Court); [2002] 2 I.R. 493 (Supreme Court).
[3]   *ibid.*

(2) the nature of the law regarding children in the jurisdiction in which it is purported the child should live;[4]

(3) whether or not the country concerned is a signatory to the Hague and/or Luxembourg Conventions;[5]

(4) whether or not there is already a system of co-operation between the child care authorities in the proposed jurisdiction, and the health boards in their role as child care authorities in this jurisdiction, or can such a system be readily established;

(5) if the child is placed abroad, whether or not access to the child by the natural parent or parents will be a practical possibility in terms of distance and expense;

(6) whether or not there is a reasonable possibility of using either undertakings or mirror orders to make the position of the child and of the relevant health board more secure.

It should be noted that the provisions of the Protection of Children (Hague Convention) Act 2000, discussed in Chap.12, will need to be considered when it comes into force. The provisions of the revised Brussels II Regulation,[6] also discussed in detail in Chap.12, should be consulted where the child is to be placed within the EU.

Children with medical or psychiatric needs

7–06   It is open to the health board, in appropriate cases, to place a child in a hospital or other institution providing care for children suffering from a physical or mental disability.[7] It is suggested that every effort should nonetheless be made to give children with special needs, where possible, the opportunity to live in a regular home environment. Where this is not possible, the board, it is submitted, might consider (under s.36(1)(d) of the 1991 Act) appointing lay visitors, perhaps from the panel of foster parents. These persons would periodically visit the child in the institution in which he or she is based, with the possibility of providing some occasional respite in the form of supervised day trips or weekend breaks.

Mental Health Act 2001

7–07   Children attending special schools and institutions do not fall within the Education (Welfare) Act 2000 discussed in Chapter 3. Children suffering from mental disorders are covered by the Mental Health Act 2001. The function

---

[4] For example, whether the principle that the welfare of the child is paramount applies or is it likely that the order of the Irish court will be recognised and enforced.

[5] Council Regulation No.2201/2003, Concerning Jurisdiction and the Recognition and Enforcement of Judgments in Matrimonial Matters and Matters Relating to Parental Responsibility Repealing Regulation (EC) [2003] O.J. L3381, 1347–2000.

[6] See Chap.10.

[7] s.36(3).

of this legislation was to provide a mechanism by which standards of care and treatment in the mental health service could be monitored, inspected and regulated. The Mental Health Act 2001 provides for the voluntary and involuntary detention of children, defined as those less than 18 years of age.

A parent may admit a child for voluntary treatment in an approved centre as a voluntary patient. However, if the parent decides to discharge the child, and the consultant psychiatrist, a registered medical practitioner or a registered nurse of the staff of the approved centre is of the opinion that the child is suffering from a mental disorder, the child may be detained and placed in the custody of the appropriate health board.[8] The health board may then return the child to both parents; to either of them; to a person acting in *loco parentis*; or may make an application to the District Court for an order authorising the detention of the child under s.25 of the Mental Health Act 2001. Such applications may be dealt with in a similar manner to the emergency care orders under the Child Care Act 1991.[9]

Involuntary admission of children

7–08   A health board also has the power to apply to the District Court for an order authorising the detention of a child in an approved centre, where it appears to the health board that a child is suffering from a mental disorder and requires treatment which he or she is unlikely to receive unless an order is made.[10] The health board may not make an application for detention unless the child has been examined by a consultant psychiatrist who is not a relative of the child. A report of the results of the examination must be furnished by the health board to the Court.[11] There are limited circumstances where the health board may make an application for the detention order without a prior examination of the child by a psychiatrist. These are confined to where:

(a) the parents of the child refuse permission for the examination; or

(b) the parents cannot be identified or found.[12]

7–09   In these circumstances the court may direct the health board to arrange for the examination of the child where it is of the view that the child is suffering from a mental disorder. The court may set down directions as to the time in which the report is to be obtained.[13] The psychiatrist can then carry out the examination and prepare the report for the court, commenting on whether or not the child is suffering from a mental disorder.

7–10   Where the court is satisfied that the child is suffering from a mental disorder on the basis of the psychiatric opinion and any other evidence that

---

[8] Mental Health Act 2001, s.23(2).
[9] Mental Health Act 2001, s.23(4) applies the criteria detailed in the Child Care Act 1991, s.13(4).
[10] Mental Health Act 2001, s.25(1).
[11] Mental Health Act 2001, s.25(2).
[12] Mental Health Act 2001, s.25(3).
[13] s.25(4).

may be adduced, an order that the child be admitted and detained for treatment can be made. This detention must be in a specified approved centre for a period not exceeding 21 days. Involuntary admission orders can be extended for a further period not exceeding three months, and following that for periods not exceeding six months.[14] Extensions may only be granted where the child has been seen by a psychiatrist and the court is satisfied that the child still suffers from a mental disorder.[15]

Medical examinations

7–11   Difficulty arises where a child refuses to submit to an examination by a psychiatrist. It would seem that an application for involuntary admission could not be made in such circumstances. In order to utilise s.25, the health board must have a psychiatric report, or must obtain a court order where there is parental objection or where there is no parent to consent. This power is purely statutory. Therefore it is submitted that the health board cannot apply for involuntary admission, where it has a child in need of treatment and admission who refuses to submit to an examination by a psychiatrist, even where the parents consent.

7–12   Section 25(14) of the 2001 Act incorporates the provisions of s.27 of the Child Care Act 1991 in terms of procuring a report on a child. The Court must take into consideration the wishes of the parties, but is not bound by those wishes.

   However, if no such report can be produced because the child refuses to submit to an examination, the health board cannot proceed. That said, pursuant to ss.34 and 35 of the 1991 Act, the health board may obtain a Care Order. Section 47 of the 1991 Act will then allow the health board to seek directions on any matter impacting on the welfare of the child where he or she is in the care of a health board. Significantly, reference to a psychiatric examination, treatment or assessment under the 1991 Act does not include reference to treatment under the Mental Health Act 2001.[16] Pursuant to s.25(12) and (13) of the Mental Health Act 2001, psycho-surgery and electroconvulsive therapy may not be performed on a child without the consent of the court, although the term "psycho-surgery" is not defined.[17]

7–13   All applications relating to a child made under the Mental Health Act 2001 must view the paramount consideration as the welfare of the child. In addition, as far as is practicable, due consideration must be given to the wishes of the child having regard to his or her age and understanding. To further protect the child's interests, the court has the power to join the child as a party to the proceedings and appoint a solicitor to represent the child. Alternatively,

[14] s.25(9) and (10).
[15] s.25(11).
[16] s.25(15).
[17] s.25(12) and (13).

the court may appoint a guardian *ad litem* for the child not made party to the proceedings, where it considers that it is in the interests of the child to do so.[18]

7–14 There may be difficulties for the solicitor appointed to represent a child under the Mental Health Act 2001. The role of a solicitor is discussed further at Chapter 8, Pt IV. However, of direct concern when appointed under the Mental Health Act 2001 is the capacity of the child to give instructions. An issue may arise where there appears to be a conflict between the wishes of the child expressed to the solicitor, and the objective welfare of the child. How is this conflict reconciled? The best course of action available to the solicitor is to apply for directions to the court.

7–15 The Mental Mental Act 2001 incorporates the provisions of the 1991 Act in terms of the effect of appeals from orders made under the Mental Health Act 2001. An appeal of an order cannot act as a stay unless so ordered by the court which granted the order or the court to which the appeal is directed. The court may also of its own motion vary or discharge the order made; any condition or direction attaching to the order; or may substitute a care or supervision order in place of the involuntary detention order.

7–16 To further bring domestic legislation into harmony with Ireland's international obligations, the Mental Health Act 2001 seeks to provide children suffering from a mental disorder with quality care and protect against unnecessary detention. That said, the efficacy of the Act may be undermined by its failure to address significant issues, such as children refusing a psychiatric examination, and the lack of practical guidelines for those appointed to represent the child's interests.

Access to children in care

7–17 In all cases where a child is in the care, voluntary or otherwise, of a health board, it is possible to make provision for the granting of reasonable access to the child's parents and other relatives. Section 37 of the 1991 Act obliges the board, in such cases, to facilitate reasonable access to the child by his or her parents, by any person acting *in loco parentis* in respect of the child, or by any other person who has a bona fide interest in the child. The latter may include a grandparent or grown-up sibling. Such access as is permitted may include provision to allow the child to reside temporarily with the designated person. For instance, a child residing with foster parents may be permitted to spend the last weekend of every month with his natural father, or to stay overnight, once a month, with his grandparents.

The health board has a primary duty to facilitate access to the parents and to other persons to whom the child is closely connected. In practice, this duty is not always fulfilled. It seems, for instance, from primary research conducted by the author, that the managers and staff of residential centres are not always

---

[18] See Chap.8.

conscious of the importance of this provision. It may be necessary that such access be supervised. This is especially crucial where allegations of sexual abuse have been made against a parent. Investigation and validation of such allegations can take a considerable time. Unfortunately, however, provisions for such supervised access for a parent "under suspicion" seem, to date, to be practically non-existent.

7–18   Some persons may be unhappy with the access arrangements made. If so, it is open to that person, or indeed any person, to apply to the court for appropriate directions. In this case, the court may make an order, in such terms as it considers appropriate, regarding access to the child by that person. This order may, however, be varied or discharged on application by any person. It is also open to the court, on the application of the health board only, to preclude access by a named person. This may be done only where the court deems it necessary to do so in order to safeguard or promote the child's welfare. The order precluding access may, furthermore, be varied or discharged by the court on the application of any person. It may be possible, however, for the child himself or herself to seek the direction of the court on this, or on any other matter relating to access, under s.47 of the 1991 Act.[19]

It is noteworthy that the terms of s.37 reflect a rather parent-centred attitude to access. The section speaks of access "by" a parent "to" a child, whereas surely it is the reverse that should concern the court. Is it not more apt to speak of the *child's* right of access *to* his or her parents and other relatives? If the primary concern of the court is with the welfare of the child, should not this section be worded accordingly? The divergence is subtle, no doubt, but revealing.

7–19   The importance of ease of contact for parents with children in residential care cannot be overstated. Research has demonstrated that child care placements are more successful where there is regular access between the child in care and the natural parents. Schapiro in his research demonstrated a positive correlation between regular access and discharge from care.[20] Milner in his research in the United States identified a similar pattern.[21] The importance of access between natural parents and their children in care has therefore been a consistent finding of research studies.

The active promotion of access has been a feature of child care in other jurisdictions for some time. In Sweden, for example, ss.1(1) and (2) of the Social Services Act 1980 requires the placement of a child in a residential unit

---

[19] See *Eastern Health Board v Judge McDonnell and Others (Notice Parties)*, unreported, High Court, McCracken J., March 5, 1999.

[20] Schapiro, "Land Availability and Fertility in the United States" (1982) 42, 3 *Journal of Economic History* 577–600. See also Lasson, *Where's my Mum? A Study of the Forgotten Children in Long-Term Care* (Repart Publications, London, 1980) and Millham, Bullock, Hosie and Hark, *Lost in Care: The Problems of Maintaining Links between Children in Care and their Families* (Gower, London, 1986).

[21] Milner, "An Ecological Perspective on Duration of Foster Care" (1987) LXVI, 2 *Child Welfare League*.

to be carried out in such a way as to permit the child to have close contact with his relatives and to be able to visit his home.

7–20 Before leaving this topic, it is worth noting developments in the international legal arena. In *Eriksson v Sweden*,[22] the European Court of Human Rights held that the natural family relationship is not terminated by reason of the fact that a child is taken into care. The enjoyment by a child and a parent of each other's company, it said, is a fundamental element of family life. The curtailment or denial of access would thus be a *prima facie* violation of Art.8 of the European Convention on Human Rights. It would, furthermore, be deemed an unjustified violation thereof unless it could be shown to be in accordance with law, that such denial of access had an aim or aims that is or are legitimate under Art.8(2) and was "necessary in a democratic society". Access, according to the court, is an automatic right of the child in care, not to be denied unless there is clear evidence that it is contrary to the welfare of the child. This approach is also to be found in the UN Convention on the Rights of the Child 1989, Art.9(3) of which makes specific provision for:

> "the right of the child who is separated from one or both parents to maintain public relations and direct contact with both parents on a regular basis unless it is contrary to the child's best interests."

7–21 From this flow two prevailing principles to be observed when considering access arrangements:

(i)   the appropriateness, or otherwise, of making access arrangements should be considered primarily by reference to the welfare of the child;

(ii) access to parents and other relatives should invariably be considered to be in the best interests of the child, unless the contrary is clearly demonstrated.

Termination of care

7–22 There are certain situations where a child may be deemed no longer to be in the care of the health board:

(a)   first and foremost, a child who has reached the age of 18 is no longer deemed to be a "child" for the purposes of the Act. Thus the jurisdiction of the health board in respect of that child is ended. A child who marries is likewise deemed no longer to be the responsibility of the board;

(b)   where a child has voluntarily been placed in the care of the health board (under s.4), such care will be terminated by the decision of the parents to resume custody;[23]

(c)   where under s.18(8) of the 1991 Act, a care order is discharged by the court;

---

[22] (1990) 12 E.H.R.R. 200.
[23] s.4(2).

(d) where an emergency care order made under s.13 or an interim care order
      created by means of s.17 expires and is not renewed.

It goes without saying that where, on appeal or judicial review, a care order is
reversed or quashed, the effect of such appeal or review shall be to terminate
the health board's lawful custody of the child in respect of which the order has
been made.

Removal from placement

7–23 Where a child has been placed in accordance with s.36 of the 1991
Act, he or she may be removed from such placement under the provisions of
s.43. This allows the health board to terminate any placement of a child,
seemingly with little comeback for the persons having custody, for the time
being, of the child. The removal of a child from custody has the effect of
bringing to an end any contract between the health board and the
aforementioned person(s) in respect of the child's care.

Should any person, for the time being having custody of a child, refuse to
comply with the request, or alternatively ignore it, the board may seek the
direction of the court. The court may thus order this person to return the child
to the custody of the board. The court, nonetheless, has a discretion in this
regard. It may refuse to grant the order if it considers that it is not in the best
interests of the child to do so.[24]

7–24 Where an order is made, however, any person who fails to comply
therewith may be guilty of contempt of court. If this person unlawfully retains
custody of the child following the making of an order under s.43(2), it is
possible, furthermore, that such person may be found guilty of an offence
under s.43(3) of the Act. This is conditional on the person having been shown
a copy of the order in question, or having been required by the health board or
a person acting on its behalf to deliver up the child. The health board will be
deemed, however, to have satisfied this latter condition where the person in
question was present at the court sitting at which the order was made. A person
so convicted faces a maximum penalty of six months' imprisonment or a fine
of IR£500 (€630), or both, at the discretion of the court.

The unlawful removal of a child from care

7–25 Where a child is unlawfully removed from the care of the board or of
any person having lawful custody of the child, s.46 allows the board to take
steps to restore the child to the lawful custody of any person. This will include
a situation where a child, having been in the lawful custody of a person for a
temporary period, has been prevented from returning to a place of lawful
custody at the end of that lawful period.

The health board is empowered by s.46(2) to request the assistance of An
Garda Síochána in searching for a child unlawfully detained with a view to his

---

[24] s.43(2).

or her return to lawful custody. To this end the Gardaí may take all reasonable measures to secure his or her return. It is possible, furthermore, to obtain an order of the court regarding the child's return.[25] This allows the court to order that a named person produce or return a child to the custody of the board. This may be done only where the judge is satisfied by information on oath that there are reasonable grounds for believing that the child can be produced by the person named in the application. An application under subs.(3) may be made *ex parte*.[26] In addition to the possibility of conviction for contempt of court, a failure or refusal to comply with such order will amount to an offence under s.46(4). This, again, is conditional on the person having been shown a copy of the order in question or having been required by the health board or a person acting on its behalf to comply with the requirement. The health board will be deemed, however, to have satisfied this condition where the person in question was present at the court sitting at which the order was made.[27] A person so convicted faces a maximum penalty of six months' imprisonment, or a fine of IR£500 (€630), or both, at the discretion of the court.

7–26 A warrant can be issued permitting a member of An Garda Síochána to enter a place in which, it is reasonably believed, the child is being detained.[28] Such a place may include a house or any other place, including a building or part thereof, and any tent, caravan or other temporary or moveable structure. It is possible also to make an order in respect of a vessel, vehicle, aircraft or hovercraft in which it is suspected a child is being detained. Upon the making of such an order, a member of the Gardaí, accompanied by any person deemed necessary (including other gardaí), may enter and search the place stated in the order, using such force as is necessary in the circumstances.

It is possible for an order under subs.(3) or (6) to be made, should the urgency of the case so require, other than at a public sitting of the District Court.[29] Such an order or warrant will usually be issued by a justice of the district in which the person or place specified in the information is to be found.[30] Where this is not possible, however (where the justice is not "immediately available"), an order may be made or a warrant issued by any district justice.

Application for directions

7–27 Where a child is in the care of the health board, any person may apply to the court for directions as to any matter affecting the child's welfare. It is also possible for the court to issue such directions on its own initiative. The court should consider the prospect of such directions as it thinks proper, with reference always to the predominant requirement that the child's welfare be promoted. Such directions as are given may, however, be varied or discharged by the court, should it see fit.

---

[25] s.46(3).
[26] s.46(7).
[27] s.46(5).
[28] s.46(6).
[29] s.46(8).
[30] s.46(9).

Aftercare

7-28   Where a child reaches the age of 18, he or she is no longer technically deemed to be in care. Few parents, however, see fit to sever all links with their children on their reaching the age of majority. In a similar vein, the health board (notwithstanding s.2(1) of the 1991 Act) is empowered, should it see fit, to make continuing provision for persons formerly in its care. Section 45 allows the board to assist such persons until they have reached the age of 21, should it be satisfied that such assistance is needed. This may include:

(a) making provision for visits to the former child or other practical assistance;

(b) making arrangements to assist the completion of education by the former child and the provision of maintenance to assist him or her while completing this education. Such arrangements may be continued after the child has reached the age of 21 should it be necessary to facilitate the completion of that person's education;

(c) placing the former child in a suitable trade, calling or business and paying such fees as are required to facilitate such placement (presumably this refers, *inter alia*, to a vocational apprenticeship);

(d) arranging appropriate accommodation (including hostel accommodation). This may involve consulting and co-operating with local and voluntary housing authorities with a view to securing appropriate accommodation.

These provisions are facilitative only, and not mandatory. The reality is that a health board, hard pressed and under-resourced, may choose to devote its scant resources to children in need rather than to aftercare for persons who are now no longer "children" for the purposes of the Act. This would be unfortunate. The Age of Majority Act 1985 notwithstanding, a person's vulnerability may not end simply by attaining the age of 18.

Conclusion

7-29   Despite the undoubtedly improved legal structure effected by the 1991 Act, the child care system in Ireland cannot easily be defended. The realities of under-resourcing and under-staffing, and the present shortage of well-qualified child care professionals, means that in many cases there are not adequate facilities for the accommodation of children in need. The currently high number of homeless children highlights this, a situation described by a representative of one voluntary agency as "nothing short of a national disgrace".[31] It is not uncommon for judges considering an application under the 1991 Act to find that there is nowhere to house a child in need. Judge Hubert Wine of the Dun Laoghaire District Court and Kelly J. for the High Court are of particular note for their respective condemnations of what an *Irish Times* editorial referred to as "... [the State's] persistent failure to provide services for young people who need protection."[32]

---

[31] Ivan Mahoney for *Focus Ireland*, in Sheridan, "Ireland's Shame", *Issues* 1, 1.

[32] "Editorial", *The Irish Times*, July 11, 2000.

PART II

CHILD SEXUAL ABUSE

7–30   The term "child sexual abuse" is a relatively recent addition to legal and social discourse. It is defined in the Department of Health guidelines entitled *Children First* as occuring "when a child is used by another person for his or her gratification or sexual arousal, or that of others".[33] Prosecutions for the sexual abuse of children have risen significantly in recent years. This may not necessarily signpost an increase in the incidence of child sexual abuse but rather a more frequent reporting of the offence. Cases of sexual abuse of children are very difficult to prove. The prosecution is frequently left with little other than the victim's testimony. Indeed, the conduct of child sexual abuse cases reflects the current uncertainty attaching to the law in this area.

Standard of proof

7–31   In cases of child sexual abuse, applications by health boards to remove children from the custody of their parents are normally contested by the civil standard of proof on the balance of probability. That said, the court is always alert to the inalienable rights of parents in relation to their children under Arts 41 and 42 of the Constitution. The general law and trial procedures relating to child sexual abuse are discussed in Chapters 2 and 4.

Protections for Persons Reporting Child Abuse Act 1998

7–32   Allegations of child sexual abuse take a considerable length of time to complete and the procedures set out in *Guidelines on Procedures for the Identification, Investigation and Management of Child Abuse* all take time.[34] In addition, once the allegation has been made, the Gardaí are notified in accordance with the *Guidelines on the Notification of Suspected Cases of Child Abuse between Health Boards and Gardaí*.[35] Ultimately, if the allegations transpire to be "unfounded" or not established, there is very little which the "wronged party" can do from a practical point of view.

The Protection for Persons Reporting Child Abuse Act 1998 protects those who report their opinion that a child has been abused, once the report is made to "an appropriate person".[36] The Act defines these as members of the Garda Síochána or designated officers of a health board.

7–33   The operative section is s.3(1). It provides that a reporter "shall not be liable in damages in respect of the communication" of his or her opinion that a child is or has been abused. The immunity is contingent upon the person

---

[33] Department of Health, *Children First: National Guidelines for the Protection and Welfare of Children* (Government Publications, Dublin, 1999) at p.6.
[34] See Department of Health Guidelines Revised, 1997.
[35] Department of Health, 1995.
[36] No. 49 of 1998.

acting reasonably, and in good faith, in forming the opinion and in communicating it. This is a test with which the courts have long been familiar. Such a test, however, runs the risk of giving "a licence to prurient members of the general public to cast stones at their neighbours with impunity".[37]

Parents who make false allegations can, however, expect serious censure. In the case of *S. v S.*, the Supreme Court upheld the award of custody of three children to the husband in a case where the High Court judge had considered that the wife had attempted to make false and bogus allegations against the husband of improper sexual behaviour.[38] That said, the higher standard prescribed by the Law Reform Commission in its report on child sexual abuse would perhaps have been preferable:

> "We recommend that express statutory immunity from legal proceedings should be given to any person who bona fide and with due care reports a suspicion of child sexual abuse to the appropriate authority".[39]

7–34   Given the seriousness of any allegations involved it may be that this higher standard is necessary. Despite creating the offence of false reporting in s.5, which is committed where a person makes a statement knowing it to be false, the law must protect against the "busybody" as much as a malicious reporter.

In this regard, a constitutional balance between the rights to a good name and fair procedures on the one hand, and those relating to the protection of children on the other, must be maintained. The temptation is to err on the child's side but to overweigh the balance is a mistake. Also, over-reporting does not assist the health boards. Resources are limited enough, without being diverted to investigate spurious claims. On the whole, however, this Act is a necessary complement to existing child care provisions. It remains to be seen how it will interact with any mandatory reporting regime that may be introduced.

Child sexual abuse guidelines

7–35   Increasing concern about child sexual abuse led to the issue by the Minister for Health in 1978 of the first guidelines to help professionals isolate, identify, investigate and treat child abuse. Revised guidelines have been issued intermittently in the intervening period, the most recent in 1999. These guidelines, under the name of *Children First: National Guidelines for the Protection and Welfare of Children*, were drawn up by a Working Group established in February 1998.

The guidelines are designed to be applicable to everybody, but especially to professionals and bodies involved with children. The aim is to assist people in identifying and reporting child abuse, primarily to a health board. The guidelines profess to be informed by the principles underlying the 1991 Act and the 1989 UN Convention on the Rights of the Child, specifically that the

---

[37] LRC 32–1990, p.6.
[38] [1992] I.L.R.M. 733.
[39] LRC 32–1990, p. 11.

child's welfare is paramount, but also to have regard to the needs of families and to the child's wishes. In some ways the guidelines could be seen as an enactment of Art.19 of the ECHR, whereby parties are to take appropriate measures to protect children. It is planned to put them on a statutory basis, something that may well amount to mandatory reporting by the backdoor.

7–36 The guidelines cover child abuse, which has been given a wide meaning. There are four kinds specified in the report: neglect, emotional abuse, physical abuse and sexual abuse. The indicators and symptoms of each are well described in plain language. A three-stage guide for the recognition of abuse is set out. Firstly, to consider the possibility of abuse, including looking for signs of distress and behavioural problems. The second stage is looking for signs of abuse. It is explained that these can be physical, behavioural or developmental, and some indicators are listed. Finally, there is the recording of information. It is stressed that as much detail of the abuse as possible should be recorded.

The grounding principle in reporting suspected abuse is the well-being of the child. It is stressed that the report should be made without delay to the health board. The health board must treat all reports seriously and evaluate the complaint. The decision taken must strike a balance between protecting the child and avoiding unnecessary intervention. It is specified that anonymous reports can be investigated depending on the content and circumstances. The procedures to be followed by the health board thereafter are also set out, as are procedures for co-operation with the Gardaí.

In summary, the guidelines are a comprehensive set of procedures for dealing with complaints of child abuse. They are an excellent set of principles for members of the public and for those involved with children. However, the guidelines are not legally binding, and are therefore of limited legal value in that professionals dealing with children are not obliged to enforce them.

Mandatory reporting

7–37 The Law Reform Commission[40] and Kilkenny Incest Report[41] recommended the introduction of mandatory reporting for certain persons, such as psychologists, doctors, psychiatrists, social workers, health board workers, teachers and probation officers. The Government has not yet introduced legislation to implement this recommendation.

Mandatory reporting laws will not solve the problem of under-reporting child sexual abuse and should not be seen as a panacea. There are arguments in favour of and against mandatory reporting laws. For example, it is difficult for professionals to build and foster a confidential relationship with their patients/clients when it is known to all parties that the professional will be required under law to report suspected abuse to the relevant authorities.

---

[40] *ibid.*, Chap.1.
[41] *Kilkenny Incest Investigation; Report presented to Minister for Health by South Eastern Health Board* Pl. 9812 (Dublin, 1993).

Sex Offenders Act 2001[42]

7–38 Legislation for a register of sex offenders was introduced in the form of the Sex Offenders Act 2001. The word "register", however, does not appear in the text of the Act. This Act provides for the post-release monitoring of convicted sex offenders; post-related supervision of sex offenders; garda powers to preclude sex offenders from doing anything the court considers necessary for the purpose of protecting the public from serious harm; making it an offence for a convicted sex offender to apply for or assume a job with children, and legal representation for victims of rape where the defence seeks to adduce evidence of their prior sexual history. "Sex offenders" are defined in Pt 5 of the Act as persons convicted after the commencement of the Act (which was June 30, 2001) of an offence for which the court deems the appropriate punishment to be imprisonment.

Part 2 of the Sex Offenders Act 2001 provides for certain notification requirements that must be complied with by persons convicted of a sexual offence. In particular, under s.9 of the Act, a convicted sex offender must notify the Gardaí of their name and home address, any other address within the State at which they are staying for a particular period, and any change of name or address within 10 days of such change.

7–39 Under s.16, a "sex offender order" may be sought from the court *ex parte* by a garda not below the rank of Chief Superintendent, where a person has been convicted at home or abroad of a sexual offence. The threshold for the granting of such an order is that the court is satisfied, on the balance of probabilities, that the person has acted on one or more occasions to give reasonable grounds for believing that an order is necessary to protect the public from serious harm. The order prohibits the sex offender from doing anything the court considers necessary for the protection of the public from serious harm. A sex offender order may remain in force indefinitely, and breach of the order attracts a maximum penalty of five years' imprisonment.

Section 26 of the Act provides that sex offenders must notify any prospective employer of their conviction, if applying for any position that would require unsupervised access to children as a necessary and regular feature. The Act also applies to non-national sex offenders.

7–40 The provisions of the Sex Offenders Act 2001 are in line with the law in Britain, where sex offenders also are required to give their address to the police within 10 days of being freed from prison. The penalty for a breach of this provision is a fine of up to IR£1,500 (€1,905), a jail sentence of 12 months, or both.

A significant shortcoming in the Act is a lack of emphasis on medical help and rehabilitation of offenders. At present, the rehabilitation of sex offenders while in custody is hopelessly inadequate. The Act does little to improve the situation and must be criticised for its failure to make provision for increased treatment places for sex offenders.

---

[42] See also District Court (Sex Offenders) Rules 2002 (S.I. No. 206 of 2002).

Legal reform

7–41   It is regrettable in view of the large number of cases concerning claims of child sexual abuse recently before the courts that there has been no move to introduce a general offence of child sexual abuse. Indeed, in order to comply fully with the terms of Art.19(1) of the 1989 United Nations Convention on the Rights of the Child, Ireland should introduce such an offence. The Law Reform Commission in its *Report on Child Sexual Abuse* recommended that an offence of "child sexual abuse" be introduced.[43] It recommended the definition of child sexual abuse propounded by the Western Australia Task Force in its 1987 Report for that purpose:

"(i)   intentional touching of the body of a child for the purpose of the sexual gratification of the child or the person;

(ii)   intentional masturbation in the presence of the child;

(iii) intentional exposure of the sexual organs of a person or any other sexual act intentionally performed in the presence of the child for the purpose of sexual arousal or gratification of the older person or as an expression of aggression, threat or intimidation towards the child; and

(iv) sexual exploitation, which includes permitting, encouraging or requiring a child to solicit for or to engage in prostitution or other sexual act as referred to above with the accused or any other person, persons, animal or thing or engaging in the recording (on video-tape, film, audio tape, or other temporary or permanent material), posing, modelling or performing of any act involving the exhibition of a child's body for the purpose of sexual gratification of an audience or for the purpose of any other sexual act …"[44]

Such a change is timely, since prosecutors currently must rely on offences such as incest, unlawful carnal knowledge and sexual assault, which lack the flexibility necessary to cover all forms of sexual abuse to which children are subjected.

7–42   One of the greatest shortcomings in modern child care protection legislation has been the requirement that, before a health board can intervene to provide therapeutic or protective services, there must be a finding by the court that the child is in need of protection. This stands in contrast to the situation which exists internationally, where the main thrust of child care objectives has been developing preventative services to combat child abuse. In fact, as far back as 1976 in the Canadian jurisdiction, the preventative approach was outlined and endorsed in the case of *Kingston v Reeves* in the following terms:

"Perhaps the most important recent development in the child-care field

---

[43] LRC 32–1990.
[44] *ibid.*

has been the growing commitment to prevention work, to family rehabilitation rather than removal from the home. It is recognised that children should be permanently removed from the home only when the factors which have produced an environment of risk to the physical or mental health of the child cannot be ameliorated by help given to that child and those who care for him or her."[45]

7–43 The traditional grounds of when a child is found to be in need of protection continue to find favour in Ireland.[46] Little attention is given to a situation where a child is being emotionally abused, or is alleged to be in a substantial risk situation. One statute that has taken on board the substantial risk situation and the notion of emotional abuse is the Alberta Child Welfare Act 1984. Section 1 stipulates:

> "(2) [F]or the purposes of this Act, a child is in need of protective services if there are reasonable and probable grounds to believe that the survival, security or development of the child is endangered because of any of the following:
> [...]
> (f) the child has been *emotionally*[47] injured by the guardian of the child;
> (g) the guardian of the child is unable or unwilling to protect the child from emotional injury;...
> (3) for the purposes of this Act—
>   (a) a child is *emotionally*[48] injured—
>   (i) if there is substantial and observable impairment of the child's mental or emotional functioning that is evidenced by a mental or behavioural disorder, including anxiety, depression, withdrawal, aggression or delayed development, and
>   (ii) there are reasonable and probable grounds to believe that the *emotional*[49] injury is the result of—
>   (A) rejection,
>   (B) deprivation of affection or cognitive stimulation,
>   (C) exposure to domestic violence or severe domestic disharmony,
>   (D) inappropriate criticism, threats, humiliation, accusations or expectations of or towards the child, or
>   (E) the mental or emotional condition of the guardian of the child or chronic alcohol or drug abuse by anyone living in the same residence as the child."

---

[45] *Reports of Family Law*, Vol.23, 391 (Ont. Prov. Ct), p.393.
[46] I refer here to the tangible physical and sexual abuse grounds.
[47] Emphasis added.
[48] Emphasis added.
[49] Emphasis added.

7–44 It is recommended that the Irish legislature should put in place a preventative and protective provision similar to that enacted in Alberta. The aforementioned suggestion can be implemented without removing the child from the home. This can be achieved through supervision, which is an important preventative mechanism, and can take a variety of forms—attendance by parents at counselling, treatment for alcoholism, and medical or psychiatric attention—with reports to be made of future assessments planned.

PART III

INSTITUTIONAL ABUSE

7–45 The last decade has seen an upsurge in the reporting of cases involving victims of abuse arising in institutional settings. Many such incidents came to light during the 1990s, revealed by the Madonna House Inquiry and RTÉ's documentary series, *States of Fear*. The systematic physical and sexual abuse of children in institutions established for the care of children became an area of national concern. The Commission to Inquire into Child Abuse—also known as the Laffoy Commission after its chairwoman Ms Justice Mary Laffoy—was established in 1999 to provide a forum for victims to seek redress against those who perpetrated the abuse. The Commission was established on a statutory basis under the Commission to Inquire into Child Abuse Act 2000 and has the power to compensate victims of child abuse in residential institutions without recourse to the Court.

7–46 The Commission to Inquiry into Child Abuse Act 2000 has four main functions: to afford an opportunity to persons who have suffered abuse in childhood institutions during the relevant period to tell their stories to a committee; to investigate the abuse of children in childhood institutions in order to determine the causes, nature, circumstances and extent of such abuse; to determine the extent to which childhood institutions, management and regulatory authorities had responsibility for the abuse; and to produce and publish a report. The "relevant period" is determined as being from and including 1940 (or such earlier year as the Commission may determine) up to and including the year 1999 and such later year (if any) as the Commission may determine.[50]

7–47 The institutions referred to include industrial schools, orphanages, reformatories, children's homes, hospitals and any other places where children are cared for other than as members of their families.

---

[50] The Statute of Limitations (Amendment) Act 2000 should also be noted. It became law on June 21, 2000. Its central provision is s.2, which extends the concept of disability contained in the Statute of Limitations 1957 to accommodate circumstances of childhood sexual abuse. Section 3 of the Act addresses the issue of delay and retains the power of a court "to dismiss an action on the ground of there being such delay between the accrual of the cause of action and the bringing of the action as, in the interests of justice, would warrant its dismissal".

The Laffoy Commission had its first public sitting on June 29, 2000. However, difficulties were systemic in the Commission, culminating in the resignation of Ms Justice Laffoy in September 2003, citing slowness in paying compensation as one of the reasons for her resignation.[51] Mr Justice Sean Ryan took over chairmanship of the Commission from Ms Justice Laffoy. While the Laffoy Commission was established as an alternative to litigation, the delay in achieving redress may leave victims with little alternative other than the court civil litigation process.

Vicarious liability

7–48 The area of abuse arising in an institutional setting raises complex issues, such as vicarious liability and negligence. The Irish courts have not had the opportunity to develop a test to determine the allocation of liability in the context of institutional abuse. Due to the lack of cases in Irish courts, it may be possible to learn from other common law countries which have dealt with similar issues.

The doctrine of vicarious liability has been used by the Canadian, American and English judiciaries to impose liability on institutions for child abuse perpetrated by employees, the rationale for which may be instructive to the Irish courts.

Canada

7–49 In Canada, it is clear from the Supreme Court decisions of *Bazley v Curry*[52] and *Jacobi v Griffiths*[53] that a residential care institution may be vicariously liable for the sexual assaults committed by an employee who is allocated parental duties. The case of *Bazley v Curry*[54] was the first time the Canadian judiciary considered the applicability of vicarious liability in the context of abuse in a children's home. Mr Curry was employed as a child councillor by the Children's Foundation, which provided residential care for children aged between six and 12 years. His duties essentially involved him being entrusted with the duties and obligations of a parent in the lives of the children placed in his care.[55] In 1991 Mr Curry was convicted on 18 counts of gross indecency and two counts of buggery, some of which involved the plaintiff victim. The Canadian Supreme Court held that in child abuse cases, "special attention should be paid to the existence of a power and dependency relationship, which on its own often creates a considerable risk of wrongdoing."[56]

---

[51] Ms Justice Laffoy's letter of resignation was published in *The Sunday Tribune*, September 7, 2003.

[52] (1999) 174 D.L.R. (4th) 45 Supreme Court of Canada, [1999] 2 S.C.R. 534.

[53] (1999) 174 D.L.R. (4th) 71 Supreme Court of Canada.

[54] (1999) 174 D.L.R. (4th) 45 Supreme Court of Canada [1999] 2 S.C.R. 534.

[55] These duties ranged from ensuring appropriate hygiene, ensuring that children obeyed the house rules and got to school on time, to tucking the children in at night, accompanying them on outings and physical activities, and dealing in an age-appropriate manner with children's questions regarding sexuality.

[56] *ibid.* A similar result occurred in *B(D) v Children's Aid Society of Durham Region* (1996) 136 D.L.R. 4th 297, Ontario Court of Appeal.

The Court held that imposing vicarious liability in incidences of sexual abuse may act as a deterrent by motivating organisations with the care of children to take not only such precautions as the law of negligence requires, but all reasonably practicable steps to ensure that their children are not sexually abused. The risk-based connection is fair to employers in that a risk connected to conditions of employment will generally be foreseeable and tying vicarious liability to this risk-based connection provides an adequate and just remedy for the injured party and deters future harm.[57]

7–50 The decision in *Bazley* has subsequently been refined. In *E.B. v Order of the Oblates of Mary Immaculate in the Province of British Columbia*,[58] the British Columbia Court of Appeal held that employers are not to be regarded as "involuntary insurers responsible for every wrongful act committed by employees". There must be a strong link between what was requested of the employee and the wrongful act, so that the employer greatly increased the risk of the harm by requiring of the employee the performance of the entrusted duties.[59]

7–51 The case of *Jacobi v Griffiths*[60] is also instructive in that the Supreme Court of Canada held that whenever an employer confers on an employee a parenting role in respect of children, giving that employee unhindered access to the children in a residential centre, the employer will be vicariously responsible if the employee abuses those children during the course of his or her employment. In this particular case there was not a sufficient connection found between the nature of the employee's role and the abuse that occurred. Here the defendant, Vernon Boys and Girls Club, which operated recreational programmes for children, had employed Griffiths as a programme director. The plaintiff Jacobi children, a brother and sister who resided in Vernon, were two children who used the club facilities. Griffiths co-ordinated after-school activities for children whom he was required to supervise. In the performance of his duties he was expected to foster good communication with the children, though he was not required to deliver services of a parental nature to the children using the facilities at the club. Griffiths, however, fostered a relationship with the Jacobi children and later subjected them to sexual assaults. Griffiths was dismissed from employment, charged and convicted. Proceedings were brought against the club on behalf of the Jacobi children seeking damages for the sexual abuse by Griffiths. The Supreme Court of Canada held that the fact the club provided an opportunity to develop a rapport with the children was not a sufficient connection for vicarious liability as Griffiths had no "job created authority to insinuate himself into the intimate lives of these children".[61]

---

[57] M. Hall, "After Waterhouse: vicarious liability and the tort of institutional abuse" (2000) 22, 2 *Journal of Social Welfare and Family Law* 159–173 at 168.
[58] [2003] B.C.J. No. 1123.
[59] [2003] B.C.J. No. 1123, para.24.
[60] (1999) 174 D.L.R. (4th) 71 Supreme Court of Canada.
[61] (1999) 174 D.L.R. (4th) 71 Supreme Court of Canada.

7–52   The American judiciary has followed a similar line of reasoning to its Canadian counterparts in *DeShaney v Winnebago County Dept. of Social Services*.[62] The United States Supreme Court in that case held that the state has a duty of care towards children in its care. However, this duty only arises when the state takes a person into its custody, and so deprives that person of the ability to care for himself or herself.

England and Wales

7–53   In England and Wales, in both *Barrett v Enfield London Borough Council*[63] and *Lister v Hesley Hall Ltd*,[64] the House of Lords placed considerable weight on the decisions of *Bazley v Curry* and *Jacobi v Griffiths*; Lord Steyn in *Lister v Hesley Hall Ltd* believed they were of "high persuasive value". In that case the employers of a warden in a school boarding house were held vicariously liable for the warden's sexual abuse of boys in his care. In reaching this finding, the close relationship between the warden's wrongdoing and the nature of the parental duties assigned to him by his employees was significant.

Lister represents a significant departure from the previously narrow approach taken by the Court of Appeal in *Trotman v North Yorkshire County Council*,[65] where vicarious liability was not found against the employer of a deputy headmaster, who sexually assaulted a handicapped teenager in his care during a foreign holiday.

7–54   As well as *Lister*, several other cases evidence a swing away from the restrictive approach taken by the courts. A relevant and instructive case is *Barrett v Enfield London Borough Council*.[66] In *Barrett*, the plaintiff (then in his twenties), who had been in care from when he was a baby through to his majority, brought an action in negligence against Enfield London Borough Council claiming for personal injury. He alleged breaches by the authority of its duty to protect him from physical, emotional, psychiatric and psychological injury and to promote his welfare. In particular, he mentioned the State's failure to place him for adoption and unsatisfactory foster-care placements. He alleged that if the defendant has not breached its duties, he would not on the balance of probabilities have left the care of the local authority as a young man of 18 years with no family or attachments, who had developed a psychiatric illness causing him to self-harm and become involved in criminal activities.[67] Although no analogous case had succeeded, the House of Lords believed that it could incrementally extend the pre-existing duties of care.[68] The question of whether

---

[62] (1989) 489 U.S. 189, 103 L. ed. 2d 149, 109 S. Ct. 998.

[63] [1999] 3 W.L.R. 79 at 106.

[64] [2001] U.K.H.L. 22; [2001] 2 F.L.R. 307, 312 H.L.; [2001] 2 Wlr. 1311, 1316; [2001] 2 F.C.R. 97.

[65] [1999] L.G.R. 584.

[66] [1999] 2 F.L.R. 426; [1998] Q.B. 367; [1997] 3 All E.R. 171; [1997] 2 F.L.R. 167.

[67] [19991] 2 F.L.R. 426 at 434. The plaintiff complained of the authority's failure to arrange his adoption, unsatisfactory placements with foster parent and in community homes, lack of monitoring, and failure to manage his reintroduction to relatives.

[68] [1999] 3 All E.R. 193 at 208.

it was fair, just and reasonable to impose a duty of care was to be decided on the facts proven, not in the abstract on the basis of assumed hypothetical facts.[69] Emphasising the movement towards a broader approach, the Court of Appeal in *D, K & RK, RK & Anor*[70] held that human rights considerations applied in relation to the position of the child.[71]

There is now a strong body of international judicial opinion supporting the imposition of liability on those responsible for the abuse of children placed within their care. As well as recourse to vicarious liability, the Canadian Courts have also applied equitable doctrines in cases of child abuse.

Equitable principles

7–55 The Canadian judiciary have utilised equitable principles as a remedy for sexual abuse within the family. La Forest J., in the case of *K.(M.) v H.(M.)*,[72] observed that "it is intuitively apparent that the relationship between parent and child is fiduciary in nature".[73] Breach of fiduciary duty has been found in cases of father-daughter incest,[74] and in *J. v J.*,[75] a mother was held in breach for not taking any action to protect her daughter from sexual abuse by her father.

7–56 The extent of this duty was broadened in *Justice v Cairnie Estate*,[76] where Scott C.J.M. held that social workers could fall to be considered within the scope of the fiduciary relationship.[77] In the subsequent case of *A.(C.) v Critchley*,[78] however, McEachern C.J.B.C. held that breach of a fiduciary duty should be confined to cases where the defendant does not act honestly and in good faith, and personally takes advantage of a relationship of trust for his or her own personal advantage.

While equitable principles have proven flexible in providing a remedy in child abuse cases, the preferred approach of international jurisdictions in cases of institutional child abuse has been the imposition of vicarious liability. In Ireland, in the absence of an authoritative Supreme Court decision, it remains to be seen whether statutory authorities will be held liable where the negligent performance of their child welfare protection is proven to have facilitated abuse.

---

[69] [1999] 3 All E.R. 193; [1999] 3 W.L.R. 79 (HL); [1999] 2 F.L.R. 426. *See also Phelps v Hillingdon London Borough Council* [1999] 1 All E.R. 421; and [1999] 1 W.L.R. 500 which support this decision.
[70] *D. v East Berkshire Community Health NHS Trust, Dewsbury Healthcare NHS Trust & Anor. and Oldham NHS Trust and Anor* [2003] E.W.C.A. Civ. 1151; [2003] All E.R. (D) 547 (Jul).
[71] *Barrett* has subsequently been applied in the cases of *S v Gloucestershire County Council, L v Tower Hamlets London Borough Council* [2000] 1 F.L.R. 828, [2001] Fam. 313 C.A., [2001] 2 W.L.R. 909.
[72] (1992) 96 D.L.R. 4th 289.
[73] At p.323.
[74] *K.(M.) v H.(M.)* (1992) 96 D.L.R. 4th 289; *C v C* (1994) 114 D.L.R. 4th 151.
[75] (1993) 102 D.L.R. 4th 177.
[76] (1993) 105 D.L.R. 4th Manitoba Court of Appeal.
[77] At p.511.
[78] (1999) 1666 D.L.R. 4th 475 British Columbia Court of Appeal.

That said, children who have been subjected to abuse while in care could bring a complaint under the European Convention for the Protection of Human Rights and Fundamental Freedoms, an issue which is discussed in Chapter 12.

Conclusion

7–57 International judicial opinion and the European Court of Human Rights have established substantive rights for victims of institutional child abuse against the State. The doctrine of vicarious liability and equitable principles have been used to provide remedies for children abused while in the care of the State. While seeking justice through the courts may provide victims with compensation, it could be an expensive and protracted process. The Laffoy Commission offers the possibility of an efficient and compassionate resolution to victims of institutional abuse. However, the problems encountered by the Commission since its inception may result in victims of abuse looking to the courts for justice and compensation.

PART IV

Child Pornography and the Trafficking of Children

7–58 Child pornography is a serious and escalating problem, both in Ireland and internationally. Society today is inundated with sexually explicit materials through most modes of communication: print, audio and video. The advancement of technology means that such material can be distributed quickly and extensively as media such as the internet are not limited by geographical boundaries. A recent example of sexually explicit material being transmitted via picture-capable mobile phones illustrates the challenge posed by evolving technology.[79] Further, a study by Livingstone in 2001 suggested that 90 per cent of children had viewed pornography on the internet.[80]

It should be noted that although the term "child pornography" is widely used, a preferred terminology gaining acceptance internationally is "abuse images", "abusive images", or "images of sexually exploited children".

7–59 Professionals from a number of sectors have expressed concerns about the problem of images of sexually exploited children, and the need to protect children worldwide from victimisation in the pornography industry. In October 2002, the International Centre for Missing and Exploited Children (ICMEC) held its first forum in Dublin to debate the extent of the problem, with the ultimate aim of developing an action plan to address it at an international

---

[79] J.H. Downes, "Gardaí seek distributor of explicit image of girl on phone", *The Irish Times*, January 23, 2004.

[80] S. Livingstone, "Online Freedom and Safety for Children" (London School of Economics and Political Science, November 2001); www.ippr.org.uk/research/files/team25/project72/IPPR.pdf.

level. The campaign, titled the "Dublin Plan", agreed a 10-point action plan to address the problem of child pornography:

"(a) build public awareness of the problem of child pornography;
(b) demand that child pornography be placed high on the political agenda;
(c) create an international child pornography monitoring and oversight system;
(d) undertake extensive research to define and measure the extent of the problem;
(e) examine and evaluate best practice;
(f) develop and promote systems for identifying the victims of child pornography;
(g) develop and promote model legislation and ensure consistence of law between jurisdictions;
(h) enhance the capacity of law enforcement to investigate child pornography;
(i) promote international sharing and co-ordination between and among law enforcement, internet hotlines, the media and others;
(j) promote stronger involvement by private sector entities, including internet service providers, non-governmental organisations and others."[81]

7–60 Ireland has addressed the issue of child pornography and the trafficking of children through robust legislation in the form of the Child Trafficking and Pornography Acts 1998 to 2004[82] (the "1998 and 2004 Acts").

By criminalising the production, distribution and possession of child pornography, this Act provides very valuable protection against the pernicious activities of paedophiles. Of particular importance is the interpretation section of the Act, which specifically includes the following:

"(a) any visual representation—
    (i) that shows or, in the case of a document, relates to a person who

---

[81] International Centre for Missing and Exploited Children (M. Taylor), *Creating a Global Agenda to Combat Child Pornography* (Virginia USA, International Centre for Missing and Exploited Children, November 2003) at p.48.

[82] The Child Trafficking and Pornography (Amendment) Act 2004 (No.17 of 2004) amended the Child Trafficking and Pornography Act 1998 (No.22 of 1998) by inserting the following section after s.12 of the 1998 Act:
"13.—Nothing in this Act prevents—
    (*a*) the giving of or compliance with a direction under section 3 of the Committees of the Houses of the Oireachtas (Compellability, Privileges and Immunities of Witnesses) Act 1997, or
    (*b*) the possession, distribution, printing, publication or showing by either House of the Oireachtas, a committee (within the meaning of that Act) or any person of child pornography for the purposes of, or in connection with, the performance of any function conferred by the Constitution or by law on those Houses or conferred by a resolution of either of those Houses or resolutions of both of them on such a committee."

is or is depicted as being a child and who is engaged in or is depicted as being engaged in explicit sexual activity,

(ii) that shows or, in the case of a document, relates to a person who is or is depicted as being a child and who is engaged in or is depicted as witnessing any such activity by any person or persons, or

(iii) whose dominant characteristics is the depiction for a sexual purpose, of the genital or anal region of a child,

(b) any visual or audio representation that advocates, encourages or counsels any sexual activity with children which is an offence under any enactment, or

(c) any visual representation or description or information relating to, a child that indicates or implies that the child is available to be used for the purpose of sexual exploitation within the meaning of s.3,

irrespective of how or through what medium the representation, description or information has been produced, transmitted or conveyed and, without prejudice to the generality of the foregoing, includes any representation, description or other electronic or mechanical means...."

7–61 In summary, the 1998 and 2004 Acts protect children in three ways. First, they protect against the trafficking of children for the purpose of their sexual exploitation.[83] Secondly, they protect children from being used and thereby sexualised and abused, in the making of child pornography. Finally, they criminalise the possession of child pornography.

7–62 New offences introduced by the 1998 and 2004 Acts include child trafficking and taking a child for sexual exploitation;[84] permitting a child to be used for pornography;[85] producing and distributing child pornography;[86] and the possession of child pornography.[87] The District Court (Child Trafficking and Pornography Act 1998) Rules 1999 set down the procedure for the issue of a warrant under s.7 of the 1998 and 2004 Acts. In particular, Ord.23, r.11(1) of the District Court Rules 1997 provides that an application for such a warrant may be made to the District Court judge for the District Court district "wherein the place in respect of which the warrant is sought is situated".[88] A formidable obstacle in prosecuting child pornographers is the means by which the age of the victim (defined as a person under 17 years of age) can be proven for the purposes of the Act. This problem is circumvented by s.2(3) of the Child Trafficking and Pornography Acts 1998 and 2004, which provide that:

---

[83] A report, titled *Trafficking in Unaccompanied Minors*, published in June 2004 by the International Organisation for Migration, held that 40 children a year are being trafficked to the Republic of Ireland for either ethnic or sexual exploitation. The report also notes the increased presence of unaccompanied minors within the asylum process. In 2003, the figure was 918.

[84] s.3.

[85] s.4.

[86] s.5.

[87] s.6.

[88] S.I. No. 216 of 1999.

"In any proceedings for an offence under ss.3, 4, 5 or 6 a person shall be deemed, unless the contrary is proved, to be or have been a child or to be or have been depicted or represented as a child, at any time if the person appears to the court to be or have been a child, or to be or have been so depicted or represented at the time."

7–63   In essence, the 1998 and 2004 Acts are part of a series of legislative initiatives designed to protect children against sexual abuse and exploitation.

The 1998 and 2004 Acts were utilised in a recent investigation by Gardaí into the circulation of pornographic images of a schoolgirl through the use of camera phones. This investigation and the concern regarding the potential for mobile phones to be used inappropriately received widespread media coverage.[89] Ireland has the highest proportion of mobile phone usage in the European community and mobile connectivity to the internet, as described by the Minister for Justice, Equality and Law Reform, Mr McDowell, "means there is a PC in everyone's pocket".[90] This technology presents new challenges when compared to the internet, as it makes it more difficult to trace messages back to the original sender. Recently, Mr Dermot Ahern TD, the former Minister for Communications, the Marine and Natural Resources, stated that the Government intended to introduce a national register of the next 3G phones. As these new phones are capable of carrying video clips, it is clear that the creation of a national register is directly aimed at protecting children.

The increase of public awareness in the issue of abuse images of children has been further aided by the extensive media coverage of the arrests and trials of alleged offenders in relation to child pornography charges. These trials have raised concerns as to sentencing policy in respect of such charges and an inconsistency in the disclosure of the names of alleged offenders, both of which need to be addressed.

7–64   The Dublin Plan (see para.7–59) and the UN Optional Protocol to the 1989 UN Convention on the Rights of the Child[91] offer Ireland the opportunity to build on domestic legislation to find ways of combating the problem of child pornography. Technical advances require such initiatives to look beyond national borders and therefore must involve international co-operation to effectively protect children from victimisation.

---

[89] J. Downes, "Gardaí seek distributor of explicit image of girl on phone", *The Irish Times*, January 23, 2004.

[90] For example see: K. Holland, "Mobile camera phone girl is identified", *The Irish Times*, January 29, 2004; J. Downes, "Focus on identifying schoolgirl is criticised", *The Irish Times*, January 28, 2004; and T. Shiel, "Call for schools to ban photo phones", *The Irish Times*, February 11, 2004.

[91] This UN Protocol entered into force on February 12, 2002.

PART V

CHILD CARE SERVICES

7–65 Significant social change has altered the nature of the family in Ireland. Factors such as equal opportunities for men and women and growing economic demands have created an environment where both parents pursue careers in paid employment. This has resulted in an increasing demand for child care services, as more and more young children spend at least part of the day with a child carer. This may be in the form of private pre-school, nursery, crèche or day care, whether in the child carer's home or in the child's home. The growth in this field has been unmatched by Government regulation, which was recognised by the Department of Health and Children review group established in February 2002 to make recommendations on the law in this area. The present legal responsibilities of persons caring for children in this context can be found in the common law and primarily Pt VII of the Child Care Act 1991 (the "1991 Act").

The common law

7–66 The common law has long imposed a duty on those having care of children.[92] Under the general law of criminal or tort liability, a person who has the care of a child may be held liable where a child is assaulted, ill-treated, neglected, abandoned, or exposed in a manner likely to cause unnecessary suffering or injury to health. The person who has care of the child stands *in loco parentis*, albeit temporarily. This provides the carer with the powers of a parent so far as is reasonably necessary for the discharge of his or her duties. The duty imposed on a carer by the common law may be enlarged where the child care is both regular and lengthy in duration.

In general, a person who has temporary care of a child has no powers relating to the education or medical treatment, of the child. However, there may be a duty to avail of medical treatment, such as giving consent to medical treatment where the child does not have the capacity to give consent and an emergency arises requiring immediate action to save the life of the child.

The Child Care Act 1991

7–67 Part VII of the 1991 Act is the first attempt to regulate child care services in Ireland. The services covered include pre-school, play-group, day nursery, crèche and day-care services catering for pre-school children.[93] Section 50 of the 1991 Act facilitated the introduction of the Child Care (Pre-School) Regulations 1996 and the Child Care (Pre-School Services) (Amendment) Regulations 1997. These Regulations are concerned mainly with safeguarding the safety, health and welfare in the physical environment in which the children

---

[92] See *R. v Griffin* (1869) 11 Cox C.C. 275 and *R. v Gibbens and Proctor* (1918) 13 Cr. App. Rep. 134.

[93] s.49 of the Child Care Act 1991.

are cared for. They prescribe required safety standards, for example: those in relation to the use of fire-retardant materials;[94] a suitably equipped first-aid box; and arrangements to summon medical assistance in an emergency.[95] The emphasis of the regulations are on health and safety issues and do not, as such, ensure quality of care. Indeed, there is no specific requirement that staff have special professional training.

Child carers

7–68   There is a lack of guidance in the 1991 Act as to what is a competent child carer. The focus on the physical environment has overlooked critical issues such as who is a competent or fit child carers. Under the present situation it may fall to the courts to decide these factors. It is an area that should be clarified by statutory amendment to protect children and those using child care, by ensuring that services are provided to an acceptable standard.

Any statutory reform should be guided by the comprehensive guidelines issued by the Department of Health in England which provided the following factors when assessing a child carer:

(a) previous experience of looking after, or working with, young children or people with disabilities or the elderly;

(b) qualifications and training in a relevant field such as child care, early years' education, health visiting, nursing or other caring activities;

(c) ability to provide warm and consistent care, commitment and knowledge to treat all children as individuals and with equal concern;

(d) knowledge of, and attitude to, multicultural issues and people of different racial origins;

(e) physical health; and

(f) mental stability, integrity and flexibility.

7–69   These guidelines were expanded in 1993[96] to state that the most important issue is the general overall quality of care rather than each individual factor being used to conclude a person unfit. The House of Lords supported this approach in the case of *Sutton London Borough Council v Davis*[97] when considering the local authority's refusal to register the applicant, Mrs Davis, because of its policy that child carers undertake not to use corporal punishment on children in their care. Mrs Davis had refused to give an undertaking to this effect as the mother had authorised such action. Although lawful to adopt such a policy, this did not oblige the local authority to adopt it as a "blanket"

---

[94] Art.27 of the Child Care (Pre-School Services) Regulations 1996 addresses fire drills, heating, secure doors, gates and fencing, hazardous objects and the temperature of hot running water.

[95] Arts 5 and 6 of the Child Care (Pre-School Services) Regulations 1996.

[96] LAC (93).

[97] [1995] 1 All E.R. 53.

policy when assessing suitability of child carers to be registered. The House of Lords held that the totality of the evidence needed to be looked at.

7–70 In England and Wales, police are obliged to check that adults working in any child care setting have nothing in their backgrounds that would adversely affect their suitability to hold a position of trust in relation to children.[98] Ireland had, until very recently, no such vetting system. Health boards were not always required to check previous criminal records of persons working in child care provision. This lack of regulation compromised the welfare and safety of pre-school children.[99]

This is likely to change under new proposals announced by the Minister of State at the Department of Health and Children, Mr Brian Lenihan TD, on September 23, 2004. The proposals include a major extension of the role of the Central Garda Vetting Unit with the number of staff increasing from 13 to 30. It is therefore likely, according to the Minister, that within months, anyone wishing to be employed as a teacher or wishing to work in a school or crèche or in the voluntary sector with children will first have to obtain Garda clearance.

Child care facilities

7–71 Part VII of the 1991 Act defines pre-school service very broadly, covering almost all forms of child care or minding activities except for those expressly prevented by s.58. This section means that Pt VII will not apply where care of pre-school children is undertaken by their relatives; or where the person taking care of the pre-school children of one family does so in the child carer's home; or where a person is taking care of not more than three pre-school children of different families. This section attempts to avoid interfering with arrangements made by parents with a relative or neighbour to look after their children. Child carers have been found to be one of the most popular alternatives for parents in Ireland seeking day care.[100] This exclusion raises concerns, as there are a significant number of children being cared for in environments which are exempted from regulation and cannot be said to protect the welfare of the child.

7–72 People operating pre-school and child care services are required to notify the relevant health board of their existence in the prescribed manner, according to s.51 of the 1991 Act. Further, Art.9 of the Child Care (Pre-School Services) Regulations 1996 requires notice of the pre-school service to be furnished to the relevant health board within six months of the date of commencement of Pt VII.[101]

---

[98] See English Disqualification for Caring for Children Regulations 1991, S.I. No. 2094 of 1991.

[99] See *M.Q. v Gleeson*, unreported, High Court, Barr J., February 13, 1997.

[100] Congress Report of Survey of Childcare Practices, *Identifying Members Childcare Needs* (Irish Congress of Trade Unions, Dublin, 2002).

[101] This part of this Act is operative since December 18, 1996 by virtue of the Child Care Act 1991 (Commencement) Order, 1996 (S.I. No.349 of 1991).

7–73 Health boards are required to supervise child care services, once notified, by visiting and inspecting the premises where the service is being provided to ensure the duties imposed under s.52 of the 1991 Act are being fulfilled.[102] Section 55 gives inspectors wide-ranging powers of inspection, which powers are augmented by criminal sanction.[103]

Although a step in the right direction, the current statutory framework is limited in its effectiveness, requiring notification rather than a register of approved pre-school services. A health board in Ireland would not be civilly liable for any harm resulting to a child in a pre-school service that had been notified to the board. This can be contrasted to other jurisdictions such as England, where the local authorities can be held accountable through the registration process. In the case of *T. v Surrey County Council*,[104] a local authority was held liable for negligent misstatement when an officer of the authority informed T.'s mother that there was no reason why a child should not be placed in the particular child-minder's care when the local authority knew, or ought to have known, that there was a significant risk in placing a child in the care of that person. The court held that the officer was speaking as a professional with special knowledge and responsibility who knew, or ought to have known, that what he said related directly to the safety of the infant and would be relied upon by T.'s mother.[105] The expotential growth in the area of child care has not been matched with the development of a framework to monitor the carer and safeguard against abuse of the child. The current powers of health boards could be extended to allow registering and inspection of all child carers to provide a form of quality control over child care.

Conclusion

7–74 Growth in the child care industry has not been matched by statutory regulation to ensure a quality service is provided. The current law focuses on environment issues and safety concerns. However, it is arguable that the more important areas of quality of care and the carer's role in assisting the development of children have not been addressed. An integrated legislative policy is required to promote the interests of the child, and reassure parents or guardians that a quality service is being provided.

---

[102] s.51 of the 1991 Act.

[103] s.57 of the 1991 Act.

[104] [1994] 4 All E.R. 577.

[105] *ibid.* at 601. See also the English Care Standards Act 2000, operative since September 2001, where the Office for Standards in Education (OFSTED) has assumed responsibility from local authorities for the registration, regulation and inspection of childcare providers.

CHAPTER 8

THE INVOLVEMENT OF CHILDREN IN THE COURT PROCESS

PART I

CHILDREN GIVING EVIDENCE—PRACTICE AND PROCEDURE

8–01 A court can be an intimidating place even for a worldly adult. For a child it must be especially so. A key concern ought to be to avoid the process causing additional trauma to the children involved. Several commentators have referred to the stress involved in testifying in open court as a "revictimisation", or secondary victimisation. A child already scarred by the subject-matter of the proceedings may be further traumatised by the process of testifying in court in relation to such matters. In addition to preventing trauma, there is also a further concern of a more judicial nature. The court will also be concerned to ensure that a child giving evidence will be able to give as full, accurate and coherent an account of his or her experiences as possible. A belief that this is not always possible, added to the fear of further traumatising the child, often results in the courts failing to hear the evidence of children. The prevailing wisdom, it seems, has been that the benefit of hearing the child's evidence is generally outweighed by the danger of the child incurring "secondary trauma" as a result of being exposed to the formal questioning of legal personnel.

Both of the concerns noted above are no doubt genuine and worthy. The inevitable result, however, is that the child is often effectively silenced in such proceedings, perhaps to the detriment of his or her ultimate welfare. The right of children to be heard can no longer be sidelined, especially in the light of our obligations under the United Nations Convention on the Rights of the Child 1989. The latter convention makes it clear that in matters concerning the future safety and welfare of a child of sufficient age and maturity, the child in question has a right to have his or her views and concerns noted by the court.

8–02 The testimony of a child is obviously of particular importance in the context of cases involving child sexual abuse. Because of the nature of the offence, and the secluded context in which it usually occurs, there may be no other evidence to corroborate that of the child. Thus, the need to facilitate child witnesses becomes especially important.

The former (and widely held) view that the testimony of children is not fully to be trusted has nowadays dissipated somewhat. Clinical professionals in particular now widely accept that children do not fabricate abuse allegations and should generally be believed when making such allegations.

Problems still remain, however, in the context of the giving of evidence before a court, especially where matters of a sexual nature are concerned. Children often face having to give evidence about confusing and embarrassing events in open court. The distress is often exacerbated by the presence of the accused during the giving of such testimony.

8–03 Placed in such an environment, it is no wonder that children often fail to be able to give a full and coherent account of their experiences. The credibility of even the most honest child can be weakened by a skillful cross-examination. Aggressive questioning and the use of intimidating or embarrassing language can engender confusion and highlight childish inconsistencies that further undermine the coherence and credibility of a child's testimony. Often (and particularly in the context of child sexual abuse cases) a child lacks the vocabulary necessary to describe specifically a particular experience.

In this regard, some advances have been made. Statutory reform has allowed the family courts to reduce to a minimum the formality involved in a family case. Great efforts have been made to alleviate unnecessary formality, for instance, by prohibiting the wearing of wigs and gowns by either judges or legal representatives in family proceedings in the Circuit Family Court and High Court. This is a worthy gesture designed to normalise the atmosphere of the court in such cases. It was effected by s.33 of the Judicial Separation and Family Law Reform Act 1989, which further requires that all such proceedings be as informal as is possible in all the circumstances. It is worth noting, in addition, that the personal kindness and concern of judges and legal personnel alike frequently comes to the fore in such stressful circumstances. The courts must be careful, however, not to throw caution to the winds. Such informality as is permitted must be consistent with the administration of justice and must be without prejudice to the rights of the parties.

8–04 Procedural changes have also allowed the child to be seated in the well of the court along with the judge, counsel and solicitors and to be accompanied by a friend or relative, willing and able to support the child if needs be. Amplification equipment has been installed in some courts to facilitate greater ease of communication. Occasionally, an interpreter may be appointed to clarify or explain certain questions being asked of, or answers being made by, the child.

An additional safeguard is that of privacy. The proceedings of all family cases are exempted from the general constitutional requirement that justice be administered in public.[1] This would appear to be one of the "special and limited cases" contemplated by the Constitution in which justice may be administered otherwise than in public.

---

[1] See Art.34.1 of the Constitution and s.45(1)(b) of the Courts (Supplemental Provisions) Act 1961 (No. 39 of 1961). See also s.34 of the Judicial Separation and Family Law Reform Act 1989, s.38(6) of the Family Law Act 1995, and s.38(5) of the Family Law (Divorce) Act 1996, as amended by s.40 of the Civil Liability and Courts Act 2004.

8–05   In light of the negative impact of court hearings upon children, the overriding preference of judges has been to exclude children from legal proceedings. Indeed, both the Child Care Act 1991 ("the 1991 Act")[2] and the amended Guardianship of Infants Act 1964[3] allow the court to hear cases concerning the welfare of children in the absence of those children. While a child may apply to be present at a hearing, the court may exclude such child if, having regard to his or her age and the nature of the proceedings, it feels that it would not be in the child's interest to allow him or her to be present.

The exclusion of children from the process may, however, be to the detriment of the child's right to have his or her interests duly considered by the court. To this end, several innovative methods have been formulated to enable a child's voice to be heard in the judicial process, in some cases without requiring the child to be physically present in court.

(a) The admissibility of hearsay evidence

8–06   The rule against hearsay states that a statement initially made outside court by any person may not be repeated in court. There are indeed many exceptions to this rule but the basic thrust is described succinctly in *Cross and Tapper on Evidence* as follows:

> "[A] statement other than one made by a person while giving oral evidence in the proceedings is inadmissible as evidence of any fact stated".[4]

The rationale behind this may quite simply be that what a person says is not always good evidence of what they, in fact, do. Nonetheless, enforced to its full extent, it is obvious that such a rule would cause great hardship. In the context of child law proceedings, it may prevent evidence being given by a person who has interviewed a child as to the content of that interview. Thus, short of presenting the child as a witness, such evidence could not be admitted. In both public law and private law family proceedings, however, the rule has been eroded considerably.

8–07   In the context of public child law cases, the inclusion of hearsay evidence is permitted, albeit at the discretion of the court. The Supreme Court affirmed this proposition in *Southern Health Board v C.H.*,[5] a case involving the admissibility of a video-recorded interview with a child.

Section 23 of the Children Act 1997 ("the 1997 Act"), furthermore, permits the inclusion of hearsay evidence of any fact in all proceedings relating to the welfare of a child, public or private. The legislation also applies in cases relating to any person who has a mental disability to such an extent that independent living is not feasible. However, in all cases to which s.23 relates, several conditions apply as listed below:

---

[2]   s.30.

[3]   s.27 as inserted by s.11 of the Children Act 1997.

[4]   Tapper, *Cross and Tapper on Evidence* (9th ed., Butterworths, London, 1999), p.6.

[5]   [1996] 1 I.R. 219.

(i) the court must be satisfied that the child in question is either unable to give evidence by reason of age or that the giving of oral evidence (in person or by television link) would not be in the interests of the child's welfare;[6]

(ii) evidence of a fact will only be admitted if direct oral evidence of such fact would also have been admissible;[7]

(iii) such statement cannot be admitted if, in the opinion of the court, its inclusion would be to the detriment of the interests of justice, in particular if its inclusion would result in unfairness to any of the parties to the proceedings;[8]

(iv) prior to hearsay evidence being admitted, all interested parties to the proceedings must be given notice of the proposal to submit such evidence. This should be accompanied by such particulars of, or relating to, the evidence as are considered reasonable and practicable in all the circumstances, to allow the parties to deal with any matter arising from its being hearsay.[9] This condition does not apply where the parties, by agreement, consent that it should not apply;[10]

(v) s.23 does not apply to proceedings started before the commencement of Pt III of the 1997 Act, that is January 1, 1999.

8–08 In *Eastern Health Board v Mooney*,[11] the High Court considered the right to give hearsay evidence in proceedings initiated under the 1991 Act. The High Court case arose from a consultative case stated by the District Court in relation to the admissibility of hearsay evidence. This case pre-dated the coming into force of the equivalent provisions of the Children Act 1997; so they were not considered. That said, Carney J. provides some useful guidance in outlining the position as follows:

1. hearsay evidence can be admissible in cases initiated under the 1991 Act, where appropriate;[12]

2. where witnesses in cases initiated under the 1991 Act are competent and compellable to give the requisite evidence as direct evidence, the hearsay evidence is admissible, having regard to the circumstances of the case. That said, where witnesses are compellable, competent and available, hearsay evidence may not be appropriate or necessary;

---

[6] s.23(1).
[7] s.23(1).
[8] s.23(2).
[9] s.23(3).
[10] s.23(4).
[11] unreported, High Court, March 28, 1998.
[12] See also the judgments of *Re K. (infants)* unreported, High Court, January 18, 1996, *Southern Health Board v C.H.* [1996] 1 I.R. 219 and *Eastern Health Board v M.K. and M.K.*, unreported, Supreme Court, January 29, 1999 (in relation to the admissibility of hearsay evidence in wardship proceedings).

3.   foster parents are compellable witnesses in proceedings initiated under the 1991 Act. The District Court judge is entitled to call them of his or her own motion if, having regard to the circumstances of the case, he is of the view it is appropriate to do so.

Weight to be given to such evidence

8–09   When hearsay evidence is admitted by virtue of s.23, the court must also turn its attention to s.24 of the 1997 Act. This relates to the weight to be given to such evidence. The court is generally required to have regard to all circumstances from which any inference can be drawn as to its accuracy or otherwise, but in particular must consider the following:

(a)   was the original statement made at the time of, or as soon as possible after, the event to which it relates? Obviously, the closer to the event, the greater the likelihood of accuracy;

(b)   does the evidence involve multiple hearsay?[13]

(c)   does any person involved have any vested interest in concealing or misrepresenting the matter or matters? Take, for instance, the case of a person accused of abusing a child informally questioning that child relating to the matter. It may be the case that the court would consider inadmissible evidence of the child's answers;

(d)   to what extent, if any, was the original statement an edited account? To what extent, if any, was such statement made in collaboration with another for a particular purpose? Obviously, an edited account will be of lesser weight, particularly where the person relating it has a vested interest in the case;

(e)   were the circumstances in which the evidence was gathered such as to suggest an attempt to prevent the proper consideration of its weight?

8–10   Section 25 of the 1997 Act allows evidence regarding the credibility of the child to be admitted, notwithstanding the fact that the child is not, strictly speaking, a witness.

Section 26 of the 1997 Act allows a copy of any document—which for these purposes includes a sound recording and a video-recording—to be admitted in evidence in proceedings where s.23 allows hearsay evidence to be admitted. The document, by definition, need not be an original. Indeed, it is not necessary that the original document be still in existence. It is possible to produce a copy or facsimile thereof, and for these purposes it is not relevant how many removes there are between the copy and the original.[14] The court may prescribe such means of authentication as to it appear proper.

---

[13] For example, evidence of more than one statement made outside the confines of the court.

[14] For example, the document may be a copy of a copy.

8–11 Hearsay evidence may also be admitted in wardship proceedings. This was affirmed in *Eastern Health Board v M.K. and M.K.*,[15] where the Supreme Court referred with approval to the changes in the Children Act 1997. It noted that, provided the court is satisfied that introduction of hearsay evidence is necessary and that its content is reliable, the court may admit it. The similarity to the provisions of the Act is obvious, although the ability to give direct weight to such statements, by contrast with s.24 of the 1997 Act, remains uncertain.

(b) Evidence given by television link

8–12 The concern with preventing trauma and ensuring that a child's evidence is as coherent as possible, has motivated several other evidential reforms. One is the possibility of a child giving evidence by means of a live television/video link. This allows the evidence of a child to be broadcast live in court but from a separate room.

   This method of giving evidence was pioneered, however, not in family cases but in the field of criminal trials. The Criminal Evidence Act 1992 was the first statutory provision in this jurisdiction to allow for the giving of evidence from a room separate from the court. This evidence, is in turn, broadcast live into the court. Owing to the departure from standard courtroom proceedings, there were, inevitably, major concerns regarding the constitutionality of such provisions, the key fear being that this facility might undermine the accused's right to "face his accuser". The constitutionality of these provisions has, nonetheless, been first affirmed in the High Court in *White v Ireland*,[16] and later upheld in the Supreme Court decision of *Donnelly v Ireland*.[17] The Supreme Court made it clear, however, that sufficient other safeguards must be put in place to ensure that this method of presenting evidence does not prejudice the accused. It noted in particular that the use of the video-link in this case did not prejudice the accused's rights because the child had given evidence under oath. This begs the question, whether the video-link procedure may be used where a child has not sworn an oath. In Ireland, after all, provision is made, most notably for younger children, who do not understand the nature of such an oath, to forego it.[18] Would this preclude the giving of video-linked testimony?

8–13 Notwithstanding these concerns, the 1997 Act, building on the advances made in the criminal sphere, has now extended this live television video-link facility to civil proceedings concerning the welfare of a child. Section 21 of that Act allows for the court to permit the giving of evidence, in any such case, by means of a live television link. While the evidence will be broadcast live, there is also a further requirement that it be video-recorded (presumably for the further perusal of the judge and, where necessary, of any appellate court). One remarkable feature is that such evidence may be made from outside

---

[15] unreported, Supreme Court, January 29, 1999.
[16] [1995] 2 I.R. 268.
[17] [1998] 1 I.R. 321.
[18] See s.28 of the Children Act 1997.

the State. However, any material statement made during the proceedings by a child giving evidence outside the State will be treated as if made within the State. Thus, where the child makes a statement that he or she knows to be false or does not believe to be true, that child will be guilty of perjury or of an offence under s.28 of the 1997 Act as if such offence had been committed in Ireland.

8–14 A standard procedure associated with court proceedings is that of identification in open court. Where a person is mentioned, particularly in connection with an allegation of wrongdoing, a court may require the person mentioned to be identified by the speaker in open court. This would of course undermine the efficacy of s.21 of the 1997 Act, and to this end it is possible for a child to forego this requirement.[19] If the child gives evidence by television link, as contemplated by s.21, that he or she knew a person before the commencement of the proceedings, it will not be necessary for the child to identify such person in open court. This obviates the trauma often associated with court proceedings where alleged wrongdoers and their victims are thrown together in open court.

8–15 A further safeguard for the child is contained in s.22 of the 1997 Act. This allows evidence, given by means of a television link, to be conveyed through an intermediary. This may be done provided that the court is satisfied that, having regard to the age and mental condition of the child, evidence should be gathered through such an intermediary.[20] The benefit of this approach is that it enables questions to be put to the child in language that he or she understands. Indeed, the Act requires as much.[21] The court must also be satisfied that the intermediary is competent to perform such a task.[22] It may not be sufficient that the intermediary be experienced as a social worker *per se*. In *Eastern Health Board v M.K. and M.K.*,[23] Keane C.J. cited with approval the following extract from the judgment of Wall L.J. in the Court of Appeal in *Re N.*:[24]

> "For the court to rely on opinion evidence—even to admit it—the qualifications of the witness must extend beyond experience gained as a social worker and require clinical experience as or akin to a child psychologist or a child psychiatrist".[25]

A key fear may be that the interposition of an intermediary will blunt the opportunity for robust cross-examination of witnesses. All parties are still, of

---

[19] s.21(5).
[20] s.22(1).
[21] See s.22(2).
[22] s.22(3).
[23] [1999] 2 I.R. 99; [1999] 2 I.L.R.M. 321.
[24] [1996] 2 F.L.R. 214.
[25] See also judgment of O'Flaherty J in *Southern Health Board v C.H.* [1996] 2 I.L.R.M. 142, wherein he referred to the fact that the District Judge regarded a senior social worker with the health board as an expert on the basis that he was "a man who had considerable expertise ... dealing with sexual abuse cases involving the very young".

course, entitled to put questions to the child but only indirectly. The Supreme Court considered the use of the television link and intermediary in child law proceedings in *Eastern Health Board v M.K. and M.K.*[26] While critical of the handling of the particular interview,[27] the court seemed in principle to approve of this innovation. Two of the judges, in particular, noted that it was possible for all concerned to see the child during the interview (and, as it was recorded, to review the proceedings thereafter), thus placing all concerned in a better position to judge his or her credibility. In light of the decision in *Donnelly v Ireland*,[28] it is indeed unlikely that the new provisions in the 1997 Act will face constitutional difficulties. That said, caution is still required. The latter case underlines the particular need to ensure that such procedures as are followed do not prejudice the right of all concerned to natural justice, in particular to challenge the veracity of evidence delivered by television link.

8–16 The main practical concern surrounding these innovations, however, is one of resources. Few Irish courts have adequate facilities to carry out a remote television link. The commencement of Part III of the Children Act 1997 (in January 1999) could only have compounded these shortcomings. With this in mind, s.27 of the latter Act allows the court, where it lacks such facilities, to transfer proceedings to a Circuit or District Court building that has adequate facilities (although this can only put further pressure on already limited resources).

(c) Appointing experts

8–17 Where parties in cases involving children wish to introduce "expert evidence" it is important for both parties to agree on the appointment of an expert or to make application to the Court in advance. This position has been given the status of a practice direction in the neighbouring jurisdiction in the case of *Re G. (Minors) (Expert Witnesses)*.[29] Other cases such as *Re C. (Expert Evidence: Disclosure: Practice)*[30] give detailed specimen directions which should normally accompany such directions. Applications for leave to instruct experts should be made at an early stage in the proceedings.[31] It is important to fully instruct the expert and to ensure that the person chosen has the requisite level of expertise. In the case of the older child, their consent must be ascertained.[32] Expert witnesses who have other clinical experience of the child outside the litigation should ensure that all of their clinical material is available for inspection by the court and by other experts.[33]

---

[26] unreported, Supreme Court, January 29, 1999.
[27] See also the judgment of Butler-Sloss L.J. in *Re D (Minors)* [1998] 2 F.L.R. 10.
[28] [1998] 1 I.R. 321.
[29] [1994] 2 F.L.R. 291.
[30] [1995] 1 F.L.R. 204.
[31] See generally Burrows, *Evidence in Family Proceedings* (Family Law, Bristol, 1999) and J. Wall with Lain Hamilton, *A Handbook for Expert Witnesses in Children Act Cases* (Family Law, Bristol, 2000).
[32] See *Gillick v West Norfolk and Wisebech Area Health Authority* [1986] A.C. 112; [1986] 1 F.L.R. 224 H.L.
[33] See *Re M. (Minors) (Care Proceedings: Child's wishes)* [1994] 1 F.L.R. 749.

(d) Evidence gathered by means of a social report

8–18   Despite the strictures of the adversarial approach, it has been the frequent practice of the courts to request social reports in respect of children who are the subject of proceedings, public law and private, for some number of years. These allow evidence relating to the child's welfare to be collected without necessarily requiring the child to appear in court. This task was originally performed by the probation and welfare service on an informal basis, although since 1996, such reports have generally been prepared by social workers, the former maintaining that it lacked the resources to continue doing so adequately. That said, a pilot project commenced in 2003 involving the probation and welfare service in the preparation of social report in private divorce and judicial separation cases.

The jurisdiction to obtain a social report was put on a formal statutory footing by s.47 of the Family Law Act 1995. Section 47 of the 1995 Act empowers the Circuit Court or High Court, as the case may be, to order a social report relating to any party to proceedings or any other person to whom they relate, obviously including the children of the parties. Such reports may be requested on an application by a party to the proceedings, although it is worth noting that the court may request the procuration of such a report of its own motion without necessarily being requested to do so by a party. Section 47 may be invoked in respect of proceedings in a wide range of contexts as listed below:

(a) Guardianship of Infants Act 1964;

(b) Family Law (Maintenance of Spouses and Children) Act 1976;

(c) Family Home Protection Act 1976;

(d) Domestic Violence Act 1996;

(e) Status of Children Act 1987;

(f) Judicial Separation and Family Law Reform Act 1989;

(g) Child Abduction and Enforcement of Custody Orders Act 1991;

(h) an application for a decree of nullity; and

(i) under the Family Law Act 1995 itself.

By virtue of s.42 of the Family Law (Divorce) Act 1996, the social report facility also applies to proceedings taken under that Act. Section 26 of the Guardianship of Infants Act 1964,[34] furthermore, once in force, will allow such a report to be procured in proceedings before the District Court taken under the 1964 Act.[35]

8–19   Section 47 allows the court to appoint as author of the social report either a probation and welfare officer, or a suitably qualified person nominated

---

[34] Inserted by s.11 of the Children Act 1997.

[35] This section is one of the two sections of the Children Act 1997 not yet in force.

by a health board, or any other person named in the order.[36] In practice, as stated previously, the report is generally made by a qualified social worker.

A largely similar power is conferred on the District Court and, on appeal, the Circuit Court, in public law cases (such as proceedings to obtain a care order) by s.27 of the Child Care Act 1991. This allows the aforementioned courts to order the making of a report on any matter relating to welfare of a child to which the proceedings relate.

In deciding whether to request a report, the courts must at least pay heed to the wishes of the parties involved, although it is not required to abide by those wishes. It is the court alone that must make the final decision. A copy of the final report must, however, be presented to the parties or (where legally represented) their legal representatives. In the course of the proceedings, the court is entitled to utilise the report as evidence in the proceedings and for these purposes, the author of the report may be called as a witness by any of the parties to the proceedings or by the court itself. The cost of preparing such a report and of appearing in court shall be met by such party or parties to the case as the court decides.

A similar investigation (although arguably more far-reaching in its results) may be undertaken in certain private law proceedings by virtue of s.20 of the Child Care Act 1991. Such private law proceedings include proceedings under:

(i)   s.7, 8, 11, 11B or Pt III of the Guardianship of Infants Act 1964;

(ii) s.3(3) of the Judicial Separation and Family Law Reform Act 1989;

(iii) s.6(b) or 10(f) of the Family Law Act 1995; or

(iv) s.5(2), 11(b) or 41 of the Family Law (Divorce) Act 1996.

In any of the above proceedings, a court may make such order as is contemplated by s.20 of the Child Care Act 1991. Despite the fact that these are essentially private law proceedings, s.20 allows the court to order the carrying out of an investigation with a view to determining whether a care order or supervision order is appropriate in relation to a child who is the subject of the proceedings. The court may order such investigation of its own motion or following the request of any party to the proceedings. As a condition precedent to such an order, it must appear to the court that it may be appropriate to make one, although the court, obviously, need not have made up its mind on this point. If it comes to such a conclusion it may order the health board in whose functional area the child resides to undertake an investigation of the child's circumstances.

Following such an order, proceedings will be adjourned pending the publication of the results of the investigation. In the interim, the court may make such orders regarding the child(ren)'s care and custody as to it seem proper, including a supervision order. During the adjournment, the health board will be obliged to investigate the child's circumstances. In doing so, it must consider, in particular, whether it should apply for a care or supervision order in respect of a child; provide services or assistance for the benefit of a child or his or her family; or take any other appropriate action in relation to the child.

---

[36] s.47(1).

Once made, the report must be delivered in writing to the court. If the health board, having completed its investigation, decides not to proceed to obtain a care or supervision order, it must inform the court of its reasons for so deciding and of any service or assistance that it has provided or intends for the child or for his or her family. It is also required to appraise the court of any action that it has taken or intends to take in respect of the child. It is possible, in addition, for the court to call the person making the report to give evidence before it.

The potential consequences of this latter provision are of great significance. A practitioner advising family members on the wisdom of commencing proceedings under any of the provisions mentioned previously would be well-advised to warn his or her clients of the danger of precipitating a care or supervision order in respect of a child. The prospect of this occurring is in no way lessened by the fact that these are effectively private law proceedings.

8–20   An additional danger is that reports may, and sometimes do, tend to approach the circumstances of the family from the perspective of the adults as they relate to their children, rather than focusing on the children's interests in and of themselves. Great care is needed then to ensure that the ultimate purpose of the proceedings—to secure the welfare of the child—is not obscured or diluted.

Attachment and committal

8–21   All orders of the District Court other than judgments for the payment of money are governed by Ord.46B of the District Court Rules 1997, introduced by S.I. No. 196 of 2000. This rule concerns attachment and committal in the District Court and has specific relevance to child law, where enforcement of child law orders can be problematic.

The rules apply to all child law decisions that result in court orders and apply not only to orders made in respect of parties to the action, but also to orders made to non-parties. The latter include social workers and others requested to undertake social reports.

Where there has been a failure to comply with an order, the party entitled to the benefit of the order, or the court, may serve a notice requiring the person bound to attend court and demonstrate why he or she should not be committed for contempt. It should be noted that the court can also order attachment.

When before the court, the person in default can either be discharged on such terms and conditions as the court see fit, or committed to prison. The committal may continue for a certain period or until the person has purged his or her contempt. The person in custody may also apply to the court for discharge.

8–22   Although there is no likely injustice in enforcing orders against parties to a case, difficulty may arise in relation to those ordered to undertake a social report for the court. Instructions given to such persons in their order of appointment are sometimes vague, and they may well find complete adherence difficult. If so, r.46B may be triggered in unjust circumstances. Similarly, there may also be scope for accidental breaches of orders given under the Child Care Act 1991, where such orders are vague.

These rules increase the accountability of non-parties who are subject to orders made by the court and strengthen practitioners' ability to ensure that orders are complied with. However, to prevent the attachment and committal mechanism being invoked in unwarranted cases, it is suggested that clear directions are given, with any vagueness being clarified in court by direction. Persons conducting reports should also attempt to get fresh directions if circumstances change.

(e) Abolition of the requirement to give evidence on oath

8–23   The general requirement that a person giving evidence before a court must do so under oath or on affirmation may be foregone where the provisions of s.28 of the Children Act 1997 are satisfied.[37] Section 28 applies to all civil proceedings and not just to those contemplated by the 1997 Act itself. It permits the court to accept the evidence of a child under the age of 14 years, even where such evidence is given otherwise than on oath or affirmation. The provisions, however, also apply to any person, regardless of age who has a mental disability.[38] Any evidence given in this way may be taken as corroborating other evidence, whether the latter is sworn or unsworn.

There are, however, certain important conditions. The court must be satisfied that the child is able to give an intelligible account of all relevant events. It is further stipulated that, the absence of an oath notwithstanding, a child who gives evidence knowing it to be false or not believing it to be true shall be guilty of an offence. The child shall on conviction be treated as if guilty of perjury, and sentenced accordingly.

(f) The use of anatomically correct dolls

8–24   In many cases, especially those involving alleged sexual abuse, a child may lack the language necessary to describe his or her experiences. An innovative solution to the problem of the child's limited vocabulary is the use of anatomically correct dolls. These enable a child to convey to the court, by gesture rather than words, the nature of his or her experiences. For instance, a child allegedly the victim of sexual abuse can point to the places where he or she has been touched, thus obviating the need to mention what to the child may be embarrassing words. This was first used in the criminal case of *D.P.P. v J.T.*[39] While this case involved the alleged sexual abuse of a person who was mentally disabled, it is submitted that the court's decision is equally applicable to civil cases involving minors.

---

[37] Each of these involves the making of a promise to tell the full truth and to avoid lying in court.

[38] See also s.20(b).

[39] 3 Frewen 141.

PART II

SᴇᴘᴀRᴀᴛᴇ RᴇᴘRᴇsᴇɴᴛᴀᴛɪoɴ ғoR CʜɪʟᴅRᴇɴ: Tʜᴇ GᴜᴀRᴅɪᴀɴ *Aᴅ Lɪᴛᴇᴍ*

8–25   Although the above-mentioned reforms are welcome, there are some lingering concerns. While the overall strategy of minimising the child's exposure to the court process is a worthy one, it may be at the expense of ensuring that the child is adequately represented in court. It is suggested that the best means of obviating this shortcoming is the provision for separate legal representation of children, a facility now provided for in this state in the form of a guardian *ad litem*.

Traditionally, common lawyers have been wary of such innovations. The common law system of adjudication is typified by an adversarial approach to judicial proceedings. The net effect of this perspective is that the parties are viewed as competing against each other for the court's favour. The judge, furthermore, is limited in the inquiries he or she may initiate. In the classical adversarial model, it is the legal representatives of the parties rather than the court that dictates the direction and tenor of the proceedings. This is in sharp contrast to the more inquisitorial system operated in the civil law jurisdictions of continental Europe, a system that, with respect, lends itself much more readily to the type of proceedings being discussed here.

8–26   Of particular concern at this juncture is the fate of the child in the adversarial model of proceedings. This perspective tends to view a custody application, for instance, as a struggle between competing parents, with the child being the sought-after "prize". It jars with what is, after all, the overriding concern of the court in such cases: that the welfare of the child is paramount, taking precedence over all other considerations and interests.[40] It seems strange then that, at least until recently, very little consideration was given to the proposition that the child (himself or herself) should be represented in court.

Recent innovations have, however, tended to exhibit a will for reform in this regard. There is, indeed, already some evidence of a softening of the adversarial line in family cases. In *J.L. v J.L.*,[41] for instance, McGuinness J. (sitting as a Circuit Court judge) rejected the proposition that family cases were entirely adversarial, pointing in particular to the overriding requirement that the court look to the welfare of the child as the primary consideration.

International underpinnings of the right to representation

8–27   The primary foothold for separate representation in international child law can be found in the United Nations Convention on the Rights of the Child 1989, Article 12 of which provides that:

> "1. State parties shall assure to the child who is capable of forming his or her own views the right to express those views freely in all matters

---

[40] See s.3 of the Guardianship of Infants Act 1964.
[41] [1996] 1 Fam. L.J. 128.

affecting the child, the views of the child being given due weight in accordance with the age and maturity of the child.

2. For this purpose, the child shall in particular be provided the opportunity to be heard in any judicial and administrative proceedings affecting the child, either directly, or through a representative or an appropriate body, in a manner consistent with the procedural rules of national law."

8–28 In line with the overriding principles of Irish child law, the welfare of the child is deemed to be of crucial importance. Article 3 of the Convention underlines this preference, noting that:

"1. In all actions concerning children, whether undertaken by public or private social welfare institutions, courts of law, administrative authorities or legislative bodies, the best interests of the child shall be a primary consideration."

The wording of that article betrays, however, a subtle qualification. It refers after all to the welfare principle being not "the" primary consideration but only "a" primary consideration, suggesting that the pre-eminence of the best interests test is not guaranteed. Nonetheless, when read together with the explicit guarantees contained elsewhere in the Convention, it is hard to escape the conclusion that Ireland has made little headway in satisfying its terms. It is, perhaps, ill-advised to apply too literal an interpretation of a multi-lateral agreement, especially considering the range of official languages in which such conventions tend to be published.

8–29 The European Convention on the Exercise of Children's Rights followed its UN counterpart in 1996, although in several respects it is of more limited application. The 1996 Convention focuses predominantly on procedural rather than substantive rights, the emphasis being on such matters as the right of children to participate in, and have access to information about cases that concern their welfare. It is obvious that such provisions are aimed primarily at children of sufficient age and maturity to understand the matters under scrutiny, and are of little use to children of more tender years.[42]

The European Convention on Human Rights is also of some general relevance in this area and is considered in Chapter 12.

The birth of the guardian *ad litem* in Ireland

8–30 Ireland, by entering into several international agreements aimed at increasing the role of the child in family proceedings, has bound itself to make family courts more child-friendly. The kernel of this reform lies in the Child Care Act of 1991 and in particular in the introduction of the position of guardian *ad litem*.

---

[42] See Chap.12 for a more detailed discussion on the 1996 Convention.

The guardian *ad litem* is, effectively, an independent representative appointed by the court to represent the child's personal and legal interests in proceedings under that Act. The Children Act 1997 has further extended the range of proceedings in which the guardian *ad litem* may act, in particular, by allowing such an appointment in certain proceedings envisaged by the Guardianship of Infants Act 1964 (including custody and access cases). These proceedings are, of course, private rather than public law cases and, of necessity, the scope for state intervention will be more limited than in, say, the hearing of an application for a (public law) care order.

It is proposed to look at the guardian *ad litem* in its public and private law roles respectively.

The guardian ad litem *in public law proceedings*

8–31 It was in the public law sphere that the guardian *ad litem* first came to the fore in this jurisdiction. Section 26 of the Child Care Act 1991 allows the court to appoint a guardian *ad litem* in respect of a child involved in proceedings under Part IV (care and supervision orders), and Part VI (children in the care of health boards) of that Act. Section 25 of the 1991 Act allows the child to be added as a party to the proceedings, but where this does not occur, s.26(1) allows a guardian *ad litem* to be appointed to act on the child's behalf. This is subject to the important caveat that the court be satisfied that such appointment is both necessary in the interests of the child, and consistent with the requirements of justice. As with all child law proceedings, s.24 of the Act ranks the child's welfare as the first and paramount consideration in such cases, although the court is also required to have due regard to the rights and duties of the parents. It further notes that, in deciding whether to appoint a guardian *ad litem*, the court should, in so far as practicable, have regard to the wishes of the child. The practicability of so doing will, as always, depend on the latter's age and understanding.

Beyond that, few other guidelines are laid down to aid the court in deciding whether it is appropriate to appoint a guardian *ad litem*. Section 26(4) stipulates that should the court see fit to add a child as a party to the proceedings under s.25, any prior appointment of a guardian *ad litem* in respect of the same child shall be deemed to have ceased. In fact, it seems that s.25 (allowing a child to be a party to the case) and s.26 (allowing the appointment of a guardian *ad litem*) are mutually exclusive. This is so even where a child is added as a party not fully, but only for certain purposes specified by the court.

Qualifications

8–32 The 1991 Act as it stands lays down no criteria governing the type of person who may be appointed as a guardian *ad litem*. Stranger still, it provides no means by which such criteria may be laid down, *e.g.* by regulation. In strict theory at least, the court could appoint anybody. Nonetheless, it may probably be said with some conviction that the guardian *ad litem* should be a social worker or some other child care professional with expertise in dealing with children. This view is supported in part by the fact that the Act stipulates that the relevant health board should pay any costs incurred by a person acting in the capacity of guardian *ad litem*. It can be assumed that a responsible health board would not be expected to pay someone without qualifications or expertise to perform such a task, although, as noted above, there is nothing preventing the court from appointing such a person. It is suggested, furthermore, that the guardian *ad litem* should be familiar with the workings of the courts in cases involving children. This is all the more important considering that the Act seems not to permit the appointment of a barrister or solicitor to represent the guardian *ad litem* at the hearing. Presumably, the guardian *ad litem* should not be an employee of a health board, which is itself a party to the case. The conflict of interest arising should of necessity preclude such an appointment.

Functions and duties of the guardian ad litem

8–33   The Act is equally vague regarding the functions and role of the guardian *ad litem*. It does not specify any role or duty beyond that necessarily implied by the term guardian *ad litem*—presumably, that the person appointed would be charged with advocating a legal solution that is in the best interests of the child. Nor is there any provision in the Act allowing regulations to fill this gap.

Stranger still is the lack of any obvious provision allowing access to the child. It seems perverse in the extreme to facilitate the appointment of a representative without also permitting regular access to the person he or she is representing.

One point at least is necessarily implicit, and that is that the guardian *ad litem* is to act independently of the parents and health board with a view to promoting the welfare and wishes of the child. Beyond that, the guardian *ad litem* is probably best advised to take direction from the presiding judge. He or she should first and foremost appraise the situation of the child. It is strongly suggested that for these purposes the guardian *ad litem* should be granted permission to have access to the child with a view to ascertaining his or her needs, wishes and concerns. Adequate access to records (such as health board and social worker's reports) should, arguably, also be afforded. Presumably, the guardian *ad litem* has no role in interviewing the other parties to the case, although it is suggested that the guardian *ad litem* should be permitted to make such inquiries so as to enable him or her to determine the best interests of the child concerned.

The guardian ad litem in England and Wales: a model of best practice

8–34   The situation as described above is in marked contrast to that existing in England and Wales, where detailed guidelines govern the appointment and conduct of the guardian *ad litem*.[43] The differences are striking:

(a) an English or Welsh court, in proceedings relating to the welfare of a child, must appoint a guardian *ad litem* unless satisfied that it is not necessary to do so. The strong tenor of the legislation, in other words,

---

[43] See Timms, *Children's Representation* (Sweet and Maxwell, London, 1995); Monro and Forrester, *The Guardian ad litem* (Family Law Guide and Practice Series, Bristol, 1995).

leans heavily towards appointment. By contrast, the Irish legislation requires that the necessity of such an appointment must be established before such appointment can be made, indicating perhaps a greater scepticism regarding the role of the guardian *ad litem*;

(b) the guardian *ad litem* in England and Wales is appointed from independent panels of persons deemed to be suitable for the task. Guidelines are laid down for the selection of persons to be appointed to the independent panels. While there is no doubting the existence of comparable expertise in this jurisdiction, the appointment of guardians *ad litem* in Ireland effectively occurs on an ad hoc basis. In strict theory at least, when appointing a guardian *ad litem* in this State, no equivalent guidelines or restrictions apply;

(c) in England and Wales, the guardian *ad litem* must appoint a solicitor to act on behalf of the child. The child, if of sufficient age and understanding, may instruct the solicitor on his or her own behalf, in which case the solicitor will represent the child directly. In such a case the guardian *ad litem* will remain as independent advisor to the court. There seems to be no similar provision for legal representation in s.26 of the (Irish) Child Care Act 1991. In fact, the terms of that section seem to indicate that legal representation and the appointment of the guardian *ad litem* are mutually exclusive—in other words, the presence of one prevents the appointment of the other;

(d) the guardian *ad litem* in England and Wales is explicitly deemed to be an independent actor. In particular, he or she is independent of local authorities and health boards, a point noted by many guardians *ad litem* in that jurisdiction as being of great importance. This was clearly stated by the President of the Family Division, Sir Stephen Brown, in the neighbouring jurisdiction, in *R v Cornwall County Council ex parte G*:[44]

> "It is vital that the independence of the guardian in carrying out his or her duties on behalf of the child in any proceedings should be clearly recognised and understood. Since it is the responsibility of each local authority to establish a panel of guardians in its area and to be responsible for the payment of the expenses, fees and allowances to the guardians, and furthermore to determine within its own area the rates of payment, it is vitally important that the position of the guardian should not be compromised by any restriction placed directly or indirectly upon him or her in [the] carrying out of his or her duties. It is important that the courts and the public should have confidence in the independence of the guardians. It is important that the guardians themselves should feel confident of their independent status."[45]

8–35 It is obvious, then, that a person should not be an employee of a health

[44] [1992] 1 F.L.R. 270.
[45] See generally article by Ian Robertson and Jonathan Baker, "The reappointment of Guardians *ad litem*" [September, 1996], *Family Law*, pp.556–559. See also Walton,

board or local authority if also a party to the proceedings involving the child in question. There is no such explicit requirement of independence in Irish law, although it is arguably necessarily implicit in the nature of the role envisaged. Costello J., in the case of *Re M.H. and J.H., Oxfordshire County Council v J.H. and V.H.,*[46] noted the independent nature of a guardian *ad litem's* appointment and defined the role of the guardian *ad litem* in terms of his or her obligation to advise the Court on the child's behalf as to what is to happen.

The guardian ad litem *in private law proceedings*

8–36 Provision is also made in Irish law for the appointment by the court of a guardian *ad litem* to act on behalf of any child in private law proceedings involving:

(a) the custody of, or access to, a child; or

(b) an application for guardianship by a natural father.[47]

8–37 The circumstances in which a guardian *ad litem* may be appointed in such proceedings are, however, very clearly more limited than those contemplated in public law cases. The court must be satisfied that "special circumstances" exist necessitating the appointment of the guardian *ad litem*, a formula that obviously precludes such appointment in all but the most pressing of cases. Clearly then, the guardian *ad litem* is considered not to be as crucial to the best interests of the child in private law cases as in public law cases. Alternatively, this more restrictive perspective may reflect a concern to avoid undue state intervention in private law proceedings, an approach that, in fairness, is not borne out by the provisions of s.47 of the Family Law Act 1995.

8–38 In deciding whether to appoint a guardian *ad litem*, several criteria may be considered. These include:

(a) the age and understanding of the child in question;

(b) the findings of any social report;[48]

(c) the welfare of the child;

(d) the wishes of the child;

(e) the submissions of any other parties.

8–39 By contrast with the Child Care Act 1991, there is some guidance on the criteria upon which the guardian *ad litem* should be chosen, s.28(3) of the

---

"The Guardian *ad litem's* Independence" (1997) 1 *Family Law* at 106–108; Masson and Shaw, "The Work of Guardians *ad litem*" (1988) 1 *Journal of Social Work and Law* at 164.

[46] unreported, High Court, May 19, 1988.

[47] s.28 of the Guardianship of Infants Act 1964 to be inserted by s.11 of the Children Act 1997—this section is one of only two sections of the Children Act 1997 not yet in force.

[48] s.47 of the Family Law Act 1995.

1964 Act providing that the author of a s.47 report in respect of the child may be selected as its guardian *ad litem*. Another, and remarkably peculiar, difference is that the private law guardian *ad litem* may be legally represented[49] should the court consider it necessary in the best interests of the child. This is all the more surprising considering the comparatively more serious consequences that tend to accompany an order made under the 1991 Act.

Other than that, the two regimes appear to be largely similar. The most notable similarity lies in the lack of any detail in both Acts regarding the functions and duties of the guardian *ad litem*. Again, much of detail can only be worked out on an ad hoc, common sense basis. The primary function of the guardian *ad litem* is presumably the independent representation of the child's best interests. Beyond this, the guardian *ad litem* would be well advised to seek appropriate direction from the court, allowing, for instance, access to the child and to any relevant information relating to the child. It is suggested, also, that provision should be made to allow the guardian *ad litem* to be involved in the formulation of any settlement by the parties. Arguably, it is as crucial that the voice of the child be heard in such negotiations as it is in the hearing itself. In this regard, as in so many others, however, statutory guidance is non-existent.

8–40   It is arguable that unnecessary duplication may occur where a social report has already been submitted, and that in such circumstances, it is unlikely that a guardian *ad litem* will also be appointed. In its submission to the English *Court Welfare Services Working Group*,[50] the Association of Lawyers for Children suggests that these twin roles be fused with a view to reducing the time and expense involved in such cases, a suggestion that has much to recommend itself.

PART III

SEPARATE REPRESENTATION FOR CHILDREN: MAKING A CHILD A PARTY TO THE PROCEEDINGS

8–41   As previously stated, it is also possible to allow a child to be entered as a party to the proceedings. In public law proceedings, this is clearly an alternative to the appointment of the guardian *ad litem*. A child cannot both be a party to the proceedings, and have a guardian *ad litem* appointed to represent him or her. Considering the concern of the legislature to shield children from the legal process, it seems somewhat at odds that it should provide a facility to allow a child to be added as a party to proceedings. Nonetheless, there will obviously be some cases in which this may be appropriate. To this end, s.25 of the 1991 Act permits the court to add a child as a party to public law proceedings in which his or her welfare is at stake. The court may alternatively grant the child such rights of a party as may be specified by it. Either order may be made

---

[49] See s.28(4).
[50] (1998) *Family Law* 403.

only in proceedings to which Part IV or Part VI of the 1991 Act relate, primarily the making of care and supervision orders and the treatment of children in the care of health boards. A number of conditions apply to the making of such an order:

(a) by definition, the child must not already be a party to the proceedings;

(b) the court must be satisfied that it is necessary in the interests of the child and the interests of justice to do so. In so deciding, the court must have regard to the age, understanding and wishes of the child. In practice, this latter condition rules out such appointments in cases where children are too young to understand the proceedings or to instruct a lawyer to act on their behalf;

(c) the court may make such order as it sees fit, including an order limiting the child's participation to certain specified parts of the proceedings only.

8–42 It is not necessary, however, that such order be made on the intervention of a "next friend" of a child, the standard approach by which a child takes legal proceedings.

Once an order under s.25 is made, the court may appoint a solicitor to act as representative of the child in the proceedings. It may, furthermore, give directions as to the solicitor's duties in the case. Notwithstanding such an order, however, it is still possible to exclude the child from the proceedings under s.30(2) of the 1991 Act.

The costs of the child's legal representative are to be paid by the health board, but it is open to the latter body to apply to the court for a direction that any other party to the case should foot the bill.

8–43 The key lacuna in this provision is that, once made, it prevents or alternatively terminates the appointment of a guardian *ad litem* as envisaged by s.26. This is unfortunate, considering that a lawyer, while talented in the advocacy of law, may not necessarily be best equipped to identify and advocate the social and emotional needs of a child.

Private law proceedings

8–44 In private law proceedings there is no explicit provision allowing for the addition of a child as a party. It appears, however, that the courts possess a residual jurisdiction to do so and, furthermore, to appoint a solicitor to act on the child's behalf. The prospects of such an occurrence are, however, small, particularly considering the fact that these are private law proceedings. The best prospects of representation in such cases seem to lie with the power to appoint a guardian *ad litem*, who in turn may be legally represented, thereby providing indirect legal representation for the child.[51]

---

[51] This is only possible in private law cases. A guardian *ad litem* appointed to represent a child in public law cases, strangely, may not be legally represented.

PART IV

REPRESENTING A CHILD

8–45   The role of the guardian *ad litem* requires a child welfare professional in order to deal with both "welfare" and "wishes". The solicitor who represents the child directly has an onerous task, but one which is quite different to the guardian *ad litem*. Solicitors are generally not trained in child psychology and are never professionally qualified to tell the court what is in the best interests of their client. The solicitor does not have this dual role. The solicitor/client relationship is a professional and objective one. The commitment is a personal one, rather than one which can be delegated.[52] The solicitor has a duty to advise the client that the courts' paramount consideration will be the welfare of the child. Solicitors are obliged to follow the instructions of their client, however. There is no requirement to override his client's instructions to put forward arguments which the solicitor perceives to be in the best interests of the client. Solicitors owe a professional duty as officers of the court not to mislead the court. In general, however, the duty of the solicitor is to investigate and collate evidence, call and cross-examine witnesses, and ensure the client's instructions are presented to the court in the most persuasive manner.[53] The personal views of the solicitor as to what is best can only be used as a guide to the client on the likely approach to be taken by the court. As succinctly stated by Treyvaud J. in the Australian case of *Waghorne v Dempster*:[54]

> "Advocacy … demands that the advocate conduct his client's case objectively and without necessarily holding, and certainly not expressing, any personal opinion or view as to the case or any aspect of it. To permit otherwise would be to fly in the face of Australian and English understanding of the role of an advocate".

One of the first tasks for the solicitor taking instructions is to meet the child and explain to him or her who he or she is, how he or she was appointed, and what his or her role is. In general, the child will be acutely aware of the court proceedings, but he or she may not be aware of the role of the solicitor appointed to represent him or her in the proceedings. Interviews should be short and taken at the child's pace.

8–46   It is important for the solicitor to ascertain whether the client is capable of giving instructions. In other words, the solicitor must be satisfied that the client fully understands the nature of the proceedings and the ramifications of

---

[52] The Solicitors Family Law Association in the neighbouring jurisdiction, in its guide to good practice, provides that the solicitor should not normally delegate the preparation, supervision, conduct or presentation of the case, but should deal with it personally. In each case the solicitor must consider whether it is in the best interests of the child to instruct another advocate and then advise on whom should be instructed.

[53] Peggy Ray, paper delivered at First World Congress on Family Law and Children's Rights, July 4–9, 1993, Sydney Convention Centre.

[54] (1979) 5 F.L.R. 503.

what he or she is asking the solicitor to do on his or her behalf. If the child is severely emotionally disturbed he or she may not be capable of giving instructions.[55] If there are already child mental health professionals involved the solicitor may consult them. However, if there are none the solicitor is faced with a difficult dilemma. The direction of the court can be sought in such circumstances.

8–47 It is important to explain to the client the nature of the proceedings in question (child care, wardship and custody/access) in simple and straight-forward terms.[56] The client should be made aware of the fact that the court will make decisions about his or her future and that, by law, it must consider his or her views and wishes.[57] Where a solicitor has been appointed to represent a mature child in public law child care proceedings, the child is given party status in the proceedings. As a case progresses the child will need to know and understand the relevant factors:

- what parents and other parties want for the child;
- what the reports recommend for the child;
- an outline of the essential law relevant to the proceedings.

8–48 The child has the same right to be kept informed about the progress of the proceedings as an adult client. He or she must have sufficient information to be able to make informed decisions for himself or herself. In certain circumstances he or she may request to be present in court for the hearing of the proceedings.[58] However, in many cases the child client will want to be reassured that he of she will not have to speak or be present in court. Section 30 of the Child Care Act 1991 enables the court to proceed in the absence of the child who is the subject of the proceedings unless the court, either of its own motion or at the request of any of the parties to the case, is satisfied that it is necessary to hear the child for the proper disposal of the case.[59] The client must be told that the judge may ask to speak to him—although this does not happen very often; when it does, the judge generally speaks to the child in private and without the parents present.

Where the solicitor requires access to documentation, reports or case papers, the direction of the court must first be obtained where the child is not a party to the proceedings. Such proceedings are generally *in camera*—and the *in camera* rules apply to such papers.

Where the client must give evidence in court, the method and manner of doing so must be explained. In civil proceedings, children under 14 years no

---

[55] See *Re H. (A Minor) (Care Proceedings: Child's Wishes)* [1993] 1 F.L.R. 440, where Thorpe J. pointed out that a child had to have sufficient understanding and must be rational. This may not be so where the child is severely emotionally disturbed. If there is any doubt on this matter, expert opinion must be obtained.

[56] The Lord Chancellor's Department Leaflet No.2, available at http://www.offsol.demon.co.uk/leaf2tfr.htm, can be very usefully adapted for this purpose.

[57] See s.24 of the Child Care Act 1991 and s.25 of the Guardianship of Infants Act 1964.

[58] s.30 (2) of the Child Care Act 1991 and s.27(2) of the Guardianship of Infants Act 1964.

[59] See also s.27(1) of the Guardianship of Infants Act 1964.

longer have to give an oath or affirmation where the court is satisfied that the child is capable of giving an intelligible account of events which are relevant to the proceedings.[60] The client must be told about the consequences of telling lies or making statements which he or she knows to be false or does not believe to be true.[61]

The client must be told that the court hears the evidence from all of the relevant witnesses and then decides what is to happen. The judge will make the decision on the basis of what is best for the child. What the court decides may not be the same as what the child client wishes to happen.

The Department of Justice, Equality and Law Reform has produced some very helpful booklets describing what actually happens in court and these may be given to the client to explain the court process and personnel.

8–49   Normally a client is entitled to see relevant documentary evidence held by the solicitor. In the case of a child client, however, this does not also follow and the direction of the court may be obtained where the child client wishes to access a confidential report, which may be inappropriate for the child client to see or have a copy of.[62] Social reports are generally given to the court in the first instance, as they are reports for the benefit of the court.

PART V

OMBUDSMAN FOR CHILDREN

8–50   A further representative that will be able to represent children's interests is the Ombudsman for Children (the Ombudsman). The Ombudsman acts as an independent complaints-handler and is an advocate of children's rights. In Ireland, the Ombudsman for Children Act 2002, broadly modelled on the Ombudsman Acts of 1980 and 1984, provides for the appointment of an Ombudsman who has a dual role: to promote the rights and welfare of children in all aspects of public policy, practices, procedures and law; and to conduct investigations of complaints regarding actions by public bodies, hospitals and schools. The Ombudsman for Children Act 2002 came into force on May 1, 2004, though the Ombudsman, Ms Emily Logan, was appointed by the President in December 2003.

Appointment, terms and conditions of office

8–51   The office of the Ombudsman for Children is established pursuant to s.4 of the 2002 Act. The appointment is made by the President upon a resolution passed by Dáil Éireann and the Seanad Éireann recommending the appointment

---

[60] s.28 of the Children Act 1997.
[61] s.28(2) and (3) of the Children Act 1997.
[62] See *Re C (Expert Evidence: disclosure practice)* [1995] 1 F.L.R. 204; *Re M (Minors) (Care Proceedings: child's wishes)* [1994] 1 F.L.R. 794; *Re T and E (Proceedings: conflicting interests)* [1995] 1 F.L.R. 581.

of the person.[63] Section 4(4) of the Act provides that the Ombudsman shall hold the office for six years. The Ombudsman can only be removed from office prior to the conclusion of this term by the President following a resolution of the Dáil and Seanad in the circumstances set out by s.4(3), which it will serve to protect the independence of the office.[64]

A "child" is defined in s.20 of the 2002 Act as a person under the age of 18 years. The Ombudsman for Children Bill 2002, as introduced in the Seanad, excluded from this definition all persons who, under the stipulated age, are or have been married. The minimum age for marriage, since 1996, as stated in Chapter 1, is 18.[65] That said, parties of a younger age may marry by consent of the Circuit Court where the circumstances are such as to render such a step necessary in the interests of the parties. This exclusion was removed before the Bill was passed following representations made by children's rights advocates. It should also be noted that schools not registered under s.10 of the Education Act 1998, and private bodies and hospitals, do not fall for consideration by the Ombudsman.

8–52 The Ombudsman's functions under the Act are laid out in s.7, which include promoting generally the rights and welfare of children. In particular she shall:

"(a) advise the Minister (for Health and Children) or any other Minister of the Government, as may be appropriate, on the development and co-ordination of policy relating to children,

(b) encourage public bodies, schools and voluntary hospitals to develop policies, practices and procedures designed to promote the rights and welfare of children,

(c) collect and disseminate information on matters relating to the rights and welfare of children,

(d) promote awareness among members of the public (including children of such age or ages as she considers appropriate) of matters (including the principles and provisions of the [UN] Convention on the Rights of the Child 1989) relating to the rights and welfare of children and how these rights can be enforced,

(e) highlight issues relating to the rights and welfare of children that are of concern to children,

(f) exchange information and co-operate with the Ombudsman for Children (by whatever name called) of other states,

(g) monitor and review generally the operation of legislation concerning matters that relate to the rights and welfare of children, and

(h) monitor and review the operation of this Act and, whenever he or she thinks it necessary, make recommendations to the Minister …".

8–53 It can be seen from the foregoing that little reference is made to the

---

[63] s.4(2).
[64] s.6 (a).
[65] See Chap.1 and s.31 of the Family Law Act 1995.

protection of the rights or welfare of children. During the debate on the Ombudsman for Children Bill 2002, it was clear that the Ombudsman was not regarded as having a protective role.[66] It should be noted that the UN Convention on the Right of the Child Act 1989 recognises children as a special group requiring particular protection because of their inherent vulnerability in a world of adults.[67] The Child Care Act 1991 began the protective process for children at risk and in need of protection. The omission of the word "protection" in s.7(1) of the 2002 Act fails to expressly acknowledge a role for the Ombudsman in the protection of children and their rights. The failure to provide protection for vulnerable children in Ireland was commented on by the Committee on the Rights of the Child, established under the Convention on the Rights of the Child in February 1998 in Geneva. The Committee was criticial of the failure to provide national co-ordination not only in promoting but also in protecting the welfare of children in Ireland.

In summary, the functions set out in s.7(1) of the 2002 Act include the development of policy, monitoring and reviewing legislation, and also practices of public bodies, schools and voluntary hospitals, as well as an educational role on issues relating to children's rights and welfare. Further, the 2002 Act requires the Ombudsman to establish structures for regular consultation with representative groups of children such as the Children's Rights Alliance, Barnardos and the ISPCC. In the performance of his or her functions, the Ombudsman is required to have regard, pursuant to s.6(2) of the 2002 Act, to the views of children which, consistent with the UN Convention on the Rights of the Child, will depend on the age and understanding of the child or children in question.

Complaints against public bodies, schools and voluntary hospitals

8–54   One of the most important functions of the Ombudsman is her powers to investigate complaints made by or on behalf of children arising in the course of the administration of public bodies,[68] schools and voluntary hospitals.[69] Sections 8 and 9 provide that, subject to exceptions, the Ombudsman may investigate any action taken by or on behalf of a public body where:

> "(a)   the action has or may have adversely affected a child, and
>   (b)   the action was or may have been—
>   (i)   taken without proper authority,
>   (ii)   taken on irrelevant grounds,
>   (iii)   the result of negligence or carelessness,
>   (iv)   based on erroneous or incomplete information,
>   (v)   improperly discriminatory,

---

[66] This was seen to be properly the role of the health boards.

[67] Arts 3 and 19 of the UN Convention on the Rights of the Child provide for the right of the child to be protected.

[68] s.8.

[69] s.9. The lists of public bodies and voluntary hospitals covered are listed in the Schedules to the Act.

(vi) based on an undesirable administrative practice, or
(vii) otherwise contrary to fair or sound administration."

8–55 An "action" is defined widely in s.2(1) of the Act and "includes a decision, failure to act and an omission",[70] though the term "adversely affected" is not defined in the 2002 Act. While the Ombudsman is afforded a wide discretion, he or she can only undertake investigations where a complaint has been made to him or her or where it appears to be warranted under s.10(1)(a). An investigation may be commenced by the Ombudsman in respect of complaints made by a child, his or her parents, or by any other person who is considered suitable to represent the child by reason of relationship and/or interest in the rights and welfare of the child.[71] As the relationship may be a professional one, the Act may allow lawyers acting for children a new avenue of redress. Where the complaint is not made by a parent of the child, the Ombudsman is required to inform a parent before investigating the complaint.[72]

After a preliminary examination, the Ombudsman may either reject the complaint or continue the investigation. Complaints can be rejected or discontinued on several grounds if the Ombudsman is of the opinion that:

"(a) the complaint is trivial or vexatious,
(b) the child making the complaint, or on whose behalf the complaint is made, has an insufficient interest in the matter,
(c) the child making the complaint, or on whose behalf the complaint is made, has not taken reasonable steps to seek redress in respect of the subject matter of the complaint or, if he or she has been refused redress, or
(d) the lapse of time since the occurrence of the matter complained of makes effective redress impossible or impracticable."[73]

8–56 The Ombudsman may, under s.10(5) of the 2002 Act, use his or her discretion when determining whether to initiate, continue, or discontinue an investigation. Section 11 outlines the circumstances where no investigations may be undertaken. In particular, s.11(1)(a) provides that the Ombudsman may not investigate where the action complained of is the subject of civil legal proceedings or where there is a statutory right of appeal in the matter.

8–57 A limitation period is also imposed by s.11(1)(g) of the 2002 Act. A complainant has two years to complain to the Ombudsman from the time of the action or from the time the child involved became aware of the action, whichever is later. However, s.11(3) provides the Ombudsman with a general power to undertake an otherwise time-barred investigation where it appears to his or her "that special circumstances make it proper to do so".[74]

---

[70] s.2(1).
[71] s.10(1)(b)(ii).
[72] s.10(1)(c).
[73] s.10(2).
[74] s.11(3)(b).

8–58 Complaints excluded from s.11 include those in relation to actions taken in the administration of the asylum and immigration process, as well as in the administration of children detained in prisons. Concerns about these exclusions were raised while the Ombudsman for Children Bill was being debated. The Ombudsman for Children should be allowed to conduct investigations into actions by the public bodies most relevant to the lives of these children, including "prisons or other places for the custody and detention of children". In New Zealand, for example, where there is a specific limitation on the Children's Commissioners authority prohibiting him from investigating any decision, act or omission of any court, no such restriction applies to investigating the position regarding children in police cells.[75]

To ensure that all children, without regard to their citizenship status, have equal access to the Ombudsman for Children, s.11(1)(e)(i)[76] should be deleted when the Act is next reviewed. This is not to suggest that the Ombudsman be a court of appeal with respect to determinations made regarding an applicant's asylum or refugee status. Section 11(1)(e)(i), however, goes well beyond excluding complaints about official decisions regarding refugee status or citizenship claims. The Ombudsman is currently constrained, for example, from investigating complaints regarding the treatment of asylum-seeker children in "direct provision" under this exclusion. Indeed, this exclusion fails to incorporate the principles that underpin the *Statement of Good Practice*, produced by the *Separated Children in Europe Programme*. In particular, paragraph 2 of the *Statement of Good Practice* states:

> "Separated children are entitled to the same treatment and rights as national or resident children. They must be treated as children first and foremost. All consideration of their immigration status must be secondary."

The exclusion of children in detention from the remit of the Ombudsman by s.11(1)(e)(iii) should also be deleted in any review of the 2002 Act. This exclusion was raised in the Seanad. Minister Hanafin stated, in response to the concerns expressed at the exclusion, the following:

> "In relation to children in prison, the Senators will know that when the Children Act is enforced, it will be illegal for children to be held in inappropriate places …[I]t would not cover young people between the ages of 16 and 18 who are legitimately in a place like St Patrick's Institution by virtue of their being offenders."

It should be noted, however, that s.56 of the Children Act 2001[77] provides that a detained child can be kept in a cell where no other place is available.[78] The

---

[75] See Chap.11, paras 11–70 *et seq.*

[76] s.11(1)(e)(i) excludes from the Ombudsman for Children Act 2002 any action "taken in the administration of the law relating to asylum, immigration, naturalisation or citizenship".

[77] See Chap.11.

[78] See s.263 of the Children Act 2001.

UN Convention on the Rights of the Child (CRC) provides for the protection of the rights of children and young people in the criminal justice system. Article 37 of the CRC refers to the dignity of the child charged with an offence and guarantees detention as a measure of last resort and for the shortest appropriate period of time. This provision has been interpreted dynamically by the European Court of Human Rights. The European Convention for Human Rights, which has been incorporated into domestic law by the European Convention on Human Rights Act 2003, should also be noted, as should the recent decision of the European Court of Human Rights in *S.C. v UK*.[79]

8–59 Another limitation of concern is s.11(4), which allows a Government Minister to request that the Ombudsman shall not investigate, or shall cease an investigation into, a Minister's Department or public body whose business and functions fall under that Department. Although the Minister must make such a request in writing, setting out his or her reasons, there is no list of acceptable reasons for such a request included in the Act. This effective veto over investigations, motivated by a desire to prevent a breach of the separation of powers doctrine, threatens the independence of the Ombudsman and could prevent investigations that would be in the best interests of the child. A safeguard to protect the independence of the Office is that all such requests must be included in the Ombudsman's annual report.[80]

Investigation and examination of complaints

8–60 Where there is a complaint arising in the course of the administration of bodies covered by the Act, the procedures for investigation are a matter for the Ombudsman, though the Act generally encourages openness and communication when dealing with complaints. Under s.13, if the Ombudsman decides not to carry out an investigation or discontinue an investigation into a complaint, then he or she must provide a written statement of reasons to the child. If the decision is caused by a ministerial request under s.11(4) of the 2002 Act, a copy of the request and of the reasons for the request must also be included in the statement. If the complaint is investigated, then a statement of results must be sent to the child; the public body, school or voluntary hospital investigated; to the appropriate Government Department; and any other person considered relevant.

If the Ombudsman considers that the action "adversely affected" a child's interest and fell within the grounds set out in ss.8 or 9, then, pursuant to s.13(3) of the 2002 Act, she may recommend to the body concerned that:

> "(a) the matter in relation to which the action was taken be further considered,
> (b) measures or specified measures be taken to remedy, mitigate or alter the adverse effect of the action, or

---

[79] June 15, 2004 (Application No. 609 58/00).
[80] s.13(7).

(c) the reasons for taking the action be given to the Ombudsman for Children."

8–61 The Ombudsman may further request a reply in response to the recommendation. Section 13(4) provides that the result and any comments made by the public body, school or voluntary hospital are then required to be communicated to the child or the person who made the complaint on behalf of the child. This is subject to the principle of natural justice and constitutional due process rights, that any person subject to criticism or an adverse finding following an investigation be given an opportunity to "make representations in relation to it".[81] In this regard the Ombudsman is shielded from liability in the law of defamation for statements made in certain communications required by the Act, affording further statutory protection to the independence of the Ombudsman. To provide some teeth where a response to a recommendation is not satisfactory, the Ombudsman can include a special report on the case in the annual report to each House of the Oireachtas.[82]

Conclusion

8–62 The Ombudsman for Children will play a central role in advancing the interests and welfare of children, who are a minority voiceless group in society. The Office of the Ombudsman for Children provides us with an opportunity to look beyond individual complaints in the public domain over the past decade and will facilitate the investigation of systemic weaknesses in the practices of public bodies, schools and voluntary hospitals. However, the Ombudsman cannot be seen as a panacea for all ills. Society as a whole needs to recognise that children are autonomous beings with discrete rights.

NATIONAL CHILDREN'S OFFICE

8–63 Irish social and educational policies and practices have been reviewed by a special interdepartmental working group to ensure compliance with objectives set by the CRC, resulting in the National Children's Strategy (2000). The National Children's Office has been established to implement the Strategy, which is aimed at improving children's lives over the next ten years. It has been proactive in the implementation of the goals identified in the National Children's Strategy. This involves promoting actions under the three National Goals of the Strategy:

(1) children will have a voice;

(2) children's lives will be better understood; and

(3) children will receive quality supports and services.

---

[81] s.13(6).
[82] s.13(5) and (7).

8–64 The National Children's Office reports to the Cabinet Committee on progress, while individual departments retain responsibility for implementing the goals outlined in the National Children's' Strategy. Significantly, the office co-ordinates and monitors progress in this regard.

8–65 The National Children's Office is proving effective in educating Irish society and Government on the need not only to recognise and respect children's rights, but also to be held accountable on that commitment. The office has been a significant development and has promoted child-related thinking through "joined-up government".

CONCLUSION

8–66 Children have a right to be heard in legal and administrative proceedings affecting them. What works best? Listening to and responding to the voice of the child in legal proceedings. Hearing the voice of the child "untrammeled by professional discretion and interpretation".[83]

Hearing the voice of the child in legal proceedings is not easy. After all, our family law systems are adult- rather than child-centred. Moreover, the child's views and the welfare of the child are not synonymous. That said, if we are to treat children as objects of concern rather than subjects, we must accept the right of children to have their voices heard. We talk of the competence of young children to have their voices heard but the relevant issue may well be more the competence of professionals to listen, to understand and to communicate appropriately with young children that is more relevant.

In conclusion, we will only be successful in the project of giving children a voice when children are given the capability of being heard in all judicial and administrative proceedings affecting them, either directly, or through a representative, having regard to their age and understanding.

---

[83] See I. Butler and H. Williamson, *Children Speak: Children Trauma and Social Work* (Longmans, London, 1994).

CHAPTER 9

ADOPTION

Introduction

9–01   Adoption is the legal process by which a parent-child relationship is established between persons unrelated by birth, whereby the child assumes the same rights and duties as children in birth families. In Ireland, unlike in some other countries, adoption has the far-reaching effect of expunging all rights and duties of the natural parents in respect of the child. The adoptive parent or parents correspondingly become, for all legal purposes, the parent or parents of the child, with full parental rights and duties. This view of adoption, however, is not universally held. In some countries the adoption of a child does not, for instance, involve a complete severance of links with the child's family of origin. The Irish model, however, is the model generally accepted in Europe and is recognised as such by the European Convention on the Adoption of Children.[1]

9–02   Adoption is a controversial topic and there are many deeply held perspectives and biases on the issue. It has, as Vivienne Darling observes, "always been a highly emotional subject—it touches on sex, non-marital births, blood ties, heredity, parenting, religion, race, folklore."[2] In the triangle of interests, the child under seven years of age is the only party to the adoption not consulted or required to consent thereto. Any person connected to the process, either as a natural parent, an adoptive parent, or an adopted child, has his or her own individual perspective which is unique to the particular adoption but may also colour his or her view of the process generally.

Irish adoption legislation was introduced in 1952.[3] The Adoption Act 1952 ("the 1952 Act") provided the legal basis for adoption in Ireland and for the establishment of the Adoption Board, bringing order to the ad hoc arrangement which had operated hitherto in lieu of formal adoption procedures. The legislative framework for adoption was, at that point, closely allied to the quest for the provision of a socially acceptable family environment for children born of "irregular unions" and simultaneously providing a fresh start for the unmarried mother of the child concerned. The adoption code that was introduced by the 1952 Act was seen as a private, consensual mechanism designed to facilitate a legal transplantation of a child into the adoptive family. Adoption was perceived as a means of saving the child from the opprobrium and stigma then attached to the status of "illegitimacy". The demand by childless

---

[1]   April 24, 1967.

[2]   [1999] 4 I.J.F.L. 2.

[3]   Adoption Act 1952.

couples for children with which to form a family was, and remains, high. The 1952 Act has been amended six times, by Adoption Acts in 1964, 1974, 1976, 1988, 1991 and 1998. Two further pieces of adoption legislation were in contemplation at the time of writing this book: (a) the Adoption Information, Post Adoption Contact and Associated Issues Bill; and (b) the Bill to ratify the Hague Convention for the Protection of Children and Co-Operation in Respect of Intercountry Adoption 1993 and to update the provisions relating to the structure and functions of the Adoption Board.[4] Between 1953 and 2003, 42,440 adoption orders have been made in Ireland.

9–03 The 1952 Act itself was introduced after much soul searching and controversy, and represented a compromise between, on the one hand, those who wanted legal adoption introduced to give them a legal hold over the child and, on the other, the Christian churches who effectively controlled the "orphanages". The churches were themselves involved in the placement of children abroad for adoption by suitably religiously qualified couples, and so they could not be regarded as being opposed to adoption in principle. They feared, however, that adoption would be used as a vehicle for changing the child's religion and it was, therefore, necessary to assuage such concerns in the legislation.

9–04 Adoption draws into sharp relief the difference between a child born within a family based on marriage and a child born to parents who are not married to each other. Adoption, as originally envisaged, was for the benefit of the latter category of child only. A child born to a married family was not eligible for adoption even if the child's parents had abandoned him or her. It is only since 1988 that marital children have been eligible for adoption and then only once "freed for adoption" by order of the High Court.[5]

The legal consequences of adoption

9–05 The primary legal consequence of an adoption lies in the transformative effect it has on the respective parental rights of the parties. Notwithstanding the natural mother's or guardian's rights, the adoption acts to expunge all parental rights and obligations of that mother or guardian in respect of her child. Simultaneously, the effect of an adoption order is to vest full parental authority in the adoptive parent or parents, with full rights and duties residing in them as if the child was the child of the adopters, born to them within wedlock. Section 24 of the Adoption Act 1952 is especially clear in this regard:

> "Upon an adoption order being made:
> (a) the child shall be considered with regard to the rights and duties of parents and children in relation to each other as the child of the adopter or adopters born to him, her or them in lawful wedlock;

---

[4] The draft proposals are on the Department of Health's website on www.doh.ie/publications/hobdinf.html and www.doh.ie/publications/hobhague.html respectively.
[5] Adoption Act 1988.

(b) the mother or guardian shall lose all parental rights and be freed
from all parental duties with respect to the child."[6]

9–06   Thus, the making of the order effectively and comprehensively severs
the legal nexus between the natural parent and the child, so that the former
will retain no rights or duties at all in respect of the child. Nor can the natural
parent (unless he or she is, in fact, an adopter of the child) be liable towards,
or in respect of, the child. One consequence of the adoption order, for instance,
is the severing of any pre-existing obligation under a maintenance order unless
the mother herself is the adopter.[7] The liability of a natural father who has
been ordered to pay maintenance in respect of a child, thus, will cease absolutely
on the lawful adoption of that child by persons other than the mother herself.
However, s.3 of the Family Law (Maintenance of Spouses and Children) Act
1976, as amended by s.16(e) of the Status of Children Act 1987 and the
Adoption Act 1991, redefines "parent" as including a person who has adopted
a child under the Adoption Acts 1952 to 1991, but does not include a person
who is a parent of the child adopted under those Acts, where the person is not
an adopter of the child. In effect, therefore, following the adoption of a child
by the natural mother, the natural father is no longer a "parent", and therefore
any maintenance order previously made ceases to have effect. Nor will the
estate of a natural parent (not being an adopter of the child) be deemed liable
under the Succession Act 1965 (the Status of Children Act 1987 notwithstanding) for any legacy payable on intestacy. By the same token, however,
any order allowing either natural parent (or any other person) access to the
child will, by the same reasoning, be deemed to have lapsed upon the making
of the adoption order.[8] The Adoption Board should be provided with the option
to attach a condition to the adoption order that the non-marital father's access
continue following the making of an adoption order.[9] Any care order in respect
of the adopted child subsisting at the time of the adoption will, likewise, be
considered to have been terminated by the adoption.[10]

9–07   Section 26(1) of the 1952 Act stipulates that, should an adopter or
adopted person die intestate, the property of that person shall devolve in all
cases as if the adopted person were the child of the adopter "born in lawful
wedlock" and not the child of any other person. Section 26(2), in like manner,
states that in any will, codicil, or other disposition of real or personal property
made *inter vivos* or otherwise, a reference to the "child" or "children" of an
adopter shall be construed as including any person adopted by them. Such
reference may be express or implied. The adopted child then will be included
as a beneficiary unless the contrary intention is clearly expressed in the
disposition itself. This provision operates, however, only in relation to
dispositions made after the making of the relevant adoption order. In a

---

[6] See also s.7 of the Adoption Act 1988.
[7] Adoption Act 1952, s.31(1).
[8] See *W.O'R. v E.H.* [1996] 2 I.R. 248.
[9] See *Report of An Bord Uchtála* (2000), p.7.
[10] Adoption Act 1952, ss.31 and 33; Child Care Act 1991, s.44(2).

disposition made before the adoption order takes effect, a reference to a "child" or "children" will not generally include the adopted child. A will made before the date of an adoption order shall not be deemed to have been made after that date, by reason only of the fact that it has been confirmed by a codicil executed after the date in question.[11]

A reference to any other relationship in such dispositions shall be considered, again unless the contrary intention appears, as if the adopted child was the natural child of the adopter born within wedlock. Thus, if a deceased grandparent were, by will, to bequeath a legacy to "all my grandchildren, to be divided in equal shares amongst them", such disposition would operate in favour of a person adopted by a son or daughter of that grandparent. Again, this will only occur if the disposition in question has been effected after the relevant adoption order has been made. In the case of all such dispositions, however, it is possible to exclude this consequence, thereby denying the adopted person the benefit of a disposition, but only if an intention to do so is expressly stated. Corresponding provisions apply where there is any reference in a disposition to the child or children of the natural parents given by them for adoption to third parties. Such reference shall, unless the contrary intention appears, be construed as not being applicable to the child who has been adopted. Thus, where a natural parent of a child adopted by others wishes to create a benefit for a child, this intention must be expressly stated by reference, where possible, to the name of the child.

9–08   Similar provisions take effect where matters relating to succession duty, legacy duty, customs duty and stamp duty are being considered. In all such cases the relevant taxes should be levied in relation to the adopted person as if he or she were the natural child of adoptive parents born within wedlock.[12] For the purposes of the Workmen's Compensation Acts 1934 to 1948, like provisions apply.[13] Indeed, in most cases, where the relationship between a parent and child is implicated, it is the invariable rule to state that for those purposes an adopted child shall be treated as if he or she were the natural marital child of the adopter.[14]

9–09   By virtue of s.222 of the Finance Act 2001, an adopted child bears to a deceased natural parent, in relation to a gift or inheritance taken on or after March 30, 2001, the relationship of a "child". Consequently, an adopted child has now a Group One threshold of €456,438 in respect of any gift or inheritance from his or her adoptive parent and his or her natural parent. Practitioners should note that while s.14(d) of the Interpretation Act 2000[15] has redefined adopted child, this is unlikely to have any impact on this section.

---

[11]   s.26(4) of the Adoption Act 1952.

[12]   s.27 of the 1952 Act.

[13]   s.28 of the 1952 Act.

[14]   See, for instance, s.1(1) of the Family Home Protection Act 1976; s.3(1) of the Family Law (Maintenance of Spouses and Children) Act 1976; and s.2(1) of the Family Law Act 1995.

[15]   No. 53 of 2000.

9–10   It is difficult for a child to be adopted where its natural parents were married to each other at the time of the adoption. That said, the subsequent marriage of the natural parents of a child who has been validly adopted prior to that marriage is irrelevant to the adoption order. An adopted child is not legitimated by the subsequent marriage of his or her natural parents unless the adoption order is set aside. A subsequent change in the status of the natural parents cannot effect the status of the child in any way, the adoption having severed the link between the natural parents and the child who has been adopted.[16] This provision does not apply, however, where the child has been adopted by one of its natural parents. In such a case, the subsequent marriage of the natural parents will have the normal effect of "legitimating" the child and the Legitimacy Act 1931[17] will operate accordingly. This is the only case in which an adoption order that is otherwise valid at its inception can be rescinded. The effect of the legitimation, according to s.29(2)(b) of the 1952 Act, is that the adoption order shall "cease to be in force".

9–11   While an adoption permanently terminates the parental rights and duties of the natural parents of the child (unless one of them is himself or herself an adopter), the adoption itself may be terminated in certain limited circumstances. A child may be re-adopted, for instance, on the death of its adoptive parents.[18] Re-adoption is also possible, furthermore, where the adoptive parents are found to have been in serious dereliction of their parental duties under the provisions of the Adoption Act 1988.[19]

Categories of adoption

Adoption may be broadly classified into three categories:

1. Domestic consensual adoption

9–12   This is where a child is adopted with the consent of its natural mother and/or guardian. This type of adoption can only occur where the child is not the child of parents married to each other at the time of the child's birth.

2. Domestic non-consensual adoption

9–13   There are two situations in which an Irish adoption may be effected without consent of the parents. The first relates to s.3 of the Adoption Act 1974, the provisions of which allow a child who has been validly placed for adoption by its natural mother or guardian to be adopted notwithstanding the subsequent withdrawal of consent. The second is provided by the Adoption Act 1988, which provides for the adoption of children (including the children

---

[16] Adoption Act 1952, s.29(1).

[17] No. 13 of 1931.

[18] Adoption Act 1952, s.18.

[19] See the comments of the Supreme Court in *B. &. B. v An Bord Uchtála* [1997] 1 I.L.R.M. 15, where it was stated that an adoption order may be set aside under s.22(7) of the Adoption Act 1952. It is to be noted that s.18 of the 1952 Act permits re-adoption in some limited circumstances.

of parents married to each other), in circumstances where total abandonment of parental rights and duties has occurred.

3. Foreign adoption

9–14 The adoption of a child not of Irish residential origin may be recognised in this jurisdiction, provided that certain conditions are met.
Each of these three options is discussed further below.

Emerging trends in Irish adoption

9–15 Figure 1, below, illustrates certain trends in Irish adoption. This it does by means of five-year working averages of the relevant annual percentages. It shows, *inter alia,* the annual number of births and adoptions, the proportion of total births outside of marriage, and the percentage of adoption orders made in respect of children born outside of marriage in the same period.

Figure 1: Total births, births outside marriage and adoptions in Ireland, 1953 to 2003
(absolute figures and percentages for five year periods)

5 year period	*Total births*	*Births outside marriage*	*Percent of total births*	*Total no. of adoptions*	*Percent adopted of total births outside marriage*
1953–57	308,696	6,089	2.0	3,372	55.3
1958–62	302,040	4,989	1.7	2,844	57.0
1963–67	314,365	6,828	2.2	5,563	81.4
1968–72	324,376	8,756	2.4	6,578	75.1
1973–77	340,952	12,373	3.6	6,841	52.5
1978–82	359,782	18,242	5.1	5,708	31.3
1983–87	313,620	27,143	5.1	4,776	17.5
1988–92	263,469	39,044	5.1	3,025	7.7
1993–97	248,464	45,440	5.1	2,241	4.0
1998–03	341,064	105,006	3.2	1,842	1.8

Fig. 1: For an annual trend from 1953–2003, see the Annual Report of the Adoption Board, 2003.

9–16 The figures set out above[20] and below[21] give an overview of adoption trends from 1953 to 2003, along with corresponding figures from the Central Statistics Office, for live births and births outside marriage in the same period.

---

[20] See Fig.1.
[21] See Fig.2.

From this, it is manifestly clear that while marital fertility has generally decreased, the number of births outside marriage has increased over the years. This feature is coupled with a corresponding decrease in the percentage of non-marital children being put forward for adoption.[22] While the percentage of children born outside marriage has steadily increased, the proportion of such children who are placed for adoption has seen a steep decline. For example, in 1967, 96.9 per cent of children born outside marriage were adopted. In 1997, on the other hand, only 3.0 per cent of non-marital children were adopted and this percentage fell further to 1.36 per cent in 2003. Irish statistics would appear to suggest that this domestic shortfall is being made up through intercountry adoption.

Intercountry adoption in Ireland began as a humanitarian response to the issue of abandoned children in post-Ceausescu Romania in the early 1990s. The growth in intercountry adoption emerged in line with a dramatic fall in the number of domestic adoptions. The number of declarations to adopt abroad granted by the Adoption Board has increased every year since 1991. In 2003 168 declarations were granted, an increase of almost 69 on the previous year; 341 adoptions were recognised by the Adoption Board during 2003.

Figure 2: Births outside marriage as a percentage of total births. Percentage of children born outside wedlock and subsequently adopted.

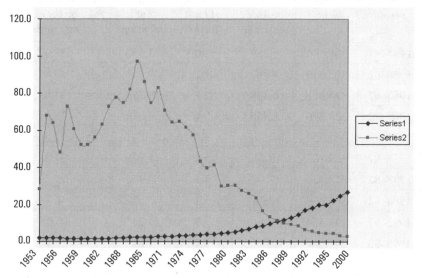

Fig. 2:   Series 1:Percentage adopted from births outside marriage.
          Series 2:Births outside marriage as a percentage of total births.

9–17   In the five-year period between 1953 and 1957, there were 3,372 adoptions orders made by the Adoption Board. In the same period, 55.3 per cent of children born outside wedlock were adopted. Only 2 per cent of children

---

[22] See Fig.2.

born were non-marital.[23] In the next five-year period, 1956 to 1962, 57 per cent of children born to unmarried parents were placed for adoption; 2,844 adoption orders were made; and only 1.7 per cent of children born were non-marital. The following five-year period, 1963 to 1967, saw the figure of births outside of marriage increasing marginally to 2.2 per cent of all births. In that period, however, 81.4 per cent of children born outside of marriage were adopted, while a total of 5,563 adoption orders were made. The highest figure for the individual years is 1967, when 96.9 per cent of children born outside of marriage were adopted. This period, together with the next five-year period, however, marks the watershed for adoption as the main care option chosen by unmarried mothers for their children.

9–18   While the next five year period, 1968–1972, saw a further increase in the number of children born to unmarried parents, to 2.7 per cent of all births, the percentage of such children being adopted was beginning to decline. In those years, 75.1 per cent of non-marital children were adopted. As Figure 1 clearly illustrates, each successive five-year period has shown a marked decline in the percentage of children born outside of marriage being placed for adoption and consequently the number of adoption orders made by the Adoption Board has fallen. The paradox is that in tandem with this decline, Ireland has seen a steady increase in births outside marriage, both in absolute terms and as a percentage of total live births.

The catalyst for change

9–19   A variety of factors may be cited as contributing to these changes in adoption practice. These included the softening of attitudes towards lone motherhood and families not based on marriage, the availability of contraception, but, perhaps most significantly, the introduction of the Unmarried Mother's Allowance in the 1970s. This made unmarried parenthood a realistic alternative to a pregnancy, which previously had tended to precipitate either a marriage or an adoption. Unmarried women were thus afforded a third and increasingly attractive option—single parenthood. In addition, it is clear from the available statistics and studies that legislation on abortion in Britain provided another alternative to an unwanted pregnancy.[24]

Adoption by relatives

9–20   In the context of domestic consensual adoption, a distinction may be drawn between non-relative adoption and adoption by relatives of the child. Non-relative adoption was originally the most common form of adoption. A study by Harold J. Abramson for the Economic and Social Research Institute

---

[23] See *Statistical Abstracts of Ireland* for statistics on births, and for adoption statistics, see annual reports of Adoption Board.

[24] See Abortion Act (England and Wales) 1967 and Mahon, Conlon, and Dillon, *Women & Crisis Pregnancy, A Report presented to the Department of Health and Children* (The Stationery Office, Dublin, 1998).

in July 1984[25] noted the relatively low proportion of adoptions effected in Ireland in favour of relatives of the child. In other jurisdictions, relative adoption seems to have proven more popular. In the United States, for instance, a study by Alfred Kadushin, *Adopting Older Children*, showed that in 1970 about half of all legal adoptions in the United States were relative adoptions. In Ireland the figure was considerably smaller, at around 10 per cent of all legal adoptions at the date of the study. Since then, as in other Western countries, there has been a marked reduction in the number of children being placed for adoption by non-relatives. This reduction in domestic non-relative adoption is primarily due, it seems, to the non-availability of children being placed for adoption. The number of adoptions by relatives, however, has increased. The term "relatives" originally embraced only persons traced through the natural mother; however, since 1998, it has been possible also to trace a family relationship through the father of the child.

Figure 3: Total adoption orders made and adoption orders made in favour of Relatives, 1994–2003

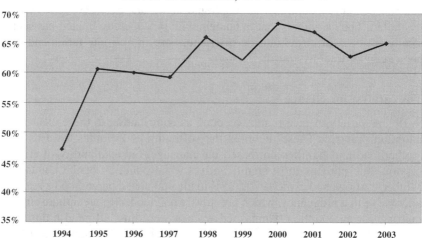

9–21 As seen above,[26] while there has been a considerable decline in the numbers of children available for adoption generally, an increasing number of the children who are being adopted are being adopted by relatives of the child. The number of family adoptions has increased from 126 in 1975 to 171 in 2003. The net effect of this trend has been to reduce even further the chances of a prospective adopter being granted an adoption in respect of a child of a non-relative. For these purposes, the term "relative" may, of course, include the child's own natural parent, as where a natural parent and his or her spouse (not being a parent of the child) jointly adopt the child of the former. Relative also includes all persons related to the child, whether traced through the mother or (since 1998) the father of the child.

---

[25] *Issues in Adoption in Ireland*: Broadsheet No.23, July, 1984.
[26] See Fig.3.

9–22   A further notable feature is the divergent profiles of the average child adopted by non-relatives as opposed to relatives. The average child adopted by strangers typically tends to be younger than the child adopted by its relatives:

Figure 4: Adoptions by age of child in 2003

	Family Adoptions	%	Non-Family Adoptions	%	Total
Under 1 year	0	0	6	7	6
Between 1 and 2 years	1	1	46	50	47
Between 2 and 3 years	0	0	11	12	11
Between 3 and 4 years	2	1	8	9	10
Between 4 and 5 years	7	4	2	2	9
Between 5 and 10 years	68	40	7	8	75
Between 10 and 15 years	79	46	3	3	82
Between 15 and 18 years	14	8	9	10	23
TOTAL	**171**	**100**	**92**	**100**	**263**

9–23   The pattern of adoption by non-relatives largely involves the adoption of babies and very young children. Non-relative adoptions appear to be primarily used to create a "family unit", approximating in so far as possible to "ordinary" family units. The adoption of older children by non-relatives is comparatively uncommon. The Adoption Board specifically noted that in 1993 it made 10 adoption orders in respect of children with "special needs", eight such orders in 1994, six in 1995, two in 1996, three in 1997 and one in 1998. The statistics also show that the majority of non-relative adopters have no children, or only adopted children in their family structure. Only a very small number of non-relative adoptive families have both natural and adopted children. As yet, the statistics show no real trend towards the adoption of older children or children with special needs, unlike the situation in the United Kingdom and the United States.

9–24   As can be seen from Figure 3, adoptions by relatives are now more common than adoptions by non-relatives. As most of these relative adoptions are by a natural parent and new spouse, it is understandable that the children concerned are more likely to be older at the date of the adoption order. In 2003, 164 of the 171 family adoptions were step-parent adoptions. Adoption is attractive as an option for natural parents for a variety of reasons. First, it is the only way of investing the spouse of the natural parent with guardianship rights in respect of the child. To achieve this, however, the natural parent must also adopt his or her own child even though he or she already has parental rights and obligations in respect of the child. The Annual Reports of the Adoption Board have pointed out this anachronism and called for the law to be changed in this regard.[27] Legislation should therefore be introduced to permit

---

[27]   See Annual Reports 1993 to 2003 and Darling, "The Changing Face of Adoption" [1999] 4 I.J.F.L. 2.

Figure 5: Adoptions by relatives—by age of child, 1993–1997

		%
Orders made in respect of boys	141	*54*
Orders made in respect of girls	122	*46*
Total	**263**	*100*
Non-Family Adoptions *Orders made in respect of children placed by:* Registered Adoption Societies (adoption placements)	21	*8*
Registered Adoption Societies (long-term foster placements)	6	*2*
Health Boards (adoption placements)	27	*10*
Health Boards (long-term foster placements)	14	*5*
Irish private placements*	2	*1*
Children placed by persons or authorities outside State	22	*8*
Total non-family adoptions	**92**	*34*
Family Adoptions Birth/natural mother and her husband	164	*62*
Birth/natural mother alone	0	*0*
Birth/natural father and his wife	1	*1*
Birth/natural father alone	0	*0*
Grandparents	1	*1*
Other relatives	5	*2*
Total family adoptions	**171**	*66*
TOTAL	**263**	*100*

*Private adoption placements within Ireland were prohibited under the Adoption Act, 1998. The orders referred to here relate to placements made before that Act came into force.

a mother to retain her guardianship of the child while at the same time permitting her spouse to acquire guardianship rights over the child. Section 51(2) of the Adoption and Children Act 2002 in Britain introduces such a provision. Adoption can also extinguish "inconvenient" ties between the child and the other natural parent. Thus it is sometimes availed of by the custodial natural parent, for instance, to effect a name change where the other parent's name was chosen at the date of registration. There is no mechanism within the existing adoption code whereby the natural parents can continue a legal parenting regime, and, at the same time, allow the custodial parent to adopt the child with his or her spouse. The Adoption Board has called for a change in the legislation to facilitate a new spouse of a natural parent obtaining joint guardianship rights with the mother, while at the same time facilitating the continuation of any factual relationship of the non-custodial natural parent with the child. The introduction of a divorce jurisdiction in Ireland in 1996 has not distorted the pattern of adoptions by relatives, and will not do so as step-parent adoptions will not arise. Under the current divorce legislation, neither parent loses guardianship on divorce.[28]

[28] s.10(2) of the Family Law (Divorce) Act 1996.

Jurisdiction to make an adoption order

Who may make an order?

9–25   An order in respect of the adoption of a child may only be effected by the Adoption Board, *An Bord Uchtála*, a body established by s.8(1) of the Adoption Act 1952. The main functions of the Adoption Board under the Acts are the making of adoption orders, the registering and supervision of adoption societies, the granting of declarations for eligibility and suitability to adopt abroad, and the recognition of foreign adoptions. This Board consists of a Chairperson (described as a "Chairman") and eight ordinary members, all of whom are appointed by the Government.[29] The Chairman must be a judge of either the Supreme Court, the High Court, the Circuit Court or the District Court, although it is also possible to appoint to such position a barrister or solicitor of at least 10 years' standing.[30] A person appointed as deputy chairman, for the purpose of deputising for the Chairman in the latter's absence, must be similarly qualified.[31] The members of the Board shall ordinarily hold office for five years, unless the member has been appointed to fill a casual vacancy.[32] In the latter case, the new appointee shall hold office until such time as the person he or she is replacing would have held office had the position not been vacated. Any member may be removed for stated misbehaviour, or otherwise resign for any reason.[33] While the Board may act in the absence of one or more of its members, it must proceed in accordance with the requirements laid down in the First Schedule to the 1952 Act.

9–26   The Adoption Board has the primary function of making or refusing adoption orders, and of registering and supervising the work of adoption societies. All organisations and societies engaged in placing children for adoption must be registered with the Adoption Board. The Adoption Board is in effect designed as a ratifying agency and a safeguard for consensual adoptions. As Walsh J. noted in *G. v An Bord Uchtála*:[34]

> "The Board has no function to settle disputes as to the custody of the child. Neither does it have any jurisdiction to adjudicate upon anything that could be said to be in controversy or dispute between the parties. ... The Board is simply concerned with what I am satisfied is the administrative function of seeing that the steps taken are not contrary to the adoption legislation, are not inimical to the welfare of the child, and that everybody concerned has had a full opportunity of considering the matter carefully. It is quite clear that the Board was not invested with any power to settle or decide any question as to the existence of a right or obligation or duty. This appears to me clearly to have been the policy and effect of the Act of 1952."

---

[29] s.8(2) and (3) of the Adoption Act 1952.
[30] s.8(4).
[31] s.8(4A) and (4B).
[32] First Schedule to the Act, clause 2.
[33] *ibid.*, clause 3.
[34] [1980] I.R. 32.

9–27   Where there is any dispute about the proposed adoption, then the High Court may be involved by one of the parties. In general terms, however, the involvement of the High Court was designed by the legislation to be the exception rather than the rule.

9–28   Doubts concerning the legal competence of *An Bord Uchtála* led to the enactment, in 1979, of the Sixth Amendment of the Constitution Act.[35] This allows the Board, or any similar body, appointed for the purpose of making adoption orders, validly to make such orders, notwithstanding the possibility that such conduct amounts to an "administration of justice", that is, the performance of a "judicial function". Normally, a judicial function may only be exercised in the courts by lawfully appointed judges.[36] While it is not clear that an adoption does indeed amount to an "administration of justice" for these purposes, it appears that even if it does, the Board may continue to act, notwithstanding the provisions of Art.34. The Amendment also supplies retrospective validation to any adoption order that may have been granted in contravention of Art.34, prior to the insertion of the Sixth Amendment.
    The Amendment reads as follows:

> "No adoption of a person taking effect, or expressed to take effect, at any time after the coming into operation of this Constitution under laws enacted by the Oireachtas and being an adoption pursuant to an Order made or an authorisation given by any person or body of persons designated by those laws to exercise such functions and powers was or shall be invalid by reason only of the fact that such person or body of persons was not a judge or a court appointed or established as such under this Constitution."

9–29   This amendment was considered essential in order to secure the validity of all adoption orders since the *McL* case.[37] In that case, a five-year adoption order was quashed by the Supreme Court, on the application of the natural mother, because the Adoption Board had made a mistake in the administrative procedure.[38] The function of the Adoption Board and its role in the making of adoption orders was raised in the High Court. It was held that the Adoption Board exercised limited civil powers of a judicial nature in accordance with the imperatives of Art.37.1 of the Constitution. Although not a court, the Board was thus empowered to make adoption orders. On appeal to the Supreme Court, this matter was not determined, since the natural mother succeeded on a non-constitutional point, and so there was a residue of doubt and uncertainty on the matter. Hence, the need for the Constitutional amendment.[39] With regard

---

[35]   Now Art.37.2 of the Constitution of Ireland 1937.

[36]   Art.34 of the Constitution.

[37]   See *M. and M. v An Bord Uchtála* [1977] I.R. 287.

[38]   See D.G. Morgan, *The Separation of Powers in the Irish Constitution* (Round Hall Sweet and Maxwell, Dublin, 1997), p.119.

[39]   See also G. Hogan and G. Whyte, *Kelly: The Irish Constitution* (4th ed., Lexis Nexis, Dublin, 2003).

to the making of adoption orders, the Board is obliged to comply strictly with the provisions of the Adoption Acts 1952 to 1998. Section 16 (1) of the 1952 Act lists the categories of person entitled to be heard on the application for an adoption order. This section has been amended by s.2(2) of the Adoption Act 1964 to include a reference to the father of the child. It has been partially repealed by s.13 and the Schedule to the Adoption Act 1974, in so far as it related to a Minister of a Religion "recognised by the Constitution". Section 7 of the Adoption Act 1988 provides that a reference to the mother of a child shall, in so far as it applies to a child of married parents (other than a child in respect of whom an adoption order is in force), be construed as including a reference to the father of the child.

9–30 Adoption applications may be heard wholly or partially in private.[40] Where the Board has notice of proceedings pending in any court with regard to the child in respect of whom an application is before the Board, it may not make an order in the matter until the proceedings have been disposed of.[41] Those persons who are entitled to be heard are also entitled to be represented by a solicitor or barrister.[42] Moreover, the Board, under s.17, is empowered to make custody orders in relation to the child on an interim basis for a probationary period not exceeding two years, and to make ancillary interim orders relating to the maintenance, education and supervision of the child.

9–31 It is quite clear from the 1952 Act that the Adoption Board was always envisaged as a private law tribunal. The procedures of the Board were laid down in the First Schedule to the Act, including detailed procedures relating to a "one judgment" rule. The Board is empowered to determine adoption applications and may summon witnesses, examine them on oath, and require the production of any document. Witnesses before the Board are entitled to the same immunities and privileges as witnesses before the High Court. At the conclusion of the hearing, the Board is required to notify the Registrar in respect of the adoption order made. It should be noted that s.27 of the Civil Legal Aid Act 1995 does not apply to hearings before the Adoption Board, and so legal aid is not available to any of the parties involved in such a hearing. The Minister for Justice, Equality and Law Reform is empowered to make an order under s.27 prescribing the Adoption Board as a tribunal to which that section applies.

9–32 Walsh J., in his foreword to Professor William Binchy's *Casebook on Irish Family Law*,[43] was critical in his analysis of the role of the Adoption Board in making legal adoptions without judicial confirmation or intervention. He pointed out that its powers are limited and that it could not decide the validity of the marriage of the couples who seek to adopt. Such an issue might determine their eligibility to adopt in the first place, and if this issue were raised later on, the invalidity of the adoption order could have very serious

---

[40] s.16(3).
[41] s.16(4).
[42] s.16(2).
[43] W. Binchy, *Casebook on Irish Family Law* (Professional Books, Abingdon, 1984), p.vii.

consequences for all concerned, in particular the child. The Adoption Board may, however, state a case for the determination of the High Court on any question of law arising out of an application for an adoption order, and such a case may be heard *in camera*.[44] The Review Committee recommended that the Adoption Board should be replaced by a specialist Adoption Court, functioning as a distinct branch of the High Court, which would be presided over by a single judge specially appointed to it, and who would sit with two assessors.[45] A system of Reginal Family Courts could also be established with jurisdiction to determine all appeals from the Adoption Board, if necessary.

9–33 The Adoption Board is obliged by statute to produce a yearly report. Section 13 of the First Schedule to the 1952 Act prescribes the contents of such an Annual Report. The Board is also obliged to keep an Adoption Societies Register, and no society can be entered on to that Register unless it exists solely for the purpose of promoting charitable, benevolent or philanthropic objectives.[46] An adoption society is under a statutory obligation to furnish the Board with details of its constitution, membership, employees, organisation and activities, and is further obliged to permit the Board to inspect all books and documents relating to adoption in its possession.[47] The Board must be satisfied that an adoption society is competent to discharge its obligations. It is empowered to cancel the registration of a society on any ground that would entitle it not to register it in the first place, or if it appears to the Board that the society is not complying with the requirements of the adoption code.[48]

9–34 Although the Board has not determined the minimum code of practice for adoption societies, it has produced guidelines which are advisory in nature.[49] Darling has expressed criticism about the lack of uniformity in the practices of the adoption societies in adoption practice. The Report of the Review Committee on Adoption Services in 1984 noted that:

"While it is implicit in the statutory provisions governing the registration of adoption societies that the Adoption Board has the responsibility to monitor their standards and performance, there is no indication that this has been done to any notable degree. The poor practice of some of the agencies may derive from this lack of critical and continuous supervision

---

[44] s.20 of the Adoption Act 1952.
[45] See *Report of the Review Committee on Adoption Services* (The Stationery Office, Dublin, 1984), paras 9.12–9.16.
[46] Adoption Act 1952, s.36.
[47] Adoption Act 1952, s.38.
[48] Adoption Act 1952, s.37.
[49] See V. Darling, "Statutory Regulations for the Operation of Adoption Societies" (1975) 1 *Children First Newsletter* at 9. See also, K. O'Halloran, *Adoption Law and Practice* (Butterworths, Dublin, 1992) p.28, where he points out that under s.5 of the Adoption Act 1952, the Adoption Board, with the consent of the Minister, may make rules for the regulation of its procedure and for any other matter referred to in the Act as prescribed. The Minister, therefore, has power in the primary legislation to empower the Adoption Board with regard to matters of professional practice.

and indicates a shortcoming in the present adoption machinery which needs to be provided for in an improved system."[50]

The Review Committee made recommendations to improve the performance of the Voluntary Adoption Societies. These recommendations have, however, never been implemented. The Annual Report of the Adoption Board in 1997 noted that the decision of some adoption societies to de-register was a natural consequence of the declining number of children being placed for adoption by birth mothers.

9–35 The powers of the Adoption Board have been augmented by the Adoption Act 1976, to include a power to request and authorise any suitable person, within or outside the State, to make enquiries and report to it on matters relating to the validity of consents. The Adoption Board is also now required to approve prospective adopters of foreign children and issue appropriate declarations, and to establish and maintain a Register of Foreign Adoptions.[51] The role of the Adoption Board is to be enlarged to that of Central Authority when the 2004 Hague Convention Bill is enacted.[52] The Central Authority is the key to the administration of the Convention within a State Party to the Convention. It will have enlarged supervisory functions with regard to other agencies and administrative bodies involved in intercountry adoption. Under the Convention, it will be obliged to set and enforce standards for their operation. This may well result in a greater "hands on" management of such agencies in domestic adoptions also. The Law Reform Commission recommended the creation of an appeal structure, through which decisions of the Central Authority could be appealed to the Circuit Court. It further recommended that the Minister for Health and Children, in consultation with the Adoption Board, should set standards of competence for all bodies administering intercountry adoption. Such standards, it held, should apply to all bodies involved in intercountry adoption, both accredited agencies and health boards.[53] A report by the Law Society of Ireland's Law Reform Committee in April 2000 entitled *Adoption Law: The Case for Reform* also acknowledged the important role performed by the Adoption Board and recommended that a system of Regional Family Courts be established with jurisdiction to determine all appeals from the Adoption Board.

Placement for adoption

9–36 The following may make a placement for adoption:

(1) a health board;

---

[50] See *Report of the Review Committee on Adoption Services* (The Stationery Office, Dublin, 1984), p.48.

[51] Adoption Act 1991.

[52] See the Adoption (Hague Convention) Bill 2004.

[53] See the recommendations in the *Report on the Implementation of the Hague Convention on Protection of Children and Co-Operation in Respect of Intercountry Adoption 1993* (LRC 58–1998).

(2) a registered adoption society;

(3) a parent of the child, but only where the child is being placed with a relative of the parent or of the child.

9–37 Generally speaking, an adoption must proceed through the auspices of a registered adoption society or health board. An adoption society may be registered for these purposes under s.36 of the Adoption Act 1952. A register of such societies is, by s.35 of the Act, required to be kept and to be open to public inspection. It is generally illegal for any body of persons to make or to attempt to make any arrangements for the adoption of a child, unless that body is a registered adoption society or health board.[54] It is also unlawful, by virtue of the original s.34(4) of the 1952 Act, for any third party to make arrangements for the adoption of a child, other than under the auspices of a registered adoption society or health board.

9–38 It was originally possible for an individual to put forward a child for adoption, or cause a child to be put forward for adoption, if that person was a parent of the child or if the person intending to adopt was a relative of the child. Since the enactment of s.7 of the Adoption Act 1998, however, it has been illegal for any person to make a private placement of a child with a view to adoption. Even a parent of the child is precluded from doing so unless the prospective adopter is a relative of the child. The Adoption Board had, for some time before the enactment, expressed its concern at the growing prevalence of such private arrangements, noting that such arrangements effectively facilitated the circumvention of the eligibility requirements in the Adoption Acts. Section 7 of the Adoption Act 1998 makes it an offence to place a child with any person for the purposes of adoption. It is also illegal for a parent of the child to place the child with anyone other than a relative of the child.[55] Such an offence attracts a penalty of imprisonment of not more than 12 months and/or a fine of no more than IR£1,500 (€1,890), an amount considerably less than the cost of the average foreign adoption.[56] No offence will be committed, however, where the child is placed under the auspices of an adoption society. Nor does the Act apply where the private placement is made by the natural parent in favour of a person who is already a relative of the child. Generally speaking, a child may not be placed by an adoption agency until it has attained the age of four weeks, although an earlier placement may proceed in certain limited circumstances outlined later.[57]

9–39 In *Eastern Health Board v E.A. and A.*,[58] the Eastern Health Board brought habeas corpus proceedings against the owners of a pregnancy counselling agency with regard to a private placement for adoption. The basis

---

[54] Adoption Act 1952, s.34.
[55] Amending s.34 of the Adoption Act 1952.
[56] See the criticisms of Darling [1999] 4 I.J.F.L. 2, who suggests that this is not a sufficient deterrent.
[57] ss.7B, 7E and 7F of the 1952 Act as inserted by s.4 of the Adoption Act 1998.
[58] [2000] 1 I.R. 430.

for the proceedings centred on the fact that, on the advice of the agency, a mother placed her child for adoption with the couple who owned the agency. Laffoy J. stated that there had been a breach of s.7 of the Adoption Act 1998 and held that there was a "glaring conflict of interest" when the person "who assumes the role of counsellor and adviser to a young girl in the later stages of a crisis pregnancy proposes himself and his wife as prospective adoptive parents of the baby and proposes taking custody of the baby within days of the baby's birth".

Other matters relating to jurisdiction

9–40 Jurisdiction for Irish adoption is based, *inter alia*, on requirements of residency and ordinary residency in the State. A child, to be the subject of a domestic order for adoption, must, at the time in question, reside in the State.[59] In the case of the child, the exact period of residence is not defined by the legislation. An adult, to be eligible to adopt, must be ordinarily resident in the State and have been so resident during the year ending at that date of the making of the adoption order.[60] Neither, in the case of the child nor of the adults, does the law stipulate Irish nationality or Irish domicile as a jurisdictional criterion. This obviates the complex and difficult task of having to ascertain the domicile of the child or of the adoptive parents.[61]

9–41 An adoption order cannot be made in favour of more than one person unless the applicants to adopt are a validly married couple living together.[62] A joint application may be made in such circumstances. Even where the prospective adoptive father is married to the birth mother, the application to adopt must be a joint one, and so the birth mother must adopt her own child jointly with her husband. In 1994, the Adoption Board's Annual Report first drew attention to this anomalous position, whereby the continuing parental relationship of the mother and child is not recognised where the birth mother or birth father is adopting the child with his or her spouse. The Board called for an amendment of the law to allow for a new type of adoption order in such situations, which would retain the birth mother's/father's original relationship with the child while creating a joint legal parental relationship for the spouse. In 1984, the *Review Committee on Adoption Services*, while acknowledging the concerns expressed about the natural mother being named as the adoptive mother of her own child, recommended no change to the legislation.[63]

---

[59] Adoption Act 1952, s.10(a).

[60] Adoption Act 1991, s.10(6).

[61] *Report on the Recognition of Foreign Adoption Decrees* (LRC 58–1989) p.5. See also Morris, *Some Recent Developments in the English Private International Law of Adoption*, Festschrift für Mann 241 at 243 (1977), who criticises English law, which made domicile the sole jurisdictional criterion in England and Wales. See also, G.H. Jones, *Adoption in the Conflict of Laws* (April, 1956) 5 I.C.L.Q. 207 to 216.

[62] Adoption Act 1991, s.10(1)(a).

[63] *Report of the Review Committee on Adoption Services* (The Stationery Office, Dublin, 1984), p.21.

9–42 The statutory conditions relating to residence, marriage, religion and minimum age stand as sentinels to the gateway of eligibility. Section 10(5) of the Adoption Act 1991 provides that the minimum age is now 21 years for each applicant. In limited circumstances, unmarried people can adopt.[64] The latter Act enabled the Board to make an order, under s.10(2), notwithstanding the marital status of the applicant, where, "in the particular circumstances of the case", that was desirable. Commentators have pointed out, however, that the child adopted by a single person will not have the constitutional buttress available to children adopted into a married unit, because the relationship between the parent and the child will not be regarded as being based on the institution of marriage.[65] See also para.9–53.

9–43 Adoption by separated and divorced people is also permitted under s.10(4) of the Adoption Act 1991. This may occur where a couple are living apart under a decree of divorce *a mensa et thoro*, or a judicial separation, or a deed of separation, or where a spouse has been deserted, either actually or constructively.[66]

9–44 Section 4 of the Adoption Act 1974 sets out the religious requirements imposed upon adoptive parents. The prospective adoptive parents, the birth parents and child must all be of the same religion unless the birth parents, knowing in advance the religious persuasion of the adoptive parents, have waived this requirement. Married couples of mixed faith can therefore adopt, provided that the birth parents consent to the placing of the child with them. As a corollary, the orphaned child of a marriage of persons of mixed faith is also eligible for adoption.

9–45 Voluntary adoption societies, under the authority of s.13(1) of the 1952 Act, often impose administrative conditions regarding upper age limits and the quality of relationships and lifestyle. These are currently endorsed by the Adoption Board. In practice, the adoption societies' guideline felt most poignantly by would-be adopters is the one relating to the upper age limit. However, the work of Rev. J. Good is particularly instructive in this regard.[67] Rev. J. Good conducted a survey of children adopted from an adoption society during the period between October 8, 1954 to October 7, 1974, to ascertain whether the latter's work had generally been successful. "In addressing envelopes," Rev. J. Good observes, "I became aware of the relatively large number of adopting parents whom I knew to have died. ... It is interesting to speculate how many adopting parents would have been rejected as unsuitable if a strict medical examination had been insisted on."[68]

---

[64] Adoption Act 1991, s.10(2).
[65] See Shatter, *Family Law* (4th ed., Butterworths, Dublin, 1997), p.11, and K. O'Halloran, *Adoption Law and Practice* (Butterworths, Dublin, 1992), p.19.
[66] Child Care Act 1991, s.10, generally brings our legislation in line with the requirements of the Council of Europe as set out in the European Convention on the Adoption of Children (April 24, 1967), Art.7.
[67] Rev. J. Good, "A Cork Society's Survey" (1970) 2 *Child Adoption*.
[68] Note that under the European Convention, unless exceptional circumstances warrant,

9–46 These upper age limits may be relaxed in the case of foreign adoptions. For instance, the Chinese Authorities tend to reflect the Chinese cultural feature of respect for older parents. Adoptive parents have recently complained that the adoption societies practice ageism in certain circumstances where the health of the prospective parents is very good, the only factor being that one of the prospective adoptive parents is over 40 years of age. They argue that many couples of such an age group naturally give birth to children at this age, a reality, they allege, that the adoption societies fail to take into account.[69]

Adoption: eligibility requirements

Children eligible for adoption

9–47 At present only the following children may be adopted under our domestic law:

1. An orphan,[70] that is, a child both of whose parents are deceased.[71] Such adoption may proceed even if the parents, while alive, were married to each other.

2. A child born outside marriage, and not subsequently "legitimated" by its parents' marriage;[72] for these purposes a child will be deemed to have been born outside marriage unless its parents were married to *each other* at the relevant time.

3. A legitimated child whose birth has not been registered under the Legitimacy Act 1931;[73] thus, where the parents of a child marry after the child's birth, an adoption may still proceed provided the child has not been registered as a "legitimate" child. In such a case, however, the consent of the natural father to the placement for adoption is required.

4. An abandoned child may be adopted in certain circumstances, regardless of the marital status of the child's parents.[74] Thus, this facility may be used even where the child's birth parents were married to each other at the time of the child's birth.

9–48 Section 10 of the 1952 Act originally confined the adoption process to

---

the lower age limit for an adopter is to be between 21 and 35, said adopter having undergone a full investigation to determine eligibility for adoption. See H.E. Bogard, "Comment, Who are the Orphans? Defining Orphan Status and the Need for an International Convention on Intercountry Adoption" (1991) 5 Emory Int'l. Rev. 571, pp.603–604.

[69] Oral submission by Mary Murray of the Irish Foreign Adoption Group at an open meeting of the Law Reform Commission on the Implementation of the Hague Convention on Protection of Children and Co-operation in Respect of Inter-Country Adoption. Trinity College, Dublin, March, 1998.

[70] Adoption Act 1952, s.10(c).
[71] Adoption Act 1952, s.3.
[72] Adoption Act 1952, s.10(c).
[73] Adoption Act 1964, s.2.
[74] Adoption Act 1988, s.3.

full orphans and what it termed "illegitimate" children (what would now be called "non-marital" children). Initially, adoption was confined to children between the ages of six months and seven years who were orphans or non-marital children.[75] The child had to be resident in Ireland.[76] The Act restricted the removal of children under seven for adoption abroad, although the removal of a child by or with the approval of the parent, guardian or relative of the child was not prohibited by the legislation.[77] Eligibility to adopt was confined to married couples living together, widows and the natural mother, natural father, and certain relatives of the child (traced at that point solely through the mother). Both of the adoptive parents had to be of the same religion as the child. This effectively meant that an inter-denominational couple could not adopt, and the child of inter-denominational parents could not be adopted.

9–49 The Adoption Act 1952 was amended by the Adoption Act 1964. The amending Act widened the category of child eligible for adoption to include certain children not originally embraced by the 1952 Act. It allowed, in particular, the adoption of children who had been legitimated by the subsequent marriage of their parents, but whose births had not been re-registered. An adoption could proceed in such circumstances, provided that the father gave his consent to both the placement and to the final adoption order, although the latter consent could be dispensed with in accordance with s.14 of the 1952 Act.[78] The Act also enabled the adoption of children over seven and obliged the Board to give due consideration to the child's wishes, having regard to the age and understanding of the child.[79] Originally the child had to be no more than seven years of age. The Adoption Act 1964 allowed a child who had not yet reached the age of nine to be adopted, provided that the child had been placed with the applicant prior to its reaching the age of seven. Both of these requirements were deleted by s.11 of the Adoption Act 1974.

9–50 Further extensions in the category of eligible children came in the form of the Adoption Act 1988, the principal feature of which is the introduction of a facility for adopting the children of married parents. Under the 1988 Act, any child, whether or not born to married parents, may be eligible for adoption where the courts have found that the parents of the child have failed in their duty for physical or moral reasons. The Adoption Act 1991 provided for the recognition of foreign adoption orders made in respect of children deemed eligible to be adopted by the law of the place where the adoption was effected.

9–51 The child to be adopted must be already "born". Section 8 of the Adoption Act 1974 amended s.15 of the Adoption Act 1952 by providing that a consent shall not be valid unless it is given after the child has attained the age of six weeks, and not earlier than three months, before the application for

---

[75] Adoption Act 1952, s.10(b).

[76] Adoption Act 1952, s.10(a).

[77] Adoption Act 1952, s.40.

[78] Adoption Act 1964, s.2, and *Re J.H. (an infant); K.C. & A.C. v An Bord Uchtála* [1985] I.L.R.M. 302 (SC).

[79] Adoption Act 1964, s.3.

adoption. However, a mother or guardian could at any time following the birth of the child agree to the placement of the child for adoption. The child must now be at least four weeks old before he or she can be placed for adoption by an adoption agency.[80] The new time requirement facilitates the pre-placement consultation process for natural fathers introduced by the 1998 Act, following the decision of the European Court of Human Rights in the case of *Keegan v Ireland*.[81] The original requirement that the child be not less than six months old before an adoption order could be made in respect of him or her was abolished in 1974.[82] In practice, however, the protracted nature of the adoption process will result in few adoption orders being granted before the child has reached that age. In addition, s.9 of the Adoption Act 1974 refers to a prescribed period during which the child must be in the care of the prospective adopters before an adoption order can be made. No such minimum period, however, has ever in fact been prescribed.

9–52 In line with other child law legislation, the meaning of "child" is confined to persons not having reached the age of majority. Thus, a person, to be eligible for being adopted, must be under 18 years of age.[83] The child must be resident in the State.[84] Where the child to be adopted is over seven years of age, the Adoption Board is required to give due consideration to his or her wishes.[85]

Persons eligible to adopt

9–53 The Adoption Acts presuppose that adopters will be married couples. Section 10(2) of the Adoption Act 1991 permits adoption by single parents, but only where the Adoption Board is satisfied that "in the particular circumstances of the case, it is desirable" to effect such an order. This Act allows for a single person, a married person acting alone,[86] or (by implication) a divorced or separated person to adopt, even where the adopter is not related to the child. Although an individual in a stable non-marital relationship may adopt under the Acts, a couple in the same circumstances may not.

The following persons are eligible to adopt a child, subject to satisfying the Board as to their suitability:

1. A married couple living together.[87]

2. The natural mother of the child in question.[88]

3. The natural father of the child in question.[89]

---

[80] Adoption Act 1998, s.7B.
[81] [1994] E.H.R.R. 342.
[82] Adoption Act 1974, s.13.
[83] Adoption Act 1988, s.6(1).
[84] Adoption Act 1952, s.10.
[85] Adoption Act 1952, s.10; Adoption Act 1964, s.3; and Adoption Act 1974, s.11.
[86] Adoption Act 1991, s.10(4), however, requires the consent of the spouse of such a person.
[87] Adoption Act 1991, s.10(1)(a).
[88] Adoption Act 1991, s.10(1)(b).
[89] Adoption Act 1991, s.10(1)(b).

4. A relative of the child. Originally, the term "relative" was confined to persons related only to the natural mother of the child.[90] A "relative" for these purposes, however, now includes a person related to either the mother or the father of the child.[91]

5. A widow.[92]

6. A widower.[93] Originally, widowers were not amongst the category of persons entitled to adopt. Section 5 of the Adoption Act 1974 attempted, somewhat, to redress this inequality. Nevertheless, the High Court, in *T.O'G. v Attorney General & Ors.*,[94] struck down s.5 of the 1974 Act on the grounds that it infringed the provisions of the Constitution. Section 5 had authorised adoption by widowers, but only in limited circumstances, the main condition being that the widower already have children in his custody. A like restriction not having been applied to widows in similar circumstances, the offending provision was struck down as having offended the guarantee of equality contained in Art.40.1 of the Constitution.

7. A single person.[95]

8. A person separated by virtue of a deed of separation, a judicial separation granted under the Judicial Separation and Family Law Reform Act 1989, or by a divorce *a mensa et thoro*, or a spouse who has been deserted.[96]

9–54 Both parties to a joint adoption application must be aware of the proposed adoption.[97] In *State (A.G.) v An Bord Uchtála*,[98] Lavery J. pointed out that an application by a wife without the knowledge of her husband had the effect of thrusting upon him the obligations of parenthood. The adoption order, thus, was declared invalid. A married person may, however, adopt solely rather than jointly with their spouse. In order to do so, the prospective adopter must obtain the consent of the other spouse. That said, no consent is required in the case of a separated couple.

The adoption order cannot be made in favour of two persons jointly unless they are a validly married couple living together, and each is aware of the application for the adoption order.[99]

9–55 While the adopter(s) must be ordinarily resident in the State during the year ending at the date of the making of the adoption order, there is no requirement for the adopters to be citizens or to hold an Irish domicile.[100] The

---

[90] Adoption Act 1952, s.3.
[91] Adoption Act 1998, s.2.
[92] Adoption Act 1991, s.10(1)(c).
[93] Adoption Act 1991, s.10.
[94] [1985] 5 I.L.R.M. 61 (HC).
[95] Adoption Act 1991, s.10(2), provided the Board is satisfied that this is "desirable".
[96] See *S.W., Applicant* [1957] I.R. 178 (HC) and Adoption Act 1991, s.10(4).
[97] See Adoption Act 1952, s.11(2).
[98] [1957] Ir. Jur. Rep. 35.
[99] *The State (A.G.) v An Bord Uchtála* [1957] Ir. Jur. Rep. 35 (SC); s.10(3), Adoption Act 1991.
[100] Adoption Act 1991, s.10(6).

lower age limits for adoptive parents have been reduced several times from their original minima.[101] Since the enactment of s.10(5) of the Adoption Act 1991, the adopters must in each case be over 21. In the case of a married couple, one of whom is the natural parent or a relative of the child, however, only one of them must be over 21.[102] While there are no legal "upper age limitations" in the legislation, in practice many adoption agencies and health boards have imposed such limits for domestic adoption.

9–56 Arguments in favour of allowing older people/couples to adopt include the fact that a woman can give birth well into her forties and even later. In addition, as the average marriage age is now close to 28 years for women and 30 years for men, it is possible that many couples will discover that they are unable to have children only in their mid- to late-thirties, when it may be too late to adopt under current practices.

Arguments against allowing older couples to adopt include maximising the adopted child's prospect of having two healthy parents until he or she becomes an adult. There is anecdotal evidence of dissatisfaction of domestic adopted persons who had older parents. In addition, birth mothers increasingly have a say in the selection of adoptive parents for their child and tend to choose younger couples. Although there are no upper age limits specified for intercountry adoption, a report commissioned in 1999 recommended a lower age limit of 25 years and an upper age limit "of not more than 42 years" for the older applicants at the time of placement.[103] This recommended age limit mirrors the age profile of birth mothers in Ireland. However, the average age of giving birth has dropped and 99.5 per cent of births in 2000 were to women aged 42 years or less.

The adoption procedure

9–57 Section 13 of the Adoption Act 1952 details the factors to be taken into account by the Adoption Board in determining the suitability of adopters. It provides that all prospective adopters must meet the following requirements:

(a) they must be of good moral character;

(b) they must have sufficient means to support the child; and

(c) they must be suitable person(s) to have parental rights and duties.

9–58 An original requirement of the adoption code was that the adopters and the child be of the same religion.[104] This former prescription had the latent effect of precluding the adoption of a child by a married couple of mixed faith, and was rightly struck down and declared to be unconstitutional by Pringle J.

---

[101] See s.5 of the Adoption Act 1964 amending s.11(3) of the Act of 1952.

[102] See Adoption Act 1991, s.10(5)(b).

[103] *Towards a Standardised Framework for Intercountry Adoption Assessment Procedures: A Study of Assessment Procedures in Intercountry Adoption* (The Stationery Office, Dublin, 1999).

[104] Adoption Act 1952, s.12.

in *M. v An Bord Uchtála.*[105] Pringle J. noted, as grounds for his judgment, the prohibition in Art.44.2.3° of the Constitution on discrimination where the grounds were religious profession, status or belief. It is also arguable that such provision indirectly infringed the constitutional right to marry, the parties to a mixed marriage being indirectly penalised for not being of the same faith. An adoption order may now be made regardless of the religious beliefs of any of the parties, provided that every person, whose consent to the making of the adoption order is required, already knows the religion (if any) of each of the prospective adopters.[106] In practice, however, the prospects of adoption can be somewhat slimmer where the prospective adoptive parents belong to a minority religious persuasion. Most adoption agencies are run by religious denominations and the preference in many cases will be for prospective adopters of the religious persuasion of the agency. It may thus, in practice, prove difficult for a couple or couples of a minority or mixed faith to adopt a child.

9–59 A rigorous assessment process precedes the placement of the child with the prospective adoptive parents. Following the completion of the assessment and the compilation of a report as to the suitability of the prospective adoptive parents by the social worker, the Adoption Board convenes an oral hearing. Arranging the oral hearing is contingent on the existence of the requisite consents, discussed below. Section 16 of the Adoption Act 1952, as substituted by s.5 of the Adoption Act 1998, states that the following persons are entitled to be heard on an application for an adoption order:

> "(a) the applicant;
> (b) the child;
> (c) the mother of the child;
> (d) the father of the child or the person who believes himself to be the father;
> (e) the guardian of the child;
> (f) the person who immediately before the placing of the child for adoption had charge of or control over the child;
> (g) a relative of the child;
> (h) a representative of a registered adoption society or health board which is or has been at any time concerned with the child;
> (i) an officer of the Adoption Board;
> (j) any other person whom the Adoption Board, in its discretion, decides to hear."

Issues of consent

Placement and consent

9–60 Placement is the process whereby a child is put forward for adoption.

---

[105] [1975] I.R. 81. *sub. nom. J.McG. and W. McG. v An Bord Uchtála & A.G.* [1974] 109 I.L.T.R. 62 (HC).
[106] Adoption Act 1974, s.4.

This is a very critical stage in the adoption consent process. Direct placement by the natural parent with a stranger is no longer permissible since the Adoption Act 1998.[107] *An Bord Uchtála* (the Adoption Board) had consistently called for the prohibition of direct placements, as the couples with whom the child was placed could circumvent the assessment process and thus effectively receive a child without first being deemed "suitable to adopt". Another cause for concern was the lack of professional counselling and support for the natural parent. It was unlawful for a third party to cause a natural mother to place her child for adoption with a couple not related to the child.[108] However, *An Bord Uchtála* noted in its 1989 Annual Report that this prohibition could be circumvented and stated that it was aware of situations where an "introduction" of a willing adoptive couple by a third party was followed by a subsequent decision by a natural mother to place the child with the couple. This was because s.34, prior to the 1998 amendment, allowed the mother herself to place the child. *An Bord Uchtála* warned in its Annual Report that it would not hesitate to refer cases where there was third-party involvement to the Director of Public Prosecutions. The grave reservation about the desirability of private adoptions was voiced in subsequent annual reports until such placements were finally prohibited in 1998.[109]

9–61   The natural parent may still place a child with a "relative", which now means a grandparent, brother, sister, uncle or aunt of the child, whether of the whole blood, or the half-blood, or by affinity, and includes the spouse of such person. The relationship to the child may now be traced through the mother or the father.[110] In effect, therefore, placements made by a parent are confined to situations where the parent alone, or with another wish to adopt their own child, or where the natural parent places their child with a "relative of the child". Where a child is in the care of relatives, for example grandparents, they may also place and apply for the adoption of that child. In all other cases it is unlawful for any body to make or attempt to make any arrangements for the adoption of a child—unless that body is a registered adoption society or a health board. It is also unlawful for any person to receive a child for the purposes of adoption unless that person is a relative of the child.[111] The adoption code provided for the making of interim orders.[112] This allows a child to be placed in the custody of prospective adoptive parents while the making of an adoption order is still being considered.

Effecting an adoption: procedural prerequisites

Consent to adoption

9–62   As a general rule, an adoption can only proceed with the "full, free and

---

[107] Adoption Act 1998, s.7.
[108] Adoption Act 1952, s.34 and the Adoption Act 1974, s.6(4).
[109] Adoption Act 1998, s.7.
[110] Adoption Act 1998, s.2.
[111] s.7 of the Adoption Act 1998, s.7.
[112] s.17 of the Adoption Act 1952 and s.8 of the Adoption Act 1964.

informed consent" of all parties whose consent is required under the legislation.[113] This requirement has a Constitutional dimension, the Courts having recognised that the act of placing a child for adoption and the subsequent consent to a final order involves a waiver by the non-marital mother of her personal right to the care and custody of her child, a right guaranteed by Art. 40.3.1° of the Constitution.

The persons whose consent is required for an adoption to take place are listed in s.14 of the Adoption Act 1952, these persons being:

(a) the natural mother of the child; the Act is specific as regards gender—the natural father has no right to object by reason only of his status as natural father of the child;

(b) any guardian of the child: this may include a natural father who has been appointed a guardian by the consent of the parties (s.2(4) of the Guardianship of Infants Act 1964) or by virtue of s.6A of the Guardianship of Infants Act 1964 (as inserted by the Status of Children Act 1987);

(c) any other person having charge of or control over the child immediately before it is placed for adoption.

No consent is required, however, where the party whose consent is sought either cannot be found or is incapable, by reason of mental infirmity, of giving such consent.[114]

9–63 The natural mother's/guardian's consent is required at two stages – when the child is placed for adoption, and before the making of the adoption order when the final consent is given. In all cases, a person whose consent is necessary must be informed of his or her right to withdraw his or her consent at any time prior to the making of the adoption order.[115]

Consent must be given in writing only.[116] A consent given orally will not, thus, amount to a valid consent for these purposes. No consent may be given, furthermore, where the child has not yet reached the age of six weeks.[117] There is an onus on the Adoption Board to be satisfied that every person whose consent is necessary, and has not been dispensed with, has given consent and understands the nature and effect of the consent and of the adoption order.[118]

9–64 The Consent to Placement procedure, where the mother or guardian proposes to place a child at the disposal of a registered adoption society, is set out in s.39 of the Adoption Act 1952.[119] The procedure requires the society to complete a form with the natural mother or guardian prior to receiving the child for adoption.[120] This form details the effect of an adoption order in simple

[113] *G. v An Bord Uchtála* [1980] I.R. 32.
[114] Adoption Act 1952, s.14(2).
[115] Adoption Act 1952, s.14(6).
[116] Adoption Act 1952, s.14(5).
[117] s.15(1).
[118] Adoption Act 1952, s.15(2).
[119] See also Adoption Rules 1990 (S.I. No. 170 of 1990).
[120] Initial Consent to Placement: Form 10.

and direct terms:

> "If an adoption order is made for the child, you will lose all your parental
> rights and will be freed from all parental duties. These rights and duties
> will be transferred permanently to the adopters. The child will thereafter
> be regarded as their child as if the child were born to them in marriage."

The Form goes on to explain about the persons whose consent is required to
the making of the order, about the power of the Adoption Board and the High
Court to dispense with consent in certain circumstances, and about the right to
withdrawal of consent at any time before the making of the adoption order,
with a view to reclaiming the child.[121]

The meaning of "consent"

9–65   It is well-established for these purposes that where a consent is required,
and not dispensed with by virtue of the 1974 Act, it must be a real and not
merely an apparent consent to the adoption. In other words, it is not enough
for the person whose consent is required merely to state, in writing, that he or
she has consented as required. It must be shown that the consent is "full, free
and informed".[122] This stipulation is closely linked to the fact that the rights
being ceded by the natural mother by virtue of the adoption are not merely
legal rights, but are, rather, rights of a constitutional origin. The mother's
personal right to the care and custody of her child being guaranteed by Art.40.3
of the Constitution, any waiver of such rights must be as free as it feasibly can
be in all the circumstances. It must, in addition, be made with as full as possible
an understanding of the consequences of both the placement and the final
adoption order.

9–66   A further relevant and instructive case is *C.A. v St Patrick's Guild
Adoption Society*, wherein Flood J. stated as follows:

> "The true test is whether in the circumstances which prevail at the time
> she makes her decision, that decision reflects her will or the will of
> somebody else".[123]

9–67   The failure to make the mother aware of her right to withdraw her
consent at any time prior to the making of the final adoption order results in
the invalidity of the adoption order.[124] Similar consequences occur where the
mother is not informed, at the time of placement, of the possibility that her
consent may be dispensed with under s.3 of the Adoption Act 1974.[125]

---

[121]   Adoption Act 1952, s.14(6).

[122]   *G. v An Bord Uchtála* [1980] I.R. 32.

[123]   unreported, High Court, Flood J., July 31, 1995.

[124]   See s.14(6) of the Adoption Act 1952 and *M. (McL.) v An Bord Uchtála* [1977] I.R.
287.

[125]   See *O.G. v An Bord Uchtála* [1991] I.L.R.M. 514, where Finlay C.J. emphasised that
the consequences of placement must be explained very clearly to the mother.

Placement is a significant step which may lead to the High Court later dispensing with the consent of the mother to the adoption.[126] While the rights of the mother should be explained clearly and correctly to her, it is not specifically necessary to explain the source of such rights, for instance that the rights being waived are constitutional rather than simply legal in nature.[127] Nor will a consent be deemed to be flawed by reason only of the fact that the person whose consent is required does not know of the identity of the prospective adopters.[128] The consent may not be a conditional one, and while the adoption agency or health board may comply with wishes expressed by the person placing the child for adoption, the fact that they fail to do so does not of itself invalidate the consent to placement.[129]

9–68 An adoption should, furthermore, be the result of the free consent of all persons whose consent is required. Parental pressure (or the perception of parental disapproval) may, for instance, so qualify the consent of a natural mother as to render the adoption order invalid.[130] In *D.G. and M.G. v An Bord Uchtála*, Laffoy J. held that there had been no valid agreement to place the child for adoption "because of fear which was a product of [the mother's] upbringing, stress, anxiety, lack of maturity and deprivation of emotional support."[131] Even circumstantial (as opposed to interpersonal) compulsion may vitiate an otherwise valid adoption order,[132] although, in this regard, not every circumstantial pressure will suffice. As McWilliam J. noted in *Mc F. v G.*,[133] all sorts of pressures and strains, physical, emotional and financial, accompany the birth of a child. Were all of these factors to be recognised as vitiating the consent to an adoption, "there could hardly be a case found in which one or other of them would not be present so that it could be argued that a consent was not valid."[134] Indeed, the very fact that financial and social changes have led to significant increases in the number of unmarried mothers keeping their children is testament to the fact that those adoptions that did occur prior to these changes were rarely effected without some degree of compulsion.[135]

Withdrawal of consent and dispensing with the final consent

9–69 When a child is placed for adoption with the full, free and informed consent of those persons whose consent to adoption is required by law, the

[126] See the comments of Keane J., as he then was, in *F. and F. v An Bord Uchtála* [1997] 1 F.L.R. 6 at 31.
[127] *M. O'C v The Sacred Heart Adoption Society* [1996] 1 F.L.R. 175 (HC); 1 F.L.R. 296 (SC) and *E.F. v An Board Uchtála*, unreported, Supreme Court, July 17, 1996.
[128] Adoption Act 1952, s.14(4).
[129] See *State (M.G.) v A.H. & M.H.* [1984] I.L.R.M. 237.
[130] *G. v An Bord Uchtála* [1980] I.R. 32.
[131] unreported, High Court, Laffoy J., May 23, 1996.
[132] See *S. v Eastern Health Board,* unreported, High Court, Finlay P., February 28, 1979.
[133] [1983] I.L.R.M. 228.
[134] *ibid.* at 232.
[135] See also the comments of Laffoy J. in *D.G. v An Bord Uchtála* [1996] 1 F.L.R. 263 at 282 and those of Flood J. in *A.C. v St. Patrick's Guild Adoption Society* [1996] 7 F.L.R. 309 at 317.

person placing the child may still withdraw his or her consent to the adoption up to the date of the making of the adoption order.[136] The prospective adoptive parents may, however, refuse to hand over custody of the child and then the dispute becomes one to be determined by the High Court. The Court must determine the custody of the child on the basis of the "best interests of the child"— otherwise known as the "paramountcy" test. If the consent to placement, however, is flawed, the child will not have been validly placed for adoption. The placement to be valid must have been made with the full, free and informed consent of the person placing the child for adoption. Where such initial (as opposed to final) consent has not been given, the voluntary adoption of the child cannot proceed and adoption can only be considered in the limited context of the Adoption Act 1988.

9–70   The first critical amendment to the Adoption Act 1952 came in 1974 as a result of the frailty of the consent procedure when viewed from the perspective of the child. Where the natural mother, having placed her child for adoption, subsequently failed to sign the consent form to the legal adoption of the child, the adoption process could not be completed. Commentators in the field of adoption work, medicine and the law had complained that the adoption code was thus too "mother centred" as opposed to "child centred".[137]

9–71   The Adoption Act 1974 empowers prospective adoptive parents to apply to the High Court to dispense with the final consent of the natural mother, or of any other person whose consent is required. This can be effected where the Court is satisfied that it is in the "best interests" of the child to do so.[138] The 1974 Act thus introduced into the adoption code the requirement that the welfare of the child was to be "the first and paramount consideration in deciding any matter, application or proceeding before the board or any court relating to the arrangements for or the making of an adoption order."[139]

9–72   The "paramountcy" test only comes under consideration, however, when the mother has voluntarily and freely placed the child for adoption. The revered nature of the mother and child relationship under the Constitution, and the nature of adoption, with the implied severance of the legal ties between the mother and child and the creation of new parental ties between the child and the adoptive family, require that the process be entered into voluntarily. The mother must consent, in writing, to the placement of the child for adoption, and also to the adoption of her child, and may still withdraw her consent at any

---

[136] Adoption Act 1952, s.14(6).
[137] See, Dr P.E. McQuaid, *An Outsider's View: Reform in the Law Relating to Children*, Lecture No. 67, 15th Joint Seminar of Society of Young Solicitors. See also the then Senator Mary Robinson, Lecture No. 68, 15th Joint Seminar of Society of Young Solicitors, *The Status of Children under the Adoption Acts*. See also, Rev. J. Good, "Legal Adoption in Ireland" (1979) 3 *Child Adoption*.
[138] Adoption Act 1974, s.3.
[139] For an analysis of the section, see the judgments of Walsh and Henchy JJ., in *G. v An Bord Uchtála* [1980] I.R. 32, O'Connor, *Key issues in Irish Family Law* (Round Hall Press, Dublin, 1988), and Shatter, *Family Law* (4th ed., Butterworths, Dublin, 1997).

time before the final adoption order is made.[140] The right given to prospective adoptive parents under the amending legislation was to apply to the High Court to dispense with the consent to the adoption order. Should the consent to the initial placement of the child for adoption be itself impeachable, then there can be no adoption. In such a case, there is no room for the exercise of any discretion by the court. The Court may only act, then, to dispense with the requirement of the final consent, and not the initial consent to placement.

9–73   Section 3 of the Adoption Act 1974 applies only where the applicant has already applied for an adoption order, and where the person whose consent is required has already agreed to the initial placement of the child for adoption. Where any person whose consent to the adoption order is required either:

(a) fails, neglects or refuses to give such consent, or

(b) withdraws such consent, it having already been given,

the High Court may order that such consent is no longer required for the making of a valid adoption order. In doing so, it must consider what is in "the best interests" of the child. If it is satisfied that the latter consideration so demands, it may give custody of the child to the applicant, while simultaneously authorising the Adoption Board to proceed with the making of an adoption order in respect of the child. Section 3 cannot be used, however, to dispense with the consent of a ward of court unless the court so permits.

Dispensing with consent applications—practice and procedure

9–74   All applications under s.3 of the Adoption Act 1974 (dispensing with consent) must be heard, at first instance, by the High Court.

Acting for a natural mother

9–75   Where a natural mother has placed her child for adoption and wants to regain custody of her child, a letter should be sent to the adoption society seeking the return of the child. A copy of the letter should be forwarded to the Adoption Board. If the child is not returned, an application for custody should be issued without delay in the District Court (at first instance), the Circuit Court or the High Court (either under the Guardianship of Infants Act 1964 by way of special summons or by issuing habeas corpus proceedings).

Acting for prospective adopters

9–76   The longer the period of time the prospective adopters have *de facto* custody of the child, the stronger their case for establishing that the best interests of the child is served by remaining with them. Therefore, prospective adopters should be advised to postpone issuing a s.3 application until they are forced to do so in response to the natural mother's application for custody. Any such application is initiated by way of special summons in the High Court grounded

---

[140] s.14(5) and (6) of the Adoption Act 1952.

on an affidavit sworn by the prospective adopters. Proceedings are served on the Chief State Solicitor as solicitors for An Bord Uchtála. The natural mother, by way of a notice of motion to the High Court, is made a notice party to the proceedings. Similarly, where the natural mother has issued custody proceedings, the prospective adopters are made a notice party to her proceedings.

Retrospective validation of certain adoptions

9–77   The Adoption Act 1976 permits the retrospective validation of certain adoptions effected without the making of a full, free and informed consent. In *McL.*, properly cited at para.9–28 as *M. and M. v An Bord Uchtála*,[141] the Supreme Court held that an adoption order was void *ab initio*. It did so on the ground that the Adoption Board had not fulfilled its statutory obligation to ensure that the natural mother knew and understood the nature and effect of giving consent to adoption, or of her right to withdraw that consent up to the making of the order. This case received extensive publicity, and came to symbolise the fear of prospective and existing adoptive parents that an adoption order might not be permanent, and that loopholes and re-interpretations in regulations and laws might force the adopting family to lose the adopted child. Abramson, in his review of the adoption statistics in the period 1953–1981, noted an abrupt decline in adoptions in the years following 1975. He clearly attributes this case and the resultant publicity as being responsible, at least in part, for that decline in the number of families willing to adopt a child.

9–78   The purpose of the Adoption Act 1976 was primarily to validate all adoptions made prior to its enactment, in so far as they might be invalid for procedural reasons. The legislation, in addition, provided that adoption orders should not be declared invalid if such a declaration was not in the best interests of the child, or that it would otherwise not be proper to do so, subject to "the rights under the Constitution of all persons concerned".[142] The Act also provided that the natural mother should be informed of her right to be heard on the application for the adoption order and be advised of the date on which the order was to be made.

9–79   The 1976 Act only applies to an order made before the passing of the Act. It is therefore solely retrospective in effect, and not prospective. A failure in consent occurring after the passing of the Act cannot be cured by the Act. The particular flaws to which the Act relates are as follows:

(a) where the person giving the consent was not aware of his or her right to withdraw the consent before the making of the final order;

(b) where the person was not aware of the date on which the order was to be made;

---

[141] [1977] I.R. 287.
[142] Adoption Act 1976, s.5.

(c) where a person was not aware of his or her right to be consulted regarding the adoption; and

(d) where the board had no information as to whether the person at (c) above was aware of those rights.

9–80   There may be a failure to comply with the requirement (under s.15 of the 1952 Act) that the Board satisfy itself that all consents have been given with a full understanding of the nature and the effect of same. Notwithstanding such failure, an adoption will be deemed to have been validly made under the 1976 Act.

The natural mother/legal guardian and the consent process

9–81   The first consent is to the placing of the child for adoption. The mother or legal guardian must be informed of the legal implications involved in "placing the child for adoption". She, or he, must be made aware of his or her legal rights, and that that the mother or guardian may withdraw his or her consent to the adoption of the child at any time before the making of the adoption order.[143] He or she must also be told that, once the child is validly placed for adoption, the High Court may dispense with his or her consent to the making of the adoption order if it is found to be in the best interests of the child to do so.

9–82   Before accepting the child for adoption, the health board or adoption society is obliged to furnish the mother or guardian placing the child with a statement explaining the consent procedures, and the legal effects of an adoption order upon the rights of the mother or guardian placing the child. This is generally achieved by the completion of a form entitled "Initial Consent to Placement" or Form 10.[144] This form details the legal effect of an Adoption Order, the procedure relating to consents, the power of the court to dispense with consent, and the procedure involved in reclaiming the child. The person placing the child must sign a receipt for the information contained in Form 10, confirming at the same time that he or she understands the information. This acknowledgement must also be signed and witnessed.

9–83   Before allowing the mother or legal guardian to sign the initial consent (the consent to placement), the adoption society or health board must be satisfied that the person signing the consent fully understands its import and significance. In this regard the case of *J.P. and S.P. v O'G. and Others*[145] is worthy of note. This case held that the duties imposed on adoption societies, as previously set out under the provisions of s.39 of the 1952 Act, need not be carried out by the servants or agents of the adoption society, provided certain other conditions are met. These conditions are that the social workers who explained the contents of the form to the natural mother ensured that the mother fully understood the

---

[143]   s.3 of the Adoption Act 1976.
[144]   s.39 of the Adoption Act 1952. Also, Adoption Rules 1990 (S.I. No 170 of 1990).
[145]   unreported, Supreme Court, February 26, 1991.

consent procedure, and provided instruction on the form to her with a view to explaining its meaning and, finally, obtained a signed receipt to that effect.

9–84 The obligation on registered adoption societies under s.39(1)(b) to ensure that the person understands the information and signs a document to that effect (Form 10) is an onerous one. However, the fact that a mother may not fully absorb all the advice and information given to her by a social worker prior to placing her child for adoption and signing Form 10 may not necessarily invalidate the placement. In *N.B. & T.B. v An Bord Uchtála*,[146] Barron J. determined that it was clear that at the time she signed the Form 10, the mother wanted her child to be placed for adoption. The social worker had explained the procedure clearly to the natural mother and read Form 10 over to her, but it was accepted that the only thing which the mother took in was that she could change her mind. Yet the mother clearly wanted the adoption process to proceed because it could not be argued that the mother agreed to the placement conditional upon a mistaken belief that her consent was a contingent one revocable by her any time prior to the making of the order. However, in *D.G. & M.G. v An Bord Uchtála*,[147] Laffoy J. reached the conclusion that it is not sufficient merely to consider whether the relevant information was conveyed by the social worker in advance of the placement. It is also necessary to consider the ability of the mother to receive the information and to intellectually process it in such a way as to lead to an understanding of the effect of an adoption order and the consequences of each step in the process leading to the adoption order. These decisions sit uneasily together and while it must be acknowledged that each case is fact dependent and therefore capable of being distinguished, the judgment of Laffoy J. appears to take a more stringent approach to the requirements of s.39(1)(b). The Supreme Court recommended in *E.F. & F.F. v An Bord Uchtála*[148] that the mother should be advised of the consequences of the process and her consent to placement "in blunt and uncompromising language". From a practical point of view, it is advisable for adoption agencies to record in detail the advice given at every stage to the mother or guardian proposing to place a child for adoption through their agency.

9–85 However, the form of consent [Form 10] does not affect the question as to whether a consent constitutes an agreement to place for adoption within the meaning of s.15(3). A duly signed Form 10 is not a statutory prerequisite showing proper compliance with s.39. It is very helpful in establishing "consent" but is not definitive in that regard, and failure to comply with the section may not vitiate an otherwise valid consent.[149]

The adoption society or health board must also request the Adoption Board to provide them with a copy of any notice received from the natural father.

---

[146] unreported, High Court, February 1983.

[147] [1996] I.F.L.R. 263 (HC).

[148] [1997] 1 F.L.R. 6.

[149] *S. v EHB & Ors*, unreported, High Court, February 1979, *McC. v An Bord Uchtála* [1982] 2 I.L.R.M. 159; *Re D.G., an Infant* [1991] 1 I.R. 49; and *P.F. v An Bord Uchtála* [1994] 3 I.R. 500.

The natural father may have notified the Board (pursuant to s.7D as inserted by the Adoption Act 1998) of his wish to be consulted in relation to any proposal by an adoption agency to place the child for adoption, or by an application by the mother or a relative of the child for an adoption order relating to the child. The agency must contact the natural father prior to the placement of the child for adoption where his identity is known to the agency. Pre-placement consultation with the father may, however, be dispensed with in limited circumstances, following consultation and agreement with the Adoption Board. This could occur, for instance, where the agency is unable to notify the father or where, due to the relationship between the natural mother and father, or the circumstances of the conception of the child, such notification is deemed to be inappropriate.[150]

9–86 Where the mother refuses to reveal the identity of the father to the adoption agency, the agency must counsel her to attempt to obtain her co-operation, indicating to her:

1.   the possibility that the adoption may thus be delayed;

2.   the possibility that the father may contest the adoption at some later date;

3.   the fact that the absence of information about the medical, genetic and social background to the father may be detrimental to the health, development or welfare of the child; and

4.   any other matter that the agency deems appropriate.

Should the mother still refuse to reveal the identity of the father, then the agency must furnish the board with a written report of the counselling that the agency has provided. The Board may only authorise the agency to place the child for adoption if it believes that all reasonably practical steps have been taken to procure the assistance of the mother, and that there is no other practical way to ascertain the father's identity.[151]

9–87 Once the appropriate consents to placement for adoption have been made, the adoption society or health board may place the child with the prospective adoptive parents. Prior to this placement, however, the child may be placed in short-term foster care. The period between the placement of the child and the adoption of the child is in effect "a legal limbo" when full authority and ultimate responsibility in respect of the child remains suspended. The natural parents or guardian have relinquished parental rights and responsibilities to the adoption society or health board.

9–88 In the time period between the placement and the making of the adoption order, the prospective adoptive parents are thus in a vulnerable situation. The natural parents or legal guardian may change their mind and withdraw the consent to the adoption. The adoptive parents must also submit to the sometimes

---

[150] s.7F(1) and (2) as inserted by the Adoption Act 1998.
[151] s.7F(4) of the Adoption Act 1952, as inserted by the Adoption Act 1998.

intrusive supervision of the placing agency, although "the purpose of such supervisory visits [is] little more than negative monitoring of the welfare standards."[152] There is, as such, no statutory requirement to carry out a programme of visits of a supervisory, or statutory, nature. Section 8 of the Adoption Act 1974, however, stipulates that an adoption order may not be granted until the child is at least six weeks old.

Section 9 of the Adoption Act 1974 refers to a prescribed period during which the child must be in the care of the prospective adopters before an adoption order can be made. To date, however, such a minimum period has never in fact been prescribed. The lack of a legally specified period after placement within which a final consent must be given, while allowing the natural mother/guardian time to decide whether or not to carry on with the adoption, can be potentially disruptive and detrimental to a child's welfare if allowed to drag on at length. The Report of the Review Committee and Adoption Services suggested:

> "that a natural parent be statutorily entitled to the return of her child at any time before she gives her consent to adoption or within three months from the date on which the child was placed for adoption, whichever is the shorter period..."[153]

The Task Force on Child Care Services had previously made a similar recommendation and also suggested the maintenance of the discretion to reduce the period in which the birth parent should be entitled to the return of her child in particular circumstances.[154] A more restrictive provision exists in Australian legislation, where consent is irrevocable after 30 days after placement, thus making the initial decision to place the child for adoption the key decision on the part of the natural mother. There is evidence to show that this is working well.

In general, the Adoption Board will not make an adoption order until the child has been in the care of the prospective adopters for at least six months.

Final Consent Form 4A

9–89   The placing agency is under an obligation to notify the Adoption Board of details of the facts and circumstances giving rise to the placement, and of the "home study" report on all parties involved. Once the placement has been made, the natural parent(s) are informed of it. Prior to the making of the adoption order by the Adoption Board, the final consent to the making of such an order (Form 4A) must be obtained by the adoption society or health board. The final consent may only be given after the child has attained the age of six weeks, and not earlier than three months before the adoption application.[155] This

---

[152] See O'Halloran, *Adoption Law and Practice* (Butterworths, Dublin, 1992), p.81.
[153] *Report of the Review Committee on Adoption Services* (The Stationery Office, Dublin, 1984), p.29.
[154] *Task Force on Child Care Services* (The Stationery Office, Dublin, 1980).
[155] s.8 of the Adoption Act 1974.

consent must be made on oath, with a full understanding of the consequences. It must be unconditional, and must not have been withdrawn at the time of the hearing. The birth mother or legal guardian must be advised of his or her right to be heard on the application for the adoption order. He or she may decide not to be heard, or consulted again, in relation to the application for the order. If he or she decides to be heard, however, he or she may be heard in person or through a solicitor or counsel. He or she must be informed of the date of the hearing.[156]

9–90 If the natural mother or legal guardian withdraws his or her consent, or simply does not complete the final consent, an application may be made to the High Court to dispense with his or her final consent, thereby enabling the Adoption Board to make an adoption order in favour of the prospective adopters.[157] On the other hand, the prospective adoptive parents could decide to return the child to the natural parent or guardian. Should he or she fail to return the child, however, the natural parent or legal guardian may apply to the High Court for custody of the child. If the consent to adoption is withdrawn by the natural parent(s), they will then be met by the "welfare" test in litigation concerning the custody of the child, provided that the initial placement was not flawed in any way. In all such cases, however, the marriage of the natural parents to each other will have the effect of creating a presumption in their favour, requiring that the child be returned to its constitutional family unless there are compelling reasons to do otherwise.[158]

Consent, consultation and natural fathers

Persons to be consulted

9–91 Upon an application being made for an adoption order, s.16 of the Adoption Act 1952 (as amended by s.13 of the 1974 Act and s.5 of the Act of 1998) requires that certain stipulated persons, but no other persons, be afforded a right to be consulted in relation to the adoption of the child. These persons are:

(a) the applicants;

(b) the child;

(c) the natural mother of the child;

(d) the natural father of the child;[159]

(e) the guardian of the child;

---

[156] Adoption Act 1976, s.3.

[157] Adoption Act 1974, s.3.

[158] See *Re J.H., an infant: K.C. & A.C. v An Bord Uchtála* [1985] I.L.R.M. 302.

[159] Initially, the natural father of the child was not, by reason of his paternity alone, automatically entitled to be heard. Sections 5 and 7 of the Adoption Act 1998, however, now extend to the latter the right to be consulted. A person who believes himself to be the father of a child, whatever the true position, may also be heard.

(f) a person having charge of, or control over, the child;

(g) a relative of the child;[160]

(h) a representative of a registered adoption society or health board which is or has been at any time concerned with the child; and

(i) an officer of the Board.

The Board is further empowered, however, to allow any other person to be heard. This, however, is a matter for its own discretion. No person, other than those to whom s.16 refers, may be permitted to address the Board without its consent. Counsel or a solicitor, however, may, in proceedings before the Board, represent all persons so permitted or entitled to be heard. It was originally stipulated by the 1952 Act that a priest, minister or authorised representative of a religion where the child, or a parent thereof, living or dead, is claimed to be, or to have been, a member of that religion was entitled to be heard. This facility, it seems, is now abolished, although the Board may consider such person an appropriate person to be consulted under s.16(1)(j) of the 1952 Act.

The rights of natural fathers

9–92   Before 1998 there was no provision requiring either the consent of, or extending the right to be consulted to, the natural father of the child. While there was an obligation to consult the natural father if, at the relevant time, he fell into one of the categories listed previously, his parental status alone conferred no such right. The Status of Children Act 1987 ("the 1987 Act") inserted a new s.6A into the Guardianship of Infants Act 1964, giving the natural father a right to apply to the court to be appointed as a guardian of his child jointly with the mother of the child. The Children Act 1997, in addition, provided for such status to be conferred by agreement with the mother, and without the necessity of a court application. Armed with such status, the father could effectively veto the adoption. In the absence of such status, however, he had no automatic footing in adoption proceedings. Indeed, until 1998 the father had no statutory right even to be informed of the proposed adoption.

The 1987 Act attempted to equalise the rights of marital and non-marital children and to rid society of the stigmatising language associated with this area. While the Act was clearly a product of pressure from groups acting for unmarried parents and their children, it also owed its inception to the decision of the European Court of Human Rights in *Johnson v Ireland*.[161] The European Court in that case held that the State had violated Art.8 of the European Convention on Human Rights.[162] The State had done so by failing to provide a regime whereby a daughter born to parents who were not married to each other could enjoy a normal family life and have proper legal links to her parents. The 1987 Act did not, however, grant automatic guardianship rights to the

---

[160] This now, by virtue of the Adoption Act 1998, includes a relative of the father of the child, as well as that of the mother.

[161] (1986) 9 E.H.R.R. 203.

[162] See Chap.12.

father, eschewing in particular the recommendations of the Law Reform Commission's *Report on Illegitimacy*.[163] Instead, it took a "mother-centred" approach by recognising the latter alone as the sole automatic guardian of her child to the exclusion of the natural father, but with provision for the father's addition as guardian.

9–93 While the 1987 Act introduced significant changes regarding the legal status of non-marital children, it did not properly address the issue of the rights of the unmarried father. Neither did it address the position of the child born into a family unit that could not rely on the Constitutional status of a family based on marriage. In a series of Supreme Court decisions, it has been declared that a family unit, as perceived by the Constitution, is based on marriage and has constitutional protections and guarantees which a family unit not based on marriage does not possess.[164]

9–94 Therefore, while it can be said that the Status of Children Act 1987 attempted to ameliorate the position of the natural father, it only did so to the point of giving him a right to apply to the court to be appointed guardian. While the legislation did not give the natural father automatic guardianship rights by virtue of his biological position, he was accorded the right to apply to the court to be appointed guardian. Section 3 of the 1987 Act specifically provided that the marital status of the parents was not to affect the relationship of the child with his father or mother. Section 12 of the 1987 Act inserted a new s.6A into the Guardianship of Infants Act 1964, authorising the Courts to appoint certain fathers as guardians. Thus, where the father objected to the mother placing the child for adoption, he could apply to the court to be appointed guardian jointly with the mother of the child. Since 1998, however, the natural father may now also be appointed a guardian with the consent of the mother without any need to apply to the court.[165] Where the mother opposes his application to be appointed as a guardian of the child, the dispute must be determined by the court. As in all such matters, the court must consider the welfare of the child to be the first and paramount consideration.

9–95 As guardian, the father's consent will be required in order for the adoption to proceed, thus giving the father an effective veto over the adoption. In the absence of being granted such guardianship status, however, the father had, until 1998, no right by virtue of his fatherhood alone even to be heard in an adoption application. A natural father, in other words, continued to enjoy no *automatic* rights. Prior to 1998, in the event of a negative response from the natural father, the tendency of the Adoption Board was to await the outcome

---

[163] Report on Illegitimacy (LRC-419-82) (Dublin, September, 1992).

[164] *State (Nicolaou) v An Bord Uchtála* [1966] I.R. 567 (SC); *G. v An Bord Uchtála* [1980] I.R. 32 (SC);, *J.K. v V.W.* [1990] 2 I.R. 437 (SC); *Keegan v Ireland* (1994) 18 E.H.R.R. 342; *W.O'R. v E.H. & An Bord Uchtála* [1996] 2 I.R. 248 reported as *O'R. (W.) v M. (E.) and the Adoption Board* [1997] 2 Fam. L.J 33 (SC).

[165] See s.2(4) of the Guardianship of Infants Act 1964, and the Guardianship of Children (Statutory Declarations) Regulations 1998 (S.I. No. 5 of 1998).

of guardianship proceedings prior to placing the child for adoption. This practice only developed, however, following the matter being considered by the Supreme Court in the case of *K. v W.*[166]

9–96 In *K. v W.*, the Irish Supreme Court observed that a natural father, while not having a constitutional right or a natural right to the guardianship of his child, did enjoy a statutory right to *apply* for guardianship by virtue of s.6A of the 1964 Act. That case concerned the adoption of a child born to an unmarried couple as the result of a planned pregnancy. Shortly before the birth of the child, however, the couple split up and the mother placed the child for adoption. The placement of the child for adoption proceeded without the consent, or even the knowledge, of the natural father. At the time, he had no right in law to be so notified, or indeed, consulted. Having subsequently discovered that the placement had been made, he applied to the Court for guardianship rights and/or custody of the child. He had the right to do this by virtue of the Status of Children Act 1987. By the time the proceedings were finally determined by the High Court, however, the child had been with the adoptive parents for 15 months, and the primacy test required that the child's welfare necessitated that the child remained with them.

9–97 Having failed in the Irish courts, the father of the child applied to the European Court of Human Rights on the basis that his rights under Arts 6 and 8 of the European Convention on Human Rights had been violated.[167] The European Court of Human Rights held that where the existence of a family tie with the child had been established ("family" not being restricted to unions based on marriage alone), the State should refrain from acting so as to sunder that tie, unless there existed a strong reason for so doing. The court considered that the fact that Irish law permitted the child to be placed secretly for adoption denied the father his right to a "fair and public hearing of an independent and impartial tribunal" under Art.6 of the Convention. His rights to such a hearing had also been violated by reason of the fact that he had no right to challenge the placement decision, nor any standing in the adoption proceedings generally. Judged in its entirety, the actions of the State had also infringed the plaintiff's right to have his family life respected and vindicated by the State (Art.8 of the Convention).

9–98 Subsequent to the judgment of the European Court of Human Rights in *Keegan v Ireland,* adoption societies and health boards espoused a policy of ascertaining details regarding the natural father and ascertaining his attitude to the matter of the adoption prior to placing the child for adoption.[168] The Annual Report of An Bord Uchtála in 1994, for instance, noted that the

---

[166] [1990] I.L.R.M. 121 and [1990] 2 I.R. 437. See also *W.O'R. v E.H. & An Bord Uchtála* [1996] 2 I.R. 248; reported as *O'R. (W.) v M.(E.) & An Bord Uchtála* [1997] 2 Fam.L.J. 33; *Keegan v Ireland* (1994) 18 E.H.R.R. 342. See also, C. Hamilton and K. Standley, *Family Law in Europe* (Butterworths, London, 1995), p.558.

[167] *Sub nom. Keegan v Ireland* (1994) 18 E.H.R.R. 342.

[168] See Darling [1999] 4 I.J.F.L. 2.

judgment of the European Court of Human Rghts had effected changes in its practice and in the practice of adoption agencies. These concessions notwithstanding, Irish adoption law continued until 1998 to refuse to recognise a natural father as a parent, or indeed even as a relative of the child. It was only the consent of a natural father of a legitimated child (as guardian) that was required by law. Although the natural father was eligible to adopt his child, his opinions on an adoption proposed by anyone else, in law at least, could safely be ignored. The enactment of the Adoption Act 1998, however, significantly redressed these shortcomings.

The Adoption Act 1998 and the consultation with natural fathers

9–99   The Adoption (No.2) Bill 1996 was introduced in order to provide a new statutory procedure for consulting the father of a child born outside marriage before that child was placed for adoption. The Bill proposed to allow the father to be heard in any application in respect of a child born to him. This would be without prejudice to his continuing statutory rights to apply for guardianship and/or custody of the child. It was thus aimed at remedying the shortcomings of Irish domestic law highlighted in the *Keegan v Ireland* decision of the European Court of Human Rights. The Bill was ultimately passed into law as the Adoption Act 1998.[169] The amending legislation empowered the father of a child to notify the Adoption Board of his wish to be consulted in relation to either:

(a) a proposal made by an adoption agency to place his child for adoption, or

(b) an application made by the natural mother or a relative of the child for an adoption order in relation to his child.[170]

For these purposes, the term "father" includes any person who believes himself to be the father of the child, whether this is the case or not.[171]

9–100   Such notice as is given must be in writing and must contain such information as is required by the Adoption Board. It may be given to the Board before the child in question is born as well as after the birth. The Adoption Act 1998 also introduced new procedures to be followed by adoption agencies before placing children for adoption. Agencies are now required to endeavour to ascertain the identity of the natural father, and must request the Adoption Board to provide them with a copy of any notice received from the natural father.

---

[169] See also the Adoption Rules 1999 (S.I. No. 315 of 1999), operative since October 8, 1999. This S.I. prescribes the forms to be used for the purpose of the Adoption Act 1998 and is to be read in conjunction with the Adoption Rules 1988 (S.I. No. 304 of 1988), the Adoption Rules 1990 (S.I. No. 170 of 1990), and the Adoption Rules 1996 (S.I. No. 223 of 1996).

[170] s.7D of the Adoption Act 1952, as inserted by s.4 of the Adoption Act 1998.

[171] s.7A of the Adoption Act 1952, as inserted by s.4 of the Adoption Act 1998.

9–101   The natural mother may decide to place her child for adoption with an adoption agency or health board. The adoption agency or health board must then go through the process of consulting the natural father with regard to the proposed placement of the child for adoption.[172] The pre-placement consultation process may be dispensed with, however, where the agency is unable to consult the father or declines to do so due to the nature of the relationship between the father and the mother, or the circumstances of the conception of the child. In such a situation, the child may be placed for adoption with the authorisation of the adoption board, but without the pre-placement consultation with the natural father.[173]

An adoption society or health board may lawfully place a child for adoption. The child concerned must have attained the age of four weeks unless:

(i)   the father indicates that he has no objection to the placement; or

(ii) the adoption agency is unable to, or does not, consult the father on the placement.[174]

9–102   Where the natural father is consulted prior to the placement for adoption, he may either consent to the placement, in which case the child may be immediately placed for adoption, or he may refuse his consent to the placement. In the latter situation, the placement is deferred for a period of 21 days, commencing on the date of the notice. This is done so as to afford the father an opportunity of applying under s.11(4) or s.6A of the Guardianship of Infants Act 1964 (as inserted by the Status of Children Act 1987). The child may not then be placed until the proceedings have been concluded. However, a party may apply to court for an order expediting the proceedings on the basis of the best interests of the child.[175]

9–103   Where the identity of the father is known or ascertained, the agency has a duty to take reasonable steps to consult him about the proposed placement. In the event of an objection by the father to the placement of the child for adoption, the matter must be deferred for 21 days to facilitate an application by the father to the Court for guardianship and/or custody of the child. Should the adoption agency not receive a notice that the father intends contesting the matter in court, or any indication from him within 21 days, the agency may proceed to place the child for adoption.[176] The legislation provides for exemptions from the requirement to consult the father, including circumstances where the relationship between the parents was such that it would be inappropriate to consult the father, or where, due to the circumstances of the conception of the child, consultation would likewise be inappropriate.[177] Thus,

---

[172] Adoption Act 1998, s.4 inserting s.7E into the Adoption Act 1952.
[173] Adoption Act 1998, s.4 inserting s.7F into the Adoption Act 1952.
[174] s.4 of the Adoption Act 1998 Act inserting s.7B, 7E(3) and 7F into the Adoption Act 1952.
[175] s.7E(3)(a), (b), (4), (5) and (6) of Adoption Act 1952, as inserted by the Adoption Act 1998.
[176] s.7E of the Adoption Act 1952.
[177] s.7F of the Adoption Act 1952.

for example, a child conceived by rape would not be subjected to the pre-placement procedure. Such exemptions, however, may only be granted by the Adoption Board. In fact, in *J.B. and D.B. v An Bord Uchtála*,[178] the natural father of the child, conceived following the rape of the mother, signed a consent to the adoption of the child by the prospective adopters.This would appear to suggest that while the Adoption Board may exempt an adoption agency from the requirement to consult the natural father in such circumstances, he should be consulted where possible.

9–104   Where the agency is to be exempted from the duty to consult the father, the authority of the Adoption Board must be obtained before the child is placed for adoption. In the event of the refusal of the mother to disclose the identity of the father, the agency is under a duty to counsel the mother as to the importance of doing so. If the mother persists in her refusal to identify the father, a report on the counselling provided must be given to the Adoption Board. The Board may then authorise the adoption, notwithstanding the failure to consult the father.[179] Section 7 of the 1998 Act amends s.3 of the Adoption Act 1952 (as amended by s.6 of the Adoption Act 1974) by providing that the relatives of a child can now also be traced through the father of the child. When first enacted, the 1952 Act was not so inclusive. Only the members of the mother's family were deemed for this purpose to constitute "relatives". Section 7 of the 1998 Act now remedies this inequity.

The constitutional rights of parents and children, and the adoption of marital children

9–105   The distinction between children who are born to married parents, and those born to parents who are not married to each other, comes into sharp relief in the area of adoption. Where a child is placed for adoption, the consent for which being later withdrawn, problems inevitably arise. The issue can then become a contest between the wishes of the natural parent(s) to regain custody of the child and the wishes of the adoptive parents to insist on an adoption order being made and their legal position as adoptive parents thus being ensured. Provided that the original consent to the agreement to place the child for adoption was valid, the Court must then regard the "best interests of the child" as being central to the resolution of the matter. In the case of a child whose parents have subsequently married, however, there is a Constitutional presumption that the "best interests of the child" are to be found within its family. There must be compelling reasons for taking a child from its family and those reasons must be clearly established.[180]

---

[178]   unreported, High Court, December 21, 1998.

[179]   s.19A of the Adoption Act 1952, as inserted by s.6 of the Adoption Act 1998.

[180]   See *Re J.H. (An Infant): K.C. and A.C. v An Bord Uchtála* [1985] I.R. 375, and W. Duncan, "The Constitutional Protection of Parental Rights in Parenthood in Modern Society" in *Parenthood in Modern Society, Legal and Social Issues for the Twenty-First Century* (J.M. Eekelaar and P. Sarcevic (eds), Martinus Nijhoff, Dordrecht, 1993) and reproduced in the Report of the Constitutional Review Group (Whitaker Report), (The Stationery Office, Dublin, 1996), pp.612–626 and see, R. Horgan, "The United

9–106 There is, therefore, a clear difference between the treatment by the Irish Courts of children born within the confines of marriage and those born outside wedlock. Such divergent treatment is arguably quite arbitrary, being based solely upon the constitutional status of the "family unit" into which children are born, rather than on concerns of a more substantive nature. By virtue of the adoption process, and the effect of the bonding or "attachment" of a baby to its carers, it is very difficult for an unmarried natural parent to succeed in regaining custody of his or her child.[181] The balance of proof is tilted considerably in favour of the birth parents, however, where they can rely on the constitutional presumption that the welfare of the child is to be found within its marital family of origin. For example, in the case of *Re J., an Infant*,[182] Henchy J. stated at 306–307:

> "The fact that the parents and the child constitute a family enables the prosecutors to invoke Article 42, section 1, of the Constitution, by which the State acknowledges that the primary and natural educator of the child is the family and guarantees to respect the inalienable right and duty of parents to provide, according to their means, for the religious and moral, intellectual, physical and social education of their children. ... The only way in which the parents' right and duty of educating this child could be supplanted would be by bringing the case within section 5 of Article 42, which provides that, in exceptional cases, where the parents for physical and moral reasons fail in their duty towards their children, the State as guardian of the common good by appropriate means shall endeavour to supply the place of the parents, but always with due regard for the natural and imprescriptible rights of the child."

9–107 Articles 41 and 42 of the Constitution remain the sentinels to the gateway of adoption. If one views adoption generally as "a second chance",[183] then it will be obvious that not all children in Ireland are entitled to avail of such a second chance. Children born into marital family units can often suffer homelessness through marital breakdown or family dysfunction. In other words, the care options available for such children are limited by the circumstances of their birth.

9–108 The rights attaching to the marital family are, it should be noted, rights enjoyed regardless of nationality or citizenship. This is because, *per* Hamilton P. in *Northants C.C. v A.B.F.*,[184] the rights guaranteed by virtue of Arts 41 and

---

Nations Convention on the Rights of the Child and Irish Family Law" (1991) 9 I.L.T. 162.

[181] *S. v Eastern Health Board*, unreported, High Court, Finlay P., February 1979. See Shatter, *Family Law* (4th ed., Butterworths, Dublin, 1997), p.476 where he notes that the approach taken in *S. v Eastern Health Board* acted as a catalyst to the concepts of bonding and attachment, playing a central role in the judicial determination of "the best interests of the child" in all subsequent cases.

[182] [1966] I.R. 295.

[183] See generally, B. Tizard, *Adoption, a Second Chance* (Open Books, London, 1977).

[184] [1982] I.L.R.M. 164.

42 of the Constitution are natural rights, universally enjoyed by all human persons. The Supreme Court seem to have accepted this point, albeit implicitly, in *T.M. and A.M. v An Bord Uchtála*.[185] Where a non-national child is born to non-national married parents, the family to which the child is born will nonetheless be regarded as a "marital family" for these purposes. Thus, the adoption of such a child would have to proceed under the provisions of the 1988 Act.

9–109 The child, however, also has personal rights under Art.40.3 of the Constitution other than the rights identified in Art.42. In the case of *In the matter of Article 26 and the Adoption (No.2) Bill 1987*,[186] Finlay C.J. held that the rights of the family guaranteed in Arts 41 and 42 of the Constitution could not operate to deny personal rights to a member of that family. It was therefore permissible for legislation to make provision for the restoration of personal rights to a member of a family, even where in the process of such restoration, the constitution of the family had to be disturbed or altered.

Adoption Act 1988

9–110 Since the Adoption Act 1988, the non-consensual adoption of a child, including but not limited to a child born in wedlock, is now possible in exceptional and very restricted circumstances. O'Halloran has suggested that the 1988 Act may be viewed as an encroachment by the State into what was originally perceived in 1952 as an area of private family law. The adoption code was originally designed "to bolster" the constitutional model of the family based on marriage. As Hogan and Whyte point out, the adoption code as originally conceived, sought to facilitate the taking of children from family units that were not based on marriage, with the intent of delivering them as securely and discreetly as possible into family units based on marriage.[187] The scheme put in place by the 1988 Act would seem, on one view at least, to have inverted this agenda.

9–111 The reality, of course, is that marital status alone is no guarantee of a family's functional success or happiness. Large numbers of marital children remain in care and cannot be adopted precisely because their parents are married. For these children, there is no "second chance". Thus, the sustenance of opposition to the provisions of the Adoption Act 1988 appears to be a denial of reality rather than an affirmation of the rights of the family based on marriage. The 1988 Act, in a small way, enables adoption to be chosen as a child care option by the State, in its discharge of the public service obligation to promote the best welfare interests of the child concerned. This choice, however, can only be made in the case of marital children where their parents have been legally branded as failures. In summary, married parents are still denied the option of choosing adoption as a long-term care option for their children. If

[185] [1993] I.L.R.M. 577.
[186] [1989] I.R. 656.
[187] G. Hogan and G. Whyte, *Kelly: The Irish Constitution* (4th ed., Lexis Nexis, Dublin, 2003).

any criticism can be levelled at the 1988 Act, then, it is that it arguably does not go far enough in securing the rights of marital children.

The provisions of the Adoption Act 1988

9–112   The profound irony of this situation is that it is easier, by means of adoption, to vindicate the interests of a child born outside marriage in being part of a caring, stable family unit than it is to secure the same rights for a child born within wedlock. The Adoption Act 1988 goes some way towards redressing this imbalance, though the stringency of its requirements is such that an adoption can only proceed in the most extreme of circumstances. It is still not possible, for instance, for two parents who are married to each other simply to waive their parental rights should they wish to give effect to an adoption. This arguably places the child of parents married to each other at a significant disadvantage relative to his or her non-marital counterpart.

While an application must, initially, be made to the Board, it must be followed by an order of the High Court permitting the adoption. Section 2 of the 1988 Act only empowers the Board to make a *conditional* adoption order in respect of a child. The second tier of the process, then, involves an application to the High Court by the health board in whose functional area the child is at the relevant time. In the absence of the permission of the High Court, or Supreme Court on appeal, the adoption cannot proceed.

9–113   The Court itself, however, may only grant such an adoption if it is satisfied of all of the following:

(a) The parents of the child must, for physical or moral reasons, have failed in their duty towards the child for a period of not less than 12 months immediately preceding the making of the application. This failure must, according to the Supreme Court in the Art.26 reference of the Adoption (No.2) Bill 1987,[188] be "total" in character. Poverty alone, or other "externally originating circumstances", will not suffice to amount to a failure for these purposes.

(b) This failure must be likely to continue without interruption until the child has reached the age of 18. The use of the term "without interruption" seems to underline the need to prove a total abdication of duty on the parents' part.

(c) It must, furthermore, amount to abandonment on the part of the parents of all parental rights, whether of constitutional or other origin, in respect of the child. In *Western Health Board v An Bord Uchtála*,[189] the Court refused to make an order in respect of a child of married parents. Lardner J. held that there had indeed been a failure on the part of the child's father. This failure had lasted at least 12 months and was likely, furthermore, to continue until the child was 18 years old. He was not satisfied, however, that the

---

[188] *In the matter of Article 26 and the Adoption (No.2) Bill 1987* [1989] I.R. 656.
[189] unreported, High Court, Lardner J., July 27, 1993.

evidence was such as to prove abandonment of parental rights on the father's part. The Supreme Court agreed,[190] noting that the failures envisaged by (a) and (b) above did not automatically amount to an abandonment of all parental rights. This largely mirrors the comments of the Supreme Court in the reference of the Adoption (No. 2) Bill 1987,[191] where it observed that a failure to carry out parental duties did not automatically, and of itself, amount to an abandonment of rights under (c).

In *T.M. & A.M. v An Bord Uchtála*,[192] the plaintiff adopters wanted the Irish Adoption Board to recognise an adoption effected in India. The child had been abandoned by unknown parents soon after its birth in Delhi. In the absence of proof that the child was born outside wedlock, or that the child was an orphan, the parents proceeded to adopt the child under the 1988 Act. For these purposes, the Supreme Court accepted that the abandonment of the child had been sufficiently comprehensive to satisfy the provisions of the Act.

In *Northern Area Health Board and W.H. and P.H. v An Bord Uchtála and P.B.*,[193] McGuinness J., in delivering the judgment of the Supreme Court, held that a failure of parental duty and "an abandonment on the part of the parents of all parental rights", while not being the same concepts in law, are and will be related in the facts of any particular case. The case concerned an application by foster parents to adopt a child they had cared for from infancy. The child was 12 years old by the date of the application and had been interviewed by the trial judge. McGuinness J. applied a purposive approach to the interpretation of the Adoption Act 1988 since it was a "remedial statue" intended to permit the adoption of children who had previously been deprived of the benefits of adoption. She held that the fact that the natural mother had infrequent visits to her daughter was "not inconsistent with the reality of her abandonment of her position as a parent". In confirming the decision of the High Court, McGuinness J. held that the mother for physical reasons and not moral reasons had "abandoned the custody and care of her daughter" to the foster parents.

(d) Finally, it is necessary to establish that because of such failure, it is appropriate that the State "as guardian of the common good, should supply the place of the parents."

9–114   Even if each of these stipulations is satisfied, it will still be necessary to establish to the court's satisfaction that, all things considered, the adoption is in the best interests of the child. In so deciding, the court must have regard to the rights, constitutional and otherwise, of all persons concerned. Section 4(1) of the Adoption Act 1988 requires the court to hear the parents of the child, although in the *Northern Area Health Board* case mentioned above,

---

[190]   unreported, Supreme Court, November 10, 1995.
[191]   [1989] I.R. 656 at 664.
[192]   [1993] I.L.R.M. 577.
[193]   [2004] 4 I.R. 252.

McGuinness J. did not hear the natural father as she was satisfied on the evidence that he had never acknowledged the child as his daughter.[194] The Court is also required to pay due regard to the wishes of the child, although the extent of such consideration will depend on the age and understanding of the latter.[195] Each and every one of these conditions, according to the Supreme Court in the Art.26 reference of the Adoption Bill 1987,[196] is an "absolutely essential proof". "Failure in any one of these proofs", it observed, "absolutely prohibits the making of an authorised order, no matter how strong might be the evidence available of its desirability from the point of view of the interests of the child".[197]

The constitutionality of the 1988 Act

9–115   The Bill that ultimately became the Adoption Act 1988 was referred to the Supreme Court by President Hillery using his powers under Art.26 of the Constitution.[198] The Court upheld its constitutionality. It should be noted that the provisions of Art.26 preclude any subsequent constitutional challenge to the terms of the Act.[199] Practitioners considering the provisions of the 1988 Act should, thus, note the essential futility of alleging that the Act or any part of it may be unconstitutional. No doubt, however, the Act passed constitutional scrutiny precisely because it is so rigorous and exacting. It is this very factor that is its biggest drawback. The procedures required by the Act have proved themselves to be "lengthy and cumbersome"[200] and the requirements are often difficult to make out.[201] It is perhaps time, then, that the privileges of the marital family in this area were reconsidered. The legislature should, arguably, consider the possible expansion of the range of circumstances in which the children of dysfunctional marital families can enjoy the security of a permanent adoption in a stable and loving family environment.[202] If a constitutional amendment is required to achieve this, it will be a price worth paying to secure for those children the rights that their non-marital counterparts already enjoy.

9–116   The rights of the child within his or her family of origin and within the adoptive family were considered in detail in a case entitled *In the Matter of*

---

[194] See also *Southern Health Board v An Bord Uchtála* [2000] 1 I.R. 182, where the Supreme Court referred to s.4(2) of the Adoption Act 1988 which states: "Where the parents concerned (or either of them), having been requested to give evidence to the Court at the hearing of an application for an order under *section 3(1)*, fail or refuse to do so, the Court may, if it so thinks fit, notwithstanding the absence of the evidence of the parents or, as the case may be, of either of them, make the order."
[195] s.3(2).
[196] *op. cit.* at 664.
[197] *ibid.*
[198] *In the matter of Article 26 and the Adoption (No.2) Bill 1987* [1989] I.R. 656.
[199] Article 34.3.3° of the Constitution.
[200] See the criticisms of Darling, [1999] 4 I.J.F.L. 2 at 4.
[201] *Western Health Board v An Bord Uchtála*, unreported, Supreme Court, November 10, 1995.
[202] See para.40 of the report of the working group on foster care which addresses the issue of adoption for children in care (Foster Care – A Child Centred Partnership, p.43, Dublin: Government Publications, May 2001).

the Adoption Acts 1952 to 1988 and in the Matter of Section 3 of the Adoption Act, 1988 and in the Matter of F.O'D. an Infant; Southern Health Board v An Bord Uchtála.[203] In the Supreme Court,[204] the Court considered the tragic plight of F.O'D., who was born in 1986 as the eleventh child of a deprived Traveller family. In December of 1987, he was taken into the care of the health board under a Fit Persons Order pursuant to the 1908 Act. He had been tied to a window with a piece of string and was cold and on the verge of serious illness. He was in the care of siblings, both parents being absent from the caravan. He was placed in foster care. When the Order was discharged by his parents, he was returned to their care in August 1989. In December of 1989, F.O'D. was brought to a local hospital by his mother suffering from a fracture and bruising. His injuries were diagnosed to be non-accidental. Having been taken into care again, he was returned to the care of the original foster parents who wished to adopt him. They applied in the ordinary way under the 1988 Act and were deemed suitable to adopt F.O'D. The application was brought by the Health Board to free F.O'D. for adoption by the foster parents. Costello J., in the High Court, authorised the making of the Adoption Order in March 1995 on the basis that the parents had failed in their duty towards F.O'D. He held that it was likely that the natural parents would continue to fail in their duty without interruption until he was 18. Further he stated that the failure constituted an abandonment by the natural parents of all their rights with respect to F.O'D.

9–117   This decision was appealed to the Supreme Court on the basis that the trial judge had erred in finding the parents responsible for the injuries to F.O'D. and that the requisite criteria had not been established showing total abandonment. It was also argued that no proper regard was given to the fact that F.O'D. and his siblings were part of a family, in this case a family with a cultural heritage quite different to the prospective adopters. It was submitted that to satisfy the requirements of the 1988 Act there must be an intention to abandon the child and that no such intention was shown in this case. The Supreme Court, in confirming the decision of the High Court, held that the findings with regard to the non-accidental injuries by the High Court were binding, being findings of fact. The neglect in the case did not just encompass physical abuse but psychological abuse also, and the parental failure would therefore continue until the child was 18. The Supreme Court was of the opinion that the first step under s.3 is to determine that the parents had failed in their duty towards the child, and that this test is a very high one, requiring strong evidence to establish such a failure. The second step is to determine that the failure will continue until the child reaches 18. The third step is to determine whether the failure constitutes an abandonment of rights. The evidence must establish that the parents, by acts or omissions, have failed in their duty to such an extent that the Court can determine that this failure constitutes an abandonment of their rights. Denham J. stated that the word "abandon" had a broader meaning than to abandon "in the ordinary meaning of the word". She held that the term "abandon" could be applied where, by their actions or

---

[203] [1995] 2 I.L.R.M. 369 (HC).
[204] [2000] 1 I.R. 165; [1999] 3 I.J.F.L at 23–24.

omissions, parents "failed in their duty so as to enable a court to deem that their failure constitutes an abandonment of parental rights."[205] The Supreme Court acknowledged that in determining the requisites of s.3, the full circumstances of the child and the wider family and siblings must be considered. However, it left such matters to be addressed by the Adoption Board, noting that in placing a child with a family of different cultural or ethnic background, it was important to ensure that a child's best interests are served. The wishes of the child must always be given consideration, as the Act is child centered. Significantly, the Supreme Court noted that a child's age and vulnerability to outside influences require the authorities to consider each case on its facts. Such a major decision cannot be left to the child to decide.

Provisions in other jurisdictions

9–118 In England and Wales, the child's welfare dictates the outcome of disputes between substitute parents and natural parents. In Northern Ireland, as stated in Chapter 5, if the child has been in the care of foster parents for a period of five years or more, the prospective adopters obtain statutory rights independent of their role as carers for the local authority.[206]

In order to provide a child with parents that he or she can identify as his or her "own", with some promise of permanence, many jurisdictions in the United States have moved to simplify the process of termination of parental rights in circumstances where the parents have abandoned their child to foster care.[207]

Guardianship as an alternative to adoption

9–119 Adoption is not always the most suitable form of care for children. Frequently, as outlined in Chapter 5, older children may wish to have continued contact with their natural families. A special guardianship order, intended to provide permanence for children for whom adoption is not appropriate, has been introduced in the Adoption and Children Act 2002 in England and Wales. It might prove useful in this jurisdiction for the children of a widow/widower who remarries as well as for the children of a single parent who marries.

---

[205] [2000] 1 I.R. 178.

[206] s.29 of the Adoption (NI) Order 1987 as amended:

"(1) While an application for an adoption order in respect of a child made by the person with whom the child has had his home for the five years preceding the application is pending, no person is entitled, against the will of the applicant, to remove the child from the applicant's [home] except with the leave of the court or under authority conferred by any enactment or on the arrest of the child.

(2) Where a person ('the prospective adopter') gives notice to the Board [or HSS trust] within whose area he has his home that he intends to apply for an adoption order in respect of a child who for the preceding five years has had his home with the prospective adopter, no person is entitled, against the will of the prospective adopter, to remove the child from the prospective adopter's [home], except with the leave of a court or under authority conferred by any enactment or on the arrest of the child, before:

   (a) the prospective adopter applies for the adoption order, or
   (b) the period of 3 months from the receipt of the notice by the Board [or HSS trust] expires, whichever occurs first."

[207] See Chap.5, para.5–53.

Court costs

9–120 Where the natural parents are refused legal aid under the Legal Aid Act 1995, the health board involved must pay court costs incurred by them which are not paid by another party to the 1988 Act proceedings.[208] Where the application to the High Court is made by the health board, the health board will meet the costs of the proceedings. However, where the health board declines to make the application, and the prospective adopters apply themselves and are successful, the health board must meet the costs incurred by them that are not met by the other party. They may also, of course, apply to the Legal Aid Board to fund the proceedings on their behalf. If they are unsuccessful in securing the assistance of either the health board or the Legal Aid Board and are then unsuccessful in their application to the High Court, they must meet their own costs. Section 44(1) of the Child Care Act 1991 should also be noted in that it allows for the continuance of the foster-care allowance after an adoption order has been granted. It provides:

"Where a child becomes adopted under the Adoption Acts, 1952 to [1998], and the child was, immediately before the adoption, being maintained in foster care by a health board with the adopter or adopters, the health board may, subject to any general directions given by the Minister and subject to such conditions as the health board sees fit, contribute to the maintenance of the child as if he continued to be in foster care."

Costs in adoption cases under s.3 of the Adoption Act 1974 are not so well provided for.[209] Prospective adopters who fail to qualify for legal aid must ordinarily pay the costs of actions to enable the adoption process to proceed. The High Court, in *J.B. and D.B. v An Bord Uchtála*; *S.M. v St. Louise's Adoption Society and An Bord Uchtála*, allowed the making of an order for costs against the Adoption Society, run by the Eastern Health Board, although it was accepted that it was not at fault in the proceedings.

Post-adoption services

9–121 Once the adopted child becomes a member of the adoptive family, the normal arrangements for health and social services apply as they do for all children. It is argued that emotional, psychological and financial support services should be put in place to assist adopted children, adoptive parents and natural parents in dealing with issues which may arise as a direct result of the adoption; for example, facilitation of ongoing access between the natural family and adopters and dealing with feelings of loss. Some of these issues may arise in the immediate aftermath of the adoption, or years later. In the case of a child adopted from abroad, discussed below, additional support may be required to deal also with issues surrounding culture, language and race.

[208] Adoption Act 1988, s.5. See also s.5(3) of the 1988 Act.
[209] See *J.B. and D.B. v An Bord Uchtála*, unreported, High Court, 1998; *S.M. v St. Louise's Adoption Society and An Bord Uchtála*, unreported, High Court, McGuinness J., January 15, 1999.

INTERCOUNTRY ADOPTIONS

Introduction

9–122 The most significant change in adoption in Ireland in recent years has been the growth of intercountry adoption.[210] Intercountry adoption in Ireland began, as previously stated, as a humanitarian response to the issue of abandoned children in Romania in the early 1990s. The Adoption Act 1991 (later amended by the Adoption Act 1998) was introduced in response to the large number of adopters who travelled to Romania at that time. The Act fulfils two functions: (a) it provides a framework for foreign adopted children to have the same rights as Irish born children; and (b) it sets up a legal framework for assessing prospective adopters prior to adoption.

A number of issues have arisen in the course of implementing the 1991 Act, as amended by the 1998 Act which are discussed in greater detail in the section on the Hague Convention. These are:

1. the recognition of simple adoptions by which the parents in the country of origin still retain some rights in relation to the adopted child,

2. the absence of an appeals mechanism on decisions to grant declarations of eligibility and suitability to adopt, and

3. the granting of country-specific declarations.

Recognition

9–123 Where an adoption is effected in a jurisdiction other than Ireland, the question of recognition arises. Such recognition is dealt with under the statutory framework put in place by the Adoption Act 1991, as amended by the Adoption Act 1998, and enables the adoptive parent or parents to be treated under Irish law as full guardians of the child. As the number of children available for adoption in this country has dwindled, the option of foreign adoption has become more attractive, especially for parents who do not necessarily meet the very tight criteria laid down by some adoption societies. The path to recognition, however, has been far from easy. The non-recognition of foreign adoptions has serious legal consequences for the parents and children involved. These adoptions remain, even today, rather controversial. There are potential constitutional difficulties, not least that the natural parents of the child might have been married (and thus have had "inalienable and imprescriptible" rights in respect of their child). Objections might also be mounted where the consent requirements may not have been as rigorous as the Supreme Court required in *G. v An Bord Uchtála*.[211] It is worth noting, in this connection, that persons other than non-nationals can enjoy the rights guaranteed under Art.41 of the Constitution.[212] These rights being universal in nature, it is generally

---

[210] In 2000, for example, the Adoption Board recognised 323 foreign adoption orders compared to 117 in 1996.

[211] [1980] I.R. 32.

[212] See *per* Hamilton P. in *Northants Co. Co. v A.B.F.* [1982] I.L.R.M. 164 (HC), and *per* O'Flaherty J. in *T.M. and A.M. v An Bord Uchtála* [1993] I.L.R.M. 577 at 589–590.

acknowledged that they may be pleaded even where the litigant is not an Irish citizen.

9–124   While the Adoption Act 1991 itself does not preclude recognition of the adoption of the children of married parents, the Constitution may, effectively, require that the public policy exceptions in ss.2 to 5 thereof be read restrictively so as to preclude such adoptions. The Supreme Court seems to suggest, in *T.M. and A.M. v An Bord Uchtála*,[213] that this would be the case. Nonetheless, it has held that for these purposes the Adoption Act 1988 can be applied to the adoption of non-national children. In *T.M.*, the plaintiffs were attempting to adopt an Indian-born child abandoned by unknown parents soon after its birth. There being no proof that the child was either non-marital or an orphan, the parents successfully proceeded to adopt the child under the provisions of the 1988 Act. The Court accepted that the abandonment of the child so soon after its birth was sufficiently comprehensive to satisfy the provisions of the 1988 Act, even if the child's parents were married to each other and still alive. The implication, however implicit, is that even in the case of a non-national child, the adoption of children born within wedlock will be restricted. Given the rights enjoyed under Art.41 of the Constitution, the adoption abroad of a child who is a member of a marital family might not be recognised unless provisions similar to those in the 1988 Act have been satisfied.

9–125   An additional complication is the inevitable socio-cultural and legal differences encountered between jurisdictions in this field. What is known as an "adoption" in one jurisdiction may not necessarily comply with our understanding of adoption in Ireland. For example, the complete severance of the legal nexus between parent and child originally required by the Adoption Act 1991 is not a universal feature of adoptions effected abroad. Some jurisdictions, such as China, allow for the termination of an adoption order in certain exceptional cases. Many other jurisdictions only allow a less than complete form of adoption, where the child continues to enjoy a qualified legal nexus to his or her natural parents, allowing the former, for instance, to enjoy succession rights on the death of the natural parents. These "simple" adoptions are a feature of some Muslim countries. Sharia law, for example, only permits an arrangement equivalent to foster care, the "*Kafala*". By this method the child, though in the custody of "adoptive" parents, continues legally, culturally and socially to be regarded as the child of his or her natural parents. Other jurisdictions' adoptions involve somewhat more substantive transfers of rights and duties on adoption, but do not have the effect of severing for all time the relationship between the natural parents and child. These "simple" adoptions were thought not to comply with the original requirement in the 1991 Act that the foreign adoption have substantially the same effect as an adoption effected in this jurisdiction, since they involved no final termination of the natural parents' parental rights and duties. While the 1998 Act goes some way towards rectifying this situation, problems still remain.

---

[213] [1993] I.L.R.M. 577.

General provisions relating to all foreign adoptions

9–126 Between 1952 and 1991, there were no statutory provisions relating to foreign adoptions. Instead, the common law rules prevailed, requiring that the adoption be recognised only where the adopters were domiciled in the place where the adoption was granted.[214] This rather rigorous requirement was widened considerably by the Adoption Act 1991.[215] In response to some of the concerns previously noted, regarding simple and terminable adoptions, the original terms of that Act have been amended considerably by the Adoption Act 1998. The Adoption Act 1991 is retrospective in effect; *i.e.* it applies to all foreign adoptions that otherwise meet the criteria, whether such adoptions have been made before, or after, the commencement of the 1991 Act.

9–127 A "foreign adoption" is defined by s.1 of the 1991 Act as the adoption of a child who, at the date on which the adoption was effected, was under 21 (if the adoption was effected before the commencement of the Act). If the adoption was effected after the commencement of the Act, this maximum age is reduced to 18. Thus, the adoption of a person who, when adopted, is of full age will generally not be recognised in this State. In order to qualify for recognition as a foreign adoption under the Adoption Acts 1991–1998, the following conditions must also be satisfied:

(a) The first requirement for recognition is that consent to the adoption of all persons necessary under the foreign law has been obtained or dispensed with. The consent to the adoption is, therefore, dealt with in accordance with the laws of the foreign jurisdiction and so the Act neatly sidesteps the complications attaching to this issue under Irish domestic adoption law. The Irish court must accept the competence of the foreign jurisdiction to determine the consent requirement. The European Convention on the Adoption of Children 1967 (see Appendix 12) is quite specific on the nature of the consent required for adoption and on the question of the dispensation with that consent on exceptional grounds.[216] As a safety net, however, the Act provides a "public policy" escape clause in the case of adoptions effected abroad by persons ordinarily resident in Ireland.[217]

Where a couple fail to comply with a requirement of local law (the "*lex loci contractus*"), even where not stipulated in Ireland, the adoption may not be recognised as a "foreign adoption" under the Irish legislative requirements. Section 10 of the 1998 Act substitutes a new paragraph (a) in the definition of "foreign adoption" under s.1 of the 1991 Act:

> "(a) the consent to the adoption of every person whose consent to the adoption was, under the law of the place where the adoption was effected, required to be obtained or dispensed with was obtained or dispensed with under that law either—

---

[214] *M.F. v An Bord Uchtála* [1991] I.L.R.M. 399.
[215] No. 14 of 1991.
[216] The European Convention, European Treaties Series, No. 58, Art.5.
[217] See s.5(1).

(i)   at the time the adoption was effected, or

(ii) at a subsequent time when, if the adoption which was initially
      granted did not have the effect in that place of terminating a
      pre-existing legal parent-child relationship, it was converted
      into an adoption having that effect by virtue of such consent
      being obtained or dispensed with under that law (the date on
      which the adoption was initially granted being construed for
      the purposes of this Act as at the time the adoption was
      effected)."

Thus, if a simple adoption can be converted into a full adoption in the
foreign jurisdiction, the adoption may be recognised as a "foreign adoption"
capable of recognition, provided the consent to the "full adoption" is
obtained or such consent to "full adoption" is lawfully dispensed with in
accordance with the laws of the foreign jurisdiction.

(b) The second condition outlined in the definition requirement of a "foreign
    adoption" is that the "adoption" made in the foreign jurisdiction is
    essentially the same as a domestic adoption. Some jurisdictions have quite
    different concepts of adoption to our own. Some recognise "simple
    adoptions", which do not sever the legal links between the birth family
    and the adopted child. As a matter of policy, the 1991 Act required that
    only adoptions which accord to our own definition of adoption should be
    recognised in Irish law. The reason for this restriction was that the incidents
    and effects of foreign and domestic orders should be the same. Irish children
    and children adopted from abroad should be entitled to the same status as
    a result of their adoption. In addition to domestic policy considerations,
    the European Convention specified the incidents and effects of adoption
    in terms of a full adoption.[218]

    The Adoption Board also examines the adoption codes of foreign
    countries to ensure that the foreign adoption code is "essentially the same"
    as the Irish adoption code. Paragraph (b) of the 1991 Act has also been
    substituted by the 1998 Act, as follows:

    "(b) the adoption has, for so long as it is in force, substantially the
         same legal effect as respects the guardianship of the child in the
         place where it was effected as an adoption effected by an adoption
         order..."

This new section is substantially different from the previous one which
stated:

    "(b) the adoption has essentially the same legal effects as respects the
         termination and creation of parental rights and duties with respect
         to the child in the place where it was effected as an adoption
         effected by an adoption order".

It is clear from the Dáil debates that the purpose of this amendment was to
facilitate the recognition of adoption orders made in jurisdictions such as
China, where adoptions may be terminated in certain defined circum-

---

[218] Arts 10, 16 and 24.

stances. The Adoption Board thought that the Chinese adoptions should be defined as "simple adoptions" because of the provisions in the Chinese adoption code making them revocable in certain circumstances. The line between the categories of "full" and "simple" adoptions may, however, sometimes become blurred. In the case of *B and B v An Bord Uchtála*,[219] the Supreme Court highlighted that adoptions traditionally viewed as "simple" adoptions might, because of their particular characteristics, be equated with full adoptions. By substituting "guardianship" for the termination and creation of parental rights, it may be argued that "simple" adoptions could now be recognised under the terms of the 1991 legislation as amended by the 1998 Act. A simple adoption may well have the same guardianship effects as an adoption order. Guardianship, however, is not necessarily an exclusive status, nor does it imply an inherent right to custody or access.

By completely removing any reference to the termination and creation of parental rights, that exclusive aspect of an Irish adoption order is removed as a yardstick for measuring the compatibility of foreign adoption codes. The Report of the Law Reform Commission on the implementation of the Hague Convention noted that:

> "The permeability of the two primary categories of adoption is also apparent in the redefinition of a recognisable adoption in the *Adoption Act 1998*. The 1991 Act, which until this year governed the recognition of simple adoptions, set out strict criteria for the recognition of foreign adoptions, requiring that, in order to be recognised here, an adoption must have essentially the same legal effect as an Irish adoption, in terminating the parental rights of the birth parents. The 1998 Act modifies this somewhat, providing that the adoption must have 'for so long as it is in force, substantially the same legal effect as respect the guardianship of the child' as an Irish adoption. This allows for the recognition of some simple adoptions in Irish Law, but it is by no means clear that it will allow for the recognition of all simple adoptions."[220]

The "conflict of laws" position with regard to the recognition of an adoption order, which is not necessarily available in the domestic adoption code, is complicated. In the case of orders obtained abroad by persons who have no connecting factor with the foreign jurisdiction, the position is regulated by the provisions of the 1991 Act, as amended, and by the issue of "public policy". The State has undertaken to implement the provisions of the Hague Convention on Protection of Children and Co-operation in Respect of Intercountry Adoption.

(c) The third policy consideration is that the foreign jurisdiction should undertake enquiries into the adopters, the child, and the parents or guardians. At the very least, this policy requirement ensures that some

---

[219] [1997] I.L.R.M. 15.
[220] *Report of the Law Reform Commission on the Implementation of the Hague Convention on Protection of Children and Co-Operation in Respect of Intercountry Adoption*, 1993 (LRC 58–1998) June, 1998, p.42.

rudimentary enquiries are made in both jurisdictions. The adopters would of necessity have to produce some "home study" report in advance of the adoption being made. The foreign jurisdiction would have to make enquiries into the position of the child and the birth family or legal guardians. The European Convention is quite precise as to the nature of the enquiries to be carried out by a competent authority in advance of an adoption being made. It is also prescriptive as to the qualifications of the persons entrusted to carry out the enquiry.[221]

(d) The fourth policy requirement is that the court, or other authority, or person by whom the adoption was effected in the foreign jurisdiction, had given due consideration to the interests and welfare of the child before making the adoption order. Due consideration is not defined in the Act. The European Convention requires the competent authority to refrain from making an adoption order unless it is satisfied that the adoption will be in the interests of the child. The UN Convention on the Rights of the Child (1989) also requires State Parties to ensure, as a paramount consideration, that the adoption is in the child's best interests.[222]

The original s.1 of the 1991 Act defined the welfare criterion as follows:
"(d) the law of the place where the adoption was affected required the court or other authority or person by whom the adoption was effected, before doing so, to give due consideration to the interests and welfare of the child..."

In contrast, the new s.1(d), as substituted by s.10(a)(iii) of the 1998 Act, states:
"(d) the adoption was affected for the purpose of promoting the interests and welfare of the child..."

The original sections appear to have been directed towards ensuring that the foreign jurisdiction went through some formal determination that the child was suitable for adoption abroad. The welfare of the child was required to be considered in advance of the decision to place the child for adoption abroad. This, of course, accorded with the provisions of the European Convention on the Adoption of Children 1967,[223] the United Nations Convention on the Rights of the Child 1989,[224] and the Recommendations of the United Nations Report on Adoption and Foster Placement of Children 1980.[225] The substituted section, without question, applies a less onerous standard. Such a standard could be achieved by asserting that the adoption was in fact carried out to promote the interests and welfare of the child, even if the foreign jurisdiction did not have a procedure in place in its laws to ensure that this was so. The amending s.10 also alters the definition of "place" in the original s.1 of the 1991 Act.

---

[211] See Arts 7–9.
[222] See United Nations Convention on the Rights of the Child, adopted by the General Assembly on November 20, 1989, Art.21.
[223] Arts 8 and 9.
[224] Art.21.
[225] Recommendations 19–23.

It can be seen that the legislative intention "as a matter of policy" appears to be to make the recognition of adoptions effected abroad easier from the point of view of the adoptive parents. It may well be argued that this also protects the interests of the children involved, as it is better that their status under the foreign order be clarified by the recognition of the foreign orders and their entry on the Register of Foreign Adoption Orders. The Law Reform Commission cogently makes this argument in favour of recognition. It also recommends that, as a matter of policy, Ireland should not use the veto under Art.17 to prevent the entrusting of the child to the adoptive parents, merely because only a simple adoption can be assured by the Convention process. The Law Reform Commission, however, is clearly opposed to automatic recognition of non-Convention simple adoptions.

(e) The final policy consideration is that no money should have changed hands in relation to the adoption. This is a central policy consideration in both the domestic adoption code and under the European Convention on the Adoption of Children. It does not prevent, however, payments made in connection with the adoption process for translations, travel requirements, medical fees and payments to lawyers.

Only foreign adoptions which satisfy all of these policy considerations are recognised under Irish law. The requirements set out by the existing legislation as a pre-requisite to recognition have proved to be exacting in practice.

The 1993 Hague Convention

9–128   The Hague Convention on the Protection of Children and Co-Operation in respect of Intercountry Adoption 1993, concluded and signed on May 29, 1993, is soon to be incorporated into Irish domestic law. When the Adoption (Hague Convention) Bill 2004 is enacted, Irish adoption law will facilitate the recognition of simple adoptions, subject to certain safeguards.

By implementing the 1993 Hague Convention, Ireland will be incorporating procedures for the recognition of "simple adoptions", provided, of course, that all parties go through the Convention procedure. Non-recognition is envisaged only in cases where it becomes clear that there has been a serious abuse. Under Art.24 of the Convention, recognition of an adoption may be refused by a Contracting State where the adoption is manifestly contrary to its public policy.[226] In general, however, non-recognition is not in the best interests of the child, since it results in continuing uncertainty as to the child's status with his or her adoptive family.[227] In the case of Convention adoptions, the child is protected by the process and procedures inherent in such adoptions. The situation is not so assured outside of a Convention adoption. The Law

---

[226] See Head 10 of the Hague Convention on the Protection of Children and Co-Operation on Intercountry Adoption Bill 2003.

[227] *The Law Reform Commission Report on the Implementation of the Hague Convention on Protection of Children and Co-operation in Respect of Intercountry Adoption 1993,* (LRC 58–1998), p.42.

Reform Commission noted that:

> "It must be acknowledged that there is a need for additional caution in relation to existing and non-Convention adoptions, since the adoption process in such cases will not have been subject to the same standards and regulation as an adoption effected under the Convention. Regulation of adoption from non-Convention countries should not become so lax as to undermine the Convention, by deterring prospective adopters from adopting through the carefully regulated Convention procedure. Nevertheless, and especially in relation to the retrospective recognition of adoptions which are already in place, it is not desirable, from the point of view of the welfare of the child, to leave such adoptions unrecognised, where recognition can be effected without undermining the rights of birth parents."[228]

The Commission recommended that the Convention procedure under Art.27 of the Convention be available to existing "simple adoptions", subject to the appropriate consents of the birth parents being obtained. It also recommended that Convention "simple adoptions", which cannot be converted to full adoptions, should have the same effect in Ireland as they have in the country where the adoption was effected. However, in the case of a simple adoption effected by persons in a third country (Ireland being neither the sending nor the receiving country), the adoption should have the same effect as it would be entitled to in the receiving country. In the case of foreign adoptions (non-Convention) by non-Irish residents, the Commission recommended that the restrictive interpretation under the Adoption Act 1991, as amended, should not be applied to adoptions under ss.2, 3 and 4 of that Act, and that adoptions should be entitled to recognition except where such recognition would be manifestly contrary to public policy. In the case of the recognition of non-Convention simple adoptions, the Commission was not so flexible, noting that:

> "We have considered the possibility of allowing for the recognition of simple adoptions, made outside the Convention process, as having the effects which they had in the State of origin. However, without the protection of the Convention safeguards and procedures, this would not be warranted. It would entail lengthy and difficult investigation into the laws and procedures of the State of origin, in situations where there might be no well-established channels of communication between the Irish and the sending State authorities. It would also be difficult to guarantee that adequate standards had been applied in the adoption process. Since the object of the Hague Convention, and Ireland's ratification of it, is to raise standards in intercountry adoption, it would be unfortunate to risk undermining these standards by relaxing the requirements for recognition of non-Convention adoptions to the extent that the Convention system would simply become redundant."[229]

---

[228] At pp.47–48.
[229] *ibid.* p.48.

9–129 The incident and effects of non-Convention simple adoptions are therefore unclear. It is not in the best interests of the children concerned that there should be a doubt as to their status and legal position in Irish law.[230] The courts, in determining the incidents and effects to be attributable to such adoptions, may well apply Convention procedures and standards outside the strict scope of the Convention. As outlined, central to the ethos of the Convention is the premise that non-recognition should not be used as a sanction. It would seem, however, that as a matter of public policy and in accordance with international obligations, there is an onus on the State to put measures in place to ensure that all simple adoptions must go through the Convention process.

Persons with a foreign domicile

9–130 As with marriage and divorce, an adoption effected in a place where either or both of the adopters are domiciled will be recognised as a matter of Irish law.[231] Similar provisions now apply where the relevant adoption is recognised by the law of the place of domicile. Thus, if the parties are domiciled in a jurisdiction other than that in which the adoption took place, it will be recognised as a matter of Irish law, provided that it would also be recognised in the place of the adopter's or adopters' domicile.

The domicile of the parties, for this purpose, shall be that held on the date of the relevant adoption order. This is subject to certain conditions. First, the adoption must be legally recognised as valid in the place in which it was effected. Second, the deeming of such adoption must not be contrary to the public policy of this State. There would be obvious objections to such recognition where, for instance, a foreign state permitted the abduction of children for the purposes of adoption. It should go without saying that the mere fact that another jurisdiction uses the term "adoption" to describe a child-care arrangement should not oblige the State to grant it recognition. Where it is obvious, for instance, that what is called adoption is meant to be a temporary measure only, such recognition might not be granted.

Persons who are habitually or ordinarily resident outside the State (Ireland)

9–131 In line with standard international principles, ss.3 and 4 of the Adoption Act 1991 allow for the like recognition of adoptions effected in places where the adopters are at the time of the adoption habitually resident or ordinarily resident. What happens where the jurisdiction in which one is domiciled, habitually resident or ordinarily resident, refuses to recognise *any* foreign adoptions, whatever the circumstances of their making? Prior to 1998, in the absence of such recognition, the adoption could not be recognised in Ireland. Section 4A of the 1991 Act, however, now allows such adoptions to be recognised. This new section was introduced by s.12 of the Adoption Act 1998. It provides that where such non-recognition stems solely from the fact

---

[230] For example, the right to citizenship, nationality and succession rights.
[231] s.2(1) of the Adoption Act 1991. See also *M.F. v An Bord Uchtála* [1991] I.L.R.M. 399.

that the place in question does not recognise any adoption contracted otherwise than in that place, the adoption may nonetheless be recognised in Ireland, unless it would be contrary to public policy to do so. A failure on the part of the place of domicile, habitual residence or ordinary residence simply to acknowledge the validity of a *particular* foreign adoption, and not *all* such adoptions, will not suffice for these purposes.

Persons ordinarily resident in the State (Ireland)

9–132 Where the adoptive parent or parents are ordinarily resident in Ireland at the relevant time, rather more rigorous requirements apply. Unless such parents can show that they were domiciled or habitually resident in another jurisdiction, the provisions of s.5 of the 1991 Act will apply. These require that in order for recognition to be granted, An Bord Uchtála must certify that certain conditions have been met.

These conditions are as follows:

(a) that the adopters would otherwise have met, at the time of the adoption, the provisions of s.10 of the 1991 Act;

(b) that the adopters were ordinarily resident in Ireland on the date of the adoption;

(c) where the adoption took place before April 1, 1992, that An Bord Uchtála has certified in writing that it is satisfied that the provisions of s.10 have been met in respect of the adoption;

(d) where the adoption took place after April 1, 1992, that An Bord Uchtála had, prior to the adoption, declared in writing that the adopters satisfy the provisions of s.10 of the Act of 1991, and that they have, furthermore, met the criteria for suitability laid down in s.13 of the Adoption Act 1952. For these purposes, the Board must have regard to a report by the health board in whose functional area the adopters ordinarily resided at the time of the adoption.

9–133 Where an adoption was effected between the dates of April 1, 1992, and July 1, 1992, special *inter regnum* provisions apply. This time period, originally applying for the three months between April 1, 1991, and July 1, 1991, was altered by one year by the 1998 Act.[232] The amending legislation stipulates that "1992" be substituted in *every* case for "1991". An adoption effected between the newly stipulated dates will be recognised in Irish law, provided that the Minister for Justice, Equality and Law Reform had received a request in writing from the adopters before the earlier of these two dates. If, having received such request, the Minister for Justice, Equality and Law Reform gave to them an assurance in writing before April 1, 1992 as to the admission to the State of a child adopted abroad, the adoption shall be deemed to be valid if the following conditions are met:

[232] s.13 of the Adoption Act 1998.

(a) such deeming is not contrary to public policy;

(b) the adopters satisfy the conditions as to eligibility laid down in s.10 of the 1991 Act;[233] and

(c) the adopters must have been ordinarily resident in the State at the date of the adoption order.

9–134 Each of the provisions in ss.3, 4, 4A and 5 of the 1991 Act are deemed to be in substitution for any rule of law providing for recognition of adoptions effected outside the State.[234] In other words, the scheme proposed by the Act of 1991, as amended, supersedes rather than supplements the common law criteria for recognition. Section 8 of the Act allows the health board, where requested, to perform an assessment of prospective adoptive parents ordinarily resident in the State at the time of the foreign adoption order. This may be done only where the adoption occurs after April 1, 1992. The report of such an assessment should, in particular, state whether and to what extent the adopters satisfy the conditions of s.13 of the Adoption Act 1952.

9–135 The board must be satisfied and declare as to both the eligibility and suitability in advance of the foreign adoption order being obtained. All applicants who can establish eligibility to adopt under s.10 are entitled to an assessment by a health board social worker. The assessment is sent to the Adoption Board, which decides whether or not to make the declaration as to suitability or otherwise. A copy of the declaration or refusal is sent to the social worker who carried out the assessment, and who then informs the prospective adopters. There is no appeal procedure at present, apart from an application to the Court by way of judicial review of the administrative action. In practice, the number of applicants declared unsuitable is small. However, there is concern that the health boards have imposed "age limitations" on persons who wish to adopt a child from abroad and have refused to perform the eligibility and suitability test for older would-be adopters.

9–136 The health board may only refer "would-be adopters" to State agencies, such as those in China, Thailand and Romania, who have a State-controlled system which can be recommended. Those who wish to adopt from other jurisdictions may act independently or through a foreign or domestic agency specialising in intercountry adoption. Such agencies are not at present regulated by the Adoption Board, although the Report of the Law Reform Commission recommends that they be accredited to act in intercountry adoptions, subject to the regulation and control of the Adoption Board acting as Central Authority under the Hague Convention 1993. The assessment of persons to deem whether they are eligible and suitable to adopt has proven to be somewhat controversial. As Vivienne Darling states, it may well be that intercountry adopters are

---

[233] As a prerequisite to recognition, An Bord Uchtála must declare in writing that such conditions have been satisfied.

[234] s.2(2) of the Act of 1991 as amended by s.11 of the Adoption Act 1998.

different from other adopters and find the assessment process irksome and intrusive:

> "It is interesting to note ... that there has never been the same level of complaint or anxiety in respect of assessment for domestic adoption although the process was essentially the same."[235]

9–137   Section 8 provides for assessments by health boards or registered adoption agencies of persons who want to adopt a foreign child. This assessment must be undertaken "as soon as practicable". The problems associated with providing assessments "as soon as practicable" were considered in the case of *McC. and McD. v Eastern Health Board*.[236] The High Court held that there was no constitutional right to decide to adopt a child and to have that decision executed within any particular time. Even if such a right existed, the court would also have to have regard to the constitutional rights of the child whose future was determined by the adoption process. The Court also held that the applicants had not established, as a matter of probability, that the health board was in breach of its statutory duty to process the application as soon as practicable. The applicants appealed this decision to the Supreme Court. It found that the phrase "as soon as practicable" did not mean as soon as possible. The health board had to consider all of its statutory obligations. The assessment procedure should not be prolonged beyond a period that was reasonably required to ensure that the interests and welfare of the child to be adopted were fully protected. Whether this was so depended on the circumstances of the particular health board area involved. In the instant case, the Supreme Court stated that the Eastern Health Board was doing its best given its circumstances.

Proof of foreign adoptions

9–138   Where an adoption was effected outside the State, a presumption arises, until the contrary is demonstrated, that the law of the place where it was effected has been complied with in full.[237] A document purporting to be a copy of a foreign adoption order, if duly authenticated, shall, without further proof being required, be deemed to be a true copy of the document unless the contrary is shown. Similar provisions apply where there are multiple documents or multiple copies. A document will be regarded as "duly authenticated" where it bears the seal of the court of authority, or person or persons, by which or by whom it was issued or executed. A document will also be "duly authenticated" where certified by either:

(i)   a person in his capacity as a judge or officer of that court, or in his capacity as that authority, or as a member or officer of that authority; or

(ii) the person or persons by whom it was issued or executed.

---

[235] [1999] 4 I.J.F.L. 2.
[236] [1997] 1 I.L.R.M. 349.
[237] s.9(4) of the Adoption Act 1991.

The Minister may also stipulate additional requirements of proof of foreign adoptions by regulations, which regulations may discriminate between different places and different classes of adoption. By virtue of s.16 of the Adoption Act 1998, all such regulations are subject to negative action clauses that allow the Oireachtas to annul the regulations in certain circumstances.

The register of foreign adoptions

9–139 All adoptions contracted abroad, but recognised in Irish law, must be registered by An Bord Uchtála upon request by the adopters.[238] For this purpose, the Board is required to establish and maintain a "Register of Foreign Adoptions". Where it is satisfied that the adoption is one to which any of ss.2, 3, 4, 4A or 5 of the 1991 Act apply, the Board is obliged to register the adoption therein. Such obligation, however, arises only on the making of an application by either the adopted person, by the adopter or adopters, or by any other person having an interest in the matter. In such circumstances, the Board may refuse to do so only in the case of an adoption made under s.5(1)(iii)(II) of the Act, that is, an adoption made after April 1, 1991, in favour of persons ordinarily resident in the State on the date of the adoption. The aforementioned exception applies only where the Board is satisfied that, since the granting of recognition, circumstances have changed such that the adopters are no longer considered to be eligible persons to adopt by reason of s.13 of the 1952 Act or s.10 of the 1991 Act.

9–140 Persons seeking an entry in the Register of Foreign Adoptions will be obliged, by virtue of s.6(4) of the 1991 Act, to furnish the Board with all relevant information reasonably required to assess the validity of the request made. Once entered, a true copy of the entry in the Register shall be deemed to be evidence of recognition of the adoption order within this State. That said, it is possible for the Board, if satisfied as to the matter in question, to remove the entry if the adoption order has been set aside, annulled or declared void. It is also open to the Board to rectify any errors that may appear on the Register.

9–141 Section 7 of the 1991 Act empowers the High Court, following an application made by an adopter, adopters, by an adopted person, or by any other person having an interest in the matter, to make one of a series of orders relating to the Register of Foreign Adoptions. The Court may, for instance, order the Board to make an entry in the Register concerning a specific adoption, or alternatively, require the correction or cancellation of an entry. A refusal to order recognition will have the consequence of deeming the adoption in question not to have been effected by a valid adoption order. Where an adoption is set aside, revoked, terminated, annulled, or otherwise deemed void under the law of the place where it was made, the Court is required to refuse to give a direction cancelling an entry in the Register, except in certain circumstances. These circumstances are where the Court is satisfied that it would be in the best interests of the child to cancel the entry.[239] Where the entry is can-

---

[238] s.6 of the 1991 Act.

[239] s.7(1A) of the 1991 Act, as inserted by s.15(b) of the Adoption Act 1998.

celled, the Court may make such declarations as appear proper regarding the guardianship, custody, maintenance and citizenship of the child in question, subject always to the overriding criterion that the Court act in the best interests of the child.

9–142   Section 14 of the 1998 Act amends s.6 of the 1991 Act in a technical sense by including a reference to the widened categories of orders recognised under the Act. It also deletes the original subs.(6) which provided for the removal from the Register of Foreign Adoptions of entries of foreign adoptions where such orders had been set aside, annulled or otherwise rendered void under and in accordance with the law of the place where it was effected, or if the court so directed in accordance with s.7. In the event of the annulment or revocation of the foreign order in the country where the order was made, therefore, there would be no automatic removal from the Register of Foreign Adoptions. In accordance with the amended s.7, application could be made to the court to consider the matter on the basis of public policy and the welfare of the child.

9–143   While the Hague Convention on Jurisdiction, Applicable Law and Recognition of Decrees relating to Adoption 1964 provided for the international validity of decrees for the annulment and revocation of adoptions,[240] the 1993 Hague Convention is silent on the question. The focus of the latter Convention is to establish a system of co-operation between receiving States and States of origin for the purpose of minimising abuse, ensuring that the interests of the child are uppermost in the adoption process and guaranteeing the recognition of adoptions made under the Convention. In the event of serious abuse in the case of a simple adoption, action taken to quash the order in the State of origin of the child could have serious consequences for the child and the adoptive parents alike. This amendment ensures, however, that the order could not be removed from the Register without judicial intervention in Ireland.

9–144   The Report of the Law Reform Committee of the Law Society of Ireland noted that:

> "The 1991 Act, and the 1998 Act, are primarily directed towards recognition rather than towards regulation. The regulatory element of the legislation, which introduced an important safeguard in inter-country adoption, was the requirement to establish 'eligibility and suitability' to adopt in advance of embarking on an inter-country adoption. This requirement may have resulted in an administrative nightmare for health boards, but it introduced an important safeguard into the inter-country adoption process for the children concerned. The 1991 Act broadened the categories of person eligible to adopt and also introduced a time controlled exception to the requirement for a prior Declaration of

---

[240] See Art.7 of the Convention (which was not signed or ratified by Ireland), and J. Unger, "Hague Conference on Private International Law: Draft Convention on Adoption" (1965) (28) M.L.R. 465.

Eligibility. The purpose of these concessions was to afford recognition to adoptions which had already been effected prior to the Act. It was intended that after July, 1991 everyone adopting from abroad would have to comply with the requirements set out in s.5. The 1998 Act has extended this period by a further year in order to afford recognition to adoptions, which did not meet the original deadline. Adoptive parents of children adopted prior to 1991 should be obliged to apply for recognition of the foreign order."

9–145 The Report recommended that:

1. measures be introduced requiring adoptive parents of children adopted abroad prior to 1991 to apply to the Adoption Board for recognition of the Foreign Order;

2. measures be introduced to the effect that the Declaration of Eligibility to adopt be limited to specific foreign jurisdictions, to include Convention countries and countries whose adoption laws have been established by the Board to be compatible with Irish law; and

3. post-adoption services, as recommended in the Report, be extended to support the adoptive parents of children adopted abroad and be funded by the State.

9–146 All international studies agree that unregulated intercountry adoption can lead to abuses. The effective control of foreign adoption is therefore essential as long as the demand for adoptable children increases and the supply decreases. Legitimate intercountry adoption, based on the best interests of the child, is beneficial to both the child and the adoptive parents. Finally, it must be reiterated that although intercountry adoption may offer a permanent home to a large number of children who are clearly in need of one, it is essential that the process is, and is seen to be, a "child-centred" one which meets the needs of the individual child being adopted.

The Adoption (Hague Convention) Bill

9–147 The 1993 Hague Convention will be incorporated into Irish law when the foregoing Bill is enacted. This widely-ratified international instrument will then have the force of law in Ireland.

At the time of writing, the Bill was still in its infancy. It is therefore likely that some of the provisions will be altered before it is enacted.

Any ambiguity in so far as the 1993 Convention is concerned will be clarified by reference to the Parra-Aranguren report (this is the explanatory report prepared by G. Parra-Aranguren in 1993 on behalf of the Permanent Bureau of the Hague Conference. This report provides a comprehensive account of the thinking and negotiation involved in producing the final text of the 1993 Convention as adopted during the 17th Session of the Hague Conference on Private International Law). The Adoption Authority, to be established under the Bill, will carry out the key functions and will replace the Adoption Board, which will be dissolved.

Applications to the Adoption Authority are to be preceded by an assessment of eligibility and suitability. This assessment will be prepared either by the health board or by a body accredited by the Adoption Authority. The period of a declaration of eligibility and suitability is to be extended from 12 months under the Adoption Act 1991 to 18 months.

In summary, adoption orders made under the 1993 Hague Convention in countries other than Ireland will be recognised in Ireland. The Adoption Authority will also have the power to establish working arrangements or bilateral agreements with Contracting States (Ireland has bilateral agreements with China, Vietnam, Belarus, Romania and Thailand). This provision offers enormous potential and mirrors Art.39 of the 1993 Hague Convention which provides for the conclusion of bilateral agreements between Contracting States regarding the implementation of the Convention. In addition, the Adoption Authority will be able to enter into agreements with non-Contracting States, though these agreements will have to be in line with the principles underpinning the 1993 Hague Convention. It should be noted that adoptions from such States can only take place where an agreement has been effected.

Each placement will have to be approved by the Adoption Authority. An upper age limit of 50 years is to apply to anyone applying for a declaration of eligibility, though this condition is subject to some limited exceptions. The age limit will not, for example, apply where the application is one concerning a child with whom there is a strong familial link; or where the applicants already have children, or have personal experience or professional expertise in caring for a child with special needs and are applying to adopt a particular child who is aged three or more or who has special needs. There is a requirement in all cases that the Adoption Authority must be satisfied that the adoption is in the best interests of the child. The original Bill provided for a maximum age gap between that of the child and the applicant (or in the case of couples, the older applicant) of 42 years, with limited exceptions. Considerable debate has revolved around the upper-age-limit provision, and whatever age limit is finally adopted must be consistent with the best interests of the child.

The criteria for suitability will reflect the capacities which form the basis for the standarised framework of assessment for adoption:

(a) good moral character;

(b) a reasonable expectation of continuing to enjoy good health and have the capacity to fulfil parental duties while the child is growing up;

(c) the capacity to promote the child's development and health;

(d) the capacity to safeguard, actively support and arrange for the necessary health, social, educational or other interventions throughout the child's life;

(e) adequate financial means to support the child;

(f) the capacity to value and support the child's need in relation to identity; and

(g) no convictions for a sexual offence.

In the case of intercountry adoptions, applicants will be required to have attended an approved course of education regarding intercountry adoption, and to demonstrate the capacity to value and support the child's needs in relation to original nationality, culture, race, language and religion.

The Adoption Authority will be able to accredit bodies to carry out assessments, mediate intercountry adoptions and provide post-placement services. An accredited body will not be able to both carry out assessments and mediate adoptions.

There will be a right of appeal on a point of law from the Adoption Authority to the Circuit Court.

Currently, adoption is possible only where the person to be adopted is under the age of 18 years. Adoption of persons aged 18 or over is thus not possible. In appropriate cases, the Adoption (Hague Convention) Bill will make it possible to adopt a child who has already reached the age of 18.

The Adoption (Hague Convention) Bill, when passed, will ensure intercountry adoption takes place in the interests of the child and with respect for his or her fundamental rights as recognised under international law.

ANONYMITY AND PRIVACY

9–148 The Adoption Act 1952 was drawn up at a time when the stigma attached to extra-marital births led to many women concealing their pregnancy. The "closed" or "clean break" adoption was, in this respect, seen as a perfect avenue of escape from the dilemma in which these women found themselves.

Secrecy is often regarded as an inevitable hallmark of "clean break" adoption. The complications that this causes, however, are manifold, especially for the adopted child wishing to learn more about his or her origins and meet his or her natural parents. The presence of such secrecy may, furthermore, serve simply to compound the stigma once thought to attach to non-marital birth. Society's silence regarding an issue can, after all, so often imply social disapproval. Many natural parents, of course, may remain anxious not to have their past experiences brought to light, especially where they now have partners and families of their own. Small wonder then that adoption professionals regard the issue of privacy and confidentiality of records to be of vital importance. The prevalent policy is, as previously stated, best described as a "clean break policy".[241] Thus, the various adoption societies remain, by-and-large, reluctant to release details of natural parentage without the consent of the birth parents involved.

The statutory position

9–149 Currently, there is no established legal right allowing access to birth records. Indeed, s.22(5) of the Adoption Act 1952 generally precludes the public inspection of the adoption index. No information therefrom may be given to any person without the consent of the Adoption Board. Section 8 of the Adoption Act 1976 similarly precludes any court from ordering the release

---

[241] See Darling, "The Changing Face of Adoption" [1999] 4 I.J.F.L. 2 at 4.

of such information, unless it is satisfied that such access is "in the best interests of the child" in question.[242]

9–150 In *C.R. v An Bord Uchtála*, the High Court held that where an adopted person seeks information under s.22(5) of the 1952 Act, the Adoption Board cannot adopt a blanket policy of refusal and must enquire as to the individual merits of each application.[243] In summary, the Adoption Board was required to inform itself of the individual circumstances of the case, which required it to consider the release of all information and not merely non-identifying information. Morris J. provided the following guidance:

> "[I]t is necessary to screen any applicant and indeed the parent he is attempting to trace and the correct manner in which this is to be performed is by passing the matter to the Adoption Society for them to process.[244] ... Having considered this advice and all other relevant matters, the decision to furnish or withhold the information must be that of the Board".[245]

The Adoption Board, in attempting to comply with this case, generally seeks a report from the adoption agency involved in the initial placement prior to deciding whether or not it is appropriate to make an order under s.22(5) of the 1952 Act. The case of *D.C. v D.M.* would appear to recommend the prevention of the disclosure or inspection of documents, save where "it is in the best interests of any child concerned to do so".[246] A similar approach was adopted by Costello J. in *P.B. v A.L.*, where disclosure was held to be "in the best interests" of the child concerned.[247]

The constitutional position

9–151 The child, according to the Supreme Court, enjoys an unenumerated constitutional right to be told the identity of his or her natural mother. This right, however, is not absolute, and must be balanced against the natural mother's right to privacy and anonymity. The parameters of this conflict were examined by the Supreme Court in the joined cases of *I.O'T. v B. and the Rotunda Girls' Aid Society* and *M.H. v Rev. G.D. and the Rotunda Girls' Aid Society*.[248] These cases involved proceedings seeking declaratory relief relating to the natural parentage of two children informally adopted. Both plaintiffs claimed that they had a constitutional right to access information relating to the circumstances of their respective births. The defendant Adoption Society contested this, claiming, presumably in the interests of the natural parents, that the records in question were confidential. While these cases concerned

[242] See *P.C. v An Bord Uchtála*, unreported, High Court, McWilliam J., April, 1980.
[243] [1994] 1 I.L.R.M. 217.
[244] At p.221.
[245] At p.222.
[246] [1999] 2 I.R. 150.
[247] [1996] 1 I.L.R.M. 154.
[248] [1998] 2 I.R. 321.

informal adoption, the Supreme Court made a num'
adoption. Keane C.J., as he then was, in considerin

> "I find it difficult to imagine an aspect of hu.
> more clearly into the constitutional areas of privac,
> of the natural mothers in the present case."[249]

Barron J. held that secrecy "has always been a paramount con.
adoption law" and while "the public attitude to absolute secrecy .
weakened there [does] not appear to have been any cases where communit.
has taken place against the wishes of the mother."[250]

The Court agreed that the right to know the identity of one's natural mother is a constitutional right guaranteed by Art.40.3. of the Constitution.[251] While this right is restricted by the Adoption Acts, such restriction may be valid, having regard to the need for the State to respect and vindicate the sometimes conflicting rights of the natural mother, being the right to privacy and confidentiality in respect of the adoption.

The task of balancing these rights falls to the Courts, who in doing so must seek to "harmonise such rights, having regard to the provisions of the Constitution, and in the event of failure to so harmonise, to determine which right is the superior, having regard to all the circumstances of the case".[252] Neither set of rights was, it said, absolute. The question of whether the veil of anonymity was to be lifted, then, was ultimately one for the Circuit Court that had stated the case for the Supreme Court's opinion. In making its decision, the Supreme Court pointed to certain criteria of which the lower court should take account:

(a) the circumstances surrounding the natural mother's loss of custody of the child;

(b) the current status and circumstances of the natural mother and the potential effect upon her of disclosure of her identity;

(c) the natural mother's own wishes and attitude regarding the disclosure, and the reasons behind these wishes and the aforementioned attitude;

(d) the current age of the natural mother and child respectively;

(e) the attitude of the child, including the reasons why he or she wishes to seek disclosure of his or her natural mother's identity;

(f) the present circumstances of the child; and

(g) the opinion of the adoptive parents or other interested persons.[253]

9–152 Given the weight of the argument attributed to privacy in *I.O'T. v B.*

---

[249] At p.373.
[250] At pp.380–381.
[251] Though, see the dissenting judgment of Keane J., as he then was.
[252] *ibid. per* Hamilton C.J. at 52.
[253] Judgment of Hamilton C.J., *ibid.* at 50.

ving person informally adopted), it is likely that even greater importance
.d be accorded to privacy in legal adoption where the link between the
.ural mother and adopted child are legally severed. In considering the right
a child formally adopted, the Supreme Court in *I.O'T. v B.* held that no
.amilial relationship can survive between a legally adopted person and his or
her natural mother:

> "[I]ts exercise is restricted in the case of children who have been lawfully
> adopted in accordance with the provisions of the Adoption Act 1952 as
> the effect of an adoption order is that all parental rights and duties of the
> natural parents are ended, while the child becomes a member of the family
> of the adoptive parents as if he or she had been their natural child."[254]

9–153 Significantly, in *Northern Area Health Board v An Bord Uchtála*,
McGuinness J. appeared to support the increasing trend towards openness in
adoption practice.[255] The learned judge stated as follows:

> "Adoption practice in general has become more open in recent years.
> The old insistence on secrecy and a complete exclusion of the natural
> mother has virtually gone and it is not uncommon for adopted children
> to continue to meet their birth parents from time to time."[256]

The European Convention on Human Rights Act 2003

9–154 The European Convention on Human Rights Act 2003, which became
part of Irish law on December 31, 2003, and which is discussed in detail in
Chapter 12, requires the decision of the European Court of Human Rights
(ECt.HR) to be taken into account by the Irish courts.

9–155 In *Gaskin v UK*,[257] the ECt.HR held that denying the applicant (who
had spent the majority of his life in care) access to his file was a breach of
Art.8 of the European Convention on Human Rights (ECHR)[258] in the absence
of an independent and impartial authority to determine the merits of the
applicant's claims.

In *Mikulic v Croatia*,[259] the ECt.HR again recognised the importance to a
child of information about his or her identity.

In *Odièvre v France*,[260] a recent decision of the ECt.HR, the applicant was
an adopted person seeking the release of information identifying her natural

---

[254] At p.348.
[255] [2002] 4 I.R. 252; [2003] 1 I.L.R.M. 481.
[256] See also the judgment in *J.B. and D.B. v An Bord Uchtála*, unreported, High Court,
1998, where McGuinness J. stated that a meeting between the natural mother and the
prospective adopters is in accordance with present-day adoption practice, where it is in
the best interests of the child who has been placed with the prospective adopters.
[257] Judgment of July 7, 1989.
[258] Art.8 of the ECHR provides for respect of one's private and family life.
[259] Judgment of February 7, 2002.
[260] Judgment of February 13, 2003.

mother. As the natural mother had expressly reserved her right to confidentiality, the ECt.HR held, by a majority of 10 votes to seven, that the Parisian Child Welfare Authority's refusal to release this information was not contrary to the ECHR, on the grounds that France had a pressing reason to respect the privacy of the natural mother. This judgment has been subject to some criticism and sits uneasily with the importance attached to the right of a child to information regarding the identity of his or her parents in both the UN Convention on the Rights of the Child 1989 and the 1993 Hague Convention on Intercountry Adoption. It addressed the French law on anonymous births which allows women to give birth anonymously[261] and is the only decision of the ECt.HR on the discrete issue of access to birth information following adoption.

9–156 In order to comply with ECHR best practice, it is necessary to balance in a proportionate manner the rights of all the parties implicated in adoption information matters—the child, its natural parents and the adoptive parents.

Assisted human reproduction (AHR) and identity

9–157 Assisted human reproduction (AHR) has not yet been the subject of legislation in Ireland. The Commission on Assisted Human Reproduction is currently examining a legislative framework and is likely to publish its report by the end of 2004.

The judgments in *Gaskin* and *Mikulic*, cited above, are instructive in considering the protection of the anonymity of the donor in AHR. Legislation in the neighbouring jurisdiction, the Human Fertilisation and Embryology Act 1990, currently requires the social parents rather than the genetic parents to be named on the child's birth certificate as the child's parents. This legislation will be amended from 2005 to allow the donor child to access information concerning his or her origins.

The ECt.HR in *X, Y and Z v UK* stated that there was considerable uncertainty as to whether the interests of a child conceived by assisted reproduction using donor gametes was best served by maintaining the anonymity of the donor, which uncertainty afforded the United Kingdom a wide margin of appreciation in *X, Y and Z*.[262]

European Convention on the Adoption of Children

9–158 Ireland ratified the European Convention on the Adoption of Children in 1968, thereby making the provisions of this international instrument binding on the State. It is currently under review, with a proposal on access to adoption records forming part of that review. Significantly, most of the countries who participated in the review of this instrument accept the principle that adopted people should have access to information held by competent authorities

---

[261] The possibility to give birth anonymously has existed in France since 1941. Germany is currently considering a legislative proposal that will allow women to give birth anonymously in German public hospitals.

[262] (1997) 2 F.L.R. 892.

concerning the identity of their parents. Accordingly, it is proposed that Art.20, paragraphs 3 and 4,[263] which currently appear in Pt III of the European Convention, should appear in Pt II. Whether the provisions are incorporated in Pt II or III of the Convention is significant, because under Art.1 of this European Convention:

"Each contracting party undertakes to ensure conformity of its law with the provisions of Part II of this Convention ...".

Article 2 of the same Convention states:

"Each Contracting Party undertakes to give consideration to the provisions set out in Part III of this Convention ...".

In effect, the provisions of Pt II are binding on States which have ratified the Convention, while the provisions of Pt III are optional.

United Nations Convention on the Rights of the Child 1989

9–159 Article 7 of the United Nations Convention on the Rights of the Child 1989 (CRC), which was ratified by Ireland on December 21, 1992, without reservation, requires the State to "respect the right of the child to preserve his or her identity (including nationality, name and family relations as recognised by law), without unlawful interference", while Art.8 recognises the right of every child to know and be cared for by his or her parents. Both provisions, when read together, have been held to require Member States to provide adopted children with information on their birth.[264] While the CRC is binding on the Member State, it is not binding on the Irish courts.

9–160 There are current proposals to amend the law in this area as part of a Bill on adoption information, post-adoption contract and associated issues. Pending the enactment of this Bill, it is recommended that information and tracing enquiries received by the Adoption Board be processed, having regard to international best practice in this area.

National contact register

9–161 It is currently possible for persons who wish to do so, to volunteer their willingness to learn of the identity of, or make contact with, their natural

---

[263] Art.20:
   3. The adopter and the adopted person shall be able to obtain a document which contains extracts from the public records attesting the fact, date and place of birth of the adopted person, but not expressly revealing the fact of adoption or the identity of his or her former parents.
   4. Public records shall be kept and, in any event, their comments reproduced in such a way as to prevent persons who do not have a legitimate interest from learning the fact that a person has been adopted or, if that is disclosed, the identity of his or her former parents.

[264] See the comments of the Committee on the Rights of the Child, the body which monitors the implementation of the CRC.

parents. A group of adopted persons themselves established in 1994 a voluntary National Contact Register,[265] facilitating such contact between adopted persons and their natural parents. Natural parents wishing, or willing, to make contact with their children may consult the register with a view to tracing their children, and *vice versa*. The Law Society of Ireland's Law Reform Committee has recommended the introduction of a similar voluntary contact register to be established and administered by the Adoption Board.[266] It suggests, however, that an Information Veto Register should also be introduced, allowing adult adopted persons and/or their natural parents, if they so wish, to prevent the disclosure of contact information.[267]

Open adoptions

9–162 When the present adoption regime was first introduced in Ireland in 1952, the stigma surrounding extra-marital births was a pervading feature of Irish society. Many women, fearing the negative social reaction of their communities and families, strongly felt the need to conceal the fact of their pregnancy. The "closed" adoption was, as previously stated, a perfect avenue of escape from the dilemma in which these women found themselves.

9–163 Over 50 years on, an increasingly popular alternative to the closed model is a type of adoption variously known as the "open" or "semi-open" adoption or "adoption with contact". Open adoption allows the natural mother, and other family members, to choose from a pool of prospective adopters. In some cases the natural mother may, in fact, meet the would-be adopters prior to the adoption order being made. In a semi-open adoption, by contrast, such access will be indirect only, the birth mother being supplied with information that does not identify the prospective adopters, and hence does not compromise the anonymity of all involved.

9–164 Many models of open adoption[268] allow the maintenance of an agreed level of contact between the child and his or her natural parents, without compromising on the fundamental legal effects of the adoption vesting full parental rights in the adoptive parents. This model presupposes the inception of an ongoing relationship between all parties concerned. The level of contact will differ, depending on the wishes and priorities of the various parties, but may include periodic visits, receipt of photographs of the child, phone calls and emails. Provision may also be made for grandparental visitation and contact, again on an agreed basis. The key advantage is that the adopted child, so often left with a profound yearning to know of his or her origins, can have pre-planned and controlled access to, and know of his or her natural parents, without comprising the legal integrity of the adoption process.

---

[265] The "Marfan" Contact Register.
[266] Law Society, *Adoption Law: The Case for Reform* (Law Society, Dublin, April 2000) at 28.
[267] *ibid.* at 25.
[268] For example, that operated in Oregon.

9–165   Several jurisdictions in the United States[269] now allow a form of open adoption that permits a degree of contact between the child and his or her natural family. Australia, New Zealand and some Canadian provinces have also long operated such schemes, with encouraging results.[270] The Law Society of Ireland's Law Reform Committee notes another advantage, being that the "use of open systems of adoption would encourage more birth parents to place a child for adoption where this would be in the best interests of the child".[271] The Committee suggests that this might result in an increase in the pool of children available for adoption, thus extending to an increased number of children "the benefits of a secure upbringing within a stable family environment".[272] Open adoption, the Committee suggests, avoids the "all-or-nothing" nature of the closed adoption. The pain of permanent separation of mother and child can be tempered, so long as there remains an agreed link between the two. It seems that at least one Irish adoption society has made use of the open adoption model, allowing pre-placement meetings between the natural mother and the adoptive parents, and encouraging the continuance of contact after placement.[273]

9–166   The key drawback of open adoption relates to the legal effects of the standard form of adoption. In Ireland, the effect of adoption is to extinguish absolutely the parental rights of the birth parents, whereas the success of an open adoption scheme depends largely on the goodwill of the adoptive parents (who, in many cases, may be anxious to foreclose the prospect of being perceived as something other than the child's primary care-takers). Where an open adoption is favoured, all parties involved should be careful to discuss thoroughly the appropriate boundaries for access arrangements prior to the adoption order being made. These agreed boundaries should then form the substance of a legally binding contract, which, subject to renegotiation and possible variation in the courts, could form the very core of an agreed parenting strategy. This way the child can have the best of both worlds. Adoption, in other words, need no longer require the permanent and absolute sundering of the precious bond between natural parent and child.

---

[269] For example Minnesota, New Mexico, Oregon and Washington State.

[270] See Mullender (ed.), *Open Adoption* (BAAF, 1991). See also Berry, "The effects of open adoption on biological and adoptive parents and the children: The arguments and the evidence" (1991) LXX *Child Welfare*, 637–651, and Berry, Cavazos Dylla, Barth and Needell, "The role of open adoption in the adjustment of adopted children and their families" (1998) 20 *Children and Youth Services* 151–171. All the latter mentioned studies report the widespread success of, and satisfaction with, models of open adoption.

[271] Law Society, *Adoption Law: The Case for Reform* (Law Society, Dublin, April 2000) at 68.

[272] *ibid.*

[273] See Darling, "The Changing Face of Adoption" [1999] 4 I.J.F.L. 2 at 3–4.

CHAPTER 10

CHILD ABDUCTION

CHILD ABDUCTION—AN INTERNATIONAL PHENOMENON

10–01 The phrase "child abduction" is often used to describe the unilateral actions of parents, guardians or close family members of a child involving the removal or retention of the child or children in contravention of the rights of parents, guardians or other persons or bodies with legal responsibilities and rights in respect of a child, such as local authorities or health boards. From time to time, high-profile cases make media headlines and focus public attention on what is a relatively common occurrence. The available statistics do not provide a complete picture or profile of the phenomenon. Information received by the Permanent Bureau of the Hague Conference in 1997 suggests that, in 1996, the total number of reported Hague Convention cases alone was approximately 1,250.[1] In the last 10 years, Ireland has been at the centre of over 1,400 child abduction cases. The Department of Justice's Central Authority dealt with 72 incidents in 2002.

10–02 Decisions regarding the care and control of a child or children following the breakdown of a marriage are often very contentious and, in many cases, the situation is aggravated by a rise in the emotional temperature of one or both of the parents. There are probably as many reasons motivating a parent to abduct or retain a child as there are different reasons for the breakdown. It is not unusual to find that the abducting parent will believe that he or she is acting in the best interests of the child, whereas the deprived parent will often interpret the actions of the other as an exercise in revenge or denial.[2] Either way, the assessment of Greif and Hegar is apposite: "Abductions occur for a variety of reasons from the narcissistic to the heroic."[3]

10–03 Whatever the motivation, the abduction of a child invariably causes distress and a certain element of psychological harm to the child. Beaumont and McEleavy state that:

> "the ability of a child to survive these events will depend on several factors: age, his or her pre-existing relationship with the abductor and the left behind parent, the manner in which the removal or retention was

---

[1] *Hague Convention Review Special Commission*, 1997.
[2] G.L. Greif and R.L. Hegar, "International Parental Abduction and its Implication for Social Work Practice: Great Britain to the U.S." 7 *Children and Society* 269 (1993). See also Greif and Hegar, *When Parents Kidnap – The Families Behind the Headlines* (Free Press, New York, 1993).
[3] *ibid.* at 270.

effected, its length, the environment in which the child was forced to live, and the support available upon recovery. Even under the most favourable circumstances, a child is likely to suffer some sense of loss at being uprooted from his or her home environment and not having contacted the left behind parent, relatives, friends and familiar places. There is equally the effect that an abduction will have on a child's education."[4]

Before the Hague and Luxembourg Conventions came into force (see para.10–09), the avenues open to a deprived parent were limited, arduous and costly. Obviously, the deprived parent faced the initial problem of ascertaining the child's whereabouts. Once the child was located, the deprived parent was then faced with the ordeal of instituting a "kidnapping case" against the abducting parent or person and, in general, the courts of the jurisdiction to which the child had been abducted were not readily disposed to ordering the return of the child without first making enquiries as to his or her welfare and best interests.[5]

Legal responses to the problem

Definitions—When does child abduction occur?

10–04   Child abduction, in simple terms, occurs when a child is removed from a person who has the legal right to custody of the child (referred to as "the custodial parent") without that person's authority or consent. The use of the term "custodial parent" should not obscure the fact that a non-parent may also be awarded custody of a child in certain circumstances and a child may be wrongfully abducted from that person's or body's care and custody also. Such a situation of wrongful removal constitutes abduction within the meaning of the relevant international Conventions and in Irish law. Both international and domestic law have dedicated provisions aimed at securing the return of the child to the jurisdiction of his or her habitual residence, and vindicating the custodial parent's rights.

10–05   An act of wrongful retention, where a child is lawfully removed from the jurisdiction of his or her habitual residence to another jurisdiction (*e.g.* for a holiday or access visit with the consent of the custodial parent) but is unlawfully retained in that jurisdiction, will also attract sanction under the relevant Conventions and in domestic law. Similarly, where a child is taken out of the jurisdiction of his or her habitual residence without the authority or consent of a person who has non-custodial rights in respect of the child (*e.g.* a legal guardian or a person who has a right of access to the child), steps may also be taken to vindicate such rights under international and domestic law.

---

[4]   Beaumont & McEleavy, *The Hague Convention on International Child Abduction* (Oxford University Press, 1999), p.12.
[5]   See, for example, *Northampton County Council v A.B.F. & M.B.F.* [1982] I.L.R.M. 164 and *Saunders v Mid-Western Health Board* [1989] I.L.R.M. 229.

10–06 As with other crisis situations involving children, the wrongful removal or wrongful retention of children causes great emotional distress to all parties involved and requires swift responses on the part of the person (or body) whose rights have been denied and their legal advisors. The object of the applicable international and domestic legal regimes is the speedy restoration of the *status quo ante*. The guiding principle is that the courts of the jurisdiction in which the child is habitually resident is the proper forum (often referred to as the *forum conveniens*) for the vindication of the rights of the child and for the determination of the best interests of the child. Accordingly, the central aim of the international and domestic legislative framework is to ensure the return of the child to the jurisdiction of his or her habitual residence as quickly as possible and, if there are any disputes, for example, regarding custody of or access to the child, these should be litigated before, and determined by the courts of the jurisdiction of the child's habitual residence and not by the courts of the jurisdiction into which a child has been abducted.

10–07 The Irish Supreme Court has indicated on a number of occasions, and most recently in the case of *M.(E.) ex parte v M.(J.)*,[6] that proceedings instituted under the Hague Convention on the Civil Aspects of International Child Abduction "are intended to be summary and completed in a speedy fashion. This is the type of case which should be on a fast-track management process."[7]

10–08 Beaumont and McEleavy suggest that "[i]n addition to the primary objective identified in Article 1 and the preamble to the [Hague] Convention, there are other issues which, while not given significant consideration by the drafters, might today be considered as subsidiary aims of the Convention. Two of these, a child's right to a have a meaningful relationship with both parents and a child's right to be heard, have evolved separately from the Child Abduction Convention. These are outlined in the United Nations Convention on the Rights of the Child and are in whole or in part furthered by the Hague Convention."[8]

International legislative responses

10–09 The rise in the number of abductions of children across international frontiers prompted the adoption of Art.11 of the United Nations Convention on the Rights of Child, which required Member States to take measures to combat child abduction. Arising from this commitment, two further Conventions were drafted to address the issue, the Hague Convention on the Civil Aspects of International Child Abduction ("the Hague Convention") and the European Convention on Recognition and Enforcement of Decisions

[6] unreported, Supreme Court, Denham J., July 9, 2003.
[7] *T.M.M. v M.D.* unreported, Supreme Court, Denham J., December 8, 1999 at pp.16–17.
[8] *op. cit.* at p.33. Note also the Recommendations of the Constitutional Review Group in respect of the revision of Art.41 of the Constitution of Ireland 1937, pp.336–337 of the Report of the Group (May 1996), and in particular Recommendation 4(vi).

Concerning Custody of Children and on Restoration of Custody of Children ("the Luxembourg Convention"), both of which were signed by the original Contracting States in 1980. Although the Irish Law Reform Commission had recommended in 1985 that Ireland should ratify and implement the Hague Convention, and should consider ratifying the Luxembourg Convention,[9] the Conventions were not brought into force in Ireland until October 1, 1991, with the enactment of the Child Abduction and Enforcement of Court Orders Act 1991. By this time both Conventions had been operating for almost 11 years.[10]

10–10 Prior to the incorporation of the principles of the Conventions into Irish law in 1991, abduction, wrongful removal and wrongful retention disputes which came before the Irish courts were dealt with in accordance with the well-established principle of comity of courts, *i.e.* the Irish courts recognised and enforced decisions and orders made by the courts in jurisdictions with comparable legal systems. While, in general, the principle of comity resulted in the Irish courts recognising the validity of a foreign order, the courts also undertook an examination of the case in the context of the statutory duty imposed by s.3 of the Guardianship of Infants Act 1964, *i.e.* the issue of the child's welfare and best interests was assessed, and there have been situations in which the Irish courts have refused to return children to the jurisdiction of their habitual residence, where to have done so would have resulted in a breach of rights guaranteed under the Irish Constitution.[11] However, the introduction of the principles of the aforesaid Conventions into Irish law in 1991 resulted in a streamlined approach to all cases of abduction, wrongful removal and wrongful retention involving children who had been habitually resident, or retained in, or removed to, the territory of Contracting States.

10–11 With regard to abduction of children, or wrongful removal from, or wrongful retention in a non-Contracting State, the pre-existing comity principles apply. With regard to children brought to or retained in this jurisdiction, it is to be anticipated that, although not bound thereby in such circumstances, the courts will be mindful of the Convention principles in determining such cases,[12] while the welfare of the child must be regarded as the first and paramount consideration.[13]

---

[9] Law Reform Commission Report on The Hague Convention on the Civil Aspects of International Child Abduction and Some Related Matters (LRC 12–1985).

[10] The Hague Convention had been signed by the original Contracting Party States on October 25, 1980, under the auspices of the Hague Conference on Private International Law. The Luxembourg Convention was initially signed on May 20, 1980, under the auspices of the Council of Europe.

[11] See *Northampton County Council v A.B.F. & M.B.F.* and *Saunders v Mid-Western Health Board*, previously discussed.

[12] *A.S. v E.H. and R.M.H.* unreported, High Court, Budd J., May 1996.

[13] Guardianship of Infants Act 1964, s.3.

The Hague and Luxembourg Conventions—general

10–12   As set out above, both Conventions are concerned with securing the expeditious return of abducted children, or children who have been wrongfully retained in, or improperly removed to, a jurisdiction to the country in which they are (or had been prior to the wrongful removal or retention) habitually resident. This general policy of return is based on the assumption that the courts of the Contracting States are all equally capable of fairly determining the issues between the parties and of protecting the welfare of children:

> "The whole jurisdiction under the Convention is, by its nature and purpose, peremptory. Its underlying assumption is that the courts of all its signatory countries are equally capable of ensuring a fair hearing to the parties and a skilled and humane evaluation of the issues of child welfare involved. Its underlying purpose is to ensure stability for children, by putting a brisk end to the efforts of parents to have their children's future where they want and when they want, by removing them from their country of residence to another jurisdiction chosen arbitrarily by the absconding parent."[14]

The Hague Convention has a greater geographical application than the Luxembourg Convention and, at present, the Hague Convention covers 74 countries worldwide.[15] The Luxembourg Convention applies to fewer countries.[16]

10–13   The two Conventions share many common features. For example, under both regimes, the welfare of the child (in each case defined as a person under the age of 16 years) is of paramount importance, and it is envisaged that the views of the child should be considered where appropriate. The expeditious processing of applications for the return of children is a common goal. Under each regime, it is envisaged that, in determining whether the child should be returned, the judicial or administrative authority in the State to which the child has been abducted, or in which the child has been retained, should not adjudicate

---

[14] *P. v P. (Minors)(Child Abduction)* [1992] 1 F.L.R. 155, cited with approval by Keane J. in *Wadda v Ireland* [1994] I.L.R.M. 126.

[15] Argentina, Australia, Austria, Bahamas, Belgium, Belize, Republic of Bosnia and Herzegovina, Brazil, Bukina-Faso, Canada, Chile, China, Colombia, Republic of Croatia, Czech Republic, Republic of Cyprus, Denmark, Ecuador, Finland, France, Federal Republic of Germany, Greece, Honduras, Republic of Hungary, Republic of Ireland, Iceland, Israel, Italy, Grand Duchy of Luxembourg, Former Yugoslav Republic of Macedonia, Malta, Republic of Mauritius, Mexico, Principality of Monaco, Netherlands, New Zealand, Norway, Panama, Poland, Portugal, Romania, Republic of Slovenia, South Africa, Spain, St. Kitts & Nevis, Sweden, Switzerland, Turkey, United Kingdom, United States of America, Uruguay, Republic of Venezuela, Federal Republic of Yugoslavia and Republic of Zimbabwe.

[16] Austria, Belgium, Republic of Cyprus, Denmark, Finland, France, Federal Republic of Germany, Greece, Republic of Ireland, Iceland, Italy, Liechtenstein, Grand Duchy of Luxembourg, Netherlands, Norway, Republic of Poland, Portugal, Spain, Sweden, Switzerland, United Kingdom of Great Britain and Northern Ireland.

on the merits of the custody or access issue. Under each system it is emphasised that a decision under the Conventions is not to be taken as a determination on the merits of the custody or access issue. Under either Convention, a person accused of abduction or retention of a child can seek to rely on a number of defined "defences". On an administrative level, each Convention proposes the establishment of Central Authorities in Contracting States to facilitate the implementation of the Conventions.

10–14 The most significant substantive difference between the two Conventions is that, in order to activate the Luxembourg Convention, an applicant must be in a position to demonstrate that he or she has a court order (a *decision* relating to custody), whereas under the Hague Convention, the focus is on a breach of *rights* of custody and it is not necessary to have a formal court order "confirming" the rights.

The Hague Convention

10–15 The Hague Convention was signed by the original Contracting Party States on October 25, 1980, and has now been ratified by 46 countries worldwide. The central principle of the Convention is that, in cases of wrongful removal or wrongful retention of children in breach of rights of custody, Contracting States are required, in almost every case, to return a child to the jurisdiction of the child's habitual residence.

Principal features of the Hague Convention

10–16 Article 1 of the Convention provides that the objectives of the Convention are "to secure the prompt return of children wrongfully removed to or retained in" a Contracting State and "to ensure that rights of custody and of access under the law of one Contracting State are effectively respected in the other Contracting States." Article 2 commits the Contracting States to taking "all appropriate measures to secure within their territories" the implementation of the said objectives of the Convention and, to this end, they "shall use the most expeditious procedures available".

10–17 The removal or retention of a child is stated to be wrongful for the purposes of the Convention where "it is in breach of rights of custody attributed to a person, an institution or any other body, either jointly or alone, under the law of the State in which the child was habitually resident immediately before the removal or retention" and "at the time of the removal or retention those rights were actually exercised, either jointly or alone, or would have been so exercised but for the removal or retention".[17] In the first instance, therefore, a person seeking the return of a child must establish that he or she enjoyed and actually exercised "rights of custody" under the law of the State in which the child was habitually resident immediately prior to the removal or retention.

---

[17] Hague Convention, Art.3.

Procedure and jurisdiction

10–18 Applications in respect of the Hague Convention may be made pursuant to Part III of the Child Abduction and Enforcement of Custody Orders Act 1991. Section 6 of the 1991 Act provides that the Hague Convention "shall have the force of law in the State and judicial notice shall be taken of it." Section 7 of the Act provides that, for the purposes of Part II of the Act, the High Court "shall have jurisdiction to hear and determine applications under ... [the Hague] Convention." Section 8 provides for the establishment of an Irish Central Authority by the Minister for Justice, Equality and Law Reform. Section 9 of the Act provides that applications pursuant to the Hague Convention for the return of a child removed to the State may be addressed to the Irish Central Authority. Where the Central Authority is satisfied that the application is one to which the Hague Convention applies, s.9(2) provides that "it shall take action or cause action to be taken under that Convention to secure the return of the child." Similarly, s.10 provides that, in respect of a child removed from the State to another Contracting State, any application may be addressed to the Irish Central Authority and, where satisfied that it is an application to which the Hague Convention applies, the Authority "shall, on behalf of the applicant, take any action required to be taken. ..."

10–19 Section 11 of the 1991 Act provides that nothing in Pt II of the Act "shall prevent a person from applying in the first instance to the [High] Court under the Hague Convention in respect of the breach of rights of custody of, or breach of rights of access to, a child removed to the State." Section 12 of the Act provides that where an application has been made or is about to be made to the Court under the Hague Convention, the High Court may give such interim directions for the purpose of securing the welfare of the child or preventing prejudice to interested persons or changes in the circumstances relevant to the determination of the application.[18] An application for such interim directions may be made *ex parte* in cases of urgency.[19]

10–20 The Central Authority is empowered by s.14 of the Act to request a probation and welfare officer to prepare a written report on a child dealing "with ... any matter relating to the child which appears to it to be relevant".[20] It is also empowered to request a health board to arrange for a suitably qualified person to prepare a report[21] "where information relating to a child has been requested under Article 7(d) of the Convention by the Central Authority of another Contracting State".[22] Section 14 also empowers the Central Authority to "request any court to which a written report relating to the child has been made to send it a copy of the report".[23]

---

[18] Child Abduction and Enforcement of Custody Orders Act 1991, s.12(1).
[19] *ibid.*, s.12(2).
[20] *ibid.*, s.14(a).
[21] *ibid.*, s.14(b).
[22] *ibid.*, s.14.
[23] *ibid.*, s.14(c).

10–21   Where an application is made to the High Court pursuant to Pt II of the Act "for the purposes of Article 15 of the Hague Convention by any person appearing to the Court to have an interest in the matter,"[24] the Court "may ... make a declaration that the removal of any child from, or his retention outside, the State was wrongful within the meaning of Article 3 of that Convention".[25] Furthermore, in the making of such an application, any other Central Authority may make a request for assistance to the Irish Central Authority on behalf of the applicant and, in such circumstances, the Irish Central Authority "shall take action or cause action to be taken"[26] to assist the applicant.

Rights of custody

10–22   Article 3 of the Convention declares that rights of custody "may arise in particular by operation of law or by reason of a judicial or administrative decision, or by reason of an agreement having legal effect under the law of that State". Article 5 defines "rights of custody" as including rights relating to the care of the person of the child and, in particular, the right to determine the child's place of residence. The fact that the legal code in another jurisdiction may utilise a different description of the concepts of custody and access is not material. For example, the terms used in the United Kingdom to describe what, in Irish law, are defined as "custody" and "access" are "parental responsibility" and "contact" respectively. In the decision of *W. v W.*,[27] Lardner J. held that the right of parental responsibility (as defined in English law) includes within it the concept of custody.

10–23   The proper scope of the term "rights of custody" received considerable attention in the High Court decision in *H.I. v M.G.*,[28] and later in the Supreme Court on appeal. The case concerned a child born in New York to an Egyptian father, the plaintiff, and an Irish mother, the defendant. Although the parties went through an Islamic marriage ceremony, the marriage was not recognised by New York law.

As a non-marital father, the plaintiff did not enjoy any automatic rights of custody, although the child's mother never disputed the matter of paternity and he acted as *de facto* joint custodian of his son for five-and-a-half-years. Following the removal by the defendant of her son to this jurisdiction, the child's father instituted proceedings pursuant to the Hague Convention. It was agreed by both parties that the issue of the presence or absence of rights of custody on the part of the child's father must be resolved as a preliminary matter. It was argued on behalf of the plaintiff that, as he was entitled to apply to the New York Courts for rights to custody of, or access to, the child once the issue of paternity was formally confirmed, he had inchoate rights in respect of the child which had been breached by the defendant's action in removing the child to Ireland.

---

[24] *ibid.*, s.15(1).
[25] *ibid.*
[26] *ibid.*, s.15(2).
[27] unreported, High Court, Lardner J., February 19, 1996.
[28] [1999] 2 I.L.R.M. 22.

In the High Court, Laffoy J. noted that the term "rights of custody" must be construed in a manner which accords with the overall objective of the Convention; in other words to spare children already suffering the effects of the breakdown of their parents' relationship the further disruption suffered when they were taken arbitrarily from their settled environment. In her view, the term should, in most cases, be given the widest possible interpretation. In this instance, the defendant acknowledged that the plaintiff was the father of the child. Laffoy J. thus concluded that the inchoate rights of the plaintiff father to custody, which would almost certainly have crystallised into established rights in the event of the approval by a New York court of the mother's acknowledgement of custody, amounted to rights of custody within the meaning of Art.3 of the Convention.

The Supreme Court reversed the finding of the learned trial judge. Delivering judgment for the majority, Keane C.J. noted that the removal of a child in circumstances in which his or her dispossessed parent or other appropriate person or body, not yet having rights of custody, had instituted custody proceedings, is wrongful within the meaning of the Convention. Likewise, in the absence of such proceedings, a removal may nonetheless be wrongful as a violation of custodial rights attributed to a *court* which has made an order prohibiting the removal of a child without the consent of the dispossessed party, or without a further order of the court itself, since the court's right to determine the custody or to seek to prohibit the removal of the child necessarily involves a determination that, at least until the circumstances change, the child's residence should continue to be in the state in question.

The Supreme Court, however, rejected the assertion that the term "rights of custody" embraced "an undefined hinterland of inchoate rights of custody not attributed in any sense by the law of the requesting state to any party asserting them or to the court itself." On the facts at issue, there were no proceedings in being in New York regarding the plaintiff father's right of custody. Neither was there a New York court order prohibiting the defendant from removing the child to another jurisdiction without the consent of the plaintiff, or without further order of the court. The plaintiff did not, therefore, enjoy anything amounting to a right of custody as defined, and the Supreme Court ruled that he could not invoke the Hague Convention to secure the return of his child.[29]

In the course of his judgment, Keane J. (as he then was) referred to the decision of the English courts in *Re B. (A Minor)(Abduction)*,[30] and quoted the following passage from the judgment of Waite L.J., with which Staughton L.J. agreed :

> "There is no difficulty about giving a broad connotation to the word 'custody' ... The difficulty lies in fixing the limits of the concept of 'rights'. Is it to be confined to what lawyers would instantly recognise as established rights ... or is it capable of being applied in a Convention

---

[29] See also *S.(A.) v H.(E.) & H.(M.)*, unreported, High Court, Geoghegan J., December 10, 1997.

[30] [1994] 2 F.L.R. 249.

context to describe the inchoate rights of those who are carrying out duties and enjoying privileges of a custodial or parental character which, though not yet formally recognised or granted by law, a court would nevertheless be likely to uphold in the interests of a child concerned? The answer to that question must, in my judgment, depend upon the circumstances of each case. If, before the child's abduction, the aggrieved parent was exercising functions in the requesting state of a parental or custodial nature without the benefit of any court order or official custodial status, it must in every case be a question for the courts of the requested state to determine whether those functions fall to be regarded as 'rights of custody' within the terms of the Convention."[31]

10–24   In the case of *W.P.P. v S.R.W.*,[32] the defendant mother had been granted sole custody of the two children of her marriage by a Santa Barbara Court in December 1994 at the conclusion of uncontested proceedings to dissolve her marriage to the plaintiff. The Californian Court had also granted visitation rights to the plaintiff, together with an order requiring him to pay child support, and it was agreed between the parties that they would discuss any "out of State trips with the children". However, by November 1997, the arrears of child support due to the defendant amounted to $45,794.90. The defendant was in severe financial difficulty as a result and filed for bankruptcy in 1995. It was the defendant's evidence that she had informed the plaintiff on a number of occasions that, because of her financial difficulties, she thought that she would have no option but to return to Ireland. On September 5, 1999, two days after the plaintiff had seen the two children, the defendant left the United States for Ireland and had not returned. She had not notified the plaintiff of her intentions to travel out of the jurisdiction and only informed him of her arrival in Ireland by telephone after the event. The plaintiff instituted proceedings pursuant to the Hague Conventions seeking an order for the return of the minors to the jurisdiction of the Californian Court, arguing that their removal was "wrongful" within the meaning of Arts 3 and 12 of the Convention.

It was agreed that the defendant was entitled to legal and physical custody of the children. The plaintiff argued that, accordingly, she was entitled to determine where the children should reside and, therefore, her move to Ireland was not "wrongful" within the meaning of the Convention. The plaintiff argued that, although entitled to the physical custody of the children, by her actions the defendant had effectively frustrated him in the exercise of his visitation rights and, therefore, the removal of the children to Ireland by the defendant constituted a breach of a right of custody (vested in the plaintiff by the Californian Court) and was "wrongful".

Keane C.J., in delivering the judgment of the Court, ruled that, as the plaintiff had a right of access to the minors at the time of their removal, the question to be answered was "whether, under the law of California, the granting of a right of access, by implication, prohibited the removal of the child without

---

[31] At pp.33–35.
[32] unreported, Supreme Court, April 14, 2000, *nem diss.*

the consent of the plaintiff or a further order of the court".[33] Having considered the affidavits submitted by the parties, Keane C.J. was of the opinion that neither afforded the Court "any conclusive guidance" on the question.[34] Keane C.J. held that, on the basis of the affidavits filed, "the defendant, as the parent having custody, was entitled to determine the minors' place of residence".[35] The question remained as to whether the defendant could unilaterally exercise that right in circumstances where the Santa Barbara Court had already awarded access to the plaintiff. Keane C.J. referred to the Explanatory Report on the Convention prepared by Madame Perez Vera, and the decision of the Canadian Supreme Court in *Thompson v Thompson*,[36] which confirm that "the primary object of the Convention was the enforcement of custody rights. By contrast, the Convention left the enforcement of access rights to the administrative channels of Central Authorities ...".[37]

The Court considered the provisions of Art.21 of the Convention. Under the heading "Rights of Access", Art.21 provides that "[a]n application to make arrangements for organising or securing the effective exercise of rights of access may be presented to the central authorities of the contracting States in the same way as an application for the return of a child." The Central Authorities are bound by Art.21 to "promote the peaceful enjoyment of access rights and the fulfilment of any conditions to which the exercise of those rights may be subject" and "shall take steps to remove, as far as possible, all obstacles to the exercise of such rights". Further, they may "either directly or indirectly initiate or assist in the institution of proceedings with a view to organising or protecting these rights and securing respect for the conditions to which the exercise of these rights may be subject."

The Court held as follows:

> "The exercise of a child's right to determine his or her place of residence may, of course, be restricted by the order of the court awarding custody to one parent by prohibiting the removal of the child from the jurisdiction of the court without the further leave of the court or the consent of the other parent. In such a case ... the removal of the child, without such leave and without the consent of the other parent may constitute a breach of a right of custody vested in the court. In this case, however, we are concerned with an order which gave the plaintiff rights of access only. It is clear, in my view, that the appropriate machinery for enforcing such rights is Article 21 of the Convention. To order the return of children and their custodial parent to the jurisdiction in which they were formerly habitually resident merely so as to entitle the non-custodial parent to exercise his rights of access is not warranted by the terms of Convention."

It ruled that the removal of the minors "was not in breach of any rights of

---

[33] At p.12.
[34] At p.15.
[35] At p.19.
[36] (1994) 3 S.C.R. 551.
[37] At p.17.

custody attributed to either the defendant or the Californian court"[38] and, accordingly, was not wrongful within the meaning of Art.3 or Art.12 of the Convention, and refused the reliefs sought by the plaintiff.

10–25 In the recent case of *C.(R.) v S.(I.)*,[39] Finlay Geoghegan J. held the removal of a child to Belgium to be a wrongful removal pursuant to s.15 of the Child Abduction and Enforcement of Custody Act 1991. She therefore granted a declaration under the Hague Convention that the removal of the child from Ireland by the respondent and his retention in Belgium was wrongful. Finlay Geoghegan J. held that although the applicant did not enjoy custody rights, he was a guardian and was entitled to be consulted in respect of all matters affecting the child. It should be noted that the applicant was granted access as part of previous judicial separation proceedings.

10–26 *Actual exercise of rights* Article 3(1)(b) of the Convention provides that the removal or retention is to be considered wrongful where "at the time of the removal or retention those rights were actually exercised, either jointly or alone, or would have been so exercised but for the removal or retention."

According to Beaumont and McEleavy, Art.3(1)(b) "is a safety mechanism … [which] was conceived as a means of ensuring that an applicant could not rely on a custody order which, although valid, had been overtaken by subsequent events, thereby rendering it 'stale'."[40] The onus is on the deprived parent to establish a *prima facie* case that, at the time of removal or retention, he or she was *actually exercising* the rights of custody which have allegedly been "breached".[41]

10–27 Judicial decisions in England,[42] the US[43] and Australia[44] suggest that, rather than defining the concept of "actual exercise" by reference to certain categories of action or activity, the courts should "… liberally find 'exercise' whenever a parent with *de jure* custody rights keeps, or seeks to keep, any sort of regular contact with his or her child".[45]

10–28 In *C.M. and O.M. v Delegacion de Malaga and Others*,[46] the second-named plaintiff, the natural mother of a child, maintained that she had placed the child in the care of the first-named defendant on a temporary basis. However,

[38] At p.20.
[39] unreported, High Court, Finlay Geoghegan J., November 11, 2003.
[40] *op. cit.*, p.83.
[41] Note the reference in Mme Pérez-Vera's report to the representations of delegates to the XIVth Session of the Permanent Conference regarding concerns in relation to the burden of proof (Report of Mme Perez-Vera, p.448 at para.73).
[42] *Re: W (Abduction: Procedure)* [1995] 1 F.L.R. 878.
[43] *Friedrich v Friedrich* 1983 F. 2d. 1396 (6th Cir 1993) and 78F. 3d. 1060 (6th Cir 1996), and *Urness v Minto* S.C. 249 (1994).
[44] *Director General, Department of Community Services Central Authority v Crowe* (1996) F.C. 92–717.
[45] Boggs C.J. in *Friedrich v Friedrich* 983 F. 2d 1396 (6th Cir 1993) and 78F. 3d 1060 (6th Cir 1996). See also, Beaumont and McEleavy, *op. cit.* at pp.85–86.
[46] [1999] 2 I.R. 363.

it was the defendants' case that she had signed a form placing the child for fostering and thereafter consenting to adoption in the future. The first-named defendant had made an official decision to the effect that that the mother had abandoned the child and, on that basis, assumed guardianship of the child. The mother sought the return of the child to Ireland. McGuinness J. held, *inter alia*, that at the material time, the mother was not exercising custody rights within the meaning of Art.3(b) of the Hague Convention.

10–29 *Status of interim orders* With regard to the application of Art.3 of the Convention in circumstances where an interim decision or order has been made in respect of the child at issue, it has been suggested by, among others, Beaumont and McEleavy[47] that "unless an express declaration is made to the contrary, a provisional award of sole custody should not be recognised as allowing a parent to remove a child to, or retain a child in, a foreign jurisdiction".[48]

Habitual residence

10–30 The definition of the term "habitual residence", for the purpose of determining the place of the child's habitual residence prior to his or her wrongful removal or retention, has been given considerable judicial attention. Laffoy J., in the decision of *ZS-A v ST*,[49] stated that the determination of the place of the child's habitual residence is a question of fact and is "not to be treated as a term of art with some special meaning" but, rather, the words are to be given their "ordinary meaning". Thus, the matter is not governed, for example, by the same rigid rules of dependency as apply in the context of the law of domicile.[50] In the case of *K.L. v L.C.*,[51] Blayney J., following the approach of the English courts, ruled that "habitual residence" is to be equated with ordinary residence. In the English case of *Barnet London Borough Council v Shah*,[52] it was held that, to establish the place of "habitual residence" of a child, there has to be "a settled purpose with a sufficient degree of continuity".

10–31 Although it takes time to establish a habitual residence, it was held in the English case of *C. v S.*[53] that it takes no time at all to terminate it. If a person leaves a place with a settled intention not to return, the loss of the former habitual residence follows, but while the habitual residence may be lost immediately on departure, a person does not acquire a new habitual residence overnight. In the *C. v S.* case, less than six months' residence was

---

[47] *op. cit.*, pp.51–52.
[48] See also J. M. Eeklaar, *The International Abduction of Children by a Parent or Guardian*, Commonwealth Secretariat, Commonwealth Law Ministers, 1980 Barbadas Meeting, Memoranda, LMM (80) 16, pp.21–22. See also *Re: F. (A Minor) (Abduction: Custody Rights Abroad)* [1995] Fam. 224; *B. v B. (Abduction: Custody Rights)* (1993) Fam. 32.
[49] unreported, High Court, August, 1996.
[50] In this regard, see *In the matter of C.M.* [1999] 2 I.L.R.M. 103.
[51] [1993] 2 Fam. L.J. 79.
[52] [1983] 2 A.C. 309.
[53] [1990] 3 W.L.R. 492.

considered sufficient to establish habitual residence. The courts will examine the intention of the party seeking to prove that a new place of habitual residence has been established. In the decision of the English Court of Appeal in *Re F.*,[54] the Court approved of the finding of a lower court that a family had acquired a new place of habitual residence after only one month in a new country.

10–32   The case of *S.(A.) v H.(E.) & H.(M.)*[55] prompted an examination of the effect of the death of the mother of a non-marital child on the child's habitual residence. In this case, a child of parents who were not married to each other but were both habitually resident in England was removed from England to Ireland by maternal relatives upon the death of the natural mother and without the consent of the natural father. Geoghegan J. held that the habitual residence of the child was not altered by such unilateral action and "[a]t all relevant times, the child E., had ... an habitual residence in England." The Court quoted with approval from the judgment of Mr. Lionel Swift, Q.C., the Deputy High Court Judge who dealt with the case in England, who had stated as follows:

> "I am not prepared to accept that a person with no jurisitic power over a person of this age can change his habitual residence within a day or two. It is not necessary to consider the position of a child kept by such a person over a significant period of time."[56]

In a similar vein, Geoghegan J. quoted from the judgment of Lord Slynn of Hadley in the House of Lords, who in turn quoted from the judgment of Dame Elizabeth Butler-Sloss in the Court of Appeal:

> "The death of a mother, the sole carer, would not immediately strip the child of his habitual residence acquired from her, at least, while he remained in the same jurisdiction. Once the child has been removed to another jurisdiction, the issue whether the child has obtained a new habitual residence whilst in the care of those who have not obtained an Order or the agreement of others will depend upon the facts. But a clandestine removal of the child on the present facts would not immediately clothe the child with the habitual residence of those removing him to that jurisdiction, although the longer the actual residence of the child in the new jurisdiction without challenge, the more likely the child would acquire the habitual residence of those who have continued to care for the child without opposition."[57]

Where habitual residence has been established in a country, it was held in the *Oundijan* case[58] that periods of absence, with an intention to return, will not change it.[59]

---

[54] [1992] 1 F.L.R. 548.

[55] unreported, Geoghegan J., December 10, 1997.

[56] See judgment of Geoghegan J. at p.6.

[57] See judgment of Geoghegan J. at p.7.

[58] [1980] 1 F.L.R. 19.

[59] See also *Hague Conference on Private International Law: Report of the Second Special*

10–33 The case of *C.M. and O.M. v Delegacion de Malaga and Others*[60] prompted a detailed examination of the concept of habitual residence. The first-named plaintiff was a child born in Spain in October 1995. The second-named plaintiff was the child's natural mother, who was an Irish citizen and was unmarried. The second-named plaintiff moved to Spain in May of 1995 and commenced discussions with the first-named defendant in respect of the placement of the child for fostering and adoption. The second-named plaintiff maintained that she only wished to place the child in temporary care and that she never wanted her to be placed for adoption. However, on December 1, 1995, the child was handed over by the second-named plaintiff to the first-named defendants and the mother signed a form consenting to foster placement and also to future adoption.

On December 18, 1995, the first-named defendant made an official decision that the second-named plaintiff had abandoned the child and assumed guardianship. The mother maintained that she never received notification of this decision. She eventually made contact with the first-named defendant in April 1996, and she sought the return of the child. She was advised that she had a right of appeal to the Spanish Family Court, and she instituted proceedings in Spain. These proceedings were ultimately dismissed by the Spanish court in September 1998. The second-named plaintiff appealed this decision, and she also instituted proceedings in Ireland seeking a declaration that the child, as an Irish citizen, was being wrongfully retained by the Spanish authorities. The defendants entered an appearance to the Irish proceedings solely for the purposes of contesting jurisdiction. It was argued on behalf of the defendants that the habitual residence of the child was Spain and that the Spanish court was the proper *forum conveniens* to determine all matters concerning the welfare of the child.

In dismissing the plaintiff's claim, McGuinness J. held that, in order for the Court to make the declarations sought by the plaintiffs, it would be necessary to establish that the child was habitually resident in Ireland, and that the second-named plaintiff was actually exercising or would have been exercising rights of custody over the child were it not for the alleged wrongful removal or retention.[61] Having reviewed the authorities, McGuinness J. ruled that:

> "it seems to me to be settled law in both England and Ireland that 'habitual residence' is not a term of art, but a matter of fact, to be decided on the evidence in this particular case. It is generally accepted that where a child is residing in the lawful custody of its parent (in the instant case the mother), its habitual residence will be that of the parent. However, the habitual residence of the child is not governed by the same rigid rules of dependency as apply under the law of domicile and the actual facts of the case must always be taken into account. Finally, a person, whether a

---

Commission Meeting to Review the Operation of the Hague Convention on the Civil Aspects of International Child Abduction (1994) 33 I.L.M. 225 and especially at pp.234–235 where the case of military personnel is examined.

[60] [1999] 2 I.R. 363.

[61] *ibid.* at p.374.

child or an adult, must, for at least some reasonable period of time, be actually present in a country before he or she can be held to be habitually resident there".[62]

The Court found, as a matter of fact that "the first plaintiff was born in Spain, was placed in the lawful custody of the first defendant in Spain and has never left Spain. The mother has returned to Ireland and has sought the return of her child. I cannot accept that the mother's decision can of itself result in the change of the child's habitual residence to Ireland when the child has never, at any stage, been present in Ireland".[63]

The Court held that the habitual residence of the child was Spain and that, on the facts as established, the second-named plaintiff was not exercising custody rights at the material time within the meaning of Art.3(b) of the Hague Convention.

On the facts, McGuinness J. ruled that "it would be inappropriate for this Court to assume jurisdiction in the instant case",[64] and, in particular, noted that the courts of the Kingdom of Spain had been seised of the matter since June 1996 and had already made a number of orders in respect of the child. The Court also ruled that the customary "*forum conveniens*" principles would indicate that evidence in regard to the child's welfare would be more readily available to the Spanish court. According to McGuinness J., "[t]here is a risk that if this Court assumes jurisdiction, inconsistent orders in regard to the child will be made ... the Spanish court has reached decisions which the second plaintiff opposes, but that is not a reason for this court to reject the jurisdiction of the Spanish court."[65] In any event, McGuinness J. commented that "[t]here is no evidence to suggest that the Spanish court would necessarily yield to declarations and orders made by this court and this court has no way of enforcing such orders in Spain".[66]

Finally, the Court considered whether there was "some over-riding factor which would cause this court to reject the Spanish jurisdiction".[67] McGuinness J. stated that, under Irish law, the second-named plaintiff could not claim the benefit of the inalienable and imprescriptible rights guaranteed under Arts 41 and 42 of the Constitution of Ireland 1937, as she was not married to the father of the child who was the subject of the proceedings but, rather, she enjoyed rights in respect of the child pursuant to Art.40.1 of the Constitution, which were alienable. Furthermore, both Irish law and Spanish law provide for dispensing with the consent of the natural mother of a child for the purposes of making an adoption order and, in the Spanish courts, "it is clear that the welfare of the child is also the paramount consideration".[68]

Accordingly, McGuinness J. made an order, as sought by the defendants,

---

[62] *ibid.* at p.381.
[63] *ibid.*
[64] *ibid.* at p.387.
[65] *ibid.* at p.388.
[66] *ibid.*
[67] *ibid.*
[68] *ibid.* at p.389.

dismissing the proceedings "as contrary to the principle of the comity of courts as the habitual residence of the infant with whom the proceedings are concerned is in Spain and there are prior proceedings before the courts of the Kingdom of Spain concerned with the substantive issues in contention herein, in respect of which the aforesaid courts of the Kingdom of Spain have *seisin*".[69]

Consent and acquiescence

10–34   A deprivation of the right to exercise custody shall not be "wrongful" if an abducting parent may show evidence of consent to the removal or retention of a child on the part of the dispossessed parent or other relevant person or body, although continued detention without the consent or contrary to the wishes of such a parent may be deemed wrongful.[70] A consent must be an unconditional one. Thus, a consent conferred by a dispossessed father upon his estranged wife for the purposes of the removal of their children from England to Ireland in order to enable them to set up a new home and life there, when granted on the understanding and condition that he would follow them to their new home in order to effect a reconciliation, shall not suffice.[71] Similarly, Morris J. concluded in *D.C. v V.L.C.*[72] that a statement by one spouse to the effect that the other spouse should leave and take their child with him, for example in the course of an argument, did not constitute a consent to leave the jurisdiction.

10–35   In the case of *I.K. v J.K.*,[73] Morris J. dealt with the issues of consent and acquiescence. The defendant argued that, as the plaintiff "knew that she was leaving and did nothing about it", he "therefore must be deemed to have consented".[74] Morris J. rejected this argument and ruled that a letter written by the plaintiff to the defendant, the contents of which demonstrated that the plaintiff was aware the defendant was making travel plans, could not be interpreted in such a manner. According to Morris J., "at most [the letter] shows that the plaintiff knew that the defendant was making plans which might or might not have included her departure or the departure of the children and this departure might have been a temporary or a permanent one. In my view it is not correct to read that part of the letter as an indication that the plaintiff was consenting to her leaving. Moreover, I am satisfied that at the time when the defendant was leaving she did not believe that the plaintiff was in fact consenting to her doing so".[75]

Furthermore, it was argued on behalf of the defendant that the plaintiff had acquiesced in the bringing of the children to Ireland by the defendant on the

---

[69] *ibid*. See also the recent decision of *Murphy J. in P.A.S. v A.F.S.*, unreported, High Court, September 13, 2004.

[70] See *N.K. v J.K.* [1994] 3 I.R. 483.

[71] See *M.D. v A.T.D.*, unreported, O'Sullivan J., March 6, 1998. On the facts, O'Sullivan J. rejected the father's argument that his consent was a conditional one of the type described above.

[72] unreported, High Court, Morris J., January, 1995.

[73] unreported, High Court, Morris J., February 25, 1998.

[74] *ibid*. at p.9.

[75] *ibid*.

basis of "(a) matters contained in letters that he wrote to her, (b) the fact that he sought relief in the District Court in this jurisdiction [and] (c) his delay in mounting these proceedings".[76]

In reviewing the evidence, Morris J. stated that the letters written by the plaintiff to the defendant:

> "must be read in the context of the general tone of the letters. They are letters clearly written by a man demonstrating extravagances of grief and love for his wife and family. It is obvious that the plaintiff was wishing to convey to his wife the fact that he would do anything to rebuild the bridges between them and was prepared to go to any lengths to make up for what he perceived to be his shortcomings. I am satisfied that nothing in these letters amounts to a statement of acceptance by the Plaintiff of the fact that his wife had improperly removed the children from their home".[77]

Morris J. concluded that, in making efforts to establish the whereabouts of the children, contacting Irish social workers and the Gardaí, the defendants' parents and a hotel where he believed he might find his wife and children, "[e]verything about the plaintiff's conduct at this time indicates a wish to get his family back".[78] The Court also ruled that "recourse to the District Court in Ireland for the purpose of obtaining access to the children in the circumstances of this case could constitute acquiescence".[79]

10–36 In the case of *M.D. v A.T.D.*,[80] the plaintiff and defendant were a married couple who had separated in July 1997 and resided in England. In August 1997, the defendant wife brought the children of the marriage to Ireland for a short holiday. The plaintiff husband alleged that, in September 1997, the defendant indicated to the plaintiff that she wished to reconcile and informed him that the best chance of effecting a reconciliation was if all parties came to live in Ireland. On that occasion and on that basis, the plaintiff argued that he gave his consent to the removal from the English jurisdiction of two children, B and H, who were living with the defendant, together with the third child, who had been living with the plaintiff, to go to live with their mother in Ireland. The plaintiff argued that this consent was given on the condition that he would follow and attempt a reconciliation with his wife and family. The defendant, however, argued that the plaintiff's consent had been unconditional.

O'Sullivan J. heard oral evidence from the plaintiff and the defendant and also, crucially, reviewed the correspondence which had passed between the parties' English solicitors. While there appears to have been a record of some discussion between the parties about a reconciliation in the correspondence from the plaintiff's solicitor to the defendant's solicitor, and in an attendance

---

[76] *ibid.* at p.10.
[77] *ibid.* at p.11.
[78] *ibid.* at p.12.
[79] *ibid.*
[80] unreported, O'Sullivan J., March 6, 1998.

note prepared by the plaintiff's solicitor, the Court found that there was "nothing about his agreement [to the children moving to Ireland] being dependent or conditional upon a reconciliation".[81] It was held that the attendance note prepared by the plaintiff's solicitor "crucially, does not support him in linking his consent to the reconciliation".[82] Furthermore, the Court found that the plaintiff had provided his consent to the arrangement without qualification on September 23, 1997, and that the discussion of the possibility of a reconciliation occurred on September 24, 1997. In all the circumstances, the Court held that the plaintiff did give his consent to the removal of all three children to Ireland.

10–37 The presence of consent does not, however, determine matters. The Supreme Court noted in *B.B. v J.B.*[83] that a trial judge shall retain a discretion to return a child to a parent who has consented to the removal or the retention of the child. The Supreme Court outlined a checklist of eight factors to which a judge exercising his or her discretion should have regard. Thus, a trial judge shall consider, *inter alia,* the following:

(a) the habitual residence of the child at the time of the removal;

(b) the law relating to his or her custody and access in the place of habitual residence;

(c) the overall policy of the Convention and its objective to secure protection for rights of access;

(d) the need to ensure respect for rights of custody and access under the law of Contracting States in the laws of other Contracting States;

(e) the circumstances of the child, including information relating to the social background of the child;

(f) the nature of the consent in question and the circumstances in which it was given;

(g) any relevant litigation in the place of the child's habitual residence;

(h) any undertaking(s) given.

10–38 This approach was followed in the case of *M.D. v A.T.D.*,[84] where the above factors were held not to represent an exhaustive list. In this case, as previously stated, the defendant wife had moved to Ireland with three children— one child from her previous marriage who was almost 18 years old; H., the defendant's child, who was almost 16 and had been legally adopted by the plaintiff, and B., a child of the parties who was four-and-a-half years of age. The plaintiff applied for an order pursuant to the Convention in respect of B. only.

---

[81] *ibid.* at p.28.
[82] *ibid.*
[83] unreported, Supreme Court, July 28, 1997.
[84] unreported, High Court, O'Sullivan J., March 6, 1998.

In respect of the issue of consent, O'Sullivan J. ruled that, even though he had held that the plaintiff had given his consent to the removal of the child, B., from the English jurisdiction, the Court still had to consider whether it was appropriate to exercise discretion under Art.13 of the Convention. Having considered the eight factors laid down in *B.B. v J.B.*, O'Sullivan J. noted that, because of the plaintiff's consent, the removal of the children was not wrongful. However, O'Sullivan J. took account of the fact that the plaintiff was a man of "very limited means"[85] and, as a result, had encountered difficulty travelling to Ireland and exercising access in respect of the child B. The Court held that "it is probable that if B. stays in [Ireland], his father will see him on relatively rare occasions".[86] The Court also took account of the fact that "[i]t may well be that at the time of giving his consent, the [plaintiff] hoped for a reconciliation and this may have precluded him from giving careful thought to the effect of the consent ... shortly after giving the consent the [plaintiff] repented of it and has now brought these proceedings".[87] Consideration was also given to the application by the plaintiff to the English courts in respect of matters of custody, access and welfare, and, in the context of this application, O'Sullivan J. was of the opinion that "it would be possible for the [defendant] ... to bring her own application for a judicial determination that she be permitted to reside with B. in [Ireland]".[88] The Court also took account of the undertakings provided to the Court by the plaintiff.

Having considered the eight factors laid down by the Supreme Court, O'Sullivan J. determined that his discretion should be exercised by the making of an Order directing the return of B. to England.[89] An "abducting parent" may seek to resist an allegation of abduction by claiming that the custodial parent acquiesced in the removal or retention of the child. The difference, in this context, between "consent" and "acquiescence" is merely one of timing. Consent precedes the wrongful taking or retention, while acquiescence follows it. Acquiescence, like consent, may be active, arising from express words or conduct, or passive, arising by inference from silence or inactivity. It must be real in the sense that the dispossessed parent or institution must be informed of his, her or its general right of objection, but precise knowledge of legal rights and remedies, including the specific remedy under the Convention, is not necessary. The test to be employed in this regard is an objective one and a court must determine whether a parent conducted himself or herself in a manner which is consistent with the seeking of a summary order for a child's return at a later date.

10–39 In *P. v B.*,[90] endorsing the test set out by Waite J. in *W. v W. (Child Abduction Acquiescence)*,[91] Budd J. in the High Court concluded that, as the

[85] *ibid.* at p.33.
[86] *ibid.*
[87] *ibid.* at p.34.
[88] *ibid.* at p.35.
[89] See also the case of *A.S. v P.S.* [1998] 2 I.R. 244.
[90] [1994] 3 I.R. 507.
[91] (1993) 3 F.L.R. 2 at 21. See also the comments of Donaldson L.J. in *Re A (Minor) (Abduction: Acquiescence)* (1992) 2 F.L.R. 11.

"abducting parent" and members of her family had informed the father of the child, that she and the child were merely returning to Ireland in order to enable her to recuperate, she had given rise to an inference that she would in due course return to the place of the child's habitual residence. A six-month lapse between the date of wrongful return and the date on which the request for return was received by the Irish authorities did not amount to a "long-term acceptance of a state of affairs" and thus, the plaintiff was not precluded from seeking relief pursuant to the Convention. The Supreme Court endorsed this approach on appeal.

10–40 In *S. v S.*,[92] the Supreme Court likewise concluded that there was no such long-term acceptance by the plaintiff father, as he had used the two months prior to the institution of proceedings to secure a reconciliation with his wife, and thus to encourage her to return with the children to their place of habitual residence.

10–41 Therefore, where an applicant can demonstrate to the court that: the child in question is under 16 years of age and was the subject of custody or access rights in favour of the applicant; that there has been a breach of those rights; and that the child was habitually resident in a Contracting State before the breach thereof, Art.12 directs that, where a period of one year has not yet elapsed since the date of the wrongful removal or retention, the Court "shall order the return of the child forthwith". Where the proceedings have been commenced after the expiration of a period of one year since the date of the wrongful removal or retention, Art.12 provides that the Court "shall also order the return of the child, unless it is demonstrated that the child is now settled in its new environment".

Delay

10–42 In *S. v S.*,[93] the Supreme Court expressed its concern about the fact that some 18 months expired between the date of the commencement of the High Court proceedings seeking the return of the children in question, and the date on which the matter concluded in the Supreme Court. Denham J., noting that delay serves to defeat the purpose of the Convention, referred to the duty on parties and professionals to proceed with all due expedition in cases of this nature. The Supreme Court decision in *P. v B. (No.2)*[94] espouses the view that a significant culpable delay on the part of the dispossessed party, and the inferences which may be raised from such a delay, are matters to which a court should have regard when considering whether to return a child to its place of habitual residence. On the facts before it, the Court concluded that a delay of over 20 months between the date of removal of the child from its place of habitual residence to this State and the institution of proceedings for return

---

[92] [1998] 2 I.R. 244.
[93] [1998] 2 I.R. 244.
[94] [1999] 2 I.L.R.M. 401.

were not adequately explained by the child's dispossessed father. Furthermore, such delay had caused the child in question to spend a critical period of her development in this State and had enabled her to put down roots in her new community. The Court concluded that the child was settled, from both a physical and psychological point of view, in her new environment. Reversing the conclusion of the trial judge, the Supreme Court refused to order the return of the child. Significantly, Denham J. expressed a similar view in July 2003 in *M.(E.) ex parte v M.(J.).*[95]

In the case of *I.K. v J.K.,*[96] the defendant wife had argued that the plaintiff husband was guilty of delay in instituting the proceedings since she had left Scotland on or about September 1, 1996, and the Central Authority in Scotland was not authorised to take the necessary steps to recover the minors until October 17, 1996. However, Morris J. noted that, in his affidavit, the plaintiff had stated that he was not able to ascertain the whereabouts of his children until October 6, 1996. According to Morris J., "[t]hat means that the period between establishing the whereabouts of the children and the signing of the appropriate authority was 11 days. In my view, that could not amount to delay".[97]

Relevant considerations

10–43   In the consideration of an application for the return of a child under the Convention, its provisions quite clearly state that the Court "shall not decide on the merits of the rights of custody until it has determined that the child is not to be returned" under the Convention[98] or unless an application under the Convention has not been lodged within a reasonable time after receipt of the notice of the wrongful removal or retention.

Accordingly, the Supreme Court has unequivocally determined that, within Hague Convention proceedings, the Irish courts are not required to make enquiries pursuant to s.3 of the Guardianship of Infants Act 1964 regarding the welfare of the child.[99] Similarly, Lardner J., in the case of *W. v W.,*[100] stated that the courts do not have to decide what would be for the long-term benefit of the child.

In the case of *M.D. v A.T.D.,*[101] O'Sullivan J. noted that the plaintiff had made an application to the English courts for a determination of matters relating to custody, access and welfare in respect of the child at the centre of the proceedings. O'Sullivan J. stated that, in reaching his decision to exercise his discretion to direct the return of the child to England, he was "bearing in mind that the question of his parents' custody of and access to B. and all matters relating to his welfare can be dealt with in the near future and also the fact that the Courts in England will have access to a range of evidence which is not

[95]   unreported, Supreme Court, July 9, 2003. See also the case of *A.S. v P.S.* [1988] 2 I.R. 244.
[96]   unreported, High Court, Morris J., February 25, 1998.
[97]   *ibid.* at p.12. See also the case of *A.S. v P.S.* [1998] 2 I.R. 244.
[98]   *ibid.*, Art.16.
[99]   *P v B* [1994] 3 I.R. 507 *per* Denham J.
[100] [1993] 2 F.L.J. 21.
[101] unreported, High Court, O'Sullivan J., March 6, 1998.

compellable in this jurisdiction and therefore will be better equipped to make a comprehensive decision in relation to his future".[102]

10–44 Similarly, Art.19 provides that "a decision under this Convention concerning the return of the child shall not be taken to be a determination of the merits of any custody issue." In considering an application pursuant to Article 13, the Court "shall take into account the information relating to the social background of the child provided by the Central Authority or other competent authority of the child's habitual residence." Thus, for example, McGuinness J. in *T.M.M. v M.D.* relied upon the negative assessments of the family environment contained in social work reports compiled by the relevant English authorities.

Defences

10–45 For a defendant in proceedings under the Convention, recourse may be had to the "defences" provided by Arts 13 and 20 of the Convention.
Article 13 provides that, notwithstanding the provisions of Art.12, the Court is not bound to order the return of the child if the person, institution or other body opposing its return establishes that:

(a) the person, institution or other body having the care of the person of the child was not actually exercising the custody rights at the time of removal or retention, or had consented to, or subsequently acquiesced in, the removal or retention; or

(b) there is a grave risk that his or her return would expose the child to physical or psychological harm or otherwise place the child in an intolerable situation.

Article 18 of the Hague Convention provides that the court of the requested State may return a child, despite the fact that the case falls within the parameters of one of the exceptions set out in Art.13. This Article itself provides that the requested State "is not bound" to order the return of the child if it is shown that the relevant circumstances exist. Thus, as Keane C.J. noted in *B.B. v J.B.*,[103] the jurisdiction to refuse to return which Art.13 confers, is permissive and the courts retain a discretion throughout. In this regard, reference should be made to the decision of the Supreme Court in the above case, wherein the Court endorsed the trial judge's finding that the dispossessed parent had in fact consented to the removal of the child, yet overturned his order refusing to return as the learned trial judge had failed to exercise the discretion which Arts 13 and 18 conferred.

10–46 (a) *"Grave Risk"* These provisions of Art.13(b) have often been invoked by abducting parents as a means of resisting an application for return. The attitude of the Superior Courts to this defence has varied and, over time,

---

[102] *ibid.* at p.42.
[103] unreported, Supreme Court, July 28, 1997.

an increasingly restrictive interpretation has been placed on the phraseology of Art.13(b) of the Convention, particularly since *C.K. v C.K.*[104] In *R.K. v J.K.*,[105] the Supreme Court stated that the "grave risk" contemplated by Art.13 of the Hague Convention was a serious risk. A similar approach was adopted by Finlay Geoghegan J. in the recent case of *E.H. v S.H.*, wherein she stated:

> "It is well settled by the decisions in this jurisdiction that the exception provided for in Article 13 of the Convention to the obligation of this court to make an order for the return of a wrongfully removed child to the jurisdiction of the Courts of his or her habitual residence must be strictly construed."[106]

In the earlier case of *M.A. v P.R.*,[107] the High Court refused to order the return of a child to a father who had behaved in an extremely violent manner towards the family, and whose behaviour had first forced his wife and children out of the family home and into a refuge prior to her departure with the children for this State. The High Court accepted that the defendant was forced to leave because she was stricken with fear and, furthermore, acknowledged that the violence inflicted by her husband was physically affecting the children and the defendant. The court accepted that there was a grave risk of further physical and psychological harm to the children if they were returned to their father.

10–47 A similar conclusion was reached by Costello J. in *R.G. v B.G.*,[108] wherein the learned judge accepted the evidence of the mother of the children that her husband drank to excess and was violent while drunk. Perhaps the most lenient application of all may be found in the *P.F. v M.F.*[109] decision, wherein the Supreme Court invoked the final clause of Art.13(b) and refused to order the return of children to their father in Massachusetts on the grounds of his previous record of gross financial irresponsibility; returning them to such an environment would, the Court concluded, expose the children in question to an intolerable situation. It is clearly arguable that, in the above cases, the Irish courts tended towards a consideration of the merits of the custody issues and, in effect, the courts began to move into territories more properly the preserve of the courts of the state of the child's habitual residence.

10–48 The decision in *C.K. v C.K.*[110] clearly envisages, however, that the defence may be successfully invoked in limited circumstances. The Court drew attention to the Preamble of the Hague Convention, which states that a child's interests are of paramount importance and that such interests are best served

---

[104] [1994] 1 I.R. 250.
[105] [2000] 2 I.R. 416.
[106] unreported, High Court, Finlay Geoghegan J., April 24, 2004. Also *A.S. v P.S.* [1998] 2 I.R. 244.
[107] unreported, High Court, Flood J., July 23, 1992
[108] [1993] 2 Fam. L.J. 55.
[109] unreported, Supreme Court, January 13, 1993.
[110] [1994] 1 I.R. 250.

by the return of the child to the jurisdiction in which he or she was habitually resident, in order to enable the courts of that jurisdiction to determine issues of custody and related matters. The court concluded that the defendant had not shown that the courts in Australia, being the jurisdiction to which it was proposed to return the children, would not adequately consider the children's welfare.

The decision of the Supreme Court in *S. v S.*[111] is in a similar vein. While acknowledging that grave risk may take many forms, and furthermore that there was a *prima facie* case of sexual abuse of one of the children by the father who sought to secure return, the Court nonetheless refused to apply the Art.13(b) defence. The Court concluded that there was no grave risk involved in returning the child in question to the jurisdiction of the courts of England and Wales, although it refused to order her return to her father pending full custody proceedings in the said courts. The evidence in the case did not sustain a finding that there would be a grave risk of psychological harm in returning the child to the family home if the plaintiff father was absent.

10–49 In the more recent case of *T.M.M. v M.D.*,[112] the plaintiff mother sought to secure the return to England of her two children, aged eight and 11 years. The children had been brought to this jurisdiction by their maternal grandparents and had been resident here for a period of one-and-a-half years by the time the matter came on for hearing in the High Court. The evidence before McGuinness J. indicated that the plaintiff had a 10-year history of alcoholism and had suffered from bouts of depression. Evidence of child neglect was borne out by a social welfare report compiled by the English authorities. McGuinness J., and the Supreme Court on appeal, concluded that there was a very real risk of physical and psychological harm to the two children and thus refused to order the return of the children. McGuinness J. distinguished this case from *S. v S.*[113] by adverting to the fact that, unlike the earlier case, there was no satisfactory carer for the children in England if they were returned there. Similarly, in the case of *E.M. v J.M.*,[114] O'Donovan J. refused to order the return of a six-year-old autistic child, wrongfully removed from the United Kingdom on the grounds that, in the short term, the United Kingdom was unlikely to be able to provide comparable services to those which the child was receiving in a specially dedicated school for autistic children in Ireland. The learned judge held that there was "a grave risk that the return of the (autistic) child would expose him to physical or psychological harm or otherwise place him in an intolerable situation". This decision was reversed by the Supreme Court on appeal. Denham J., writing the judgment of the Court, stated:[115]

"The essence of the decision of the High Court was that, while eventually if T. was returned to England he would have his autistic needs satisfied

---

[111] [1998] 2 I.R. 244.
[112] unreported, Supreme Court, Denham J., December 8, 1999 *nem diss.*
[113] [1998] 2 I.R. 244.
[114] unreported, High Court, July 18, 2002.
[115] At p.11.

in a manner comparable to the programme which exists in this State, in the short term England and Wales was unlikely to be able to provide comparable services. In those circumstances the High Court held that to return the child to England and Wales would lead to the physical or psychological harm as contemplated in Article 13. In this decision the High Court erred. While it may be that the system[s] of welfare available to T.M. are comparable in both jurisdictions and while it may well be that there might be a delay in achieving comparable care after the movement of a child and while such a disruption is to the disadvantage of the child, such a situation is not the "grave risk" provided for in Article 13 of the Hague Convention."

That said, the learned judge does not totally exclude a comparable analysis of the health systems in different jurisdictions, stating:[116]

"I wish to make it quite clear that I am not excluding for all time a situation where a comparison of health or education or other services should be excluded from a case where the grave risk exception is in issue."

10–50   The decision of O'Sullivan J. in *M.D. v A.T.D.*[117] should also be noted at this juncture. In that case, the defendant relied, *inter alia*, on the psychological harm which separation from his mother would cause to the child in question, in order to resist her husband's application to secure a return. The defendant indicated that she would not return to England as she wished to stay in this State with her other, older child (who was not the subject of an application under the Convention by the plaintiff). O'Sullivan J. rejected her attempt to rely on this provision, stating that "a court should be astute not to permit an abducting parent to set the Convention at naught by refusing to travel with a returning child."

10–51   In the case of *S.(A.) v H.(E.) and H.(M.)*,[118] Geoghegan J. noted that "in a large number of Hague Convention cases an Order for return could result in some psychological harm. It is a question of degree. It is well established by the authorities that Article 13(b) is intended to cover only serious psychological harm …".[119]

Some months later, Morris J., in the case of *I.K. v J.K.*,[120] ruled that, on the evidence proffered to the Court, the plaintiff was somewhat unstable and argumentative and his conduct "indicate[s] to me that care must be taken if an Order is made in this case".[121] However, in all the circumstances of the case, Morris J. ruled that "[o]n the other hand I do not think that the plaintiff would have any intention of harming either of the children and that many of his worst

---

[116] At p.14.
[117] unreported, High Court, March 6, 1998.
[118] unreported, Geoghegan J., December 10, 1997.
[119] *ibid.* at p.14.
[120] unreported, High Court, February 25, 1998.
[121] *ibid.* at p.13.

characteristics have been brought to the surface by the circumstances of the case and the hostility that it has generated".[122] As has become common, Morris J. proposed "to make the Order sought but this order must be hedged around by undertakings".[123]

In the case of *N.O'D. v P.B. (otherwise O'D.)*,[124] Quirke J. confirmed that, in determining the issue of grave risk, the Court is "not concerned with the interests, health or well-being of the plaintiff or the defendant, except in so far as such matters may have a bearing upon the psychological health of the two children and that in determining this issue I am solely concerned with the interests, health and well being of the children ...".[125]

In that case, the parties were granted a divorce in April 1997. Its terms provided, *inter alia*, that the defendant wife would have custody of the two children of the marriage, subject to the right of the plaintiff husband to have liberal access. Following the divorce, the defendant made various complaints against the plaintiff alleging aggressive and threatening behaviour on his part towards her. As a result, the plaintiff was charged with the indictable offensive of "aggravated stalking" and with violation of an order of protection which had been made, restraining such conduct on the part of the plaintiff. The charges came to trial a number of months after the divorce and, although the plaintiff was acquitted of the indictable offence of aggravated stalking, he was convicted of the offence of violation of the order of protection. By way of sentence, the plaintiff was placed on probation for a period of 24 months. During the first 12 months of that period the terms of probation included the imposition of a curfew, twice-weekly visits to a probation officer, appearance before the Court every two months, community service and alcohol evaluation.

Following sentence, a number of applications were made by the parties to the Domestic Relations Court relating to the plaintiff's rights of access to the children, most of which applications were made by the defendant and related to allegations of harassment and inappropriate behaviour by the plaintiff. On December 11, 1997, the defendant removed the two children of the parties from the United States to the Republic of Ireland without the plaintiff's consent or permission of the Court. The defendant claimed in evidence that the plaintiff had delivered death threats to her by telephone and it was her opinion that he was intent on killing her. She claimed that she was in fear for her life as a result of the plaintiff's threats and irrational conduct. These allegations were denied by the plaintiff. Quirke J. directed that the children of the parties should be assessed by a consultant psychiatrist and requested an opinion on the likely effect on the children of a direction that they be returned to the United States.

A consultant psychiatrist assessed the children and reported to the Court that the defendant mother feared for her life and that this was "a real fear regardless or whether or not it [was] well founded".[126] In oral evidence, the defendant testified that she was terrified of the plaintiff and that she believed

---

[122] *ibid.* at p.13.
[123] *ibid.*
[124] unreported, High Court, Quirke J., July 31, 1998.
[125] *ibid.* at p.23.
[126] *ibid.* at p.25.

that "... Eventually he will kill me ...". The defendant claimed to be "... determined not to go back" insisting that she was "... frightened for [her] ... life and for [her] ... safety".[127]

According to Quirke J., the consultant psychiatrist's evidence in respect of the effect on the children of their return to the United States unaccompanied "was of considerable importance. She made it clear that the return of the children in such circumstances would certainly give rise to a grave risk of serious psychological damage not only to K., who at four years old is heavily dependent on his mother, but also to B. who is, after all, only 6 years old notwithstanding his independent disposition".[128]

Having reviewed all the evidence and being satisfied that the US Courts had dealt with the issues arising in relation to the custody of, access to and welfare of the children "in a careful and highly competent fashion",[129] Quirke J. commented that "those Courts are at present better equipped to make fully informed and comprehensive decisions relating to the children's welfare and custodial and other interests than the Courts within this jurisdiction".[130]

Quirke J. ruled that "the only further issue which requires to be determined by this Court is the question of whether or not there is a likelihood that the defendant will refuse to accompany her children if they return to the United States as ordered by the Court, thereby surrendering her maternal and other interests in their ongoing custody, care and welfare and knowingly placing them at grave risk of psychological damage".[131] In this regard, the Court took account of the fact that "[i]f the defendant is genuinely exposed to the risk of injury or even death at the hands of the plaintiff then that risk must extend to her while she is present within this jurisdiction where her husband enjoys citizenship resources and accommodation without the restrictions which have been imposed upon him by the Circuit Court [in the United States]. Furthermore, if the defendant's fear of the plaintiff is real and as intense as she has claimed then her fear of the plaintiff will surely increase if the plaintiff is placed in a position where he feels he has been permanently deprived of access to his children".[132]

Quirke J. stated that he could not accept that the defendant's fear of the plaintiff was sufficient to prevent her from accompanying her children if they were returned to the United States and expressed his impression that her fear was not well-founded. Accordingly, and being satisfied on the evidence that the return of the children to the United States accompanied by their mother would not place them in an intolerable situation, either by reason of psychological harm or otherwise, the Court made an order under the Child Abduction and Enforcement of Court Orders Act 1991, directing that the two children should be returned to the United States.[133]

---

[127] *ibid.* at p.26.
[128] *ibid.*
[129] *ibid.* at pp.30–31.
[130] *ibid.* at pp.30–31.
[131] *ibid.* at p.31.
[132] *ibid.* at p.32.
[133] See also *Re: C (a minor) (abduction)* (1989) 1 F.L.R. 403.

10–52 (b) *The child's wishes* A Court may also refuse to return a child if it finds that the child objects to being returned and has attained an age and degree of maturity at which it is appropriate to take account of his views. Article 13(c) provides a separate and distinct ground for refusal to return on this basis and, thus, this defence may be invoked in the absence of allegations of grave risk of physical or psychological harm.

The Irish courts have, however, noted that whilst it is a separate ground, "a decision not to return a child to the country of its habitual residence is a decision of the court and care should be taken [t]hat it is not, nor does it appear to be, the decision of the child."[134] Great care must be taken in the exercise of this judicial discretion and the courts shall not rely upon a child's objections, unless satisfied that they are raised for mature and cogent reasons.[135] Whether a child objects to being returned, and furthermore whether he or she has attained an age and degree of maturity at which it is appropriate to take account of his view, are questions of fact peculiarly within the province of the trial judge, and the courts have resisted the call to adopt guidelines setting out the procedure to be employed by judges when ascertaining these facts.

In the case of *R.G. v B.G.*,[136] Costello J. elected to interview two of the three children at issue in the proceedings. Costello J. found that J.G. (aged 10) was "… a bright and intelligent little girl. I think she has reached an age and degree of maturity at which it is appropriate for me to take into account her views".[137] G.G. (aged eight) was also interviewed and found to be an "exceptionally bright child".[138] By virtue of her interaction with her older sister and with him during the interview, Costello J. opined that "she had reached an age of maturity which justifies my taking account of her views also".[139]

10–53 (c) *Article 20 defence—Fundamental principles* Article 20 supplements the Art.13 defences by providing that "[t]he return of the child under the provisions of Art.12 may be refused if this would not be permitted by the fundamental principles of the requested State relating to the protection of human rights and fundamental freedoms." However, Art.18 provides that nothing in c.III of the Convention shall limit the power of a judicial or administrative authority to order the return of the child at any time.

The present attitude of the courts, following the lead of the Supreme Court,[140] is to favour a very strict interpretation of the defences provided in the Convention. The presumption underlying the Convention (that the best interests of the child are served by the prompt return of the child to the jurisdiction of origin) is not easily surmountable, and any risks identified to the court by the defendant will often be regarded as best dealt with by the relevant authorities in the jurisdiction of origin.

---

[134] *Per* Denham J. in *T.M.M. v M.D.*, unreported, Supreme Court, Denham J., December 8, 1999 *nem. diss.*, above.

[135] *Per* Morris J. in *D.C. v V.L.C.*, above.

[136] unreported, Costello J., November 12, 1992.

[137] *ibid.* at pp.5–6.

[138] *ibid.* at p.6.

[139] *ibid.*

[140] For example, in cases such as *C.K. v C.K.* [1994] 1 I.R. 250.

Undertakings

10–54 The High Court frequently seeks undertakings from the plaintiff parent as a prerequisite to an order for return. Undertakings may be drafted in negative terms, such as those which envisage that, if a child is returned to the place of habitual residence, his or her plaintiff parent shall not reside in the family home pending the resolution of custody or other relevant matters.[141] Alternatively, undertakings may impose positive obligations such as a duty to make interim maintenance payments, or to provide accommodation for the abducting parent pending the resolution of relevant court proceedings in the place of habitual residence.[142] The provision of undertakings to the Court by one or both parties will often be regarded as adequate interim protection, pending a resolution of the custody or access issues before the Courts in the jurisdiction of origin.

In *P. v B.*, the Supreme Court agreed that the use of reasonable and enforceable undertakings, designed to ensure the welfare of the child during the transition from one jurisdiction to another, is entirely consistent with the 1991 Act and with the Hague Convention. Such undertakings, the court added, accord with the constitutional protection of the welfare of the child and they may also protect a parent in his or her role and in the exercise of his or her rights under the Constitution.

10–55 The courts have, on occasion, rejected the argument that a child should not be returned to the place of his or her habitual residence by reason of a grave risk that he or she would suffer physical or psychological harm at the hands of the plaintiff parent, and have instead insisted upon the acceptance and adoption of appropriate undertakings by that parent. Thus, as mentioned above, the Supreme Court in *S. v S.* concluded that the child in question should be returned to England but that the plaintiff parent, in respect of whom allegations of sexual abuse against the child were made, should not reside in the family home pending the resolution of proceedings before the English courts.

In the case of *I.K. v J.K.*,[143] Morris J. made an order directing the return of the child at issue in the proceedings, which order was "hedged around by undertaking" given by the plaintiff husband to provide funds to the defendant wife to enable her to purchase air tickets for the return journey to Scotland with the children, together with sundry expenses associated with the journey. In addition, he was directed to provide his wife and children with a weekly payment to cover support of the defendant and the children until a further order is made, together with an undertaking that he would not make contact with the defendant wife or the children pending a ruling from the Scottish Family Law Court.

10–56 In *T.M.M. v M.D.*,[144] on the other hand, McGuinness J. in the High

---

[141] An example thereof is found in *S. v S.* [1998] 2 I.R. 244.

[142] In that regard, see judgment of O'Sullivan J. in *P. v B.* [1994] 3 I.R. 507.

[143] unreported, High Court, February 25, 1998.

[144] unreported, Supreme Court, Denham J., December 8, 1999 (*nem. diss.*).

Court distinguished the facts before her from those in the *S. v S.* case. The learned trial judge noted the mother's difficult history of alcoholism, and also referred to the fact that the children's father had ceased to play any role in their upbringing and was, thus, clearly not a satisfactory alternative carer for the children. There was, therefore, no safe environment for the children in England. McGuinness J. accepted that the English courts would enforce any undertakings imposed but concluded, nonetheless, that there was a very real risk of physical and psychological harm which could not be met by any form of undertaking. The approach of the learned trial judge was endorsed by the Supreme Court on appeal.

10–57   In the case of *L.P. v M.N.P.*,[145] McGuinness J. had delivered an *ex-tempore* judgment on November 12, 1997, by virtue of which an order was made returning the child of the parties, E., on the basis of, *inter alia*, a number of undertakings provided by the plaintiff and the defendant. However, subsequent to the making of this order, a number of further applications were made to the Court regarding the exact effect of the undertakings, and McGuinness J. delivered a number of rulings on these issues. The child and the defendant mother then returned to Italy.

In her judgment delivered in October 1998, McGuinness J. recites that, from time to time during the following months, counsel for the defendant had been obliged to make a number of applications to the Court "concerning the virtually complete failure of the husband to abide by the various undertakings given by him".[146] Noting that "the whole question of the giving and receiving of undertakings and their enforcement was one of very considerable importance in cases arising under the 1991 Act and the Hague Convention", McGuinness J. quite correctly concluded that the use of undertakings "depended on there being legal procedures for the recognition and enforcement of undertakings in the Courts of the Country to which the child was returned".[147]

Having received replies to a number of queries directed to the Italian Central Authority, McGuinness J. stated that it was not clear from the replies "whether the common law concept that a party may give undertakings to the Court and that the failure to abide by such undertakings constitutes a contempt of court is a normal part of the Italian legal code."[148] It was noted in the instant case that the contents of the order of the Irish High Court made on February 12, 1997 was not conveyed to the Italian Court until April 23, 1997, and then was not translated until May 5, 1997. In that period the child, E., was removed from the custody of her mother.

McGuinness J. concluded that "[c]learly this Court cannot know the reasons for the lengthy delay in conveying the contents of the Order of February 12, 1997 to the Italian Court and of having it translated, nor can it know whether any attempt was made by the legal representative of the mother to have the Order legally enforced initially. The answer given by the Central Authority

---

[145] unreported, McGuinness J., October 14, 1998.
[146] *ibid.* at p.78.
[147] *ibid.* at p.81.
[148] *ibid.* at p.83.

for Italy does not in fact make it clear whether it is the Order itself which may be recognised as enforceable or whether the undertakings as apart from the Order may be recognised as enforceable. Unfortunately, it appears to me that the situation is now such that there is not useful further action that this Court can take in the matter".[149]

McGuinness J. went on to refer to the judgment of Singer J. in the English High Court case of *Re O. (Child Abduction: Undertakings)*.[150] In his judgment, the learned Singer J. stated as follows:

> "If in relation to any particular Contracting State that process revealed the absence of machinery adequate to give backing to undertakings the observance of which the English Court relied upon to relieve the children of risk of an intolerable situation, then it would be relevant to consider whether the parent proffering the undertakings generally intended to honour them".[151]

Rights of access

10–58   Rights of access are defined as including "the right to take a child for a limited period of time to a place other than the child's habitual residence". It is clear from the wording of the preamble to the Hague Convention, and the wording of Art.3 of the same Convention, that the primary objective thereof is the protection and enforcement of custody rights. By contrast, the terms of the Convention do not require the return of children and their custodial parent to the jurisdiction in which they were formerly habitually resident merely to enable the non-custodial parent to exercise his or her right of access.

In the case of *M.D. v A.T.D.*,[152] O'Sullivan J. was concerned that, due to the financial circumstances of the plaintiff father, he would not be able to exercise regular access to the child who was the subject matter of the proceedings, if the child remained living in Ireland. The Court considered the issue of access as part of the process of considering the eight factors laid down by the Supreme Court in *B.B. v J.B.*[153] In all the circumstances, it ordered the return of the child to England, commenting that the English Courts would be better equipped to make a comprehensive decision regarding the child's future.

10–59   As previously stated, Art.21 provides that "[a]n application to make arrangements for organising or securing the effective exercise of rights of access may be presented to the central authorities of the Contracting States in the same way as an application for the return of a child." The Central Authorities are bound by Art.21 to "promote the peaceful enjoyment of access rights and the fulfilment of any conditions to which the exercise of those rights may be subject" and "shall take steps to remove, as far as possible, all obstacles to the

---

[149] *ibid.* at pp.83–84.
[150] [1994] 2 F.L.R. 349.
[151] *ibid.* at 367.
[152] unreported, High Court, March 6, 1998.
[153] unreported, Supreme Court, July 28, 1997.

exercise of such rights". Further, they may "either directly or indirectly ... initiate or assist in the institution of proceedings with a view to organising or protecting these rights and securing respect for the conditions to which the exercise of these rights may be subject."

10–60   In the case of *W.P.P. v S.R.W.*,[154] the defendant mother had been granted sole custody of the two children of the marriage by a Santa Barbara court in December 1994 at the conclusion of uncontested proceedings to dissolve the marriage instituted by the defendant in the United States. The Californian court had also granted visitation rights to the plaintiff. The plaintiff instituted proceedings pursuant to the Hague Convention seeking an order for the return of the minors to the jurisdiction of the Californian court, arguing that their removal was "wrongful" within the meaning of Arts 3 and 12 of the Convention. Although it was agreed that the defendant was entitled to legal and physical custody of the children, the plaintiff argued that, by her actions, she had effectively frustrated him in the exercise of his visitation rights. Therefore, the plaintiff submitted, the removal of the children to Ireland by the defendant constituted a breach of a right of custody (vested in the plaintiff or the Californian court) and was "wrongful". The defendant argued she was entitled to determine where the children should reside and, therefore, the removal to Ireland was not "wrongful" within the meaning of the Convention.

Keane J. held that, on the basis of the affidavits filed, "the defendant, as the parent having custody, was entitled to determine the minors' place of residence".[155] Thus, the question which had to be determined was whether the defendant could unilaterally exercise that right in circumstances where the Santa Barbara Court had already awarded access to the plaintiff.

On the basis of an analysis discussed above, the court held as follows:

> "The exercise of a child's right to determine a child's place of residence may, of course, be restricted by the order of the court awarding custody to one parent by prohibiting the removal of the child from the jurisdiction of the court without the further leave of the court or the consent of the other parent. In such a case, ... the removal of the child, without such leave and without the consent of the other parent may constitute a breach of a right of custody vested in the court. In this case, however, we are concerned with an order which gave the plaintiff rights of access only. It is clear, in my view, that the appropriate machinery for enforcing such rights is Article 21 of the Convention. To order the return of children and their custodial parent to the jurisdiction in which they were formerly habitually resident merely so as to entitle the non-custodial parent to exercise his rights of access is not warranted by the terms of the Convention."

The court ruled that the removal of the minors "was not in breach of any rights

---

[154]   unreported, Supreme Court, April 14, 2000 (*nem. diss.*).
[155]   At p.19.

of custody attributed to either the defendant or the Californian court"[156] and accordingly was not wrongful within the meaning of Art.3 or Art.12 of the Convention, and refused the reliefs sought by the plaintiff.

Oral testimony

10–61   In a number of cases which have come before the Irish courts for determination, the presiding judge has deemed it necessary or appropriate to hear oral testimony from the plaintiff and defendant.[157] This trend is likely to increase with the coming into force of the revised Brussels II Regulation on March 1, 2005 (see para.10–105 and Chapter 12).

In the case of *R.G. v B.G.*,[158] Costello J. stated that, in light of the level of contradiction in the affidavits filed by the plaintiff and the defendant, it was "of vital importance for the exercise of my powers under the Convention to determine this issue of fact and I could not determine the issue of fact without hearing oral evidence of the Parties on the disputed issues; …".[159]

Contempt of court

10–62   As child abduction cases concern matters of family law, the pro-ceedings are conducted *in camera* with reporting restrictions. Where either parent (or indeed any other person) involved in child abduction proceedings gives interviews or provides information to the media, they may be guilty of contempt of court, breach of the *in camera* rule and/or the offence of scandalising the court.[160]

The Luxembourg Convention

Principal features

10–63   The Luxembourg Convention, as its long title suggests, is primarily concerned with the recognition and enforcement of custody decisions made in any of the Contracting States and, accordingly, also has a role in the restoration of custody of children. A decision relating to custody is, for the purposes of the Convention, "a decision of an authority in so far as it relates to the care of the person of the child, including the right to decide on the place of his [or her] residence, or the right of access to him [or her]".[161]

Improper removal is defined in Art.1 as meaning:

"the removal of a child across an international frontier in breach of a decision relating to his [or her] custody which has been given in a

---

[156] At p.20.
[157] See, for example, *N. O'D. v P. B. (otherwise O'D.)*, unreported, High Court, Quirke, J., July 31, 1998.
[158] unreported, High Court, Costello J., November 12, 1992.
[159] *ibid.* at p.2.
[160] *S.(P.S.) v S.(J.A.) and Independent Newspapers(Ireland) and RTÉ*, unreported, High Court, Budd J., May 19 and 22, 1995.
[161] Luxembourg Convention, Art.1.

Contracting State and which is enforceable in such a State; improper removal also includes:

(i) the failure to return a child across an international frontier at the end of a period of the exercise of the right of access to this child or at the end of any other temporary stay in a territory other than that where custody is exercised;

(ii) a removal which is subsequently declared unlawful within the meaning of Article 12."

Improper removal may also occur where it effects or results in the breach of an access order. In the case of *S.M. v A.J.B.*,[162] it was held by Morris J. that the removal of a child by the defendant from the jurisdiction of the courts of England and Wales "was a removal of the child across an international frontier, that this removal was in breach of the order of Oldham Magistrates Court of April 13, 1994 [granting the plaintiff access to the child]."

10–64 The Luxembourg Convention also establishes a Central Authority to carry out the functions provided for by the Convention, and the Central Authorities are also required to co-operate with each other and promote co-operation in a manner akin to that required pursuant to the Hague Convention.

In order that the provisions of the Convention may be activated therefore, a *decision relating to custody* made by the relevant authority in a Contracting State must be in existence. Further, like the Hague Convention, the child the subject of the decision must be under 16 years of age.

Procedure and jurisdiction

10–65 Applications for orders of recognition and enforcement may be made to the High Court pursuant to Pt III of the Child Abduction and Enforcement of Custody Orders Act 1991. Section 21(1) of the 1991 Act provides that the Luxembourg Convention "shall have the force of law in the State and judicial notice shall be taken of it." Section 23 of the Act provides that, for the purposes of Part III of the Act, the High Court "shall have jurisdiction to hear and determine applications under ... [the Luxembourg] Convention for the recognition or enforcement of a decision relating to custody." Such applications may be addressed to the Irish Central Authority and, where the Central Authority is satisfied that the application is an application to which the Luxembourg Convention applies, s.24 provides that "it shall take action or cause action to be taken under that Convention to secure the recognition or enforcement of the decision".[163]

10–66 Section 25 of the Act provides that nothing in Pt III "shall prevent a person from applying in the first instance to the [High] Court under the Luxembourg Convention for the recognition or enforcement of a decision

---

[162] [1994] 3 I.R. 491.
[163] s.24(2) of the 1991 Act.

relating to custody made by an authority in a contracting State" other than Ireland.

Section 26 of the Act provides that where an application has been made, or is about to be made to the High Court under the Luxembourg Convention for the recognition or enforcement of a decision relating to custody, the High Court may give such interim directions for the purpose of securing the welfare of the child, preventing prejudice to interested persons, or changes in the circumstances relevant to the determination of the application. An application for such interim directions may be made *ex parte* in cases of urgency.

10–67   Crucially, s.29 of the Act provides that:

> "[a] decision relating to custody in respect of which an enforcement order has been made shall be of the same force and effect and, as respects the enforcement of the decision, the Court shall have the same powers, and proceedings may be taken, as if the decision was a decision of the Court."

The Central Authority is empowered by s.30 of the Act to request a probation and welfare officer to prepare a written report "with respect to any matter relating to the child which appears to it to be relevant".[164] It is also empowered to request a health board to arrange for a suitably qualified person to prepare such a report[165] where the Irish Central Authority is requested to make enquiries about a child under Article 15(1)(b) of the Convention by the Central Authority of another Contracting State. Section 30 also empowers the Irish Central Authority to "request any court to which a written report relating to the child has been made to send it a copy of the report".[166]

10–68   Where an order of recognition of a decision relating to custody has been made by the High Court and the original decision is varied or revoked by an authority in the contracting State in which it was made, s.31(1) of the 1991 Act provides that "any person appearing to the Court to have an interest in the matter may make an application to the Court for an order for variation or revocation of the order of recognition or enforcement of that decision."

Section 32 (1) provides that a person on whom any rights are conferred by a decision relating to custody made by an Irish court, or by an authority within the meaning of the Luxembourg Convention in another Contracting State, may make an application to the Irish Central Authority under Art.4 of the Luxembourg Convention, with a view to obtaining an order of recognition or enforcement in another Contracting State.[167]

---

[164] s.30(a).
[165] s.30(b).
[166] s.30(c).
[167] s.33 of the 1991 Act sets out the documents which will be required by a person seeking recognition or enforcement of an Irish Order in a Contracting State other than Ireland.

Recognition and enforcement of orders

10–69   Where a person who has obtained a decision wishes to have that decision recognised or enforced in another Contracting State, Article 7 provides that "[a] decision relating to custody given in a Contracting State shall be recognised and, where it is enforceable in the State of origin, made enforceable in every other Contracting State."

As previously stated, s.23 of the Child Abduction and Enforcement of Custody Orders Act 1991 confers jurisdiction on the High Court to hear and determine applications for recognition and enforcement. Section 19 provides details of the types and categories of documents, which will be admissible as evidence of the original decisions of the judicial and administrative authorities of Contracting States. In particular, s.19(1)(a) provides that "a document, duly authenticated, which purports to be a copy of a decision or declaration relating to custody of a judicial or administrative authority of a [foreign] Contracting State ... shall without further proof be deemed to be a true copy of the decision or declaration unless the contrary is shown; ..."

10–70   In *S.M. v A.J.B. (Child Abduction)*,[168] the plaintiff mother and defendant father lived together in England and were not married to each other. Their son, A., was born in February 1984 and, at a later date, the relationship between the parties ended. On April 13, 1994, custody of A. was awarded to the defendant by an English court and the plaintiff was granted access to him on Saturdays between 10am and 6pm. In June 1994, the defendant removed the child from the jurisdiction of the English court and brought him to Ireland. In August 1994, the plaintiff issued proceedings against the defendant seeking an order directing the return of A. to the jurisdiction of the Courts of England and Wales pursuant to the Luxembourg Convention.

The plaintiff argued that it would not be possible to enforce the access order unless the child was returned to the jurisdiction of the courts of England and Wales. The defendant argued, *inter alia,* that there was no evidence before the High Court to prove that the English order was "enforceable in the State of origin". The defendant also argued that the recognition and enforcement of the English order did not require the return of the child to the jurisdiction of the courts of England and Wales.

Morris J. granted the reliefs sought by the plaintiff and directed the return of A. to the jurisdiction of the courts of England and Wales. Counsel for the defendant argued that Art.7 of the Luxembourg Convention requires that the High Court should be satisfied "as a matter of strict proof that the order of the Magistrate's Court in England is 'enforceable' in the State of origin".[169] He submitted that "nowhere in the affidavit of laws which has been filed on behalf of the plaintiff is there any statement to that effect. He argued that in default of such a statement, there is no evidence before the court that the order of the Magistrates Court is enforceable, and that [the] court should not make the order sought". Morris J. ruled that this would not be "a realistic or proper

[168] [1994] 3 I.R. 491.
[169] *ibid.* at 495.

approach to the consideration of the effect of a court order made in England, valid on its face and made with apparent jurisdiction". Accordingly, it was held that the Order of the English court, being valid on its face and made with apparent jurisdiction, was "enforceable in the State of origin" within the meaning of Article 7 of the Luxembourg Convention. Article 12 of the Convention provides that "[w]here, at the time of the removal of a child across an international frontier, there is no enforceable decision given in a Contracting State relating to his custody, the provisions of this Convention shall apply to any subsequent decision, relating to the custody of that child declaring the removal to be unlawful, given in a Contracting State at the request of any interested person."

10–71 In the case of *P.M. v V.M.*,[170] a paternal grandmother instituted proceedings, pursuant to the Luxembourg Convention, seeking the return of her grandchild, who had been in her care prior to the removal of the child from England to Ireland by the mother, the defendant. The facts were that the child had been placed in the plaintiff grandmother's care by Bromley Social Services and, with the consent of the child's parents, the plaintiff had applied to the English courts for a residence order in respect of the child. While these proceedings were pending, the mother removed the child from the jurisdiction of England and Wales to Ireland on or after March 16, 1997.

Pursuant to proceedings issued by the grandmother in England on April 1, 1997, an order was made by the English High Court granting the grandmother a residence order, as well as an order directing the return of the child to England and Wales and a declaration that the removal was unlawful. The order was made *ex parte* and the mother was only notified of the making of the application after the event when she was served with the order on April 5, 1997.

On foot of the High Court order, the grandmother issued proceedings in Ireland pursuant to Article 12 of the Luxembourg Convention. In the High Court, it was argued on behalf of the plaintiff that the decision made by the Bromley Family Proceedings Court placing the child in the care of the grandmother was a decision relating to custody of the child, and this decision was in existence at the time of the removal. Kinlen J. rejected this argument, ruling that the originating proceedings for the purposes of the application before the Irish High Court were those initiated on April 1, 1997. He refused to make an order recognising and enforcing the order of the English High Court, following the decision of the President of the High Court in *C.D. and D.D. (minors): S.D. v R.B.*,[171] on the basis that the requirements of the 1991 Act had not been satisfied, as the defendant mother had not been notified of the application before the English courts and, therefore, could not have been expected to appear or be represented.

On appeal, the Supreme Court upheld the High Court decision and refused the relief sought on the basis that the originating summons was not served on the child's mother in sufficient time to enable her to arrange to be present at

---

[170] unreported, Supreme Court, February 20, 1998 (*nem. diss*).
[171] [1996] 3 I.R. 524.

the hearing before the English High Court, or to arrange for legal representation, and endorsed the decision in *S.D. v R.B.*[172]

Disputes regarding access rights

10–72 An order granting the non-custodial father access to his child constitutes a decision relating to custody for the purposes of the Luxembourg Convention. In the case of *R.J. v M.R.*,[173] the plaintiff father and the defendant mother, who were British citizens, lived together in England from August 1988 until January 1992. They were not married to each other. Their daughter, J., was born in September 1989. The defendant left their home in January 1992, taking J. with her. The plaintiff obtained an order from the English courts in March 1992 granting him access to J. A number of days later, on April 3, 1992, the defendant and J. disappeared. The plaintiff then obtained an order from the English courts on April 6, 1992, prohibiting the removal of J. from the jurisdiction of the English court. In December 1992, the defendant and J. were located in Ireland. A request was made for the return of J. to England by the Child Abduction Unit of the Lord Chancellor's Department to the Irish Department of Justice on December 6, 1992. On December 18, 1992, the plaintiff issued proceedings seeking, *inter alia*, an order directing the return of J. to the jurisdiction of the courts of England and Wales pursuant to the Luxembourg Convention.

In the High Court, the defendant argued that the Court should refuse to recognise the access order granted by the English court on the grounds that, firstly, recognition or enforcement of the access order would be contrary to the fundamental principles of Irish law relating to the family and children. Secondly, there had been a change in circumstances such that the enforcement of the access decision would no longer be in accordance with the welfare of the child. The High Court rejected the arguments, ruling that "there is nothing manifestly incompatible with the fundamental principles of law relating to the family and children in this country in granting access to the natural father of a child, particularly where the parents have cohabitated continuously since the birth of the child and where the child is in no danger from the father".[174]

Carroll J. also rejected the defendant's argument that there had been a change of circumstances beyond merely a change in residence so that the effects of the original decision were no longer in accordance with the welfare of the child. In particular, Carroll J. stated that she did not "accept that, after less than nine months in this country a child aged 4 would not adapt back to the environment she has always known. ... The lapse of time and change of circumstances has not been such that it could be said that the effects of the original decision are no longer in accordance with the welfare of the child. It is for the child's benefit to have contact with her father. Through him she will have contact with his extended family".[175]

---

[172] *ibid.*
[173] [1994] 1 I.R. 271.
[174] *ibid.* at 280.
[175] *ibid.*

The High Court decision was upheld on appeal and the Supreme Court noted, *per curiam,* that s.11 of the Guardianship of Infants Act 1964, as amended by s.13 of the Status of Children Act 1987, granted the right to natural fathers to apply to the Irish courts for custody of and access to their children. The Chief Justice, Finlay C.J., commented that, having regard to the 1964 Act, as amended, "an order ... granting access to the father of this child, whose parents have not married each other, is not in any way inconsistent with the fundamental principles of the law relating to children in Ireland".[176]

Recognition of orders

10–73   Where a child has been unlawfully removed or retained, and an order is granted to the deprived parent under the Hague or Luxembourg Conventions, such an order is, in effect, an order recognising the custody/access decision given by the relevant authority in a Contracting State and enforcing it by ordering the return of the child. However, the Luxembourg Convention, as implemented by Pt III of the Child Abduction and Enforcement of Custody Orders Act 1991, also provides a facility whereby a person or body in whose favour a decision relating to custody has been made by the relevant authority in a Contracting State, may apply to the Irish High Court for an order recognising the decision in this jurisdiction. Such orders are commonly referred to as "mirror orders".

A common situation which may prompt such a person or body to make an application is where one parent has been granted custody of a child, with access granted to the other parent and with permission for the custodial parent to leave the jurisdiction of the Court which has made the decision and take up residence in another jurisdiction. Another common situation is where a child has been placed in the care of a local authority by order of a court, with permission that the child may be placed with relatives in another jurisdiction, but with the local authority retaining legal responsibility for the child. In such circumstances, it is in the interests of the "access parent" in the first example, and the local authority in the second, to have a mirror order granted by the court of the jurisdiction in which the child will be residing. The purpose of such an application is, in so far as possible, to ensure that the courts of the jurisdiction in which the child originally resided retain the right to deal with all issues relating to the child, despite the fact that the child's habitual residence will have changed. In this way, it may be possible to prevent or frustrate attempts by the custodial parent or placement relatives to make an application to the courts of the "new" jurisdiction, seeking to alter the custodial/access arrangements by arguing that the court of the "new" jurisdiction is the appropriate judicial authority to deal with issues relating to the welfare of the child, on the grounds that the child is now habitually resident within its jurisdiction.

It is noteworthy in this context that, by virtue of s.29 of the Act, the powers of the High Court in respect of the custody/access decision of a foreign court, the proceedings of which may be taken in the Irish courts on foot of the decision,

---

[176] *ibid.* at p.290.

are expressly limited to those related to "the enforcement of the decision", *i.e.* the Court ought not "look behind" the foreign order.

Refusal of orders of recognition and/or enforcement

10–74   Articles 9 and 10 outline the circumstances in which an application for recognition and enforcement may be refused:[177]

(a) Where procedural defects exist, *e.g.* if a decision in respect of custody or access was made in the absence of the defendant or his or her legal representative, or if the defendant was not duly served with the initiating document in sufficient time to enable him or her to arrange his or her defence (unless service was not effected due to the defendant's concealment of his or her whereabouts).[178] A relevant and instructive case is *C.D. and D.D. (Minors): S.D v R.S.*[179] This approach was endorsed in *M.(P.) v M.(V.)*,[180] when Costello P. refused to endorse the decision of the English courts regarding the custody of two children brought to this jurisdiction by their mother. The High Court, however, found that notice of the proceedings before the English courts had not been properly served on the mother and that she had been made aware of the impending court hearing a mere two days before it took place. She was not therefore in a position to secure legal assistance and representation nor arrange her own travel to the proceedings. The learned judge noted that the child's father had been aware of the whereabouts of the mother and had nonetheless failed to inform her of these matters.[181]

(b) If the effects of the decision are manifestly incompatible with the fundamental principles of the law relating to the family and children in this State.[182]

(c) Where, by reason of a change in circumstances (including the passage of time, not including a mere change in the residence of the child after an improper removal), the effects of the original decision are manifestly no longer in accordance with the welfare of the child.[183]

(d) Where, at the time when the proceedings were instituted in the State of origin, the child was an Irish national, or was habitually resident here and no such connection existed with the State of origin.[184]

---

[177] Note also that proceedings for recognition and enforcement may be adjourned on grounds set out in Art.10(2).
[178] Art.9(1).
[179] [1996] 3 I.R. 524.
[180] unreported, High Court, Kinlen J., November 4, 1997; unreported, Supreme Court, February 20, 1998.
[181] See also *S.(A.) v H.(E.)*, unreported, High Court, Budd J., May 8, 1996, and *P.M. v V.M.*, unreported, Supreme Court, February 20, 1998, in which this approach to the procedural requirements of the Luxembourg Convention was endorsed by the Supreme Court.
[182] Art.10(10)(a). See, for example, *R.J. v M.R.* [1994] 1 I.R. 271 (H.C., S.C.).
[183] Art.10(1)(b).
[184] Art.10(1)(c)(i).

(e) Where, at the time when the proceedings were instituted in the State of
origin, the child was both an Irish national and a national of the State of
origin and was habitually resident in Ireland.[185]

(f) Where the decision is incompatible with a decision given in Ireland, or a
decision enforceable here having been given in a third State, pursuant to
proceedings commenced before the submission of a request for recognition
or enforcement, and if the refusal is in accordance with the welfare of the
child.[186]

10–75 In accordance with the judicial stance taken in respect of the
interpretation of the Hague Convention, the courts have taken a restrictive
approach to the interpretation of the circumstances in which an application for
the return of a child under the Convention will be refused.[187] The applicable
standard of proof is one of "high probability", "something more than the
probability appropriate for ordinary proof in civil actions".[188]

If, at the time of the removal, there is no custody order in force, Article 12
of the Convention provides that the Luxembourg Convention may apply to an
order made after the removal, if it also contains a declaration that the removal
was wrongful.

10–76 In the case of *C. v B.*,[189] s.34(1) of the Child Abduction and
Enforcement of Custody Orders Act 1991 fell to be considered by the Supreme
Court. This section provides that where "a court in the State makes a decision
relating to the custody of a child who has been removed from the State that
court may also, on an application made by any person for the purposes of
Art.12 of the Luxembourg Convention, make a declaration that the removal of
the child from the State was unlawful if it is satisfied that the applicant has an
interest in the matter and that the child has been taken from or sent or kept out
of the State without the consent of any of the persons having the right to
determine the child's place of residence under the law of the State".

The Supreme Court ruled that the phrase "a court" was not defined by the
1991 Act, whereas the words "the court" are clearly different[190] and refer
exclusively to the High Court by virtue of s.2 of the 1991 Act. The Supreme
Court held that s.34(1) of the 1991 Act applies to "a court" which makes a
decision relating to the custody of a child and then gives it consequential
jurisdiction to make the declaration. It was held that, accordingly, the High
Court had no jurisdiction pursuant to s.34(1) of the 1991 Act to make an order
declaring that the removal of the minor at issue in the proceedings was unlawful,
as it had made no decision relating to custody in the case. As a custody order
had previously been made by the District Court, the Supreme Court ruled that

---

[185] Art.10(1)(c)(ii).

[186] Art.10(1)(d).

[187] See, for example, *R.J. v M.R.* [1994] 1 I.R. 271 (H.C., S.C.) and *S.M. v A.J.B.* [1994] 3
I.R. 491 (H.C.).

[188] *R.J. v M.J.*, *ibid.*

[189] [1996] 1 I.L.R.M. 63.

[190] *ibid.* at 68.

a declaration pursuant to s.34(1) of the 1991 Act "may be made only, in this instance, by the District Court".[191]

The Supreme Court also ruled that the declaration made by the High Court to the effect that the removal of the child constituted a breach of the plaintiff's custody rights "was not a decision relating to custody ... and not being such it did not give jurisdiction to make an order declaring that the removal of the minor from the State was unlawful".

Onus of proof

10–77 In the case of *S.M. v A.J.B.*,[192] it was held by Morris J. that, where a defendant relied on Art.10(1)(b) of the Luxembourg Convention, the word "manifestly" in Art.10(1)(b) placed an onus of proof upon him or her to establish to a standard of proof higher than that required in civil actions that the order of the English court was no longer in accordance with the welfare of the child at issue in the proceedings.

In *R.J. v M.R.*,[193] the Supreme Court ruled that the word "manifestly" in Art.10(1)(a) and (b) placed an onus of proof upon the party objecting to the return of the child in reliance upon those provisions to establish his or her case to a high degree of probability.

Amendment of pleadings

10–78 It is noteworthy that in the case of *S.(A.) v H.(E.) and H.(M.)*[194] proceedings were instituted under the Luxembourg Convention. The plaintiff applied to amend the proceedings to include a claim under the Hague Convention. Budd J., in acceding to the plaintiff's application, quoted with approval from the case of *Cropper v Smith*:[195]

> "[I]t is a well established principle that the object of the Courts is to decide the rights of the parties, and not to punish them for mistakes they make in the conduct of their cases by deciding otherwise than in accordance with their rights. I know of no kind of error or mistake which, if not fraudulent or intended to overreach, the Court ought not to correct, if it can be done without injustice to the other party".

Form of request does not limit jurisdiction

10–79 In the case of *R.J. v M.R.*,[196] Carroll J. in the High Court ruled that the case before her fell to be dealt with pursuant to Art.10 of the Luxembourg Convention and ordered that the child, J., should be returned to the jurisdiction of the courts of England and Wales. On appeal to the Supreme Court, it was argued by the defendant/appellant that, since the request for the return of the

---

[191] *ibid.* at 69.
[192] [1994] 3 I.R. 491.
[193] [1994] 1 I.R. 271 (H.C., S.C.).
[194] unreported, High Court, Budd J., May 8, 1996.
[195] (1884) 26 Ch. D. 700.
[196] [1994] 1 I.R. 271 (H.C., S.C.).

child transmitted by the Lord Chancellor's Department in England to the Irish Department of Justice was a request formulated pursuant to the Hague Convention, it was not open to the trial judge to make an order pursuant to the provisions of the Luxembourg Convention.

It was held by the Supreme Court in dismissing the appeal that, *inter alia*, s.25 of the Child Abduction and Enforcement of Custody Orders Act 1991:

> "must ... inevitably be construed as giving a clear right to an Applicant who has obtained an order relating to the custody of a child in another Contracting State to seek as a plaintiff relief from the courts within this State. Any interpretation limiting the jurisdiction of the court to enforce the Luxembourg Convention merely by reason of the form or timing of a request from a Central Authority in respect of the same child would be a completely unjustified ouster of the ordinary jurisdiction of the court".[197]

Conclusion

10–80   Given the more limited "defences" available to defendants and the narrower margin of discretion available to the courts in proceedings instituted under the Luxembourg Convention, it would appear to be in the interests of a person seeking the return of a child wrongfully or improperly removed, or retained, to institute proceedings under the Luxembourg Convention as opposed to the Hague Convention, where it is possible to do so.

However, as demonstrated by the decision of the High Court in *C.D. and D.D. (minors): S.D. v R.S.*,[198] and the Supreme Court in *P.M. v V.M.*,[199] it is imperative that there is strict compliance with the provisions of the 1991 Act. Almost certainly, failure to satisfy the procedural requirements of Arts 9 and 10 of the Convention will be fatal to an application.

CHILD ABDUCTION AND IRISH LAW

Child Abduction and Enforcement of Custody Orders Act 1991

10–81   As indicated above, the Child Abduction and Enforcement of Custody Orders Act 1991 brought both the Hague and Luxembourg Conventions into force in Irish law on October 1, 1991. Applications under the Act may be made to the High Court directly or through the Irish Central Authority. It is clear that the Conventions do not oust the jurisdiction of the Court, as s.11 of the 1991 Act expressly provides that nothing in Pt II of the Act (the Part dealing with the Hague Convention) "shall prevent a person from applying in the first instance to the Court, whether or not under the Hague Convention, in respect of the breach of rights of custody of, or breach of rights of access to, a child

---

[197]   *ibid.* at 289.
[198]   [1996] 3 I.R. 524.
[199]   unreported, Supreme Court, February 20, 1998 (*nem. diss.*).

removed to the State". Section 25 of the 1991 Act contains a similar provision in respect of applications pursuant to the Luxembourg Convention.

The Court referred to in the 1991 Act is the High Court.[200] In addition to applications for the return of children to their country of habitual residence and for the recognition and enforcement of foreign court orders, applications may be made to the High Court for interim directions[201] and for a stay on any other proceedings pending before the Courts.[202]

10–82 Section 36 of the 1991 Act provides that, where, in proceedings under Pt II or Pt III of the 1991 Act, for orders retaining a child, or recognising or enforcing a decision in respect of a child, "there is not available to the Court adequate information as to the whereabouts of the child, the Court may order any person who, it has reason to believe, may have relevant information to disclose it to the Court."

Section 37 empowers a member of an Garda Síochána to detain a child "who[m] he reasonably suspects is about to be or is being removed from the State" in breach of, *inter alia*, custody or access orders, an order made relating to the wardship of the child, orders made under child protection legislation, and certain orders made under the 1991 Act. Significantly, the Gardaí are also empowered to detain a child in such circumstances "while proceedings for one of those orders are pending or an application for one of those orders is about to be made". Accordingly, this power may be invoked quite strategically by, for example, a person who wishes to prevent an abduction by: obtaining an Irish order prohibiting the removal of the child from the jurisdiction; and/or directing the surrender of the child's passport; and/or the delivery of the child into the custody of a specified person; or if necessary, by an application to have the child admitted to wardship.

Child abduction rules

10–83 Section 38(2) of the Child Abduction and Enforcement of Custody Orders Act 1991 provides that Rules of Court may be made for the expeditious hearing of an application under the Hague and Luxembourg Conventions. These rules were made in 2001.

S.I. No. 94 of 2001 sets down the rules regarding child abduction and inserts Ord.133 into the Rules of the Superior Courts. The principal rule governing applications for the return of a child removed to or from the State is r.2. It provides that all applications shall be brought by way of special summons as follows:

---

[200] s.2.

[201] ss.12 and 15.

[202] s.13.

The High Court

Family Law

In the Matter of the Child Abduction and Enforcement of
Custody Orders Act, 1991

and In the Matter of the _____ Convention (as the case
may be)

and in the Matter of [X], a minor,

Between

AB,

applicant

and

CD,

respondent.

Under r.2, an affidavit verifying proceedings is required and is to have regard
to the matters detailed in Art.8 of the Hague Convention 1980.[203] The affidavit
should, where possible, be accompanied by the following:

(a) information on the identity of the applicant, the child and the person alleged
to have removed or retained the child;

(b) where available, the child's birth certificate;

(c) the grounds on which the application for the return of the child is based;

(d) all available information as to the child's whereabouts and the identity of
the person with whom the child is presumed to be.

10–84   Rule 4 provides that a respondent may deliver a replying affidavit
and that replying affidavit must be served on the applicant within seven days
of the grounding affidavit having been served upon the respondent. The replying
affidavit must detail the grounds of defence being relied upon in opposition to
the applicant's application.[204] Rule 4(3) enables the applicant to file a further
affidavit replying to any issue or matter alluded to by the respondent within
seven days after the service upon the applicant of the respondent's affidavit.

Rule 5 requires the court to facilitate an early hearing, which is to be
conducted on the basis of affidavit evidence only, save in exceptional
circumstances where the court may "direct or permit oral evidence to be
adduced".

---

[203] r.3(1).
[204] r.4(2).

Interface with other Irish statutes

10–85 Other Irish statutes which may interface with an abduction, removal or retention situation are the Guardianship of Infants Act 1964, as amended,[205] the Family Law Act 1995[206] and the Non-Fatal Offences Against the Persons Act 1997.[207]

Child abduction as an offence

10–86 The act of child abduction has been categorised as a criminal offence by virtue of ss.16 and 17 of the Non-Fatal Offences Against the Person Act 1997. A breach of ss.16 or 17, upon summary conviction, may lead to a fine not exceeding £1,500 or imprisonment for up to 12 months, or both, or, upon conviction on indictment, may lead to a fine or imprisonment for up to seven years, or both.

Sharia Law, Forthcoming Changes and New Provisions

10–87 It would appear that parental child abduction is a growing problem in the Irish Muslim community. At the centre of this problem are tensions between Irish and Sharia law. Sharia law, a form of Islamic religious law, is an all encompassing religious law, which governs all family relationships in the Islamic world independent of any state interference. Under Sharia law, a Muslim parent is required, without exception, to bring his or her children up as Muslims. The Muslim parent may therefore argue that he or she is justified, should conflict arise, in using this as an excuse to abduct his or her children for the purpose of taking them back to an Islamic state. That said, there is no moral or legal justification for the use of culture for the purpose of the abduction of a child.

On August 22, 2002, Morocco became the first Muslim State to ratify the Hague Child Protection Convention 1996. This is a significant development and one that, it is hoped, will facilitate closer co-operation between Morocco and the other State parties to the Convention in solving the complex problem of child abduction.

The revised Brussels II

10–88 The revised Brussels II, discussed in detail in Chapter 12, will bring about a fundamental change in the procedure for dealing with intra-EC Member State child abduction cases, even though the 1980 Hague Convention will continue to apply.[208] It will also cover children aged 16 and over, unlike the

---

[205] In particular, s.3 and s.11 of the Guardianship of Infants Act 1964, as amended.

[206] In particular, s.47 of the Family Law Act 1995, which provides for the procurement of social reports.

[207] In particular, s.16 and s.17 of the Non-Fatal Offences Against the Person Act 1997.

[208] Council Regulation No.2201/2003 Concerning Jurisdiction and the Recognition and Enforcement of Judgments in Matrimonial Matters and Matters Relating to Parental Responsibility Repealing Regulation (EC) No. 1347/2000, [2003] O.J. L338/1.

1980 Hague Convention. At their council meeting of November 29, 2002, the EU justice ministers addressed the relationship between the revised Brussels II and the 1980 Hague Convention on the Civil Aspects of International Child Abduction 1980 (1980 Hague Convention). It was agreed that the courts in the State of the child's habitual residence are to have jurisdiction to make rulings on custody and access rights.[209] The exception to this, which is further elaborated upon in Chapter 12, is where the child has been living with the non-custodial parent for over a year, and the custodial parent has made no request for his or her return. Recital paragraph 17 in the revised Regulation provides that the 1980 Hague Convention will continue to apply in child abduction cases, but will be complemented by Art.11 of the revised Regulation.[210]

Under the revised Brussels II, the courts of the requested Member State can continue to refuse to return a child by invoking the defences provided by the 1980 Hague Convention. Article 11(1) provides that paragraphs 2 to 8 of Art.11 will apply when dealing with applications for the return of a child "wrongfully removed or retained in a Member State other than the Member State where the child was habitually resident immediately before the wrongful removal or retention".

10–89 Article 11(2) requires the court to which an application has been made to issue a judgment on custody without delay, and, in doing so, the child must be heard unless it is inappropriate because of his age and maturity.[211] This mirrors obligations arising under Art.6 of the European Convention for the Protection of Human Rights and Fundamental Freedoms 1950 (ECHR) and Art.12 of the UN Convention on the Rights of the Child 1989. That said, Recital paragraph 19 should be noted, more of which later. It provides: "the hearing of the child plays an important role in the application of this Regulation, although this instrument is not intended to modify national procedures applicable." Article 11(3) of the revised Regulation provides that the court shall, unless exceptional circumstances make this impossible, issue its order no later than six weeks after it is seised of the application.[212]

10–90 Article 11(4) provides that a non-return order pursuant to Art.13(b) of the 1980 Hague Convention cannot be made if it is established that adequate

---

[209] See Art.10 of Council Regulation No.2201/2003.

[210] "(17) In cases of wrongful removal or retention of a child, the return of the child should be obtained without delay, and to this end the Hague Convention of October 25, 1980, would continue to apply as complemented by the provisions of this Regulation, in particular Art.11. The courts of the Member State to or in which the child has been wrongfully removed or retained should be able to oppose his or her return in specific, duly justified cases. However, such a decision could be replaced by a subsequent decision by the court of the Member State of habitual residence of the child prior to the wrongful removal or retention. Should that judgment entail the return of the child, the return should take place without any special procedure being required for recognition and enforcement of that judgment in the Member State to or in which the child has been removed or retained."

[211] See Art.13 of the 1980 Hague Convention.

[212] See Art.11 of the 1980 Hague Convention.

arrangements have been made to protect the child after his return.[213] This will
have less of an impact in common law jurisdictions, where undertakings and
mirror orders have been used for some time to ensure measures are taken in
order to protect the child after return.[214] The legal basis for making mirror
orders, however, is a matter for concern, though it has been suggested that
Art.20 of the revised Regulations might be sufficient to address this issue. It
will however bring about a fundamental change in the civil law of Member
States, where a judge may only order what is provided by statute. In fact,
undertakings are unknown in the civil law system. Uncertainty surrounds who
has to demonstrate that adequate arrangements have been made to secure the
child's protection after his return.

Significantly, as regards the return of the child, a court cannot refuse to
return a child unless the person who requested the return of the child has been
given an opportunity to be heard.[215] This may lead to an increase in oral
evidence in child abduction cases, which as the Practice Guide states, might
include the applicant being heard in his home state through a video-link facility.

10–91   Under Art.11(6), if a court issues an order for non-return under Art.13
of the 1980 Hague Convention, the court must send a copy of the court order
on non-return and a transcript of the proceedings, as well as any other relevant
documents, to the competent court in the Member State where the child was
habitually resident immediately before the wrongful removal or retention. The
latter court must receive all the mentioned documents within one month from
the date of the non-return order.

The court seised of the case in the Member State where the child was
habitually resident immediately before the wrongful removal or retention is
expected to notify and invite the parties, including the local authority/health
board, to make submissions within three months of the date of the notification,
so that the court can consider the question of custody.[216] Where a court is not
already seised in the child's state of habitual residence, the court or central
authority that receives the information must notify and invite the parties to
make submissions. If neither parent files custody or access proceedings within
three months of notification, the child will be left in the state to which he or
she has been removed. The child will also remain in the state to which he has
been removed if, following custody proceedings in the state of the child's
habitual residence, custody is awarded to the abducting parent.

10–92   If there are custody proceedings, and should the order involve the
return of the child, it will take precedence over a non-return order made under

---

[213] See s.4 and Annex IV of the revised Brussels II, which requires a judge in the requested
Member State, in ordering the child's return, to include in any certificate issued details
of any protective measures in favour of the child to be taken to ensure the protection of
the child after its return to the Member State of habitual residence. Also, Art.36 of the
1980 Hague Convention.
[214] See paras. 10–66 and 10–90.
[215] See Art.11(5) of the revised Brussels II.
[216] Art.11(7).

Art.13 of the 1980 Hague Convention.[217] An abducting parent would not be in a position to challenge the recognition of this order as it comes within the automatic recognition procedure provided for in Art.42. An order for the return of a child made under Art.11(8) of the revised Brussels II is recognised and enforceable in another Member State without any declaration of enforceability and without any opportunity for the recognition of such an order to be challenged. The only requirement necessary to avail of this expedited recognition is that the judgment be certified in the Member State of origin to make sure that it has satisfied the minimum grounds of procedural fairness.[218] The court in the Member State where the child was habitually resident before the wrongful removal or retention must also take into account "the reasons for and evidence underlying the (non-return) order issued pursuant to Art.13 of the 1980 Hague Convention".[219] Article 42 places a premium on the removal of all intermediate steps to the recognition of judgments.

The provisions on the rights of the child in this part of the revised Regulation are very much to be welcomed, though they stop short of requiring necessary procedural changes in the Member States' domestic law.

10–93 In summary, the effect of this section of the revised Regulation will be to change the application of the 1980 Hague Convention within the EU. It will allow courts in the Member States to which the child has been abducted to make non-return orders, but leave the courts of the child's habitual residence to make final orders requiring the return of the child. In effect, this approach undermines mutual trust between the Member States and will do little to promote co-operation between the courts of the Member State.

While it is the case that the 1980 Hague Convention is not being "communitarised" by the revised Brussels II, it must be acknowledged that a different regime will apply to abduction within Member States and outside such states. This is regrettable in that it will change the dynamic and operation of the 1980 Hague Convention within the European Union. While the revised Brussels II will, in reality, take precedence where the child is within the EU, the 1980 Hague Convention applies where the child is outside the European Union.[220] This should make for some interesting forum shopping by personal litigants.

PROCEDURE

10–94 Applications for Orders pursuant to the 1991 Act are made to the High Court and are initiated by way of special summons, grounded on an

---

[217] Art.11(8). The justification advanced for this approach has been that the main objective of the 1980 Hague Convention is, after all, that the state of a child's habitual residence is the jurisdiction best equipped to adjudicate on any dispute relating to the child and not the state to which the child has been abducted.
[218] Art.42(2).
[219] Art.42(2)(c).
[220] Art.60(e).

affidavit. Usually, a notice of motion is also prepared mirroring the summons.[221] Circumstances usually dictate that the proceedings are first brought before the Court by way of an *ex parte* application on foot of the summons and affidavit seeking an order restraining a named person (usually the defendant), or any person having notice of the order from removing the child or children, who are subject matter of the proceedings, from the jurisdiction, pending the determination of the proceedings. If it is sought, liberty is usually granted in the context of such an application to the solicitor for the plaintiff to notify named persons (usually the Commissioner of An Garda Síochána, port and airport authorities) of the making of the Order.[222]

10–95 In general, and in addition to the above-mentioned restraining order, the plaintiff will be granted liberty to serve short notice of a Motion for interlocutory relief, and the matter will be made returnable for a number of days following the application. In relation to applications for recognition of an Order, or in other cases as appropriate, if the proposed defendant or appropriate notice parties reside outside the jurisdiction, it will be necessary in the first instance to bring an *ex parte* application seeking liberty to issue and serve the special summons and all other subsequent and ancillary documentation outside the jurisdiction. This application is made by way of *ex parte* Docket, grounded on an affidavit. Where the proposed defendant is not an Irish citizen, liberty to serve a notice of the special summons should be sought. In the usual way, where there are difficulties in effecting service, an *ex parte* application may be made for substituted service.

10–96 When the matter comes before the court on foot of the notice of motion, an application may then be made for an early hearing date. In accordance with the directions of the Supreme Court in relation to cases under the 1991 Act, all efforts must be made to ensure that the case proceeds to hearing with due expedition. At this stage in many cases, the defendant will appear to the motion and seek time to put in a replying affidavit. It may be appropriate for either or both of the parties to indicate to the court that an affidavit of laws will be necessary and time may be granted to facilitate the preparation of same. It may also be appropriate to seek to have a psychological assessment of the child or children carried out or to apply to have a written report prepared pursuant to s.47 of the Family Law Act 1995 "on any question affecting the welfare of a party to the proceedings or any other person to whom they relate" from such person or body and on such terms as the court may direct.

10–97 The special summons, meanwhile, will be returnable to the Master's Court and the return date will usually be approximately four or five weeks after the date of issue. Given that speed is of the essence, the High Court will usually effectively treat the notice of motion as a notice of trial and the application will very often be determined prior to the return date allocated to the special summons.

---

[221] See Appendix 13.
[222] *ibid.*

10–98   If the defendant or the notice parties are not present in court, the plaintiff must be in a position to prove service of all the pleadings to the satisfaction of the court. The plaintiff must also ensure that all of the relevant court orders (*i.e.* the Order(s) sought to be enforced or recognised), or duly authenticated and acceptable copies of same, are available for the court, as well as, where applicable, court welfare (or similar) reports prepared for the Courts of the jurisdiction in which the Orders were granted. Other proofs include certificates of enforceability from the Central Authority of the Requesting State, the birth certificates for the child or children who are subject matter of the proceedings, and, where relevant, any other court orders granted in respect of the parties or the children.

When the matter comes on for hearing, the court may direct that it is necessary or appropriate to hear the oral evidence of the parties. It is also open to each of the parties to serve a notice of intention to cross-examine on the other side in respect of the affidavits filed.

Practice direction

10–99   Following the comments of the Supreme Court on the delay in bringing the child abduction action to completion in *E.M. v J.M.*,[223] a practice direction was issued on July 17, 2003. The practice direction included the recommendations of the Supreme Court in *E.M. v J.M.* in respect of the listing of appeals for mention the Friday after lodgment. It also incorporates the new methods outlined by the Supreme Court for speeding up appeals, and states:

> "As from July 21, 2003 in all cases in which a notice of appeal from a judgment of the High Court in proceedings under the [Child Abduction and Enforcement of Custody Orders Act 1991] is lodged, the case will be listed for mention on the following Friday. The practitioners engaged in the appeal must be in a position to indicate to the court, when the case is called on that day, what steps have been taken in order to ensure the expeditious hearing of the appeal. The court will give directions at that time as to the filing of written submissions and an early date will be fixed for the hearing of the appeal.
>
> The Practice Direction is being issued in order to ensure that the State complies with those provisions of The Hague Convention requiring promptness and expedition in the disposal of proceedings under the Convention.
>
> In the event of the notice of appeal being lodged during the vacation, the appeal will be listed for mention on the first Friday of the following term."

---

[223] unreported, Supreme Court, July 9, 2003.

RECOMMENDATIONS FOR REFORM

1. Child abduction within the State

10–100   Section 16 of the Non-Fatal Offences Against the Person Act 1997 established a new offence of abduction of a child under the age of 16 out of the State by his or her parent or guardian. While this section makes abduction out of the State an offence, it does not appear to cover taking a child within the State. The latter situation can only be dealt with through normal custody proceedings. Section 16 of the 1997 Act should, therefore, be amended without delay but in a manner that will not prejudice domestic violence victims who leave the family home to escape the violence. Similarly, s.36 of the Child Abduction and Enforcement of Custody Orders Act 1991 should be amended. This section, which gives the court the power to order the disclosure of a child's whereabouts, is confined to child abductions out of the State but does not appear to cover a situation where a child is not taken out of the country.

2. Domestic violence

10–101   The 1980 Hague Convention can operate unjustly when applied to domestic violence victims who abduct to escape the violence—it should be noted that domestic violence causes children real harm. The courts of the Member States are only now awakening to the injustices that can result from applying the 1980 Hague Convention to domestic violence victims.[224] Greater efforts must be made to be sensitive to the 1980 Hague Convention's remedy of return in circumstances where the abductor is a victim of domestic violence.

3. Rights of non-marital fathers

10–102   The rights of non-marital fathers under the 1980 Hague Convention present particular difficulties and need to be addressed, given the fact that in a number of countries, including Ireland, they do not have an automatic right to custody equivalent to those of the married parents.

4. Delay

10–103   Time is of the essence in child abduction cases. Article 11 of the 1980 Hague Convention states that applications should be resolved within a six-week period. In *S. v S.*[225] and *M.(E.) ex parte v M.(J.)*,[226] Denham J., in noting that delay has the potential to defeat the purpose of the Convention, stated that parties and professionals should display special diligence in expediting child abduction proceedings. The current delay in the procurement and completion of social reports in Ireland and the difficulties encountered in retaining guardians *ad litem* must surely fall to be considered in this context.

---

[224] See *Re F. (Child Abduction: Risk if Returned)* [1995] 2 Fam. L. Rep. 31.
[225] [1998] 2 I.R. 244.
[226] unreported, Supreme Court, Denham J., July 9, 2003.

5. Mediation

10–104 It is obviously desirable for all parties that, if at all possible, a solution be reached by means other than court proceedings. To this end, mediation should be actively promoted to assist in securing the return of the child to the parent who has the legal right to custody.

CONCLUSION

10–105 Relative to other international instruments, the 1980 Hague Convention is generally regarded as a successful Convention. In particular, it should be noted that the number of cases where returns are refused on the basis of one of the exceptions having been proven is very low. It would seem, however, that the progress achieved by the 1980 Hague Convention could be imperilled by a competing European Union instrument. In so far as the proposed new Council Regulation, known as the revised Brussels II, will impact on the client, any material conflict in substance or practice between the revised Brussels and the 1980 Hague Convention, which instruments have the same subject matter, but a different geographical scope, is likely to cause difficulty, uncertainty and increased costs. The advantages brought about by an added tier of legislation in the form of the revised Regulation are not obvious, though the pitfalls and tripwires are many.

CHAPTER 11

CHILDREN IN CONFLICT WITH THE LAW AND MISCELLANEOUS MATTERS

11–01   The Children Act 2001,[1] together with the Children Act 1941[2] and the Children's (Amendment) Act 1957,[3] deals with the treatment of unruly children or those children with special needs and those found to be in breach of the criminal law. The 2001 Act contains 271 sections, designed primarily to overhaul the Children Act 1908. It was signed by President McAleese on July 8, 2001, though several of the provisions of the Act are not yet in force.[4] The National Children's Office has the lead role in relation to co-ordinating the implementation of the Children Act 2001. Part 10 (with the exception of s.159(1) which is already in force) of the 2001 Act is to enter into force by the end of 2004. The Act may not be fully in force until 2007.

11–02   The Children Act 2001 repeals the Children Act 1908. It establishes a children's court and sets out provisions for the disposal of children and young persons after conviction. The 2001 Act is primarily concerned with matters of juvenile justice, with the exception of Pt 3, which amends the Child Care Act 1991. It has 13 parts, which will be discussed in detail. The 2001 Act is the culmination of three decades of debate[5] and attempts to put a modern statutory framework for dealing with juvenile justice in place. It adopts neither a welfare nor a justice model of youth justice. Rather, it reflects a rights-based approach, imported in large measure from international imperatives. It provides for family welfare conferences and other new provisions to deal with unruly children or those children with special needs. A comprehensive strategy on restorative cautioning and conferencing is introduced. Broadly speaking, the 2001 Act supports the philosophy that children in conflict with the law must be treated as children first. It is based on the premise that detention should be used only as a last resort and should only be considered after a range of community-based measures (detailed in Pt 9 of the Act) have been exhausted.

---

[1]   S.I. No. 24 of 2001.
[2]   S.I. No. 12 of 1941.
[3]   S.I. No. 28 of 1957.
[4]   See Children Act 2001 (Commencement) Order 2002 (S.I. No. 151 of 2002); Children Act 2001 (Part 11) (Commencement) Order 2003 (S.I. No. 527 of 2003); Children Act 2001 (Commencement) Order 2004 (S.I. No. 468 of 2004); Child Care Act 1991 (Commencement) Order 2004 (S.I. No. 547 of 2004); and Children Act 2001 (Commencement) (No.2) Order 2004 (S.I. No. 548 of 2004).
[5]   See the Kennedy Report (1970), the Henchy Report (1974), the Task Force on Child Care Services (1980), the Whitaker Report (1985) and the Report of the Dáil Select Committee on Crime (1992).

11–03   While the provisions of the 2001 Act signpost a movement towards a more progressive juvenile justice system, a number of shortcomings in the Act should be noted. The Act does not acknowledge the socio-economic context that encourages deviant behaviour in children. The concept of the family conference is imported from New Zealand, a jurisdiction which views the family as the solution to the problems of the child in conflict with the law. The Children Act 2001 sees the family as the primary cause of the problems encountered by troublesome children. For example, ss.111 to 114 of the 2001 Act attempt to sanction failed parenting. A similar approach is not adopted when the State is fulfilling a parenting role. In fact, the State as a parent has had a disturbing history. It is a question of double standards. While the Children Act 2001 sends a clear message to parents regarding care, it does not send a similar message to the State. In summary, the State is effectively immune from prosecution.

11–04   The District Court (Children) Rules 2004[6] amend the District Court Rules 1997[7] to facilitate applications under the various sections of the Children Act 2001. These rules came into operation on October 14, 2003, and are to be found in the Appendix.

PART I

PRELIMINARY

11–05   The word "child" has been defined in s.3(1) of the 2001 Act, in line with the definition of a child under the Child Care Act 1991,[8] to mean "a person under the age of 18 years".

Types of conferencing

11–06   Three types of conferencing are provided for under the Children Act 2001. The first is the family welfare conference, which is provided for in Pt 2 of the Act and in the Children (Family Welfare Conference) Regulations 2004.[9] It is to be convened by the health board and deals with young people who are not offenders, but whose behaviour presents a serious risk either to themselves or others. Where it appears to a health board that a child in its area is in need of special care and protection, a family welfare conference must be convened under Pt 2 of the 2001 Act before the board can apply for a special care order under Pt 3, more of which later. The family welfare conference provisions were commenced on September 23, 2004, with the exception of ss.7(1)(a), 10(2) and 13(2).[10]

---

[6]   S.I. No. 539 of 2004.
[7]   S.I. No. 93 of 1997.
[8]   S.I. No. 17 of 1991.
[9]   S.I. No. 549 of 2004.
[10]   See Children Act 2001 (Commencement) (No.2) Order 2004 (S.I. No. 548 of 2004).

The second type of conference is the Garda conference, as the garda juvenile liaison scheme is now to be known.[11] The Garda conference has been in force since May 1, 2002.

The third type of conference is a family conference, which is convened under Pt 8 of the Act by the Probation and Welfare Service where a child is charged with an offence and the court considers that a family conference is desirable. It is a valuable link between the child care/welfare system and the criminal law. The family conference provisions, ss.78 to 87, were commenced on July 29, 2004.[12]

PART II

Family Welfare Conferences

Introduction

11–07   Part 2 of the Children Act 2001 establishes for the first time on a statutory basis provisions for early intervention at an inter-agency level for children at risk by the holding of a family welfare conference. The concept of a family welfare conference has been imported from the family group conference, a term which originally came from New Zealand, where it forms an integral part of the youth justice system. Health boards are empowered under the Act to establish family welfare conferences in appropriate cases in respect of children at risk who have not committed offences, and children before the court for their criminal behaviour but whom the court considers may need care and protection. Family welfare conferences provide a useful framework within which a child, his or her family and the appropriate agencies can find solutions to the problems that have led to the child's vulnerable situation. It empowers families to come to their own solutions in co-operation with the relevant professionals. The emphasis is on consensus and partnership, in line with the approach adopted in the New Zealand family group conference, from which this approach was imported. One of the most significant and progressive elements of the family welfare conference is that children will be present at the conference. Two core principles underlying the family welfare conference are that the child's interests are paramount and that, in so far as is possible, the child is best looked after within his or her own family.

11–08   The Children (Family Welfare Conference) Regulations 2004, which came into force on September 24, 2004, provide a framework and context for the holding of family welfare conferences. They prescribe certain matters pertaining to the administration and operation of family welfare conferences.

---

[11] See Pt 4 of the Children Act 2001.
[12] See Children Act 2001 (Commencement) Order 2004 (S.I. No. 468 of 2004) and District Court (Children) (No.2) Rules 2004 (S.I. No. 666 of 2004).

Family welfare conference

11–09 A family welfare conference is convened under s.7 of the 2001 Act by a co-ordinator appointed by the health board. The co-ordinator[13] will act as chairperson of the family welfare conference. Section 7 also identifies the circumstances in which a family welfare conference may be convened. It can be triggered in two ways: on the direction of the court, where it considers that a child before it on a criminal charge may be in need of special care or protection, or where it appears to a health board that a child in its functional area may require special care or protection.

The basic purpose of the family welfare conference is to produce a plan for the future care, protection and development of the child. This will involve the family taking responsibility for the child, and coming up with proposals for the plan with the assistance of the professionals attending the conference. Section 8 sets out the functions of the family welfare conference. It can decide whether a child is in need of special care and protection which he or she is unlikely to receive unless a special care order is made. If it decides that the child is in need of a special care order, it shall recommend to the health board that it seek such an order. If it does not so decide, it may make recommendations to the health board on the care and protection requirements of the child, including the seeking of a supervision order or a care order under the Child Care Act 1991, or the provision of services and assistance to the child and his family. The family welfare conference is designed to ensure that children who require special care and protection will only be sent to a special care unit as a last resort.

11–10 One of the fundamental principles of the family welfare conference is that agreement should be unanimous. Therefore, s.8(2) requires any recommendations made by a family welfare conference to be unanimous, unless the co-ordinator regards the objection of any participant unreasonable. Where unanimity cannot be achieved, s.8(3) provides that the matter revert to the health board for determination.[14]

11–11 In convening a family welfare conference, the co-ordinator should discuss with all the parties the persons he believes should be permitted to participate in this conference. The guiding test for participation is the welfare of the child, which is defined in Art.4 of the Family Welfare Conference Regulations 2004. By virtue of s.9 of the 2001 Act, a variety of different people are entitled to attend a family welfare conference, including:

- the child and his parents or guardians;[15]
- any guardian *ad litem* appointed;[16]

---

[13] See Art.3 of the 2004 Family Welfare Conference Regulations for a definition of "co-ordinator".

[14] See also Art.7(5) of the Family Welfare Conference Regulations 2004.

[15] s.9(1)(a) and (b).

[16] s.9(1)(c).

- other relatives, as determined by the co-ordinator, following consultation with the child and his parents or guardians;[17] and
- an officer or officers of the health board.[18]

11–12   Under s.9(1)(f), the co-ordinator can permit other persons to attend whom, "in the opinion of the co-ordinator…" could make a positive contribution to the conference. This subsection could facilitate the presence of a solicitor at the family welfare conference. Section 9(2) of the 2001 Act should be noted. It provides:

> "If, before or during a family welfare conference, the co-ordinator is of the opinion that the presence or continued presence of any person is not in the best interests of the conference or the child, the co-ordinator may exclude that person from participation or further participation in the conference."

The foregoing is an important provision in that someone contributing negatively to a conference should be excluded from it.

11–13   Attendance at a family welfare conference is considered in Art.6(1) of the Family Welfare Conference Regulations 2004. Article 6(2) is to be noted in that it opens up the possibility of a researcher attending a conference to undertake evidence and research.

11–14   Section 10 of the 2001 Act deals with the procedure at the family welfare conference and provides that each family welfare conference will generally set down its own procedures and time frame. Article 7(2) of the Family Welfare Conference Regulations 2004 requires, as far as is reasonably practicable, the co-ordinator to inform each person entitled to attend a conference, in writing, of the procedures and objectives of the conference. Section 11 requires the health board to provide such administrative services as are necessary. Section 12 requires the co-ordinator to notify the recommendations of the conference to the participants and any other body or persons the co-ordinator deems appropriate. Section 13 sets out how the health boards are to give effect to the recommendations of a family welfare conference. It may either apply for a special care order, a care order, a supervision order or provide appropriate services and assistance for the child and his family. Section 14(1) provides that no evidence shall be admissible in court regarding any information, statement or admission disclosed in the course of the family welfare conference. It states:

> "No evidence shall be admissible in any court of any information, statement or admission disclosed or made in the course of a family welfare conference."

---

[17] s.9(1)(d).
[18] s.9(1)(e).

Section 14(2) renders admissible, of necessity, the recommendation or decision of a family welfare conference.

11–15   The family welfare conference as a participate model of child care is very much to be welcomed. That said, a more pro-active approach is needed in that family welfare conferences will only be convened when crisis intervention is necessary. This part of the Act errs in terms of omission in that it does not facilitate early intervention in families with difficulties.

PART III

CHILDREN IN NEED OF SPECIAL CARE OR PROTECTION

Special care orders

Introduction

11–16   The Children Act 2001 introduces a "special care order", designed to provide for children in need of special care or protection. This part of the Act was commenced on September 23, 2004,[19] with the exception of s.23D, which allows for an emergency special care order. The concept of special care orders is imported from New Zealand and is designed to maximise the use of a child's social and family support networks at a time of crisis in his or her life.

Part 3 of the Children Act amends the Child Care Act 1991 by inserting a new Part IVA into the 1991 Act. The latter Act was widely criticised for failing to make provision for secure placements for unruly children in need of care. The High Court partly filled the gap, using its inherent jurisdiction over children to order secure detention.[20] Prior to this, unruly children could only be so detained by being "criminalised", that is, by being charged with an offence so that the courts could have jurisdiction over them. The new approach was sanctioned by the Supreme Court in *D.G. v Eastern Health Board*.[21] There, the Court ruled that, though the High Court's jurisdiction involved the deprivation of the child's right to liberty, this was justified by the requirement that the child's welfare be promoted as a paramount consideration. Where the child's welfare required that he or she be placed in secure detention, such detention was, the Court said, permissible. The child did not need to be charged or convicted in relation to a criminal offence in order for him or her to be detained for his or her own best interests.

11–17   The Supreme Court decision in *D.G. v Eastern Health Board*[22] was

---

[19] See Children Act 2001 (Commencement) (No.2) Order 2004 (S.I. No. 548 of 2004).

[20] See *F.N. v Minister for Health* [1995] 1 I.R. 409; *D.B. v Minister for Justice* [1999] 1 I.R. 29, and *T.D. v Minister for Education, Ireland, the Attorney General, the Eastern Health Board and the Minister for Health and Children*, unreported, High Court, Kelly J., February 25, 2000.

[21] [1998] 1 I.L.R.M. 241.

[22] *ibid.*

subsequently appealed to the European Court of Human Rights, which issued its judgment on May 16, 2002.[23] The case challenged the legality of detaining in St. Patrick's Institution a 16-year-old non-offending child with serious behavioural problems. Article 5 of the European Convention on Human Rights (ECHR) guarantees the right to liberty and security, though this right is not an absolute right. It provides as follows:

1.   Everyone has the right to liberty and security of person. No one shall be deprived of his liberty save in the following cases and in accordance with a procedure prescribed by law:

      ...

      (d) the detention of a minor by lawful order for the purpose of educational supervision or his lawful detention for the purpose of bringing him before the competent legal authority;

      ...

5.   Everyone who has been the victim of arrest or detention in contravention of the provisions of this Article shall have an enforceable right to compensation.

This Article has been invoked in cases involving disturbed children, for whom there are at present insufficient high support units in Ireland and where, in many cases, these children are held in penal institutions for want of appropriate accommodation. Ireland was found to be in breach of Art.5 of the ECHR. The European Court of Human Rights held that the detention of the child in St. Patrick's Institution in *D.G.* was in contravention of rights guaranteed under Art.5.1 of the ECHR. The court ruled that the Irish State acted unlawfully in failing to provide the disturbed child with a safe, suitable therapeutic unit and upheld the claim that the child's human rights were violated and his right to compensation denied. It noted, in particular, the fact that St Patrick's was not "an interim custody measure for the purpose of an educational supervisory regime which was followed speedily by the application of such a regime".

Child Care Act 1991

11–18   The new Part IVA of the Child Care Act 1991 is introduced by s.16 of the 2001 Act and came into force on September 23, 2004, with the exception of s.23(1).[24] For this purpose, s.16 has introduced several new sections to be inserted into the 1991 Act. Section 23A of the 1991 Act is arguably the most important of these. It imposes a duty on the relevant health board to apply for a special care order, or an interim care order, in all cases where it appears that a child who resides or is found in its area needs special care and attention that he or she is unlikely to receive unless the court makes such an order. Before applying for the order, however, the board must arrange for the convening of a family welfare conference under Pt 2, ss.7 to 15 of the Children Act 2001. The

---

[23] See *D.G. v Ireland*, ECHR, judgment of May 16, 2002 and Chap.12.
[24] See Children Act 2001 (Commencement) (No.2) Order 2004 (S.I. No. 548 of 2004).

purpose of the family conference is to formulate an action plan for the child and to consider whether a special care order ought to be applied for. The principles underlying the conference are that the child's interests are paramount and that in so far as it is practicable the child is best looked after within his or her own family. If, on completion of its deliberations, a health board wishes to proceed with an application for a special care order, the views of the special residential services board, established in Pt 11, must be sought.[25]

11–19   Where a health board seeks an interim special care order, it is required to arrange a family welfare conference if such a conference is not already in place, or the board must be in the process of seeking the views of the special residential services board. The philosophy of the Children Act 2001 is that the application for a special care order should only be used as a last resort. Special secure units are the ultimate level of care for a child, in that the Act also permits boards to provide alternative arrangements or other accommodation for the child in need of special care or protection as part of the programme for the care, education and treatment of the child, from family support services to special fostering arrangements to ordinary residential care.

11–20   As with care orders and supervision orders, only the health board, the statutory body with responsibility for promoting the welfare of children at risk, can make the final decision as to whether to apply for a special care order. The parents of a child may, under s.23A(3), request the health board to make an application for a special care order in respect of a child. Should the board refuse to accede to this request, it is required to inform the parents in writing of such refusal.

11–21   Special care orders are only to be granted when the conditions set out in s.23B of the 1991 Act have been satisfied. These stipulate that the court may make an order where it is satisfied that:

(i)   the child's behaviour poses a real and substantial risk to his or her health, safety, development or welfare; and

(ii) the child requires special care or protection which he or she is unlikely to receive unless the court makes such an order.

11–22   Section 23B therefore gives health boards the power to detain a child in a special care unit on receipt of a court order, where his behaviour is such that it poses a real and substantial threat to his health, safety, development or welfare, and he is in need of special care and protection. The application is

---

[25] Part 11 of the Children Act 2001 provides for the establishment of the special residential services board to co-ordinate residential services for children placed in special care units under Pt 3 of the 2001 Act or detained in detention schools under Pt 10. Non-offending children with behavioural problems who are the subject of special care orders and child offenders are to be placed in separate residential accommodation. Part 11 came into force on November 7, 2003. Part 11 needs to be implemented before Pts 2 and 3 of the Children Act 2001.

made by the health board in the District Court. That said, Pt 3 of the Children Act 2001 will not deprive the High Court of the constitutional jurisdiction it has developed in this area since *F.N. v Minister for Health*.[26] Both jurisdictions will operate concurrently.

Section 23(B)(2) states that a special care order authorises a health board to provide appropriate care, education and treatment for the child in need of special care or protection. Section 23B(3) additionally empowers the board to take such steps as are reasonably necessary to prevent a child in special care from causing injury to himself or others or from escaping from a special care facility. Section 23(B)(5) requires the board to seek a discharge of the special care order in respect of a child where the circumstances which led to the making of the original order no longer exist.

Once made, the order has the effect of committing the child to the care of the health board which applied for the order. The child is to be kept in a special care unit, as defined by s.23K, for a specified period of between three and six months. During this time, the board is required to provide for the care, education and training of the child. On the expiry of the order, it is possible for the board to apply for an extension to it, but only where the conditions that gave rise to the original order still exist.

11–23 The Act also provides for the making of an interim special care order pending the making of a special care order.[27] This can be made for a period of up to 28 days, although a longer period may be chosen if the health board and parents agree. Where action is urgently required and an interim special care order cannot be awaited, s.23D, which has not yet been commenced, allows an emergency special care order to be made. Such order permits the Gardaí to deliver a child into the care of the health board. All orders made under the new provisions are necessarily intended to be interlocutory in nature. Section 23F allows a court on its own motion, or on the application of any person, to vary or discharge any special care order. This permits a parent or guardian to seek a discharge of a special care order. In discharging a special care order, the court can make a supervision order in respect of the child. It is unlikely that the European Court of Human Rights judgment in *D.G. v Ireland*[28] will impact on the constitutionality of special care orders, given the wide interpretation afforded by the European Court to educational supervision. A relevant and instructive case is that of *Koniarska v U.K.*,[29] where the European Court held that placing a child in secure accommodation was not contrary to the ECHR as it amounted to "educational supervision" within the meaning of Art.5 of the ECHR.

11–24 Section 16 of the 2001 Act is unfortunately vague. There is, for example, no satisfactory definition of "substantial risk", or of "health", "safety", "development" of "welfare". Without further clarification, the precise meaning

---

[26] [1995] 1 I.R. 409.
[27] s.23C.
[28] ECHR, judgment of May 16, 2002.
[29] ECHR, judgment of October 12, 2000.

of these terms will have to be worked out on an ad hoc basis in the courts. The fact that such provisions, furthermore, lie in the middle of a criminal justice Act is worrying. Modern legislation, by contrast with the Children Act 1908, deliberately separates child care proceedings from juvenile criminal proceedings, the obvious logic being that action seeking to promote the welfare of the child should at all costs avoid "criminalising" the child. The Children Act 2001, by including special care orders in the midst of measures designed to combat child criminality, arguably blurs this valuable distinction. It is at least arguable that the provision for special care orders should have been contained in a separate amending Act.

11–25   Children in schools of detention may, in some material respects, be in a better position than children taken into special care units. For example, s.179(3) of the Children Act 2001 provides that children in places of detention are to be advised of the institution's rules and routines on admission. It states:

> "A notice containing an abridged version of the rules shall be displayed in a conspicuous place in each children detention school, and a child on admission to such a school shall be given a document which contains information relating to the rules and the daily routine in the school and is written in language appropriate to the age of the children catered for in the school."

Further, s.186(1) of the 2001 Act provides that an inspector shall carry out regular inspections which are to take place at least once every six months of each children detention school. It states:

> "The inspector shall carry out regular inspections (which shall be at least once every six months) of each children detention school and place provided under s.161, paying particular attention to the conditions prevailing in them, the treatment of children detained there, the facilities available to the children and such other matters as the Minister may direct."

However, the same protections do not apply to children admitted to special care units regarding discipline, while s.23K(7)(f) merely refers to a periodic inspection of special care units by authorised persons. Detailed regulations have now been made under s.23(K)(6) regarding the establishment and operation of the special care units,[30] similar to those already in force in relation to residential care centres.[31] The Social Services Inspectorate, set up in 1999, has also drawn up national standards for special care units which provide the basis on which their inspectors form judgments about the quality of care provided in special care units. The regulations, together with the national standards, will assist in ensuring that children placed in special care units

---

[30] See Child Care (Special Cases) Regulations 2004 (S.I. No. 550 of 2004).
[31] See S.I. No. 259 of 1995.

receive the proper care and protection they need. That said, children who have committed crimes are in a better position than those children in need of special care or protection. A similar issue arises in respect of the length of time a child may be detained in a high support unit. It is clear from the foregoing that children in need of special care and protection by definition will not be the subject of criminal proceedings and, therefore, will not have the same protection as children before the courts on criminal charges. For this reason, detailed regulations governing the operation of special care units are critically important, not only to ensure the appropriate services are provided for the child, but also to protect his civil rights.

Child Care (Special Care) Regulations 2004

11–26   Section 23K of the Child Care Act 1991, as inserted by s.16 of the Children Act 2001, specifically requires the Minister for Health and Children to formulate regulations with respect to the operation of special care units. These were enacted on September 24, 2004, as the Child Care (Special Care) Regulations 2004.[32] For the purposes of these regulations, the term "special care unit" refers to "a residential centre provided and operated by a health board, voluntary body or any other person on behalf of a health board and approved by the Minister for Health and Children". In summary, the Child Care (Special Care) Regulations 2004 create a statutory framework for the provision of care in special care units.

11–27   In addition to the greater duties placed on the health board in respect of children in its care, the health board must be satisfied that the following standards are met in each special care unit over which it has jurisdiction.

11–28   Care practices and operation policies   Article 4 of the Child Care (Special Care) Regulations 2004 requires a health board to ensure that appropriate and suitable care practices, operational policies and rules are in place in respect of each special care unit within its functional area, taking into account the number of children accommodated at the unit and the nature of their needs.

11–29   Management and staffing   The health board should be satisfied that there is an adequate number of suitably qualified and experienced staff available to work at each unit within its functional area.[33] Article 5(7) is a welcome provision and requires the vetting of the staff prior to appointment.

11–30   Accommodation   Appropriate and suitable accommodation is to be provided.[34] Whether such accommodation is adequate will be dependent on the number of children residing in the unit and their respective needs. The health board is obliged, in particular, to ensure that there is:

---

[32] S.I. No. 550 of 2004.
[33] Art.5.
[34] Art.6.

(a) a room for each child;

(b) adequate and suitable furniture;

(c) a sufficient number of lavatories, wash basins, baths and showers, with sufficient water, hot and cold. As far as possible such arrangements should respect the need for privacy;

(d) adequate facilities for laundry;

(e) adequate light, heat and ventilation;

(f) sufficiently clean premises, appropriately decorated and maintained in good structural order;

(g) adequate recreation facilities; and

(h) an appropriate and adequate level of security so as to ensure that children can be safely detained in the special care unit.

11–31   Food and cooking facilities   Article 7 requires a health board to ensure, in respect of each special care unit in its functional area, that adequate amounts of food are supplied, having regard to the nutritional needs of the children at the unit. Such food should be property prepared, wholesome and nutritious. There should be a sufficient element of variety and choice. The staff should be particularly mindful of any dietary requirements and proscriptions.

11–32   Fire and safety precautions   Without prejudice to the detailed requirements of the Fire Services Act 1981, Art.8 sets down specific stipulations as to fire safety. Adequate arrangements should be made to ensure that the facilities are otherwise specifically safe, having regard to the structure and fabric of the unit.[35] The requirements detailed in Art.9 are in addition to the obligations imposed by the Safety, Health and Welfare at Work Act 1989. It should be noted that s.12 of the 1989 Act imposes an obligation on the manager of a specific care unit to prepare or have caused to be prepared a safety statement. A safety statement specifies the manner in which health and safety shall be secured in the special care unit.

11–33   Access arrangements   Article 11 imposes an obligation to ensure that adequate arrangements have been made to enable the child to have appropriate access to his parents or guardian, relatives, guardians *ad litem*, and to other persons with a genuine interest in the child.

11–34   Health care   Children at the unit should have access to a general practitioners and psychological services. It should be possible, furthermore, to refer a child, if required, for medical, psychiatric, counselling, therapeutic, dental, opthalmic or other specialist treatment or assessment.

---

[35] Art.9.

11–35   Education   Article 13 provides that adequate arrangements should be in place in each special care unit to ensure access by children placed in the unit to appropriate educational facilities. It is clear from the judgment of the European Court of Human Rights in *Koniarska v UK*,[36] previously discussed, that the legality of detaining a child in a special care unit is contingent on the provision of "educational supervision".

11–36   Religion, ethnicity and culture   Appropriate arrangements should be in place to facilitate the child in practising his or her religion.[37] The individual needs, as well as the ethnic and cultural identity, of each child must also be considered.

11–37   Managing behaviour   Article 15 provides that any breaches of the rules of the special care unit are to be managed in a way that is reasonable, having regard to any directions made under s.19 of the Child Care Act 1991. It should be noted that corporal punishment is outlawed, as is any treatment that could be regarded as cruel, inhuman or degrading.

11–38   Notification of significant events   Each special care unit must notify the health board of any significant event which has an adverse effect on a child who has been placed in the special care unit.[38] The special care unit is also specifically required to notify the child's parents or guardian of any significant event.

11–39   Restraint and single separation   Article 17 provides that a child shall not be physically restrained, save in exceptional circumstances and then only by staff who have received appropriate training in the use of physical restraint. Similarly, Art.18 prevents a child from being locked in a room on his own in any unit, other than his bedroom during usual bedtime hours, save in exceptional circumstances and then only by staff who have received training in the use of procedures to confine or separate a child.

11–40   Complaints procedure   Article 19 provides for the putting in place of procedures for the timely investigation of complaints made by children.

11–41   Care record, register and case record   In respect of every child in a special care unit, the manager is obliged to maintain a case record.[39] Each health board is required to keep a register of all children placed in a special care unit.[40] The health board is additionally required to maintain an up-to-date case record.[41]

---

[36] Judgment of October 12, 2000.
[37] Art.14.
[38] Art.11.
[39] Art.20.
[40] Art.24.
[41] Art.25.

11–42   Care plan   The placement of a child in a special care unit, except in emergency situations, must be preceded by the creation of a care plan in respect of that child.[42] The care plan must be a living document and has to have a reality for the child. The Mid-Western Health Board has conducted very useful research in this area.

11–43   Review of cases   Article 28 requires that regular reviews should be undertaken in respect of each child placed in a special care unit. In particular, in the first month after placement, and once every month thereafter, the care plan drawn up in respect of each child should be reviewed by an authorised officer. Article 29 also makes provision for the initiation of a special review.

11–44   Certification of unit   A special care order cannot be made unless a special care unit has been certified by the Minister for Health and Children.[43]

The Child Care (Special Care) Regulations 2004 introduce a regulated special care system and provide important protections for the child. Such protections include the monitoring of standards and regular reviews.

Conclusion

11–45   The creation of a formal duty to make special provision for troubled youth in care is welcome.[44] The Springboard initiative, made up of 15 pilot projects throughout the country, is also worthy of mention. It is designed to facilitate early intervention so as to prevent children at risk from engaging in various forms of anti-social behaviour, by providing a pro-active, inter-agency response to support these children and their families. It involves the establishment of formal collaborative structures (involving relevant state agencies, the voluntary sector and the local community) and the identification of a local centre to act as a focal point for the delivery of services to children. Such centres will act as a resource for both parents and children. It is hoped that this legislative reform, however, will be matched by financial resources, aimed at enhancing the number and quality of suitable places available for such children.

PART IV

DIVERSION PROGRAMME

Introduction

11–46   Part IV of the Children Act 2001, ss.17 to 51, places the former Juvenile Liaison Scheme, introduced in Dublin in 1963, on a statutory footing

---

[42] Art.26.

[43] Art.32.

[44] It is in marked contrast to the provision in the Residential Treaties Act 2004, which gives local authorities the power to seek an exclusion order against a child who has been found guilty of anti-social behaviour.

and renames it the Diversion Programme. This section of the Act was commenced on May 1, 2002. It is supported by a new principle, that children must admit responsibility for their acts before admittance to the scheme and is therefore a good example of restorative justice. The primary purpose of the programme is "to divert from committing further offences any child who accepts responsibility for his or her criminal behaviour".[45] Diversion may be achieved by way of administering a caution, formal or informal, to the child and, where appropriate, by placing the child under the supervision of a juvenile liaison officer and convening a conference which will provide a forum for the child, his parents and other family members, possibly other interested persons and, where appropriate, a victim to discuss the child's offending and the reasons for it. The conference, to be known as the Garda conference, is convened by the Garda Síochána and involves the formulation of an action plan for the child in respect of whom it has been convened. The provision for an action plan is a key feature of restorative conferencing. It provides an opportunity to confront the child with the consequences of his offending in the presence of the victim and allows the child to apologise and make reparation to the victim.

Diversion programme

11–47   Section 18 of the 2001 Act states that, unless the interests of society require otherwise, any child who has committed an offence and accepts responsibility for his criminal behaviour must be considered for admission to the Diversion Programme. The objective of the programme, contained in s.19, is to divert from committing further offences any child who accepts responsibility for his criminal behaviour. A statutory obligation is imposed on the Garda Síochána to operate a Diversion Programme. A director, defined in s.20 as "a member of the Garda Síochána not below the rank of Superintendent", operates the programme, which is under the control and general supervision of the Commissioner of the Garda Síochána. Section 22 requires a report to be prepared by the member of the Garda Síochána dealing with the child. This report must then be sent to the director of the Diversion Programme with a recommendation as to any further action, including admission to the Diversion Programme, that should be taken. Section 23 provides that a child must admit responsibility for his criminal behaviour before being admitted to the scheme and must also consent to be cautioned. If a child is to be admitted to the Diversion Programme, a written notice is furnished to the parents or guardians of the child by the juvenile liaison officer, acting on the instructions of the director of the Diversion Programme, specifying the fact that the child is to be cautioned under the programme (s.24).

11–48   Section 25 provides for the administration of a caution, whether informal or formal. An informal caution is given where no previous caution has been administered or where any previous caution or cautions have also been informal. The formal or informal caution is either given in a Garda station

---

[45] s.19(1).

or the child's residence or, in exceptional circumstances, at another place. It must take place in the presence of the parents or guardians. Section 26 facilitates restorative cautioning and provides that where a formal caution is being administered to a child offender who has been admitted to the Diversion Programme, the victim may be present. It is a mini-conference type response in circumstances where a full conference is not warranted and where the child offender can be confronted with the consequences of his offending and be invited to apologise or make some form of reparation to the victim. Section 27 details the length of the supervisory periods associated with the different types of caution. A formal caution entails a 12-month period under the supervision of a juvenile liaison officer from the date of the administration of the caution. Where a child has received an informal caution he shall not be placed under the supervision of a juvenile liaison officer, save in exceptional circumstances and then for no longer than six months. Section 27(1)(d) provides that the supervision period may be varied by the director of the Diversion Programme. The level of supervision to be applied in the case of any child is to be determined by the juvenile liaison officer who shall have regard to the matters set out in s.28(2) of the 2001 Act.

Garda conference

11–49   Section 29 provides that a convened conference may be held in respect of a child who has been formally cautioned and is being supervised by a juvenile liaison officer. It is the decision of the director of the Diversion Programme as to whether or not a conference is to be convened.[46] The Garda conference, as it is known, incorporates within its parameters modern restorative justice measures. It is an integral part of the Diversion Programme. Section 29(1) sets out the functions of the conference. One to the key functions of the conference is to mediate between the child offender and the victim. It will be convened by the Garda Síochána. The conference venue will be determined by the facilitator. Attendance at the conference is governed by s.32 of the 2001 Act and will usually consist of the child, his parents or guardians, and the facilitator, who will generally be the juvenile liaison officer.[47] Other persons permitted to attend the conference include the relatives of the child, a person nominated by the health board for the area in which the child normally resides, a victim, and any other person who may be of benefit to the conference. Section 35 provides that parties must be given sufficient notification of the conference while s.36 requires the facilitator to take all reasonable steps to ascertain the views of interested parties who may be unable or unwilling to attend the conference. The conference is to regulate its own procedure.[48]

11–50   The conference will discuss why the child became involved in the criminal behaviour and will discuss how, through family support and community

---

[46] s.31. The views of the victim must be considered when deciding whether or not to hold a conference.

[47] See s.31(4) of the 2001 Act.

[48] s.37.

involvement, the child might be diverted from crime. It will also formulate an action plan for the child in respect of whom it has been convened.[49] The action plan may provide for the making of an apology, other reparation to the victim, a curfew, or participation by the child in appropriate sporting and recreational activities. The primary focus of the Garda conference is on issues of accountability rather than child welfare, though the action plan is to be welcomed in that it involves the child in the decision-making process.

11–51   The facilitator is required to complete a report of the conference as soon as practicable after the conference has concluded and must submit it to the director of the Diversion Programme. The director may recommend that the period of supervision be varied as a result of the conference.[50] Section 48 provides that any admission of responsibility made by a child for the purposes of admission to the Diversion Programme shall not be admissible against the child in any civil or criminal proceedings. One matter of concern in relation to this section is what would happen if a child did admit responsibility, but, because of the gravity of the offence, is refused admission to the Diversion Programme. This contingency does not seem to be covered by the immunity provided in s.48. Section 50 states that evidence obtained in the course of the Garda conference is not admissible in any court, while s.51 makes it an offence to publish any report of the proceedings of the Garda conference.

PART V

CRIMINAL RESPONSIBILITY

11–52   Section 52 of the 2001 Act will raise the age of criminal responsibility from seven—the lowest age in Europe—to 12. This means that children under the age of 12 years will no longer have the legal capacity to commit offences. Section 52(2) states that there is a rebuttable presumption that a child between 12 and 14 years is incapable of committing an offence, based on the idea that the child did not have the legal capacity to know that the act or omission was wrong. This places the common law presumption of *doli incapax* on a statutory footing. Section 52, once in force, will provide a psychological "window of opportunity" for children between 10 and 14, as set out in Daniel Goleman's book *Emotional Intelligence*. Section 53 provides that if a child under the age of 12 years is found by a member of the Garda Síochána to be engaged in an activity which, if the child was over 12 years, would constitute criminal activity, the member must take the child to his parents or, if the member has reasonable grounds for believing the child is not receiving adequate care or attention, to the health board. Any person who aids or abets a child in committing what would, but for his age, be criminal acts, can be charged under s.54 and tried as a principal offender. A commencement date has yet to be set for Pt 5 of the 2001 Act.

---

[49] s.39.
[50] s.41.

PART VI

Treatment of Child Suspects in Garda Síochána Stations

11–53 Part 6 deals with the treatment of child suspects in Garda Síochána stations. It obliges the Gardaí to have due regard to the dignity of children and their vulnerability owing to their age and level of maturity. This part of the Act, with the exception of ss.59 and 61(1)(b), came into force on May 1, 2002.

Section 56 provides that a detained child shall be kept separate from a detained adult, and shall not, unless there is no other place available, be kept in a cell. This section is disappointing in that there still exists the prospect of children who are detained in Garda custody being held with adults.

11–54 When a child is arrested, he or she must be informed, in language appropriate to his or her age and understanding, of the details of the alleged offence, that he or she is entitled to consult a solicitor, and that his or her parent or guardian has been told.[51] Section 58 states that if the parents cannot or will not attend, the child is to be told of his or her "entitlement to have an adult relative or other adult reasonably named by him or her given the information specified in s.58(1)(a) and requested to attend at the station without delay". Section 59(1) provides that where the member in charge of the garda station in which a child is detained has reasonable cause to believe that the child may be in need of care or protection, the member must inform the local health board for the area and the health board shall then be obliged to send a representative to the station "as soon as practicable". This section is one of two sections of Pt 6 of the 2001 Act not yet in force.

11–55 Section 61 sets out the details regarding the interviewing of children. The 2001 Act provides that a child may not be interviewed unless in the presence of his or her parent or guardian, subject to s.62(2) and (3). Significantly, s.61(4) permits the member in charge of the garda station to remove an adult from where a child is being questioned or a written statement is being taken where the member has reasonable grounds for believing that the conduct of the adult amounts to an obstruction of the course of justice. Section 61(7) defines parent or guardian for the purposes of s.61 as including the adult reasonably named by the child under s.58. In the absence of the parent or guardian, or the other adult reasonably named by the child, the member in charge can nominate another adult. Little guidance is provided as to what "reasonably named" means. This is likely to cause confusion and affords a wide discretion to the member in charge of the garda station in deciding whether to allow the adult named by the child to attend the interview. Section 62(1) provides that a parent or guardian must be given a copy of the charge sheet and is to be notified in writing, as soon as practicable, as to the date of the child's first appearance in court. Under s.63, a child who cannot contact a parent or guardian can name another adult, not being a member of the Garda Síochána.

---

[51] s.57.

11–56 Section 67 is significant in that it changes from 17 to 18 years the age at which a person is regarded as a child. This section brings s.5 of the Criminal Justice Act 1984, which provides for access to a solicitor and notification of detention, in line with the Age of Majority Act 1985.[52] By virtue of s.2 of the 1985 Act, a person reaches full age on attaining 18 years of age.

11–57 Section 70(b) and (c) of the 2001 Act enables the Minister for Justice, Equality and Law Reform to make regulations governing the role of any of the adults present at the interviewing of children in garda stations. These regulations will provide useful guidance as to whether the adult present during the questioning of the child in a garda station is there to ensure procedures are complied with, to ensure the child is properly treated, or to offer support to the child. Section 70(1)(c) enables the Minister for Justice, Equality and Law Reform to make more general regulations concerning such other matters as may be necessary for the purposes of allowing the part of the 2001 Act dealing with the treatment of child suspects in garda stations to have full effect.

PART VII

CHILDREN'S COURT

11–58 The former Juvenile Court has been abolished and, in its place, s.71 of the 2001 Act establishes a new Children's Court. Section 71 also provides that the Children's Court will now deal with persons under 18 years of age. All sections in Pt 7 of the 2001 Act commenced on 1 May, 2002.

11–59 Order 37, rule 6 of the District Court (Children) Rules, 2004,[53] should be noted in the context of persons in a position to attend sittings of the Children Court:

> "[A]ll persons shall be excluded from sittings of the Children Court except—
> (a) officers of the court,
> (b) the parents or guardian of the child concerned,
> (c) an adult relative to the child, or other adult who attends the court pursuant to section 91(6) of the Act,
> (d) persons directly concerned in the proceedings,
> (e) bona fide representatives of the press,
> (f) such other persons (if any) as the Court may at its discretion permit to remain. However the order or decision of the Court (if any) in any such proceedings shall be announced in public."

---

[52] S.I. No. 2 of 1985.
[53] S.I. No. 539 of 2004.

PART VIII

PROCEEDINGS IN COURT

11–60 Part 8 details the rights of children before the court charged with criminal offences. It gives a central new role to the Children's Court in implementing the restorative justice provisions in the Children Act 2001. Part 8 is generally to be welcomed in that it facilitates rehabilitation by vesting in the Children's Court the power to adjourn a case and refer it to the health board, thereby serving as a useful link between the child care system and the Children's Court.

11–61 Section 77 of the Act, which is not yet in force, allows the court to adjourn the criminal proceedings where it considers that a child's real problem is a need of care or protection. In such cases the local health board will be directed by the Children's Court to convene a family welfare conference in respect of the child and report back to the court on what action, if any, it intends to take. For example, the health board may apply for a care order, a supervision order or a special care order for the child. Following the outcome of the family welfare conference, the court will have the discretion as to whether it should dismiss the charge against the child.[54]

11–62 Sections 78 to 87 of the 2001 Act were recently commenced[55] and provide for the introduction of a court-directed and supervised family conference, which is to be convened by the Probation and Welfare Service. The family conference is similar to the garda conference in many respects and will generally arise where the Gardaí consider they have no option other than to prosecute. Section 78(1) states that where a child has accepted responsibility for his criminal behaviour and it appears to the court that an action plan for the child may be appropriate, the court will have the power to adjourn the case to convene a family conference as an alternative at that point to proceeding to a finding. This subsection is to be criticised in that its primary focus is on issues of accountability rather than the best interests of the child. The action plan formulated by the family conference will be supervised by the court and is enforceable. The court will, on the resumption of the case following completion of the action plan, have the discretion to decide whether or not to proceed to a finding. Section 83 is worthy of particular note as it makes provision for the Probation and Welfare Service to report back to the court and, where it appears to the court that the child has failed to comply with an action plan, it may resume the proceedings in respect of which the child is charged.

11–63 Section 88(2) provides that persons remanded in custody who are under the age of 16 years are to be sent to a designated junior remand centre, while s.88(3) states that children over the age of 16 years are to be sent to a

---

[54] s.77(3).
[55] See Children Act 2001 (Commencement) Order 2004 (S.I. No. 468 of 2004) and District Court (Children) (No.2) Rules 2004 (S.I. No. 666 of 2004).

designated remand centre. In this jurisdiction, remanding young offenders in custody has been the subject of considerable debate, due to the fact that children on remand have been mixed with children being detained. Section 88(5) of the 2001 Act is to be criticised in that it empowers the Minster for Justice, Equality and Law Reform, with the agreement of the Minister for Education and Science, to designate as a junior remand centre any place, including part of any children's detention school, which in his opinion is suitable for children who are remanded in custody. If the remand centre is part of a children's detention school, it is difficult to see how children on remand can be kept apart from those in detention.

11–64   Section 5 of the Bail Act 1997 has been amended by s.89 of the 2001 Act. This section came into force on 1 May, 2002 (along with ss.90 to 94 of the Act). It provides that the payment of monies into court under the 1997 Act does not apply to persons under 18 years of age.

11–65   Section 91 concerns the attendance in court by the parents or guardians. It requires the parents to attend all stages of proceedings in court where a case is being heard against their child. Failure by the parents or guardians, without reasonable excuse, to attend such proceedings shall, subject to s.91(5), be treated as if it were contempt of court. Section 91(5) enables parents to be excused from attending court if the court is of the opinion that the interests of justice would not be served by such attendance. The court has the power, where the parents fail to attend the proceedings, to adjourn the proceedings and issue a warrant commanding the parents to be produced before the court.

PART IX

POWERS OF COURTS IN RELATION TO CHILD OFFENDERS

11–66   Part IX sets out the powers of a court on a finding of guilt of a child. Those powers must be exercised in accordance with the principles set out in s.96 of the 2001 Act relating to the exercise of criminal jurisdiction over children, one of which is the need to adopt and implement alternatives to formal criminal prosecution, wherever possible, in order to divert young offenders away from the criminal justice system. A range of imaginative community sanctions are available to a court, including probation and training orders, orders for day care, orders for supervision, and mentor orders. Of the 10 community sanctions provided in the Children Act 2001, eight are new. Their purpose is to ensure an appropriate and suitable sanction for the young person accused of an offence. These sanctions give tangible effect to the principle in the 2001 Act that detention is to be an option of last resort, to be ordered only in respect of serious offences of violence or the repeated commission of other serious offences.

11–67   Part IX introduces, *inter alia*, the parental supervision order, the parental compensation order and the imposition of a detention order, and makes provision for the introduction of rules governing places of detention. It establishes the rights of children before the courts charged with criminal offences. Significantly, s.96 provides that criminal proceedings cannot be used solely to provide any assistance or services needed to care for or protect a child. On a finding of guilt, before a court decides how it will deal with the child, it will usually request a probation officer's report. The only situation where a report will not be requested is where the court is imposing a minor penalty such as a small fine, or where it already has available to it an up-to-date report on the child. It should be noted that where the court is not in a position to impose detention in a children's detention school due to lack of space, it will, as an alternative, be empowered to impose an appropriate community sanction.

Sentencing

11–68   Section 96 of the Children Act 2001 sets out the matters a court should have regard to when dealing with a child offender at the sentencing stage. The various orders available to a court are detailed in s.98. They include a reprimand for the child, non-custodial orders, or detention. On a finding of guilt, the court will have the power to request a victim impact report.

Fines, costs or compensation

11–69   Sections 108 to 110 of the 2001 Act give the courts the power to impose fines, costs and compensation. In particular, s.108 provides that fines, where appropriate, are not to exceed half the fine for an adult committing the same offence.

11–70   Order 37, r.12 of the District Court (Children) Rules 2004,[56] provides:

> "12.   Where the court orders an accused child to pay a fine, costs, or compensation and the child is in default, the Court may, on the application of the prosecutor therefor, issue a warrant in the Form 37.22, Schedule B, for the arrest of the child to be brought before the Court to answer such default. Alternatively, application may be made by the prosecutor for an order under section 110 of the [2001] Act. Such application shall be preceded by the issue and service, at least four days before the date upon which the application is to be heard, on the accused, the parents or guardian of the accused and any other person directly affected by the order, of a notice in the Form 37.23, Schedule B. The order of the Court on the hearing of the application shall be in the Form 37.24, Schedule B."

---

[56] S.I. No. 539 of 2004.

Parental control mechanisms

11–71   The Children Act 2001 imposes responsibilities and obligations on parents to participate in their children's welfare. The court may, under s.111 of the 2001 Act, make a parental supervision order. This order gives the court the power to instruct parents to undergo treatment for substance or alcohol abuse and/or to attend a course in parenting skills (where such facilities are reasonably available). Failure to comply with a parental supervision order can be treated as contempt of court under s.112 of the 2001 Act.

11–72   Section 113 of the Children Act 2001 provides that parents, rather than their child, can be ordered to pay compensation in the event of the child committing an offence. Before making a compensation order, the court must be satisfied of the parents' ability to pay and that a wilful failure on the part of the parents to take care of or control their child contributed to the child's offending. This provision, which enables the court to compel parents to pay compensation to the victim of an offence committed by their child, seeks to bring home to parents the fact that their responsibilities extend to the consequences of negative actions on the part of their child. Similarly, s.114 focuses on parental responsibilities and gives the courts the power to order the parent or guardian of a child offender to enter into a recognisance to exercise proper or adequate control over the child.

The use of parental control mechanisms in the Children Act 2001 demonstrate a reluctance to acknowledge the social context that contributes to a child's delinquent behaviour, such as poverty, drug addiction or disadvantage.

Community sanctions

11–73   Section 115 of the Children Act 2001 provides community-based sanctions which greatly increase the non-custodial options available to the court and will assist in ensuring that custodial sentencing is treated as a measure of last resort. The 2001 Act provides for the following non-custodial options:

(a) a community service order for a child of 16 or 17 years of age,

(b) a day care centre order,

(c) a probation order,

(d) a probation (training or activities) order,

(e) a probation (intensive supervision) order,

(f) a probation (residential supervision) order,

(g) a suitable person (care and supervision) order,

(h) a mentor (family support) order,

(i) a restriction on movement order, and

(j) a dual order.

11–74 Sections 118 and 123 provide for day centre orders and have enormous potential. It is planned to implement and commence the suitable person (care and supervision) order and the mentor (family support) order by the end of 2004. Sections 133 to 136 deal with restriction on movement orders on child offenders. These orders facilitate the imposition of curfews or barring orders from premises or their vicinities or a particular locality. The restriction on movement order came into force on May 1, 2002.

11–75 Order 37, rules 10 and 11 of the District Court (Children) Rules 2004[57] should be noted:

"10. An order imposing a community sanction shall be in the Form 37.17, Schedule B. Any application made under section 136 of the [2001] Act shall be preceded by the issue and service, at least four days before the date upon which the application is to be heard, on the accused, the parents or guardian of the accused, and any other person directly affected by the order, of a notice in the Form 37.18, Schedule B.

11. Where it appears to the court, on application in that behalf by a member of the Garda Síochána that a child has failed, without reasonable cause, to comply with an order in force imposing a community sanction or any condition to which such order is subject, there shall be issued a summons to the child to appear before it in the Form 37.19, Schedule B. Unless the Court has excused the parents and/or guardian of the child from appearing, pursuant to section 90(5) of the [2001] Act, such summons to appear shall also be addressed to the parents and/or guardian of the child. If the child shall fail to appear in answer to said summons, the Court may issue a warrant in the Form 37.20, Schedule B for his or her arrest. The order of the Court on the hearing of the application shall be in the Form 37.21, Schedule B."

Detention

11–76 Section 143 of the Children Act 2001 provides that detention cannot be imposed unless the court is satisfied that it is the only suitable manner of dealing with the child and, in the case of a child under 16 years of age, a place in a children detention school is available. Children detention schools are to replace industrial and reformatory schools. These are places of detention for convicted child offenders between 12 and 16 years of age. Places of detention are for child offenders between 16 and 18 years of age. The court must, pursuant to s.143(2), provide reasons for making a detention order in open court. Section 144 gives the court the power to defer the making of a detention order on the evidence of the parents and others, though no reference is made to the child. Provision is made in s.145 of the 2001 Act for the court, where it wishes to make a detention order but no place is available and it would not be appropriate

---

[57] S.I. No. 539 of 2004.

to defer the making of the order, to impose the most appropriate community-based sanction. Section 153 allows the retention of Saint Patrick's institution which is, in reality, part of Mountjoy Prison. This would appear to be contrary to the philosophy underpinning the Act, which outlaws the use of prisons for children. For example, s.156 provides that no sentence of imprisonment may be passed on a child. This section repeals the use of imprisonment on foot of certificates of unruliness issued under the Children Act 1908. Sections 95 to 107, 111 to 112, 115 to 132 and 137 to 156 of the 2001 Act are not yet in force.

PART X

Children Detention Schools

11–77   Part X establishes children detention schools, which will be under the control of the Minister for Education and Science. It updates the system of juvenile detention, replacing the nineteenth-century categorisations of detention centres into "industrial" and "reformatory" schools, and replacing them with "children detention schools", to be used by the courts where detention is considered the only suitable option for dealing with a child. Children detention schools will therefore be used by the courts where detention is considered to be the only suitable means of dealing with children aged between 12 and 16 years who have been found guilty of criminal offences. Part 10 emphasises the principal role of children detention schools in promoting the reintegration of the children referred to them back into society through the provision of appropriate educational and training programmes and appropriate facilities in which to deliver these programmes. It also provides for the certification of children detention schools, as well as the number, age and the sex of children who may be detained in each children detention school at any time. Sections 185 to 189 set out an inspection system for children detention schools. In summary, Pt 10 of the Children Act 2001 deals primarily with the management and objectives of the children detention schools. All sections of Pt 10 are to be commenced by the end of 2004, although the only provision currently in force is s.159(1).

11–78   Two issues of concern should be noted in Pt 10. Firstly, the directors of children detention schools are not in a position to refuse to admit children on the direction of the courts. Consequently, the pressure on accommodation may lead to overcrowding and the mixing of children with different needs, with the attendant implications in terms of cross-contamination. Secondly, the Children Act 2001 provides for the segregation of children detained on criminal charges and others. Only children detained on criminal charges can be detained in day care and other juvenile centres. Section 161(5) of the 2001 Act, however, states, "Any such place need not cater exclusively for children found guilty of offences". A children detention school need not therefore provide exclusively for children who have committed criminal offences. This, in itself, is a grievous breach of international standards, which require the separation of child offenders and those children needing special care and attention. In fact, it is at variance with the ethos that underlies the Children Act 2001, which provides that children committed for criminal offences should only be detained in certain detention centres, while those committed for other reasons should not.

PART XI

SPECIAL RESIDENTIAL SERVICES BOARD

11–79   Part 11 provides for the establishment, functions and membership of the Special Residential Services Board. The Board is designed to ensure the efficient, effective and co-ordinated delivery of services for children in respect of whom children detention orders or special care orders have been made. As previously stated, the advice of the Board must be sought before applying for a special care order. The Board is also to advise the Ministers for Health and Children and Education and Science on policy matters pertaining to the remand and detention of children. It is to be noted that the Board was already operating with a full membership on an administrative basis prior to the commencement of Pt 11 of the 2001 Act on November 7, 2003. The implementation of Pt 11 was made contingent on Pt 10 commencing while Pt 3 of the 2001 Act was made dependent on the Special Residential Services Board being in place.

PART XII

PROTECTION OF CHILDREN

11–80   Part 12 of the Children Act 2001 re-enacts and updates provisions of the Children Act 1908 for the protection of children in relation to the offences of cruelty to children, begging, allowing children to be in a brothel and causing or encouraging a sexual offence on a child. The provisions on cruelty and neglect have been updated and the penalty has been increased. Significant changes have been introduced regarding the sending out of children to beg. The evidential burden is now on the person who sends the child out to beg, receive alms or induce the receiving of alms, making successful prosecutions less troublesome. The law on encouraging or causing a sexual offence upon a child under 17 years of age has been updated in several important respects, most notably in relation to increased penalties.

11–81   The offence of cruelty to children has been updated and the penalty substantially increased. Section 246 of the Children Act 2001, which covers cruelty to or the neglect of children, provides that the expression "a child's health or well-being" includes "the child's physical, mental or emotional health or well-being". Cruelty can therefore now be defined as frightening, bullying or threatening a child. This important addition to the definition of cruelty arises from a recommendation of the Select Committee on Social Affairs in its 1997 report on non-fatal offences against the person in respect of children. The effect of the change, which came into force on May 1, 2002, is that the meaning of a child's well-being in s.246 of the 2001 Act is expanded to include mental and emotional well-being.

11–82 Section 247 re-enacts the offence of causing or procuring a child to beg. This section makes it an offence for any person, including a parent or a person having the custody, charge or care of a child, to ask, allow, cause or procure a child to beg, receive alms or induce the receiving of alms. This applies in any street, public place or house-to-house visit, whether or not there is "any pretence" of singing, playing, performing or offering anything for sale. Significantly, a child is presumed to be in the street, public place or in any house with the consent of the parent, unless the contrary is proven. Section 247 reverses the burden of proof so that parents now have to satisfy the court that they did not allow the child out to beg. Changing the burden of proof should make a difference in terms of convictions. A person found guilty of an offence under s.247 shall be liable on summary conviction to a fine not exceeding, in the case of a first offence, £250 (€317), or in the case of a second or any subsequent offence, £500 (€635). This section commenced on May 1, 2002.

11–83 Section 250 of the Children Act 2001, which came into force on May 1, 2002, amends s.6 of the Criminal Law (Sexual Offences) Act 1993. It raises the penalty for soliciting a child for the purpose of prostitution. Section 252 of the 2001 Act specifically prohibits the publication or broadcast of any report or picture that would identify a child who is the subject of any proceedings under the Children Act 2001, or where a child is a witness in any such proceedings. In s.252(2), the court is given a discretion to dispense to any specified extent with the requirement of anonymity if it is satisfied that it is appropriate to do so in the interests of the child. It is therefore open to the trial judge to make an order sanctioning the dispensation of the anonymity requirements, though he or she must furnish an explanation in open court as to why he or she is satisfied to waive the preservation of the child's anonymity. This section is in force since May 1, 2002.

PART XIII

Miscellaneous

11–84 Section 258 introduces a limited "clean slate" in respect of offences committed by children. It provides for the non-disclosure of findings of guilt in respect of most offences committed by children. In fact, it is one of the most important matters to be included in the Children Act 2001 and is consistent with the Act's emphasis on rehabilitation. The conditions that must be satisfied are that:

(a) the offence (not being one tried by the Central Criminal Court) was committed before the age of 18 years,

(b) at least three years have elapsed since the finding of guilt, and

(c) the person has not been dealt with for an offence in that three-year period.

This section was commenced on May 1, 2002.

11–85 Section 263 makes provision for the temporary detention of a child in a garda station or other place for a period not exceeding 24 hours. This section has not yet been commenced. Section 264 permits the Minister for Justice, Equality and Law Reform to conduct research into any matter connected with children who are considered at risk of committing offences, or who have committed offences, or who appear before the courts charged with offences. This section was commenced on May 1, 2002.

11–86 Section 17 of the Child Care Act 1991 makes provision for an interim care order. In its original form, s.17(2) of the 1991 Act provided that an interim care order required the child to remain in the care of the health board for a period not exceeding eight days. This has been amended by s.267(1)(a) of the Children Act 2001 and an interim order can now be made for a period not exceeding 28 days. This section was commenced on May 1, 2002.[58] It has prompted the Court Services to withdraw the second health board day, every second week, in the Children's Court in Dublin.

Problems are likely to arise in the application of s.267(1)(a). It may be recalled that similar problems arose regarding *ex parte* applications under the Children Act 1908 and the Summary Jurisdiction Rules, where a substantial time-lag could elapse between the health boards taking *ex parte* proceedings under that legislation to take a child to a place of safety, and a hearing enabling the parents to challenge the order under s.20 of the 1908 Act. In the case of *State (D.C.) v Midland Health Board,* Keane J., as he then was, noted that the time-lag could constitute an impermissible violation of parental rights.[59] That said, in that case the difficulty did not result from a frailty in the Act or Rules but from the absence of a summons server for the particular area. The time-lag, therefore, could have been circumvented and the legislation was not held to be constitutionally unsound. A recent challenge to the Domestic Violence Act 1996 on the basis that the return date given in a case where the court granted a barring order *ex parte* was too long was upheld by the Supreme Court.[60] Specifically, the Court held that the failure to prescribe a fixed period of a relatively short duration during which an interim barring order made *ex parte* was in force deprived the applicant of his right to fair procedures to an extent which was disproportionate, unreasonable and unnecessary. Keane C.J. summarised the position in the following terms:

"The court is satisfied that the procedures prescribed by subs.(1), (3) and (4) of the 1996 Act, in failing to prescribe a fixed period of relatively short duration during which an interim barring order made *ex parte* is to continue in force deprive the respondents of *audi alteram partem* in a

---

[58] See also S.I. No. 151 of 2002.

[59] [1990] 7 Fam. L.J. 10 (HC).

[60] See *D.K. v C. and Others* unreported, Supreme Court, October 9, 2002.

manner and to an extent which is disproportionate, unreasonable and unnecessary".[61]

Significantly, the core provision of the amending legislation, the Domestic Violence (Amendment) Act 2002, provides that the interim *ex parte* barring order shall have effect for a period not exceeding eight working days. In summary, if an interim order is to be facilitated under Irish child care law, it ought to be strictly limited in time. Similar comments apply in respect of the interim special care order (under s.23C of the Child Care Act 1991) previously discussed.

11–87 The definition of a children's residential centre under the Child Care Act 1991 excluded an institution for the care and maintenance of physically or mentally handicapped children but this, as previously stated, has been deleted by s.267(1)(b) of the Children Act 2001.[62]

11–88 Section 270 of the Children Act 2001 addresses the safety of children at an entertainment event where the number of children who attend the event exceeds 100 and access to any part of the building in which children are accommodated is by stairs, escalator, lift or other mechanical means. Where this section is applicable, the organiser of the event is obliged to supervise the movement of persons and provide a sufficient number of trained adult attendants to ensure that no more people enter the event area so as to exceed its accommodation limits. The organiser of the event is further required to take other precautions to ensure the safety of the children. It should also be noted that the occupier of a building who rents the premises for such a purpose is required to take all reasonable steps to ensure the requirements of this section are met. The provisions of s.270 are enforced by the Garda Síochána, who have the power to inspect any premises where they believe an event anticipated by s.270 is taking place or about to take place. Fines for a first offence have an upper limit of €635 and/or up to six months in prison, while a second offence attracts a maximum fine of €1,905 and/or up to 12 months in prison. Both of these sections came into force on May 1, 2002.

The New Zealand experience—a cause for reflection?

11–89 As stated previously, New Zealand legislation has been adapted in Irish reform of the youth justice and child protection system. The Children, Young Persons and Their Family Act 1989 introduced innovative ways of dealing with children and young people who came before the courts. The Act marked a significant transfer of power from the State, exercised principally by the courts, to the community. This was achieved through the Family Group Conference, as a way of providing community involvement to negotiate a plan for tackling a child's needs and, in the case of offending, the consequences

---

[61] At p.32.
[62] See Chap.6, para.6–45.

and causes of a young person's offending.[63] The Act acknowledges the importance of upholding the child's rights and the need to protect the child,[64] and in the 15 years since its implementation, has been largely successful in doing so. However, there are also weaknesses that have been identified, and as the Children Act 2001 is implemented, it is important to ask what lessons Ireland can learn from the New Zealand experience.

11–90   There have been concerns by the New Zealand public, fuelled by the media, that youth offending, particularly violent crime, is increasing. However, as pointed out by the Principal Youth Court Judge, this must be seen in light of a general increase in offending and the growing population, currently just over four million. In fact, youth offending has remained around 22 per cent of total offending since the implementation of the Act.[65] Significantly though, there was a dramatic decrease in the number of cases coming before the courts and the number of young offenders imprisoned.[66] This is largely attributable to the manner in which the police have embraced the spirit of the legislation, as 76 per cent of all cases of youth offending are dealt with by alternative action, through diversion, warnings or other community-based approaches.[67] However, like Ireland, one of the weaknesses of the New Zealand system is the lack of reliable statistical information. Currently there is no centralised collection of data, hampering Government agencies in accurately identifying strategies which are working, regional variations and areas that could be improved.

11–91   Family Group Conferences have often been described as the "lynchpin" of the New Zealand system. They are a mechanism allowing the child and his or her extended family and the community to have a voice in addressing the needs of the child concerned. A family group conference is required in care and protection cases involving children and young people before the Family Court, and is also invoked in the Youth Court where the young person has been charged with an offence.[68] With full participation and co-operation by participants and effective guidance by the facilitator, the family group conference can be a valuable tool in developing a creative and individual plan to address the care and protection for a child, or young person's offending.

---

[63] FWM, J. McElrea, "Education, Discipline and Restorative Justice" (December, 1996) 2, 4 *Butterworths Family Law Journal* 91–94.
[64] Children, Young Persons and Their Families Act 1989, s.13(a).
[65] Judge A. Becroft, "Past lessons and future challenges", Paper for the Australian Juvenile Justice Conference, Sydney, December 1–2, 2003. http://www.courts.govt.nz/youth/ for more information.
[66] G. Maxwell, "Achieving Effective Outcomes in Youth Justice: Implications of new research from Principles, Policy and Practice", Crime and Justice Research Centre, Victoria University of Wellington, June 2003, p.8.
[67] Final Report "Police Youth Diversion", Crime and Justice Research Centre, Victoria University of Wellington, January 2002.
[68] The Youth Court only deals with child offending when the child (a person under 14) is charged with murder or manslaughter (Children, Young Persons and Their Families Act 1989, s.272(1)). All other cases of child offending are dealt with by the Family Court, reflecting the philosophy that offending by children must be considered within the context of their family environment.

However, the success of a family group conference can be undermined by several factors. In a number of care and protection cases, Judge Inglis of the Family Court has identified the potential dangers of family group conference making decisions where there is an imperfect grasp of the facts, or where the decisions are based on expediency or unduly emphasise family loyalty.[69] As Inglis J. noted, "with the best of intentions, an overriding emphasis on family unity may serve only to lock the child into an unsatisfactory and dysfunctional family situation".[70] The Mason Inquiry[71] into the 1989 Act also heard of instances of children being "harangued", or "intimidated"; of conferences being hijacked by family members; and the Department of Social Welfare scapegoating various participants.[72] These concerns highlight the need for courts to carefully evaluate plans prepared by a family group conference, as it is the court's duty to ensure that the interests of the child are safeguarded. Further, there is a danger that the plans reached may not be realistic or capable of achievement. This was identified by the Children and Young Persons Service, and it is now a matter of policy that a plan must expressly include such details as where the child is to live, with whom and for how long, what tasks are to be done, and by whom, as well as address the matter of a review."[73]

11–92 In relation to the family group conference in the Youth Justice system, Judge Becroft noted some weaknesses that could detract from the effectiveness of the decisions reached. The first of these included time-frames being breached. Not only does this reduce a young person's confidence in the system, it can also result in the conference being invalid and deny the court's jurisdiction. Further, poor attendance at the family group conference sometimes means that only the police, the facilitator (Youth Justice Co-Ordinator), young person and one parent attend. This undermines the legislative intention that the young person's family in the broadest sense be involved in resolving the consequences and providing solutions for that person's offending. Importantly, if the victim of the offending is not present, the young person does not get the opportunity to hear the victim's experience and effects of the offending.[74]

11–93 Another weakness is poorly prepared, resourced and monitored family

---

[69] *Re Children* CYPF 031/020/90 (No.1) (1990) 6 F.R.N.Z. 55 at 57 (the concerns were repeated in later judgment in the same case, *Re Children* CYPF 031/020/90 (No.2) (Family Court, Levin, March 21, 1990) at 5–6). Similar sentiments are expressed in His Honour's judgement in *Re Children* CYPF 041/002/89 (Family Court Napier, June 13, 1990), *Re Children* CYPF 054/014/90 (Family Court, Palmerston North, June 6, 1990 at 10), and *D-GSW v H.* (Family Court, Palmerston NA, CPYF 26/27/90, September 28, 1990 at 8).

[70] *Re L.* (Family Court, Hawera MFP 021/006/90, November 22, 1991) at 5.

[71] Inquiry under s.47 of the Health and Disability Services Act 1993 in respect of certain mental health services: report of the Ministerial Inquiry to the Minister of Health (1996), Wellington.

[72] M. Freeman, "The Importance of Children's rights perspective in litigation" (1996) 2 B.F.L.J. 84.

[73] CYPS Care and Protection Handbook (1996), Vol.2 at p.47.

[74] Judge A. Becroft, "Past lessons and future challenges", Paper for the Australian Juvenile Justice Conference, Sydney, December 1–2, 2003 at p.32.

group conference plans. A Youth Justice Co-ordinator is able to harness many different resources to ensure all relevant information is available to the conference, including professional advisors, and psychological, education and health assessments. However, often these resources are not available to the family group conference and can result in a "sameness" of plans or a young person not receiving the necessary help to implement the plan.[75] Although the conference may address the consequences of the offending, lack of resources and monitoring may mean that the causes of the young person's offending may not be addressed.

11–94   At the heart of many of these weaknesses is the issue of inadequate resources to properly implement the principles of the legislation. There are not enough social workers to organise, implement and monitor family group conferences or the funding to provide resources that would enable a family group conference to accurately identify and address causative factors that led to the child being brought to the attention of the welfare or justice system. As Ian Hassell, the then Commissioner for Children, observed, "the rhetoric of family responsibility can readily lead to the reduction of the support of the state sector which is essential to the well-being of many families".[76] Further, the principles of the legislation require that the conference is child-oriented. The danger is that the child's right to be heard is not respected, reducing his or her involvement in any plan prepared by the conference and thereby weakening his or her commitment to the decisions reached by the group. The challenge for Ireland is to learn from the New Zealand experience, and build on the strengths of an inclusive community approach to tackling welfare and justice issues in relation to children.

Conclusion

11–95   The provisions in the Children Act 2001 relating to family welfare conferences and the juvenile liaison scheme (which has been restructured and renamed the Diversion Programme) are positive steps forward. The latter introduces a system based on restorative justice. The benefits of restorative justice are well documented. It provides an opportunity to turn young offenders away from crime. Replacing the categorisations of reformatories and industrial schools with children detention schools, under the control of boards of management, and the establishment of a special residential services board to co-ordinate the provision of care for children in detention, are all evidence of a more long-term approach to the solution of the problem of youth crime.

11–96   The Children Act 2001 has enormous potential, yet that potential will only be realised with adequate resources. In this regard, the delay in the implementation of the early intervention sections of the Act, and in particular

---

[75] *ibid.*

[76] Briefing Paper (1991). Appraisal of First Year of the Operation of the 1989 Act. Another appraisal is Hudson J. *et al.* (1996). Family Group Conferences, Sydney, Federation Press.

Pt 2 of the 2001 Act, is to be regretted. Early intervention is critical to the success of the Children Act 2001 and means galvanising resources and proper care plans for families in crisis, while children are still of an age to be rescued from permanent alienation.

11–97   Lord Laming's 15-month investigation into Victoria Climbié's death, and his subsequent report,[77] published in January 2003, makes 108 recommendations. The inquiry's main recommendations centre on inter-agency co-operation and a lack of social work resources. It broadly mirrors the problems highlighted in the 1980s Cleveland inquiry, chaired by Dame Elizabeth Butler-Sloss and the other 70 public inquiries in England and Wales since 1945. Interestingly, the success of the Children Act 2001 will depend upon both inter-agency co-operation and ample resources.

---

[77] The Victoria Climbié Inquiry. Report of an Inquiry by Lord Laming.

CHAPTER 12

INTERNATIONAL AND EUROPEAN COMMUNITY LAW

Introduction

12–01   Internationally, the traditional ideal-typical nuclear family is becoming an endangered species. Notwithstanding this, the designation of the family in Art.41 of the Irish Constitution as a private realm, which is virtually impenetrable, still endures, as can be seen from the Supreme Court case of *North Western Health Board v H.W. and C.W.*[1] In the face of such a restrictive interpretation of the "family", Irish litigants have sought redress under international law through international human rights treaties. However, our dualist approach to international law generally makes international human rights treaties binding on the State, though not on the courts, as such treaties have traditionally not been incorporated into Irish law.[2] This has changed, to a limited extent, with the incorporation of the European Convention on Human Rights and Fundamental Freedoms (ECHR) into domestic law.

United Nations Convention on the Rights of the Child 1989

12–02   Ireland ratified the United Nations Convention on the Rights of the Child 1989 without reservation on September 21, 1992. Again, by virtue of Ireland's dualist nature, the provisions do not form part of the domestic law. The Convention gives recognition to children's rights in their widest sense. Article 3 of the Convention states, *inter alia*:

(1) In all actions concerning children, whether undertaken by public or private social welfare institutions, courts of law, administrative authorities or legislative bodies, the best interest of the child shall be a primary consideration.

(2) State parties undertake to ensure the child such protection and care as is necessary for his or her well-being, taking into account the rights and duties of his or her parents, legal guardians, or other individuals legally responsible for him or her, and, to this end, shall take all appropriate legislative and administrative measures.

---

[1]   [2001] 3 I.R. 635.
[2]   Most of the other Member States of the Council of Europe adopt a monist approach to international law, where international law is automatically applicable in domestic law, without the need for any implementing legislation.

12–03   While this article requires only that the children's interests be *a* primary consideration, not *the* primary consideration, it must also be read alongside the series of explicit rights which the Convention protects. These include: "the inherent right to life" (Art.6); "the right from birth to a name, the right to acquire a nationality and, as far as possible, the right to know and be cared for by his or her parents" (Art.7); "the right of the child to preserve his or her identity, including nationality" (Art.8); "the right of the child who is separated from one or both parents to maintain personal relations and direct contact with both parents on a regular basis, except if it is contrary to the child's best interests" (Art.9(3)); "the right (of a child who has the capacity to form his or her own views) to express those views freely in all matters affecting the child, the views of the child being given due weight in accordance with the age and maturity of the child" (Art.12); "the right to freedom of expression" (Art.13); "the right of the child to freedom of thought, conscience and religion" (Art. 14(1)); "the right of the child to freedom of association and to freedom of peaceful assembly" (Art.15); "the right to the protection of the law against arbitrary or unlawful interference with the child's privacy, family home or correspondence and unlawful attacks on the child's honour and reputation" (Art.16); "the right of every child to a standard of living adequate for the child's physical, mental, spiritual, moral and social development" (Art.27); "the right of the child to education" (Art.28); and "the right of every child alleged as, accused of, or recognised as having infringed the penal law to be treated in a manner consistent with the promotion of the child's sense of dignity and worth" (Art.40). Taking cognisance of the foregoing rights, and in particular Art.12, it can be seen that the United Nations Convention on the Rights of the Child 1989, is soundly based on a defensible concept of children's rights. The law in Ireland, however, falls far short of such a concept.

Participation

12–04   Article 12 of the United Nations Convention on the Rights of the Child 1989, provides for the separate representation of children:

1.   State parties shall assure to the child who is capable of forming his or her own views the right to express those views freely in all matters affecting the child, the views of the child being given due weight in accordance with the age and maturity of the child.
2.   For this purpose, the child shall in particular be provided the opportunity to be heard in any judicial and administrative proceedings affecting the child, either directly, or through a representative or an appropriate body, in a manner consistent with the procedural rules of national law.

12–05   Article 9 of the same Convention provides for the participation by children in separation and divorce processes:

1.   State parties shall ensure that a child shall not be separated from his or her parents against their will, except when competent authorities

subject to judicial review determine, in accordance with applicable law and procedures, that such separation is necessary for the best interests of the child. Such determination may be necessary in a particular case such as one involving abuse or neglect of the child by the parents, or one where parents are living separately and a decision must be made as to the child's place of residence.

2. In any proceedings pursuant to paragraph 1 of the present article, all interested parties shall be given an opportunity to participate in the proceedings and make their views known.

12–06   The failure of the State to bring into force s.28 of the Guardianship of Infants Act 1964, amounts to a breach of Art.9 of the 1989 Convention. The positive effect of child participation in the separation and divorce process is detailed in the work of the developmental psychology expert, E. Singer.[3]

European Convention on the Exercise of Children's Rights 1996

12–07   Ireland has signed but not ratified the European Convention on the Exercise of Children's Rights 1996.[4] Article 1(1) of the Convention provides that the object of the Convention is to:

"promote [children's] rights, to grant them procedural rights and to facilitate the exercise of these rights by ensuring that children are, themselves or through other persons or bodies, informed and allowed to participate in proceedings affecting them before a judicial authority."

12–08   In some respects, the 1996 Convention is of more limited application than its 1989 counterpart. It focuses predominantly on procedural rather than substantive rights, the emphasis being on such matters as the right of children to participate in, and access information about, cases that concern their welfare. For example, Art.5 of the 1996 Convention states:

"Parties shall consider granting children additional procedural rights in relation to proceedings before a judicial authority offering them, in particular:
(a) the right to apply to be assisted by an appropriate person of their choice in order to help them express their views;
(b) the right to apply themselves, or through other persons or bodies,

---

[3]   E. Singer, "Kinderen als morele personen: Argumenten vanuit een ontwikkelings-psychologisch perspectief" in: C. Van Nijnatten and S. Sevenhuijsen (eds.), *Dubbelleven; Nieuwe perspectieven voor kinderen na echtscheiding* (Thela Thesis, Amsterdam, 2001), 31–40.

[4]   European Treaty Series No. 160. The European Convention on the Exercise of Children's Rights was opened for signature at Strasbourg on January 25, 1996, and Ireland was one of the seven signatories to the Convention on that date. It came into force on July 1, 2000, following ratification by Greece (September 11, 1997), Poland (November 28, 1997) and Slovenia (March 28, 2000) in accordance with Article 21(3) of the 1996 Convention.

for the appointment of a separate representative, in appropriate cases a lawyer;

(c) the right to appoint their own representative;

(d) the right to exercise some or all of the rights of parties to such proceedings.

12–09   Clearly, these provisions are aimed primarily at children of sufficient age and maturity to understand the matters under scrutiny. That said, in appropriate cases, a child should have a person to help the expression of his or her views. Articles 4 and 9 of the European Convention on the Exercise of Children's Rights provide for the appointment of such a special representative. The absence of a facility for children in Ireland to articulate their views, particularly where a case is settled in advance of the hearing, is a serious problem.

European Convention on Human Rights and Fundamental Freedoms

Introduction

12–10   Of special significance in discussing our international obligations towards children are the relevant provisions of the European Convention on Human Rights and Fundamental Freedoms (ECHR). The civil and political rights enshrined in the ECHR emphasise individual and familial freedom and autonomy and protection from excessive state interference. The ECHR is not child-focused in the same way as the United Nations Convention on the Rights of the Child 1989. It does not recognise children as a special group requiring particular protection because of their inherent vulnerability in a world of adults. The rights contained in the ECHR are as available to children as to adults, however, and there is an increasing awareness that the ECHR has potential as an important resource in the promotion of child rights. Whilst it must be acknowledged that only a small body of ECHR case law deals with cases from the perspective of the child, it has been utilised very effectively to protect children in the context of their family life with their parents.

12–11   The incorporation of the ECHR into Irish law has been by way of statute. As a result of incorporation, the provisions of the ECHR have become part of our domestic law. It is now possible to take proceedings in the Irish courts alleging a breach of the ECHR. Previously, to assert any rights under the ECHR, an injured party had first to exhaust all domestic remedies before bringing the case to the European Court of Human Rights (ECt.HR) in Strasbourg, with the costs and delays associated with that process.

There is little doubt that inconsistencies will arise between, on the one hand, Irish child law and practice and, on the other, the standards required by the ECHR. That said, the significance of this development has been over-stated in the arena of Irish child law. The indirect or interpretative mode of incorporation preserves the domestic primacy of the Constitution.[5] Conse-

---

[5]   See s.2 of the European Convention on Human Rights Act 2003.

quently, Art.41 of the Constitution will continue to act as an impediment to the effective implementation of the legal entitlements of children under the ECHR. In particular, incorporation of the ECHR at sub-constitutional level will ensure that child rights remain subordinate to parental rights. (If there is a conflict between a provision of the Constitution and the ECHR, the Constitution prevails). Therefore in the child law arena there will continue to be cases where a remedy for a breach of a ECHR right cannot be procured in the Irish courts, with the only avenue at the disposal of such litigants being an application to the Strasbourg court.

EUROPEAN CONVENTION ON HUMAN RIGHTS ACT 2003

12–12 The European Convention on Human Rights Act 2003 (the "2003 Act") was signed by the President on June 30, 2003, and came into force on December 31, 2003. Section 1 of the 2003 Act provides that Arts 2 to 14 of the ECHR and Protocols 1, 4, 6 and 7 are to be incorporated into Irish law.

The new regime

12–13 Section 2 of the 2003 Act requires the Irish courts to interpret Irish law in a manner compatible with the State's obligations under the ECHR "in so far as is possible". All courts are now obliged to interpret and apply any statutory provision or rule of law in accordance with the ECHR and take judicial notice of the decisions of its institutions. Where this is not possible and where no other legal remedy is adequate and available, the superior courts may make declarations of incompatibility in relation to legislation and awards of damages (and other remedies) against "organs of the State" who behave in a manner contrary to the State's obligations under the ECHR.

Every organ of the State, pursuant to s.3(1) of the 2003 Act, is required to perform its functions in a manner compatible with the ECHR. The definition of "organ of the State" specifically excludes the courts.[6] Section 3(2) of the 2003 Act states:

> "3.—(2) A person who has suffered injury, loss or damage as a result of a contravention … may, if no other remedy in damages is available, institute proceedings to recover damages in respect of the contravention in the High Court (or, subject to subsection (3), in the Circuit Court) and the Court may award to the person such damages (if any) as it considers appropriate."

12–14 The effect of this provision is that if a person has suffered injury, loss or damage as a result of a breach of s.3(1), he may take an action for damages, but only if no other remedy in damages is available. It excludes proceedings

---

[6] This subsection deals with jurisdiction limitations. It does, however, appear to include health boards.

taken in the District Court. This is a matter of particular concern in the child law area, as the District Court has principal jurisdiction for proceedings instituted under the Child Care Act 1991. Section 3(5) of the 2003 Act states that proceedings for violation of a ECHR right must be brought within one year of the contravention. This one-year period may be extended by a court order if the court considers it appropriate to do so in the interests of justice.

12–15   Section 4 of the 2003 Act requires a court to take judicial notice of both the ECHR provisions and the decisions of the institutions of the ECHR. It further requires a court to "take due account of the principles laid down by … decisions" of the institutions of the ECHR when applying the ECHR provisions.

12–16   Section 5 of the 2003 Act provides that where the High Court, or the Supreme Court on appeal, rules that there is an incompatibility between domestic law and the Convention, a declaration of incompatibility may be granted by that court. It should, however, be noted that demonstrating that no other legal remedy is "adequate or available" is a condition precedent to invoking this section. Further, legal aid is not available to the applicant seeking a declaration of incompatibility. Where the courts issue a declaration of incompatibility, it is a matter for the Government to consider the steps to be taken to remedy the incompatibility, as such a declaration will not, for constitutional reasons, affect the validity, enforcement or continuing operation of the national law in question. Section 5(4) creates a new compensatory scheme for a person who has been granted a declaration of incompatibility by the courts. Such a person may apply to the Government for payment of *ex gratia* compensation in respect of any injury, loss or damage he or she may have suffered as a result of the incompatibility. This section has been criticised for failing to provide a mechanism whereby the level of compensation awarded can be appealed.

12–17   Section 6 of the 2003 Act provides that, before a court decides whether to make a declaration of incompatibility, the Attorney General must be given notice of the proceedings in accordance with the rules of court. In summary, the remedies available to a litigant under the 2003 Act are confined to a declaration of incompatibility (and possible *ex gratia* compensation) and an action for damages against an "organ of the State" (*i.e.* a health board).

The District Court

12–18   Sections 2 and 4 of the 2003 Act apply in the District Court. Consequently, decisions of the ECt.HR are now relevant in public and private law cases dealt with in this court. The District Court must also interpret legislation in a manner harmonious with the State's obligations under the ECHR. This it must do, however, "in so far as is possible" and "subject to the rules of law relating to interpretation and application". No remedy is available in the District Court for breach of a ECHR right. District Court issues likely to be informed by ECt.HR jurisprudence include placing children in care, access issues in respect of children placed in care, the representation of children in proceedings and expert reports in cases involving children.

Protection

12–19 There is an obligation, imposed by Art.3, ECHR, to protect children from harm and ill-treatment. In *Z and Ors v UK*,[7] the ECt.HR called into question the approach of the English courts to the liability of public authorities. It held that a local authority has a positive duty to see that measures are taken to protect a child at risk. The ECt.HR noted, in particular, the local authority's failure to assign a senior social worker or guardian *ad litem* in respect of the child at the centre of that case. In *K.L. v UK*, the Commission on Human Rights declared admissible a case in which children, placed in care following abuse by their parents, argued a breach by the local authority of its duty to comply with its positive obligations under Art.3 to take steps to protect them.[8]

12–20 In *A. v UK*,[9] the ECt.HR, considering the caning of a nine-year-old boy by his stepfather and the defence of "reasonable chastisement" in the law of the UK, concluded that the State had failed to protect the applicant from punishment amounting to inhuman or degrading treatment within the meaning of Art.3, ECHR. The Court held that cognisance should be taken of the following criteria when considering whether the punishment is reasonable:

- the nature and context of the child's behaviour;
- the duration of the behaviour;
- the physical and mental consequences of the behaviour of the child; and
- the age and personal characteristics of the child.

It is clear from the judgment of the ECt.HR in this case that the State has a positive duty to take measures to ensure that no one private individual is subjected to torture, inhuman or degrading treatment at the hands of other private individuals. On this point, the court held that States are:

> "[r]equired to take measures designed to ensure that individuals within their jurisdiction are not subjected to torture or inhuman or degrading treatment or punishment, including such ill treatment administered by private individuals. Children and other vulnerable individuals, in particular, are entitled to State protection, in the form of effective deterrence against such serious breaches of personal integrity".[10]

---

[7] (2001) 2 F.L.R. 612.

[8] (1998) 26 E.H.R.R. C.D. 113. See also *E. v UK* [2003] 1 F.L.R. 348, where the ECt.HR held that there has been a breach of Art.3 where there had been no effective remedy for the continuous assaults suffered by four children at the hands of their stepfather, due to maladministration by a local authority.

[9] (1999) 27 E.H.R.R. 611.

[10] See, however, *Costello-Roberts v UK* (1993) 19 E.H.R.R. 112, where three "whacks" on the bottom administered by a headmaster to a seven-year-old boy was not found to amount to a violation of Art.3, ECHR.

12–21 In *D.P. & J.C. v UK*,[11] the ECt.HR held that in cases involving serious child abuse, the State will only be liable where the local authority (*i.e.* health board) knew, had reason to suspect, or ought to have known that abuse was going on.

The right to liberty and security

12–22 Article 5, ECHR guarantees the right to liberty and security, though this is not an absolute right. It has been invoked in cases involving disturbed children, for whom there are at present insufficient high support units in Ireland and where, in many cases, they are held in penal institutions for want of appropriate accommodation. Ireland has recently been held to be in breach of Art.5, ECHR in *D.G. v Ireland*.[12] The case, as previously stated in Chapter 11,[13] challenged the legality of detaining in St. Patrick's Institution a 16-year-old non-offending child with serious behavioural problems. The ECt.HR held that the detention of the child in St Patrick's Institution was in contravention of rights guaranteed under Art.5(1), ECHR. The ECt.HR ruled that the State acted unlawfully in failing to provide the disturbed child with a safe, suitable therapeutic unit and upheld the claim that the child's human rights were violated and his right to compensation denied.[14]

Legal aid

12–23 In *Airey v Ireland*,[15] the European Court of Human Rights held that Art.6 of the ECHR imposed obligations upon a State which may only be discharged by providing legal representation.[16] This decision does not create a right to free legal aid in all civil cases, but rather imposes a duty upon the State to act, which depends on the nature of the rights under consideration.[17] It is likely that the requirement to provide free legal aid will arise more frequently in relation to children than in relation to adults.

Public hearing

12–24 In general, Irish law is committed to the administration of justice in public. This principle is guaranteed by the Constitution. Article 34(1) of the Constitution states:

---

[11] [2003] 1 F.L.R. 50 (ECHR).

[12] Judgment of May 16, 2002.

[13] See para.11–14.

[14] See, however, *Koniarska v UK*, judgment of October 12, 2000, where the court held that placing a child in secure accommodation was not contrary to the ECHR as it amounted to "educational supervision" within the meaning of Art.5 of the ECHR.

[15] (1979–80) 2 E.H.R.R. 305.

[16] See also *Dombo Beheer BV v Netherlands* (1994) 18 E.H.R.R. 213, and *P., C. and S. v UK* (2002) 35 E.H.R.R. 1075.

[17] Interestingly, Ireland entered a reservation in respect of legal aid on September 3, 1953. A reservation gives a State certain immunity from a challenge on ECHR grounds.

"Justice shall be administered in courts established by law by judges, and, save in such special and limited cases as may be prescribed by law, shall be administered in public."

12–25 By way of exception to this general principle, however, family law cases and cases involving children are amongst the categories of cases which may by law be shielded from such public and media scrutiny. In general, the public and the media are not admitted to family proceedings. The Courts (Supplemental Provisions) Act 1961 provides that justice may be administered otherwise than in public in specified circumstances. Section 45(1) of the 1961 Act states:

"Justice may be administered otherwise than in public in any of the following cases:

(a) applications of an urgent nature for relief by way of habeas corpus, bail, prohibition or injunction;
(b) matrimonial causes and matters;
(c) lunacy and minor matters;
(d) proceedings involving the disclosure of a secret manufacturing process."

Individual family law statutes provide that the "*in camera* rule" is mandatory in most family law matters.[18]

12–26 Of special significance in discussing the "*in camera* rule" is Art.6, ECHR. In *Werner v Austria*,[19] the ECt.HR stated that "the holding of court hearings in public constitutes a fundamental principle enshrined in paragraph 1 of Art.6", save where there is "a pressing social need" and the reasons advanced for the restriction are "relevant and sufficient". The right to a public hearing mirrors, of course, the explicit obligations under Art.6, ECHR, but it is also a right that arises under the guarantee of freedom of expression enshrined in Art.10, ECHR.

12–27 The decision of the ECt.HR in *B. and P. v UK*[20] states that a rigid interpretation of a mandatory "*in camera* rule" may be in breach of the ECHR if it is disproportionate. This case related to two fathers who wanted their residence applications concerning their sons to be heard in public, with a public pronouncement of the judgment. They pleaded breach of Arts 6 and 10, ECHR. The ECt.HR noted the existence of a judicial discretion in English domestic

---

[18] See s.34 of the Judicial Separation and Family Law Reform Act 1989, s.38(5) of the Family Law (Divorce) Act 1996; s.25(1) and (2) of the Family Law (Maintenance of Spouses and Children) Act 1976; s.29 of the Child Care Act 1991; s.38(6) of the Family Law Act 1995; and s.16(1) of the Domestic Violence Act 1996. There is no mandatory provision in the Guardianship of Infants Act 1964 or Family Home Protection Act 1976. That said, the discretionary provision of s.45 of the Courts (Supplemental Provisions) Act 1961 applies to such applications.

[19] Judgment of November 24, 1997.

[20] Judgment of April 24, 2001.

law to hear Children Act proceedings in public if merited by the special features of the case. As both cases were routine and "run of the mill" in their nature, the hearings "*in camera*" did not give rise to a violation of Art.6(1) of the ECHR. Neither was there a breach of Art.10, ECHR on the ground that the fathers could not share information revealed in the cases with others, as the restrictions imposed were to protect the rights of others, to prevent the disclosure of information received in confidence and to maintain the authority of the judiciary. The restriction of disclosure was proportionate to these aims. In the Irish context, the absolute and mandatory nature of the "*in camera* rule" in the 1989 and 1996 Acts is clearly inconsistent with the requirements of Art.6(1), ECHR.

12–28   This shortcoming has been addressed in the Civil Liability and Courts Act 2004. Section 40(3) of the Act, to come into force on March 31, 2005, allows for the publication of reports of family law proceedings so long as the report does not identify the parties or any child to which the proceedings relate. It provides as follows:

> "40(3)—Nothing contained in a relevant enactment shall operate to prohibit—
>
>> (a) the preparation by a barrister at law or a solicitor or a person falling within any other class of persons specified in regulations made by the Minister and publication of a report of proceedings to which the relevant enactment relates, or
>>
>> (b) the publication of the decision of the Court in such proceedings, in accordance with rules of court, provided that the report or decision does not contain any information which would enable the parties to the proceedings or any child to which the proceedings relate to be identified. ..."

Reform of the "*in camera* rule" is necessary but involves a sensitive balancing act between the right to privacy and the right to a fair, transparent and accountable system of justice.

The right of the child to initiate legal proceedings

12–29   The child's right to initiate proceedings is implied in the right of access to a court under Art.6, ECHR. In *Golder v UK*,[21] the ECt.HR explicitly refers to the right of the child to bring proceedings, although in the later case of *Ashingdane v UK*,[22] the ECt.HR held that the right of access to court could be restricted.

---

[21] ECt.HR, February 21, 1975, series A Vol.18, para.39.
[22] ECt.HR, May 28, 1985, series A, Vol.93.

The right to participate in legal proceedings

12–30   Articles 6 and 8, ECHR afford certain procedural safeguards applicable in court proceedings in a Contracting State. The right of the individual to participate in legal proceedings is one of those procedural safeguards, a conclusion underlined by the ECt.HR in *T v UK*[23] and *V v UK*.[24] Both cases concerned whether two 11-year-old boys who were tried for murder in an adult court had received a fair trial within the meaning of Art.6, ECHR. The cases turned on whether the boys had participated effectively in their own criminal trial and the court held in the circumstances that they had not. The provision of separate and impartial representation to children was, in these cases, deemed to be essential to the conduct of certain criminal proceedings involving children. A similar approach was adopted by the ECt.HR in the recent case of *S.C. v UK*,[25] where the ECt.HR held that there had been a violation of Art.6(1) of the ECHR. Considering the far-reaching nature of many public law proceedings involving children, a similar approach is likely in relation to applications by a health board for orders for care or supervision of a child and perhaps even in civil proceedings generally. Failure to hear children, aged four and six years, was a feature of the decision in *Kutzner v Germany*,[26] even though expert evidence was obtained by the court in that case prior to its decision to take the children into care.

At best the child's right in Ireland to representation in court applications affecting him or her is discretionary. The net result of such discretion is a chaotic system of representation for children with significant variations as to its operation throughout the State. The provisions for the separate representation of children in Irish public and private law proceedings are primarily for the children themselves and the entitlement accrues to them under the ECHR, not as some kind of dispensation.

Right to a fair trial

12–31   One of the procedural safeguards afforded by the ECHR is the right to a fair trial.[27] Article 6(1) provides:

> "In the determination of his civil rights and obligations or of any criminal charge against him, everyone is entitled to a fair and public hearing within a reasonable time by an independent and impartial tribunal established by law".[28]

12–32   In *Ruiz-Mateos v Spain*,[29] the ECt.HR stated that "as a matter of general principle the right to a fair adversarial trial means the opportunity to have

---

[23] December 16, 1999 (Application No.24724/94).

[24] December 16, 1999 (Application No.24724/94).

[25] June 15, 2004 (Application No.60958/00).

[26] February 26, 2002 (Application No.46544/99).

[27] See *V v UK*, December 16, 1999 (Application No.24888/94) and *S.C. v UK*, June 15, 2004 (Application No.60958/00).

[28] See also *Barbera, Messegue and Jabardo v Spain* (2000) 11 E.C.H.R. 360.

[29] (1993) 16 E.H.R.R. 505.

knowledge of and comment on the observations filed or evidence adduced by the other party". The three central requirements of a fair trial are a hearing in the presence of the parties, all evidence should be produced to the parties, and the opportunity to challenge evidence, which includes the right to cross-examine witnesses.[30] In children's cases, however, the Court has determined that some relaxation of the composition of a typical court and its procedures may be required.[31]

12–33 The right to a fair trial mirrors, of course, the explicit obligations under Art.6, ECHR, but it is also arguably a part of the procedural safeguards in Art.8. The inextricable link between the rights expressed in Art.6 and the inherent safeguards of Art.8 is underlined by the decision in *Keegan v Ireland.*[32] In that case, involving primarily the question of a non-marital father's right to be consulted in relation to the adoption of his child, the court held that the father's rights under Arts 6 and 8, ECHR had been violated. The court, at p.362, para.51 in particular, noted that:

> "[t]he fact that Irish law permitted the secret placement of the child for adoption without the applicant's knowledge or consent, leading to the bonding of the child with the proposed adopters and to the subsequent making of an adoption order, amounted to an interference with his right to respect for family life."

Article 8, ECHR was applicable, the ECt.HR emphasised, despite the fact that the natural parents of the child were never married to each other. For two years prior to the making of the adoption order, the mother and father had been living in a stable relationship and that essentially formed a family for ECHR purposes. Alluding to Art.6, ECHR, the ECt.HR held that the father's right to "a fair and public hearing by an independent and impartial tribunal" had also been violated. Effectively, the father had "no rights under Irish law" to challenge the decision to place his child for adoption, either before the Adoption Board or before the courts. In summary, he had "no standing in the adoption procedure generally".[33] The applicant was awarded £12,000 in pecuniary and non-pecuniary loss and approximately £38,000 in respect of his domestic and Strasbourg legal costs and expenses. The Adoption Act 1998, in amending the Adoption Act 1952, has now introduced consultation procedures for natural fathers in the adoption process, and also details the circumstances when such procedures need to be applied.

---

[30] *X. v Austria*, Application No.5362/72, (1972) 42 C.D. 145.

[31] See *McMichael v UK* (1995) 20 E.H.R.R. 205, though in that case the failure to disclose social reports to the applicants amounted to a violation of Art.6(1), ECHR. Also *L. v UK* (2000) 2 F.L.R. 322 where a breach of Art.6(1), ECHR was held in respect of the provision of documents at case conferences when not all participants see them. This case also considered the obtaining of information from Adoption Agencies and Local Authorities.

[32] (1994) 18 E.H.R.R. 342.

[33] *ibid.* at 364.

Family life

12–34   One cannot avoid noting the enormous potential of the ECHR to protect and promote the rights of children. Article 8(1), ECHR guarantees as a basic right the right to respect for private and family life, home and correspondence. Article 8(2) sets out the limits of permissible interference with the enjoyment of these rights by the State. The ECHR (unlike the Irish Constitution) makes no distinction between the family life of a marital and non-marital family.[34]

12–35   Family life constitutes not only relations between parents and their children, but also extends to grandparents and grandchildren.[35] For other relationships, it is necessary to produce evidence of a real and close family tie. In summary, the existence of family life is a question of fact and degree.[36] Family life, for example, has been held by the ECt.HR to include the relationship between the adopted child and adoptive parents,[37] and that between a foster parent and a foster child. The position of a non-marital father lacking a legal filiation link (through marriage or recognition) was considered in *R.S. Yousef v The Netherlands*.[38]

Same-sex unions

12–36   In *Dudgeon v United Kingdom*[39] and *Norris v Ireland*,[40] the ECt.HR described sexual life as the most intimate aspect of a person's private life for the purposes of Art.8, ECHR.[41] The ECt.HR has not, however, been prepared to extend the concept of "family life" to include a same-sex relationship.

12–37   In *Kerkhoven, Hinke & Hinke v The Netherlands*,[42] the European Commission on Human Rights held that a stable relationship between two women and a child born to one of them (by donor insemination) did not amount

---

[34] See *Marckx v Belgium* (1980) 2 E.H.R.R. 330, *Johnston v Ireland* (1987) 9 E.H.R.R. 203, and *Keegan v Ireland* (1994) 18 E.H.R.R. 341; see also *Berrehab v The Netherlands* (1989) 11 E.H.R.R. 322, where the European Court of Human Rights (ECt.HR) held that the traditional family relationship between a divorced man and his marital child did not cease to exist on the separation or divorce of the parents; *Kroon v The Netherlands* (1994) 19 E.H.R.R. 263 where the relationship between a man and a child conceived during an extra-marital affair, which amounted to a long-term relationship wherein the parties had four children by the time of the application, constituted a family within the meaning of Art.8 of the ECHR; *Boyle v UK* (1995) 19 E.H.R.R. 179, where family life was held to exist between an uncle and a nephew; and *Boughanemi v France*, ECt.HR, April 24, 1996, Reports of Judgments and Decisions 1996.II, 594, para.35, where family life was held to exist where the father could show a close relationship to the child. Also *Elsholz v Germany*, Application No.25735/94, July 13, 2000.

[35] *Marckx v Belgium* (1979–80) 2 E.H.R.R. 330.

[36] *X., Y. and Z. v UK* [1997] 2 F.L.R. 892.

[37] *X. v France* (1982) 5 E.H.R.R. 302.

[38] [2003] 1 F.L.R. 210.

[39] (1982) 4 E.H.R.R. 149.

[40] (1991) 13 E.H.R.R. 186.

[41] See also *X. v UK* (1997) 24 E.H.R.R. 143.

[42] Application No.15666/89, May 19, 1992.

to family life within the meaning of Art.8 of the ECHR. It should also be noted that the Court of First Instance of the Court of Justice of the European Communities in *D and Sweden v Council of Ministers*,[43] citing *Lisa Grant v Southwest Trains*,[44] held that, though the ECt.HR had extended privacy to protect private homosexual relations, the European Commission on Human Rights had stated that the right to respect for "family life" did not extend to homosexual relations.

In *Frette v France*, the ECt.HR held that it was not incompatible with the ECHR to exclude a single, homosexual male applicant from the adoption eligibility process on the grounds of his sexuality.[45] The Court stated:

> "If account is taken of the broad margin of appreciation to be left to States in this area and the need to protect children's best interests to achieve the desired balance, the refusal to authorise **adoption** did not infringe the principle of proportionality."

It can be seen from the foregoing that the protection to be offered to the child in the *de facto* family as defined within the jurisprudence of the ECt.HR is varied, and there is a wide margin of appreciation allowed to the contracting Parties. More than in any other area of law, the development of conflict is likely between the Irish domestic concept of the family and concepts set down by the ECt.HR.

Delay

12–38 Article 6 of the ECHR provides:

> "In the determination of his civil rights and obligations, everyone is entitled to a ... hearing within a reasonable time by [a] ... tribunal. ..."

12–39 Recently, in *Price and Lowe v United Kingdom*,[46] the ECt.HR held unanimously that the length of the civil proceedings (which began on February 12, 1986, and ended on March 30, 1998) amounted to a violation of Art.6(1), ECHR. The ECt.HR stated as follows:

> "The Court has held on a number of occasions that a principle of domestic law or practice that the parties to civil proceedings are required to take the initiative with regard to the progress of the proceedings, does not dispense the State from complying with the requirement to deal with cases in a reasonable time.[47] In the light of the preceding comments, ...,

---

[43] Case T–264/97, Court of Justice of the European Communities, Court of First Instance, January 28, 1999.

[44] unreported, February 17, 1998.

[45] [2003] 2 F.L.R 9.

[46] No.43186/98, judgment of July 29, 2003.

[47] See *Buchhotz v Germany*, judgment of May 6, 1981, Series No.43, p.16, §50; *Guinco v Portugal*, judgment of July 10, 1984, Series A, No.81, p.17, §32; *Capuana v Italy*, judgment of June 25, 1987, Series A No.119, p.11, §25; *Mitchell and Holloway v United Kingdom*, No.44808/98, judgment of December 17, 2002.

the Court finds that the proceedings in the present case were not dealt with within a 'reasonable time', as required by Art.6 of the Convention."[48]

The prospects of a fair hearing may be diminished by significant delay in child law proceedings.[49] This may result in a breach of Arts 6 or 8 of the ECHR or, as in *W v UK*,[50] of both. Article 7 of the European Convention on the Exercise of Children's Rights 1996, requires that:

"[I]n proceedings affecting a child, the judicial authority shall act speedily to avoid any unnecessary delay and procedures shall be available to ensure that its decisions are rapidly enforced."

12–40   Mindful that "justice delayed" is often "justice denied", or at least diminished, the jurisprudence of the ECt.HR has tended to lean towards requiring that the national authorities display special diligence in expediting proceedings involving children. Indeed, in *H v UK*,[51] the ECt.HR stated that exceptional diligence is required where the maxim "justice delayed is justice denied" is fully applicable. This might arise where custody and access proceedings are initiated by parents of children in the care of health boards as such proceedings are decisive for the parents' future relations with their children and have a "particular quality of irreversibility". The ECt.HR in *H v UK* alluded in particular to delay such that the elapse of time has the effect of determining the issue. Denham J., as stated in Chapter 10, expressed a similar view in *M.(E.) ex parte M.(J.)*,[52] a Hague Convention case (*i.e.* child abduction case) where time is of the essence.

12–41   In *Nuutinen v Finland*,[53] the ECt.HR held that Art.6, ECHR had been violated by the five years and five months duration of the custody and access proceedings. The current delay in the procurement and completion of s.20 reports in Ireland and the difficulties encountered in retaining guardians *ad litem* must surely fall to be considered in this context. If it transpires that a child is seriously neglected or ill-treated due to a delay in the procurement of a s.20 report, for example, a breach of Art.3, ECHR may also arise.[54] In *Glaser v UK*,[55] the ECt.HR stated that it is essential that custody and access cases be

---

[48] At p.4.

[49] In *Eastern Health Board v M.K. and M.K.* [1999] 2 I.R. 99; [1999] 2 I.L.R.M. 321, Denham J. expressed her concern at the considerable delay (three years) which had occurred in that case: "Time is of the essence in child custody cases. Childhood exists for only a short and finite time. Custody and care arrangements of themselves create dynamics which have a profound effect on children and their families. The long-term effects can be immense. Consequently, I voice my unease at the length of time, the delay, which exists between the judgment of the High Court and the appeal."

[50] (1988) 10 E.H.R.R. 29 at 65.

[51] (1988) 10 E.H.R.R. 95.

[52] unreported, Supreme Court, July 9, 2003.

[53] ECt.HR, June 27, 2000.

[54] *See Z. and D. v UK*, no. 29392/95, Comm. Rep. 10.9.99.

[55] ECt.HR, September 19, 2000.

dealt with speedily. The ECt.HR ruled that neither the volume of work nor shortage of resources will justify excessive delay.

Consultation and access to reports

12–42 Parents should be adequately consulted on and informed of all matters pertaining to their children. Failure to do so will amount to a breach of Art.8, ECHR unless the exempting provisions of Art.8(2) apply. In *McMichael v UK*,[56] the ECt.HR ruled that a parent cannot, without good reason, be denied access to reports or documents relating to his or her child. To do so would be to deny the parent his right to participate in the decision-making process relating to his child.

12–43 Denying a parent access to reports or documents may constitute a breach of Art.6, ECHR which guarantees the right to a "fair and public hearing". This necessarily involves the right of access to reports or documents, save where this is other than in the best interests of the child. The principle of proportionality will apply in the provision of reports or documents. It should be stated that while there is no absolute right to reports or documents, ECt.HR jurisprudence dictates that a decision to disclose should be considered speedily. Moreover, this decision should be made by an independent authority such as a Court. In *T.P. and K.M. v UK*,[57] for example, the ECt.HR held that parents, defending serious allegations regarding children, should, where possible, be afforded full access to information as to their factual basis. The ECt.HR adopted a similar approach in *Venema v The Netherlands*[58] where a care order was made in respect of a child on a suspicion that she was a victim of Munchausen Syndrome by Proxy.

Care order

12–44 The right to family life cannot be interfered with, unless such interference is in accordance with law and has an aim or aims that is or are legitimate.[59] The interference must also be shown to be "necessary in a democratic society". As a core principle, then, the ECHR requires that the contracting parties refrain from arbitrary interference in the lives of individuals in the State. Thus, where the State intervenes in the life of a family, for instance by taking a child into care, the State must show that its intervention is in accordance with the law, for the furtherance of a legitimate aim or aims and necessary in a democratic society.

12–45 In a case against Finland, the ECt.HR held that as the care order was not the only option available to the local authority in that case for securing the

---

[56] (1995) 20 E.H.R.R. 205.
[57] (2001) 2 F.L.R. 549.
[58] December 17, 2002 (Application No.35731/97).
[59] Art.8(2), E.C.H.R.

children's protection, the reasons used to justify it were insufficient and amounted to a violation of Art.8, ECHR.[60] In *Venema v The Netherlands*[61] in 2002, the ECt.HR stated as follows:

> "[I]t is for the respondent State to establish that a careful assessment of the impact of the proposed care measure on the parents and the child was carried out prior to the implementation of a care measure".

The impact of the foregoing judgments is that where health boards fail to use a care order as a measure of last resort, a violation of a core provision of the ECHR may arise.[62]

Access

12–46   Where a child is validly taken into care, Art.8 of the ECHR guarantees that parents and children have access to each other. Thus, any restriction on access must be justified by reference to Art.8(2), ECHR.[63] There is, in addition, a positive duty on the health board to facilitate access between the parent and child.[64] The ECt.HR has taken the view that as the mutual enjoyment by a child and a parent of each other's company constitutes a fundamental element of family life, access should only be denied where there is clear evidence that it is contrary to the best interests of the child. This approach now forms part of Art.9(3) of the United Nations Convention on the Rights of the Child 1989, which provides for:

> "the right of the child who is separated from one or both parents to maintain public relations and direct contact with both parents on a regular basis, except if it is contrary to the child's best interests."

The ECt.HR has also stated access to be the right of the child.[65]

12–47   In protecting individual rights, the State is under an obligation to prevent interference by others with a view to undermining these rights.[66] This is a positive duty placed on the State. In *Hokkanen v Finland*, for instance, the ECt.HR ruled that the Finnish government had a positive obligation to facilitate

---

[60] December 17, 2002 (Application No.35731/97).

[61] See also *E.P. v Italy* (2001) 31 E.H.R.R. 17.

[62] *K. and T. v Finland*, judgment of April 27, 2000.

[63] See for instance, *Hendriks v Netherlands* (1983) 5 E.H.R.R. 223; *W. v UK* (1988) 10 E.H.R.R. 29; *R. v UK* (1988) 10 E.H.R.R. 74; *O. v UK* (1988) 10 E.H.R.R. 82, *H. v UK* (1988) 10 E.H.R.R. 95; *Olsson v Sweden* (1989) 11 E.H.R.R. 259, and *McMichael v UK* (1995) 20 E.H.R.R. 205.

[64] See *Eriksson v Sweden* (1990) 12 E.H.R.R. 183.

[65] See *Hoppe v Germany* [2003] 1 F.L.R. 384.

[66] See *Airey v Ireland* (1980) 2 E.H.R.R. 305; *X. and Y. v The Netherlands* (1985) 8 E.H.R.R. 235; *Johnston v Ireland* (1987) 9 E.H.R.R. 203; *Keegan v Ireland* (1994) 18 E.H.R.R. 342, and *Hokkanen v Finland* (1994) 19 E.H.R.R. 139.

parental access to a child, including ensuring that third parties (in this case the maternal grandparents) did not impede the child's right to access.[67]

12–48 The ECt.HR has stated that a care order is intended to be temporary in nature and that its implementation must be guided always by the ultimate aim of family reunion. Contact between parents and children in care is vital therefore, in order to maintain the family relationship. In *Olsson v Sweden*,[68] the ECt.HR noted that there was a positive obligation on each State to take appropriate measures to facilitate reunion between children and their parents. In that case, three children from one family (the Olssons) had been placed in foster care with different foster parents living a considerable distance from each other and from the parents of the children. As a result of the geographical distance between them, contact between the children themselves and between the parents and the children was made virtually impossible. This, the ECt.HR concluded, constituted a breach of Art.8, ECHR, the State having failed to make adequate provision for intra-familial contact. The administrative difficulties (such as the apparent shortage of appropriate foster families) asserted in a defence by the State were deemed not to be of sufficient weight to prevent a ruling against it.[69] Little guidance is given, however, as to what is an acceptable distance by which children and their parents can be separated.

Procedural rights in child law cases—some recent trends

12–49 In *Elsholz v Germany*,[70] the ECt.HR considered the hearing of children in access proceedings. The court held that an expert should have been appointed to interpret the child's evidence:

> "Moreover, taking into account the importance of the subject-matter, namely, the relations between a father and his child, the Regional Court should not have been satisfied, in the circumstances, by relying on the file and the written appeal submissions without having at its disposal psychological expert evidence in order to evaluate the child's statements."

12–50 *Elsholz* is an important ruling by the ECt.HR that emphasises the need to obtain psychological analysis of children's evidence. In *Sommerfeld v Germany*,[71] the ECt.HR criticised the German national court for not obtaining a psychological report, in order to assess the apparently entrenched views of a 13-year-old child not to see her father.

The Chamber's decision was overturned by the Grand Chamber, which held that the national court could rely on the directly expressed wishes of a 13-

---

[67] (1994) 19 E.H.R.R. 139. See, however, *Nuutinen v Finland*, ECt.HR, June 27, 2000, Reports of Judgments and Decisions (2001).

[68] (1989) 11 E.H.R.R. 259.

[69] See *Implementation Handbook for the Convention on the Rights of the Child*, prepared for UNICEF by Rachel Hodgkin and Peter Newell, New York, 1998, 152.

[70] ECt.HR, July 13, 2000.

[71] October 11, 2001 (Application No.31871/96).

year-old.[72] That said, the December 2003 French decision of *Palau-Martinez* highlights the need for expert evidence in the making of decisions on custody and access matters.[73]

12–51   The decision of the ECt.HR in *Sahin v Germany*[74] is worthy of particular note. In that case, a father's application for access (in respect of his five-year-old child) was rejected on the basis that expert evidence supported the termination of access. The domestic court did not hear the child as it relied on the experts' view that the hearing of the child in court would impose a psychological strain on the child, since the child could gain the impression that her statements would be decisive. The ECt.HR, however, held that the domestic court should only have considered the best interests of the child after having direct contact with the child. In particular, the European Court stated that complete information on the relationship between the father and the child was an indispensable prerequisite for establishing a child's true wishes and thereby striking a fair balance between the interests at stake.

12–52   This case was later referred to the Grand Chamber where the Chamber's decision was overturned. The Grand Chamber held that the regional court had not overstepped the margin of appreciation in relying on the expert's statements "about the risks inherent in questioning a child". Notwithstanding the fact that hearing a child between four and five years of age did not amount to a violation of Art. 8, ECHR, the Grand Chamber held that the hearing of a child in court depends "on the specific circumstances of each case, having due regard to the age and maturity of the child concerned."[75]

Discrimination

12–53   Article 14, the right not to be discriminated against, has been less effective than some of the other ECHR provisions in that it can only be pleaded in conjunction with another article in the ECHR.[76] It has, on occasion, been used to challenge the substantive outcome of child custody/access disputes.[77] Article 14 states:

> "The enjoyment of the rights and freedoms set forth in the Convention shall be secured without discrimination on any ground, such as sex, race, colour, language, religion, political or other opinion, national or social origin associated with the national minority, property, birth or other status."

12–54   In the case of *Hoffman v Austria*, the ECt.HR found a violation of

---

[72] [2003] 2 F.C.R. 619.

[73] *Affaire Palau-Martinez v France*, December 16, 2003 (Application No.64927/01).

[74] (2002) 1 F.L.R. 119.

[75] Judgment of July 8, 2003, para.73.

[76] This is likely to change when Protocol 14 to the ECHR comes into force.

[77] See *Keegan v Ireland* (1994) 18 E.H.R.R. 34, *Hoffman v Austria* (1994) 17 E.H.R.R. 293, and the *Palau-Martinez* decision in December of 2003.

Art.14, ECHR as the legislation under consideration provided a blanket ban on awarding custody to a person who had changed his or her religion.[78] Ireland has not yet ratified the non-discrimination protocol.[79]

CONCLUSION

12–55 The ECHR has been criticised as being too conservative. Much of the early jurisprudence suffers from the now-dated assumption that shielding "the family" from state interference automatically protects children. There is, however, a clear power imbalance between adults and children in cases of conflict.[80] Recent jurisprudence of the ECt.HR has unambiguously recognised and addressed the power imbalance inherent in disputes between parents and children.[81] The net result of this development is that the ECHR is now proving to be a potent instrument in the promotion of child rights, a fact borne out by recent statistics from England and Wales indicating that the majority of Convention cases in family law involved children cases. There is no doubt that the coming into force of the European Convention on Human Rights Act 2003 on December 31, 2003, will have a positive impact on child law in Ireland.

The Charter of Fundamental Rights of the European Union

12–56 The Charter of Fundamental Rights of the European Union was adopted on December 7, 2000, with its principal aim being the maintenance of the human rights protection currently afforded by European Union law, national law and international law.[82] In s.4 of the preamble to the Charter, it is stated that:

> "[i]t is necessary to strengthen the protection of fundamental rights in the light of changes in society, social progress and scientific and techno-logical developments by making those rights more visible in a Charter."

Significantly, the Charter is declaratory rather than legally binding, rendering it of little direct assistance to the individual litigant. That said, the case law of the European Court of Justice (ECJ) is certain to be affected by this development.[83]

---

[78] See also *Salgueiro da Silva Mouta v Portugal* (2001) 31 E.H.R.R. 1055, which directly follows the *Hoffman* case.

[79] Protocol 12.

[80] See for example *Nielson v Denmark* (1989) 11 E.H.R.R. 175, where the majority of the ECt.HR held that the rights of a 12-year-old boy under Art.5, E.C.H.R. had not been infringed by his detention and placement in a psychiatric ward at the request of his mother.

[81] See *Hokkanen v Finland* [1996] 1 F.L.R. 289 and *A. v UK (human rights: punishment of child)* [1998] 2 F.L.R. 959.

[82] O.J. C364 Vol.43, December 18, 2000.

[83] See, for example, *Carpenter v Secretary of State for the Home Department*, September 13, 2001.

12–57   The Charter does not create new family and child rights, but is generally confined to restating rights available under existing international instruments. Chapter II guarantees the right to respect for private and family life[84] and the right to marry and found a family. Equality between men and women and the protection of children[85] are covered in Chapter III. Chapter V protects the right of access to documents. The right to a fair trial is provided for in Chapter VI. Chapter VII explains the relationship between the Charter of Fundamental Rights of the European Union and the ECHR. This Chapter allows the ECJ to depart from the interpretation afforded by the ECt.HR of a right protected by the ECHR. Article 51 of the Charter, however, provides:

> "Nothing in this charter shall be interpreted as restricting or adversely affecting human rights and fundamental freedoms as recognised, in their respective fields of application, by international law and international agreements to which the Union, the Community or all Member States are party, including the European Convention for the Protection of Human Rights and Fundamental Freedoms, and by the Member States' constitutions."

12–58   With the adoption of the Charter of Fundamental Rights of the European Union, we see the emergence of two separate systems of human rights protection in Ireland. The Irish courts are bound by EU law to follow the jurisprudence of the ECJ but are also bound under international law to follow the jurisprudence of the ECt.HR. To which system should the domestic courts defer? This growing tension between EU law and international law can be seen in the cases of *Pellegrini v Italy*[86] and *Sahin v Germany*[87].[88] The issues raised in *Pellegrini* and *Sahin* are especially important for the member states of the European Union who are obliged by virtue of Art.19 of Council Regulation 1347/00 (discussed later in this chapter) to give effect to each other's judgments in civil proceedings relating to divorce, legal separation or marriage annulment and parental responsibility on the occasion of those proceedings. The importance derives from the fact that individuals may seek to invoke the provisions of the ECHR to prevent the automatic recognition of a judgment under Council Regulation 1347/00. The time is therefore now ripe to clarify the position by establishing a hierarchy of courts.

---

[84]   Art.9.
[85]   See also Arts 24 and 31 of the Charter.
[86]   Application No.30882/96, July 20, 2001.
[87]   (2003) 2 F.L.R. 671.
[88]   See also Case C–60/00 *Carpenter v Secretary of State for the Home Department*, September 13, 2001, Case C–459/99 *Mouvement contre le racisme, l'antisémitisme et la Xénophobie ASBL v The Belgian State*, July 25, 2002, and the opinion of A.-G. Geelhoed in Case C–413/99 *Baumbast and R. v Secretary of State for the Home Department*, July 5, 2001.

THE REVISED BRUSSELS II REGULATION

Introduction

12–59 The Brussels II Convention, signed on May 28, 1998,[89] was arguably the most dramatic development in the field of family law since the establishment of the EEC. The Convention came as a surprise to many[90] as it was the first time that the EU had introduced a legal measure directly concerning family law. However, in many ways this Convention or something like it was inevitable. Since the 1992 completion of the internal market, the EU has been increasingly turning away from economic concerns and towards extending European law into other areas. Initiatives have been mooted in the areas of property law[91] and succession.[92] In the Borras Report it was stated that the Brussels II Convention was a "first step ... and it may open the way to other texts on matters of family law and succession".[93]

From Convention to Regulation

12–60 The impact of the so-called Brussels II Convention was further extended by its adoption as a Regulation of the European Community on March 1, 2001.[94] A Regulation is the EC legislative measure of the most binding nature. Once it has been duly enacted and promulgated, it generally is directly applicable throughout the European Union. This means that it automatically has the full force of law in every Member State, without the need for any action by that Member State. Moreover, as EC law is superior to national law within the scope of EC law, any national law that conflicts with the Regulation in any Member State is deemed to be unenforceable to the extent of such conflict.[95] A judge who comes across such a conflict must always enforce the EC measure over the national measure, even, for example in the Irish context, if neither the Irish Parliament nor the Superior Courts have yet invalidated the Irish measure.

12–61 The Regulation came into force on March 1, 2001. The impact of this

---

[89] O.J. C–221(1).

[90] For a treatment of the difficulties associated with the introduction of a Convention of this nature see, P. Beaumont and G. Moir, "Brussels Convention II: A New Private International Law Instrument in Family Matters for the European Union of the European Community", 20 (3) E.L.R. 268 (1995), and A. Reed, "A New Brussels Convention II on Family Law Matters for the European Union", 18(9) *J. Soc. Wel. & Fam.* L 381 (1996).

[91] The future "Brussels III".

[92] The future "Brussels IV".

[93] *The Explanatory Report on the Convention drawn up on the basis of Article K.3 of the Treaty on European Union, on Jurisdiction, Recognition and Enforcement of Judgments in Matrimonial Matters,* prepared by A. Borras (1988) O.J. C221/28 at para.1.

[94] Council Regulation 1347/2000 O.J. L160/19 on jurisdiction and the recognition and enforcement in matrimonial matters and in matters of parental responsibility for the children of both spouses.

[95] See C–6/64 *Costa v ENEL* [1964] E.C.R. 585, C–106/77 *Simenthal* [1978] E.C.R. 629, and *Campus Oil v Minister for Industry and Energy* [1982] I.R. 82.

metamorphosis from Convention to Regulation was highly significant in several respects. It brought the Convention directly into the corpus of EC law. As such it enjoyed the status of supremacy accorded to all binding EU laws.[96] It rendered the measure directly applicable as a matter of EC law. In other words, the measure became part of the national law of the various Member States without the need for incorporation by the individual states.

12–62   The Regulation applies to the Member States of the European Union, excluding Denmark, but including the 10 new Member States,[97] who must accept all existing EC Regulations as a condition of entry to the European Union. The Regulation does not apply to either the Channel Islands or the Isle of Man, although Gibraltar is covered by its terms.

12–63   The Regulation applies to all civil proceedings seeking the following:

* a divorce, legal separation and an annulment of marriage; and
* a declaration or other order concerning parental responsibility in respect of the children of both spouses, which declaration is sought in connection with proceedings for a divorce, legal separation and an annulment of marriage.

12–64   The aims of the Regulation were two-fold: first, to standardise the rules regarding the jurisdiction of courts in divorce, legal separation and annulment proceedings; and second, to give priority among courts with jurisdiction to the court first hearing the case. The latter has prompted parties with property abroad to litigate earlier in an attempt to secure jurisdiction in their state of choice. It has militated against the statutory provisions encouraging parties to engage in mediation, and other forms of alternative dispute resolution.

Revised Brussels II

12–65   "Complete automatic enforcement" is the basis of the new Council Regulation repealing Brussels II. It has become known as Brussels II *bis*, although it is referred to here as the "the revised Brussels II".[98] It came into force, according to Art.72, on August 1, 2004, though will apply in its entirety from March 1, 2005.[99] As with Brussels II, the revised Brussels II applies to the Member States of the European Union (excluding Denmark) but including the 10 new EU Member States. Transitional provisions are dealt with by Art.64 which states that "[t]he provisions of this Regulation shall apply only to legal proceedings instituted to documents formally drawn up or registered as

---

[96] See C–6/64 *Costa v ENEL* [1964] E.C.R. 585, C–106/77 *Simenthal* [1978] E.C.R. 629, and *Campus Oil v Minister for Industry and Energy* [1982] I.R. 82.

[97] Cyprus, Czech Republic, Estonia, Hungary, Latvia, Lithuania, Malta, Poland, Slovak Republic and Slovenia, who joined the EU on May 1, 2004.

[98] Council Regulation No.2201/2003 Concerning Jurisdiction and the Recognition and Enforcement of Judgments in Matrimonial Matters and Matters Relating to Parental Responsibility Repealing Regulation (EC) No.1347/2000 [2003] O.J. L338/1.

[99] The current Brussels II will cease to operate from March 1, 2005, and the revised Brussels II becomes directly applicable on that date.

authentic instruments and to agreements concluded between the parties" on or after March 1, 2005. It should, however, be noticed that for recognition and enforcement, Art.64(2) and (3) provides that the revised Brussels II will apply to judgments given under the current Regulation. A fully automatic enforcement regime takes no account of the fact that circumstances change rapidly in child matters. Indeed, the interlocutory nature of a parental responsibility order makes it unsuitable for automatic recognition and enforcement.

Interpretation

12–66   In approaching and interpreting the revised Brussels II, it is impossible to overestimate the importance of the Brussels convention (now Regulation[100]), and the considerable body of interpretative case law emanating principally from the ECJ, but also from the courts of the Member States. The Borras Report expressly provides that identical terms in the current Brussels II and the Brussels Convention must be given the same meaning and that the case law of the European Court of Justice (ECJ) on the Brussels Convention and Regulation should be taken into account.

No explanatory report accompanies the revised Brussels II, in that this instrument originated as Community legislation. The lack of an equivalent to the Borras Report accompanying the new Regulation is a major deficiency. The recitals, 33 in number, have therefore added weight (in the absence of an explanatory report) as a guide to interpreting the Regulation. That said, the Commission is currently preparing a Practice Guide on the application of the revised Regulation to the provisions concerning parental responsibility. This Guide will not be legally binding but will be of considerable assistance to practitioners.

Scope of the revised Regulation

12–67   The revised Brussels II makes few changes to the provisions on divorce, though it does make clear that the Regulation is confined to the status issue, and does not apply to ancillary orders.[101] The principal changes are in relation to children where the expression "parental responsibility" is greatly extended. The current Regulation confines parental responsibility to the children of both spouses in connection with a divorce, legal separation and marriage annulment and protective measures concerning those children that were taken at the time of the dissolution of a marriage. The revised Brussels II brings about significant changes in respect of jurisdiction, recognition and enforcement for measures pertaining to the protection of children.

---

[100] Council Regulation 44/2001 of December 22, 2000, on Jurisdiction and the Recognition and Enforcement of Judgments in Civil and Commercial Matters.

[101] Recital para.8 of the revised Brussels II provides:
"As regards judgments on divorce, legal separation or marriage annulment, this Regulation should apply only to the dissolution of matrimonial ties and should not deal with issues such as the grounds for divorce, property consequences of the marriage or any other ancillary measures."

12–68   Article 1(2) of the revised Regulation provides some instruction on the scope of parental responsibility. It "may, in particular, deal with:

(a) rights of custody and rights of access;

(b) guardianship, curatorship and similar institutions;

(c) the designation and functions of any person or body having charge of the child's person or property, representing or assisting the child;

(d) the placement of a child in a foster family or in institutional care;

(e) measures for the protection of the child relating to the administration, conservation or disposal of the child's property."

12–69   It should be noted that Art.1(3) excludes the application of the Regulation to the establishment or contesting of a parent-child relationship, adoption and "measures taken as a result of criminal offences committed by children".

12–70   Article 2 defines "parental responsibility" to mean "all rights and duties relating to the person or the property of a child which are given to a natural or legal person by judgment, by operation of law or by an agreement having legal effect". It also provides that the term is to include "rights of custody and rights of access". Article 2(4) provides that agreements between the parties which are enforceable in one Member State shall be regarded as judgments for the purpose of recognition and enforcement in all other Member States.

The revised Regulation will apply not merely in private law, but also in public law cases. It will cover both biological and adopted children of the couple, as well as stepchildren and non-marital children. The revised Brussels II will apply to all civil matters relating to the "attribution, exercise, delegation, restriction or termination of parental responsibility".[102] It will apply not only to Court judgments but also agreements so long as they are enforceable in the Member State of origin (*i.e.* the Member State in which they are concluded).

Curiously, "child" is not defined in the revised Brussels II, leaving the term to be defined by national law. Neither the Practical Guide nor the Regulation deals with whether the revised Regulation applies to unborn children.[103]

The interrelationship between the revised Brussels II and the 1996 Hague Convention on the Protection of Children is detailed in Art.61 and will be important to watch. The current Regulation, which merely covers parental responsibility on a particular occasion, takes precedence over the 1996 Convention which governs private international law matters with regard to children at a global level. While parental responsibility is widely defined in the revised Regulation, conflict may occur between the instruments due to the differences in geographical scope. This is likely to lead to uncertainty and increased costs for the individual litigant.

---

[102]   See Art.1(1)(b) of Council Regulation 2201/2003.

[103]   See Art.2 of the 1996 Hague Convention which defines child to exclude its application to unborn children. Also *B. v H. (Habitual Residence)* [2002] 1 F.L.R. 388.

Jurisdiction

12–71   The new rules governing jurisdiction on divorce, legal separation and marriage annulment broadly mirror the current Brussels II provisions. Article 3 of the revised Regulation governs the issue of jurisdiction. A court will have the power or jurisdiction to litigate a matter relating to divorce, legal separation or marriage annulment in the following cases:

- where the spouses at the time of the application are "habitually resident" in the territory over which the court has jurisdiction, or
- where the spouses were last "habitually resident" together in the territory over which the court has jurisdiction, provided that one of the parties remains "habitually resident" there, or
- where the respondent to the action is "habitually resident" in the territory over which the court has jurisdiction, or
- if both parties make a joint application, where either spouse is "habitually resident" in the jurisdiction, or
- where the applicant has been "habitually resident" in the territory for at least one year immediately prior to the application being made, or
- where the applicant has been "habitually resident" in the territory, once he or she has resided there for six months before the application and is domiciled in that State.

12–72   It is important to note that these grounds are exclusive, so that a Member State cannot take jurisdiction if the case does not fall within one of the grounds, even if both parties enter an appearance. This is copperfastened by Art.17, which provides that each State will automatically carry out a jurisdiction examination. The range of grounds set out are alternatives, without any order of precedence.

12–73   Each of the above-mentioned grounds is broadly based on the "habitual residence" of one or both parties. The term "habitual residence" is not defined in the revised Regulation and should be interpreted in a manner similar to the one adopted by the ECJ in relation to other instruments, an approach that may cause some difficulty, more of which later.[104] There is, however, an alternative avenue based on either the nationality or domicile of the parties. In the case of all Member States except Ireland and the United Kingdom, nationality is the relevant criterion. In the case of the jurisdictions of Ireland, Northern Ireland, England and Wales and Scotland, the concept of domicile is used for these purposes.

12–74   Article 5 of the revised Regulation provides that the forum with jurisdiction for the initial separation shall maintain jurisdiction for conversion of the separation into divorce, subject to the caveat that such conversion is possible under the domestic law of the Member State in question. Unlike the

---

[104] See p.11.

revised Brussels I,[105] the revised Brussels II forecloses the possibility of a pre-selection of jurisdiction,[106] except in respect of matters relating to parental responsibility. That said, a number of practitioners in the Member States are now inserting "full and final settlement" clauses in separation agreements which include a provision to the effect that a stated ground of jurisdiction, in Art.3 of the revised Regulation, for example, is to apply in the event of a divorce. While this a practice has many advantages, it is likely to cause some difficulty, as the revised Regulation does not include a provision providing for jurisdiction founded exclusively on the agreement of the parties. It could also result in the case been heard in a Member State in which neither of the spouses has a meaningful connection.

12–75   It is clear from the foregoing that the Member State courts assuming jurisdiction pursuant to Art.3 of the revised Brussels II are obliged to follow a fixed set of principles which are designed to ensure that there is an adequate connection between the foreign court and the spouses. That said, the recognising court is not in a position to consider the adequacy of the connection between the spouses and the foreign court. A key concern, certainly in Ireland, is whether these jurisdictional rules provide an adequate protection against forum shopping, and against circumventing the mandatory four-year waiting period[107] established under Irish domestic divorce law.[108]

12–76   The interaction between Arts 6 and 7 of the revised Brussels II will be interesting to watch. Article 6 provides:

> "A spouse who:
>   (a) is habitually resident in the territory of a Member State; or
>   (b) is a national of a Member State, or, in the case of the United

---

[105]   See Art.23 of the revised Brussels I.

[106]   See Art.12 of the revised Regulation.

[107]   s.5(a) of the Family Law (Divorce) Act 1996 provides that an Irish court may grant a divorce where "at the date of the institution of the proceedings, the spouses have lived apart from one another for a period of, or periods amounting to, at least four years during the previous five years...".

[108]   In Ireland, at common law and under the Domicile and Recognition of Foreign Divorces Act 1986 (No. 24 of 1986), a divorce could be refused recognition on the following grounds:
    (a) insufficient connection between the spouses and the jurisdiction granting the divorce;
    (b) recognition of the foreign divorce being contrary to public policy (*i.e.* a foreign divorce obtained by collusion, fraud and duress);
    (c) where an estoppel arises against the recognition of the divorce at the request of the party seeking recognition;
    (d) foreign divorce obtained in breach of *audi alteram partem*.
    S.5(6) of the Irish Domicile and Recognition of Foreign Divorces Act 1986 provided that the common law defences were to be preserved:
        "Nothing in this section shall affect a ground on which a court may refuse to recognise a divorce, other than such a ground related to the question whether a spouse is domiciled in a particular country, or whether the divorce is recognised in a country where a spouse is domiciled."

> Kingdom and Ireland, has his or her 'domicile' in the territory of one of the latter Member States,

may be sued in another Member State only in accordance with Articles 3, 4 and 5."

Yet Art.7(1) states that where no court of a Member State has jurisdiction pursuant to Arts 3, 4 and 5, jurisdiction is to be determined, in each Member State, by the national law of that State. Take, for example Tony (domiciled in Wales) and his wife Máire (Irish domiciled), who married during a working holiday in Turkey (a third State). The marriage breaks down after a short period of time. Tony returns to Cardiff. Article 3 of the revised Regulation requires a minimum of six months' residence in Cardiff before applying for a divorce. Under Art.7(1) of the revised Regulation, however, Tony could apply immediately for a divorce under the English residual jurisdiction rules.[109] This situation is made possible by the fact that Art.6 does not take precedence over Art.7. It is clear that the conflict evident in the application of both provisions has the potential to undermine the aims of the revised Brussels II.

The above anomaly needs to be considered in the context of the exclusive nature of Arts 3 to 5 of the revised Regulation. Such an approach derives support from para.48 of the Borras Report.[110] The consequence of attributing exclusive jurisdiction to Arts 3 to 5 of the revised Regulation would prevent the Wales court from assuming jurisdiction until after six months' residence. Further, such an approach would appear to be consistent with the language in Art.7(2) of the revised Brussels II, which provides:

> "As against a respondent who is not habitually resident and is not either a national of a Member State or, in the case of the United Kingdom and Ireland, does not have his 'domicile' within the territory of one of the latter Member States, any national of a Member State who is habitually resident within the territory of another Member State may, like the national of that State, avail himself of the rules of jurisdiction applicable in that State."

In the final analysis, this logjam will be resolved by the ECJ.

Jurisdiction and parental responsibility

12–77 Article 8(1) of the revised Regulation governs the issue of jurisdiction

---

[109] Tony could rely on s.5(2)(b) of the Domicile and Matrimonial Proceedings Act 1973 (which allows jurisdiction on the basis of the domicile of either spouse) as he is domiciled in Wales.

[110] Para.48 provides as follows:
"Taking into account the grounds of jurisdiction laid down in Arts 2 to 6 of the Convention [Arts 3 to 5 of the revised Regulation], [Art.8] para.1 [of the current Regulation (Art.7(1) of the revised Regulation)] sets the boundary between grounds of an exclusive nature established by the Convention and the principle of applying internal rules of jurisdiction, thus demonstrating the geographical limits of the Convention" (1998) O.J. C–221/44.

in matters of parental responsibility and is modelled on Art.5 of the 1996 Hague Convention. It attributes jurisdiction to the State of the child's habitual residence and provides as follows:

> "The courts of a Member State shall have jurisdiction in matters of parental responsibility over a child who is habitually resident in that Member State at the time the court is seised."

While alternative grounds of jurisdiction are provided for matrimonial matters, no alternative grounds for jurisdiction are provided in respect of parental responsibility matters, which is a welcome development.

Essentially, jurisdiction is to be based on the child's habitual residence at the time the court is seised. This is a significant departure from the current Regulation, where parental responsibility is linked to the divorce. It is to be noted that Art.16(1) defines seised broadly as lodging the documents or equivalent documents that institutes the proceedings.[111] There are, however, a number of limited exceptions.

12–78   One such exception is to allow jurisdiction in respect of access to a court in the child's former habitual residence, for three months following the child's acquisition of a new habitual residence, for the purpose of modifying a judgment on access rights issued in the former State of habitual residence. This is provided the holder of the access rights continues to have his or her habitual residence in that State.[112] This appears to be a sensible transitional provision but seems to be founded on the assumption that a child automatically acquires habitual residence on moving to the new State. What then is the meaning of the term "habitual residence"? Habitual residence has not been defined in the revised Regulation. It has long been argued that there is no need for such a definition and that the words should bear their ordinary and natural meaning and are not a term of art.[113],[114] As previously stated, in the absence of a definition, habitual residence will be interpreted in a manner similar to that adopted by the ECJ in relation to other Community instruments. In *Robin Swaddling v Adjudication Officer*,[115] the ECJ held, in considering the applicant's entitlement for social security, that the length of residence in the Member State in which payment of the benefit at issue is sought, cannot be regarded as an intrinsic element of the concept of residence. While this interpretation of habitual residence may be distinguished on its facts, and the outcome justified

[111] Under the current Regulation, the question of when a court is seised is left to national law. Generally, in civil law countries, the court is seised when the defendant is served, whereas in common law countries, the court is seised when proceedings are issued. See Case 129/83 *Zelger v Salinitri (No.2)* [1984] E.C.R. 2397 and *Dresser UK Ltd v Falcongate Freight Management Ltd* [1992] 2 All E.R. 450. This rule gave an advantage to the common law courts.

[112] Art.9.

[113] *C.M. and O.M. v Delegacion de Malaga and Others* [1999] 2 I.R. 363.

[114] See Rogerson, I.C.L.Q. 49 (2000) 86, 87; McClean (Morris), p.34 justifying this policy.

[115] Case C–90/97 [1999] E.C.R. I–1100. See also *Gingi v Secretary of State for Work and Pensions* [2002] 1 C.M.L.R. 20.

as serving a different purpose, if it were applied to the revised Brussels II it would signpost a significant departure from the current interpretation of the word in the United Kingdom and Ireland.

12–79 The term "habitual residence" has been interpreted in both the United Kingdom and Ireland to mean not only an intention to reside but also implies a physical presence in the jurisdiction for an appreciable period of time.[116] In the case of *C.M. and O.M. v Delegacion de Malaga and Others*,[117] discussed in Chapter 10 for example, McGuinness J. held habitual residence to be a factual concept based on residence for a reasonable length of time. The learned judge summarised the position as follows:

> "[I]t seems to me to be settled law in both England and Ireland that 'habitual residence' is not a term of art, but a matter of fact, to be decided on the evidence in this particular case. It is generally accepted that where a child is residing in the lawful custody of its parent (in the instant case the mother), its habitual residence will be that of the parent. However, the habitual residence of the child is not governed by the same rigid rules of dependency as apply under the law of domicile and the actual facts of the case must always be taken into account. Finally, a person, whether a child or an adult, must, for at least some reasonable period of time, be actually present in a country before he or she can be held to be habitually resident there."[118]

12–80 Whether the approach adopted by the ECJ in *Swaddling* will be applied in the future remains to be seen. Will it be that the ECJ approach will apply over the approach adopted by the national law of the Member States? Article 59 of the new Brussels I addresses the issue in the context of domicile. It provides:

> "1. In order to determine whether a party is domiciled in the Member State whose courts are seised of a matter, the court shall apply its internal law.
>
> 2. If a party is not domiciled in the Member State whose courts are seised of the matter, then, in order to determine whether the party is domiciled

---

[116] The question of residence is "essentially a question of fact" in each case. (See Lord Buckmaster in *I.R.C. v Lysaght* [1928] A.C. 234 at p.248.) In *Levene v I.R.C.*, Viscount Cave L.C. nevertheless, referred with approval to an Oxford English definition of residence as "to dwell permanently, or for a considerable time, to have one's settled usual abode, to live in or at a particular place". At present, modern Irish tax law defines a resident generally as a person who has spent 183 days or more in the State in any one year, or an aggregate of 280 days or more over two consecutive years. (Taxes Consolidation Act 1997, s.819(1) and (2).) For the purposes of the aforementioned aggregate, the individual must have remained in the State for at least 30 days in aggregate in each of the consecutive years.

[117] [1999] 2 I.R. 363.

[118] At p.381. See also *Re J. (A Minor)(Child Abduction: Custody Rights)* [1990] 2 A.C. 562.

in another Member State, the court shall apply the law of that Member State."

No such provision is included in the revised Regulation in respect of habitual residence. This would suggest that habitual residence is not to be determined according to national law, but requires a supra-national Community-wide approach.

12–81   If the Irish and English definition of habitual residence is adopted, the Art.9 exception in the revised Regulation may be redundant as the child may have abandoned his or her previous habitual residence[119] but may not have yet acquired a new habitual residence. Article 9 is, it would appear, contingent on the child acquiring "a new habitual residence".[120]

12–82   There is the possibility of conflicting judgments where a child acquires habitual residence in the new Member State before the three months elapse in circumstances where the court in the new Member State has already made an order under Art.13 of the revised Regulation. The latter order is entitled to benefit from the automatic recognition procedure provided for in Art.41 of the revised Regulation.[121] In the interests of clarity and certainty, the revised Regulation should have left the definition of habitual residence as a matter of national law.

Article 10 of the revised Regulation, based on Art.7 of the 1996 Hague Convention, provides that in the case of a "wrongful removal or retention", the courts of the State of the child's former habitual residence continues to have jurisdiction until the child has acquired a habitual residence in another Member State and either:

"(a)   each person, institution or other body, having rights of custody has acquiesced in the removal or retention; or

(b)   the child has resided in that other Member State for a period of at least one year after the person, institution or other body, having rights of custody has had or should have had knowledge of the whereabouts of the child and the child is settled in his or her new environment and at least one of the following conditions are met:

(i)   within one year no requests for return has been lodged or has been withdrawn; or

(ii)   the case before the court in the Member State of the child's former habitual residence has been closed pursuant to Art.11(7); or

(iii) a custody judgment that does not entail the child's return has been made in the State of the child's former habitual residence."

12–83   The other exceptions to attributing jurisdiction to the courts of the

---

[119]   A person may cease to be habitually resident in a particular Member State in a single day. See *Fam. Law* 1997, 27 (Dec), 782–783.

[120]   *Per* Art.9(1).

[121]   See p.23.

Member State in which the child is habitually resident at the time the court is seised are confined to a provision on prorogation of jurisdiction[122] and cases involving the wrongful removal or retention of a child.[123]

Agreement with third-party States

12–84 No provision has been made in the revised Regulation for agreements with third States. Article 16 of the current Regulation enables a Member State to enter into an agreement with a non-Member State. Any such agreement can provide that a Member State does not have to "recognise a judgment given in another Member State" where jurisdiction is "founded on grounds ... other than those specified in Articles 2 to 7". Community law will, under the revised Regulation, determine third-party negotiations so that individual Member States will no longer be in a position to negotiate agreements with third-party States to the extent that such agreements will affect the revised Brussels II rules.

Prorogation of jurisdiction

12–85 Article 12 of the revised Regulation, modelled on Art.10 of the 1996 Hague Convention, provides for prorogation of jurisdiction and thereby addresses one of the criticisms levelled at the current Regulation. Under Article 12(1) of the revised Brussels II, the forum exercising jurisdiction in respect of matrimonial proceedings has jurisdiction "in any matter relating to parental responsibility connected with that application" where at least one of the spouses has parental responsibility in relation to that child and "the jurisdiction of the courts has been accepted expressly or otherwise in an unequivocal manner by the spouses and by the holders of parental responsibility at the time the court is seised, and is in the superior interests of the child". The use of "the superior interests" rather than "the best interests" of the child is to be regretted in that it signposts a departure from the approach adopted in the 1989 UN Convention on the Rights of the Child. It should be noted that the Practice Guide states that no such departure was intended. What practical impact this will have is difficult to assess in the absence of detailed guidance on the matter.

12–86 The jurisdiction of a State over parental responsibility under Art.12(1) is linked with the substantive application and thus will cease when the judgment allowing or refusing the application for divorce, separation or annulment has become final.[124] Where those proceedings have finished but where proceedings in relation to parental responsibility are still pending, the State retains jurisdiction until they also end.[125] Article 12(3) provides that the courts of a Member State will have jurisdiction in relation to parental responsibility in proceedings other than divorce, legal separation or marriage annulment, where the child has a substantial connection with that Member State (by, for example, being a national of that state), or where one of the spouses having parental

---

[122] Art.12.
[123] Art.10.
[124] Art.12(2)(a).
[125] Art.12(2)(b).

responsibility is habitually resident in that Member State. In this regard, that jurisdiction must be accepted by both spouses to be in the best interests of the child. This will prevent parallel proceedings being brought and conflicting custody decisions, in that only the courts of one Member State will have jurisdiction.

12–87   Article 13, which broadly mirrors Art.6 of the 1996 Hague Convention, provides that if a child's habitual residence cannot be established and jurisdiction cannot be determined under Art.12, then the Member State in which the child is present shall by default assume jurisdiction. Therefore, for Art.13 to apply, it must be proven that jurisdiction cannot be established on the basis of prorogation.

12–88   Article 14 provides that where no court of a Member State has jurisdiction in matters relating to parental responsibility pursuant to Arts 8–13, jurisdiction shall be determined in each Member State by the laws of that state. It seems likely that the Art.14 residual rules of jurisdiction will be invoked more often than was, perhaps, anticipated by the drafters, given the extent and breadth of the jurisdiction rules in the Regulation. This may result in proceedings being brought on the basis of nationality, for example, notwithstanding the fact that the child is resident thousands of miles away in a different country. Alarmingly, such a judgment would be entitled to recognition and enforcement under the revised Brussels II.

Transfer to a court better placed to hear the case

12–89   When, in a matter with which the revised Brussels II is concerned, a court's jurisdiction has been invoked, it is generally not open to that court to deny a hearing on the grounds that another forum may be more appropriate. Provided that the court has lawful jurisdiction (under the above-mentioned rules) to hear the case, it must proceed with the hearing of the case, save in very limited circumstances.

One notable feature of the current Regulation is the absence of discretion caused by the non-availability of the principle of *forum non conveniens*. This preclusion has the potential to cause difficulty and could result in the custody/access issue being considered in a jurisdiction other than that in which a child resides.

12–90   Article 15 of the revised Brussels II is a welcome provision facilitating a court with jurisdiction under the Regulation to transfer the case to a court in another Member State better placed to hear it and is similar to Arts 8 and 9 of the 1996 Hague Convention. This provision is significant in that it, for the first time, in an EC instrument on jurisdiction, facilitates discretion. It allows for the transfer of a case, in whole or in part, from the court having jurisdiction to a court of another Member State with which the child has a particular connection, where the court seised of the case is satisfied that the court of the other Member State "would be better placed to hear the case or a specific part thereof" and that this would be in the best interests of the child. Where the court seised is so satisfied, it may stay proceedings on a *forum conveniens* basis[126] or it may invite the court of another Member State to assume jurisdiction.[127] The transfer can be requested by either a spouse or on the court's own initiative or "upon application from a court of another Member State with which the child has a particular connection".[128] Article 15(1) makes clear that any transfer will only arise "by way of exception", and is more confined than the analogous provision in the 1996 Hague Convention. Only one transfer is allowed under this provision. The necessary connection for a case to be transferred is confined in Art.15(3) to:

- a Member State in which the child had a formal habitual residence or is a national; or
- a Member State in which one of the spouses having parental responsibility is habitually resident; or
- a Member State in which "property of the child is located".

12–91 Articles 15(4) and 15(5) set down strict time limits and require the second court to accept jurisdiction within six weeks "of their seisure".

12–92 Article 15 requires the court of the Member States to co-operate either directly or through the central authorities designated under Art.53. The Practice Guide contains valuable information on the procedure for making a transfer. It recommends the use of the European Judicial Atlas in Civil Matters to ascertain where the competent court of another Member State is. The Guide actively encourages judicial cooperation in relevant cases and states:

"The judges will wish to keep their parties and their legal advisors informed, but it will be a matter for the judges to decide for themselves what procedures and safeguards are appropriate in the context of the particular use".

12–93 Article 15 is a useful provision allowing for the transfer of a case to a court of another Member State on the ground of *forum conveniens* though it is far too narrowly drawn. It is to be regretted that the drafters of the revised Brussels II have not, in large measure, addressed the concerns expressed by family law practitioners on the *lis pendens* rules which have created a "first-come first-served principle". This will continue to make speed of the essence in Brussels II applications. The danger then is that the parties to a transnational marital breakdown will be lured into a "race" to see who can get to court first. Art.19(1) of the revised Regulation provides that where the same action is taken in the courts of two or more countries, all but the first court to be seised of the case must stay proceedings pending the first court's decision. That first court thus has exclusive jurisdiction in the case. The revised Regulation is

---

[126] Art.15(4).
[127] Art.15(5).
[128] Art.15(2).

quite inflexible in this regard insofar as matrimonial proceedings are concerned, with Art.15 only allowing the transfer of jurisdiction to another Member State, "by way of exception",[129] where it is in the best interests of the child. Instead of encouraging conciliation and mediation, the limited availability of "one of the most civilised of legal principles"[130] will prompt parties to litigate earlier to secure jurisdiction in their home State. This militates against the recent statutory provisions in Ireland encouraging parties to engage in mediation and other forms of alternative dispute resolution.

Lis pendens

12–94 The revised Brussels II applies in civil proceedings relating to divorce, legal separation or marriage annulment. Each of these applications/actions is considered to be the same cause of action, although unlike Art.11 of the current Regulation, the revised Brussels II does not use this term. It merely refers to divorce, legal separation or marriage annulment. Where a case might potentially be taken in either or any of two or more states, Art.19 of the revised Brussels II must be considered. Art.19, unlike Arts 11(1) and (2) of the current Regulation, no longer contains discrete provisions addressing competing matrimonial proceedings between the same parties which do and do not involve the same cause of action. It provides that when proceedings relating to divorce, legal separation or marriage annulment have already been commenced in the courts of one Member State, a court in a different Member State must "stay its proceedings until such time as the jurisdiction of the court first seised is established". Article 19(3) provides that the court second seised must decline jurisdiction in favour of the court first seised. It is to be noted that Art.15 of the revised Regulation, which to a limited degree allows a court having jurisdiction under the Regulation to transfer jurisdiction to another Member State, attempts to mitigate the worst excesses of the strict *lis pendens* rule outlined above.

Provisional and protective measures

12–95 Article 12 of the current Regulation is imported from Art.24 of the 1968 Brussels Convention (now Regulation) and provides that a court in a contracting State may, even if it does not have jurisdiction under the Regulation, take emergency steps to protect either assets or persons. This provision becomes Art.20 in the revised Regulation.

The current Art.12 provision goes much further than Art.24 of the Brussels Convention (now Regulation) in that the latter provision is confined to matters within the scope of the Brussels Convention. The measures envisaged in Art.12 related to both persons and property, and thus touch on matters outside the scope of the Regulation. This is no longer the case as Art.1(2)(e) of the revised Brussels II now covers measures for the protection of a child's property.

---

[129] Art.15(1).
[130] Lord Goff, describing the principle of *forum non conveniens* in *Airbus Industries GIE v Patel and Others* [1998] 2 All E.R. 257 at 271.

12–96 Article 20 of the revised Brussels II refers to "measures in respect of persons or assets in that State as may be available under the law of that Member State". It is clear from the Brussels Convention (now Regulation) jurisprudence that this includes all national injunctive or provisional measures. The Article makes these available as if the case was one proceeding before the national court.

In the context of the Brussels Convention (now Regulation), the most important interim measure has been the Mareva injunction. The classic use of this was seen in *Republic of Haiti v Duvalier*.[131] Proceedings were started in the French courts against ex-President Jean Paul Duvalier by the new Government of Haiti to recover state assets ($120 million) allegedly mis-appropriated by him and members of his family. The plaintiffs sought a Mareva injunction from the English High Court to restrain the defendants from disposing of any assets in England. Staughton L.J. held that he had the power to grant such an injunction.

12–97 The issue has arisen whether a court can grant protective measures in respect of a defendant who is domiciled outside the contracting states. In *X. v Y.*,[132] proceedings were commenced in France against a Saudi Arabian executive who had defaulted on a loan. An application was made in England for a Mareva injunction. The court held that Art.24 of the Brussels Convention (now Regulation) was not limited to cases where the defendant was domiciled in a Contracting State.

12–98 In *Wermuth v Wermuth*, Thorpe J. afforded a strict interpretation to Art.12 of the current Brussels II. He stated:

> "We must not take or be seen to take opportunities for usurping the function of the judge in the other member state. Once another jurisdiction is demonstrated to be apparently first seised, this jurisdiction must defer, by holding itself in waiting in case that apparent priority should be disproved or declined."[133]

This approach seems to be more rigid than that adopted in respect of the equivalent provision in the Brussels Convention (now Regulation).

12–99 A new paragraph 20(2), inserted in the revised Brussels II, limits the application of Art.20 to matters falling within the scope of the revised Regulation and appears more vague though narrower than the current Art.12. It provides as follows:

> "The measures referred to in paragraph 1 shall cease to apply when the court of the Member State having jurisdiction under this Regulation as to the substance of the matter has taken the measures it considers appropriate."

---

[121] [1989] 1 All E.R. 456.
[132] [1989] 3 All E.R. 689.
[133] [2003] 1 W.L.R. 942.

Access

12–100   Section 4 of the revised Regulation will bring about fundamental changes to access rights, the most significant of which is the removal of the need of "exequator".[134] The removal of all the intermediate steps to the recognition of access orders was an agreed objective at the European Council meeting at Tampere in Finland in October 1999. Article 41 is, in part, the realisation of the objective to create a common judicial area and incorporates elements of the French proposal for adopting a Council Regulation on the mutual enforcement of judgments on rights of access to children.[135] In particular, Art.41(1) provides that an access judgment that has been certified in the Member State of origin is to be treated for enforcement purposes as if it were handed down in the Member State of enforcement.

12–101   Significantly, Art.41(2) provides that the judge of origin should only issue a certificate where all the parties and the child (having regard to his or her age and maturity) have been given an opportunity to be heard. Where a judgment is given in default, certain special considerations apply. The person defaulting must have been served "with the document (instituting proceedings) or with an equivalent document in sufficient time and in such a way as to enable that person to arrange for his or her defense ...". A judge cannot refuse to issue a certificate, however, where the person defaulting has accepted the decision unequivocally.

Article 41(3) provides:

> "Where the rights of access involve a cross-border situation at the time of the delivery of the judgment, the certificate should be issued *ex officio* when the judgment becomes enforceable, even if only provisionally. If the situation subsequently acquits a cross-border character the certificate shall be issued at the request of one of the parties".

The certificate referred to above must be in the standard form contained in Annex III.

12–102   With respect to rights of access, the revised Regulation applies not merely to access orders made during matrimonial proceedings but generally. The access provisions of the revised Regulation apply not only to parents but also to grandparents and those *in loco parentis*. Article 48(1) of the revised Regulation is a welcome provision and mirrors Art.11(2) of the 1980 European Convention on the Custody of Children and on Restoration of Custody of Children.[136] It provides:

---

[134] "Exequator" means an intermediate measure whereby a court decree is given enforceable quality.

[135] (2000) O.J. C–234 (7).

[136] "[T]he competent authority of the State addressed may fix the conditions for the implementation and exercise of the right of access taking into account, in particular, undertakings given by the parties on this matter."

"The courts of the Member State of enforcement may make practical arrangements for organising the exercise of rights of access, if the necessary arrangements have not or have not sufficiently been made in the judgment delivered by the courts of the Member State having jurisdiction as to the substance of the matter and provided the essential elements of this judgment are respected."

12–103　As with the current Regulation,[137] the revised Brussels II takes precedence over the European Convention of May 20, 1980, on Recognition and Enforcement of Decisions concerning Custody of Children and on Restoration of Custody of Children. Application to enforce any custody order made in a Member State will be made under the revised Brussels II. The opportunity for Member States to enter reservations under Arts 17 and 18 of the 1980 European Custody Convention reduced its potential. Reservations will not be possible under the revised Brussels II.

It should be noted that unlike those seeking enforcement under the 1980 Hague Convention, applicants seeking to enforce a custody order under the revised Regulation will not automatically receive free legal aid. In short, the means test and merits test will apply.[138] A person seeking to enforce an access order is required to produce the certificate referred to above and a copy of the judgment.

12–104　A new Council of Europe Contact Convention is currently in preparation, which will contain a procedure for advanced recognition and enforcement thereby enabling courts in the Contracting States to make mirror orders. Twelve countries signed the Convention on the first day it was available for signature.

Recognition

12–105　One of the most common problems when dealing with foreign divorce, separation and parental responsibility judgments is how to enforce them. This is an area of law that has been very sensitive to Ireland due to its specific socio-cultural implications. As in the current Regulation, the revised Regulation provides that a judgment given in the courts of one Member State is to be recognised in all other Member States without any special procedure.[139] Article 2(4) of the revised Regulation defines judgment as "a divorce, legal separation or marriage annulment, as well as a judgment relating to parental responsibility, pronounced by a court of a Member State, whatever the judgment may be called, including a decree, order or decision". The existence of a final judgment relating to divorce, legal separation or marriage annulment in another Member State is declared to be sufficient for updating the civil status records

---

[137] See Art.37 of Council Regulation 1347/2000 O.J. L160/19.

[138] See Art.50.

[139] Art.21(1). Recognition is restricted to the dissolution of the marriage bond (*i.e.* annulment, legal separation or divorce), Art.2(4).

of a Member State.[140] An interested party[141] can contest recognition of the foreign judgment.[142]

12–106 Article 49 of the revised Regulation provides for the recognition and enforcement of an order for costs and expenses. Similarly, recognition and enforcement will apply to "documents which have been formally drawn up or registered as authentic instruments and are enforceable in one Member State and also agreements between the parties that are enforceable in the Member State in which they were concluded".[143] Recognition is restricted to the dissolution of the marriage bond (*i.e.* annulment, legal separation or divorce) and does not apply to other matters.[144] Thus, judgments refusing a divorce or other relief are not entitled to recognition under the Regulation.[145]

12–107 Article 24 of the revised Regulation prevents a review of the jurisdiction of the court of origin. Further, Art.25 states that the recognition of a judgment relating to a divorce, legal separation or a marriage annulment is not to be refused because the law of the recognising Member State would not allow the relevant order on the same facts. This is effectively a limit on the use of the public policy defence to recognition. It is allied to Art.26 on non-reviewability.

Defences to recognition of a judgment in a matrimonial matter

12–108 There are a very limited number of defences to automatic recognition, which is not surprising given the fact that the defences rest uneasily with the EC's objective of facilitating the automatic recognition of judgments.

Article 22 of the revised Brussels II details the grounds upon which a judgment relating to a divorce, legal separation or marriage annulment shall not be recognised.

12–109 Contrary to public policy A court in one Member State shall not recognise any decision that is "manifestly contrary to the public policy" of the Member State.[146] Such a conflict must be extremely profound in order to justify refusal. It is not sufficient, for instance, simply to state that the decision is one that the courts of Ireland, for example, could not make or would not have made. Nor is it sufficient to refuse recognition on the grounds of legislative differences alone. This provision mirrors Art.23(2)(d) of the 1996 Hague Convention.

The case of *Vervaeke v Smith*[147] is perhaps the best example of a case

---

[140] Art.21(2).
[141] An "interested party" includes spouses, children and in some states a relevant public authority, and need not be resident in the jurisdiction. See Borras Report, (1998) O.J. C221/27, para.80.
[142] Art.21(3).
[143] Art.46 of the revised Regulation.
[144] Art.21.
[145] See Borras Report (1998) O.J. C221/48, para.60.
[146] Art.22(a).
[147] [1983] 1 AC 145, [1982] 1 All E.R. 144.

involving public policy grounds. There, the House of Lords refused to recognise a Belgian annulment decree on the grounds that the decree had been obtained using falsified evidence. That said, the ECJ has made it clear in *Krombach v Bamberski*[148] and *Hoffman v Krieg*[149] that the public policy ground is to be used sparingly and only in exceptional cases. Under the revised Brussels I, even fraud does not allow the invocation of the public policy defence.[150] The Borras Report, with some justification, refers to this ground of non-recognition in the original Brussels Convention (now Regulation) as being of little practical significance.[151] This approach can be gleaned from Art.24 of the revised Brussels II, which provides that an alleged fraud going to jurisdiction will not give rise to any right of review under the revised Brussels II:

> "The jurisdiction of the court of the Member State of origin may not be reviewed. The test of public policy referred to in Articles 22(a) and 23(a) may not be applied to the rules relating to jurisdiction set out in Articles 3 to 14."

12–110   Natural justice Where a judgment was given in default of appearance of one of the parties, certain special conditions apply. A court may refuse to recognise such a judgment where the respondent was:

> "not served with the document which instituted the proceedings or with an equivalent document in sufficient time and in such a way as to enable the respondent to arrange for his or her defence unless it is determined that the respondent has accepted the judgment unequivocally".[152]

The reasoning here is that such failure may constitute a breach of natural justice, a failure to give all parties to the case an opportunity to be heard.

12–111   A court cannot refuse to recognise a judgment where the respondent has clearly indicated that he or she has accepted the judgment of the court without any conditions or complaint ("unequivocally"). While there is no discrete provision for the application of the doctrine of estoppel under the revised Brussels II, it seems from the wording of Art.22(b) that a person who had previously benefited from recognition of a divorce would not be able to avail of the Art.22(b) defence because he or she would be deemed to have "accepted the judgment unequivocally". The Irish Supreme Court has recently considered and rejected the application of estoppel to the issue of marital status in the case of *C.K. v J.K.; F.McG. (notice party)*.[153]

Natural justice is the most commonly used defence under the Brussels

---

[148] Case 7/98 [2000] E.C.R. I–1935.

[149] Case 145/86 [1988] E.C.R. 645.

[150] See *Societé d'Information Service Realisation (SISRO) v Ampersand Software BV*, July 29, 1993, *The Times*.

[151] (1998) O.J. C221/27 at para.69.

[152] Art.22(b).

[153] unreported, Supreme Court, March 31, 2004.

Convention (now Regulation) and has given rise to the greatest number of difficulties. The ECJ, in considering the equivalent provision under the Brussels Convention (now Regulation), has held that due service consists of two elements—service according to the rules of the first court and service in time.[154]

12–112   Irreconcilable judgments   For divorce, legal separation or marriage annulment, the revised Brussels II excludes recognition of a judgment which is irreconcilable with a judgment given in a dispute between the same parties in the Member State in which recognition is sought.[155] A court, for instance, would obviously not be required to recognise a foreign divorce in respect of parties whose marriage has already been annulled by the courts of the juris-diction in which recognition is sought. Pre-eminence is given to the judgment of the recognising court. There is no requirement that the judgment of the recognising state pre-date the judgment for which recognition is sought.

12–113   In cases where a judgment is irreconcilable with an earlier judgment of another Member State or a non-Member State involving the same parties, a similar principle applies.[156] In such a case, the earlier judgment is to be enforced in preference to the later, on condition that the earlier judgment meets the conditions necessary for recognition in the Member State in which recognition is sought. Thus in *Hoffman v Krieg*,[157] where the ECJ considered the Brussels Convention (now Regulation) equivalent, a German judgment awarding maintenance on desertion was clearly irreconcilable with a subsequent Dutch divorce. This ground does not, however, prevent matrimonial proceedings being taken within a Member State while identical proceedings are currently in being in a non-Member State.

The ECJ has taken a very narrow and restrictive approach to the foregoing defences.[158] Indeed, as previously stated, the very existence of any of the grounds of non-recognition seems at odds with the EC objective of removing all obstacles to the recognition of judgments.

The substance of the decision cannot be questioned

12–114   Proceedings to obtain recognition may not question the decision on the basis of the substance of that decision.[159] In this respect the recognition process is somewhat like judicial review. Once the court has established that none of the criteria for the non-recognition set out above have been satisfied, it must recognise the judgment in question. It cannot question the decision on the basis, for instance, that the domestic judge would not have reached the same decision on the facts. Indeed, the domestic court cannot challenge the decision on the basis that such a judgment would have been unobtainable in

---

[154] See Case 166/80 *Klomps v Michel* [1981] E.C.R. 1593 and Case 305/88 *Isabelle Lancray v Peters and Sickert* [1990] 1 E.C.R. 2725.
[155] Art.22(c).
[156] Art.22(d).
[157] Case 145/86 [1988] E.C.R. 645.
[158] See, for example, *Solo Kleinmotoren Gmbh v Boch* [1994] E.C.R. 2237.
[159] Art.26.

the home state. Article 25 makes it clear that differences in applicable law cannot be invoked as a ground for non-recognition.[160]

Stay of proceedings

12–115   Article 27 provides that a court can stay proceedings for recognition and enforcement if there is an appeal against that judgment. In Case 3/77 *Industrial Diamond Supplies v Riva*,[161] the ECJ held that "appeal" means an appeal, the outcome of which may result in the annulment or amendment of the judgment that is the subject matter of the recognition or enforcement proceedings.

Recognition of parental responsibility judgments

12–116   In parental responsibility cases, the revised Brussels II takes a somewhat different approach.[162] It provides that in such cases, a court can refuse recognition of a judgment if it is irreconcilable with a later judgment of the Member State in which recognition is sought.[163] This is justified as orders relating to parental responsibility may be subject to reconsideration in the light of new circumstances. Thus, a judgment of the state addressed is not entitled to automatic priority. The same approach applies in the case of a conflict between two judgments from other Member States.[164] The later in time will prevail. In the case of a judgment of a non-Member State, it will only be recognised if it is a judgment of the state in which the child is habitually resident and also fulfils any other conditions necessary for it to be recognised in the state addressed.[165] Article 23(g) of the revised Brussels II inserts an additional ground of non-recognition for parental responsibility judgments which mirrors Art.23(2)(f) of the 1996 Hague Convention. It provides that a judgment placing a child in care[166] in another Member State (other than one seised of the application) will only be recognised if the authority facilitating such a placement has adhered to the procedure outlined in Art.56. For example, the authority must first consult with the Central Authority or other competent authority in the Member State where the placement is to take place.

Enforcement

12–117   The enforcement provisions are limited to judgments relating to parental responsibility. For judgments relating to matrimonial matters, recognition procedures are sufficient.[167] Article 28 provides that an enforceable

---

[160] See *Interdesco SA v Nullfire Ltd* [1992] 1 L1. Rep. 180, where the ECJ considered a similar provision in the Brussels Convention.
[161] [1977] E.C.R. 2175; see also *Petereit v Babcock International Holdings* [1990] 1 W.L.R. 450.
[162] Art.23.
[163] Art.23(e).
[164] Art.23(f).
[165] Art.23(f).
[166] In either institutional care or in foster care.
[167] Art.21.

judgment from one Member State can be declared enforceable in another Member State on the application of an interested party[168].[169] That said, under the revised Brussels II, a declaration of enforceability is not required for an access order or an order for the return of the child under Art.11(8) of the revised Regulation.[170] There is no possibility of recognition being challenged so long as either judgment is certified in the Member State of origin as having been obtained in accordance with the grounds of procedural fairness detailed in Art.41(2) and Art.42(2) of the Regulation. This new approach to the enforcement of access and non-return orders may cause considerable difficulty. Custody and access decisions, which are interlocutory in nature, are unsuitable for automatic recognition and enforcement. The removal of all intermediate steps to the recognition of access judgments may therefore be inappropriate.

Procedure

12–118 Once jurisdiction has been secured, the required steps for effective service should be taken without delay. Service should be in accordance with Council Regulation (EC) 1348/2000.[171] The service requirements for each of the Member States are to be found on the Europa website. The Central Body has the responsibility for ensuring the supply of information to the transmitting agencies and seeking solutions to any problems that may arise during the transmission of documents for service. The Central Body in Ireland is the Master of the High Court. Article 30(1) of the revised Regulation provides that the national law of the enforcing State will govern the application procedure for enforcement. The applicant must provide an address for service within the jurisdiction of the court seised.[172] If the law of the enforcing State does not provide for the furnishing of such an address, the applicant must appoint a representative *ad litem*.

Articles 37 and 39 specify the documents to be produced in an application for either recognition or enforcement, or an application contesting such recognition. The applicant must produce an authentic copy of the judgment and, in the case of enforcement documents, establish that according to the Member State of origin, the judgment is enforceable and has been served. Where appropriate, the applicant is required to produce a document showing that he or she is in receipt of legal aid in the Member State of origin.

12–119 In the case of default proceedings, an original or a true copy of the

---

[168] An "interested party" includes spouses, children and in some states a relevant public authority, and need not be resident in the jurisdiction. See Borras Report (1998) O.J. C221/27, para.80.

[169] A judgment on the exercise of parental responsibility will be enforceable in all Member States by a mere declaration, save for the United Kingdom where judgments will only be enforceable following formal registration in England and Wales, Scotland or in Northern Ireland.

[170] See Arts 41(1) and 42(1).

[171] See Council Regulation (EC) No.1348/2000 of May 29, 2000, on the service in the Member States of judicial and extrajudicial documents in civil or commercial matters.

[172] Art.30(2).

document instituting the proceedings is required, which will establish that the party in default was correctly served, or any document indicating that the defendant accepted the judgment unequivocally. A person requiring the updating of civil status records must produce a document indicating that the judgment is not subject to appeal in the Member State where the judgment was given.

12–120　When the required documents are not available to the court, Art.38 allows the court, before recognition is sought, to specify a time during which they must be produced or, alternatively, to vary the documents required. If the court considers that it has sufficient information before it, it may dispense with the documentary requirements.

　　If the enforcing court requires it, a translation of the documents must be furnished. The translation is to be certified by a person qualified to do so in one of the Member States. Article 29 specifies the courts in the Member States to which application is to be made.

Partial enforcement

12–121　Article 36(1) provides that a court may order partial enforcement in circumstances where enforcement has been requested in respect of several matters, but cannot be authorised in all of them. An applicant may request partial enforcement of a judgment under Art.36(2).

Appeal against an order for enforcement

12–122　Article 33 provides a party against whom enforcement is ordered with a right of appeal. Such an appeal must be made within one month of service of the judgment where the defendant is habitually resident in the Contracting State in which the decision permitting enforcement is given. Where he is not habitually resident in that particular state, he has two months to appeal. Time runs either from the date of service of the decision on him or at his residence. No extension of time is permitted. Article 34 sets out the courts to which an appeal may be addressed.

　　Appeal proceedings may be stayed, on the application of the appellant, if the judgment is being appealed in the Member State of origin, or if the time for such an appeal has not yet expired.[173]

Legal aid

12–123　Article 50 provides that if the applicant, in his state of origin, has benefited from complete or partial legal aid, or exemption from costs or expenses, he will also be entitled in the enforcing state to benefit from the most favourable legal aid, or the most extensive exemption from costs and expenses. The applicant for enforcement or recognition must produce a document showing that he or she is entitled to legal aid in the state of origin.

---

[173] Art.35.

As with the current Regulation, the revised Brussels II provides that the entitlement to legal aid will apply in respect of the *ex parte* stage.

Security for costs

12–124   Article 51 provides that security for costs cannot be required of an applicant to enforce a foreign judgment, on the ground that the applicant is a foreign national, or is not domiciled or habitually resident in the state in which enforcement is sought. This reflects the equivalent provision in the current Regulation.

Central authorities

12–125   Article 53 requires each Member State to establish a central authority to which central authorities from other Member States, or holders of parental responsibility, will be able to request co-operation or assistance with the application of the revised Brussels II. Such co-operation or assistance is broadly defined in Article 55 and is to be provided free of charge.[174] It includes both facilitating communications between courts, administrative authorities and agreement between holders of parental responsibility. The foregoing will be complemented by the European Judicial Network in civil and commercial matters,[175] which will facilitate judicial co-operation between the Member States in cross-border family issues.

The voice of the child in the revised Brussels II Regulation

12–126   A judgment under the current Brussels II will not be recognised if it was given without the child having been afforded the opportunity to be heard, "in violation of fundamental principles of procedure of the Member State in which recognition is sought", or without a similar opportunity being given to any other person claiming that the judgment infringes his or her right of parental responsibility. This mirrors an equivalent provision in the 1996 Hague Convention. Member States rules set out how the child should be heard. The Borras Report provides that these rules "must include the rules in the United Nations Convention of 20 November 1989 on the Rights of the Child and in particular Art.12 thereof …".[176] Article 12 of the 1989 Convention provides:

1.   States parties shall assure to the child who is capable of forming his or her own views the right to express those views freely in all matters affecting the child, the views of the child being given due weight in accordance with the age and maturity of the child.

2.   For this purpose, the child shall in particular be provided the opportunity to be heard in any judicial and administrative proceedings

---

[174] Art.57(3).
[175] Council Decision of May 28, 2001 (2001/470/EC) applicable since December 1, 2002.
[176] (1998) O.J. C–221/52 at para.73.

affecting the child, either directly, or through a representative or an appropriate body, in a manner consistent with the procedural rules of national law.

12–127   Brussels II, however, makes little reference to children and is confined to parental responsibility in respect of the natural and adopted children of both spouses.[177] The status of the child in the revised Regulation is, however, significantly enhanced. To this end, the hearing of the child plays an important role in the application of the revised Regulation. This is a welcome departure from the invisibility of children in the current Regulation. In particular, Art.11(2) requires the child to be heard during child abduction proceedings "unless this appears inappropriate having regard to his or her age or degree of maturity".[178] This is in line with Art.13 of the 1980 Hague Convention, which allows a court to refuse to return a child if the child objects to being returned, having regard to his or her age and maturity. Article 41(2)(c) establishes the child's status in access proceedings:

> "The judge of origin shall issue the certificate only if:
>
> (c) the child was given an opportunity to be heard, unless a hearing was considered inappropriate, having regard to his or her age or degree of maturity".

12–128   The child is to be heard in accordance with the arrangements detailed in Art.11 of EC Council Regulation 1206/2001 of May 28, 2001, on co-operation between the courts of the Member States in the taking of evidence in civil or commercial matters.[179] While it is, according to recital para.19, left to Member States' discretion to provide a framework for representing the interests and wishes of the child, this discretion must be exercised in a manner compatible with the provisions of the 1989 United Nations Convention on the Rights of the Child (UNCRC). Research undertaken by the European Forum for Child Welfare in 2001, which took the form of an examination of the implementation of Art.12, UNCRC in six Member States,[180] identified significant shortcomings and divergent age-based restrictions in giving effect to the right of the child to be heard in family law proceedings. The author participated in this research, the findings of which highlight the absence of an automatic right for the child to be heard in private law proceedings in Ireland, which is compounded by the fact that s.28 of the Guardianship of Infants Act 1964, as introduced by s.11 of the Children Act 1997, has not yet come into force. In public law cases, while s.26 of the Child Care Act 1991 allows for the appointment of a guardian *ad litem,* the practical reality is that the absence of a legal infrastructure for the operation of the guardian *ad litem* has lead to a reluctance to engage children in decisions regarding their own future.

---

[177] See Art.3(2)(b) and Art.15(2).
[178] See also Art.42(2)(a).
[179] (2001) O.J. L174, June 27, 2001.
[180] Austria, Greece, Netherlands, Ireland, Italy and the United Kingdom.

12–129   While the revised Brussels II establishes the general right of the child to be heard in family proceedings, child-consultation procedures remain an issue of national law. This is to be regretted and will result in the child's right to be heard being dependent on the Member State in which he or she is habitually resident. The vulnerable position of the migrant child arising out of the divergent child-consultation procedures between the Member States should be addressed in advance of the seven-year review of the revised Regulation required under Art.65. This would ensure greater uniformity between Member States and have a significant impact on honouring not only the terms but also the spirit of Art.12 of the 1989 UNCRC.

Conclusion

12–130   Considering the controversy that accompanied the introduction of the current Regulation, it is surprising that these new developments have attracted so little attention. The greatly extended scope of the expression "parental responsibility" is to be welcomed, as is the limited availability of the principle of *forum non conveniens*. The revised Brussels II is likely to increase transfrontier judicial co-operation and represents a more equitable balance between placing a premium on ease of access to the courts of other Member States at the expense of whether the court with first jurisdiction is the most appropriate venue for the parties' case.

12–131   One unfortunate matter is that a comprehensive family law Regulation was not negotiated on this occasion to cover all aspects of child and matrimonial jurisdiction. As it now stands, issues of status and matrimonial jurisdiction will be dealt with by different Regulations. The revised Brussels II is therefore unlikely to achieve the uniformity realised by the original Brussels Convention. This is, in part, due to the fact that the conditions that heralded the success of the original Brussels Convention are no longer present. Indeed, reaching agreement in the future will be more difficult, in that a number of features of the family law systems in the newer Member States do not appear to be compatible with the family law systems of the original Member States. It will now require consensus among 24, possibly 25, Member States.

THE HAGUE CHILD PROTECTION CONVENTION 1996

12–132   The Hague Child Protection Convention 1996 ("the 1996 Convention") came into force on January 1, 2001.[181] The 1996 Convention has a potentially much wider scope than any of the other Hague Conventions affecting children. Its ambit is wider than that proposed under the revised Brussels II. Ireland has already passed the implementing legislation in the form of the Protection of Children (Hague Convention) Act 2000,[182] although this Act is

---

[181] This is when Slovakia's ratification took effect, thereby providing the third ratification (Monaco ratified in May 1997 while the Czech Republic ratified in March 2000).

[182] S.I. No. 37 of 2000.

not yet in force. The EU Council at its November 29, 2002 meeting approved a draft Decision authorising the Member States to sign the 1996 Convention. A Declaration attached to the Decision states that the 1996 Convention is to enter into force the same time as the revised Brussels II Regulation.

12–133 As regards jurisdiction, there are a number of rules dealing with different aspects of the 1996 Convention, but the main rule, contained in Art.5, is to ascribe jurisdiction to the State of the child's habitual residence, and jurisdiction will change with any changes in habitual residence. That application of the law of the state of habitual residence is unaffected by a wrongful removal or retention unless circumstances similar to the exceptions to parental child abduction in the 1980 Hague Convention are applicable. Article 7 provides that, in cases of wrongful removal or retention, jurisdiction remains in the State of the child's former habitual residence, unless there has either been acquiescence or one year has elapsed since the wrongful removal and the child is settled in his or her new environment. Authorities can decline jurisdiction upon the basis of *forum non conveniens*.[183] The emergency jurisdiction provided for by Art.11 is likely to prove useful in that the State where the child or his or her property is situate has jurisdiction to take necessary measures of protection.

As with other modern child Conventions, it will be incumbent on each Member State to establish a Central Authority to assist co-operation between states to fulfil the purposes of the 1996 Convention. Article 32 could be useful in the context of child abduction in that it provides that the authorities of another state may, for specified reasons, request the central authority of a child's habitual residence to begin measures to protect a child's person. It should be noted, however, that the 1996 Hague Protection Convention makes no provision for costs to be met by a contracting state.

12–134 In summary, as previous stated, the interrelation between the 1980 Hague Convention, the revised Brussels II Regulation and the 1996 Hague Convention will be interesting to watch.[184]

OVERVIEW AND CONCLUSION

12–135 Irish family law is unique in that it has resisted the steady erosion of parental rights that characterise international family law systems. By ratifying the 1989 United Nations Convention on the Rights of the Child on September 21, 1992, without reservation, Ireland accepted its international obligations

---

[183] The doctrine of *forum non conveniens* is a distinctive feature of the law relating to jurisdiction in common law systems and affords the court a discretionary power to refuse to take jurisdiction if there is some other available forum which prima facie is clearly more suitable for the trial of the case. See Arts 8 and 9 of the 1996 Hague Convention.

[184] For example, in theory, while Art.50 of the 1996 Hague Convention provides that it "shall not effect" the application of the 1980 Hague Convention, the practical reality may be more complex.

towards children. Article 41 of the Irish Constitution, however, continues to act as an impediment to the effective implementation of children's legal entitlements under the 1989 Convention.

12–136   The European Convention on Human Rights Act 2003 and the other international and European Community instruments, considered in this chapter, are likely to create a significant paradigm shift in legal culture in family law. In relation to the law on children, they will consolidate the four main aims of the United Nations Convention on the Rights of the Child 1989, the standard-setter on children's rights, which have been identified as prevention, protection, provision and participation. Where family law and child law issues conflict in terms of rights, it will be necessary to balance the rights of different family members. The approach when Art.8, ECHR is invoked in relation to private family law will be to balance the rights of all family members, with the interests of the child being decisive where the way is not clear.[185]

---

[185] See *Yousef v The Netherlands* [2003] 1 F.L.R. 210.

APPENDIX 1

FAMILY LAW IN IRELAND: CODE OF PRACTICE*

Introduction

There is concern that solicitors and court procedures might add to the distress and anger that can arise when relationships break down. Solicitors should deal with matters in a way designed to preserve people's dignity and to encourage them to reach agreement. The result will often be to achieve the same or more satisfactory solutions than going to court but at less cost both in terms of emotion and money.

Solicitors act as representatives of the client, but are also officers of the Court and citizens having special responsibilities for the quality of justice.

As a representative of clients, the solicitor performs various functions. As an adviser, the solicitor provides a client with an informed understanding of the client's legal rights and obligations and explains their practical implications. As an advocate, the Solicitor forthrightly asserts the client's position under the rules of the adversarial system. As a negotiator, the solicitor seeks a result advantageous to the client but consistent with the requirement of honest dealings with others.

In all professional functions, the solicitor must uphold the duties owed to clients in accordance with the Law Society's rules of professional conduct and must also demonstrate respect for the Constitution and the legal system and for those who serve it, including judges, other lawyers and public officials.

The Constitution is strongly supportive of the family. In family law cases therefore solicitors should fulfil their professional duties in a manner conducive to the best interests of their client but also mindful of the best interests of the family as a whole.

The solicitor's responsibilities as a representative of clients and as an officer of the court are usually harmonious. However, conflicting responsibilities can be encountered. The Code of Practice suggests methods by which such conflicts may be resolved.

The Law Society recommends that all solicitors practising family law should follow this code. Our members should explain the code to their clients, as it will form the basis of the approach that they adopt.

Keeping the code is not a sign of weakness. It does not expose the client to disadvantage. The approach the solicitor adopts should be firm and fair.

---

*Reproduced with the kind permission of the *Family Law and Civil Legal Aid Committee* (2nd ed., *The Law Society of Ireland*, 2000).

Solicitors are not prevented from taking immediate and decisive action where necessary. Even when there are ongoing discussions, court proceedings may be started and continue at the same time in case negotiations do not produce an agreement.

The code is not a straitjacket. Its guidelines cannot be absolute rules. It may be necessary to depart from the code if professional rules or duties require it.

General

1. At an early stage, you should explain to your client the approach you adopt in family law work.

2. You should encourage your client to see the advantages to the parties of a constructive and non-confrontational approach as a way of resolving differences. You should advise, negotiate and conduct matters so as to help the parties settle their differences as quickly as possible and reach agreement, while allowing them time to reflect, consider and come to terms with their new situation.

3. If there are contentious issues concerning children, you should advise your client that the court will, by law, prioritise the best interests of the child. You should make sure that your client understands that the best interests of the child should be put first. You should explain that where a child is involved, your client's attitude to the other spouse will affect the family as a whole and the child's relationship with his or her parents.

4. You should encourage the attitude that the dispute is not a contest in which there is a winner and a loser, but rather that it is a search for fair solutions. You should avoid using words or phrases that suggest or cause a dispute where there is no serious dispute. You should stress the need for your client to be open and honest in all aspects of the case and you must explain what could happen if your client is not open and honest.

5. Emotions are often intense in relationship disputes. You should avoid inflaming them in any way. You should take great care when considering the effect your correspondence could have on other parties and on your own client. Your letters should be clear and free of jargon. Remember that clients may see assertive letters between solicitors as aggressive declarations of war. Your correspondence should aim to resolve issues and to settle the matter, not to further inflame emotions or to antagonise.

Mediation

6. You should make sure that your client knows about other available services (such as mediation and counselling) which may bring about a settlement and may help your client and any other parties involved. You should explore, with your client, the possibility of a reconciliation and, where appropriate, give every encouragement in that regard.

Relationship with a Client

7. You should make sure that you are objective and do not allow your emotions or personal opinions to influence your advice.

8. When advising your client you must explain all options. The client must understand the consequences of any decision the client has to make. The decision is to be made by your client; you cannot decide.

9. You must make your client aware of the legal costs at all stages and comply fully with your obligations under section 68 of the Solicitors (Amendment) Act, 1994. The benefits and merits of any steps taken must be balanced against the costs. The right of your client to apply for Civil Legal Aid should also be made clear.

Dealing with other Solicitors

10. In all dealings with other solicitors, you should show courtesy and try to maintain a good working relationship.

11. You should try to avoid criticising the other solicitors involved in a case.

Dealing with a person who does not have a Solicitor

12. When you are dealing with someone who is not represented by a solicitor, you should take even greater care to communicate clearly and try to avoid any technical language or jargon that is not easily understood.

13. You should strongly recommend an unrepresented person to consult a solicitor and also advise that person that he or she may have an entitlement to Civil Legal Aid.

Court Proceedings

14. When taking any step in the proceedings, the long-term effect on your client and other family members must be balanced with the likely short-term benefit to the case.

15. If the purpose of taking a particular step in proceedings may be misunderstood or appear hostile, you should consider explaining it, as soon as possible, to your colleague.

16. Before filing proceedings, you and your client should consider whether the other party or his or her solicitor should be contacted in advance with a view to coming to an agreement and minimising misunderstandings.

17. You should discourage your client from naming any third parties unless there are very good reasons to do so.

Children

18. You should encourage your client to put the child's welfare and interests first.

19. You should encourage your client to co-operate with the other parent when making decisions concerning the child, and advise parents it is often better to make arrangements for the child between themselves, through their solicitors or through a mediator rather than through a court hearing.

20. In any letters you write, you should keep disputes about arrangements for the child separate from disputes about money. They should usually be referred to in separate letters.

21. You must remember that the interests of the child may not reflect those of either parent. In special circumstances, in private law cases, it may be appropriate for the child to be represented separately by a guardian *ad litem*.

22. A guardian *ad litem* should have the expertise and knowledge derived from working in the field of child protection and child welfare.

23. Specially trained solicitors should provide legal representation for the child, working with or without a guardian *ad litem*.

24. You should only accept instructions from a child if you have the necessary training and expertise in this field.

25. You must continually assess the child's competence to give instructions.

26. You should make sure that the child has enough information to make informed decisions. The solicitor should advise and give information in a clear and understandable manner and be aware that certain information may be harmful to the child.

27. Dual representation for the child is desirable in health board cases. A guardian *ad litem* and a solicitor for the child should both be appointed, unless there are compelling reasons why the child should not be so represented.

28. The child's rights to welfare and to representation are not easily separated, but that ought not to be an insurmountable problem.

29. You should not show favour towards either parent, the health board or any other person involved in the court proceedings.

30. Where expert reports on a child have been obtained in proceedings and where the normal solicitor/client relationship would dictate that a copy of this report should be made available to the client, this position should prevail wherever possible having regard to the age and understanding of the child client. However, where it is the view of the expert that the report should not, for whatever reason, be made available to the child client, then the solicitor should make the child client aware of the existence of the report. The content of the report should not be communicated to the child client, or a copy given to the child client. The direction of the court should be sought with regard to the matter.

Expert Witnesses

31. Whether either party or their solicitor wishes to have a child medically examined or assessed for the purposes of producing evidence in court, the parties shall in the first instance seek the agreement of the other party to the proceedings so as to secure an agreed referral to a mutually acceptable expert. Solicitors for both sides should agree on the issues to be notified to the agreed expert and the areas where direction and advice is being sought from the expert. In default of agreement the matter should be referred to the court for its direction.

Conflict of Interest

32. Where a solicitor has acted for parties in non-contentious matters, and subsequently one or other of the parties return to that solicitor seeking advice, then the solicitor has a duty to ensure that the other party has no objection to the retainer and that, in the course of the work done for the parties, the solicitor has acquired no information which could lead to a possible conflict of interest.

33. It is inappropriate for a solicitor or a firm of solicitors to represent both parties in any matrimonial/relationship dispute.

APPENDIX 2

GUIDE TO GOOD PRACTICE FOR SOLICITORS ACTING FOR CHILDREN*

*The text of the following guide is published with the kind permission of Mary L'Anson and the Solicitors Family Law Association (SFLA) in the U.K.

INTRODUCTION

The SFLA endorses the UN Convention on the Rights of the Child,[1] and in particular Article 12.

*ARTICLE 12

> "1. States Parties shall assure to the child who is capable of forming his or her own views the right to express those views freely in all matters affecting the child, the views of the child being given due weight in accordance with the age and maturity of the child."
>
> "2. For this purpose, the child shall in particular be provided the opportunity to be heard in any judicial and administrative proceedings affecting the child, either directly or through a representative or an appropriate body, in a manner consistent with the procedural rules of national law."[2]

A. PURPOSE OF THE GUIDE

1. This guide is intended primarily for solicitors acting for or contacted by children in:
   (1) private law proceedings; and
   (2) in public law proceedings when there is or may be a conflict between the Guardian ad litem and the "mature" child.
2. This Guide should be read in conjunction with:
   (i) the SFLA Code of Practice
   (ii) Good Practice in Family Law on Disclosure (SFLA 1996);
   (iii) the following Law Society Family Law Committee's Guidance:
       (a) for solicitors working with Guardians ad litem (to be found

---

[1] United Nations Conventions on the Rights of the Child adopted by the United Nations General Assembly on November 20, 1989, and entered into force on September 2, 1990.
[2] See also the European Convention for the Protection of Human Rights and Fundamental Freedoms Art.6 and Human Rights Act 1998 Arts 5, 8 and 14.

in "Acting for Children" by Christine Liddle, September 1992);

  (b) the Law Society's Guidance on Confidentiality and Privilege—and Advocacy in the Guide to the Professional Conduct of solicitors 7th and 8th Editions, and amendments thereto;

  (c) the Law Society's Guidance Acting for Children in Private Proceedings under the Children Act 1989 in the Guide to the Professional Conduct of solicitors, and amendments thereto;

  (d) the selected bibliography at the end of this Guide;

  (e) any up-dating guidance from time to time published.

B. PERSONAL COMMITMENT

1. Acting for a child directly involves a high degree of personal commitment, expertise, knowledge and training. Each member of the Children Panel must give an undertaking as to the conduct of cases. This undertaking is in the following terms:-

"1. Subject to paragraph 2, I will not normally delegate the preparation, supervision, conduct or presentation of the case, but will deal with it personally.

2. In each case I will consider whether it is in the best interests of the Child to instruct another advocate in relation to the presentation and preparation of the case.

3. If it is in the best interests of the child or necessary to instruct another advocate:-

3.1 I will consider and advise the Guardian ad litem (and the child if of appropriate age and understanding) who should be instructed in the best interests of the child;

3.2 I will obtain an undertaking from that advocate to:-

(a) attend and conduct the matter personally, unless an unavoidable professional engagement arises; and

(b) take all reasonable steps to ensure that so far as is reasonably practicable, a conflicting professional engagement does not arise."

2. Any solicitor contemplating acting for a child must be prepared to make such a commitment. Because of the difficult nature of these cases it is also advisable not to take instructions from children directly unless the solicitor has a significant amount of experience in the field. It is not possible to join the Children Panel until a solicitor is qualified for at least three years. This should be regarded as a minimum unless the solicitor's early experience has exceptionally provided him with the requisite expertise. The professional and emotional challenges which these cases present should not be underestimated.

3. If it is necessary to instruct another advocate it would be advisable to use a solicitor on the Children Panel or counsel experienced in dealing with children's cases. Although there is no specialist Children Panel at the Bar, it is important that counsel (and their clerks) are prepared to make the commitment to the child that is required by the undertaking above. Ideally a conference (at an appropriate place and time for the

child) prior to any court hearing at which counsel will appear should
be arranged in order that the child will know and feel comfortable
with his representative.

C. DEFINITION OF GUARDIAN AD LITEM

The term "Guardian ad litem" when applied in children's proceedings has a
number of different meanings:

(1) Guardian ad litem appointed from the Panel in specified proceedings
    (mostly public law) under Section 41 of the Children Act 1989 will
    be referred to in this Guidance as "Guardian ad litem".

(2) "Guardian ad litem" and "Next Friend" acting under FPR 1991 r. 9.2
    and 9.5 for children taking or defending proceedings (subject to FPR
    1991 r.9.2(A)) will be referred to as "Private Law Guardian".

(3) (a) The Official Solicitor may be appointed (subject to his consent)
        to act as Guardian ad litem for a child in non-specified proceedings
        (FPR 1991 r.9.5) or in specified proceedings under s.41 (only in
        the High Court) and is referred to as "the Official Solicitor".[3]
        The Official Solicitor acts broadly in the same capacity as a
        Guardian ad litem from the Panel (see para (1) above) in specified
        proceedings.

    (b) There have been occasions when Children Panel solicitors have
        been appointed to act as a Guardian ad litem or next friend for a
        child in non-specified proceedings (FPR 1991 r.9.5). It has been
        held that they are appropriate persons for such appointment (but
        see section D.3 (4) below).[4]

(4) Guardian ad litem appointed in adoption proceedings, (see Section
    S).

(5) In Inherent Jurisdiction Cases as distinct from Wardship (notably
    medical consent cases and publicity cases) "Guardian ad litem" and
    "Next Friend" may sometimes be known (probably incorrectly) as
    "Litigation Friends" under the Civil Procedure Rules 1998.

(6) Guardians ad litem in FLA (96) proceedings (see section R).

D. GENERAL PRINCIPLES

1. A solicitor should be sensitive to issues of gender, race, sexuality,
   culture and religion, both in dealing with the child as client and the
   issues in any particular case.

2. A solicitor must retain a professional and objective relationship with
   the client and not allow his or her own emotional response to either
   the child or any issue in the case to interfere with that professional
   relationship.

3. It is important for practitioners to recognise the extent and limitations
   of their professional duty towards children as clients and how that
   duty differs from other professionals involved.[5]

---

[3] See Practice Direction, December 1998 (January, 1991) *Family Law* 52.

[4] *L. v L.* [1994] 1 F.L.R. 156.

[5] Family Proceedings Rules 1991, r.4.11 and r.4.12 and Family Proceedings Courts
     (Children Act 1989) Rules 1991, r.11 and r.12.

(1) In cases in which the Official Solicitor represents a child, he has a duty to communicate their wishes to the court but is not obliged to follow instructions if they do not coincide with his assessment of the child's best interests. The role is therefore a hybrid one.

(2) A Guardian ad litem appointed in specified proceedings (usually public law cases) has a duty to advise the court what is in the child's best interests from their professional point of view, and again has a duty to communicate the child's wishes to the court. The Guardian ad litem will appoint a solicitor whose client is the child.

(3) The solicitor takes instructions from the Guardian ad litem only if the child is not sufficiently mature to instruct direct or, when the child is sufficiently mature, the child's instructions do not conflict with the Guardian ad litem's views. The mature child who is in conflict with the Guardian ad litem will give instructions to his solicitor and they must be followed (as with any other client) even if contrary to the client's interests as perceived by the solicitor.

(4) A solicitor acting as Guardian ad litem or next friend as a result of an appointment under FPR 1991 r.9.5 is under a duty to act in the child's best interests. This will normally be an appointment in relation to children without sufficient maturity to instruct direct under FPR 1991 r.9(2)(A). In these circumstances solicitors should be cautious about accepting such an appointment. Although these situations are rare, they place the solicitor in a difficult professional position. It is strongly advisable therefore to obtain expert assistance in determining what is the child's best interests. It is also important to recognise that the role requires more than simply communicating the child's underlined wishes. Among the courses of action that could be taken are:

(a) obtaining the help of an experienced panel Guardian or child psychiatrist as an expert, for which legal aid authority should be available;

(b) consider asking the Official Solicitor to become involved.
A solicitor so appointed should also be sensitive to the dilemma of being both advocate and witness. Instructing another advocate for the hearing is likely to be the most practical problem to this problem.

N.B. As with any client the solicitor must remember his duty to the Legal Aid Board in the case of wholly unreasonable instructions from a child client.[6]

4. In cases where the solicitor takes instructions from a child direct in private proceedings, he should follow the child's instructions, and his view of what should be done in the child's best interests is only relevant for the purposes of advising the client of the likely approach of the Court and outcome of the proceedings. As a vulnerable client a child may be anxious to please adults in positions of authority. The solicitor

---

[6] Civil Legal Aid (General) Regulations 1989, r.67.

must be sure the child understands the issues in the case and gives instructions freely, and further be careful when advice given by the solicitor is followed, that those instructions reflect the child's wishes and feelings.

5. In almost all cases where the Official Solicitor has been appointed he will act as his own solicitor. Very rarely the Official Solicitor may instruct a solicitor in private practice to act for him as his solicitor e.g. where a solicitor has an established relationship with the child. In this situation, it is not the child who is the client, but the Official Solicitor as his Guardian ad litem.

6. The manner in which the child's instructions are carried out should be in accordance with the SFLA Code of Practice having particular regard to the need to maintain the continuing relationships within the family and with other professionals who will remain involved with the child (social workers, child psychiatrists etc).

7. A child as client should always be given the same respect afforded to an adult as client.

E. SEEING THE CHILD

1. As a general principle, when acting for a child direct, the solicitor will always meet the child. Consideration should be given to the most appropriate setting and style for such a meeting. Interviews should be short and taken at the child's pace. In those cases involving young children, or those under profound disability, the Solicitor should not assume that they do not have to see their clients. Once seen, the child will remain "live" as an individual client for the solicitor throughout the proceedings. Clearly the number of visits with a child will depend on the level of that child's understanding of his current situation.

2. When making arrangements to see the child it is advisable to bear in mind the child's age and familiarity with meetings. For example a child or young person who has had a long history of being looked after or in care may be experienced in attending meetings. For such a young person a meeting in the office may not present such difficulties as may be faced with a less experienced child of any age. In public law proceedings the Guardian ad litem will probably introduce the solicitor to the child having had one or two earlier visits. Most visits are likely to be out of office hours, at home or in the foster home. A bag of toys may be useful to break the ice although solicitors should be sensitive to the risk of the over-interpretation of play. Play or behaviour which causes concern should be considered in light of the Law Society's guidance on confidentiality (see Section J).

3. It should not be forgotten that leave of the court is required for solicitors to see any case papers if you are seeing a child who is not yet a party.[7] This will apply to private law proceedings where it remains unusual for a child to be made a party as a matter of course. (If a child is already a party, he and therefore his Solicitor, is entitled to see case

---

[7] Family Proceeding Rules 1991, r.4.23.

papers [but see Section K]).

4. In private law matters, although caution should be exercised, in practice it is likely to be necessary to interview the child early on, even in the absence of the case papers, in order to establish a preliminary view as to the child's understanding or maturity. It may then be appropriate to proceed further to a more detailed assessment (see below-Section F).

5. When a child approaches a solicitor direct he/she ought to be seen immediately, if possible. It should be established whether the parent/ carers know the child is at the office and discussion should take place with the child as to whether or not they should be told. If the child wishes simply to obtain independent advice on a particular issue, without the knowledge of his or her parents/carers, this wish should be respected (subject to The Law Society guidance referred to at paragraph 2 above). Subject to those instructions, if there are current proceedings in which solicitors are involved, consideration should be given to informing all of the solicitors as soon as possible that you are seeing the child.

6. When receiving a referral from either a parent involved in proceedings or any other adult party or their solicitors, a solicitor should question why the referral is being made. This may involve contacting that party or speaking to that solicitor to establish whether the child is seen as a potential ally to buttress an existing application or is being used to circumvent legal aid eligibility limits. The solicitor should then consider whether it is a justifiable case in which the child needs, and should have independent representation, or whether an application in fact needs to be made i.e. where the child is Applicant as opposed to the child being a Respondent.

7. It is important when taking instructions from a young person that there is sufficient time allowed to ensure instructions can be given in a relaxed and unhurried manner. This is particularly important at Court hearings.

F. ASSESSING UNDERSTANDING

1. From the outset the solicitor will need to assess the child's under- standing and capacity to give instructions. Maturity can be assessed on the child's ability to understand the nature of the proceedings and to have an appreciation of the possible consequences of the applications before the court both in the long and short term.

2. The duty to assess a child's understanding is the solicitor's duty and it continues throughout the case. As the proceedings progress the child will need to understand (and the solicitor to explain) such factors as:
   - what parents and other parties want for the child;
   - what the Guardian ad litem and other experts recommend for the child;
   - an outline of the essential law relevant to the proceedings.

3. If a solicitor is acting on the direct instructions of a child in specified proceedings, he cannot then represent the Guardian ad litem before the court if there is a conflict between them. If he is in doubt as to the child's capacity to give instructions, and what the child is saying is in

conflict with the Guardian ad litem the solicitor should seek the advice of one of the other professionals involved in the case such as a child psychiatrist, social worker or teacher, or approach an independent expert (e.g. child psychiatrist/psychologist). When making these consultations the solicitor should remain sensitive to the duty of confidentiality to the child. Ultimately, if the solicitor cannot decide on the child's level of understanding an application can be made to the court. Usually this would be an application on notice.

4. In addition, in private law proceedings, the court must consider the child's understanding when a child seeks leave to apply or be joined as a respondent in any private Children Act 1989 proceedings or wardship. The court is then the final arbiter as to whether or not the child has the understanding to pursue his application.[8] Note that this is a different and lower test of understanding than that required to discharge an existing Guardian ad litem (see below). It should be noted that the Courts are generally unlikely to grant leave under Rule 9.2A unless it is proposed that the child be legally represented.[9]

5. During the currency of private law proceedings a child can apply for leave to have separate representation under Family Proceedings (Amendment No. 3) Rules 1997 amending r.9.2A(2). With effect from 1st October 1997, the regime in private law proceedings becomes the same as that in public law proceedings. A Guardian ad litem (usually the Official Solicitor) can remain as Guardian ad litem notwithstanding the appointment by the child of a solicitor. In such circumstances, the Official Solicitor will not need leave to continue to act as his own solicitor as well as acting as the child's Guardian ad litem. In *Re C.T.*[10] Waite L.J. said that doubts about the child's capacity should be "resolved by a swift, pragmatic enquiry conducted in a manner which involved the minimum of delay and the least possible distress to the child concerned. It would be very unsatisfactory if such issues themselves became the subject of detailed medical or other professional investigation." In any such consideration by the court it has been held that "the solicitor's judgement is to be respected and to be given great weight." It will be important that the child understands that his solicitor's judgement may be overruled by the court.

6. If it appears that a child's decision-making ability has become impaired, the solicitor should re-assess the child's capacity and consult with the Guardian ad litem, the Official Solicitor (usually only in private law proceedings in the High Court or county court), or other professional involved (see para. 3 above) being careful not to breach the child's confidentiality or prejudice his case. If need be, application may be made to the court on notice for the leave to instruct a solicitor direct to be rescinded or for other suitable directions. In private law

[8] *Re S.C. (A minor) (Leave to seek a Residence order)* [1994] 1 F.L.R. 96.
[9] *In Re S. Independent Representation* [1993] 2 W.L.R. 801.
[10] *Re C.T. (A minor)(Wardship: Representation)* [1993] 2 F.L.R. 278 at p.289D.

proceedings this may result in the discharge of the child as a party.

G. CHILDREN AS APPLICANTS

1. If a solicitor is asked by a child to make an application, his first consideration must be whether the child is able, having regard to his understanding, to give instructions in relation to the proceedings (see section F above). It is good practice to file a statement by the solicitor setting out this belief with the application. Applications by children for leave must be determined by the High Court and so should if possible be started there. Applications on behalf of children may be made in the County Court or High Court only. If the application is made within existing proceedings in a lower court the whole case may be transferred back down once the leave application has been determined in the High Court.

2. Potential conflicts of interest must be carefully considered and where appropriate the child should be helped to find another solicitor to represent him (see Section B2 and 3 above). For example, it could never be right for a parent's solicitor to issue an application on behalf of a child.

3. Solicitors should be cautious in advising children to make applications as this may expose them to considerable pressure from the other parties, which the child may not appreciate in advance. Any appropriate cases are those where the issue is sufficiently serious and there is no adult with whom the child's interest coincide (See Section E6 above)

4. Where the solicitor is in doubt about a child's capacity or has concluded that whilst he does not have capacity he may have a case that needs putting, an approach may be made to the Official Solicitor for advice or to see if he would be prepared to take the matter on as Next Friend in the absence of any other appropriate person.

H. GENERAL CONDUCT OF THE CASE

1. A solicitor should ensure a mature child as client has sufficient information to be able to make informed decisions However the solicitor should be aware that the client may feel under pressure to agree to a course of action in a wish to please and later regret such a decision. It is important to proceed at the child's pace and allow the child to change course or ultimately withdraw. It is easy for the solicitor effectively to take over the litigation and the solicitor should be sensitive to this risk.

2. If a child is to give evidence he will file a statement. Though this will be prepared by the solicitor it need not be in the child's words although it must absolutely represent the child's evidence as to fact, their views on the issues and their wishes. The statement should contain a declaration that the child understands his duty to tell the truth[11] (see Section P).

3. At the conclusion of proceedings the child should be advised of his

---

[11] Children Act 1989, s.96(2).

right of appeal if appropriate. The Court of Appeal has deplored hopeless appeals in family cases. "Legal advisers should not be carried away by the enthusiasm, frustration and hurt of their lay client".[12] This applies equally to the solicitor for the child.

I.   COMMUNICATION WITH A CHILD AND OTHER PARTIES
   1.   In relation to correspondence, the solicitor must keep the child informed by the means most appropriate to his or her level of understanding. If the case goes on over an extended period of time, regular contact with the child should be maintained either by visits or letters. The frequency of such contact will depend on the circumstances of the case and the age of the child.
   2.   The solicitor should be particularly vigilant when acting for children to maintain even-handedness in correspondence with adult parties and their solicitors, and the local authority.
   3.   If in public law proceedings, the child's solicitor finds himself in conflict with the Guardian ad litem, the duty of confidentiality is owed to the client (the child) and unless the child consents to the disclosure of information to the Guardian ad litem, or any other person, no such information should be disclosed (subject to the Law Society's guidance on confidentiality.)

J.   CONFIDENTIALITY
   1.   When acting for a mature child the duty of confidentiality exists as it does for the adult client[13]; this duty always exists save in the exceptional circumstances summarised below. Where a Guardian ad litem is appointed it is important to ensure that the mature child consents to information being given to the Guardian ad litem (who is not a client): even if no conflict exists consent should still be obtained.
   2.   There are conflicting public and professional interests in
      (a) protecting confidentiality to enable the client to confide absolutely in professional advisers;
      (b) in acting in the clients best interests and in particular in protecting children from harm;
      (c) in following instructions from the client and in observation of the duty not to mislead the court by act or omission.
   3.   The Law Society[14] has issued guidance on the circumstances where it may be necessary to breach confidentiality in relation to a child against the clients' wishes.
      (a) Where a crime has been or is likely to be committed e.g. kidnapping, child abduction, child abuse be it neglect, physical, sexual or emotional; the solicitor has to consider whether the risk of the above to the child's life or health, mental or physical, is sufficiently serious to justify a breach of the duty of confidentiality.

[12] *Re N. (Minors) (Residence)* [1995] 2 F.L.R. 230.
[13] *R. v Derby Magistrates Court ex parte B.* [1996] 1 F.L.R. 513.
[14] *The Guide to Professional Conduct of Solicitors* (7th and 8th eds.).
[15] *Re D.H. (A Minor) (Child Abuse)* [1994] 1 F.L.R. 679. *Oxfordshire County Council v M.*

    (b) The duty to disclose reports even if adverse obtained in the course of proceedings.[15]

    (c) The duty not to mislead the Court in its exercise of discretion under the Children Act on the application of S. 1 CA 89 and therefore to consider disclosure of adverse material not obtained within the course of proceedings.[16]

    (d) Where the solicitor is witness-summonsed or subpoenaed and the court directs a solicitor to disclose documentation or divulge information.[17]

4. The child client has the right to be aware of when and how the solicitor's duty of confidentiality may be breached. The child client's right to terminate the solicitor's retainer should also be explained.

5. If a solicitor's retainer is terminated the duty of confidentiality remains subject to the exceptions above.

6. A solicitor who is considering breaching confidentiality under the provisions above should always first seek advice from an experienced colleague and the professional ethics staff at the Law Society.

7. A solicitor, regardless of any advice given to him, must him/herself be able to justify a breach of confidentiality to the OSS, Law Society Disciplinary Tribunal or a court.

K. CHILD'S ACCESS TO DOCUMENTS

1. Under the professional rules solicitors are generally under a duty to allow clients unfettered access to any relevant documentary evidence which the solicitor holds, save where such evidence would adversely affect the client's physical or mental condition.[18] However, as a matter of good practice, there may be exceptional cases such as serious child sexual abuse when the nature of the document is such that it would be inappropriate for clients to be sent a copy of the document for their retention. When representing a child, solicitors should be particularly careful about showing documents to the child and, if in any doubt as to whether a document should be disclosed, should seek the opinion of the Guardian ad litem (if any) or other professional involved in the case. Speaking to a senior colleague or another Children Panel solicitor may also be of help. Ultimately directions can be sought from the court as to disclosure.[19]

2. An example of particular difficulty is when a solicitor is acting for several children where the extent of access to the evidence afforded varies. The solicitor should warn children to whom documents are disclosed, that those documents are strictly confidential and should

---

[1994] 1 F.L.R. 175, *Re L* [1996] 1 FLR 731 and *Essex County Council v R.* [1993] 2 F.L.R. 826.

[16] *Vernon v Bosley (No.2)* [1997] 1 All E.R. 614. See also Practice Direction [1995] 1 F.L.R. 456 and RSC O.24, r.4 and CCr O.20, r.12.

[17] *Ramsbottom v Senior 1869, Re B.* [1995] 1 F.L.R. 774. See also Children Act 1989, s.50(3)(1), Family Law Act 1996, s.33(1).

[18] *The Guide to the Professional Conduct of Solicitors* (8th ed.).

[19] *Re. B. (A Minor)* [1993] 1 F.L.R. 191 20.

not be shown to those who are not entitled to see them. Care should be exercised before copies of documents are given to child clients to keep. It is likely to be inappropriate to send a child client copies of documentation through the post.

3. A solicitor acting for a child should be aware that if a local authority holds personal information about their client, the child has a right of access to that information unless public interest immunity applies. There are similar regulations that give a right of access to education and health records.[20]

L. DEALING WITH CONFLICT OF INTERESTS

1. In public law proceedings the solicitor may find the mature child giving instructions which conflict with those of the Guardian ad litem. In these circumstances if the Guardian ad litem requires legal representation, an application for leave for separate representation will be made by the Guardian ad litem who should seek guidance from the Panel manager as to payment of his legal fees. Reference should be made to the suggested draft letter to the child at Appendix B.

2. Where a solicitor is representing more than one child in the proceedings, he must be aware of the possibility of a conflict arising not only between a child and the Guardian ad litem, but also between the children. An initial question for determination is how many of the children are of sufficient understanding to instruct the solicitor direct.

3. If there is a conflict, either between one or more mature children, or between a mature child and the Guardian ad litem in relation to other children, the solicitor must consider whether he can continue to act for any of the children involved in the light of information received at the time. It is impossible for an advocate to support both the care plan and at the same time challenge that plan on behalf of one dissenting child.[21] If the solicitor takes the view that he must cease acting for all or some of the children, he should inform the children, the Guardian ad litem and the court of the position, so that separate representation can be arranged. The solicitor has to decide which children he will continue to represent and should help the mature children seek alternative representation.

M. INSTRUCTING EXPERTS

1. Solicitors must be aware of the need to advise child clients of their statutory right to refuse consent to medical or psychiatric assessment or treatment. The child should be warned that in certain circumstances the court may override their decision.[22]

2. In proceedings under the Children Act 1989 solicitors are under a duty to disclose expert and other reports commissioned in the course

---

[20] See Access to Personal Files Act 1987: Access to Personal Files (Social Services) Regulations 1989 Circular No.:LAC(89) 2, Reg.9.

[21] *Re P. (Representation)* [1996] 1 F.L.R. 486.

[22] *South Glamorgan County Council v Ward B* [1993] 1 F.L.R. 574.

of proceedings, therefore the child like any other client should be cautioned before instructing an expert of the risks involved in seeking reports which may contain adverse information or opinion. The position is less clear in relation to reports and documentation obtained other than in the course of litigation. However, the child client again needs to be cautioned that a solicitor is an officer of the Court and an advocate cannot mislead the court by act or omission and therefore such documents may have to be disclosed. (See Section I above).

3. Careful consideration should be given by the solicitor before discussing with the child the selection of the expert and the letter of instruction. The child should be reminded that any expert instructed should be unbiased.

4. A solicitor who wishes to instruct an independent social worker in any capacity (either as an expert or in an advisory capacity) should be aware that they have been given a mixed reception by the courts.

5. Detailed guidance on the use and instruction of experts can be found in the final report from the Children Act Advisory Committee (1994/ 5), in section 5 of the Handbook of Best Practice in Children Act Cases 1997 and in the cases listed below.[23]

6. As a matter of practice solicitors should not instruct experts without fees in full having been authorised by the Legal Aid Board.[24] Such authority will not be granted without leave of the court having been obtained.

N. MEDIATION

1. It is possible (although unlikely) that a solicitor taking instructions from a child direct will become involved in mediation in private proceedings. This may take the form of a conciliation appointment within the court system or a series of appointments through a private service. Through representation the child obtains an adult and powerful voice. It is essential that this voice is not used inappropriately and that the solicitor does not undermine or destroy trust between the child and the family, or interfere in the line of communication between them. The solicitor may assist in re-establishing trust and communication but this must be done in such a way as to enable the solicitor to disengage when appropriate to do so.

2. During the course of formal mediation in private law proceedings, privilege applies to any information given or obtained during the mediation session. An exception to this rule applies to information which discloses abuse to a child.[25]

---

[23] *Re C. (Expert Evidence: Disclosure practice)* [1995] 1 F.L.R. 204; *Re M. (Minors) (Care Proceedings: Child's wishes)* [1994] 1 F.L.R. 749; *Re T. and F. (Proceedings: Conflicting Interests)* [19951 1 F.L.R.

[24] Legal Aid Board, Notes for Guidance at 7–18 (D).

[25] *Re D.* [1993] 1 F.L.R. 932.

O. IN COURT
  1. A child is entitled to attend court hearings if he wishes to do so, subject
  to the overriding discretion of the judge to bar any party from the
  hearing.[26] A child should be warned that he may be excluded.[27] This
  issue may need to be dealt with at a directions hearing before the
  Judge who will hear the case. The solicitor should be sensitive to the
  fact a child may not wish to be in close physical proximity to certain
  parties in and outside the court.
  2. Rather than the child giving oral evidence, the solicitor may wish to
  consider with the child whether he would like to write a letter to the
  judge, which can then be read in court. If the child wishes to see the
  Judge, a meeting can be arranged for the child to meet the magistrates
  or Judge. This will not be usual and will depend on local practice.
  Before meeting the Judge the child should be made aware that the
  conversation with the Judge will not be confidential. In the County
  Court and High Court the Judge may wish to see the child in private
  in his or her room. The solicitor or Guardian ad litem will usually
  accompany the child-the solicitor should ensure the child is
  comfortable with whoever accompanies the child.
  3. If the child attends the hearing, the solicitor should warn the child
  that they may hear evidence which may be upsetting and the solicitor
  should be sensitive to the child's emotional state throughout the
  hearing.
  4. The solicitor should offer to show the client the court room and make
  sure that there are arrangements for the child if the child asks to leave
  the hearing. Suitable arrangements should be made for someone to sit
  with the child. In domestic violence cases, arrangements must be made
  to ensure that the child does not meet the other parties in waiting
  rooms or outside court either before or after the hearing.
  5. In any court hearing, the solicitor should be extremely careful about
  their approach to other advocates and be even handed in their approach
  to them and their clients. It is important that the whole of the case and
  especially examination in Court and cross-examination is conducted
  in language which is understood by the child (if present in court) and
  that cross-examination is not aggressive.
  6. Every effort should be made to keep the hearing strictly to the issues
  and as short as possible.

P. THE CHILD AS WITNESS
  1. A child's evidence may be given in civil proceedings (including family
  proceedings) if the court considers that the child understands the duty
  to speak the truth and that he has sufficient understanding to justify

---

[26] Family Proceedings Rules 1991, r.4.16 and Family Proceedings Courts (Children Act
1989), Rules 1991, r.16 (and under s.95 in proceedings under Pt IV and Pt V of the
Children Act 1989).
[27] *Re A. (Care: Discharge application by a child)* [1995] 1 F.L.R. 599 and *Re W (A minor)
(Secure Accommodation)* [1994] 3 F.C.R. 248.

the giving of evidence.[28]

2. Whether or not a mature child should give evidence in court is a matter which will have to be considered carefully by the solicitor with the child. His evidence can be given by a third party relying on the rule that hearsay evidence is admissible in family proceedings.[29] However where the child's evidence is particularly relevant to the issues in the case the fact that hearsay evidence is not as cogent as real evidence will need to be borne in mind when considering with the child whether he will give evidence.

3. In any consideration of whether the child should give evidence the solicitor should ensure that it is the child who decides whether or not to give evidence. If the child has filed a statement, the child should be warned he may have to give evidence and be cross-examined. The solicitor should bear in mind that there will be instances where it is therapeutic or enabling for the child to have the opportunity to give evidence. In practice this is more likely to apply in private law proceedings.

4. The solicitor should consider and advise upon the likelihood of the child giving evidence before the hearing. The child is likely to be worried about speaking in court and needs to know if this is likely. In relation to the substantive evidence to be given by a child it is important not to coach a child but it would be acceptable to give the child an idea of the kind of questions which will be asked, and that it is alright for them to say they cannot remember (if this is the case) or that they do not understand the question. Generally the more information the child can be given about what is likely to happen the easier it will be for him to give evidence in a relaxed manner, with the minimum of trauma. Opening evidence in chief should be by way of gentle questions dealing with non-contentious issues to enable the child to relax.

5. If the child is to give evidence he should be reassured about the privacy of the proceedings but told of the other people who will be in the court room. This includes court staff and in particular ushers who may be wearing black gowns and in respect of whom the child may have wholly unrealistic ideas. The solicitor should tell the child where he will be sitting and if possible show the child in advance. It is the solicitor's duty to check what arrangements are made for the child to give evidence (e.g. behind a screen) if it is appropriate in the circumstances of the case. The solicitor may need to seek directions from the Judge at an early stage in the proceedings. The solicitor should establish with other advocates whether or not they anticipate extensive cross-examination and encourage them to consider the child's natural anxiety about giving evidence, in the hope that they may limit their cross-examination to the pertinent issues.

6. The solicitor should also do all he can to minimise the time the child

---

[28] S.96(1) and (2) of the Children Act 1989.
[29] Children (Admissibility of Hearsay Evidence) Order 1990.

has to wait outside the court as this will naturally increase the child's anxiety. Arrangements should be made to use the care room or children's suite at the court (if the court is so equipped).

Q. SECURE ACCOMMODATION
1. The solicitor will probably only have a few hours notice of his appointment to act for a child on a secure accommodation application. The solicitor will need to consider how instructions will be obtained and try to ensure the child is brought to Court as early as possible (see paragraph E (7)).
2. It is likely that the solicitor's first meeting with the child will be at court. The solicitor will have to assess initially whether the child is of sufficient age and understanding to give instructions. If the solicitor decides the child is capable of giving instructions it is likely he will part company with the guardian.
3. It is essential that a solicitor dealing with a secure accommodation application has regard to the Department of Health Guidance,[30] the Secure Accommodation Regulations[31] and the Guidance in particular must be read in conjunction with current case law which has made it clear, among other things, that the child's welfare although relevant, is not paramount in these proceedings.[32]
4. Once the statutory criteria are met, the only area left to the court's discretion is the length of order and whether an order should be interim or final. This has implications for the Guardian ad litem's role in these cases.[33] Interim orders can be used to provide some flexibility to enable the Guardian ad litem to make further enquiries and to consider and be consulted on the local authority care plan.

R. DOMESTIC VIOLENCE
1. Under the Family Law Act 1996 minors aged 16–18 can apply for Part IV orders (as can those under 16 with leave of the Court). Such applications for leave are to be made in the High Court, although may be transferred down.

N.B. Rule 9.2 A does not apply and therefore a minor has to proceed or defend by Next Friend or private law Guardian (FPR 3.8(10)).

2. The criterion for any leave application is that the Court is satisfied that the applicant has sufficient understanding to make the application.
3. Proceedings for a non-molestation injunction may often involve other adults. A solicitor acting for a child in such circumstances may need

---

[30] Department of Health, *The Children Act 1989, Guidance and Regulations* (HMSO 1991), Vol.1 Court Orders.
[31] Children and Young Persons, The Children (Secure Accommodation) Regulations 1991 and the Children and Young Persons, The Children (Secure Accommodation) (No.2) Regulations 1991.
[32] *Re M. (a minor) (Secure Accommodation Order)* [1995] 1 F.L.R. 413. *Re W. (a minor) (Secure Accommodation Order)* [1993] 1 F.L.R. 692. *Re B. (a minor)* [1994] 2 F.L.R. 707. *Re C. v Humberside County Council and another* [1994] 2 F.L.R. 759.
[33] *Hereford and Worcester County Council v S* [1993] 1 F.C.R. 653.

to take particular care that the child is not being used to buttress another party's application.

4. A child (i.e. a person under 18) may apply for a non-molestation order if they can establish they are a relative or a person who lives in the same household as the respondent.

5. Applications by children for Occupation Orders are likely to be very rare unless they are married or qualify under s.33 as a person entitled to occupy the house in question e.g. by beneficial interest or estate in the family home or a contractual right to occupy their parents' home.

S. ADOPTION

1. Adoption proceedings, although within the definition of family proceedings under the Act, are not specified within the meaning of s.41(6). The child is not a party in either the Family Proceedings Court or County Court,[34] but is a party in the High Court. In the County Court, if a Guardian ad litem is appointed and requires representation, it is the Guardian ad litem who can apply to be joined as a party, not the child. [35] The solicitor's role is therefore different from that in specified proceedings where the child is his client.

N.B. FPR R.9.2 A does not apply in adoption proceedings.

2. In the High Court, normally the Official Solicitor will be appointed as Guardian ad litem if the matter is contested or where certain other factors apply.[36] If a Panel guardian is appointed, he must be legally represented in the High Court.

3. In either case it is the child's means which are relevant currently for the purposes of determining Legal Aid eligibility. There is now a stringent merits test.

T. LEGAL AID

1. The legal aid scheme provides legal aid for children defined as follows.
   (1) Legal Help is available for children under 16;
   (2) representation is available for "minors", i.e. children under 18.

2. Legal aid for children is provided in the following ways:[37]
   (1) Legal Help If the child is seeking advice or assistance in connection with proceedings covered by FPR 1991 r.9.2A (i.e private law proceedings where the child is competent) then the child has an absolute right to seek that advice as if he were an adult. Otherwise the solicitor must have the authority of the Area Director to advise the child (unless the firm holds a franchise) and the merits of that advice must be established.
   (2) Representation in "Special Children Act proceedings" There is non means, non merits tested legal aid for certain public law proceedings (care/supervision order proceedings, applications for

---

[34] Adoption Rules 1984, r.15(3).
[35] *Re G. (A minor) (Adoption: Parental Agreement)* [1990] 2 F.L.R. 429.
[36] See Practice Direction [1986] 2 F.L.R. 170.
[37] Legal Aid Handbook Current Edition.

emergency protection and child assessment orders, applications for discharge of emergency protection orders and applications for secure accommodation for the child alone). In other public law proceedings the normal rules for the grant of legal aid apply.

(3) Representation in other family proceedings Save for those proceedings set out in paragraph 2 above, a child's application for legal aid is assessed as for any adult: the merit of their case is considered and their means (not those of their parent or other carer) are relevant to the financial assessment. The child's solicitor signs the application and the means form for a child under 16. For a child over 16, the child signs the appropriate financial form applicable to the adult client. The Solicitor should note that different procedure and rules apply to adoption applications. A child cannot be a separate party in Magistrates Court or County Court adoptions but is a party in High Court adoptions. The Official Solicitor, is usually invited to act on behalf of the child in such cases, although Panel guardians can be appointed and then appoint a solicitor to act. It should further be noted that in complicated County Court adoptions, Guardians ad litem may be able to receive separate legal advice upon a Direction from the Judge. (See Section S).

U. ENDING THE RELATIONSHIP

1. A solicitor should ensure that he remains accessible to the child and is sympathetic yet professional. Over-dependence by either the child or the solicitor on the other should be discouraged: it should, however, be noted that some children may wish to keep in touch with their solicitor from time to time. Care should always be exercised in such a situation because the solicitor client relationship has ended and continued communication might compromise the solicitor's representation of that child in any future or subsequent proceedings.

2. It is important that the solicitor prepares the child for the end of the relationship and begins telling the child, before the end of the case, that the solicitor's role will shortly be over.

3. Rule 9.2A(9) Family Proceedings Rules 1991 provides that where a solicitor acts for a child direct under r. 9.2A i.e. without a guardian or next friend and the conditions provided for in that rule cease to apply, the solicitor must inform the court immediately. The conditions are:

> ... the minor is able, having regard to his understanding, to give instructions in relation to the proceedings[38]; or [the solicitor] has accepted instructions from the minor to act for him in the proceedings and, where the proceedings have begun, is so acting.[39]

This means that if the child loses capacity to give instructions the

---

[38] Family Proceeding Rules, r.9.2A(1)(b)(i).
[39] Family Proceeding Rules, r.9.2A(1)(b)(ii).

court should be informed (see above F.6); and where instructions are withdrawn by the child, the court must be informed.

4. In specified proceedings the child may wish to terminate his solicitor's appointment under r.4.12(3). This rule only applies to solicitors appointed under the provisions of s.41(3) (appointment by the court) or r.4.11(2)(a) (appointment by Guardian ad litem). The child must apply to the court for an order terminating the appointment and the solicitor should assist the child in doing so e.g. by the provision of information as to the right to apply and assistance in relation to procedure.

5. The solicitor ought to warn the child that the court may be reluctant to allow the child to participate as a party in the proceedings without a next friend or Guardian ad litem if the child is not legally represented.[40] The solicitor and the Guardian ad litem have the right to make representations in their own right to the court, but should consider whether to do so would be in the child's best interests.

6. Rule 4.12(4) provides for the termination of a solicitor's appointment by a Guardian ad litem. As above, an application must be made by the Guardian ad litem to the court and the solicitor (and the child if of sufficient understanding) has the right to make representations.

7. If such applications are made every effort should be made to ensure they do not interfere with the determination of the central issues in the case, and that such applications (under either rule) are dealt with in as amicable a way as possible.

8. When the solicitor's role is over, the solicitor should ensure the child has access to information both in terms of his right to complain about matters concerning his welfare in care (if appropriate),[41] and/or of his right to make further applications to the court. This should be done in person and confirmed by letter to which the child could refer at a later stage. It is important however not to undermine the re-establishment of family relationships which may have been under pressure during the course of proceedings.

9. The Solicitor should always consider sending details with his closing letter to the child client of the SFLA/NCH Web Site for Children.[42]

Mike Hinchliffe, Tim O'Regan, Prue Murdoch, Peggy Ray, Joan Vis
Members of the SFLA Children Committee

---

[40] *Re S. (Independent Representation)* [1993] 2 W.L.R. 801 at p.810B, Sir Thomas Bingham M.R.
[41] Children Act 1989, s.26.
[42] Available from Mary L'Anson (SFLA 01689 850227).

APPENDIX A (A Guide to Good Practice)

SELECTED BIBLIOGRAPHY—SFLA GUIDE TO GOOD PRACTICE
1997

1. Children Act 1989 and Family Proceedings Rules 1991 (County Court) and Family Proceedings Courts (Children Act 1989) Rules 1991 (to include all amendment regulations)
2. The Care of Children, Principles and Practice in Regulations and Guidelines, Department of Health
3. Children Act 1989 Guidance and Regulations Volumes 1 to 9, Department of Health
4. Working Together-under the Children Act 1989, 2nd edition, HMSO 1999
5. Framework for the Assessment of Children in Need, DoH, final draft 1999
6. Legal Aid Handbook (Current Edition)
7. Children Law and Practice, Hershman and McFarlane, Jordans
8. Clark, Hall & Morrison on Children, Butterworths
9. The Child as Client, King & Young, Family Law, 1992
10. Acting for Children, Christine Liddle, Law Society, 1992
11. Report of the Inquiry into Child Abuse in Cleveland 1987, HMSO, 1991
12. Local Authority Circular, 1998 (20), DoH
13. Local Authority Circular, 1999 (29), DoH
14. The Guide to the Professional Conduct of Solicitors (Seventh and Eighth Editions) Law Society
15. GMC Guidance-Confidentiality
16. The Children Act Advisory Committee Annual Reports 1992 to 1997
17. The Children Act Advisory Committee Handbook of Best Practice in Children Act Cases, 1997
18. Family Law Advisors Board Annual Reports 1998 and 1999
19. Expert Witness Pack, 2nd edition, Jordans 2000

RECOMMENDED PERIODICALS

1. Family Law, Jordans Publishing Ltd.
2. Seen and Heard, NAGALRO
3. Practitioner's Guide to Child Law Newsletter
4. SFLA Newsletter
5. ALC Newsletter
6. The Children Panel Newsletter (Published by the Law Society)
7. Family Law Reports, Jordans
8. Family Court Reporter, Butterworths
9. Family Law News, Law Society
10. Focus (Legal Aid Board)

APPENDIX B (A Guide to Good Practice)

DRAFT LETTER TO CHILD/YOUNG PERSON WHEN CONFLICT ARISES WITH GUARDIAN AD LITEM

WHAT IT MEANS WHEN YOU AND YOUR GUARDIAN AD LITEM DISAGREE

Dear C

As you know, X was appointed by the court as your Guardian ad litem and his/her job is to find out all about your situation and tell the court what he/she thinks is the best plan for the future at the end of the case as well as what you think about that plan.

X appointed me to be your solicitor and my job is to represent your views to the court.

At first it seemed possible for you, X and me to be a team but recently it has become clear from what you have told me that you do not agree with X.

I think you are old enough to give me instructions yourself and therefore I am willing to go on representing you and not the Guardian ad litem in court. The Judge will need to know what you want before he makes a decision. X will probably instruct a new solicitor to represent him/her. It would be a good idea if you could telephone me when you receive this letter so that we can make arrangements for me to meet you again soon.

APPENDIX 3

GUIDELINES FOR DRAFTING A NOTICE RESTRICTING LIABILITY UNDER THE OCCUPIERS' LIABILITY ACT 1995

Notices should clearly specify the relevant information. This includes identifying the category of entrant and what duty the occupier intends to exclude. It is clear from section 5(3) of the Occupiers' Liability Act, 1995 that the effect of a proper notice can only operate to reduce the duty of care owed to visitors to that lower and more restricted duty which is owed to recreational users and trespassers.

APPENDIX 4

APPLICATIONS FOR CUSTODY AND ACCESS AND OTHER PROCEEDINGS UNDER THE GUARDIANSHIP OF INFANTS ACT 1964

Recommended checklist of information to be gathered prior to the commencement of proceedings in respect of a child or children under the Guardianship of Infants Act 1964

[This list is adapted from a list prepared by Elizabeth Vogt of Messrs. Vogt and Pinnloes, Attorneys at Law, Santa Barbara, California, U.S.A. It is used with the kind permission of the original authors.]

Basic primary information

The practitioner should first seek answers to the following questions:
- What are the names and ages of the children of the parties?
- Is there a case history involving the child(ren)'s care or welfare? If so, details of prior court applications or proceedings, if any, should be obtained, together with details of any orders made in respect of the child(ren) at such proceedings.
- In particular, have there been any care proceedings or other steps taken under the Child Care Act 1991 in respect of any child of the parties?
- Why does the client seek custody of the children?
- For what reasons does the opposing party seek custody or, where relevant, object to your client obtaining custody?
- To what extent, if any, do the client and opposing party agree on matters relating to the child's welfare? In particular, is there any agreement (and if so, what) on education, religion, discipline, moral values, schooling, extra curricular activities and the time to be spent with each parent?

Ascertaining who is the primary caretaker at present

The practitioner should then seek to ascertain which parent is the primary caretaker of the child or children at present. In determining this, the practitioner should find out who does the following, in each case mindful of the fact that both parents may share these tasks either equally or otherwise:
- Wakes the child and gets up with the child in the morning
- Dresses or helps the child to dress (if necessary)
- Makes breakfast for the child

- Packs a school lunch
- Drops the child to school and collects him or her afterwards
- Helps the child with homework
- Reads the child stories and plays games with him or her
- Bathes the child (where necessary)
- Toilet trains (or has toilet trained) the child
- Puts the child to bed
- Buys the child's clothes
- Takes the child to the hairdresser/barber
- Attends parent/teacher meetings as the child's parent
- Participates in the child's school activities
- Supervises the playtime of the child
- Stays home when the child is sick
- Takes the child to the optician, dentist or doctor when needs be
- Takes the child to religious services or other religious events
- Supervises the child's television viewing
- Talks to the child when problems or issues present themselves—*i.e.* does the child tend to turn to one parent rather than the other?

It goes without saying that the exact questions to be asked will depend on the situation of the child, in particular his or her age and level of maturity. The practitioner should also endeavour to determine:
- The quality of each parent's relationship with the child
- The degree to which each parent supports and has supported or undermines and has undermined the other's relationship with the child
- The nature, quality and reliability of current and past child care arrangements.

The needs and welfare of the child

Information relating to the child's needs and resources should be obtained, in particular information regarding:
- The special health needs of any child, in particular whether the child has any disability, physical or mental
- The general health of each child, in particular whether the child has any medical condition or allergies that need regular attention
- The academic performance and behaviour of the child in school, including any recent changes therein
- The apparent effect on the child of the breakdown in his or her parents' relationship, if any
- Any custody preferences expressed by the child, including the basis for such preferences and the strength thereof
- What special interests does the child have involving either or both parents?

The character, abilities and resources of each parent

- How much time has each parent for the care of the child?
- What are the respective career/vocational goals of each parent?
- What is the state of each parent's physical health?

- What is the state of each parent's mental health?
- What are the other respective strengths and weaknesses of each of the parents?
- What plans, if any, has each parent for the education, religious upbringing and general development of the child or children?
- Is the sexual conduct of either parent at issue? If so:
  - How many partners has the parent had and in what time-frame?
  - Is the child aware of such conduct?
  - Has the child been exposed to sexual conduct?
  - Is there any evidence of harm flowing from such conduct?
  - Does the parent plan to marry the partner at issue?
- Has either parent admitted or been found to have abused either another parent or a child, physically, mentally or sexually? Has either parent been accused of doing so?
- Has either parent a criminal record? If so, are any of the offences relevant to the matter of the child's custody?

Other matters

- What is the quality of the child's relationship with others—*e.g.* his siblings, grandparents, extended family and friends?
- Are there any potential witnesses who should be contacted to verify certain matters, *e.g.* neighbours, childcare providers (including babysitters), teachers, professionals, doctors, psychologists, probation officers, clergy, friends or relatives?

APPENDIX 5

SCHEDULE C, O.58, r.5(1)

AN CHUIRT DUICHE   **THE DISTRICT COURT**

No.58.15
GUARDIANSHIP OF CHILDREN ACTS, 1964 TO 1997
section 11B(2)
NOTICE OF APPLICATION FOR LEAVE TO MAKE AN
APPLICATION UNDER SECTION 11B(1)

*Dublin Metropolitan District
*Dublin Court Area of   *District No.

.... Applicant

....Respondent

TAKE NOTICE that application will be made at the sitting of the District
Court to be held at .... on the .... day of .... 20 ......
at ...... a.m./p.m. under section 11B(2) of the Act in respect of ....
...... born on .... born on ....
child(ren) residing at .... by the above-named applicant
of .... in the court *(area and) district aforesaid
            *[being a relative of the said child(ren)]
            *[who has acted in *loco parentis* to the said child(ren)]

and to whom section 11 of the Act does not apply,

for an order giving leave to the applicant to make an application under section
11B(1) of the Act.

Dated this .... day of .... 20 ......

Signed ....
            Applicant/Solicitor for the Applicant
To
of
To
of

*Delete inapplicable words

APPENDIX 6

SCHEDULE C, O.58, r.4(5)(3)

AN CHUIRT DUICHE   **THE DISTRICT COURT**

No.58.19
GUARDIANSHIP OF CHILDREN ACTS, 1964 TO 1997

NOTICE OF APPLICATION UNDER SECTION 11B FOR AN ORDER GIVING ACCESS

*Dublin Metropolitan District
*Dublin Court Area of   *District No.

.... Applicant
....Respondent
TAKE NOTICE that application will be made at the sitting of the District
Court to be held at .... on the .... day of .... 20 ......
at ...... a.m./p.m. under section 11B(2) of the Act in respect of ....
...... born on .... born on ....
child(ren) residing at .... by the above-named applicant
of .... in the court *(area and) district aforesaid
         *[being a relative of the said child(ren)]
         *[who has acted in *loco parentis* to the said child(ren)]

and to whom section 11 of the Act does not apply,

for an order giving the applicant to the said child(ren).

Dated this .... day of .... 20 ......

Signed ....
         Applicant/Solicitor for the Applicant
To
of
To
of

*Delete inapplicable words

APPENDIX 7

GUARDIANSHIP OF CHILDREN (STATUTORY DECLARATION) REGULATIONS, 1998

S.I. No. 5 of 1998

[...]

1. These regulations may be cited as the Guardianship of Children (Statutory Declaration) Regulations, 1998.

2. These Regulations shall come into operation on 1st day of February, 1998.

3. A statutory declaration referred to in paragraph (*e*) of section 2(4) (inserted by the Children Act, 1997 (No. 40 of 1997)) of the Guardianship of Infants Act, 1964 (No. 7 of 1964) shall be in the form set out in the Schedule to these Regulations.

SCHEDULE

Statutory Declaration of Father and Mother in relation to Joint Guardianship of Child

THE MAKING OF THIS DECLARATION WILL SERIOUSLY AFFECT THE LEGAL POSITION OF BOTH PARENTS. IT IS ADVISABLE TO OBTAIN LEGAL ADVICE BEFORE MAKING THIS DECLARATION.

THIS DECLARATION IS AN IMPORTANT DOCUMENT AND ON COMPLETION SHOULD BE KEPT IN A SAFE PLACE.

In the matter of a declaration under paragraph (*e*) of section 2(4) (inserted by the Children Act, 1997) of the Guardianship of Infants Act, 1964—

We—

_____ of
(father's name)

_____
(father's address)

and

_____ of
                    (mother's name)

_____
                    (mother's address)

do solemnly and sincerely declare and say as follows:

1. We have not married each other.

2. We are the father and mother of _____ who was born
                                              (child's name)
    on   day of   , 200   .

3. We agree to the appointment of _____ as a guardian of
                                              (father's name)

    _____.
                    (child's name)

4. We have entered into arrangements regarding the custody of [and access
    to]*_____.
                    (child's name)

Strike out as necessary.

We make this solemn declaration conscientiously believing the same to be
true by virtue of the Statutory Declarations Act, 1938, and pursuant to paragraph
(*e*) of section 2(4) (inserted by the Children Act, 1997) of the Guardianship of
Infants Act, 1964.

Signed _____ (Father)

Signed _____ (Mother)

DECLARED BEFORE ME BY

_____ who are personally known to me or (who are

identified to me by

_____ who is personally known to me at

_____

this day of   , 20   .

_____
       (Peace Commissioner/Commissioner for Oaths/Notary Public)

APPENDIX 8

EXTRACTS FROM THE CODE OF PRACTICE FOR DEALING WITH COMPLAINTS OF BULLYING AND HARASSMENT IN VEC WORKPLACES*

To all Staff

The Irish Vocational Education Association (IVEA), the Teachers' Union of Ireland (TUI), the Association of Secondary Teachers, Ireland (ASTI), IMPACT and the Services, Industrial, Professional & Technical Union (SIPTU) subscribe fully to this Code of Practice and are committed to creating an environment within every Vocational Education Committee (VEC) that is free of bullying and harassment and which promotes personal integrity and dignity. Unions and management have jointly agreed this Code to help promote such an environment in all VECs.

VECs recognise that bullying and harassment can seriously damage working and social conditions for staff and students. This Code outlines behaviour that would be considered inappropriate or unacceptable and provides procedures for the making of and dealing with complaints.

While all staff and students of VECs are responsible for creating a work and learning environment free of threat, harassment and intimidation, particular responsibility lies with principals and management to ensure that proper standards are maintained.

This policy is not intended to stifle normal healthy relationships amongst staff but, rather, is intended to promote a healthy working and learning environment. This process is an agreed industrial relations process and should not be understood to be a legal process. This Code (and complaints procedure) should be formally adopted and implemented by all VECs as a matter of policy.

Introduction

TUI, ASTI, IMPACT, SIPTU and IVEA are committed to ensuring a workplace environment that is characterised by mutual respect, tolerance and affirmation.

---

*Issued by the TUI, ASTI, SIPTU, IVEA and IMPACT.

Harassment and bullying is behaviour that is destructive to a positive working atmosphere and will not be tolerated. VEC staff have the right to work in an environment free from any form of harassment, bullying or intimidatory behaviour. If someone experiences offensive behaviour and makes a complaint through this complaints procedure, s/he will be protected from any victimisation resulting from the complaint.

Breach of this policy on bullying and harassment may be grounds for disciplinary action ranging from a verbal warning up to and including dismissal for serious offences.

Bullying and harassment are not "new", nor is the behaviour that they describe. What is perhaps "new" is the use of the words in the context of work and the recent recognition of the adverse effects of such behaviour on the victim and the organisation in which s/he works. Employees working in a climate of fear and resentment cannot give of their best. The adverse effects of bullying are manifest in increased absenteeism, low morale, poor performance levels and increased staff turnover. The learning institution may suffer a loss of effectiveness and creative input. It is possible that the image and wider reputation of the school, college, centre or office will also suffer.

Harassment undermines the confidence and dignity of individuals affected by it. It tarnishes the work atmosphere when bullying is tolerated or is accepted as the norm. Harassment and bullying can occur in any kind of workplace and this policy aims to inform VEC staff as to their rights and responsibilities.

Prevention

The best way to eliminate bullying in the workplace is to foster an environment which discourages such behaviour. All employees have an important role to play in creating an environment where bullying is unacceptable. An individual's responsibility extends to an awareness of the impact of personal behaviour that could cause offence to other staff members and make them feel uncomfortable or threatened. In addition to ensuring that their own behaviour is not in any way offensive, employees should make clear to others that bullying is unacceptable and should support colleagues suffering such treatment.

All management personnel have a particular responsibility to ensure that the workplace is kept free from all forms of harassment and bullying so that staff may go about their work free from the threat of harassment or intimidation. As in all matters of discipline, safety and welfare, it is primarily the responsibility of management to establish and sustain proper standards in the workplace. VEC management will respond promptly to complaints of harassment or bullying and will deal with all complaints in an expeditious and supportive manner.

Definition of Bullying and Harassment

Bullying can be defined as a destructive and malicious attempt to target a particular individual or individuals.

- It should not be confused with workplace inter-personal conflicts which may, in themselves, be damaging and stressful but which do not necessarily constitute bullying.
- It should not be confused with the reasonable conduct of their duties by school/college/centre/office management staff.
- It should not be confused with industrial relations difficulties, which should be handled using the appropriate industrial relations procedures.

Bullying and harassment is behaviour that is unprovoked, unwelcome, persistent and is intimidatory or offensive to the recipient. It can take the form of verbal, physical or psychological attack and can be openly aggressive or subtle. Generally, bullying and harassment is taken to mean repeated and persistent behaviour. The impact of bullying and harassment can be devastating; it can affect a person's work performance, health and personal life outside of work.

Bullying is frequently perceived to be a problem between someone in authority and a subordinate. However, bullying can occur between any members of staff. A bully may pick on one person or may turn his/her attention onto a group; a bully may bully a colleague or someone senior to him/her. Groups can bully individuals or other groups. In addition, the bullying of one student by another, while not specifically dealt with in this document, is a serious offence and should be dealt with under the Code of Discipline within schools/colleges/centres.

While the following examples of bullying and harassment are not exhaustive, it is important to be mindful of the fact that if a person behaves inappropriately to another and the victim can make a case that injury has been caused, then in such instances harassment may be deemed to exist.

Bullying can include:

- Open aggression, threats, shouting abuse or obscenities directed towards a colleague.
- Horseplay, offensive gestures and unwanted physical contact.
- Derogatory or offensive nicknames.
- Subjecting a colleague to constant humiliation, sneering, ridicule or using a person as a constant butt of jokes.
- Maligning or spreading malicious gossip about a colleague.
- Subjecting a colleague to unreasonable scrutiny with persistent unwarranted criticism about minor matters.
- Undermining a person's authority, work or achievements.
- Removing, for no justifiable reason, areas of work responsibility from an individual.
- Setting impossible and unreasonable objectives for an employee, or constantly changing the work requirements without telling him/her and criticising or reprimanding him/her for not meeting these objectives or requirements.
- Deliberately withholding information that an employee needs to do his/her job effectively.

- Shunning or marginalising a colleague, excluding him/her from discussions, decisions etc. or refusing to deal directly with him/her in the workplace.
- Deliberately blocking another staff member's professional development/ progression.

Procedures for Dealing with Complaints of Bullying and Harassment in VEC Workplaces

Purposes of Complaints Procedure

- To provide a fair, consistent and expeditious mechanism to process complaints of bullying and harassment against staff.
- To do so in a manner that affords all concerned full rights in accordance with natural justice.
- To outline the principles for both the employer, the staff member and their representatives in the event of complaints of bullying and harassment being made against staff.

Specifically this procedure may be utilised:

- To investigate complaints of bullying/harassment made by staff against other members of staff.
- To investigate complaints of bullying/harassment made by staff against holders of management responsibility.
- To investigate complaints of bullying/harassment made by holders of management responsibility against staff.

Exclusions

- Complaints of bullying/harassment made by staff against students. Such complaints will be treated in accordance with the appropriate student Code of Discipline.
- Complaints of bullying/harassment made by a student(s) against a staff member will be dealt with under appropriate guidelines and/or other agreed codes of practice.
- Matters of the professional competence of teachers which cannot be dealt with at school/college/centre level or which are referred to the Department of Education and Science for investigation under the terms of circular letter 43/85.
- Anonymous complaints.
- Frivolous and vexatious complaints which do not impinge on the work of the staff member.
- Complaints which are the subject of legal proceedings.

Note 1

Claims of harassment under the nine grounds set out in the Employment Equality Act, 1998, may be taken *under* the provisions of that Act. Section 32 of the Act defines these grounds as follows:

– Gender	– Race
– Age	– Sexual Orientation
– Disability	– Religion
– Marital Status	– Membership of the Traveller Community
– Family Status	

Note 2

It is recognised that staff may experience bullying/harassment from other persons calling to schools/colleges/centres/offices of the VEC. While the procedures herein do not seek to address such situations, VECs are committed to putting procedures in place in all workplaces for the protection of staff in such circumstances.

Informal Procedures

STAGE 1 – INFORMAL

1.1 A staff member who feels that s/he has been bullied or harassed should immediately ask the person harassing them to stop. It may be possible and sufficient for the employee concerned to explain clearly to the person/s engaging in the unprovoked conduct that the behaviour in question is unwelcome, that it offends them, or makes them uncomfortable and that it interferes with their work. A person who wishes to make a complaint (hereinafter referred to as the complainant) should make an appointment to discuss the matter with the staff members (hereinafter referred to as the subject/s of the complaint) with a view to resolving the complaint.

1.2 If the complainant feels that s/he cannot directly address the subject/s of the complaint engaging in the unprovoked conduct, s/he should ask a Designated Person to do so on his/her behalf. In each school/college/centre/office all staff, acting jointly for this purpose, shall elect two Designated Persons (male and female) for a period of two years. The names of the nominees shall be forwarded to the employer for ratification. If the harassment complained of does not cease, or if, in the first instance, it is of such a nature that the complainant (normally following discussion with a Designated Person) considers that it should be reported, the matter should proceed to stage 1.3. The procedures at stage 1 should normally be concluded within **5 working days** of the reporting of the matter to the Designated Person.

1.3 If the matter is unresolved at stage 1.2, the complainant should approach the Officer of First Recourse (normally understood to be a Deputy Principal in a school/college context and in a centre/office, to be a member of the senior management team) who would endeavour to resolve the complaint through an informal process as in stage 1.2. If the Officer of First Recourse is a party to the complaint, another agreed person shall be appointed to this position.

Formal Procedures

STAGE 2 – INVESTIGATION

2.1 If the issue is not resolved at stage 1, the complainant should lodge the complaint in writing, with the Investigating Officer of Second Recourse, hereinafter referred to as the Investigating Officer (normally understood to be the Principal Teacher in a school, the senior member of the management team in a centre and a senior member of the management team in an office). An allegation shall be investigated by the Investigating Officer. Where the Investigating Officer is a party to the complaint, an allegation shall be investigated by a person nominated by the employer in agreement with the relevant union. The Investigating Officer shall be responsible on behalf of management for investigating any complaint of bullying/ harassment and recommending action.

2.2 Investigations of any complaint will be handled with sensitivity and with due respect to both the complainant and the subject/s of the complaint. It is understood that all complaints will be investigated with minimum delay. In the case of a formal complaint, it is anticipated that all parties concerned will co-operate fully with the investigation undertaken. Failure by any party to co-operate will not prevent the processing of an investigation to conclusion. The Investigating Officer should acknowledge and note that the complaint has been received by dealing with the matter as follows:
   (a) Supply the staff member/s complained of with a copy of the written complaint and invite his/her written response.
   (b) Arrange meeting(s) with the parties to the complaint either separately or jointly with a view to resolving the complaint. Such meeting(s) should normally take place within **10 working days** of receipt of the written complaint as specified in 2.1.

2.3 The complainant and the subject of the complaint may each be accompanied by a colleague or another person of his/her choice. The discretion to afford representation by the relevant union to either party rests with the relevant union.

2.4 If the matter is resolved to the satisfaction of all parties concerned, the Investigating Officer shall confirm this in writing to all parties to the complaint and indicate that the matter is concluded.

2.5 In all other cases, the Investigating Officer shall convey the outcome of his/her investigation in writing to the parties to the complaint normally within **10 working days** of the meeting(s) referred to in 2.2(b). This notification of outcome shall indicate whether the Investigating Officer considers the complaint to be upheld, unfounded, or unfounded and malicious. Notification to all parties shall include reference to the right of the parties to make a formal presentation of case to the Complaints Consideration Committee of the VEC as provided for in 2.7. In cases where complaints have been made against more than one person, a separate report will issue in respect of each person against whom a complaint is made.

2.6 Within the same time-frame, the Investigating Officer shall furnish a full report, attaching all relevant documentation in a sealed envelope, to the Chief Executive Officer of the VEC, marked for the attention of the Complaints Consideration Committee (appointed by the CEO and established for this purpose). This report may include a recommendation that the Complaints Consideration Committee considers disciplinary sanctions. The role of the Investigating Officer in the process concludes upon the presentation of his/her report to the CEO of the VEC.

2.7 The Complaints Consideration Committee established will normally consist of three persons: a nominee of management, a nominee of the relevant union and an independent chairperson agreed between both management and union. However, where more than one union is involved in the complaint, each union will be invited to make a nomination to this Committee. The Committee in these circumstances will consist of an equal number of union and management nominees.

STAGE 3 – COMPLAINTS CONSIDERATION COMMITTEE

3.1 (a) The Complaints Consideration Committee will normally convene within **10 working days** (of receipt by the Committee of the Investigating Officer's report) to consider the report and accompanying documentation (as referred to in 2.6) forwarded for its attention. Within **3 working days** of its meeting, the CEO will arrange to have the parties provided with a copy of the Investigating Officer's report and documentation (as in 2.6) and invite each party to make a formal presentation of his/her case to a further meeting of the Committee The meeting shall be convened no earlier than **7 working days** from the date of issue of the invitation to address the Committee.

(b) The subject of the complaint may be accompanied and represented by a colleague or another person of his/her choice. The discretion to afford representation by the relevant union rests with the relevant union.

(c) The complainant may be accompanied and represented by a colleague or another person of his/her choice. The discretion to afford representation by the relevant union rests with the relevant union.

(d) The Committee may, at its discretion, be assisted by a person drawn from an agreed national panel of experts established through agreement between TUI, ASTI, IMPACT, SIPTU and IVEA.

(e) All meetings/hearings of the Committee will normally take place within **30 working days** of the receipt by the Committee of the Investigating Officer's report.

(f) When the Complaints Consideration Committee has completed its deliberations, the Committee's findings shall be conveyed in writing, by the Committee to the subject/s of the complaint, the complainant and the CEO, normally within **5 working days** of the findings being set down. Notification in writing to both the complainant and the subject/s of the complaint will advise of the right to appeal the findings to the CEO (as outlined in stage 4). The subject/s of the complaint will be advised of any recommended disciplinary sanctions and may also appeal this aspect of the findings to the CEO (as outlined in stage 4).

3.2 Where no appeal is lodged, the CEO shall consider the recommendation(s) of the Complaints Consideration Committee and normally decide in accordance therewith. The implementation of the decision by the CEO shall conclude the process.

3.3 If the CEO forms the view, having considered the findings and recommendations of the Committee, that consideration should be given to increased sanctions over and above those recommended by the Committee, stage 4 will commence and the person/s against whom the sanction is proposed be so notified.

STAGE 4 – APPEAL TO CEO

4.1 Where stage 4 is invoked (as per stage 3.1 (f), the CEO will afford an opportunity to the parties to the complaint to present their case. The complainant and the subject of the complaint may be accompanied and represented by a colleague or another person of his/her choice. The discretion to afford representation by the relevant union rests with the relevant union.

Where stage 4 is invoked (as per stage 3.3), the CEO will afford an opportunity to the subject of the complaint to present his/her case.

The subject of the complaint may be accompanied and represented by a colleague or another person of his/her choice. The discretion to afford representation by the relevant union rests with the relevant union.

4.2 The CEO shall consider the report and recommendations, if any, of the Complaints Consideration Committee and the case as presented at Stage 4.1 and make a decision. The implementation of the decision shall normally complete the process and shall be communicated to all parties concerned.

Disciplinary sanctions

Disciplinary sanctions may include:
(i)   An oral warning
(ii)   A written warning
(iii)   A final written warning
(iv)   With holding/refusal of an increment(s)
(v)   Demotion
(vi)   Suspension
(vii) Dismissal

The steps in the procedure should be progressive (e.g. oral warning, written warning, a final written warning etc.). There may be instances where more serious action is warranted at an earlier stage.

Where the subject of the complaint is an Officer of the VEC, within the meaning of the Vocational Education Act, 1930 (as amended) and where the CEO, following his/her investigation, considers that suspension may be warranted, the CEO shall refer the matter to the VEC Committee for consideration.

Written warnings will be placed on an individual's record and may be removed after an agreed specified period of time with the employee advised accordingly.

Any proposed disciplinary sanctions will be processed in accordance with the terms of the Vocational Education Act, 1930, Vocational Education (Amendment) Acts 1944 and 2001, relevant sections of the Regional Technical Colleges Act, 1992 and other relevant employment legislation.

Protection and Support

Staff shall be protected from intimidation, victimisation or discrimination for filing a complaint or assisting in an investigation. Retaliation against a member of staff for complaining about bullying/harassment is considered a disciplinary offence. A malicious complaint made by a staff member will be treated as misconduct under the disciplinary procedures herein.

Assistance in the Event of Bullying and Harassment

Every effort will be made to assist, if they so wish, persons who are victims of bullying/harassment to deal with the problem and where requested, the services of a counsellor will be made available by the VEC. Persons who bully/harass others may be requested to attend counselling to prevent further incidences of harassment occurring. Access to such counselling may be made available by the VEC.

Record Keeping

At all stages of the complaints procedure a clear record should be kept of:

- The investigation undertaken.
- All communications to/by the complainant, the subject/s the complaint, the Officer of First Recourse, the Investigating Officer, the Complaints Consideration Committee, the Chief Executive Officer and the VEC.
- The steps and all the decisions taken.

Where a complaint has been rejected or deemed unfounded, a statement to that effect shall conclude the record in the personnel file of the complainant. All records in respect of a rejected/unfounded complaint shall be removed from the personnel file of the subject/s of the complaint. A statement of the outcome of the investigation will conclude all other files.

Review

This complaints procedure shall be reviewed after two years.

APPENDIX 9

GUIDELINES FOR DRAFTING A SAFETY STATEMENT

Summary

1. The Safety Statement says:
   (a) What the principal teacher wants to achieve in the area of safety, health and welfare at the school—it includes a statement of general policy on safety and health, which is signed by the principal teacher and is dated.
   (b) Who is to do it—the means by which everyone in the school is made aware of the things they are expected to do to help achieve a safe and healthy school.
   (c) How is it to be done—arrangements and procedures to manage safety and health.
   (d) When and what is to be checked—planned review and revision as required.

2. The completed Safety Statement must be relevant to the school, the location and the type of pupil/student.

3. It must be brought to the notice of all school staff, as must any revisions.

4. Representatives of the school staff must be consulted in good time on matters affecting safety and health.

5. Although the general contents are specified by the Safety, Health and Welfare at Work Act, 1989 ("the Act"), there is no legally required format for a safety statement. The Health and Safety Authority ("HSA") have published extensive guidance on the subject.[1]

It is also good practice for the Safety Statement to:

6. Stress the need for co-operation before the policy can be effective.

7. Draw the attention of teachers and pupils to their own responsibilities.

8. Cover the safety and health of visitors and also to cover the safety and health of teachers where they could be affected by the work of visitors.

9. Cover occupational health matters such as stress, bullying, harassment, fatigue, eyestrain and musculoskeletal disorders.

---

[1] See www.hsa.ie.

Introduction

Under section 12 of the 1989 Act, every employer must as soon as possible prepare or cause to be prepared a statement in writing which is known as a Safety Statement. This statement specifies the manner in which safety, health and welfare shall be secured in the workplace. The purpose of the document is to require employers to assess the workplace over which they have control and to identify the hazards to safety, health and welfare in that place of work. The risks posed by these hazards are then assessed, eliminated where possible, or reduced to acceptable levels. Arrangements are then made to manage the remaining risks at the workplace.

Why do I need a Safety Statement?

The safety statement is a management tool for managing workplace health and safety. Failure to comply with the section 12 Safety Statement requirement is a criminal offence. Civil liability may also attach.

Key components of a Safety Statement

There are four main components to a Safety Statement, and these are required under the guidance documentation published by the HSA.

1. **General Policy Statement**—This spells out the commitment of the school to safety and health. The reduction/elimination of accidents and the protection of health should be expressly stated as a key feature of the school's activities and measure of success.

2. **Organisation**—Defining whom does what, and details the duties/responsibilities of persons in relation to workplace safety, health and welfare. The principal teacher will normally have overall responsibility for health and safety within the school, with specific specialised teachers having responsibility for their particular areas.[2]

3. **Arrangements**—Should characterise the particular arrangements established to achieve the targets set out in the general statement, such as first aid, training and fire precautions. This will also include a listing of all significant hazards and associated policies and procedures for eliminating or reducing the associated risks. Specific risk assessments, examining in more detail the hazards involved in practical classes, will be necessary. Class-specific safety statements might contain the following:
    *   class rules for staff and pupils;
    *   identifying specific preventative measures for specific hazards;
    *   schedules, procedures and checklists for monitoring equipment;
    *   emergency and reporting procedures;
    *   drills for emergency procedures; and
    *   local first aid arrangements.

---

[2] For example, the teachers of physical education, art and science.

Art classes

It is important to appreciate that the teaching of art presents a number of potential hazards which require a tailored health and safety policy resulting from a risk assessment. [See the discussion on the Chemical Agents Regulations in Chapter 3.]

Physical education classes

A list of the principles of safe practice associated with physical education should be developed. For example, one such principle should be not to embark on or to proceed with an activity where there is an inherent hazard which cannot be reasonably managed so that safety could be compromised. An excellent source of reference is the Millennium edition of *Safe Practice in Physical Education*. It should also be noted the GAA at its Annual Congress in Killarney on April 17, 2004 passed a motion which will require the compulsory wearing of helmets with face guards for all hurlers up to and including Minor level from January 2005.

School tours

The principal teacher must ensure that all out-of-school visits comply with the guidelines set down by the Department of Education and Science or board of management and with the school's own health and safety policies. This will involve:
- evaluating the objectives of the out-of-school visit—safety must take precedence over educational or other objectives;
- selecting an appropriately qualified teacher as the leader, preferably a teacher who has experience in managing groups;[3]
- furnishing consent forms to parents and ensuring that a completed form is received in respect of each pupil;
- having emergency procedures in place for the trip; and
- ensuring that there is an adequate staff-to-pupil ratio.[4]

Pupils should also be aware of their responsibilities. In addition to the general requirements mentioned above, there are particular considerations that relate to foreign out-of-school visits.

Minibuses

Some schools use their own transport for various trips but should ensure that this is not a casual arrangement. The principal teacher is primarily responsible for ensuring that the minibus is properly maintained, but may delegate this duty to a competent person.

---

[3] In *O'Meara v Gallivan* the Court stated that schools must employ competent staff to supervise school tours. See also *R. v (Paul) Ellis* (2003) Manchester Crown Court, where a school teacher was found guilty of manslaughter after a pupil drowned in a river during an activity weekend.

[4] The required staff-to-pupil ratio is set out in the Code of Practice— *Child Protection in the Youth Work Sector*.

4. Review—All Safety Statements should be subject to periodic review to minimise the risk of the policy falling out of date and failing to address either legal standards or practical issues which arise within the school.

IT IS NOT POSSIBLE TO PROVIDE A GENERIC SAFETY STATEMENT AS THE RISKS IN EACH SCHOOL WILL VARY DEPENDING ON THE SIZE OF THE SCHOOL AND THE TYPES OF CLASSES TAUGHT.

APPENDIX 10

FORM OF FOSTER CARE CONTRACT

THIS AGREEMENT made this .... day of .... 20 ...... BETWEEN the .... (hereinafter called "the health board") of the first part and .... (hereinafter called "the foster parents") of the second part,
WITNESSETH that the said foster parents hereby accept the care of .... (hereinafter called "the child").

The foster parents hereby covenant and agree with the health board that they will:

1. Take the child into their home and care for the child on behalf of the health board.
2. Fulfil all of the duties imposed on them under Article 16 of the Child Care (Placement of Children in Foster Care) Regulations 1995 in respect of the child.
3. Co-operate with the health board in the care and upbringing of the child.

And the health board hereby covenants and agrees with the foster parents that it will:

1. Pay the foster parents an allowance of not less than the amount currently specified by the Minister for Health in respect of the child.
2. Provide such additional financial or other assistance, including support services, as the health board considers necessary to enable the foster parents to take care of the child.
3. Facilitate the implementation of the plan prepared by the health board for the care and upbringing of the child.

Signed by _____ and _____
         Foster Parents   Chief Executive Officer of Health Board (or other officer to whom this function has been delegated).

APPENDIX 11

APPLICATION FOR REGISTRATION AS A CHILDREN'S RESIDENTIAL CENTRE

I, the applicant, hereby declare that the information given by me in this application is correct to the best of my knowledge.

Signature of applicant:

Date:

Information to be enclosed with application form

1. Please attach an example of any brochure or advertisement to be used for the centre.

2. Please attach plans of the interior design of the centre giving details of the dimensions of all rooms intended for residents' use, also indicating owners/staff rooms.

3. Please supply the name and address of the G.P./medical officer who will be responsible for the medical examination of residents.

4. Please attach a two-week menu plan to cover breakfast, lunch and dinner.

5. Please attach written confirmation from a chartered engineer or a properly and suitably qualified architect with experience in fire-safety design and management.

Additional information may be requested in support of application

Proprietors should be able to provide the relevant health board with:
  (i) a copy of the certificate of planning permission for the centre, and
  (ii) samples of job description/contracts of staff and written statements to staff on Health and Safety at Work.

APPENDIX 12

EUROPEAN CONVENTION ON THE ADOPTION OF CHILDREN

Strasbourg 4th IV 1967

PREAMBLE

The Member States of the Council of Europe, signatory hereto,

Considering that the aim of the Council of Europe is to achieve a greater unity between its members for the purpose, among others, of facilitating their social progress;

Considering that, although the institution of the adoption of children exists in all member countries of the Council of Europe, there are in those countries differing views as to the principles which should govern adoption and differences in the procedure for effecting, and the legal consequences of, adoption; and

Considering that the acceptance of common principles and practices with respect to the adoption of children would help to reduce the difficulties caused by those differences and at the same time promote the welfare of children who are adopted,

Have agreed as follows:

PART I

UNDERTAKINGS AND FIELD OF APPLICATION

ARTICLE 1

Each Contracting Party undertakes to ensure the conformity of its law with the provisions of Part II of this Convention and to notify the Secretary General of the Council of Europe of the measures taken for that purpose.

ARTICLE 2

Each Contracting Party undertakes to give consideration to the provisions set out in Part III of this Convention, and if it gives effect, or if, having given effect, it ceases to give effect to any of these provisions, it shall notify the Secretary General of the Council of Europe.

ARTICLE 3

This Convention applies only to legal adoption of a child who, at the time when the adopter applies to adopt him, has not attained the age of 18, is not and has not been married, and is not deemed in law to have come of age.

PART II

ESSENTIAL PROVISIONS

ARTICLE 4

An adoption shall be valid only if it is granted by a judicial or administrative authority (hereinafter referred to as the "competent authority").

ARTICLE 5

1. Subject to paragraphs 2 to 4 of this article, an adoption shall not be granted unless at least the following consents to the adoption have been given and not withdrawn:
    (a) the consent of the mother and, where the child is legitimate, the father; or if there is neither father nor mother to consent, the consent of any person or body who may be entitled in their place to exercise their parental rights in that respect;
    (b) the consent of the spouse of the adopter.

2. The competent authority shall not:
    (a) dispense with the consent of any person mentioned in paragraph 1 of this article, or
    (b) overrule the refusal to consent of any person or body mentioned in the said paragraph 1,
save on exceptional grounds determined by law.

3. If the father or mother is deprived of his or her parental rights in respect of the child, or at least of the right to consent to an adoption, the law may provide that it shall not be necessary to obtain his or her consent.

4. A mother's consent to the adoption of her child shall not be accepted unless it is given at such time after the birth of the child, not being less than six weeks, as may be prescribed by law, or, if no such time has been prescribed, at such time as, in the opinion of the competent authority, will have enabled her to recover sufficiently from the effects of giving birth to the child.

5. For the purposes of this article "father" and "mother" mean the persons who are according to law the parents of the child.

ARTICLE 6

1. The law shall not permit a child to be adopted except by either two persons married to each other, whether they adopt simultaneously or successively, or by one person.

2. The law shall not permit a child to be again adopted save in one or more of the following circumstances:
   (a) where the child is adopted by the spouse of the adopter;
   (b) where the former adopter has died;
   (c) where the former adoption has been annulled;
   (d) where the former adoption has come to an end.

ARTICLE 7

1. A child may be adopted only if the adopter has attained the minimum age prescribed for the purpose, this age being neither less than 21 nor more than 35 years.

3. The law may, however, permit the requirement as to the minimum age to be waived:
   (a) when the adopter is the child's father or mother, or
   (b) by reason of exceptional circumstances.

ARTICLE 8

1. The competent authority shall not grant an adoption unless it is satisfied that the adoption will be in the interest of the child.

2. In each case the competent authority shall pay particular attention to the importance of the adoption providing the child with a stable and harmonious home.

3. As a general rule, the competent authority shall not be satisfied as aforesaid if the difference in age between the adopter and the child is less than the normal difference in age between parents and their children.

ARTICLE 9

1. The competent authority shall not grant an adoption until appropriate enquiries have been made concerning the adopter, the child and his family.

2. The enquiries, to the extent appropriate in each case, shall concern, *inter alia*, the following matters:

(a) the personality, health and means of the adopter, particulars of his home and household and his ability to bring up the child;

(b) why the adopter wishes to adopt the child;

(c) where only one of two spouses of the same marriage applies to adopt a child, why the other spouse does not join in the application;

(d) the mutual suitability of the child and the adopter, and the length of time that the child has been in his care and possession;

(e) the personality and health of the child, and subject to any limitations imposed by law, his antecedents;

(f) the views of the child with respect to the proposed adoption;

(g) the religious persuasion, if any, of the adopter and of the child.

3. These enquiries shall be entrusted to a person or body recognised for that purpose by law or by a judicial or administrative body. They shall, as far as practicable, be made by social workers who are qualified in this field as a result of either their training or their experience.

4. The provisions of this article shall not affect the power or duty of the competent authority to obtain any information or evidence, whether or not within the scope of these enquiries, which it considers likely to be of assistance.

ARTICLE 10

1. Adoption confers on the adopter in respect of the adopted person the rights and obligations of every kind that a father or mother has in respect of a child born in lawful wedlock.

   Adoption confers on the adopted person in respect of the adopter the rights and obligations of every kind that a child born in lawful wedlock has in respect of his father or mother.

2. When the rights and obligations referred to in paragraph 1 of this article are created, any rights and obligations of the same kind existing between the adopted person and his father or mother or any other person or body shall cease to exist. Nevertheless, the law may provide that the spouse of the adopter retains his rights and obligations in respect of the adopted person if the latter is his legitimate, illegitimate or adopted child.

   In addition the law may preserve the obligation of the parents to maintain (in the sense of *l'obligation d'entretenir* and *l'obligation alimentaire*) or set up in life or provide a dowry for the adopted person if the adopter does not discharge any such obligation.

3. As a general rule, means shall be provided to enable the adopted person to acquire the surname of the adopter either in substitution for, or in addition to, his own.

4. If the parent of a child born in lawful wedlock has a right to the enjoyment of that child's property, the adopter's right to the enjoyment of the adopted person's property may, notwithstanding paragraph 1 of this article, be restricted by law.

5. In matters of succession, in so far as the law of succession gives a child born in lawful wedlock a right to share in the estate of his father or mother, an adopted child shall, for the like purposes, be treated as if he were a child of the adopter born in lawful wedlock.

ARTICLE 11

1. Where the adopted child does not have, in the case of an adoption by one person, the same nationality as the adopter, or in the case of an adoption by a married couple, their common nationality, the Contracting Party of which the adopter or adopters are nationals shall facilitate acquisition of its nationality by the child.

2. A loss of nationality which could result from an adoption shall be conditional upon possession or acquisition of another nationality.

ARTICLE 12

The number of children who may be adopted by an adopter shall not be restricted by law.

A person who has, or is able to have, a child born in lawful wedlock, shall not on that account be prohibited by law from adopting a child.

If adoption improves the legal position of a child, a person shall not be prohibited by law from adopting his own child not born in lawful wedlock.

ARTICLE 13

1. Before an adopted person comes of age the adoption may be revoked only by a decision of a judicial or administrative authority on serious grounds, and only if revocation on that ground is permitted by law.

2. The preceding paragraph shall not affect the case of:
    (a) an adoption which is null and void;
    (b) an adoption coming to an end where the adopted person becomes the legitimated child of the adopter.

ARTICLE 14

When the enquiries made pursuant to Articles 8 and 9 of this Convention relate to a person who lives or has lived in the territory of another Contracting Party, that Contracting Party shall, if a request for information is made, promptly endeavour to secure that the information requested is provided. The authorities may communicate directly with each other for this purpose.

ARTICLE 15

Provision shall be made to prohibit any improper financial advantage arising from a child being given up for adoption.

ARTICLE 16

Each Contracting Party shall retain the option of adopting provisions more favourable to the adopted child.

PART III

SUPPLEMENTARY PROVISIONS

ARTICLE 17

An adoption shall not be granted until the child has been in the care of the adopters for a period long enough to enable a reasonable estimate to be made by the competent authority as to their future relations if the adoption were granted.

ARTICLE 18

The public authorities shall ensure the promotion and proper functioning of public or private agencies to which those who wish to adopt a child or to cause a child to be adopted may go for help and advice.

ARTICLE 19

The social and legal aspects of adoption shall be included in the curriculum for the training of social workers.

ARTICLE 20

1. Provision shall be made to enable an adoption to be completed without disclosing to the child's family the identity of the adopter.

2. Provision shall be made to require or permit adoption proceedings to take place *in camera*.

3. The adopter and the adopted person shall be able to obtain a document which contains extracts from the public records attesting the fact, date and place of birth of the adopted person, but not expressly revealing the fact of adoption or the identity of his former parents.

4. Public records shall be kept and, in any event, their contents reproduced in such a way as to prevent persons who do not have a legitimate interest from learning the fact that a person has been adopted or, if that is disclosed, the identity of his former parents.

PART IV

FINAL CLAUSES

ARTICLE 21

1. This Convention shall be open to signature by the member States of the Council of Europe. It shall be subject to ratification or acceptance. Instruments of ratification or acceptance shall be deposited with the Secretary General of the Council of Europe.

2. This Convention shall enter into force three months after the date of the deposit of the third instrument of ratification or acceptance.

3. In respect of a signatory State ratifying or accepting subsequently, the Convention shall come into force three months after the date of the deposit of its instrument of ratification or acceptance.

ARTICLE 22

1. After the entry into force of this Convention, the Committee of Ministers of the Council of Europe may invite any non-member State to accede thereto.

2. Such accession shall be effected by depositing with the Secretary General of the Council of Europe an instrument of accession which shall take effect three months after the date of its deposit.

ARTICLE 23

1. Any Contracting Party may, at the time of signature or when depositing its instrument of ratification, acceptance or accession, specify the territory or territories to which this Convention shall apply.

2. Any Contracting Party may, when depositing its instrument of ratification, acceptance or accession or at any later date, by declaration addressed to the Secretary General of the Council of Europe, extend this Convention to any other territory or territories specified in the declaration and for whose international relations it is responsible or on whose behalf it is authorised to give undertakings.

3. Any declaration made in pursuance of the preceding paragraph may, in respect of any territory mentioned in such declaration, be withdrawn according to the procedure laid down in Article 27 of this Convention.

ARTICLE 24

1. Any Contracting Party whose law provides more than one form of adoption shall have the right to apply the provisions of Article 10, paragraphs 1, 2, 3 and 4, and Article 12, paragraphs 2 and 3, of this Convention to one only of such forms.

2. The Contracting Party exercising this right, shall, at the time of signature or when depositing its instrument of ratification, acceptance or accession, or when making a declaration in accordance with paragraph 2 of Article 23 of this Convention, notify the Secretary General of the Council of Europe thereof and indicate the way in which it has been exercised.

3. Such Contracting Party may terminate the exercise of this right and shall give notice thereof to the Secretary General of the Council of Europe.

ARTICLE 25

1. Any Contracting Party may, at the time of signature or when depositing its instrument of ratification, acceptance or accession, or when making a declaration in accordance with paragraph 2 of Article 23 of this Convention, make not more than two reservations in respect of the provisions of Part II of the Convention.

    Reservations of a general nature shall not be permitted; each reservation may not affect more than one provision.

    A reservation shall be valid for five years from the entry into force of this Convention for the Contracting Party concerned. It may be renewed for successive periods of five years by means of a declaration addressed to the Secretary General of the Council of Europe before the expiration of each period.

2. Any Contracting Party may wholly or partly withdraw a reservation it has made in accordance with the foregoing paragraph by means of a declaration addressed to the Secretary General of the Council of Europe, which shall become effective as from the date of its receipt.

ARTICLE 26

Each Contracting Party shall notify the Secretary General of the Council of Europe of the names and addresses of the authorities to which requests under Article 14 may be addressed.

ARTICLE 27

1. This Convention shall remain in force indefinitely.

2. Any Contracting Party may, in so far as it is concerned, denounce this Convention by means of a notification addressed to the Secretary General of the Council of Europe.

3. Such denunciation shall take effect six months after the date of receipt by the Secretary General of such notification.

ARTICLE 28

The Secretary General of the Council of Europe shall notify the member States of the Council and any State which has acceded to this Convention of:

(a) any signature;

(b) any deposit of an instrument of ratification, acceptance or accession;

(c) any date of entry into force of this Convention in accordance with Article 21 thereof;

(d) any notification received in pursuance of the provisions of Article 1;

(e) any notification received in pursuance of the provisions of Article 2;

(f) any declaration received in pursuance of the provisions of paragraphs 2 and 3 of Article 23;

(g) any information received in pursuance of the provisions of paragraphs 2 and 3 of Article 24;

(h) any reservation made in pursuance of the provisions of paragraph 1 of Article 25;

(i) the renewal of any reservation carried out in pursuance of the provisions of paragraph 1 of Article 25;

(j) the withdrawal of any reservation carried out in pursuance of the provisions of paragraph 2 of Article 25;

(k) any notification received in pursuance of the provisions of Article 26;

(l) any notification received in pursuance of the provisions of Article 27 and the date on which denunciation takes effect.

In witness whereof the undersigned, being duly authorised thereto, have signed this Convention.

Done at Strasbourg, this 24th day of April 1967, in English and in French, both texts being equally authoritative, in a single copy which shall remain deposited in the archives of the Council of Europe. The Secretary General of the Council of Europe shall transmit certified copies to each of the signatory and acceding States.

APPENDIX 13

CHILD ABDUCTION—PRECEDENTS AND GUIDELINES

The following precedents and guidelines are provided by way of general example and general assistance only and will not necessarily deal with all of the issues which may arise in individual cases. In the usual way, pleadings should be tailored to reflect the specific facts and requirements of each individual case.

APPLICATION FOR THE RETURN OF A CHILD TO ENGLAND PURSUANT TO THE HAGUE CONVENTION

SPECIAL SUMMONS

THE HIGH COURT
Record No.

IN THE MATTER OF THE CHILD ABDUCTION AND ENFORCEMENT OF CUSTODY ORDERS ACT, 1991 AND IN THE MATTER OF [Insert name], A MINOR

Between:

[Insert name]

Plaintiff

And

[Insert name]

Defendant

Draft /

SPECIAL SUMMONS

SPECIAL INDORSEMENT OF CLAIM

THE PLAINTIFF'S CLAIM IS FOR:

1. An Order for the production of the minor named in the title hereto before this Honourable Court and, further and in particular, an Order directing the Defendant herein to produce the said minor before this

Honourable Court;

2. An Order prohibiting the removal of the said minor from the jurisdiction of this Honourable Court by the Defendant, his/her servants and agents, or any person acting on his/her behalf or any person having notice of the making of this said Order pending the determination of the   within proceedings and/or pending further Order of this Honourable Court.

3. An Order pursuant to Part II of the above entitled Act for the return forthwith of the said minor to the jurisdiction of his/ her habitual residence, namely the jurisdiction of the Courts of England and Wales, the said jurisdiction (and more particularly England) being the minor's habitual residence within the meaning of Article 3 of the Convention of the Civil Aspects of International Child Abduction (hereinafter referred to as "the Hague Convention").

4. A Declaration pursuant to Section 15(1) of the above entitled Act that the Defendant herein has wrongfully retained the said minor in the jurisdiction of this Honourable Court within the meaning of Article 3 of the Hague Convention *or* A Declaration pursuant to Section 15(1) of the above entitled Act that the Defendant herein has wrongfully removed the said minor to the jurisdiction of this Honourable Court within the meaning of Article 3 of the Hague Convention.

5. If necessary, an Order pursuant to Section 12 of the above entitled Act for such interim directions as to this Honourable Court shall seem just and proper for the purpose of securing the welfare of the minor named in the title hereto and/or for the purpose of preventing prejudice to the said minor and/or prejudice to the Plaintiff herein, or in relation to any changes in the circumstances relevant to the determination of the within proceedings.

6. [*If applicable*—Further and in particular, an Order granting the Plaintiff access to the said minor in this jurisdiction on the return date for the hearing of the Notice of Motion herein and/or the Summons herein and/or at such other dates or times and upon such terms, if any, as to this Honourable Court shall seem just and proper.]

7. [*If applicable*—Such Order or Orders as may be deemed necessary by this Honourable Court to give effect to Article 21 of the Hague Convention, including an Order or Directions regarding the making of arrangements for organising or securing the effective exercise by the Plaintiff of his/her rights of access to the minor named in the Title hereto in accordance with the said Order of [insert Court].]

8. [*If applicable*—An Order pursuant to Section 13 of the above entitled Act staying any proceedings in respect of the said minor in being within the jurisdiction of this Honourable Court.]

9. An Order directing the Defendant herein to forthwith do all such things and take all such steps as may be necessary to procure and facilitate

the return of the said minor to the jurisdiction of the Courts of England and Wales.

10. Liberty to notify the Commissioner of An Garda Síochána and/or the Port or Airport authorities within the State of the making of any Orders by this Honourable Court in the within proceedings;

11. Such further or other Orders as to this Honourable Court shall seem just and proper and, in particular, such directions as to the service of these proceedings as to this Honourable Court shall seem just and proper.

12. An Order providing for the costs of these proceedings, including an Order for the costs and expenses incurred by the Plaintiff herein pursuant to and as provided for in Article 26 of the Hague Convention.

Signed: _____
       [Solicitor for the Plaintiff]

SCHEDULE OF AFFIDAVITS

1. Affidavit of [Insert name] sworn on the [insert date] and filed on the [date]/ to be filed [Delete as applicable]

This Summons was issued by [Solicitor for the Plaintiff] whose registered place of business is [insert], Solicitor for the Plaintiff [insert name] who resides at [insert] and is [insert occupation].

This summons was personally served by me on the Defendant [insert name] of [insert address] at [insert time] on the [insert date].

Indorsed on the [insert date]

Signed: _____
       [Insert Name and Address]

GROUNDING AFFIDAVIT

The Grounding Affidavit, in addition to the "usual averments" regarding means of knowledge and reference to the pleadings, should *inter alia* set out the basis upon which the application is being made, the grounds for the application, details of the Order(s) sought to be enforced and the circumstances of the removal or retention. It should also deal with such issues as the habitual residence of the child prior to the wrongful removal or retention, the absence of consent to the removal or retention and the exercise by the Plaintiff of the rights claimed to be the subject of the breach, where applicable.

The Deponent should also be in a position to depose that the effects of the Order(s) sought to be enforced are not incompatible with the fundamental principles of law relating to the family and children applicable within the jurisdiction of the High Court and that the enforcement of the Order by the High Court would be in the best interests of the minor named in the Title. There should also be an averment to the effect that there are no proceedings pending in respect of the child in any other Contracting State.

The Affidavit should also contain an averment that the Order is enforceable in the State in which it was granted and a Certificate of Enforceability issued by the appropriate authority should be exhibited.

Where the Orders sought to be enforced were granted in the absence of the Defendant, it is imperative that the grounding Affidavit contains averments in respect of the notification afforded to the Defendant of the application(s) and the details regarding service of the relevant papers.

Finally, the Deponent should be in a position to depose that the Plaintiff is entitled to apply for the relief sought in the Special Summons.

Obviously, the Affidavit should contain all other necessary and appropriate averments depending upon the facts of the particular case.

NOTICE OF MOTION

THE HIGH COURT
Record No.

IN THE MATTER OF THE CHILD ABDUCTION AND ENFORCEMENT OF CUSTODY ORDERS ACT, 1991 AND IN THE MATTER OF [Insert name], A MINOR

Between:

[Insert name]

Plaintiff

And

[Insert name]

Defendant

Draft /

NOTICE OF MOTION

TAKE NOTICE that on the [insert date] at 11 o'clock in the forenoon or at the first available opportunity thereafter, Counsel for the Plaintiff herein will make an application to this Honourable Court sitting at the Four Courts, Inns Quay, in the County of the City of Dublin for an Order or Orders in the following terms:

   1. An Order for the production of the minor named in the title hereto

before this Honourable Court and, further and in particular, an Order directing the Defendant herein to produce the said minor before this Honourable Court;

2. An Order prohibiting the removal of the said minor from the jurisdiction of this Honourable Court by the Defendant, his/ her servants and agents, or any person acting on his /her behalf or any person having notice of the making of this said Order pending the determination of the within proceedings and/or pending further Order of this Honourable Court.

3. An Order pursuant to Part II of the above entitled Act for the return forthwith of the said minor to the jurisdiction of his/ her habitual residence, namely the jurisdiction of the Courts of England and Wales, the said jurisdiction (and more particularly England) being the minor's habitual residence within the meaning of Article 3 of the Convention of the Civil Aspects of International Child Abduction (hereinafter referred to as "the Hague Convention").

4. A Declaration pursuant to Section 15 (1) of the above entitled Act that the Defendant herein has wrongfully retained the said minor in the jurisdiction of of this Honourable Court within the meaning of Article 3 of the Hague Convention *or* A Declaration pursuant to Section 15 (1) of the above entitled Act that the Defendant herein has wrongfully removed the said minor to the jurisdiction of this Honourable Court within the meaning of Article 3 of the Hague Convention.

5. If necessary, an Order pursuant to Section 12 of the above entitled Act for such interim directions as this Honourable Court shall deem fit for the purpose of securing the welfare of the minor named in the title hereto, for the purpose of preventing prejudice to the said minor and/or prejudice to the Plaintiff herein, or in relation to any changes in the circumstances relevant to the determination of the within proceedings.

6. [*If applicable*—Further and in particular, an Order granting the Plaintiff access to the said minor in this jurisdiction on the return date for the hearing of the within Notice of Motion and/or at such other dates or times and upon such terms, if any, as to this Honourable Court shall seem just and proper.]

7. [*If applicable*—Such Order or Orders as may be deemed necessary by this Honourable Court to give effect to Article 21 of the Hague Convention, including an Order or Directions regarding the making of arrangements for organising or securing the effective exercise by the Plaintiff of his/her rights of access to the minor named in the Title hereto in accordance with the said Order of [insert Court].]

8. [*If applicable*—An Order pursuant to Section 13 of the above entitled Act staying any proceedings in respect of the said minor in being

within the jurisdiction of this Honourable Court.]

9. An Order directing the Defendant herein to forthwith do all such things and take all such steps as may be necessary to procure and facilitate the return of the said minor to the jurisdiction of the Courts of England and Wales.

10. Liberty to notify the Commissioner of An Garda Síochána and/or the Port or Airport authorities within the State of the making of any Orders by this Honourable Court in the within proceedings.

11. Such further or other Orders as to this Honourable Court shall seem just and proper and, in particular, such directions as to the service of these proceedings as to this Honourable Court shall seem just and proper.

12. An Order providing for the costs of these proceedings, including an Order for the costs and expenses incurred by the Plaintiff herein pursuant to and as provided for in Article 26 of the Hague Convention.

AND TAKE NOTICE that the within application will be grounded upon the pleadings already had herein, the Order of this Honourable Court made on the [insert date] granting liberty for short service of the within Notice of Motion, the Affidavit of [insert name of Deponent] sworn on the [insert date] and the exhibits referred to therein, the within Notice of Motion and the Affidavit of Service thereof, such further or other evidence as may be required, the nature of the case and the reasons to be offered.

Dated: _____

Signed: _____
      [Solicitor for the Plaintiff]
      [Address]

To: [Defendant/Solicitor for the Defendant]

And To: [Law Registrar]

NOTICE OF INTENTION TO CROSS-EXAMINE

THE HIGH COURT
Record No.

IN THE MATTER OF THE CHILD ABDUCTION AND ENFORCEMENT OF CUSTODY ORDERS ACT, 1991 AND IN THE MATTER OF [Insert name], A MINOR

Between:

[Insert name]

Plaintiff

And

[Insert name]

Defendant

Draft /

NOTICE OF CROSS-EXAMINATION OF DEPONENTS AT TRIAL

TAKE NOTICE that the Plaintiff/Defendant herein intends at the trial of this action to cross-examine the several deponent(s) named and described in the Schedule hereto on his/her/their affidavit(s) therein specified.

AND ALSO TAKE NOTICE that you are hereby required to produce the said deponent(s) for such cross-examination before the Court as aforesaid.

Dated this [insert date].

Signed: _____

[Solicitor for the Plaintiff]

To: [Defendant/Solicitor for the Defendant]

SCHEDULE

NAME OF DEPONENT	ADDRESS(ES) AND DESCRIPTION	DATE WHEN AFFIDAVIT(S)FILED

APPLICATION FOR THE RECOGNITION AND ENFORCEMENT OF AN ACCESS ORDER PURSUANT TO THE LUXEMBOURG CONVENTION

SPECIAL SUMMONS

THE HIGH COURT
Record No.

IN THE MATTER OF THE CHILD ABDUCTION AND ENFORCEMENT OF CUSTODY ORDERS ACT, 1991 AND IN THE MATTER OF [Insert name], A MINOR

Between:

[Insert name]

Plaintiff

And

[Insert name]

Defendant

Draft /

SPECIAL SUMMONS
SPECIAL INDORSEMENT OF CLAIM

THE PLAINTIFF'S CLAIM IS FOR:

1. An Order pursuant to Part III of the above entitled Act for the recognition and enforcement of the Order of [insert Court] made by [insert name of Judge] on [insert date] [if applicable insert "by consent of the Parties hereto"] in [insert name of country], a Contracting State within the meaning of the *European Convention on Recognition and Enforcement of Decisions Concerning Custody of Children and on Restoration of Custody of Children* (hereinafter referred to as "the Luxembourg Convention").

2. [*If necessary*—An Order prohibiting the removal of the said minor from the jurisdiction of this Honourable Court by the Defendant, his/her servants and agents, or any person acting on his /her behalf or any person having notice of the making of this said Order pending the determination of the within proceedings and/or pending further Order of this Honourable Court.]

3. [*If necessary*—An Order pursuant to Section 26 of the above entitled Act for such interim directions as this Honourable Court shall deem fit for the purpose of securing the welfare of the minor named in the title hereto, for the purpose of preventing prejudice to the said minor and/or prejudice to the Plaintiff herein, or in relation to any changes

(including the prevention of any changes) in the circumstances relevant to the determination of the within proceedings.]

4. [*If applicable*—Further and in particular, an Order granting the Plaintiff access to the said minor in this jurisdiction on the return date for the hearing of the Notice of Motion herein and/or the Summons herein and/or at such other dates or times and upon such terms, if any, as to this Honourable Court shall seem just and proper.]

5. [*If applicable*—An Order pursuant to Section 28(2) of the above entitled Act staying any proceedings in respect of the said minor which are pending within the jurisdiction of this Honourable Court.]

6. Such Order or Orders as may be deemed necessary by this Honourable Court to give effect to Article 11 of the Luxembourg Convention, including an Order or Directions regarding the fixing of conditions for the implementation and exercise by the Plaintiff of his / her rights of access to the minor named in the Title hereto in acordance with the said Order of [insert Court].

7. Such further or other Orders as to this Honourable Court shall seem just and proper and, in particular, such directions as to the service of these proceedings as to this Honourable Court shall seem just and proper.

8. An Order providing for the costs of these proceedings.

Signed: _____

[Solicitor for the Plaintiff]

SCHEDULE OF AFFIDAVITS

1. Affidavit of [insert name] sworn on the [insert date] and filed on the [date].

This Summons was issued by [Solicitor for the Plaintiff] whose registered place of business is [insert], Solicitor for the Plaintiff [insert name] who resides at [insert] and is [insert occupation].

This summons was personally served by me on the Defendant [insert name] of [insert address] at [insert time] on the [insert date].

Indorsed on the [insert date].

Signed: _____

[Insert Name and Address]

GROUNDING AFFIDAVIT

In addition to the usual averments, the grounding Affidavit should exhibit duly authenticated copies of the foreign Orders which the Plaintiff wishes to have recognised and enforced, as well as birth and marriage certificates as appropriate. It should also contain averments in respect of, *inter alia,* the parentage of the child the subject matter of the proceedings, the citizenship status of the parents and child, a brief summary of the background to the case, the nature of the proposed application and the grounds therefor, and an averment to the effect that there are no other custody/child care proceedings pending in any other Contracting State.

The Deponent should also be in a position to depose that the effects of the Order sought to be recognised are not incompatible with the fundamental principles of law relating to the family and children applicable within the jurisdiction of the High Court and that, in all the circumstances, the recognition and/or enforcement of the Order by the High Court would be in the best interests of the minor named in the Title.

The Affidavit should also contain an averment that the Order is enforceable in the State in which it was granted and a Certificate of Enforceability issued by the appropriate authority should be exhibited.

Where the Orders sought to be recognised and enforced were granted in the absence of the Defendant, it is imperative that the grounding Affidavit contains averments confirming that the Defendant was duly notified of the applications and was served with the relevant papers.

Finally, the Deponent should be in a position to depose that the Plaintiff is entitled to apply for the relief sought in the Special Summons.

Obviously, the Affidavit should contain all other necessary and appropriate averments depending upon the facts of the particular case.

NOTICE OF MOTION

In the same manner as set out in respect of the previous example, the Notice of Motion should recite a claim for the same reliefs as those contained in the Endorsement of Claim on the Special Summons.

APPLICATION FOR THE RECOGNITION OF AN ORDER PURSUANT TO THE LUXEMBOURG CONVENTION (A "MIRROR ORDER") WHERE THE DEFENDANT RESIDES OUT OF THE JURISDICTION AND IS NOT AN IRISH CITIZEN

EX PARTE DOCKET

THE HIGH COURT
2000 No. Sp

In The Matter Of The Courts Of Justice Acts, 1924–1961 And In The Matter Of The Courts (Supplemental Provisions) Acts, 1961–1981

And In The Matter Of Intended Proceedings Pursuant To The Child Abduction And Enforcement Of Custody Orders Act, 1991 And In The Matter Of [insert name], A Minor

Between:

[Insert name]

Plaintiff

And

[Insert name]

Defendant

Draft /

EX PARTE DOCKET

TAKE NOTICE that on the   day of   2000 at 11.00 o'clock in the forenoon or at the first available opportunity thereafter, Counsel on behalf of the Intended Plaintiff herein will apply to this Honourable Court sitting at the Four Courts, Inns Quay, in the County of the City of Dublin for Orders in the following terms:

1. Liberty to issue the Special Summons and Notice of Motion herein;

2. An Order pursuant to Order 11, Rule 1(i) of the Rules of the Superior Courts, 1986, as amended, granting liberty to the intended Plaintiff to serve Notice of the said Special Summons on the intended Defendant at [insert address] by way of personal service, and liberty to serve the Notice of Motion herein, together with all grounding and ancillary documentation and further pleadings and correspondence on the intended Defendant at [insert address] by way of registered pre-paid post;

3. [*If necessary*—An Order pursuant to Order 10, Rule 1 of the Rules of the Superior Courts, 1986, as amended, granting liberty to the Intended Plaintiff to serve the aforesaid notice of Special Summons and/or the

said Notice of Motion and/or any grounding or ancillary documentation and further pleadings, upon the Intended Defendant by way of substituted service upon the Intended Defendant at his place of work, being [insert address of the Intended Respondent's place of work, or such other place as appropriate] with such further Directions with regard to service as may be necessary;]

4. An Order pursuant to Order 11, Rule 7 of the Rules of the Superior Courts, 1986, as amended, limiting the time within which the Intended Defendant may enter an appearance in the within proceedings;

5. Such further or other Order as to this Honourable Court shall seem just and proper;

6. An Order providing for the costs of and incidental to the application herein.

AND FURTHER TAKE NOTICE that the said application will be grounded upon the Ex-Parte Docket herein, the grounding Affidavit of [insert name] sworn on the [insert date], such further or other evidence as may be required, the nature of the case and the reasons to be offered.

Dated the   day of   , 2000.

Signed: _____

          [Solicitor for the Plaintiff]

To: [Family Law Registrar]

GROUNDING AFFIDAVIT FOR APPLICATION FOR SERVICE OUT OF THE JURISDICTION

In the usual way, the grounding Affidavit should exhibit the draft proceedings and duly authenticated copies of the foreign Orders which the Plaintiff wishes to have recognised and enforced. It should also contain averments in respect of, *inter alia,* the parentage of the child the subject matter of the proceedings, the citizenship status of the parents and child, a brief summary of the background to the case, the nature of the proposed application and the grounds therefor, and an averment to the effect that there are no other custody/child care proceedings pending in any other Contracting State in respect of the child.

Where the Orders sought to be enforced were granted in the absence of the proposed Defendant, it is imperative that the grounding Affidavits contain averments confirming that the proposed Defendant was duly notified of the applications and was served with the relevant papers.

Finally, the Deponent should be in a position to depose that the intended Plaintiff has a good cause of action and is entitled to apply for the relief sought in the draft Special Summons and draft Notice of Motion and that the intended Defendant is a necessary and proper party to the intended proceedings and, finally, that it would be fit and proper that an Order would be granted in terms of the Ex-Parte Docket.

Obviously, the Affidavit should contain all other necessary and appropriate averments depending upon the facts of the case.

SPECIAL SUMMONS

THE HIGH COURT
2000 No. Sp

In The Matter Of The Child Abduction And Enforcement Of Custody Orders Act, 1991 And In The Matter Of [insert name], A Minor

Between:

[Insert name]

Plaintiff

And

[Insert name]

Defendant

Draft /

SPECIAL SUMMONS
SPECIAL INDORSEMENT OF CLAIM

THE PLAINTIFF'S CLAIM pursuant to the above entitled Act is for:

1. An Order pursuant to Part III of the above entitled Act of 1991 providing for the recognition of the decision relating to the infant named in the Title hereto made on the [insert date] by [insert name of Judge], of the [insert Court and country], a contracting State within the meaning of the above entitled Act and the European Convention on Recognition And Enforcement Of Decisions Concerning Custody Of Children And Restoration Of Custody Of Children (hereinafter referred to as "the Luxembourg Convention");

2. If necessary, an Order for such interim Directions pursuant to Section 26 of the above entitled Act as to this Honourable Court shall seem just and proper, for the purpose of securing the welfare of the said infant or for the prevention of prejudice to interested persons or in relation to any changes in circumstances relevant to these proceedings;

3. [*If necessary*—An Order prohibiting the removal of the said minor from the jurisdiction of this Honourable Court by the Defendant, his/her servants and agents, or any person acting on his/her behalf or any person having notice of the making of this said Order pending the determination of the within proceedings and/or pending further Order

of this Honourable Court.]

4. [*If applicable*—An Order pursuant to Section 28(2) of the above entitled Act staying any proceedings in respect of the said minor which are pending within the jurisdiction of this Honourable Court.]

5. Such further or other Order as to this Honourable Court shall seem just and proper and, in particular, such Order or Orders as may be necessary as to the procedure to be adopted in the service of these proceedings;

6. Costs of and incidental to these proceedings.

SCHEDULE OF AFFIDAVITS

Affidavit of [insert name of Deponent]

This Summons was issued by [insert name], Solicitor for the Plaintiff, whose registered place of business is at [insert address], for and on behalf of the Plaintiff, who resides at [insert address] and is a [insert occupation].

This Summons was served by me at [insert address] on the Defendant [insert name] on the [insert date].

Indorsed on the [insert date].

Signed: _____
         [Solicitor for the Plaintiff]

To: [Defendant/Solicitor for Defendant]

And To: [Family Law Registrar]

GROUNDING AFFIDAVIT

In addition to the usual averments, the grounding Affidavit should exhibit duly authenticated copies of the foreign Orders which the Plaintiff wishes to have recognised, as well as birth and marriage certificates as appropriate. It should also contain averments in respect of, *inter alia,* the parentage of the child the subject matter of the proceedings, the citizenship status of the parents and child, a brief summary of the background to the case, the nature of the proposed application and the grounds therefor, and an averment to the effect that there are no other custody/child care proceedings pending in any other Contracting State.

The Deponent should also be in a position to depose that the effects of the Order sought to be recognised are not incompatible with the fundamental principles of law relating to the family and children applicable within the jurisdiction of the High Court and that the recognition and/or enforcement of the Order by the High Court would be in the best interests of the minor named in the Title.

The Affidavit should also contain an averment that the Order is enforceable in the State in which it was granted and a Certificate of Enforceability issued by the appropriate authority should be exhibited.

Where the Orders sought to be recognised or enforced were granted in the absence of the Defendant, it is imperative that the grounding Affidavit contains averments confirming that the Defendant was duly notified of the applications and was served with the relevant papers.

Finally, the Deponent should be in a position to depose that the Plaintiff is entitled to apply for the relief sought in the Special Summons.

Obviously, the Affidavit should contain all other necessary and appropriate averments depending upon the facts of the particular case.

NOTICE OF SPECIAL SUMMONS

THE HIGH COURT
2000 No. Sp

In The Matter Of The Child Abduction And Enforcement Of Custody Orders Act, 1991 And In The Matter Of [insert name], A Minor

Between:

[Insert name]

Plaintiff

And

[Insert name]

Defendant

Draft /

NOTICE OF SPECIAL SUMMONS

To: [insert Defendant's name] of [insert address]

TAKE NOTICE that the Plaintiff, [insert name] of [insert address], [insert occupation] has begun an action against you by originating Special Summons issued on and dated the [insert date], which Summons is endorsed as follows:-

THE PLAINTIFF'S CLAIM pursuant to the above entitled Act is for:-

1. }

2. }   [Repeat body of the Special Summons]

3. }

AND FURTHER TAKE NOTICE that you are required within   weeks after the service of this Notice upon you, exclusive of the day of service, to enter in person or by Solicitor for you, an appearance in the Central Office of the High Court of Ireland at the Four Courts, Dublin, Ireland in the above action.

AND FURTHER TAKE NOTICE that in default of your so doing, the Plaintiff may proceed therein and judgment may be given in your absence.

AND FURTHER TAKE NOTICE that this Notice is served upon you pursuant to a Order made by the High Court of Ireland on the   day of   2000.

Dated the   day of   , 2000.

Signed: _____
             [Solicitor for the Plaintiff]

To: [Defendant/Solicitor for Defendant]

And To: [Family Law Registrar]

NOTICE OF MOTION

THE HIGH COURT
2000 No. Sp

In The Matter Of The Child Abduction And Enforcement Of Custody Orders Act, 1991
And In The Matter Of [insert name], A Minor

Between:

[Insert name]

                                                                  Plaintiff
And

[Insert name]

                                                                  Defendant

Draft /

NOTICE OF MOTION

TAKE NOTICE that on the   day of   at 11.00 o'clock in the forenoon or at the earliest opportunity thereafter, Counsel on behalf of the Plaintiff herein will apply to this Honourable Court sitting at the Four Courts, Inns Quay, in the County of the City of Dublin for an Order or Orders in the following terms:-

1. An Order pursuant to Part III of the above entitled Act of 1991 providing for the recognition of the decision relating to the infant named in the Title hereto made on the [insert date] by [insert name of Judge], of the [insert Court and country], a Contracting State within the meaning of the above entitled Act and the European Convention on Recognition and Enforcement of Decisions Concerning Custody of Children and Restoration of Custody of Children (hereinafter referred to as "the Luxembourg Convention");

2. If necessary, an Order for such interim Directions pursuant to Section 26 of the above entitled Act as to this Honourable Court shall seem just and proper, for the purpose of securing the welfare of the said infant or for the prevention of prejudice to interested persons or in relation to any changes in circumstances relevant to these proceedings;

3. Such further or other Order as to this Honourable Court shall seem just and proper and, in particular, such Order or Orders as may be necessary as to the procedure to be adopted on the service of these proceedings;

4. Costs of and incidental to these proceedings.

AND FURTHER TAKE NOTICE that the within application will be grounded upon the pleadings already had herein, the Affidavit of [insert name of Deponent] sworn on the [insert date], the within Notice of Motion and an Affidavit of service thereof, such further or other evidence as may be required, the nature of the case and the reasons to be offered.

Signed: _____
[Solicitor for the Plaintiff]

To: [Defendant/Solicitor for Defendant]

And To: [Family Law Registrar]

ALL PORTS LETTER

Date

The Sergeant in Charge
An Garda Síochána
(address)

Re: (Title of proceedings, give record number)
In the matter of (name of child/children, dates of birth), An
Infant/Infants

Dear Sergeant,

We act on behalf of X, the natural father/mother of the above named infant/s who is in the process of commencing proceedings (or is/are the subject matter of the above proceedings). We enclose herewith recent photograph(s) and (if relevant) a copy of the Order made by His Honour Judge (name) this (date) (please give a description of the child/children).

We request you (on foot of this Order) to initiate an All Ports Alert in accordance with the Child Abduction and Enforcement of Custody Orders Act 1991. We understand that Ms/Mrs/Mr (name respondent) is an (state nationality if relevant) and our client is fearful that the child will be removed from the Jurisdiction of the Honourable District Family Court to (name possible destination) and we therefore ask that you exercise your powers under section 37 of the Child Abduction and Enforcement of Custody Orders Act 1991.

Our client resides at (insert address) and the Respondent resides at (state last known address). As you will see, the Order provides for the notification of An Garda Síochána by all means including by telephone.

We await hearing from you in due course.

Yours faithfully

APPENDIX 14

DISTRICT COURT (CHILDREN) RULES 2004
(S.I. No. 539 of 2004)

The District Court Rules Committee, in exercise of the powers conferred on them by section 91 of the Courts of Justice Act, 1924, section 72 of the Courts of Justice Act, 1936, section 17 of the Interpretation Act, 1937 [as applied by section 48 of the Courts (Supplemental Provisions) Act, 1961], and section 34 of the Courts (Supplemental Provisions) Act, 1961, do hereby, with the concurrence of the Minister for Justice, Equality and Law Reform, make the following Rules of Court:

1. These rules may be cited as the District Court (Children) Rules, 2004.

2. These rules shall come into operation on the 14th day of October 2004 and shall be read together with all other District Court rules for the time being in force.

Order 33

3. There shall be substituted in rule 1 and rule 6 of Order 33 and in each of the Forms numbered 33.2, 33.4, 33.6, 33.8 and 33.10 in Schedule B of the District Court Rules, 1997 (S.I. No. 93 of 1997) the words "Section 98 of the Children Act, 2001" for the words "Section 99 of the Children Act, 1908" in each place in such rules and Forms in which the said words occur and there shall be substituted in each of the said Forms the words the "Children Act 2001" for the words the "Children Acts, 1908 to 1989". In each of the said Forms, the words the "Children Court" shall be substituted for the words the "District Court" wherever those words appear.

Order 37

4. Order 37 of the District Court Rules, 1997 (S.I. No. 93 of 1997) is hereby amended by the substitution therefor of the Order appearing in Schedule 1 to these Rules.

5. The Forms numbered 37.1, 37.2 and 37.8 in Schedule 2 hereof shall be substituted for the Forms bearing those numbers respectively in Schedule B of the District Court Rules, 1997 (S.I. No. 93 of 1997). The Forms numbered 37.16 to 37.26 inclusive in Schedule 3 hereof shall be added to the Forms in Schedule B of the District Court Rules, 1997 (S.I. No. 93) of 1997).

Order 84

6.   Order 84 of the District Court Rules, 1997 (S.I. No.93 of 1997) is hereby amended by the substitution in rule 12 thereof of the words "Form 84.18" for the words "Form 18".

SCHEDULE 1

ORDER 37

PROCEEDINGS INVOLVING CHILDREN

1.   (1)   In this Order:
     "the Act" means the Children Act, 2001 (No. 24 of 2001);
     "the Court" means the Children Court.
    (2)   Subject to the Act, a Judge may adjourn business from a sitting of the District Court to a sitting of the Children Court for the same district and vice versa.
    (3)   Nothing in this Order shall prevent the Court, subject to the Act, from making any order when sitting as the Children Court which it could make at a sitting of the court sitting as the District Court and vice versa.
    (4)   Any reference in any Form to the "District Court" instead of the "Children Court" shall be taken as a reference to the Children Court and shall not invalidate such Form.

2.   (1)   Save as otherwise provided in this Order, in criminal proceedings in the Children Court, the provisions of Orders 13 to 336 shall apply, as modified or extended by the provisions of this Order.
    (2)   Rule 7 of Order 23 and rules 1 and 2 of Order 24 shall not apply in proceedings in the Children Court.

3.   Forms No. 37.1 to 37.26 Schedule B shall be the Forms to be used in criminal proceedings in the Children Court. Where no suitable Form is provided for in this Order, the Forms provided for in Orders 13 to 36 of these Rules may be used in proceedings in the Children Court, entitled in the "Children Court" and otherwise modified as required by the circumstances of the case or as provided in this Order.

4.   The procedure to be followed and the forms to be used in any application in relation to a compensation order made under the Criminal Justice Act, 1993 which involves a child are prescribed in Order 33 of these Rules.

5.   Subject to the Act and the preceding rules of this Order, the provisions of the Summary Jurisdiction Rules 1909 (S.R. & O. 952) dated July 31, 1909, made under section 133(7) of the Children Act, 1908, shall, by operation of section 5(1) of the Children Act, 2001, with any necessary modifications, apply to proceedings under the Act.

6.   Notwithstanding any provision of Order 14, all persons shall be excluded

from sittings of the Children Court except—

(a) officers of the court,

(b) the parents or guardian of the child concerned,

(c) an adult relative to the child, or other adult who attends the court pursuant to section 91(6) of the Act,

(d) persons directly concerned in the proceedings,

(e) bona fide representatives of the press,

(f) such other persons (if any) as the court may at its discretion permit to remain. However the order or decision of the Court (if any) in any such proceedings shall be announced in public.

7. Where the Court imposes one or more of the conditions specified in section 90(1) of the Act on the release on bail of a child, such condition shall be endorsed on the recognisance.

8. Where an accused child is before the court charged with an indictable offence with which the court has jurisdiction to deal summarily if the accused does not object, the judge shall inform the accused child of his or her right to be tried by a jury and if the accused child (inquiry having been made of him or her by the judge) consents to the case being tried summarily, and, the case is not one of an offence which is required to be tried by the Central Criminal Court or manslaughter and the court is of opinion that the offence constitutes a minor offence fit to be tried summarily (or, where the child, having had the opportunity to have the assistance of his or her parent or guardian, adult spouse, an adult relative accompanying him or her, wishes to plead guilty, to be dealt with summarily), the court, having taken account of the age and level of maturity of the child concerned and any other facts that it considers relevant, may take the accused child's plea and try him or her summarily.

9. Where an accused child is before the court charged with an offence which is required to be tried by the Central Criminal Court or with manslaughter and wishes to plead guilty and the Court is satisfied that he or she understands the nature of the offence and the facts alleged, then, if the accused child signs a plea of guilty the judge may by order (Form 37.16, Schedule B) and with the consent of the Director of Public Prosecutions (which consent may be conveyed as provided in rule 4 of Order 24), or, where appropriate, of the Attorney-General, send him or her forward for sentence with that plea to the court to which, if he or she had pleaded not guilty, the accused could lawfully have been sent forward for trial.

10. An order imposing a community sanction shall be in the Form 37.17, Schedule B. Any application made under section 136 of the Act shall be preceded by the issue and service, at least four days before the date upon which the application is to be heard, on the accused, the parents or guardian of the accused, and any other person directly affected by the order, of a notice in the Form 37.18, Schedule B.

11. Where it appears to the court on application in that behalf by a member of the Garda Síochána that a child has failed, without reasonable cause, to

comply with an order in force imposing a community sanction or any condition to which such order is subject, there shall be issued a summons to the child to appear before it in the Form 37.19, Schedule B. Unless the Court has excused the parents and/or guardian of the child from appearing, pursuant to section 90(5) of the Act, such summons to appear shall also be addressed to the parents and/or guardian of the child. If the child shall fail to appear in answer to said summons. the Court may issue a warrant in the Form 37.20, Schedule B for his or her arrest. The order of the Court on the hearing of the application shall be in the Form 37.21, Schedule B.

12. Where the court orders an accused child to pay a fine, costs, or compensation and the child is in default, the Court may, on the application of the prosecutor therefor, issue a warrant in the Form 37.22, Schedule B, for the arrest of the child to be brought before the Court to answer such default. Alternatively, application may be made by the prosecutor for an order under section 110 of the Act. Such application shall be preceded by the issue and service, at least four days before the date upon which the application is to be heard, on the accused, the parents or guardian of the accused and any other person directly affected by the order, of a notice in the Form 37.23, Schedule B. The order of the Court on the hearing of the application shall be in the Form 37.24, Schedule B.

SCHEDULE 2

Schedule B, O.37, r.1   **No. 37.1**

CHILDREN ACT, 2001, SECTION 64

SUMMONS TO CHILD OR TO PARENT OR GUARDIAN, OR TO BOTH

Children Court Area of   **District No.**

E.F.

of ....
                                   Prosecutor

[A.B. of

.... and]

C.D. of

....
                                    Accused

Information has been laid this day by

....

(or complaint has been this day made by

for that (you) A.B., being a child on the .... day of ....,
20...................,

at   (in the court area and district aforesaid), did

And Information has further been laid by

(or), (And complaint has further been made

by ....)

for that you C.D., are the parent (or guardian) of the said child or young person.

You are therefore (each of you) hereby summoned to appear before the Children
Court at .... on the .... day of ....,
20 .... at the hour of   a.m./p.m. to answer to the said information (or)
(complaints).

Signed...
Judge of the Children Court

To   of

To   of

AND TAKE NOTICE that under section 91 of the Children Act, 2001, unless
excused by the Court, the parents or guardian of a child are required to attend
at all stages of any proceedings against the child for an offence and where the
parents or guardian fail or neglect without reasonable excuse to attend, a warrant
for the arrest of the parents or guardian may be issued or such failure to attend
may be treated as a contempt in the face of the court and punished accordingly.

Schedule B, O.37, r.1   **No. 37.2**

SUMMONS TO CHILD OR TO PARENT OR GUARDIAN OF A CHILD

Children Court Area of   **District No.**

E.F.

of ....
                                        Prosecutor

[A.B. of

.... and]

C.D. of

....
                                        Accused

Whereas A.B., a child within the meaning, of the Children Act, 2001, of whom you are stated to be the parent or guardian having the possession and control of such child is charged that:

[here set forth the offence charged]

You are therefore (each of you) hereby summoned to appear before the Children Court at .... on the .... day of ....,

20 ...., at the hour of   a.m./p.m. and during all proceedings

of the case.

                              Signed...
                              Judge of the Children Court
                              (or) Children Court Clerk

AND TAKE NOTICE that under section 91 of the Children Act, 2001, unless excused by the Court, the parents or guardian of a child are required to attend at all stages of any proceedings against the child for an offence and where the parents or guardian fail or neglect without reasonable excuse to attend, a warrant for the arrest of the parents or guardian may be issued or such failure to attend may be treated as a contempt in the face of the court and punished accordingly.

Schedule B, O.37, r.1   **No. 37.8**

CHILDREN ACT, 2001, SECTION 113

ORDER TO PARENT OR GUARDIAN TO PAY COMPENSATION

Children Court Area of   **District No.**

Whereas A.B., hereinafter called the accused, being above the age of seven years and a child, has been this day charged for that he/she on the .... day of ...., 20 ...., within the Court area (and district) aforesaid did:

And whereas the Court is of the opinion that the charge is proved, but does not proceed to a conviction of the accused.

It is ordered that C.D., the parent (or guardian) of the accused do pay the sum of €   for compensation and €   for costs (by instalments of €   for every   days, the first instalment to be paid)

*forthwith *on the   day of   20   .

And in default of payment it is ordered that (the sums due under this Order be levied by distress and sale of the said C.D.'s goods and in default of sufficient distress that the said C.D. be imprisoned at the Prison at   and there kept for the space of   unless the said sums (and all costs and charges of the said distress) be sooner paid.

Dated this .... day .... 20 ... .

Signed ....
Judge of the Children Court

SCHEDULE 3

Schedule B, O.37, r.10   **No. 37.16**

CHILDREN ACT, 2001, SECTION 75(5)

ORDER SENDING FORWARD ON A PLEA OF GUILTY

Children Court Area of   **District No.**

....

Prosecutor

....

Accused

WHEREAS the above-named accused is before the Court charged that

AND WHEREAS the Court is satisfied that the accused understands the nature of the offence and the facts alleged;

AND WHEREAS the accused has signed a plea of guilty;

AND the Director of Public Prosecutions consents to the accused being sent forward for sentence

THE COURT HEREBY ORDERS that he/she be sent forward for sentence

*Delete whichever inapplicable

on the aforesaid charge to the *next   sitting of the ....Court ....
                       *present

at .... *in custody
                             *on conditional release as set out hereunder

(THE COURT FURTHER ORDERS that until the said conditions of release are fulfilled the accused be detained in custody).

*Delete where inapplicable

Dated this .... day .... 20 ... .

                          Signed...
                          Judge of the Children Court

Consent to and Conditions of Release

The Court hereby consents to the above named accused being conditionally released on the following conditions:

(1) his/her entering into a recognisance himself/herself in the sum of €_____ *and one sufficient surety in the sum of €_____ (of which €_____ cash to be lodged) or two sufficient sureties in the sum of €_____ each (of which €_____ cash to be lodged by each) or in lieu such surety or sureties lodgement of the sum of €_____ be accepted.

(2) the accused is not to commit any offence and be of good behaviour and *to sign on daily/weekly at _____ Garda station between a.m. ___ and _____ p.m. and

(3) [insert any condition specified under section 90(1) of the Children Act, 2001].

Dated this ………… day ………… 20 … .

Signed..
Judge of the Children Court

Schedule B, O.37, r.10   **No. 37.17**

CHILDREN ACT, 2001, SECTION 133

ORDER FOR COMMUNITY SANCTION—RESTRICTION ON MOVEMENT ORDER

Children Court Area of   **District No.**

E.F.

of ....
Prosecutor

[A.B. and

C.D. ....
Accused

Before the Children Court at

Within the Children Court area aforesaid

A.B., of ……………, hereinafter called the accused, who appears to the said Court to be a child and who resides at …………… in the county (or county borough) of ……………, is this day convicted *(the accused having been informed of his/her right to be tried by a jury and having had the assistance of his/her *parent *guardian *adult spouse *adult relative having consented to

be dealt with summarily) that he/she, on the .... day of ....20 ...,
at within the ....aforesaid did (here state the offence).

And having heard the evidence adduced

And having explained in open Court and in language appropriate to the level
of understanding of the accused (a) why a community sanction is being imposed,
(b) the terms of the sanction and any conditions to which it is being made
subject, (c) the expectation of the Court that the accused will be of good conduct
while the community sanction is in force and the possible consequences for
the accused of his/her failure to comply with the sanction and any such
conditions and *(d) the expectation of the Court that the *parents *guardian of
the accused will help and encourage the accused to comply with the sanction
and any such conditions and not commit further offences

IT IS HEREBY ORDERED that the accused between the .... day of
.... 20 ...... and the .... day of ...., 20 ...

*REMAIN AT the residence of

at

between the hours of   p.m. each day and   a.m. on the following
day

*STAY AWAY from   (*between the hours of   and
) (on   days)

And this Order shall remain in force from the .... day of
.... 20 ...... and the .... day of ...., 20 ...

*AND IT IS FURTHER SPECIFIED for the purposes of this Order and for
the purposes of section 117 of the Act that:

[specify any condition]

Dated this .... day .... 20 .... .

                              Signed..
                              Judge of the Children Court

To:

To: [Parent/guardian of the accused]

At

And to: the Member in Charge Garda Síochána at

And to: Judge   (being the Judge for the time being assigned to the district in which the child is to reside)

At the Children Court Office

Schedule B, O.37, r.10   No. 37.18

CHILDREN ACT, 2001, SECTION 136

NOTICE OF APPLICATION FOR AN ORDER ON FAILURE TO COMPLY WITH COMMUNITY SANCTION — RESTRICTION ON MOVEMENT ORDER

Children Court Area of   **District No.**

E.F.

of ....
Prosecutor

A.B. ....
Accused

....
Applicant

WHEREAS this Court on the .... day of ....20 ...... made an order imposing a community sanction on the accused, namely (specify order made)

TAKE NOTICE that the above-named applicant will apply at the sitting of the Children Court to be held at

....

On the .... day of ....20 ...... at ...... a.m./p.m. for an order pursuant to section 136 of the above-mentioned Act

*directing

that ....

*revoking the said order

and ....

on the following grounds:

Dated this .... day .... 20 ... .

Signed..
Applicant/Solicitor for applicant

To ....

of ....

*Delete words inapplicable

Schedule B, O.37, r.11   **No. 37.19**

CHILDREN ACT, 2001, SECTION 136

SUMMONS TO APPEAR TO ANSWER NON-COMPLIANCE WITH ORDER IMPOSING COMMUNITY SANCTION

Children Court Area of   **District No.**

E.F.

of...
Prosecutor

[A.B. of

.... and]

C.D. of

....
Accused

WHEREAS on application by

....

a member of the Garda Síochána that you A.B., being a child, have failed, without reasonable cause, to comply with the order of this Court made on the .... day of ....20 ......that

or a condition to which said Order is subject.

Therefore you the said A.B.,(and you, C.D. being the *parent *guardian having custody and control of the said A.B., and each of you) are hereby summoned to appear before the Children Court at .... on the .... day of ....20 ...... at the hour of ...... a.m./p.m. to answer to this summons.

Signed ....
Judge of the Children Court

To   of

To   of

AND TAKE NOTICE that under section 91 of the Children Act, 2001, unless excused by the Court. the parents or guardian of a child are required to attend at all stages of any proceedings against the child for an offence and where the parents or guardian fail or neglect without reasonable excuse to attend, a warrant for the arrest of the parents or guardian my be issued or such failure to attend may be treated as a contempt in the face of the court and punished accordingly.

Schedule B, O.37, r.11   **No. 37.20**

CHILDREN ACT, 2001, SECTION 136(3)

WARRANT TO ARREST

Children Court Area of   **District No.**

WHEREAS on application by

....

a member of the Garda Síochána that you A.B., being a child, have failed, without reasonable cause, to comply with the order of this Court made on the .... day of ....20 ......that

or a condition to which said Order is subject.

AND WHEREAS the said A.B has failed to appear in answer to the summons to appear issued herein on the .... day of ....20 ....

THIS IS TO AUTHORISE YOU to whom this warrant is addressed to arrest the said .... and bring him/her before the *next sitting of this Court on the .... day of ....200 ......

Signed ....
Judge of the Children Court

To Superintendent ....
of the Garda Síochána at ....

....

Schedule B, O.37, r.11   **No. 37.21**

CHILDREN ACT, 2001, SECTION 136

ORDER ON FAILURE TO COMPLY WITH COMMUNITY SANCTION – RESTRICTION ON MOVEMENT ORDER

Children Court Area of   **District No.**

E.F.,

of ....

Prosecutor

A.B. and

C.D.,

....

Accused

Before the Children Court at

Within the Children Court area aforesaid

WHEREAS on application by

....

a member of the Garda Síochána that you A.B., being a child, have failed, without reasonable cause, to comply with the order of this Court made on the .... day of ....20 ......that

or a condition to which said Order is subject

And having heard the evidence adduced.

IT IS HEREBY ORDERED:

*[that you, the said A.B. be and are hereby directed to comply with the said Order of this Court and every condition to which it is subject as follows:
]

*[that the said Order be and is hereby revoked and there be substituted therefore the following Order under section 133) of the above-named Act:
]

*[that the said Order be and is hereby revoked and that it be instead ordered as follows: (here insert order dealing with the case in any other way in which it could be dealt with before the Order was made)]

*[that you be remanded on bail of   to the sitting of the Children Court at .... on the .... day of ....20 ...... at the hour of ...... a.m./p.m.

Dated this .... day .... 20 ... .

                                        Signed..
                                        Judge of the Children Court

To:

To: [Parent/guardian of the accused]

At

And to: the Member in Charge

Garda Síochána at

[And to: the Children Court Office at]

Schedule B, O.37, r.12   No. 37.22

CHILDREN ACT, 2001, SECTION 110

WARRANT TO ARREST

Children Court Area of   **District No.**

WHEREAS on application by

....

A member of the Garda Síochána

that you A.B., being a child, has failed to comply with the order of this Court made on the .... day of ....20 ......

that

[AND WHEREAS the said A.B has failed to appear in answer to the application on notice issued herein on the .... day of ....20 ......]

THIS IS TO AUTHORISE YOU to whom this warrant is addressed to arrest the said .... and bring him/her before the *next sitting of this Court on the .... day of ....20 ......

Dated this .... day .... 200 ... .

Signed..
Judge of the Children Court

To Superintendent ....

of the Garda Síochána at ....

....

Schedule B, O.37, r.12   **No. 37.23**

CHILDREN ACT, 2001, SECTION 110

NOTICE OF APPLICATION FOR DEFAULT ORDER

Children Court Area of   **District No.**

E.F.

of ....

Prosecutor

A.B. ....

Accused

....

Applicant

WHEREAS this Court on the .... day of .... 20 ...... made
an order requiring the accused to pay *a fine of €   *compensation of
€   *and costs of €

Such amount(s) to be paid

and whereas the accused has defaulted in payment of same in accordance with
the terms of said Order

TAKE NOTICE that the above-named applicant will apply at the sitting of the
Children Court to be held at

....

On the .... day of ....20 ...... at the hour of ...... a.m./p.m.
for an order pursuant to section 110 of the Children Act 2001:

*[reducing the amount of said fine]

*[extending the time allowed for the payment of said amount(s)]

*[imposing a community sanction under the Children Act 2001]

Dated this ………… day ………… 200 … .

Signed..

Applicant/Solicitor for applicant

To …………………………………

of …………………………………

*Delete words inapplicable

Schedule B, O.37, r.12   No. 37.24

CHILDREN ACT, 2001, SECTION 110

ORDER ON DEFAULT OF COMPLIANCE WITH ORDER TO PAY FINE/COMPENSATION

Children Court Area of   **District No.**

E.F.

of ....

Prosecutor

A.B. and

C.D., ...

Accused

Before the Children Court at

Within the Children Court area aforesaid

WHEREAS on application by

....

a member of the Garda Síochána that you A.B., being a child, have failed to comply with the order of this Court made on the ………………………… day of …………, 20 …… requiring you to pay *a fine of € *compensation of €   *and costs of €

Such amount(s) to be paid

And having heard the evidence adduced

IT IS HEREBY ORDERED that,

*[the amount of said fine be reduced to €   and that such reduced
amount be paid   ]

*[that the time allowed for the payment of said amount(s) be extended up to
the   day   of   20   ]

*[that you between the .... day of .... 20 ...... and the
.... day of ...., 20 ... *REMAIN AT the residence of
at between the hours of   p.m. each day and   a.m. on the
following day

*STAY AWAY from   (*between the hours of   and

) (on   days)

And this Order shall remain in force from the .... day of
.... 20 ...... and the .... day of ...., 20 ...

*AND IT IS FURTHER SPECIFIED for the purposes of this Order and for
the purposes of section 117 of the Act that (here insert any condition to which
the Order is subject)]

Dated this .... day of .... 20 ... .

                          Signed ....
                          Judge of the Children Court

To:

To: [Parent/guardian of the accused]

At

And to: the Member in Charge

Garda Síochána at

Schedule B, O.37, r.1 　　　　　　**No. 37.25**

CHILDREN ACT, 2001, SECTION 114

ORDER TO PARENT OR GUARDIAN TO ENTER RECOGNISANCE

Children Court Area of 　　　　　　　　　　**District No.**

Whereas A.B., hereinafter called the accused, being above the age of seven years and a child, has been this day charged for that he/she on the ....
day of .... 20 ......, at ...... within the Court area (and district) aforesaid did:

And whereas the Court is satisfied of the guilt of the accused.

It is ordered, with his/her consent, that C.D., the parent (or guardian) of the accused do forthwith to the satisfaction of this court give security in the sum of € 　　　to 　　　exercise proper and adequate control over the said accused for the term of 　　　[not exceeding three years] now next ensuing.

Dated this .... day of .... 20 ... .

　　　　　　　　　　Signed...
　　　　　　　　　　Judge of the Children Court

Schedule B, O.37, r.1 　　　　　　**No. 37.26**

PROBATION OF OFFENDERS ACT, 1907

CHILDREN ACT, 2001, SECTION 114

RECOGNISANCE

Children Court Area of 　　　　　　　　　　**District No.**

E.F.,

of ....
　　　　　　　　　　Prosecutor

A.B., ...
　　　　　　　　　　Accused

I 　　　　　　　　　　of

Being the *parent *guardian of the above-named accused acknowledge myself to owe to the State the sum following, that is to say, the sum of 　　　euro, to the use of the Minister for Finance if I shall fail to exercise proper and adequate control over the accused

....

Surety

Acknowledged before me this   day of   20

                                                    Signed...
                                                    Judge of the Children Court

The condition of the above written recognisance is such that whereas a complaint was made that the said

the .... day of ....20 ...... did

and at the Court held at

in the said district on the .... day of ....20 ...... the Court found that the charge was proved but was of the opinion (having regard to   ) that it was expedient to release the accused, and ordered that he/she be discharged conditionally on his/her parent or guardian, with his/her consent, entering into a recognisance, in the sum of €   , to exercise proper and adequate control over the accused.

If, therefore, the above bounden parent or guardian shall comply with the provisions of said Order during the period of   next ensuing then the said recognisance shall be void, or else to stand in full force and effect.

Given this 19th day of January 2004

Peter Smithwick   Chairman

Uinsin Mac Gruairc

John P. Brophy

Thomas E. O'Donnell

Mary C. Devins

Sean McMullin

Hugh O'Neill

Noel Rubotham

Elizabeth Hughes   Secretary

I concur in the making of the foregoing rules

Dated this 14th day of September 2004

                                        L.S.

Michael McDowell, Minister for Justice, Equality and Law Reform

APPENDIX 15

DISTRICT COURT (CHILDREN) (NO.2) RULES 2004
(S.I. No. 666 of 2004)

The District Court Rules Committee, in exercise of the powers conferred on them by section 91 of the Courts of Justice Act, 1924, section 72 of the Courts of Justice Act, 1936, section 17 of the Interpretation Act, 1937 [as applied by section 48 of the Courts (Supplemental Provisions) Act, 1961], and section 34 of the Courts (Supplemental Provisions) Act, 1961, do hereby, with the concurrence of the Minister for Justice, Equality and Law Reform, make the following Rules of Court:

1. These rules may be cited as the District Court (Children) (No.2) Rules, 2004.

2. These rules shall come into operation on the 3rd day of November 2004 and shall be read together with all other District Court rules for the time being in force.

3. Order 37 of the District Court Rules, 1997 (S.I. No. 93 of 1997) is hereby amended by the insertion therein of the following immediately after rule 12 thereof:

> "13. An order pursuant to section 78(1) of the Act directing the Probation and Welfare Service to arrange for the convening of a family conference shall be in the Form 37.27, Schedule B. Where such order is made, the proceedings shall be adjourned to a date not less than seven days after the expiry of the period of 28 days prescribed in section 79 of the Act. For the purposes of convening a family conference pursuant to section 78 of the Act, the Clerk shall provide, the probation and welfare service with such information and copies of such documents in respect of the child and/or in respect of the offence alleged as may be directed by the Court.

> 14. An order of the Court pursuant to section 82(1)(b) or section 82(2)(a) of the Act in respect of an action plan ordering that the child concerned comply with it and be supervised by a probation and welfare officer while it is in operation shall be in the Form 37.28 Schedule B. On such order being made, the proceedings shall be adjourned to a date fixed by the Court for review of compliance with the action plan in accordance with Section 84 of the Act. The probation and welfare officer who convened the relevant family conference shall be at liberty

in such case to apply to the Court for the purposes of section 83 of the Act. Such application shall be preceded by the issue and service of a notice of application in the Form 37.29, Schedule B which shall be served not later than seven days before the date fixed for the hearing of such application on: (a) the prosecuting Garda; (b) the child and (c) the parent(s) or guardian of the child or if the whereabouts of the parent(s) or guardian are unknown, on any adult relative of the child or other adult who has, under section 91(6) of the Act of 2001, accompanied the child during the proceedings."

4. The Forms numbered 37.27 to 37.29 inclusive in Schedule 1 hereof shall be added to the Forms in Schedule B of the District Court Rules, 1997 (S.I. No. 93 of 1997).

Schedule B, O.37, r.13   **No. 37.27**

CHILDREN ACT, 2001, SECTION 78(1)

Children Court Area of   **District No.**

....
Prosecutor

and

....
Accused

Whereas the child named above is charged that on the .... day

of .... 20 ...... at ....

within the court (area and) district aforesaid he/she did *(here state the offence)

AND

The said child accepts responsibility for *his/*her criminal behaviour, having had a reasonable opportunity to consult with *his/*her parents or guardian and obtained any legal advice sought by or on behalf of *him/*her, and

It appears to the Court that it is desirable that an action plan for the child should be formulated at a family conference, and

The said child and *the said child's parents or guardian *members of the said child's family *relatives of the said child who in the opinion of the Court could make a positive contribution at a family conference, agree to attend such a conference and to participate in its proceedings.

THE COURT HEREBY DIRECTS under section 78 of the above-named Act that the Probation and Welfare Service arrange for the convening of a family conference in respect of the child as follows:

The said family conference to be convened by a probation and welfare officer appointed for that purpose by the principal probation and welfare officer to be held not later than 28 days after the date of this direction.

Where an action plan is formulated at the conference, the probation and welfare officer appointed shall lodge a copy of the action plan with the Clerk at least four days before the date to which the proceedings are adjourned.

*IT IS FURTHER DIRECTED that the said family conference consider the following matters relating to the child:

*AND IT IS FURTHER DIRECTED that

And the within proceedings are adjourned to ....

Dated this .... day of .... 20 ... .

Signed..
Judge of the Children Court

Schedule B, O.37, r.14   **No. 37.28**

CHILDREN ACT, 2001, SECTION 82

Children Court Area of   **District No.**

....
Prosecutor

and

....
Accused

Whereas the child named above is charged that on the .... day

of .... 20 ...... at ....

within the court (area and) district aforesaid he/she did *(here state the offence)

AND

The said child accepts responsibility for *his/*her criminal behaviour, having had a reasonable opportunity to consult with *his/*her parents or guardian and obtained any legal advice sought by or on behalf of *him/*her, and

The Court having directed the convening of a family conference in respect of the child and adjourned the proceedings to this date and.

*The probation and welfare officer appointed to convene the family conference having submitted an action plan.

*The Court having been informed that the family conference did not reach agreement on an action plan and the Court, being of the opinion that an action plan would be desirable and have a reasonable prospect of success, having formulated an action plan.

It is ordered that the action plan *as submitted *as submitted and amended by the Court *as formulated by the Court and a copy of which is annexed to this Order, be and is hereby approved.

And it is further ordered that the child shall comply with the action plan and shall be Supervised by a probation and welfare officer,   , while the said action plan is in operation.

And it is further ordered that the proceedings be listed for review on the day of   20   .

Dated this ………… day of ………… 20 … .

Signed...
Judge of the Children Court

Schedule B, O.37, r.14   **No. 37.29**

CHILDREN ACT, 2001, SECTION 83

Children Court Area of   **District No.**

....
Prosecutor

and

....
Accused

Whereas the child named above is charged that on the …… day of …………
……… under section 82 of the above-named Act that the above-named child do comply with an action plan which had been submitted to the Court pursuant

to section 81 of the said Act.

And whereas it is alleged that the said child has, without reasonable cause, failed to comply with the terms of the said action plan.

TAKE NOTICE that the above named applicant probation and welfare officer will apply at the sitting of the Children Court to be held at .... on the .... day of .... 20 ......at ....am/pm for an order that the proceedings in respect of the offence with which the child is charged be resumed.

Dated this .... day of .... 20 .... .

Signed ....
                    Probation and Welfare Officer

To   of

And to: Children Court Clerk, Children Court

Given this 27th day of September 2004

Peter Smithwick   Chairman

John P. Brophy

Mary C. Devins

Thomas E. O'Donnell

Noel Rubotham

Damian Colgan

Elizabeth Hughes   Secretary

I concur in the making of the foregoing rules

Dated this 20th day of October 2004

                                        L.S.

Michael McDowell, Minister for Justice, Equality and Law Reform

APPENDIX 16

EUROPEAN CONVENTION ON THE EXERCISE OF CHILDREN'S RIGHTS

Strasbourg, January 25, 1996

PREAMBLE

The Member States of the Council of Europe and the other States signatory hereto,

Considering that the aim of the Council of Europe is to achieve greater unity between its members;

Having regard to the United Nations Convention on the Rights of the Child and in particular Article 4 which requires States Parties to undertake all appropriate legislative, administrative and other measures for the implementation of the rights recognised in the said Convention;

Noting the contents of Recommendation 1121 (1990) of the Parliamentary Assembly on the rights of the child;

Convinced that the rights and best interests of children should be promoted and to that end children should have the opportunity to exercise their rights, in particular in family proceedings affecting them;

Recognising that children should be provided with relevant information to enable such rights and best interests to be promoted and that due weight should be given to the views of children;

Recognising the importance of the parental role in protecting and promoting the rights and best interests of children and considering that, where necessary, States should also engage in such protection and promotion;

Considering, however, that in the event of conflict it is desirable for families to try to reach agreement before bringing the matter before a judicial authority,

Have agreed as follows:

CHAPTER I

SCOPE AND OBJECT OF THE CONVENTION AND DEFINITIONS

ARTICLE 1

Scope and object of the Convention

1. This Convention shall apply to children who have not reached the age of 18 years.

2. The object of the present Convention is, in the best interests of children, to promote their rights, to grant them procedural rights and to facilitate the exercise of these rights by ensuring that children are, themselves or through other persons or bodies, informed and allowed to participate in proceedings affecting them before a judicial authority.

3. For the purposes of this Convention proceedings before a judicial authority affecting children are family proceedings, in particular those involving the exercise of parental responsibilities such as residence and access to children.

4. Every State shall, at the time of signature or when depositing its instrument of ratification, acceptance, approval or accession, by a declaration addressed to the Secretary General of the Council of Europe, specify at least three categories of family cases before a judicial authority to which this Convention is to apply.

5. Any Party may, by further declaration, specify additional categories of family cases to which this Convention is to apply or provide information concerning the application of Article 5, paragraph 2 of Article 9, paragraph 2 of Article 10 and Article 11.

6. Nothing in this Convention shall prevent Parties from applying rules more favourable to the promotion and the exercise of children's rights.

ARTICLE 2

Definitions

For the purposes of this Convention:

(a) the term "judicial authority" means a court or an administrative authority having equivalent powers;

(b) the term "holders of parental responsibilities" means parents and other persons or bodies entitled to exercise some or all parental responsibilities;

(c) the term "representative" means a person, such as a lawyer, or a body appointed to act before a judicial authority on behalf of a child;

(d) the term "relevant information" means information which is appropriate to the age and understanding of the child, and which will be given to enable the child to exercise his or her rights fully unless the provision of such information were contrary to the welfare of the child.

CHAPTER II

PROCEDURAL MEASURES TO PROMOTE THE EXERCISE OF CHILDREN'S RIGHTS

A. Procedural rights of a child

ARTICLE 3

Right to be informed and to express his or her views in proceedings

A child considered by internal law as having sufficient understanding, in the case of proceedings before a judicial authority affecting him or her, shall be granted, and shall be entitled to request, the following rights:

(a) to receive all relevant information;

(b) to be consulted and express his or her views;

(c) to be informed of the possible consequences of compliance with these views and the possible consequences of any decision.

ARTICLE 4

Right to apply for the appointment of a special representative

1. Subject to Article 9, the child shall have the right to apply, in person or through other persons or bodies, for a special representative in proceedings before a judicial authority affecting the child where internal law precludes the holders of parental responsibilities from representing the child as a result of a conflict of interest with the latter.

2. States are free to limit the right in paragraph 1 to children who are considered by internal law to have sufficient understanding.

ARTICLE 5

Other possible procedural rights

Parties shall consider granting children additional procedural rights in relation to proceedings before a judicial authority affecting them, in particular:
   (a) the right to apply to be assisted by an appropriate person of their choice in order to help them express their views;
   (b) the right to apply themselves, or through other persons or bodies, for the appointment of a separate representative, in appropriate cases a lawyer;

(c) the right to appoint their own representative;

(d) the right to exercise some or all of the rights of parties to such proceedings.

B. Role of judicial authorities

ARTICLE 6

Decision-making process

In proceedings affecting a child, the judicial authority, before taking a decision, shall:

(a) consider whether it has sufficient information at its disposal in order to take a decision in the best interests of the child and, where necessary, it shall obtain further information, in particular from the holders of parental responsibilities;

(b) in a case where the child is considered by internal law as having sufficient understanding:
   • ensure that the child has received all relevant information;
   • consult the child in person in appropriate cases, if necessary privately, itself or through other persons or bodies, in a manner appropriate to his or her understanding, unless this would be manifestly contrary to the best interests of the child;
   • allow the child to express his or her views;

(c) give due weight to the views expressed by the child.

ARTICLE 7

Duty to act speedily

In proceedings affecting a child the judicial authority shall act speedily to avoid any unnecessary delay and procedures shall be available to ensure that its decisions are rapidly enforced. In urgent cases the judicial authority shall have the power, where appropriate, to take decisions which are immediately enforceable.

ARTICLE 8

Acting on own motion

In proceedings affecting a child the judicial authority shall have the power to act on its own motion in cases determined by internal law where the welfare of a child is in serious danger.

ARTICLE 9

Appointment of a representative

1. In proceedings affecting a child where, by internal law, the holders of parental responsibilities are precluded from representing the child as a result of a conflict of interest between them and the child, the judicial authority shall have the power to appoint a special representative for the child in those proceedings.

2. Parties shall consider providing that, in proceedings affecting a child, the judicial authority shall have the power to appoint a separate representative, in appropriate cases a lawyer, to represent the child.

C. Role of representatives

ARTICLE 10

1. In the case of proceedings before a judicial authority affecting a child the representative shall, unless this would be manifestly contrary to the best interests of the child:
   (a) provide all relevant information to the child, if the child is considered by internal law as having sufficient understanding;
   (b) provide explanations to the child if the child is considered by internal law as having sufficient understanding, concerning the possible consequences of compliance with his or her views and the possible consequences of any action by the representative;
   (c) determine the views of the child and present these views to the judicial authority.

2. Parties shall consider extending the provisions of paragraph 1 to the holders of parental responsibilities.

D. Extension of certain provisions

ARTICLE 11

Parties shall consider extending the provisions of Articles 3, 4 and 9 to proceedings affecting children before other bodies and to matters affecting children which are not the subject of proceedings.

E. National bodies

ARTICLE 12

1. Parties shall encourage, through bodies which perform, *inter alia*, the

functions set out in paragraph 2, the promotion and the exercise of children's rights.

2. The functions are as follows:
    (a) to make proposals to strengthen the law relating to the exercise of children's rights;
    (b) to give opinions concerning draft legislation relating to the exercise of children's rights;
    (c) to provide general information concerning the exercise of children's rights to the media, the public and persons and bodies dealing with questions relating to children;
    (d) to seek the views of children and provide them with relevant information.

F. Other matters

ARTICLE 13

Mediation or other processes to resolve disputes

In order to prevent or resolve disputes or to avoid proceedings before a judicial authority affecting children, Parties shall encourage the provision of mediation or other processes to resolve disputes and the use of such processes to reach agreement in appropriate cases to be determined by Parties.

ARTICLE 14

Legal aid and advice

Where internal law provides for legal aid or advice for the representation of children in proceedings before a judicial authority affecting them, such provisions shall apply in relation to the matters covered by Articles 4 and 9.

ARTICLE 15

Relations with other international instruments

This Convention shall not restrict the application of any other international instrument which deals with specific issues arising in the context of the protection of children and families, and to which a Party to this Convention is, or becomes, a Party.

CHAPTER III

STANDING COMMITTEE

ARTICLE 16

Establishment and functions of the Standing Committee

1. A Standing Committee is set up for the purposes of this Convention.

2. The Standing Committee shall keep under review problems relating to this Convention. It may, in particular:
   (a) consider any relevant questions concerning the interpretation or implementation of the Convention. The Standing Committee's conclusions concerning the implementation of the Convention may take the form of a recommendation; recommendations shall be adopted by a three-quarters majority of the votes cast;
   (b) propose amendments to the Convention and examine those proposed in accordance with Article 20;
   (c) provide advice and assistance to the national bodies having the functions under paragraph 2 of Article 12 and promote international co-operation between them.

ARTICLE 17

Composition

1. Each Party may be represented on the Standing Committee by one or more delegates. Each Party shall have one vote.

2. Any State referred to in Article 21, which is not a Party to this Convention, may be represented in the Standing Committee by an observer. The same applies to any other State or to the European Community after having been invited to accede to the Convention in accordance with the provisions of Article 22.

3. Unless a Party has informed the Secretary General of its objection, at least one month before the meeting, the Standing Committee may invite the following to attend as observers at all its meetings or at one meeting or part of a meeting:
   • any State not referred to in paragraph 2 above;
   • the United Nations Committee on the Rights of the Child;
   • the European Community;
   • any international governmental body;
   • any international non-governmental body with one or more functions mentioned under paragraph 2 of Article 12;
   • any national governmental or non-governmental body with one or more functions mentioned under paragraph 2 of Article 12.

The Standing Committee may exchange information with relevant organizations dealing with the exercise of children's rights.

ARTICLE 18

Meetings

1. At the end of the third year following the date of entry into force of this Convention and, on his or her own initiative, at any time after this date, the Secretary General of the Council of Europe shall invite the Standing Committee to meet.

2. Decisions may only be taken in the Standing Committee if at least one-half of the Parties are present.

3. Subject to Articles 16 and 20 the decisions of the Standing Committee shall be taken by a majority of the members present.

4. Subject to the provisions of this Convention the Standing Committee shall draw up its own rules of procedure and the rules of procedure of any working party it may set up to carry out all appropriate tasks under the Convention.

ARTICLE 19

Reports of the Standing Committee

After each meeting, the Standing Committee shall forward to the Parties and the Committee of Ministers of the Council of Europe a report on its discussions and any decisions taken.

CHAPTER IV

AMENDMENTS TO THE CONVENTION

ARTICLE 20

1. Any amendment to the articles of this Convention proposed by a Party or the Standing Committee shall be communicated to the Secretary General of the Council of Europe and forwarded by him or her, at least two months before the next meeting of the Standing Committee, to the member States of the Council of Europe, any signatory, any Party, any State invited to sign this Convention in accordance with the provisions of Article 21 and any State or the European Community invited to accede to it in accordance with the provisions of Article 22.

2. Any amendment proposed in accordance with the provisions of the preceding paragraph shall be examined by the Standing Committee which

shall submit the text adopted by a three-quarters majority of the votes cast to the Committee of Ministers for approval. After its approval, this text shall be forwarded to the Parties for acceptance.

3.   Any amendment shall enter into force on the first day of the month following the expiration of a period of one month after the date on which all Parties have informed the Secretary General that they have accepted it.

CHAPTER V

FINAL CLAUSES

ARTICLE 21

Signature, ratification and entry into force

1.   This Convention shall be open for signature by the member States of the Council of Europe and the non-member States which have participated in its elaboration.

2.   This Convention is subject to ratification, acceptance or approval. Instruments of ratification, acceptance or approval shall be deposited with the Secretary General of the Council of Europe.

3.   This Convention shall enter into force on the first day of the month following the expiration of a period of three months after the date on which three States, including at least two member States of the Council of Europe, have expressed their consent to be bound by the Convention in accordance with the provisions of the preceding paragraph.

4.   In respect of any signatory which subsequently expresses its consent to be bound by it, the Convention shall enter into force on the first day of the month following the expiration of a period of three months after the date of the deposit of its instrument of ratification, acceptance or approval.

ARTICLE 22

Non-member States and the European Community

1.   After the entry into force of this Convention, the Committee of Ministers of the Council of Europe may, on its own initiative or following a proposal from the Standing Committee and after consultation of the Parties, invite any non-member State of the Council of Europe, which has not participated in the elaboration of the Convention, as well as the European Community to accede to this Convention by a decision taken by the majority provided for in Article 20, sub-paragraph (d) of the Statute of the Council of Europe, and by the unanimous vote of the representatives of the Contracting States entitled to sit on the Committee of Ministers.

2.   In respect of any acceding State or the European Community, the

Convention shall enter into force on the first day of the month following the expiration of a period of three months after the date of deposit of the instrument of accession with the Secretary General of the Council of Europe.

ARTICLE 23

Territorial application

1.   Any State may, at the time of signature or when depositing its instrument of ratification, acceptance, approval or accession, specify the territory or territories to which this Convention shall apply.

2.   Any Party may, at any later date, by a declaration addressed to the Secretary General of the Council of Europe, extend the application of this Convention to any other territory specified in the declaration and for whose international relations it is responsible or on whose behalf it is authorised to give undertakings. In respect of such territory the Convention shall enter into force on the first day of the month following the expiration of a period of three months after the date of receipt of such declaration by the Secretary General.

3.   Any declaration made under the two preceding paragraphs may, in respect of any territory specified in such declaration, be withdrawn by a notification addressed to the Secretary General. The withdrawal shall become effective on the first day of the month following the expiration of a period of three months after the date of receipt of such notification by the Secretary General.

ARTICLE 24

Reservations

No reservation may be made to the Convention.

ARTICLE 25

Denunciation

1.   Any Party may at any time denounce this Convention by means of a notification addressed to the Secretary General of the Council of Europe.

2.   Such denunciation shall become effective on the first day of the month following the expiration of a period of three months after the date of receipt of notification by the Secretary General.

ARTICLE 26

Notifications

The Secretary General of the Council of Europe shall notify the member States of the Council, any signatory, any Party and any other State or the European Community which has been invited to accede to this Convention of:

(a) any signature;

(b) the deposit of any instrument of ratification, acceptance, approval or accession;

(c) any date of entry into force of this Convention in accordance with Articles 21 or 22;

(d) any amendment adopted in accordance with Article 20 and the date on which such an amendment enters into force;

(e) any declaration made under the provisions of Articles 1 and 23;

(f) any denunciation made in pursuance of the provisions of Article 25;

(g) any other act, notification or communication relating to this Convention.

In witness whereof, the undersigned, being duly authorised thereto, have signed this Convention.

Done at Strasbourg, the 25th January 1996, in English and French, both texts being equally authentic, in a single copy which shall be deposited in the archives of the Council of Europe. The Secretary General of the Council of Europe shall transmit certified copies to each member State of the Council of Europe, to the non-member States which have participated in the elaboration of this Convention, to the European Community and to any State invited to accede to this Convention.

APPENDIX 17

COUNCIL REGULATION (EC) No.2201/2003

of 27 November 2003 concerning jurisdiction and the recognition and enforcement of judgments in matrimonial matters and the matters of parental responsibility, repealing Regulation (EC) No.1347/2000

THE COUNCIL OF THE EUROPEAN UNION,

Having regard to the Treaty establishing the European Community, and in particular Article 61(c) and Article 67(1) thereof,

Having regard to the proposal from the Commission, [1]

Having regard to the opinion of the European Parliament, [2]

Having regard to the opinion of the European Economic and Social Committee, [3]

Whereas:

(1) The European Community has set the objective of creating an area of freedom, security and justice, in which the free movement of persons is ensured. To this end, the Community is to adopt, among others, measures in the field of judicial cooperation in civil matters that are necessary for the proper functioning of the internal market.

(2) The Tampere European Council endorsed the principle of mutual recognition of judicial decisions as the cornerstone for the creation of a genuine judicial area, and identified visiting rights as a priority.

(3) Council Regulation (EC) No. 1347/2000[4] sets out rules on jurisdiction, recognition and enforcement of judgments in matrimonial matters and matters of parental responsibility for the children of both spouses rendered on the occasion of the matrimonial proceedings. The content of this Regulation was substantially taken over from the Convention of 28 May 1998 on the same subject matter. [5]

---

[1] OJ C 203 E, August 27, 2002, p.155.
[2] Opinion delivered on September 20, 2002 (not yet published in the Official Journal).
[3] OJ C 61, March 14, 2003, p.76.
[4] OJ L 160, June 30, 2000, p.19.
[5] At the time of the adoption of Regulation (EC) No. 1347/2000 the Council took note of the explanatory report concerning that Convention prepared by Professor Alegria Borras (OJ C 221, July 16, 1998, p.27).

(4) On 3 July 2000 France presented an initiative for a Council Regulation on the mutual enforcement of judgments on rights of access to children. [6]

(5) In order to ensure equality for all children, this Regulation covers all decisions on parental responsibility, including measures for the protection of the child, independently of any link with a matrimonial proceeding.

(6) Since the application of the rules on parental responsibility often arises in the context of matrimonial proceedings, it is more appropriate to have a single instrument for matters of divorce and parental responsibility.

(7) The scope of this Regulation covers civil matters, whatever the nature of the court or tribunal.

(8) As regards judgments on divorce, legal separation or marriage annulment, this Regulation should apply only to the dissolution of matrimonial ties and should not deal with issues such as the grounds for divorce, property consequences of the marriage or any other ancillary measures.

(9) As regards the property of the child, this Regulation should apply only to measures for the protection of the child, i.e. (i) the designation and functions of a person or body having charge of the child's property, representing or assisting the child, and (ii) the administration, conservation or disposal of the child's property. In this context, this Regulation should, for instance, apply in cases where the parents are in dispute as regards the administration of the child's property. Measures relating to the child's property which do not concern the protection of the child should continue to be governed by Council Regulation (EC) No. 44/2001 of 22 December 2000 on jurisdiction and the recognition and enforcement of judgments in civil and commercial matters.[7]

(10) This Regulation is not intended to apply to matters relating to social security, public measures of a general nature in matters of education or health or to decisions on the right of asylum and on immigration. In addition it does not apply to the establishment of parenthood, since this is a different matter from the attribution of parental responsibility, nor to other questions linked to the status of persons. Moreover, it does not apply to measures taken as a result of criminal offences committed by children.

(11) Maintenance obligations are excluded from the scope of this Regulation as these are already covered by Council Regulation No. 44/2001. The courts having jurisdiction under this Regulation will generally have jurisdiction to rule on maintenance obligations by application of Article 5(2) of Council Regulation No. 44/2001.

(12) The grounds of jurisdiction in matters of parental responsibility established in the present Regulation are shaped in the light of the best interests of the child, in particular on the criterion of proximity. This means that jurisdiction should lie in the first place with the Member State of the child's habitual residence, except for certain cases of a change in the child's residence or pursuant to an agreement between the holders of parental responsibility.

(13) In the interest of the child, this Regulation allows, by way of exception and under certain conditions, that the court having jurisdiction may transfer a

---

[6] OJ C 234, August 15, 2000, p.7.
[7] OJ L 12, January 16, 2001, p.1. Regulation as last amended by Commission Regulation (EC) No. 1496/2002 (OJ L 225, August, 22, 2002, p.13).

case to a court of another Member State if this court is better placed to hear the case. However, in this case the second court should not be allowed to transfer the case to a third court.

(14) This Regulation should have effect without prejudice to the application of public international law concerning diplomatic immunities. Where jurisdiction under this Regulation cannot be exercised by reason of the existence of diplomatic immunity in accordance with international law, jurisdiction should be exercised in accordance with national law in a Member State in which the person concerned does not enjoy such immunity.

(15) Council Regulation (EC) No. 1348/2000 of 29 May 2000 on the service in the Member States of judicial and extrajudicial documents in civil or commercial matters[8] should apply to the service of documents in proceedings instituted pursuant to this Regulation.

(16) This Regulation should not prevent the courts of a Member State from taking provisional, including protective measures, in urgent cases, with regard to persons or property situated in that State.

(17) In cases of wrongful removal or retention of a child, the return of the child should be obtained without delay, and to this end the Hague Convention of 25 October 1980 would continue to apply as complemented by the provisions of this Regulation, in particular Article 11. The courts of the Member State to or in which the child has been wrongfully removed or retained should be able to oppose his or her return in specific, duly justified cases. However, such a decision could be replaced by a subsequent decision by the court of the Member State of habitual residence of the child prior to the wrongful removal or retention. Should that judgment entail the return of the child, the return should take place without any special procedure being required for recognition and enforcement of that judgment in the Member State to or in which the child has been removed or retained.

(18) Where a court has decided not to return a child on the basis of Article 13 of the 1980 Hague Convention, it should inform the court having jurisdiction or central authority in the Member State where the child was habitually resident prior to the wrongful removal or retention. Unless the court in the latter Member State has been seised, this court or the central authority should notify the parties. This obligation should not prevent the central authority from also notifying the relevant public authorities in accordance with national law.

(19) The hearing of the child plays an important role in the application of this Regulation, although this instrument is not intended to modify national procedures applicable.

(20) The hearing of a child in another Member State may take place under the arrangements laid down in Council Regulation (EC) No. 1206/2001 of 28 May 2001 on cooperation between the courts of the Member States in the taking of evidence in civil or commercial matters.[9]

(21) The recognition and enforcement of judgments given in a Member State should be based on the principle of mutual trust and the grounds for non-recognition should be kept to the minimum required.

---

[8] OJ L 160, June 30, 2000, p.37.
[9] OJ L 174, June 27, 2001, p.1.

(22) Authentic instruments and agreements between parties that are enforceable in one Member State should be treated as equivalent to 'judgments' for the purpose of the application of the rules on recognition and enforcement.

(23) The Tampere European Council considered in its conclusions (point 34) that judgments in the field of family litigation should be 'automatically recognised throughout the Union without any intermediate proceedings or grounds for refusal of enforcement'. This is why judgments on rights of access and judgments on return that have been certified in the Member State of origin in accordance with the provisions of this Regulation should be recognised and enforceable in all other Member States without any further procedure being required. Arrangements for the enforcement of such judgments continue to be governed by national law.

(24) The certificate issued to facilitate enforcement of the judgment should not be subject to appeal. It should be rectified only where there is a material error, i.e. where it does not correctly reflect the judgment.

(25) Central authorities should cooperate both in general matter and in specific cases, including for purposes of promoting the amicable resolution of family disputes, in matters of parental responsibility. To this end central authorities shall participate in the European Judicial Network in civil and commercial matters created by Council Decision 2001/470/EC of 28 May 2001 establishing a European Judicial Network in civil and commercial matters.[10]

(26) The Commission should make publicly available and update the lists of courts and redress procedures communicated by the Member States.

(27) The measures necessary for the implementation of this Regulation should be adopted in accordance with Council Decision 1999/468/EC of 28 June 1999 laying down the procedures for the exercise of implementing powers conferred on the Commission.[11]

(28) This Regulation replaces Regulation (EC) No. 1347/2000 which is consequently repealed.

(29) For the proper functioning of this Regulation, the Commission should review its application and propose such amendments as may appear necessary.

(30) The United Kingdom and Ireland, in accordance with Article 3 of the Protocol on the position of the United Kingdom and Ireland annexed to the Treaty on European Union and the Treaty establishing the European Community, have given notice of their wish to take part in the adoption and application of this Regulation.

(31) Denmark, in accordance with Articles 1 and 2 of the Protocol on the position of Denmark annexed to the Treaty on European Union and the Treaty establishing the European Community, is not participating in the adoption of this Regulation and is therefore not bound by it nor subject to its application.

(32) Since the objectives of this Regulation cannot be sufficiently achieved by the Member States and can therefore be better achieved at Community level, the Community may adopt measures, in accordance with the principle of subsidiarity as set out in Article 5 of the Treaty. In accordance with the principle of proportionality, as set out in that Article, this Regulation does not

---

[10] OJ L 174, June 27, 2001, p.25.
[11] OJ L 184, July 17, 1999, p.23.

go beyond what is necessary in order to achieve those objectives.

(33) This Regulation recognises the fundamental rights and observes the principles of the Charter of Fundamental Rights of the European Union. In particular, it seeks to ensure respect for the fundamental rights of the child as set out in Article 24 of the Charter of Fundamental Rights of the European Union,

HAS ADOPTED THE PRESENT REGULATION:

CHAPTER I

SCOPE AND DEFINITIONS

Article 1

Scope

1. This Regulation shall apply, whatever the nature of the court or tribunal, in civil matters relating to:
    (a) divorce, legal separation or marriage annulment;
    (b) the attribution, exercise, delegation, restriction or termination of parental responsibility.

2. The matters referred to in paragraph 1(b)may, in particular, deal with:
    (a) rights of custody and rights of access;
    (b) guardianship, curatorship and similar institutions;
    (c) the designation and functions of any person or body having charge of the child's person or property, representing or assisting the child;
    (d) the placement of the child in a foster family or in institutional care;
    (e) measures for the protection of the child relating to the administration, conservation or disposal of the child's property.

3. This Regulation shall not apply to:
    (a) the establishment or contesting of a parent-child relationship;
    (b) decisions on adoption, measures preparatory to adoption, or the annulment or revocation of adoption;
    (c) the name and forenames of the child;
    (d) emancipation;
    (e) maintenance obligations;
    (f) trusts or succession;
    (g) measures taken as a result of criminal offences committed by children.

Article 2

Definitions

For the purposes of this Regulation:

1. the term 'court' shall cover all the authorities in the Member States with jurisdiction in the matters falling within the scope of this Regulation pursuant to Article 1;

2. the term 'judge'shall mean the judge or an official having powers equivalent to those of a judge in the matters falling within the scope of the Regulation;

3. the term 'Member State' shall mean all Member States with the exception of Denmark;

4. the term 'judgment' shall mean a divorce, legal separation or marriage annulment, as well as a judgment relating to parental responsibility, pronounced by a court of a Member State, whatever the judgment may be called, including a decree, order or decision;

5. the term 'Member State of origin' shall mean the Member State where the judgment to be enforced was issued;

6. the term 'Member State of enforcement' shall mean the Member State where enforcement of the judgment is sought;

7. the term 'parental responsibility' shall mean all rights and duties relating to the person or the property of a child which are given to a natural or legal person by judgment, by operation of law or by an agreement having legal effect. The term shall include rights of custody and rights of access;

8. the term 'holder of parental responsibility' shall mean any person having parental responsibility over a child;

9. the term 'rights of custody' shall include rights and duties relating to the care of the person of a child, and in particular the right to determine the child's place of residence;

10. the term 'rights of access' shall include in particular the right to take a child to a place other than his or her habitual residence for a limited period of time;

11. the term 'wrongful removal or retention' shall mean a child's removal or retention where:
    (a) it is in breach of rights of custody acquired by judgment or by operation of law or by an agreement having legal effect under the law of the Member State where the child was habitually resident immediately before the removal or retention;
    and
    (b) provided that, at the time of removal or retention, the rights of custody were actually exercised, either jointly or alone, or would have been so exercised but for the removal or retention. Custody shall be

considered to be exercised jointly when, pursuant to a judgment or by operation of law, one holder of parental responsibility cannot decide on the child's place of residence without the consent of another holder of parental responsibility.

CHAPTER II

JURISDICTION

SECTION 1

Divorce, legal separation and marriage annulment

Article 3

General jurisdiction

1. In matters relating to divorce, legal separation or marriage annulment, jurisdiction shall lie with the courts of the Member State:
   (a) in whose territory: —the spouses are habitually resident, or
      — the spouses were last habitually resident, insofar as one of them still resides there, or
      — the respondent is habitually resident, or
      — in the event of a joint application, either of the spouses is habitually resident, or
      — the applicant is habitually resident if he or she resided there for at least a year immediately before the application was made, or
      — the applicant is habitually resident if he or she resided there for at least six months immediately before the application was made and is either a national of the Member State in question or, in the case of the United Kingdom and Ireland, has his or her 'domicile' there;
   (b) of the nationality of both spouses or, in the case of the United Kingdom and Ireland, of the 'domicile' of both spouses.

2. For the purpose of this Regulation, 'domicile' shall have the same meaning as it has under the legal systems of the United Kingdom and Ireland.

Article 4

Counterclaim

The court in which proceedings are pending on the basis of Article 3 shall also have jurisdiction to examine a counterclaim, insofar as the latter comes within the scope of this Regulation.

Article 5

Conversion of legal separation into divorce

Without prejudice to Article 3, a court of a Member State that has given a judgment on a legal separation shall also have jurisdiction for converting that judgment into a divorce, if the law of that Member State so provides.

Article 6

Exclusive nature of jurisdiction under Articles 3, 4 and 5

A spouse who:
    (a) is habitually resident in the territory of a Member State; or
    (b) is a national of a Member State, or, in the case of the United Kingdom and Ireland, has his or her 'domicile' in the territory of one of the latter Member States, may be sued in another Member State only in accordance with Articles 3, 4 and 5.

Article 7

Residual jurisdiction

1.   Where no court of a Member State has jurisdiction pursuant to Articles 3, 4 and 5, jurisdiction shall be determined, in each Member State, by the laws of that State.

2.   As against a respondent who is not habitually resident and is not either a national of a Member State or, in the case of the United Kingdom and Ireland, does not have his 'domicile' within the territory of one of the latter Member States, any national of a Member State who is habitually resident within the territory of another Member State may, like the nationals of that State, avail himself of the rules of jurisdiction applicable in that State.

SECTION 2

Parental responsibility

Article 8

General jurisdiction

1.   The courts of a Member State shall have jurisdiction in matters of parental responsibility over a child who is habitually resident in that Member State at the time the court is seised.

2.   Paragraph 1 shall be subject to the provisions of Articles 9, 10 and 12.

Article 9

Continuing jurisdiction of the child's former habitual residence

1.   Where a child moves lawfully from one Member State to another and acquires a new habitual residence there, the courts of the Member State of the child's former habitual residence shall, by way of exception to Article 8, retain jurisdiction during a three-month period following the move for the purpose of modifying a judgment on access rights issued in that Member State before the child moved, where the holder of access rights pursuant to the judgment on access rights continues to have his or her habitual residence in the Member State of the child's former habitual residence.

2.   Paragraph 1 shall not apply if the holder of access rights referred to in paragraph 1 has accepted the jurisdiction of the courts of the Member State of the child's new habitual residence by participating in proceedings before those courts without contesting their jurisdiction.

Article 10

Jurisdiction in cases of child abduction

In case of wrongful removal or retention of the child, the courts of the Member State where the child was habitually resident immediately before the wrongful removal or retention shall retain their jurisdiction until the child has acquired a habitual residence in another Member State and:

(a)   each person, institution or other body having rights of custody has acquiesced in the removal or retention; or

(b)   the child has resided in that other Member State for a period of at least one year after the person, institution or other body having rights of custody has had or should have had knowledge of the whereabouts of the child and the child is settled in his or her new environment and at least one of the following conditions is met:

   (i)   within one year after the holder of rights of custody has had or should have had knowledge of the whereabouts of the child, no request for return has been lodged before the competent authorities of the Member State where the child has been removed or is being retained;

   (ii) a request for return lodged by the holder of rights of custody has been withdrawn and no new request has been lodged within the time limit set in paragraph (i);

   (iii) a case before the court in the Member State where the child was habitually resident immediately before the wrongful removal or retention has been closed pursuant to Article 11(7);

(iv) a judgment on custody that does not entail the return of the child has been issued by the courts of the Member State where the child was habitually resident immediately before the wrongful removal or retention.

Article 11

Return of the child

1.   Where a person, institution or other body having rights of custody applies to the competent authorities in a Member State to deliver a judgment on the basis of the Hague Convention of 25 October 1980 on the Civil Aspects of International Child Abduction (hereinafter 'the 1980 Hague Convention'), in order to obtain the return of a child that has been wrongfully removed or retained in a Member State other than the Member State where the child was habitually resident immediately before the wrongful removal or retention, paragraphs 2 to 8 shall apply.

2.   When applying Articles 12 and 13 of the 1980 Hague Convention, it shall be ensured that the child is given the opportunity to be heard during the proceedings unless this appears inappropriate having regard to his or her age or degree of maturity.

3.   A court to which an application for return of a child is made as mentioned in paragraph 1 shall act expeditiously in proceedings on the application, using the most expeditious procedures available in national law.

Without prejudice to the first subparagraph, the court shall, except where exceptional circumstances make this impossible, issue its judgment no later than six weeks after the application is lodged.

4.   A court cannot refuse to return a child on the basis of Article 13b of the 1980 Hague Convention if it is established that adequate arrangements have been made to secure the protection of the child after his or her return.

5.   A court cannot refuse to return a child unless the person who requested the return of the child has been given an opportunity to be heard.

6.   If a court has issued an order on non-return pursuant to Article 13 of the 1980 Hague Convention, the court must immediately either directly or through its central authority, transmit a copy of the court order on non-return and of the relevant documents, in particular a transcript of the hearings before the court, to the court with jurisdiction or central authority in the Member State where the child was habitually resident immediately before the wrongful removal or retention, as determined by national law. The court shall receive all the mentioned documents within one month of the date of the non-return order.

7.   Unless the courts in the Member State where the child was habitually resident immediately before the wrongful removal or retention have already

been seised by one of the parties, the court or central authority that receives the information mentioned in paragraph 6 must notify it to the parties and invite them to make submissions to the court, in accordance with national law, within three months of the date of notification so that the court can examine the question of custody of the child.

Without prejudice to the rules on jurisdiction contained in this Regulation, the court shall close the case if no submissions have been received by the court within the time limit.

8.   Notwithstanding a judgment of non-return pursuant to Article 13 of the 1980 Hague Convention, any subsequent judgment which requires the return of the child issued by a court having jurisdiction under this Regulation shall be enforceable in accordance with Section 4 of Chapter III below in order to secure the return of the child.

Article 12

Prorogation of jurisdiction

1.   The courts of a Member State exercising jurisdiction by virtue of Article 3 on an application for divorce, legal separation or marriage annulment shall have jurisdiction in any matter relating to parental responsibility connected with that application where:
     (a) at least one of the spouses has parental responsibility in relation to the child;
     and
     (b) the jurisdiction of the courts has been accepted expressly or otherwise in an unequivocal manner by the spouses and by the holders of parental responsibility, at the time the court is seised, and is in the superior interests of the child.

2.   The jurisdiction conferred in paragraph 1 shall cease as soon as:
     (a) the judgment allowing or refusing the application for divorce, legal separation or marriage annulment has become final;
     (b) in those cases where proceedings in relation to parental responsibility are still pending on the date referred to in (a), a judgment in these proceedings has become final;
     (c) the proceedings referred to in (a) and (b) have come to an end for another reason.

3.   The courts of a Member State shall also have jurisdiction in relation to parental responsibility in proceedings other than those referred to in paragraph 1 where:
     (a) the child has a substantial connection with that Member State, in particular by virtue of the fact that one of the holders of parental responsibility is habitually resident in that Member State or that the child is a national of that Member State; and
     (b) the jurisdiction of the courts has been accepted expressly or otherwise

in an unequivocal manner by all the parties to the proceedings at the time the court is seised and is in the best interests of the child.

4. Where the child has his or her habitual residence in the territory of a third State which is not a contracting party to the Hague Convention of 19 October 1996 on jurisdiction, applicable law, recognition, enforcement and cooperation in respect of parental responsibility and measures for the protection of children, jurisdiction under this Article shall be deemed to be in the child's interest, in particular if it is found impossible to hold proceedings in the third State in question.

Article 13

Jurisdiction based on the child's presence

1. Where a child's habitual residence cannot be established and jurisdiction cannot be determined on the basis of Article 12, the courts of the Member State where the child is present shall have jurisdiction.

2. Paragraph 1 shall also apply to refugee children or children internationally displaced because of disturbances occurring in their country.

Article 14

Residual jurisdiction

Where no court of a Member State has jurisdiction pursuant to Articles 8 to 13, jurisdiction shall be determined, in each Member State, by the laws of that State.

Article 15

Transfer to a court better placed to hear the case

1. By way of exception, the courts of a Member State having jurisdiction as to the substance of the matter may, if they consider that a court of another Member State, with which the child has a particular connection, would be better placed to hear the case, or a specific part thereof, and where this is in the best interests of the child:
   (a) stay the case or the part thereof in question and invite the parties to introduce a request before the court of that other Member State in accordance with paragraph 4; or
   (b) request a court of another Member State to assume jurisdiction in accordance with paragraph 5.

2. Paragraph 1 shall apply:

(a) upon application from a party; or

(b) of the court's own motion; or

(c) upon application from a court of another Member State with which the child has a particular connection, in accordance with paragraph 3.

A transfer made of the court's own motion or by application of a court of another Member State must be accepted by at least one of the parties.

3.   The child shall be considered to have a particular connection to a Member State as mentioned in paragraph 1, if that Member State:

(a) has become the habitual residence of the child after the court referred to in paragraph 1 was seised; or

(b) is the former habitual residence of the child; or

(c) is the place of the child's nationality; or

(d) is the habitual residence of a holder of parental responsibility; or

(e) is the place where property of the child is located and the case concerns measures for the protection of the child relating to the administration, conservation or disposal of this property.

4.   The court of the Member State having jurisdiction as to the substance of the matter shall set a time limit by which the courts of that other Member State shall be seised in accordance with paragraph 1.

If the courts are not seised by that time, the court which has been seised shall continue to exercise jurisdiction in accordance with Articles 8 to 14.

5.   The courts of that other Member State may, where due to the specific circumstances of the case, this is in the best interests of the child, accept jurisdiction within six weeks of their seisure in accordance with paragraph 1(a) or 1(b). In this case, the court first seised shall decline jurisdiction. Otherwise, the court first seised shall continue to exercise jurisdiction in accordance with Articles 8 to 14.

6.   The courts shall cooperate for the purposes of this Article, either directly or through the central authorities designated pursuant to Article 53.

SECTION 3

Common provisions

Article 16

Seising of a Court

1.   A court shall be deemed to be seised:

(a) at the time when the document instituting the proceedings or an equivalent document is lodged with the court, provided that the applicant has not subsequently failed to take the steps he was required to take to have service effected on the respondent;

or

(b) if the document has to be served before being lodged with the court, at the time when it is received by the authority responsible for service, provided that the applicant has not subsequently failed to take the steps he was required to take to have the document lodged with the court.

Article 17

Examination as to jurisdiction

Where a court of a Member State is seised of a case over which it has no jurisdiction under this Regulation and over which a court of another Member State has jurisdiction by virtue of this Regulation, it shall declare of its own motion that it has no jurisdiction.

Article 18

Examination as to admissibility

1. Where a respondent habitually resident in a State other than the Member State where the action was brought does not enter an appearance, the court with jurisdiction shall stay the proceedings so long as it is not shown that the respondent has been able to receive the document instituting the proceedings or an equivalent document in sufficient time to enable him to arrange for his defence, or that all necessary steps have been taken to this end.

2. Article 19 of Regulation (EC) No. 1348/2000 shall apply instead of the provisions of paragraph 1 of this Article if the document instituting the proceedings or an equivalent document had to be transmitted from one Member State to another pursuant to that Regulation.

3. Where the provisions of Regulation (EC) No. 1348/2000 are not applicable, Article 15 of the Hague Convention of 15 November 1965 on the service abroad of judicial and extrajudicial documents in civil or commercial matters shall apply if the document instituting the proceedings or an equivalent document had to be transmitted abroad pursuant to that Convention.

Article 19

Lis pendens and dependent actions

1. Where proceedings relating to divorce, legal separation or marriage annulment between the same parties are brought before courts of different Member States, the court second seised shall of its own motion stay its

proceedings until such time as the jurisdiction of the court first seised is established.

2.   Where proceedings relating to parental responsibility relating to the same child and involving the same cause of action are brought before courts of different Member States, the court second seised shall of its own motion stay its proceedings until such time as the jurisdiction of the court first seised is established.

3.   Where the jurisdiction of the court first seised is established, the court second seised shall decline jurisdiction in favour of that court.

In that case, the party who brought the relevant action before the court second seised may bring that action before the court first seised.

Article 20

Provisional, including protective, measures

1.   In urgent cases, the provisions of this Regulation shall not prevent the courts of a Member State from taking such provisional, including protective, measures in respect of persons or assets in that State as may be available under the law of that Member State, even if, under this Regulation, the court of another Member State has jurisdiction as to the substance of the matter.

2.   The measures referred to in paragraph 1 shall cease to apply when the court of the Member State having jurisdiction under this Regulation as to the substance of the matter has taken the measures it considers appropriate.

CHAPTER III

RECOGNITION AND ENFORCEMENT

SECTION 1

Recognition

Article 21

Recognition of a judgment

1.   A judgment given in a Member State shall be recognised in the other Member States without any special procedure being required.

2.   In particular, and without prejudice to paragraph 3, no special procedure shall be required for updating the civil-status records of a Member State

on the basis of a judgment relating to divorce, legal separation or marriage annulment given in another Member State, and against which no further appeal lies under the law of that Member State.

3. Without prejudice to Section 4 of this Chapter, any interested party may, in accordance with the procedures provided for in Section 2 of this Chapter, apply for a decision that the judgment be or not be recognised.

The local jurisdiction of the court appearing in the list notified by each Member State to the Commission pursuant to Article 68 shall be determined by the internal law of the Member State in which proceedings for recognition or non-recognition are brought.

4. Where the recognition of a judgment is raised as an incidental question in a court of a Member State, that court may determine that issue.

Article 22

Grounds of non-recognition for judgments relating to divorce, legal separation or marriage annulment

A judgment relating to a divorce, legal separation or marriage annulment shall not be recognised:

(a) if such recognition is manifestly contrary to the public policy of the Member State in which recognition is sought;

(b) where it was given in default of appearance, if the respondent was not served with the document which instituted the proceedings or with an equivalent document in sufficient time and in such a way as to enable the respondent to arrange for his or her defence unless it is determined that the respondent has accepted the judgment unequivocally;

(c) if it is irreconcilable with a judgment given in proceedings between the same parties in the Member State in which recognition is sought; or

(d) if it is irreconcilable with an earlier judgment given in another Member State or in a non-Member State between the same parties, provided that the earlier judgment fulfils the conditions necessary for its recognition in the Member State in which recognition is sought.

Article 23

Grounds of non-recognition for judgments relating to parental responsibility

A judgment relating to parental responsibility shall not be recognised:

(a) if such recognition is manifestly contrary to the public policy of the Member State in which recognition is sought taking into account the best interests of the child;

(b) if it was given, except in case of urgency, without the child having been given an opportunity to be heard, in violation of fundamental principles of procedure of the Member State in which recognition is sought;

(c) where it was given in default of appearance if the person in default was not served with the document which instituted the proceedings or with an equivalent document in sufficient time and in such a way as to enable that person to arrange for his or her defence unless it is determined that such person has accepted the judgment unequivocally;

(d) on the request of any person claiming that the judgment infringes his or her parental responsibility, if it was given without such person having been given an opportunity to be heard;

(e) if it is irreconcilable with a later judgment relating to parental responsibility given in the Member State in which recognition is sought;

(f) if it is irreconcilable with a later judgment relating to parental responsibility given in another Member State or in the non-Member State of the habitual residence of the child provided that the later judgment fulfils the conditions necessary for its recognition in the Member State in which recognition is sought.

or

(g) if the procedure laid down in Article 56 has not been complied with.

Article 24

Prohibition of review of jurisdiction of the court of origin

The jurisdiction of the court of the Member State of origin may not be reviewed. The test of public policy referred to in Articles 22(a) and 23(a) may not be applied to the rules relating to jurisdiction set out in Articles 3 to 14.

Article 25

Differences in applicable law

The recognition of a judgment may not be refused because the law of the Member State in which such recognition is sought would not allow divorce, legal separation or marriage annulment on the same facts.

Article 26

Non-review as to substance

Under no circumstances may a judgment be reviewed as to its substance.

Article 27

Stay of proceedings

1. A court of a Member State in which recognition is sought of a judgment given in another Member State may stay the proceedings if an ordinary appeal against the judgment has been lodged.

2. A court of a Member State in which recognition is sought of a judgment given in Ireland or the United Kingdom may stay the proceedings if enforcement is suspended in the Member State of origin by reason of an appeal.

SECTION 2

Application for a declaration of enforceability

Article 28

Enforceable judgments

1. A judgment on the exercise of parental responsibility in respect of a child given in a Member State which is enforceable in that Member State and has been served shall be enforced in another Member State when, on the application of any interested party, it has been declared enforceable there.

2. However, in the United Kingdom, such a judgment shall be enforced in England and Wales, in Scotland or in Northern Ireland only when, on the application of any interested party, it has been registered for enforcement in that part of the United Kingdom.

Article 29

Jurisdiction of local courts

1. An application for a declaration of enforceability shall be submitted to the court appearing in the list notified by each Member State to the Commission pursuant to Article 68.

2. The local jurisdiction shall be determined by reference to the place of

habitual residence of the person against whom enforcement is sought or by reference to the habitual residence of any child to whom the application relates.

Where neither of the places referred to in the first subparagraph can be found in the Member State of enforcement, the local jurisdiction shall be determined by reference to the place of enforcement.

Article 30

Procedure

1. The procedure for making the application shall be governed by the law of the Member State of enforcement.

2. The applicant must give an address for service within the area of jurisdiction of the court applied to. However, if the law of the Member State of enforcement does not provide for the furnishing of such an address, the applicant shall appoint a representative ad litem.

3. The documents referred to in Articles 37 and 39 shall be attached to the application.

Article 31

Decision of the court

1. The court applied to shall give its decision without delay.

Neither the person against whom enforcement is sought, nor the child shall, at this stage of the proceedings, be entitled to make any submissions on the application.

2. The application may be refused only for one of the reasons specified in Articles 22, 23 and 24.

3. Under no circumstances may a judgment be reviewed as to its substance.

Article 32

Notice of the decision

The appropriate officer of the court shall without delay bring to the notice of the applicant the decision given on the application in accordance with the procedure laid down by the law of the Member State of enforcement.

Article 33

Appeal against the decision

1. The decision on the application for a declaration of enforceability may be appealed against by either party.

2. The appeal shall be lodged with the court appearing in the list notified by each Member State to the Commission pursuant to Article 68.

3. The appeal shall be dealt with in accordance with the rules governing procedure in contradictory matters.

4. If the appeal is brought by the applicant for a declaration of enforceability, the party against whom enforcement is sought shall be summoned to appear before the appellate court. If such person fails to appear, the provisions of Article 18 shall apply.

5. An appeal against a declaration of enforceability must be lodged within one month of service thereof. If the party against whom enforcement is sought is habitually resident in a Member State other than that in which the declaration of enforceability was given, the time for appealing shall be two months and shall run from the date of service, either on him or at his residence. No extension of time may be granted on account of distance.

Article 34

Courts of appeal and means of contest

The judgment given on appeal may be contested only by the proceedings referred to in the list notified by each Member State to the Commission pursuant to Article 68.

Article 35

Stay of proceedings

1. The court with which the appeal is lodged under Articles 33 or 34 may, on the application of the party against whom enforcement is sought, stay the proceedings if an ordinary appeal has been lodged in the Member State of origin, or if the time for such appeal has not yet expired. In the latter case, the court may specify the time within which an appeal is to be lodged.

2. Where the judgment was given in Ireland or the United Kingdom, any form of appeal available in the Member State of origin shall be treated as an ordinary appeal for the purposes of paragraph 1.

Article 36

Partial enforcement

1. Where a judgment has been given in respect of several matters and enforcement cannot be authorised for all of them, the court shall authorise enforcement for one or more of them.

2. An applicant may request partial enforcement of a judgment.

SECTION 3

Provisions common to Sections 1 and 2

Article 37

Documents

1. A party seeking or contesting recognition or applying for a declaration of enforceability shall produce:
   (a) a copy of the judgment which satisfies the conditions necessary to establish its authenticity; and
   (b) the certificate referred to in Article 39.

2. In addition, in the case of a judgment given in default, the party seeking recognition or applying for a declaration of enforceability shall produce:
   (a) the original or certified true copy of the document which establishes that the defaulting party was served with the document instituting the proceedings or with an equivalent document; or
   (b) any document indicating that the defendant has accepted the judgment unequivocally.

Article 38

Absence of documents

1. If the documents specified in Article 37(1)(b) or (2) are not produced, the court may specify a time for their production, accept equivalent documents or, if it considers that it has sufficient information before it, dispense with their production.

2. If the court so requires, a translation of such documents shall be furnished. The translation shall be certified by a person qualified to do so in one of the Member States.

Article 39

Certificate concerning judgments in matrimonial matters and certificate concerning judgments on parental responsibility

The competent court or authority of a Member State of origin shall, at the request of any interested party, issue a certificate using the standard form set out in Annex I (judgments in matrimonial matters) or in Annex II (judgments on parental responsibility).

SECTION 4

Enforceability of certain judgments concerning rights of access and of certain judgments which require the return of the child

Article 40

Scope

1. This Section shall apply to:
   (a) rights of access;
   and
   (b) the return of a child entailed by a judgment given pursuant to Article 11(8).

2. The provisions of this Section shall not prevent a holder of parental responsibility from seeking recognition and enforcement of a judgment in accordance with the provisions in Sections 1 and 2 of this Chapter.

Article 41

Rights of access

1. The rights of access referred to in Article 40(1)(a) granted in an enforceable judgment given in a Member State shall be recognised and enforceable in another Member State without the need for a declaration of enforceability and without any possibility of opposing its recognition if the judgment has been certified in the Member State of origin in accordance with paragraph 2.

Even if national law does not provide for enforceability by operation of law of a judgment granting access rights, the court of origin may declare that the judgment shall be enforceable, notwithstanding any appeal.

2. The judge of origin shall issue the certificate referred to in paragraph 1 using the standard form in Annex III (certificate concerning rights of access)only if:

(a) where the judgment was given in default, the person defaulting was served with the document which instituted the proceedings or with an equivalent document in sufficient time and in such a way as to enable that person to arrange for his or her defense, or, the person has been served with the document but not in compliance with these conditions, it is nevertheless established that he or she accepted the decision unequivocally;

(b) all parties concerned were given an opportunity to be heard; and

(c) the child was given an opportunity to be heard, unless a hearing was considered inappropriate having regard to his or her age or degree of maturity.

The certificate shall be completed in the language of the judgment.

3. Where the rights of access involve a cross-border situation at the time of the delivery of the judgment, the certificate shall be issued ex officio when the judgment becomes enforceable, even if only provisionally. If the situation subsequently acquires a cross-border character, the certificate shall be issued at the request of one of the parties.

Article 42

Return of the child

1. The return of a child referred to in Article 40(1)(b) entailed by an enforceable judgment given in a Member State shall be recognised and enforceable in another Member State without the need for a declaration of enforceability and without any possibility of opposing its recognition if the judgment has been certified in the Member State of origin in accordance with paragraph 2.

Even if national law does not provide for enforceability by operation of law, notwithstanding any appeal, of a judgment requiring the return of the child mentioned in Article 11(b)(8), the court of origin may declare the judgment enforceable.

2. The judge of origin who delivered the judgment referred to in Article 40(1)(b) shall issue the certificate referred to in paragraph 1 only if:

(a) the child was given an opportunity to be heard, unless a hearing was considered inappropriate having regard to his or her age or degree of maturity;

(b) the parties were given an opportunity to be heard; and

(c) the court has taken into account in issuing its judgment the reasons for and evidence underlying the order issued pursuant to Article 13 of the 1980 Hague Convention.

In the event that the court or any other authority takes measures to ensure the protection of the child after its return to the State of habitual residence, the certificate shall contain details of such measures.

The judge of origin shall of his or her own motion issue that certificate using the standard form in Annex IV (certificate concerning return of the child(ren)).

The certificate shall be completed in the language of the judgment.

Article 43

Rectification of the certificate

1. The law of the Member State of origin shall be applicable to any rectification of the certificate.

2. No appeal shall lie against the issuing of a certificate pursuant to Articles 41(1) or 42(1).

Article 44

Effects of the certificate

The certificate shall take effect only within the limits of the enforceability of the judgment.

Article 45

Documents

1. A party seeking enforcement of a judgment shall produce:
    (a) a copy of the judgment which satisfies the conditions necessary to establish its authenticity;
    and
    (b) the certificate referred to in Article 41(1) or Article 42(1).

2. For the purposes of this Article,
    — the certificate referred to in Article 41(1) shall be accompanied by a translation of point 12 relating to the arrangements for exercising right of access,
    — the certificate referred to in Article 42(1) shall be accompanied by a translation of its point 14 relating to the arrangements for implementing the measures taken to ensure the child's return.

The translation shall be into the official language or one of the official languages of the Member State of enforcement or any other language that the Member State of enforcement expressly accepts. The translation shall be certified by a person qualified to do so in one of the Member States.

SECTION 5

Authentic instruments and agreements

Article 46

Documents which have been formally drawn up or registered as authentic instruments and are enforceable in one Member State and also agreements between the parties that are enforceable in the Member State in which they were concluded shall be recognised and declared enforceable under the same conditions as judgments.

SECTION 6

Other provisions

Article 47

Enforcement procedure

1. The enforcement procedure is governed by the law of the Member State of enforcement.

2. Any judgment delivered by a court of another Member State and declared to be enforceable in accordance with Section 2 or certified in accordance with Article 41(1) or Article 42(1) shall be enforced in the Member State of enforcement in the same conditions as if it had been delivered in that Member State.

In particular, a judgment which has been certified according to Article 41(1) or Article 42(1) cannot be enforced if it is irreconcilable with a subsequent enforceable judgment.

Article 48

Practical arrangements for the exercise of rights of access

1. The courts of the Member State of enforcement may make practical arrangements for organising the exercise of rights of access, if the necessary arrangements have not or have not sufficiently been made in the judgment delivered by the courts of the Member State having jurisdiction as to the substance of the matter and provided the essential elements of this judgment are respected.

2. The practical arrangements made pursuant to paragraph 1 shall cease to apply pursuant to a later judgment by the courts of the Member State having jurisdiction as to the substance of the matter.

Article 49

Costs

The provisions of this Chapter, with the exception of Section 4, shall also apply to the determination of the amount of costs and expenses of proceedings under this Regulation and to the enforcement of any order concerning such costs and expenses.

Article 50

Legal aid

An applicant who, in the Member State of origin, has benefited from complete or partial legal aid or exemption from costs or expenses shall be entitled, in the procedures provided for in Articles 21, 28, 41, 42 and 48 to benefit from the most favourable legal aid or the most extensive exemption from costs and expenses provided for by the law of the Member State of enforcement.

Article 51

Security, bond or deposit

No security, bond or deposit, however described, shall be required of a party who in one Member State applies for enforcement of a judgment given in another Member State on the following grounds:

(a) that he or she is not habitually resident in the Member State in which enforcement is sought; or

(b) that he or she is either a foreign national or, where enforcement is sought in either the United Kingdom or Ireland, does not have his or her 'domicile'in either of those Member States.

Article 52

Legalisation or other similar formality

No legalisation or other similar formality shall be required in respect of the documents referred to in Articles 37, 38 and 45 or in respect of a document appointing a representative ad litem.

CHAPTER IV

COOPERATION BETWEEN CENTRAL AUTHORITIES IN MATTERS OF PARENTAL RESPONSIBILITY

Article 53

Designation

Each Member State shall designate one or more central authorities to assist with the application of this Regulation and shall specify the geographical or functional jurisdiction of each.

Where a Member State has designated more than one central authority, communications shall normally be sent direct to the relevant central authority with jurisdiction. Where a communication is sent to a central authority without jurisdiction, the latter shall be responsible for forwarding it to the central authority with jurisdiction and informing the sender accordingly.

Article 54

General functions

The central authorities shall communicate information on national laws and procedures and take measures to improve the application of this Regulation and strengthening their cooperation. For this purpose the European Judicial Network in civil and commercial matters created by Decision No. 2001/470/EC shall be used.

Article 55

Cooperation on cases specific to parental responsibility

The central authorities shall, upon request from a central authority of another Member State or from a holder of parental responsibility, cooperate on specific cases to achieve the purposes of this Regulation. To this end, they shall, acting directly or through public authorities or other bodies, take all appropriate steps in accordance with the law of that Member State in matters of personal data protection to:

(a) collect and exchange information:
    (i)   on the situation of the child;
    (ii) on any procedures under way; or
    (iii) on decisions taken concerning the child;

(b) provide information and assistance to holders of parental responsibility seeking the recognition and enforcement of decisions on their territory, in particular concerning rights of access and the return of the child;

(c) facilitate communications between courts, in particular for the application of Article 11(6) and (7) and Article 15;

(d) provide such information and assistance as is needed by courts to apply Article 56; and

(e) facilitate agreement between holders of parental responsibility through mediation or other means, and facilitate cross-border cooperation to this end.

Article 56

Placement of a child in another Member State

1. Where a court having jurisdiction under Articles 8 to 15 contemplates the placement of a child in institutional care or with a foster family and where such placement is to take place in another Member State, it shall first consult the central authority or other authority having jurisdiction in the latter State where public authority intervention in that Member State is required for domestic cases of child placement.

2. The judgment on placement referred to in paragraph 1 may be made in the requesting State only if the competent authority of the requested State has consented to the placement.

3. The procedures for consultation or consent referred to in paragraphs 1 and 2 shall be governed by the national law of the requested State.

4. Where the authority having jurisdiction under Articles 8 to 15 decides to place the child in a foster family, and where such placement is to take place in another Member State and where no public authority intervention is required in the latter Member State for domestic cases of child placement, it shall so inform the central authority or other authority having jurisdiction in the latter State.

Article 57

Working method

1. Any holder of parental responsibility may submit, to the central authority of the Member State of his or her habitual residence or to the central authority of the Member State where the child is habitually resident or present, a request for assistance as mentioned in Article 55. In general, the request shall include all available information of relevance to its enforcement. Where the request for assistance concerns the recognition or enforcement of a judgment on parental responsibility that falls within the scope of this Regulation, the holder of parental responsibility shall

attach the relevant certificates provided for in Articles 39, 41(1) or 42(1).

2.   Member States shall communicate to the Commission the official language or languages of the Community institutions other than their own in which communications to the central authorities can be accepted.

3.   The assistance provided by the central authorities pursuant to Article 55 shall be free of charge.

4. Each central authority shall bear its own costs.

Article 58

Meetings

1.   In order to facilitate the application of this Regulation, central authorities shall meet regularly.

2.   These meetings shall be convened in compliance with Decision No. 2001/ 470/EC establishing a European Judicial Network in civil and commercial matters.

CHAPTER V

RELATIONS WITH OTHER INSTRUMENTS

Article 59

Relation with other instruments

1.   Subject to the provisions of Articles 60, 63, 64 and paragraph 2 of this Article, this Regulation shall, for the Member States, supersede conventions existing at the time of entry into force of this Regulation which have been concluded between two or more Member States and relate to matters governed by this Regulation.

2.   (a) Finland and Sweden shall have the option of declaring that the Convention of 6 February 1931 between Denmark, Finland, Iceland, Norway and Sweden comprising international private law provisions on marriage, adoption and guardianship, together with the Final Protocol thereto, will apply, in whole or in part, in their mutual relations, in place of the rules of this Regulation. Such declarations shall be annexed to this Regulation and published in the Official Journal of the European Union . They may be withdrawn, in whole or in part, at any moment by the said Member States.
     (b) The principle of non-discrimination on the grounds of nationality between citizens of the Union shall be respected.
     (c) The rules of jurisdiction in any future agreement to be concluded

between the Member States referred to in subparagraph (a) which relate to matters governed by this Regulation shall be in line with those laid down in this Regulation.

(d) Judgments handed down in any of the Nordic States which have made the declaration provided for in subparagraph (a) under a forum of jurisdiction corresponding to one of those laid down in Chapter II of this Regulation, shall be recognised and enforced in the other Member States under the rules laid down in Chapter III of this Regulation.

3. Member States shall send to the Commission:
   (a) a copy of the agreements and uniform laws implementing these agreements referred to in paragraph 2(a) and (c);
   (b) any denunciations of, or amendments to, those agreements or uniform laws.

Article 60

Relations with certain multilateral conventions

In relations between Member States, this Regulation shall take precedence over the following Conventions in so far as they concern matters governed by this Regulation:

(a) the Hague Convention of 5 October 1961 concerning the Powers of Authorities and the Law Applicable in respect of the Protection of Minors;

(b) the Luxembourg Convention of 8 September 1967 on the Recognition of Decisions Relating to the Validity of Marriages;

(c) the Hague Convention of 1 June 1970 on the Recognition of Divorces and Legal Separations;

(d) the European Convention of 20 May 1980 on Recognition and Enforcement of Decisions concerning Custody of Children and on Restoration of Custody of Children; and

(e) the Hague Convention of 25 October 1980 on the Civil Aspects of International Child Abduction.

Article 61

Relation with the Hague Convention of 19 October 1996 on Jurisdiction, Applicable law, Recognition, Enforcement and Cooperation in Respect of Parental Responsibility and Measures for the Protection of Children

As concerns the relation with the Hague Convention of 19 October 1996 on Jurisdiction, Applicable law, Recognition, Enforcement and Cooperation in Respect of Parental Responsibility and Measures for the Protection of Children, this Regulation shall apply:

(a) where the child concerned has his or her habitual residence on the territory of a Member State;

(b) as concerns the recognition and enforcement of a judgment given in a court of a Member State on the territory of another Member State, even if the child concerned has his or her habitual residence on the territory of a third State which is a contracting Party to the said Convention.

Article 62

Scope of effects

1. The agreements and conventions referred to in Articles 59(1), 60 and 61 shall continue to have effect in relation to matters not governed by this Regulation.

2. The conventions mentioned in Article 60, in particular the 1980 Hague Convention, continue to produce effects between the Member States which are party thereto, in compliance with Article 60.

Article 63

Treaties with the Holy See

1. This Regulation shall apply without prejudice to the International Treaty (Concordat)between the Holy See and Portugal, signed at the Vatican City on 7 May 1940.

2. Any decision as to the invalidity of a marriage taken under the Treaty referred to in paragraph 1 shall be recognised in the Member States on the conditions laid down in Chapter III, Section 1.

3. The provisions laid down in paragraphs 1 and 2 shall also apply to the following international treaties (Concordats) with the Holy See:
   (a) 'Concordato lateranense' of 11 February 1929 between Italy and the Holy See, modified by the agreement, with additional Protocol signed in Rome on 18 February 1984;
   (b) Agreement between the Holy See and Spain on legal affairs of 3 January 1979.

4. Recognition of the decisions provided for in paragraph 2 may, in Italy or in Spain, be subject to the same procedures and the same checks as are applicable to decisions of the ecclesiastical courts handed down in accordance with the international treaties concluded with the Holy See referred to in paragraph 3.

5. Member States shall send to the Commission:

(a) a copy of the Treaties referred to in paragraphs 1 and 3;

(b) any denunciations of or amendments to those Treaties.

CHAPTER VI

TRANSITIONAL PROVISIONS

Article 64

1. The provisions of this Regulation shall apply only to legal proceedings instituted, to documents formally drawn up or registered as authentic instruments and to agreements concluded between the parties after its date of application in accordance with Article 72.

2. Judgments given after the date of application of this Regulation in proceedings instituted before that date but after the date of entry into force of Regulation (EC) No. 1347/2000 shall be recognised and enforced in accordance with the provisions of Chapter III of this Regulation if jurisdiction was founded on rules which accorded with those provided for either in Chapter II or in Regulation (EC) No. 1347/2000 or in a convention concluded between the Member State of origin and the Member State addressed which was in force when the proceedings were instituted.

3. Judgments given before the date of application of this Regulation in proceedings instituted after the entry into force of Regulation (EC) No. 1347/2000 shall be recognised and enforced in accordance with the provisions of Chapter III of this Regulation provided they relate to divorce, legal separation or marriage annulment or parental responsibility for the children of both spouses on the occasion of these matrimonial proceedings.

4. Judgments given before the date of application of this Regulation but after the date of entry into force of Regulation (EC) No. 1347/2000 in proceedings instituted before the date of entry into force of Regulation (EC) No. 1347/2000 shall be recognised and enforced in accordance with the provisions of Chapter III of this Regulation provided they relate to divorce, legal separation or marriage annulment or parental responsibility for the children of both spouses on the occasion of these matrimonial proceedings and that jurisdiction was founded on rules which accorded with those provided for either in Chapter II of this Regulation or in Regulation (EC) No. 1347/2000 or in a convention concluded between the Member State of origin and the Member State addressed which was in force when the proceedings were instituted.

CHAPTER VII

FINAL PROVISIONS

Article 65

Review

No later than 1 January 2012, and every five years thereafter, the Commission shall present to the European Parliament, to the Council and to the European Economic and Social Committee a report on the application of this Regulation on the basis of information supplied by the Member States. The report shall be accompanied if need be by proposals for adaptations.

Article 66

Member States with two or more legal systems

With regard to a Member State in which two or more systems of law or sets of rules concerning matters governed by this Regulation apply in different territorial units:

(a) any reference to habitual residence in that Member State shall refer to habitual residence in a territorial unit;

(b) any reference to nationality, or in the case of the United Kingdom 'domicile', shall refer to the territorial unit designated by the law of that State;

(c) any reference to the authority of a Member State shall refer to the authority of a territorial unit within that State which is concerned;

(d) any reference to the rules of the requested Member State shall refer to the rules of the territorial unit in which jurisdiction, recognition or enforcement is invoked.

Article 67

Information on central authorities and languages accepted

The Member States shall communicate to the Commission within three months following the entry into force of this Regulation:

(a) the names, addresses and means of communication for the central authorities designated pursuant to Article 53;

(b) the languages accepted for communications to central authorities pursuant to Article 57(2);

and

(c) the languages accepted for the certificate concerning rights of access pursuant to Article 45(2).

The Member States shall communicate to the Commission any changes to this information.

The Commission shall make this information publicly available.

Article 68

Information relating to courts and redress procedures

The Member States shall notify to the Commission the lists of courts and redress procedures referred to in Articles 21, 29, 33 and 34 and any amendments thereto.

The Commission shall update this information and make it publicly available through the publication in the Official Journal of the European Union and any other appropriate means.

Article 69

Amendments to the Annexes

Any amendments to the standard forms in Annexes I to IV shall be adopted in accordance with the consultative procedure set out in Article 70(2).

Article 70

Committee

1. The Commission shall be assisted by a committee (committee).

2. Where reference is made to this paragraph, Articles 3 and 7 of Decision 1999/468/EC shall apply.

3. The committee shall adopt its rules of procedure.

Article 71

Repeal of Regulation (EC) No. 1347/2000

1. Regulation (EC) No. 1347/2000 shall be repealed as from the date of application of this Regulation.

2. Any reference to Regulation (EC) No. 1347/2000 shall be construed as a reference to this Regulation according to the comparative table in Annex V.

Article 72

Entry into force

This Regulation shall enter into force on 1 August 2004.

The Regulation shall apply from 1 March 2005, with the exception of Articles 67, 68, 69 and 70, which shall apply from 1 August 2004.

> This Regulation shall be binding in its entirety and directly applicable in the Member States in accordance with the Treaty establishing the European Community.

Done at Brussels, 27 November 2003.

For the Council

The President

R. CASTELLI

ANNEX I

CERTIFICATE REFERRED TO IN ARTICLE 39 CONCERNING JUDGMENTS IN MATRIMONIAL MATTERS[12]

1. Member State of origin

2. Court or authority issuing the certificate
   2.1. Name
   2.2. Address
   2.3. Tel./fax/e-mail

3. Marriage
   3. 1. Wife
         3.1.1. Full name
         3.1.2. Address
         3.1.3. Country and place of birth
         3.1.4. Date of birth

---

[12] Council Regulation (EC) No. 2201/2003 of 27 November 2003 concerning jurisdiction and the recognition and enforcement of judgments in matrimonial matters and the matters of parental responsibility, repealing Regulation (EC) No. 1347/2000.

    3.2. Husband
        3.2.1. Full name
        3.2.2. Address
        3.2.3. Country and place of birth
        3.2.4. Date of birth
    3.3. Country, place (where available)and date of marriage
        3.3.1. Country of marriage
        3.3.2. Place of marriage (where available)
        3.3.3. Date of marriage
        4. Court which delivered the judgment

4.1. Name of Court
    4.2. Place of Court

5.   Judgment
    5.1. Date
    5.2. Reference number
    5.3. Type of judgment
        5.3.1. Divorce
        5.3.2. Marriage annulment
        5.3.3. Legal separation
    5.4. Was the judgment given in default of appearance?
        5.4.1. No
        5.4.2. Yes[13]

6.   Names of parties to whom legal aid has been granted

7.   Is the judgment subject to further appeal under the law of the Member State of origin?
    7.1. No
    7.2. Yes

8.   Date of legal effect in the Member State where the judgment was given
    8.1. Divorce
    8.2. Legal separation

Done at ...., date ....

Signature and/or stamp

---

[13] Documents referred to in Article 37(2) must be attached.

ANNEX II

CERTIFICATE REFERRED TO IN ARTICLE 39 CONCERNING JUDGMENTS ON PARENTAL RESPONSIBILITY[14]

1. Member State of origin

2. Court or authority issuing the certificate
   2.1. Name
   2.2. Address
   2.3. Tel./Fax/e-mail

3. Person(s)with rights of access
   3.1. Full name
   3.2. Address
   3.3. Date and place of birth (where available)

4. Holders of parental responsibility other than those mentioned under 3[15]
   4.1.
      4.1.1. Full name
      4.1.2. Address
      4.1.3. Date and place of birth (where available)
   4.2.
      4.2.1. Full Name
      4.2.2. Address
      4.2.3. Date and place of birth (where available)
   4.3.
      4.3.1. Full name
      4.3.2. Address
      4.3.3. Date and place of birth (where available)

5. Court which delivered the judgment
   5.1. Name of Court
   5.2. Place of Court

6. Judgment
   6.1. Date
   6.2. Reference number
   6.3. Was the judgment given in default of appearance?
      6.3.1. No
      6.3.2. Yes[16]

7. Children who are covered by the judgment[17]
   7.1. Full name and date of birth

---

[14] Council Regulation (EC) No. 2201/2003 of 27 November 2003 concerning jurisdiction and the recognition and enforcement of judgments in matrimonial matters and the matters of parental responsibility, repealing Regulation (EC) No. 1347/2000.
[15] In cases of joint custody, a person already mentioned under item 3 may also be mentioned under item 4.
[16] Documents referred to in Article 37(2) must be attached.
[17] If more than four children are covered, use a second form.

    7.2. Full name and date of birth
    7.3. Full name and date of birth
    7.4. Full name and date of birth

8. Names of parties to whom legal aid has been granted

9. Attestation of enforceability and service
    9.1. Is the judgment enforceable according to the law of the Member State of origin?
        9.1.1. Yes
        9.1.2. No
    9.2. Has the judgment been served on the party against whom enforcement is sought?
        9.2.1. Yes
            9.2.1.1. Full name of the party
            9.2.1.2. Address
            9.2.1.3. Date of service
        9.2.2. No

10. Specific information on judgments on rights of access where 'exequatur' is requested under Article 28. This possibility is foreseen in Article 40(2).
    10.1. Practical arrangements for exercise of rights of access (to the extent stated in the judgment)
        10.1.1. Date and time
            10.1.1.1. Start
            10.1.1.2. End
        10.1.2. Place
        10.1.3. Specific obligations on holders of parental responsibility
        10.1.4. Specific obligations on the person with right of access
        10.1.5. Any restrictions attached to the exercise of rights of access

11. Specific information for judgments on the return of the child in cases where the 'exequatur'procedure is requested under Article 28. This possibility is foreseen under Article 40(2).
    11.1. The judgment entails the return of the child
    11.2. Person to whom the child is to be returned (to the extent stated in the judgment)
        11.2.1. Full name
        11.2.2 Address

Done at ...., date ....

Signature and/or stamp

ANNEX III

CERTIFICATE REFERRED TO IN ARTICLE 41(1)CONCERNING JUDGMENTS ON RIGHTS OF ACCESS[18]

1. Member State of origin

2. Court or authority issuing the certificate
   2.1. Name
   2.2. Address
   2.3. Tel./fax/e-mail

3. Person(s)with rights of access
   3.1. Full name
   3.2. Address
   3.3. Date and place of birth (where available)

4. Holders of parental responsibility other than those mentioned under 3[19] [20]
   4.1.
     4.1.1. Full name
     4.1.2. Address
     4.1.3. Date and place of birth (where available)
   4.2.
     4.2.1. Full name
     4.2.2. Address
     4.2.3. Date and place of birth (where available)
   4.3. Other
     4.3.1. Full name
     4.3.2. Address
     4.3.3. Date and place of birth (where available)

5. Court which delivered the judgment
   5.1. Name of Court
   5.2. Place of Court

6. Judgment
   6.1. Date
   6.2. Reference number

7. Children who are covered by the judgment[21]
   7.1. Full name and date of birth
   7.2. Full name and date of birth

---

[18] Council Regulation (EC) No. 2201/2003 of 27 November 2003 concerning jurisdiction and the recognition and enforcement of judgments in matrimonial matters and the matters of parental responsibility, repealing Regulation (EC) No. 1347/2000.

[19] In cases of joint custody, a person already mentioned under item 3 may also be mentioned in item 4.

[20] Please put a cross in the box corresponding to the person against whom the judgment should be enforced.

[21] If more than four children are concerned, use a second form.

    7.3. Full name and date of birth
    7.4. Full name and date of birth

8. Is the judgment enforceable in the Member State of origin?
    8.1. Yes
    8.2. No

9. Where the judgment was given in default of appearance, the person defaulting was served with the document which instituted the proceedings or with an equivalent document in sufficient time and in such a way as to enable that person to arrange for his or her defence, or the person has been served with the document but not in compliance with these conditions, it is nevertheless established that he or she accepted the decision unequivocally

10. All parties concerned were given an opportunity to be heard

11. The children were given an opportunity to be heard, unless a hearing was considered inappropriate having regard to their age or degree of maturity

12. Practical arrangements for exercise of rights of access (to the extent stated in the judgment)
    12.1. Date and time
        12.1.1. Start
        12.1.2. End
    12.2. Place
    12.3. Specific obligations on holders of parental responsibility
    12.4. Specific obligations on the person with right of access
    12.5. Any restrictions attached to the exercise of rights of access

13. Names of parties to whom legal aid has been granted

Done at ...., date ....

                                      Signature and/or stamp

ANNEX IV

CERTIFICATE REFERRED TO IN ARTICLE 42(1)CONCERNING THE RETURN OF THE CHILD[22]

1. Member State of origin

2. Court or authority issuing the certificate
    2.1. Name
    2.2. Address
    2.3. Tel./fax/e-mail

3. Person to whom the child has to be returned (to the extent stated in the judgment)
    3.1. Full name
    3.2. Address
    3.3. Date and place of birth (where available)

4. Holders of parental responsibility[23]
    4.1. Mother
        4.1.1. Full name
        4.1.2. Address (where available)
        4.1.3. Date and place of birth (where available)
    4.2. Father
        4.2.1. Full name
        4.2.2. Address (where available)
        4.2.3. Date and place of birth (where available)
    4.3. Other
        4.3.1. Full name
        4.3.2. Address (where available)
        4.3.3. Date and place of birth (where available)

5. Respondent (where available)
    5.1. Full name
    5.2. Address (where available)

6. Court which delivered the judgment
    6.1. Name of Court
    6.2. Place of Court

7. Judgment
    7.1. Date
    7.2. Reference number

8. Children who are covered by the judgment[24]
    8.1. Full name and date of birth

---

[22] Council Regulation (EC) No. 2201 of 27 November 2003 concerning jurisdiction and the recognition and enforcement of judgments in matrimonial matters and the matters of parental responsibility, repealing Regulation (EC) No. 1347/2000.

[23] This item is optional.

[24] If more than four children are covered, use a second form.

    8.2. Full name and date of birth
    8.3. Full name and date of birth
    8.4. Full name and date of birth

9.   The judgment entails the return of the child

10. Is the judgment enforceable in the Member State of origin?
    10.1. Yes
    10.2. No

11. The children were given an opportunity to be heard, unless a hearing was considered inappropriate having regard to their age or degree of maturity

12. The parties were given an opportunity to be heard

13. The judgment entails the return of the children and the court has taken into account in issuing its judgment the reasons for and evidence underlying the decision issued pursuant to Article 13 of the Hague Convention of 25 October 1980 on the Civil Aspects of International Child Abduction

14. Where applicable, details of measures taken by courts or authorities to ensure the protection of the child after its return to the Member State of habitual residence

15. Names of parties to whom legal aid has been granted

Done at ...., date ....

Signature and/or stamp

ANNEX V

COMPARATIVE TABLE WITH REGULATION (EC) No. 1347/2000

Articles repealed	Corresponding Articles of new text	Articles repealed	Corresponding Articles of new text
1	1, 2	27	34
2	3	28	35
3	12	29	36
4		30	50
5	4	31	51
6	5	32	37
7	6	33	39
8	7	34	38
9	17	35	52
10	18	36	59
11	16, 19	37	60, 61
12	20	38	62
13	2, 49, 46	39	
14	21	40	63
15	22, 23	41	66
16		42	64
17	24	43	65
18	25	44	68, 69
19	26	45	70
20	27	46	72
21	28	Annex I	68
22	21, 29	Annex II	68
23	30	Annex III	68
24	31	Annex IV	Annex I
25	32	Annex V	Annex II
26	33		

ANNEX VI

Declarations by Sweden and Finland pursuant to Article 59(2)(a) of the Council Regulation concerning jurisdiction and the recognition and enforcement of judgments in matrimonial matters and matters of parental responsibility, repealing Regulation (EC) No. 1347/2000.

Declaration by Sweden:

> Pursuant to Article 59(2)(a) of the Council Regulation concerning jurisdiction and the recognition and enforcement of judgments in matrimonial matters and matters of parental responsibility, repealing Regulation (EC) No. 1347/2000, Sweden hereby declares that the Convention of 6 February 1931 between Denmark, Finland, Iceland, Norway and Sweden comprising international private law provisions on marriage, adoption and guardianship, together with the Final Protocol thereto, will apply in full in relations between Sweden and Finland, in place of the rules of the Regulation.

Declaration by Finland:

> Pursuant to Article 59(2)(a) of the Council Regulation concerning jurisdiction and the recognition and enforcement of judgments in matrimonial matters and matters of parental responsibility, repealing Regulation (EC) No. 1347/2000, Finland hereby declares that the Convention of 6 February 1931 between Finland, Denmark, Iceland, Norway and Sweden comprising international private law provisions on marriage, adoption and guardianship, together with the Final Protocol thereto, will apply in full in relations between Finland and Sweden, in place of the rules of the Regulation.

INDEX

Welfare of the child—*contd.*
  emergency situations—*contd.*
    notification requirements
      4–54—4–56
    power of Garda Síochána to take
      child into safety
      4–37—4–40
  emotional welfare 2–18
  foster care 5–16
  generally 2–05—2–07
  health boards *see* **Health boards**
  intellectual welfare 2–14
  jurisdictional issues 4–07—4–09
  keeping siblings together 2–25
  meaning 2–05, 4–11—4–12
  medical examinations, consent to
    4–49—4–53
  moral welfare 2–12—2–13
  parental capacity 2–21
  parents in same-sex relationships
    2–13

Welfare of the child—*contd.*
  physical welfare 2–15
  placement with relatives 5–81
  religious welfare 2–08—2–11
  residential care 6–12
  social welfare 2–16
  State, duties of 4–01—4–06
  "tender years" principle
    2–19—2–20
  voluntary care 4–34—4–35
  wishes of the child 2–22—2–24
Will
  appointment of guardian by 2–47,
    2–51, 2–52
Work *see* **Employment**
Work equipment
  health and safety 3–81—3–83

Young person
  definition 4–04